QUANTITATIVE AND EMPIRICAL ANALYSIS OF NONLINEAR DYNAMIC MACROMODELS

CONTRIBUTIONS
TO
ECONOMIC ANALYSIS

277

Honorary Editors:
D.W. JORGENSON
J. TINBERGEN†

Editors:
B. BALTAGI
E. SADKA
D. WILDASIN

ELSEVIER

Amsterdam – Boston – Heidelberg – London – New York – Oxford – Paris
San Diego – San Francisco – Singapore – Sydney – Tokyo

QUANTITATIVE AND EMPIRICAL ANALYSIS OF NONLINEAR DYNAMIC MACROMODELS

Edited by

Carl Chiarella
School of Finance and Economics, University of Technology, Sydney, Australia

Reiner Franke
Institute of Monetary Economics, Technical University, Vienna, Austria

Peter Flaschel
Faculty of Economics, Bielefeld University, Bielefeld, Germany

Willi Semmler
Department of Economics, New School University, New York, U.S.A.

ELSEVIER

Amsterdam – Boston – Heidelberg – London – New York – Oxford – Paris
San Diego – San Francisco – Singapore – Sydney – Tokyo

Elsevier
Radarweg 29, PO Box 211, 1000 AE Amsterdam, The Netherlands
The Boulevard, Langford Lane, Kidlington, Oxford OX5 1GB, UK

First edition 2006

Library of Congress Cataloguing-in-Publication Data
A catalog record for this book is available from the Library of Congress

British Library Cataloguing in Publication Data
A catalogue record for this book is available from the British Library

ISBN-13: 978-0-444-52122-4
ISBN-10: 0-444-52122-4
ISBN: 0573-8555 (Series)

For information on all Elsevier publications
visit our website at books.elsevier.com

Printed and bound in The Netherlands

06 07 08 09 10   10 9 8 7 6 5 4 3 2 1

Working together to grow
libraries in developing countries

www.elsevier.com | www.bookaid.org | www.sabre.org

ELSEVIER   BOOK AID International   Sabre Foundation

INTRODUCTION TO THE SERIES

This series consists of a number of hitherto unpublished studies, which are introduced by the editors in the belief that they represent fresh contributions to economic science.

The term 'economic analysis' as used in the title of the series has been adopted because it covers both the activities of the theoretical economist and the research worker.

Although the analytical methods used by the various contributors are not the same, they are nevertheless conditioned by the common origin of their studies, namely theoretical problems encountered in practical research. Since for this reason, business cycle research and national accounting, research work on behalf of economic policy, and problems of planning are the main sources of the subjects dealt with, they necessarily determine the manner of approach adopted by the authors. Their methods tend to be 'practical' in the sense of not being too far remote from application to actual economic conditions. In addition they are quantitative.

It is the hope of the editors that the publication of these studies will help to stimulate the exchange of scientific information and to reinforce international cooperation in the field of economics.

The Editors

CONTENTS

**CHAPTER 3   THREE WAGE-PRICE MACRO MODELS AND
                THEIR CALIBRATION   49**
                Reiner Franke

**CHAPTER 4   THE DECOMPOSITION OF THE
                INFLATION–UNEMPLOYMENT RELATIONSHIP
                BY TIME SCALE USING WAVELETS   93**
                *Marco Gallegati, Mauro Gallegati,
                James B. Ramsey and Willi Semmler*

CHAPTER 5   NEW KEYNESIAN THEORY AND THE NEW PHILLIPS CURVES: A COMPETING APPROACH   113
Peter Flaschel and Ekkehart Schlicht

PART II.   DYNAMIC AD-AS ANALYSIS: QUALITATIVE FEATURES, NUMERICS AND ESTIMATION

CHAPTER 6   KEYNESIAN THEORY AND THE AD–AS FRAMEWORK: A RECONSIDERATION   149
Amitava Krishna Dutt and Peter Skott

CHAPTER 11   A HIGH-DIMENSIONAL MODEL OF REAL-FINANCIAL MARKET INTERACTION: THE CASCADE OF STABLE MATRICES APPROACH   359
Carl Chiarella, Peter Flaschel, Reiner Franke and Willi Semmler

CHAPTER 12   CURRENCY CRISIS, FINANCIAL CRISIS, AND LARGE OUTPUT LOSS   385
Peter Flaschel and Willi Semmler

List of Contributors

Toichiro Asada   Faculty of Economics, Chuo University, Hachioji, Tokyo, Japan

Pu Chen   Faculty of Economics, Bielefeld University, Bielefeld, Germany

Carl Chiarella   School of Finance and Economics, University of Technology, Sydney, Australia

Amitava Krishna Dutt   Department of Economics and Policy Studies, University of Notre Dame, Notre Dame, IN, USA

Peter Flaschel   Faculty of Economics, Bielefeld University, Bielefeld, Germany

Reiner Franke   Institute for Monetary Economics, Technical University, Vienna, Austria

Marco Gallegati   DEA and SIEC, Università Politecnica delle Marche, Ancona, Italy

Mauro Gallegati   DEA and SIEC, Università Politecnica delle Marche, Ancona, Italy

Xue-Zhong He   School of Finance and Economics, University of Technology, Sydney, Australia

Hing Hung   School of Finance and Economics, University of Technology, Sydney, Australia

Hans-Martin Krolzig   Department of Economics, University of Kent, Keynes College, Canterbury, England

James B. Ramsey   Department of Economics, New York University, New York, NY, USA

Ekkehart Schlicht   Department of Economics, Ludwig-Maximilians-University, Munich, Germany

Willi Semmler

Department of Economics and SCEPA, New School for Social Research, New York, NY, USA and Center for Empirical Macroeconomics, Bielefeld University, Germany

Peter Skott

Department of Economics, University of Massachusetts, MA, USA

Wenlang Zhang

Economic Research Division, Research Department, Hong Kong Monetary Authority

CHAPTER 1

Introduction

Carl Chiarella, Peter Flaschel, Reiner Franke and Willi Semmler

This book represents an ongoing research agenda the aim of which is to contribute to the Keynesian paradigm in macroeconomics. A currently dominant research strategy in macroeconomics is based on the dynamic general equilibrium (DGE) model. Its essential features are the assumption of intertemporal optimizing behavior of economic agents, competitive markets and price mediated market clearing through flexible wages and prices.

New Keynesian economics has over recent times, to a large extent, also adopted this framework, even though it makes use of the concepts of monopolistic competition and sticky wages and sticky prices. An excellent example of a fully developed macromodel of this type is the recent work by Woodford, 2003. In contrast to traditional Keynesian macromodels, recent New Keynesian variants also assume dynamically optimizing agents and market clearing.

The research perspective represented by the collection of articles in this book revives the Keynesian perspective. It is well known that the DGE model has not so far been very successful in capturing certain stylized dynamics on labor, product and financial markets. In this book, we attempt to pursue a modeling approach that may help to give a better account of those features. In the current approach we do not assume, as in the perfect competition or monopolistic variants of the DGE model, the clearing of all markets. Although occasionally we assume that some markets may be cleared, for example the financial market, other markets, for example the labor market definitely do not.

In the tradition of Keynesian macroeconomics we stress, more than the DGE paradigm, that macroeconomics should be concerned with the dynamic interaction of the major three markets of modern market economies – the labor market, the product market and the monetary and financial sector. In the interaction of all these three major markets there may be nonlinear feedback mechanisms at work which do not necessarily lead to temporary market clearing

CONTRIBUTIONS TO ECONOMIC ANALYSIS
VOLUME 277   ISSN: 0573-8555
DOI:10.1016/S0573-8555(05)77001-2

and nor, in addition, to convergence to a (unique) steady state growth path. As a further point, the alternative approach, that develops from the paradigm put forward in this book also seeks to contribute to the empirical and quantitative analysis of the working of advanced macroeconomics.

In reference to the aforementioned three major markets, the book is divided into four parts. The first (core) part of the analysis concentrates on the joint role of labor and product markets when the transmission mechanisms from employment to price dynamics on the product market are studied. We thus propose to study wage and price Phillips-curves separately. In order to properly separate the labor and product market effects in the employment–inflation nexus we distinguish between wage and price Phillips-curves and study each separately. In particular we allow for both backward as well as forward-looking expectations, for time-varying labor market institutions and for a time-varying NAIRU. We also consider possible nonlinearities in the relationships, study long-run relationships through an error correction model, and study short-, medium- and long-run relationships by using Wavelet analysis. This is all pursued through empirical estimates and quantitative evaluations using time series data for the US and some Euro-area countries. This provides us with essential insight into the working of the macroeconomic feedback mechanisms further studied in the subsequent parts of the book. Using the information from the estimated characteristics of the labor and the goods market and the wage and price Phillips-curves, we can study the extent to which these mechanisms are stabilizing or destabilizing for the macroeconomy.

In Part II of the book, the dynamics of the second important core sector, the product market, are studied by integrating fully demand side effects – and the feedback channels that they create – into the interaction of the markets for labor and for goods. Here the main question pursued is, whether, when (sluggish) price adjustments occur in the product market, the traditional Keynesian IS curve can consistently be replaced by dynamic AS-AD curves, and can successfully be defended against its earlier criticisms. We also pose the question as to whether the wage and price Phillips-curves of Part I can be consistently integrated into such an AS-AD framework. In this part we also pursue the estimation and numerics of such dynamic AS-AD analysis. We investigate a fairly general Keynesian AS-AD model, with more advanced feedback structures than in the currently fashionable New Keynesian approaches, using both analytical and numerical tools. Our approach is also put to an empirical test by using VAR estimation as well as calibration methods. This helps us to determine the signs and sizes of the parameters that characterize our integrated approaches to labor, product and financial market interactions. Finally an extended model also containing dynamic AD components is calibrated to a number of stylized facts of business cycles.

Part III deals in more detail with the third core sector of modern macroeconomics, the monetary and financial sector and its interaction with the real side, which in Part II is only present by way of the money market and a

Taylor-type interest rate policy rule. We first elaborate on a more differentiated financial sector that is usually represented in an LM schedule of the macroeconomy. We extend the money by stock or equity market flow dynamics, leading to an advanced seven-dimensional (7D) model of the real-financial interaction. However, in this part we not only use a flow approach to the working of risk-bearing financial markets, but also a Tobin-kind stock approach. An asset or portfolio approach is pursued, leading to even higher dimensional dynamic systems, yet confirming the insights gained from the simpler flow approaches. A fairly complete portfolio-based framework is set up thereby. Heterogenous agents, heterogeneous expectations and stochastic factors in the financial sector are also considered when we study the dynamics of such models of the real-financial interaction. Furthermore, this part lays stress on the real-financial interaction with respect to capital accumulation. The focus here is mainly on the theoretical numerical simulation properties of the model. However, an outlook for an empirical framework is also given in this part. On the technical side, this part deals with techniques for local stability analysis and its loss via the so-called Hopf bifurcations in such higher dimensional dynamic models that are an inescapable feature of advanced models of the real-financial interaction.

Part IV studies monetary policy in closed and open economies within the developed framework. Modern macroeconomics nowadays adopts the practice-originating in the work by John Taylor–of replacing the LM schedule by an interest-rate reaction function of the monetary authority. Indirect targeting of inflation rates, through money growth (as in the LM schedule), is thereby replaced by direct inflation targeting using short-term interest rates as monetary instruments. The study of modern monetary policy is pursued in this part of the book by studying the stability/instability implications of the Taylor rule for macroeconomic analysis of closed and open economies. In the final chapter the inflationary process is also studied in a two-country setup where the question can be posed – and is investigated theoretically and numerically–as to whether the international transmission of inflation leads to phase synchronization or not and, should the latter result be obtained, what the reasons are.

Overall, by stressing traditional Keynesian macrodynamics from a modern quantitative and empirical point of view, this book not only revitalizes the framework in a dynamic context of multi-market interactions but also provides an account of the empirical and quantitative relevance of this framework for the new and challenging issues in macroeconomics that are currently under discussion.

Reference

Woodford, M. (2003), *Interest and Prices*, Princeton: Princeton University Press.

PART I
PHILLIPS CURVE APPROACHES AND
THE WAGE–PRICE SPIRAL

CHAPTER 2

Wage–Price Phillips Curves and Macroeconomic Stability: Basic Structural Form, Estimation and Analysis

Peter Flaschel* and Hans-Martin Krolzig

Abstract

In this paper we introduce a small Keynesian model of economic growth, which is centered around two advanced types of Phillips curves, one for money wages and one for prices, both being augmented by perfect myopic foresight and supplemented by a measure of the medium-term inflationary climate updated in an adaptive fashion. The model contains two potentially destabilizing feedback chains, the so-called Mundell and Rose-effects. We estimate parsimonious and congruent Phillips curves for money wages and prices in the US over the past five decades. Using the parameters of the empirical Phillips curves, we show that the growth path of the private sector of the model economy is likely to be surrounded by centrifugal forces. Convergence to this growth path can be generated in two ways: a Blanchard–Katz-type error-correction mechanism in the money-wage Phillips curve or a modified Taylor rule that is augmented by a term, which transmits increases in the wage share (real unit labor costs) to increases in the nominal rate of interest. Thus the model is characterized by local instability of the wage–price spiral, which however can be tamed by appropriate wage or monetary policies. Our empirical analysis finds the error-correction mechanism being ineffective in both Phillips curves, suggesting that the stability of the post-war US macroeconomy originates from the stabilizing role of monetary policy.

*Corresponding author.

CONTRIBUTIONS TO ECONOMIC ANALYSIS
VOLUME 277   ISSN: 0573-8555
DOI:10.1016/S0573-8555(05)77002-4

Keywords: wage and price Phillips curves, real interest effect, real wage effect, instability, Taylor rules

JEL classifications: E24, E31, E32, J30

1. Introduction

1.1. The Phillips curve(s)

Following the seminal work in Phillips (1958) on the relation between unemployment and the rate of change of money-wage rates in the UK, the 'Phillips curve' was to play an important role in macroeconomics during the 1960s and 1970s, and modified so as to incorporate inflation expectations, survived for much longer. The discussion on the proper type and the functional shape of the Phillips curve has never come to a real end and is indeed now at least as lively as it has been at any other time after the appearance of Phillips (1958) seminal paper. Recent examples for this observation are provided by the paper of Gali *et al.*, 2001, where again a new type of Phillips curve is investigated, and the paper by Laxton *et al.*, 1999 on the typical shape of the expectations augmented price inflation Phillips curve. Blanchard and Katz (1999) investigate the role of an error-correction wage share influence theoretically as well as empirically and Plasmans *et al.*, 1999 investigate on this basis the impact of the generosity of the unemployment benefit system on the adjustment speed of money wages with regard to demand pressure in the market for labor.

Much of the literature has converged on the so-called '*New Keynesian Phillips curve*', based on Taylor (1980) and Calvo (1983). Indeed, McCallum (1997) has called it the "*closest thing there is to a standard formulation*". Clarida *et al.* 1999 have used a version of it as the basis for deriving some general principles about monetary policy. However, as has been recently pointed out by Mankiw (2001): "*Although the new Keynesian Phillips curve has many virtues, it also has one striking vice: It is completely at odd with the facts*". The problems arise from the fact that although the price level is sticky in this model, the inflation rate can change quickly. By contrast, empirical analyses of the inflation process (see, *inter alia*, Gordon, 1997) typically give a large role to 'inflation inertia'.

Rarely, however, at least on the theoretical level, is note taken of the fact that there are in principle two relationships of the Phillips curve type involved in the interaction of unemployment and inflation, namely one on the labor market, the Phillips (1958) curve, and one on the market for goods, normally not considered a separate Phillips curve, but merged with the other one by assuming that prices are a constant mark-up on wages or the like, an extreme case of the price Phillips curve that we shall consider in this paper.

For researchers with a background in structural macroeconometric model building it is, however, not at all astonishing to use two Phillips curves in the place of only one in order to model the interacting dynamics of labor and goods market adjustment processes or the wage–price spiral for simplicity. Thus, for example, Fair (2000) has recently reconsidered the debate on the NAIRU from this perspective, though he still uses demand pressure on the market for labor as proxy for that on the market for goods (see Chiarella and Flaschel, 2000 for a discussion of his approach).

In this paper we, by contrast, start from a traditional approach to the discussion of the wage–price spiral, which uses different measures for demand and cost pressure on the market for labor and on the market for goods and which distinguishes between temporary and permanent cost pressure changes. Despite its traditional background – not unrelated however to modern theories of wage and price setting, see Appendices A.2 and A.3 – we are able to show that an important macrodynamic feedback mechanism can be detected in this type of wage–price spiral that has rarely been investigated in the theoretical as well as in the applied macroeconomic literature with respect to its implications for macroeconomic stability. For the US economy, we then show by detailed estimation, using the software package PcGets of Hendry and Krolzig (2001), that this feedback mechanism tends to be a destabilizing one. We finally demonstrate on this basis that a certain error correction term in the money-wage Phillips curve or a Taylor interest rate policy rule that is augmented by a wage gap term can dominate such instabilities when operated with sufficient strength.

1.2. Basic macro feedback chains. A reconsideration

1.2.1. The Mundell effect

The investigation of destabilizing macrodynamic feedback chains has indeed never been at the center of interest of mainstream macroeconomic analysis, though knowledge about these feedback chains dates back to the beginning of dynamic Keynesian analysis. Tobin has presented summaries and modeling of such feedback chains on various occasions (see in particular Tobin, 1975, 1993). The well-known Keynes effect as well as Pigou effect are however often present in macrodynamic analysis, since they have the generally appreciated property of being stabilizing with respect to wage inflation as well as wage deflation. Also well-known, but rarely taken serious, is the so-called Mundell effect based on the impact of inflationary expectations on investment as well as consumption demand. Tobin (1975) was the first who modeled this effect in a 3D dynamic framework (see Scarth, 1996 for a textbook treatment of Tobin's approach). Yet, though an integral part of traditional Keynesian IS-LM-PC analysis, the role of the Mundell is generally played down as for example in Romer (1996, p. 237) where it only appears in the list of problems, but not as part of his presentation of traditional Keynesian theories of fluctuations in his Chapter 5.

Figure 2.1 provides a brief characterization of the destabilizing feedback chain underlying the Mundell effect. We consider here the case of wage and price inflation (though deflation may be the more problematic case, since there is an obvious downward floor to the evolution of the nominal rate of interest and the working of the well-known Keynes effect which, however, in the partial reasoning that follows is kept constant by assumption).

For a given nominal rate of interest, increasing inflation (caused by an increasing activity level of the economy) by definition leads to a decrease of the real rate of interest. This stimulates demand for investment and consumer durables even further and thus leads, via the multiplier process to further increasing economic activity in both the goods and the labor markets, adding further momentum to the ongoing inflationary process. In the absence of ceilings to such an inflationary spiral, economic activity will increase to its limits and generate an ever accelerating inflationary spiral eventually. This standard feedback chain of traditional Keynesian IS-LM-PC analysis is however generally neglected and has thus not really been considered in its interaction with the stabilizing Keynes- and Pigou effect, with works based on the seminal paper of Tobin (1975) being the exception (see Groth, 1993, for a brief survey on this type of literature).

Far more neglected is however a – in principle – fairly obvious real wage adjustment mechanism that was first investigated analytically in Rose (1967) with respect to its local and global stability implications (see also Rose, 1990). Due to this heritage, this type of effect has been called Rose effect in Chiarella and Flaschel (2000), there investigated in its interaction with the Keynes- and the

Figure 2.1.   Destabilizing Mundell effects

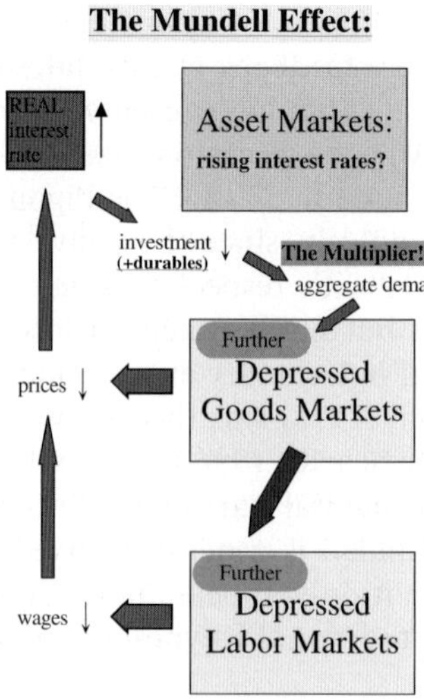

The Mundell Effect:

Mundell effect, and the Metzler inventory accelerator, in a 6D Keynesian model of goods and labor market disequilibrium. In the present paper we intend to present and analyze the working of this effect in a very simple IS growth model – without the LM curve as in Romer (2000) – and thus with a direct interest rate policy in the place of indirect money supply targeting and its use of the Keynes effect (based on stabilizing shifts of the conventional LM-curve). We classify theoretically and estimate empirically the types of Rose effects that are at work, the latter for the case of the US economy.

1.2.2. Stabilizing or destabilizing Rose effects?

Rose effects are present if the income distribution is allowed to enter the formation of Keynesian effective demand and if wage dynamics is distinguished from price dynamics, both aspects of macrodynamics that are generally neglected at least in the theoretical macroeconomic literature. This may explain why Rose effects are rarely present in the models used for policy analysis and policy discussions.

Rose effects are however of great interest and have been present since long – though unnoticed and not in full generality – in macroeconometric model building, where wage and price inflation on the one hand and consumption and investment behavior on the other hand are generally distinguished from each other. Rose effects allow for at least four different cases depending on whether consumption demand responds stronger than investment demand to real wage changes (or vice versa) and whether – broadly speaking – wages are more flexible than prices with respect to the demand pressures on the market for labor and for goods, respectively. The Figures 2.2 and 2.3 present two out of the four possible cases, all based on the assumption that consumption demand depends positively and investment demand negatively on the real wage (or the wage share if technological change is present).

In Figure 2.2 we consider first the case where the real wage dynamic taken by itself is stabilizing. Here we present the case where wages are more flexible with respect to demand pressure (in the market for labor) than prices (with respect to demand pressure in the market for goods) and where investment responds stronger than consumption to changes in the real wage. We consider again the case of inflation. The case of deflation is of course of the same type with all shown arrows simply being reversed. Nominal wages rising faster than prices means that real wages are increasing when activity levels are high. Therefore, investment is depressed more than consumption is increased, giving rise to a decrease in aggregate as well as effective demand. The situation on the market for goods – and on this basis also on the market for labor – is therefore deteriorating, implying that forces come into being that stop the rise in wages and prices eventually and that may – if investigated formally – lead the economy back to the position of normal employment and stable wages and prices.

Figure 2.2.   Normal Rose effects

Figure 2.3.   Adverse Rose effects

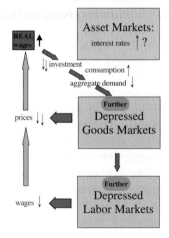

The stabilizing forces just discussed however become destabilizing if price adjustment speeds are reversed and thus prices rising faster than nominal wages (see Figure 2.3). In this case, we get falling real wages and thus – on the basis of the considered propensities to consume and invest with respect to real wage changes – further increasing aggregate and effective demand on the goods market which is transmitted into further rising employment on the market for labor and thus into even faster rising prices and (in weaker form) rising wages. This adverse type of real wage adjustment or simply adverse Rose effect can go on for ever if there is no nonlinearity present that modifies either investment or consumption behavior or wage and price adjustment speeds such that normal Rose effects are established again, though of course supply bottlenecks may modify this simple positive feedback chain considerably.[1]

Since the type of Rose effect depends on the relative size of marginal propensities to consume and to invest and on the flexibility of wages versus that of prices we are confronted with a question that demands for empirical estimation. Furthermore, Phillips curves for wages and prices have to be specified in more detail than discussed so far, in particular due to the fact that also cost pressure and expected cost pressure do matter in them, not only demand pressure on the market for goods and for labor. These specifications will lead to the result that also the degree of short-sightedness of wage earners and of firms will matter in the following discussion of Rose effects. Our empirical findings in this regard will be that wages are considerably more flexible than prices with respect to demand pressure, and workers roughly equally short-sighted as firms with respect to cost pressure. On the basis of the assumption that consumption is more responsive than investment to temporary real wage changes, we then get that all arrows and hierarchies shown in Figure 2.3 will be reversed. We thus get by this twofold change in the Figure 2.3 again *an adverse Rose effect* in the interaction of income distribution dependent changes in goods demand with wage and price adjustment speeds on the market for labor and for goods.

1.3. Outline of the paper

In view of the above hypothesis, the paper is organized as follows. Section 2 presents a simple Keynesian macrodynamic model where advanced wage and price adjustment rules are introduced and in the center of the considered model and where – in addition – the income distribution and the real rate of interest matter in the formation of effective goods demand. We then investigate the stability implications of this macrodynamic model for the case of a stabilizing Rose effect resulting from the dominance of investment behavior in effective

---

[1] The type of Rose effect shown in Figure 2.3 may be considered as the one that characterizes practical macro-wisdom, which generally presumes that prices are more flexible than wages and that IS goods market equilibrium – if at all – depends negatively on real wages. Our empirical findings show that both assumptions are not confirmed, but indeed both reversed by data of the US economy, which taken together however continues to imply that empirical Rose effects are adverse in nature.

demand and the sluggishness of price dynamics and inflationary expectations. Since the steady growth path is found to be unstable even under the joint occurrence of stable Rose and weak Mundell effects, a standard type of interest rate policy rule[2] is therefore subsequently introduced to enforce convergence to the steady state, indeed also for fast revisions of inflationary expectations and thus stronger destabilizing Mundell effects. Section 3 investigates empirically whether the type of Rose effect assumed in Section 2 is really the typical one. We find evidence (in the case of the US economy) that wages are indeed more flexible than prices. Increasing wage flexibility is thus bad for economic stability (while price flexibility is not) when coupled with the observation that consumption demand responds stronger than investment demand to temporary real wage changes.

In Section 4, this type of destabilizing Rose effect is then incorporated into our small macrodynamic model and the question of whether and which type of interest rate policy can stabilize the economy in such a situation is reconsidered. We find that a standard Taylor interest rate rule is not sufficient due to its specific tailoring that only allows to combat the Mundell-type feedback chain – which it indeed can fight successfully. In case of a destabilizing Rose or real wage effect the tailoring of such a Taylor rule must be reflected again in order to find out what type of rule can fight such Rose effects. We here first reintroduce wage share effects considered by Blanchard and Katz (1999) into the money-wage Phillips curve which – when sufficiently strong – will stabilize a system operating under a standard Taylor rule. Alternatively, however, the Taylor rule can be modified to include an income distribution term, which enforces convergence in the case where the wage share effect in the money wage Phillips curve is too weak to guarantee this.

We conclude that the role of income distribution in properly formulated wage–price spirals represents an important topic that is very much neglected in the modern discussion of inflation, disinflation and deflation.

2. A model of the wage–price spiral

This section briefly presents an elaborate form of the wage–price dynamics or the wage–price spiral and a simple theory of effective goods demand, which however gives income distribution a role in the growth dynamics derived from these building blocks. The presentation of this model is completed with respect to the budget equations for the four sectors of the model in the Appendix A.1 to this paper. The wage–price spiral will be estimated, using US data, in Section 3 of the paper.

---

[2] The discussion of such interest rate or Taylor policy rules originates from Taylor (1993), see Taylor (1999a), for a recent debate of such monetary policy rules and Clarida *et al.*, 2000 for an empirical study of Taylor feedback rules in selected OECD countries.

2.1. The wage–price spiral

At the core of the dynamics to be modeled, estimated and analyzed in this and the following sections is the description of the money, wage and price adjustment processes. They are provided by the following Equations (2.1) and (2.2):

$$\hat{w} = \beta_{w_1}(\bar{U}^l - U^l) - \beta_{w_2}(u - u_o) + \kappa_w(\hat{p} + n_x) + (1 - \kappa_w)(\pi + n_x) \tag{2.1}$$

$$\hat{p} = \beta_{p_1}(\bar{U}^c - U^c) + \beta_{p_2}(u - u_o) + \kappa_p(\hat{w} - n_x) + (1 - \kappa_p)\pi \tag{2.2}$$

In these equations for wage inflation $\hat{w} = \dot{w}/w$ and price inflation $\hat{p} = \dot{p}/p$, we denote by U^l and U^c the rate of unemployment of labor and capital, respectively, and by n_x the rate of Harrod-neutral technological change. u is the wage share, $u = wL^d/pY$.

Demand pressure in the market for labor is characterized by deviations of the rate of unemployment U^l from its NAIRU level $\bar{U}^l$. Similarly demand pressure in the market for goods is represented by deviations of the rate of underemployment U^c of the capital stock K from its normal underemployment level $\bar{U}^c$, assumed to be fixed by firms. Wage and price inflation are therefore first of all driven by their corresponding demand pressure terms.

With respect to the role of the wage share u, which augments the Phillips curves by the terms $\beta_{w_2}(u - u_o)$ and $\beta_{p_2}(u - u_o)$, we assume that increasing shares will dampen the evolution of wage inflation and give further momentum to price inflation (see Franke, 2001, for details of the effects of a changing income distribution on demand driven wage and price inflation). As far as the money-wage Phillips curve is concerned, this corresponds to the error-correction mechanism in Blanchard and Katz (1999). In Appendix A.2, we motivate this assumption within a wage-bargaining model. A similar, though less strong formulation has been proposed by Ball and Mofitt (2001), who – based on fairness considerations – integrate the difference between productivity growth and an average of past real wage growth in a wage-inflation Phillips curve.

In addition to demand pressure we have also cost-pressure terms in the laws of motions for nominal wages and prices, of crossover type and augmented by productivity change in the case of wages and diminished by productivity change in the case of prices. As the wage–price dynamics are formulated we assume that myopic perfect foresight prevails, of workers with respect to their measure of cost pressure, $\hat{p}$, and of firms with respect to wage pressure, $\hat{w}$. In this respect we follow the rational expectations school and disregard model-inconsistent expectations with respect to short-run inflation rates. Yet, in the present framework, current inflation rates are not the only measuring root for cost pressure, so they enter wage and price inflation only with weight $\kappa_w \in [0, 1]$ and $\kappa_p \in [0, 1]$, respectively, and $\kappa_w\kappa_p < 1$. In addition, both workers and firms (or at least one of them) look at the inflationary climate surrounding the perfectly foreseen current inflation rates.

A novel element in such cost-pressure terms is here given by the term π, representing the inflationary climate in which current inflation is embedded. Since the inflationary climate envisaged by economic agents changes sluggishly, information about macroeconomic conditions diffuses slowly through the economy (see Mankiw and Reis, 2002), wage and price are set staggered (see Taylor, 1999b), it is not unnatural to assume that agents, in the light of past inflationary experience, update π by an adaptive rule. In the theoretical model,[3] we assume that the medium-run inflation beliefs are updated adaptively in the standard way:

$$\dot{\pi} = \beta_{\pi}(\hat{p} - \pi) \tag{2.3}$$

In two Appendices A.2 and A.3 we provide some further justifications for the two Phillips curves here assumed to characterize the dynamics of the wage and the price level. Note that the inflationary climate expression has often been employed in applied work by including lagged inflation rates in price Phillips curves, see Fair (2000) for example. Here however it is justified from the theoretical perspective, separating temporary from permanent effects, where temporary changes in both price and wage inflation are even perfectly foreseen. We show in this respect in Section 4 that the interdependent wage and price Phillips curves can however be solved for wage and price inflation explicitly, giving rise to two reduced-form expressions where the assumed perfect foresight expressions do not demand for forward induction.

For the theoretical investigation, the dynamical Equations (2.1)–(2.3) representing the laws of motion of w, p and π are part of a complete growth model to be supplemented by simple expressions for production, consumption and investment demand and – due to the latter – also by a law of motion for the capital stock. These equations will allow the discussion of the so-called Mundell and Rose effects in the simplest way possible and are thus very helpful in isolating these effects from other important macrodynamic feedback chains, which are not the subject of this paper. The econometric analysis to be presented in the following section will focus on the empirical counterparts of the Phillips curves (2.1) and (2.2) while conditioning on the other macroeconomic variables which enter these equations.

2.2. Technology

In this and the next subsection we complete our model of the wage–price spiral in the simplest way possible to allow for the joint occurrence of Mundell and Rose effects in the considered economy.

---

[3] In the empirical part of the paper we will simplify these calculations further by measuring the inflationary climate variable π as a 12 quarter moving average of $\hat{p}$.

For the sake of simplicity we employ in this paper a fixed proportions technology:[4]

$$y^p = Y^p/K = \text{const.}, \quad x = Y/L^d, \quad \hat{x} = \dot{x}/x = n_x = \text{const.}$$

On the basis of this, the rates of unemployment of labor and capital can be defined as follows:

$$U^l = \frac{L - L^d}{L} = 1 - \frac{Y}{xL} = 1 - yk$$

$$U^c = \frac{Y^p - Y}{Y^p} = 1 - \frac{Y}{Y^p} = 1 - y/y^p$$

where y denotes the output–capital ratio Y/K and $k = K/(xL)$ a specific measure of capital intensity or the full employment capital–output ratio. We assume Harrod-neutral technological change: $\hat{y}^p = 0, \hat{x} = n_x = \text{const.}$, with a given potential output–capital ratio y^p and labor productivity $x = Y/L^d$ growing at a constant rate. We have to use k in the place of K/L, the actual full employment capital intensity, in order to obtain state variables that allow for a steady state later on.

2.3. Aggregate goods demand

As far as consumption is concerned we assume Kaldorian differentiated saving habits of the classical type ($s_w = 1 - c_w = 1 - c \geqslant 0, s_c = 1$), i.e., real consumption is given by:

$$C = cuY = c\omega L^d, \quad u = \omega/x, \quad \omega = w/p \quad \text{the real wage} \tag{2.4}$$

and thus solely dependent on the wage share u and economic activity Y. For the investment behavior of firms we assume

$$\frac{I}{K} = i((1 - u)y - (r - \pi)) + n, \quad y = \frac{Y}{K}, \quad n = \hat{L} + \hat{x} = n + n_x \quad \text{trend growth} \tag{2.5}$$

The rate of investment is therefore basically driven by the return differential between $\rho = (1 - u)y$, the rate of profit of firms and $r - \pi$, the real rate of interest on long-term bonds (consols), only considered in its relation to the budget restrictions of the four sectors of the model (workers, asset-holders, firms and the government) in Appendix A.1 to this paper.[5]

---

[4] We neglect capital stock depreciation in this paper.

[5] We consider the long-term rate r as determinant of investment behavior in this paper, but neglect here the short-term rate and its interaction with the long-term rate – as it is for example considered in Blanchard and Fisher (1999, Section 10.4) – in order to keep the model concentrated on the discussion of Mundell and Rose effects. We thus abstract from dynamical complexities caused by the term structure of interest rates. Furthermore, we do not consider a climate expression for the evolution of nominal interest, in contrast to our treatment of inflation, in order to restrict the dynamics to dimension 3.

This financial asset is needed for the generation of Mundell (or real rate of interest) effects in the model, which as we will show later can be neutralized by a Taylor-rule.

Besides consumption and investment demand we also consider the goods demand G of the government where we however for simplicity assume $g = G/K$ =const., since fiscal policy is not a topic of the present paper.

2.4. The laws of motion

Due to the assumed demand behavior of households, firms and the government we have as representation of goods–market equilibrium in per unit of capital form $(y = Y/K)$:

$$cuy + i((1 - u)y - (r - \pi)) + n + g = y \tag{2.6}$$

and as law of motion for the full employment capital–output ratio $k = K/(xL)$:

$$\hat{k} = i((1 - u)y - (r - \pi)) \tag{2.7}$$

Equations (2.1) and (2.2) furthermore give the two laws of motion (2.8) and (2.9) in reduced form, with $\kappa = (1 - \kappa_w \kappa_p)^{-1}$:

$$\hat{u} = \kappa[(1 - \kappa_p)\{\beta_{w_1}(\bar{U}^l - U^l) - \beta_{w_2}(u - u_o)\}$$
$$- (1 - \kappa_w)\{\beta_{p_1}(\bar{U}^c - U^c) + \beta_{p_2}(u - u_o)\}] \tag{2.8}$$

$$\hat{p} = \pi + \kappa[\beta_{p_1}(\bar{U}^c - U^c) + \beta_{p_2}(u - u_o) + \kappa_p\{\beta_{w_1}(\bar{U}^l - U^l) - \beta_{w_2}(u - u_o)\}] \tag{2.9}$$

The first equation describes the law of motion for the wage share u, which depends positively on the demand pressure items on the market for labor (for $\kappa_p < 1$) and negatively on those of the market for goods (for $\kappa_w < 1$).[6] The second equation is a reduced form price Phillips curve, which combines all demand pressure related items on labor and goods market in a positive fashion (for $\kappa_p > 0$). This equation is far more advanced than the usual price Phillips curve of the literature.[7] Inserted into the adaptive revision rule for the inflationary climate variable it provides as further law of motion the dynamic equation:

---

[6] The law of motion (2.8) for the wage share u is obtained by making use in addition of the following reduced form equation for $\hat{w}$, which is obtained simultaneously with the one for $\hat{p}$ and of a very similar type:

$$\hat{w} = \pi + \kappa[\beta_{w_1}(\bar{U}^l - U^l) - \beta_{w_2}(u - u_o) + \kappa_w\{\beta_{p_1}(\bar{U}^c - U^c) + \beta_{p_2}(u - u_o)\}]$$

[7] Note however that this reduced form Phillips curve becomes formally identical to the one normally investigated empirically (see Fair, 2000 for example) if $\beta_{w_2}, \beta_{p_2} = 0$ holds and if Okun's law is assumed to hold (i.e., the utilization rates of labor and capital are perfectly correlated). However, even then the estimated coefficients are far away from representing labor market characteristics solely.

$$\dot{\pi} = \beta_{\pi}\kappa[\beta_{p_1}(\bar{U}^c - U^c) + \beta_{p_2}(u - u_o) + \kappa_p\{\beta_{w_1}(\bar{U}^l - U^l) - \beta_{w_2}(u - u_o)\}]$$

$$(2.10)$$

We assume for the time being that the interest rate r on long-term bonds is kept fixed at its steady-state value r^o and then get that Equations (2.7), (2.8) and (2.10), supplemented by the static goods market equilibrium Equation (2.5), provide an autonomous system of differential equations in the state variables u, k and π.

It is obvious from Equation (2.8) that the error correction terms β_{w_2}, β_{p_2} exercise a stabilizing influence on the adjustment of the wage share (when this dynamic is considered in isolation). The other two β-terms (the demand pressure terms), however, do not give rise to a clear-cut result for the wage share subdynamic. In fact, they can be reduced to the following expression as far as the influence of economic activity, as measured by y, is concerned (neglecting irrelevant constants):

$$\kappa[(1 - \kappa_p)\beta_{w_1}k - (1 - \kappa_w)\beta_{p_1}/y^p]y$$

In the case where output y depends negatively on the wage share u we thus get partial stability for the wage share adjustment (as in the case of the error correction terms) if and only if the term in square brackets is negative (which is the case for β_{w_1} sufficiently large). We have called this a normal Rose effect in Section 1, which in the present case derives – broadly speaking – from investment sensitivity being sufficiently high and wage flexibility dominance.

In the case where output y depends positively on u, where therefore consumption is dominating investment with respect to the influence of real wage changes, we need a large β_{p_1}, and thus a sufficient degree of price flexibility relative to the degree of wage flexibility, to guarantee stability from the partial perspective of real wage adjustments. For these reasons we will therefore call the condition[8]

$$\alpha = (1 - \kappa_p)\beta_{w_1}k_o - (1 - \kappa_w)\beta_{p_1}/y^p \genfrac{}{}{0pt}{}{<}{>} 0 \rightleftharpoons \begin{Bmatrix} \text{normal} \\ \text{adverse} \end{Bmatrix} \text{Rose effects} \quad (\alpha)$$

the critical or α condition for the occurrence of *normal (adverse) Rose effects*, in the case where the flexibility of wages (of prices) with respect to demand pressure is dominating the wage–price spiral (including the weights concerning the relevance of myopic perfect foresight). In the next section we will provide estimates for this critical condition in order to see which type of Rose effect

---

[8] Note here that $1/k = xL/K$ and $y^p = Y^p/K$ are approximately of the same size, since full employment output and full capacity output generally do not depart too much from each other.

might have been the one involved in the business fluctuations of the US economy in the post-war period.

Note finally with respect to Equations (2.9) and (2.10) that $\dot{\pi}$ always depends positively on y and thus on π, since y always depends positively on π. This latter dependence of accelerator type as well as the role of wage share adjustments will be further clarified in the next subsection.

2.5. The effective demand function

The goods–market equilibrium condition (2.6) can be solved for y and gives

$$y = \frac{n + g - i(r_o - \pi)}{(1 - u)(1 - i) + (1 - c)u} = \frac{n + g + i(\pi - r_o)}{1 - i + (i - c)u} \tag{2.11}$$

We assume $i \in (0, 1), c \in (0, 1)$ and consider only cases where $u < 1$ is fulfilled which, in particular, is true close to the steady state. This implies that the output–capital ratio y depends positively on π. However, whether y is increasing or decreasing in the labor share u depends on the relative size of c and i.

In the case of $c = 1$, we get the following dependencies:

$$y_u = \frac{(n + g - i(r_o - \pi))(i - 1)}{[(1 - u)(1 - i)]^2} = \frac{y}{1 - u}$$
$$\rho_u = -y - (1 - u)y_u = 0$$

As long as y is positive and u smaller than 1, we get a positive dependence of y on u. The rate of profit ρ is independent of the wage share u due to a balance between the negative cost and the positive demand effect of the wage share u.[9]

Otherwise, i.e., if the consumption propensity out of wage income is strictly less than 1, $c < 1$, we have that

$$y_u = \frac{(c - i)y}{(1 - i)(1 - u) + (1 - c)u} \geqslant 0 \quad \text{if} \quad c \geqslant i \tag{2.12}$$
$$\rho_u = -y + (1 - u)y_u < 0 \tag{2.13}$$

where the result for the rate of profit $\rho = (1 - u)y$ of firms follows from the fact that y_u clearly is smaller than $y/(1 - u)$.

Therefore, if a negative relationship between the rate of return and the wage share is desirable (given the investment function defined in Equation (2.7)), then

---

[9] We note that the investment function can be modified in various ways, for example by inserting the normal-capacity-utilization rate of profit $\rho^n = (1 - u)(1 - \bar{U}^c)y^p$ into it in the place of the actual rate ρ, which then always gives rise to a negative effect of u on this rate ρ^n and also makes subsequent calculations simpler. Note here also that we only pursue local stability analysis in this paper and thus work for reasons of simplicity with linear functions throughout.

for the workers consumption function, the assumption $c < 1$ is required: $C/K = cuy, c \in (0, 1)$.

2.6. Stability issues

We consider in this subsection the fully interacting, but somewhat simplified 3D growth dynamics of the model, which consist the following three laws of motion (2.14)–(2.16) for the wage share u, the full employment capital–output ratio k and the inflationary climate π:[10]

$$\hat{u} = \kappa[(1 - \kappa_p)(\beta_{w_1}(\bar{U}^l - U^l) - \beta_{w_2}(u - u_o)) - (1 - \kappa_w)\beta_{p_1}(\bar{U}^c - U^c)] \qquad (2.14)$$

$$\hat{k} = i((1 - u)y - (r - \pi)) \qquad (2.15)$$

$$\dot{\pi} = \beta_\pi \kappa[\beta_{p_1}(\bar{U}^c - U^c) + \kappa_p(\beta_{w_1}(\bar{U}^l - U^l) - \beta_{w_2}(u - u_o))] \qquad (2.16)$$

where $U^l = 1 - yk$ and $U^c = 1 - y/y^p$

During this section, we will impose the following set of assumptions:[11]

(A.1) The marginal propensity to consume is strictly less than the one to invest: $0 < c < i$ (the case of a profit-led aggregate demand situation or briefly of a profit-led economy).

(A.2) The money-wage Phillips curve is not error-correcting w.r.t. the wage share: $\beta_{w_2} = 0$.

(A.3) The parameters satisfy that $u_o \in (0, 1)$ and $\pi_o \geqslant 0$ hold in the steady state.

(A.4a) The nominal interest rate r is constant: $r = r_o$ (the case of an interest rate peg).

(A.4b) There is an interest rate policy rule in operation that is of an active type: $r = \rho_o + \pi + \beta_r(\pi - \bar{\pi})$ with $\beta_r > 0$, ρ_o the steady-state real rate of interest, and $\bar{\pi}$ the inflation target.

Assumption (A.1) implies that (i) $y_u < 0$ as in (2.12), (ii) $U_u^l > 0$ and $U_u^c > 0$ since the negative effect of real wage increases on investment outweighs the positive effect on consumption, and (iii) $\rho_u < 0$ with $\rho = (1 - u)y$ (the alternative scenario with $c > i$ is considered in Section 4). (A.2) excludes the potentially stabilizing effects of the Blanchard–Katz-type error-correction mechanism (i.e., will be discussed in Section 4.2 for the money-wage Phillips curve). (A.3) ensures the existence of an interior steady state. Assumptions (A.4a) and (A.4b) stand for

---

[10] We therefore now assume – for reasons of simplicity – that $\beta_{p_2} = 0$ holds throughout, a not very restrictive assumption in the light of what is shown in the remainder of this paper. Note here that two of the three laws of motion (for the wage share and the inflationary climate) are originating from the wage–price spiral considered in this paper, while the third one (for the capital–output ratio) represents by and large the simplest addition possible to arrive at a model on the macro level that can be considered complete.

[11] In Section 4 we will relax these assumptions in various ways.

different monetary regimes and determine the nominal interest rate in (2.15) and in the algebraic equation for the effective demand which supplements the 3D dynamics.

For the neutral monetary policy defined in (A.4a), we have that output y is an increasing function of the inflationary climate π:

$$y = \frac{n + g + i(\pi - r_o)}{(1 - u)(1 - i) + (1 - c)u} \tag{2.17}$$

By contrast, assumption (A.4b), the adoption of a Taylor interest rate policy rule, implies that the static equilibrium condition is given by

$$y = \frac{n + g - i(\rho_o + \beta_r(\pi - \bar{\pi}))}{(1 - i)(1 - u) + (1 - c)u} \tag{2.18}$$

which implies a negative dependence of output y on the inflationary climate π.[12]

Proposition 1. (The unique interior steady-state position). *Under assumptions (A.1)–(A.4a), the interior steady state of the dynamics (2.14)–(2.16) is uniquely determined and given by*

$$y_o = (1 - \bar{U}^c)y^p, \quad k_o = (1 - \bar{U}^l)/y_o, \quad u_o = 1/c + (n + g)/y_o,$$
$$\rho_o = (1 - u_o)y_o$$

Steady-state inflation in the constant nominal interest regime (A.4a) is given by:

$$\pi_o = r_o - (1 - u_o)y_o$$

and under the interest rule (A.4b) we have that:

$$\pi_o = \bar{\pi}, \quad r_o = \rho_o + \bar{\pi}$$

holds true.

The proof of Proposition 1 is straightforward. The proofs of the following propositions are in the mathematical Appendix A.5. ■

The steady-state solution with constant nominal interest rate (A.4a) shows that the demand side has no influence on the long-run output-capital ratio, but influences the income distribution and the long-run rate of inflation. In the case of an adjusting nominal rate of interest (A.4b), the steady-state rate of inflation is determined by the monetary authority and its steering of the

---

[12] Note that our formulation of a Taylor rule ignores the influence of a variable representing the output gap. Including the capacity utilization gap of firms would however only add a positive constant to the denominator of the fraction just considered and would therefore not alter our results in a significant way. Allowing for the output gap in addition to the inflation gap may also be considered as some sort of double counting.

nominal rate of interest, while the steady-state rate of interest is obtained from the steady rate of return of firms and the inflationary target of the central bank.

Proposition 2. (Private sector instability). *Under assumptions* (A.1)–(A.4a), *the interior steady state of the dynamics* (2.14)–(2.16) *is essentially repelling (exhibits at least one positive root), even for small parameters* β_{p_1} *and* β_π.

A normal Rose effect (stability by wage flexibility and instability by price flexibility in the considered case $c < i$) and a weak Mundell effect (sluggish adjustment of prices and of the inflationary climate variable) are thus not sufficient to generate convergence to the steady state.[13]

Proposition 3. (Interest rate policy and stability). *Under assumptions* (A.1)–(A.3), *the interest rule in* (A.4b) *implies asymptotic stability of the steady state for any given adjustment speeds* $\beta_\pi > 0$ *if the price flexibility parameter* β_{p_1} *is sufficiently small.*

As long as price flexibility does not give rise to an adverse Rose effect (dominating the trace of the Jacobian of the dynamics at the steady state), we get convergence to the steady state by monetary policy and the implied adjustments of the long-term real rate of interest $r - \pi$ which increase r beyond its steady-state value whenever the inflationary climate exceeds the target value $\bar{\pi}$ and *vice versa*. The present stage of the investigation therefore suggests that wage flexibility (relative to price flexibility), coupled with the assumption $c > i$ and an active interest rate policy rule is supporting macroeconomic stability. The question, however, is whether this is the situation that characterizes factual macroeconomic behavior.

An adverse Rose effect (due to price flexibility and $c < i$) would dominate the stability implications of the considered dynamics: the system would then lose its stability by way of a Hopf-bifurcation when the reaction parameter β_r of the interest rate rule is made sufficiently small. However, we will find in the next section that wages are more flexible than prices with respect to demand pressure on their respective markets. We thus have in the here considered case $c < i$ that the Rose effect can be neglected (as not endangering economic stability), while the destabilizing Mundell effect can indeed be tamed by an appropriate monetary policy rule.

---

[13] In the mathematical Appendix A.5, it is shown that the carrier of the Mundell effect, $\hat{\pi}_\pi$, will always give the wrong sign to the determinant of the Jacobian of the dynamics at the steady state.

3. Estimating the US wage–price spiral

In this section we analyze US post-war data to provide an estimate of the two Phillips curves that form the core of the dynamical model introduced in Section 2. Using *PcGets* (see Hendry and Krolzig, 2001), we start with a general, dynamic, unrestricted, linear model of $\hat{w} - \pi_t$ and $\hat{p} - \pi_t$ which is conditioned on the explanatory variables predicted by the theory and use the general-to-specific approach to find an undominated parsimonious representation of the structure of the data. From these estimates, the long-run Phillips curves can be obtained which describe the total effects of variables and allow a comparison to the reduced form of the wage–price spiral in (2.1) and (2.2).

3.1. Data

The data are taken from the Federal Reserve Bank of St. Louis (see http://www.stls.frb.org/fred). The data are quarterly, seasonally adjusted and are all available from 1948:1 to 2001:2. Except for the unemployment rates of the factors labor, U^l, and capital, U^c, the log of the series are used (see Table 2.1).

For reasons of simplicity as well as empirical reasons, we measure the inflationary climate surrounding the current working of the wage–price spiral by an unweighted 12-month moving average:

$$\pi_t = \frac{1}{12} \sum_{j=1}^{12} \Delta p_{t-j}$$

Table 2.1. Data

Variable	Transformation	Mnemonic	Description of the Untransformed Series
U^l	UNRATE/100	UNRATE	Unemployment rate
U^c	1-CUMFG/100	CUMFG	Capacity utilization: manufacturing. Percent of capacity
w	log(COMPNFB)	COMPNFB	Nonfarm business sector: compensation per hour, 1992 = 100
p	log(GDPDEF)	GDPDEF	Gross national product: implicit price deflator, 1992 = 100
$y - l^d$	log(OPHNFB)	OPHNFB	Nonfarm business sector: output per hour of all persons, 1992 = 100
u	$\log\left(\frac{COMPRNFB}{OPHNFB}\right)$	COMPRNFB	Nonfarm business sector: real compensation per hour, 1992 = 100

Note: w, p, l^d, y and u now denote the logs of wages, prices, employed labor, output and the wage share (1992 = 1) so that first differences can be used to denote their rates of growth. Similar results are obtained when measuring the wage share as unit labor costs (nonfarm business sector) adjusted by the GNP deflator.

This moving average provides a simple approximation of the adaptive expectations mechanism (2.3) considered in Section 2, which defines the inflation climate as an infinite, weighted moving average of past inflation rates with declining weights. The assumption here is that people apply a certain window (12 quarters) to past observations, here thus of size 12, without significantly discounting their observations.

The data to be modeled are plotted in Figure 2.4. The estimation sample is 1955:1–2001:2, which excludes the Korean war. The number of observations used for the estimation is 186.

3.2. The money-wage Phillips curve

Let us first provide an estimate of the wage Phillips curve (2.1) of this paper: We model wage inflation in deviation from the inflation climate, $\Delta w - \pi$, conditional on its own past, the history of price inflation, $\Delta p - \pi$, measured by the same type of deviations, overall labor productivity growth, $\Delta y - \Delta l^d$, the unemployment rate, U^l, and the log of the labor share, $u = w + l^d - p - y$, by means of the Equation (2.19):

$$\Delta w_t - \pi_t = v_w + \sum_{j=1}^{5} \gamma_{wwj}(\Delta w_{t-j} - \pi_{t-j}) + \sum_{j=1}^{5} \gamma_{wpj}(\Delta p_{t-j} - \pi_{t-j})$$

$$+ \sum_{j=1}^{5} \gamma_{wxj}(\Delta y_{t-j} - \Delta l_{t-j}^d) + \sum_{j=1}^{5} \gamma_{wuj} U_{t-j}^l + \alpha_w u_{t-1} + \varepsilon_{wt} \qquad (2.19)$$

Figure 2.4.   Price and wage inflation, unemployment and the wage share

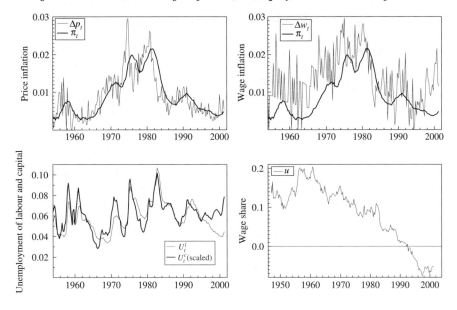

where ε_{wt} is a white noise process. The general model explains 43.7% of the variation of $\Delta w_t - \pi_t$ reducing the standard error in the prediction of quarterly changes of the wage level to 0.467%:

RSS   0.003551 $\hat{\sigma}$ 0.004653 R^2 0.4373 $\bar{R}^2$ 0.3653

ln L 1011   AIC -10.6298 HQ -10.4752 SC -10.2482

Almost all of the estimated coefficients of (2.19) are statistically insignificant and therefore not reported here. This highlights the idea of the general-to-specific (*Gets*) approach (see Hendry, 1995, for an overview of the underlying methodology) of selecting a more compact model, which is nested in the general but provides an improved statistical description of the economic reality by reducing the complexity of the model and checking the contained information. The *PcGets* reduction process is designed to ensure that the reduced model will convey all the information embodied in the unrestricted model (which is here provided by Equation (2.19)). This is achieved by a joint selection and diagnostic testing process: starting from the unrestricted, congruent general model, standard testing procedures are used to eliminate statistically insignificant variables, with diagnostic tests checking the validity of reductions, ensuring a congruent final selection.

In the case of the general wage Phillips curve in (2.19), *PcGets* reduces the number of coefficients from 22 to only 3, resulting in a parsimonious money-wage Phillips curve, which just consists of the demand pressure U^l_{-1}, the cost pressure $\Delta p_{t-1} - \pi_{t-1}$ and a constant (representing the integrated effect of labor productivity and the NAIRU on the deviation of nominal wage growth from the inflationary climate),[14]

$$\Delta w_t - \pi_t = \underset{(0.00163)}{0.0158} + \underset{(0.101)}{0.266}(\Delta p_{t-1} - \pi_{t-1}) - \underset{(0.0271)}{0.193}\, U^l_{t-1} \qquad (2.20)$$

without losing any relevant information:

RSS   0.003941 $\hat{\sigma}$ 0.004641 R^2 0.3755 $\bar{R}^2$ 0.3686

ln L 1001   AIC -10.7297 HQ -10.7087 SC -10.6777

An F-test of the specific against the general rejects only at a marginal rejection probability of 0.5238. The properties of the estimated model (2.20) are illustrated in Figure 2.5. The first graph (upper left-hand side) shows the fit of the model over time; the second graph (upper right-hand side) plots the fit against the actual values of $\Delta w_t - \pi_t$; the second graph (lower left-hand side) plots the residuals and the last graph (lower right-hand side) the squared residuals. The diagnostic test results shown in Table 2.2 confirm that (2.20) is a valid congruent reduction of the general model in (2.19).

---

[14] We have $E(\hat{p} - \pi) = 0$, $E(\hat{w} - \pi) = 0.0045$ and $\bar{U}^l = E(U^l) = 0.058$.

Figure 2.5. Money-wage Phillips curve

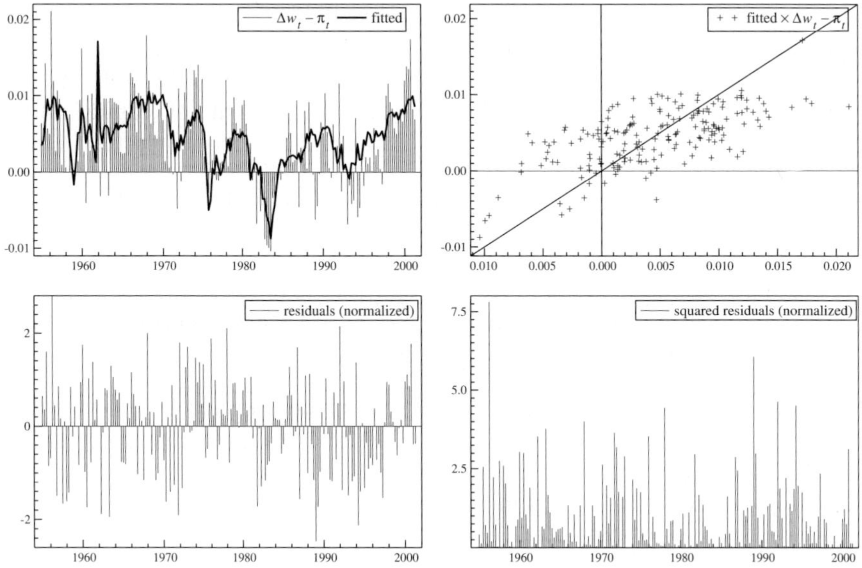

Table 2.2. Diagnostics

Diagnostic Test	Wage Phillips Curve		Price Phillips Curve	
	2.19	2.20	2.21	2.22
$F_{\text{Chow}(1978:2)}$	0.993 [0.5161]	0.866 [0.7529]	0.431 [0.9999]	0.421 [1.0000]
$F_{\text{Chow}(1996:4)}$	0.983 [0.4829]	0.771 [0.7315]	0.635 [0.8672]	0.551 [0.9288]
$\chi^2_{\text{normality}}$	0.710 [0.7012]	0.361 [0.8347]	0.141 [0.9322]	0.483 [0.7856]
$F_{\text{AR}(1-4)}$	1.915 [0.1105]	1.276 [0.2810]	2.426 [0.0503]	1.561 [0.1869]
$F_{\text{ARCH}(1-4)}$	1.506 [0.2030]	0.940 [0.4421]	1.472 [0.2133]	3.391 [0.0107]
F_{hetero}	0.615 [0.9634]	1.136 [0.3411]	0.928 [0.6072]	1.829 [0.0346]

Note: Reported are the test statistic and the marginal rejection probability.

With respect to the theoretical wage Phillips curve (2.1)

$$\hat{w} = \beta_{w_1}(\bar{U}^l - U^l) - \beta_{w_2}(u - u_o) + \kappa_w(\hat{p} + n_x) + (1 - \kappa_w)(\pi + n_x)$$

we therefore obtain the quantitative expression

$$\hat{w} = 0.0158 - 0.193U^l + 0.266\hat{p} + 0.734\pi$$

We notice that the wage share and labor productivity do play no role in this specification of the money-wage Phillips curve. The result on the influence of the wage share is in line with the result obtained by Blanchard and Katz (1999) for the US economy.

3.3. The price Phillips curve

Let us next provide an estimate of the price Phillips curve (2.2) for the US economy. We now model price inflation in deviation from the inflation climate, $\Delta p - \pi$, conditional on its own past, the history of wage inflation, $\Delta w - \pi$, overall labor productivity growth, $\Delta y - \Delta l^d$, the degree of capital under-utilization, U^c by means of the Equation (2.21), and the error correction term, u:

$$\Delta p_t - \pi_t = v_p + \sum_{j=1}^{5} \gamma_{ppj}(\Delta p_{t-j} - \pi_{t-j}) + \sum_{j=1}^{5} \gamma_{pwj}(\Delta w_{t-j} - \pi_{t-j})$$
$$+ \sum_{j=1}^{5} \gamma_{pyj}(\Delta y_{t-j} - \Delta l^d_{t-j}) + \sum_{j=1}^{5} \gamma_{puj} U^c_t + \alpha_p u_{t-1} + \varepsilon_{pt} \qquad (2.21)$$

where ε_{pt} is a white noise process. The general unrestricted model shows no indication of misspecification (see Table 2.2) and explains a substantial fraction (63.8%) of inflation variability. Also note that the standard error of the price Phillips curve is just half the standard error in the prediction of changes in the wage level, namely 0.259%:

RSS	0.001072	$\hat{\sigma}$	0.002589	R^2	0.6376	$\bar{R}^2$	0.5810
ln L	1122	AIC	−11.7843	HQ	−11.6015	SC	−11.3334

There is however a huge outlier ($\hat{\varepsilon}_{pt} > 3\hat{\sigma}$) associated with the oil price shock in 1974 (3) so a centered impulse dummy, I(1974:3), was included.

Here, the model reduction process undertaken by *PcGets* limits the number of coefficients to 9 (while starting again with 22) and results in the following price Phillips curve:

$$\Delta p_t - \pi_t = \underset{(0.0011)}{0.00463} + \underset{(0.0413)}{0.12}(\Delta w_{t-1} - \pi_{t-1}) + \underset{(0.0397)}{0.0896}(\Delta w_{t-3} - \pi_{t-3})$$
$$+ \underset{(0.0691)}{0.254}(\Delta p_{t-1} - \pi_{t-1}) + \underset{(0.0653)}{0.196}(\Delta p_{t-4} - \pi_{t-4})$$
$$- \underset{(0.0634)}{0.18}(\Delta p_{t-5} - \pi_{t-5}) - \underset{(0.0232)}{0.0467}(\Delta y_{t-1} - \Delta l^d_{t-1})$$
$$- \underset{(0.00551)}{0.0287} U^c_{t-1} + \underset{(0.00262)}{0.00988} I(1974:3)_t$$

$$(2.22)$$

RSS	0.001161	$\hat{\sigma}$	0.002562	R^2	0.6074	$\bar{R}^2$	0.5897
ln L	1114	AIC	−11.8870	HQ	−11.8238	SC	−11.7309

The reduction is accepted at a marginal rejection probability of 0.7093. The fit of the model and the plot of the estimation errors are displayed in Figure 2.6.

Figure 2.6.   Price Phillips curve

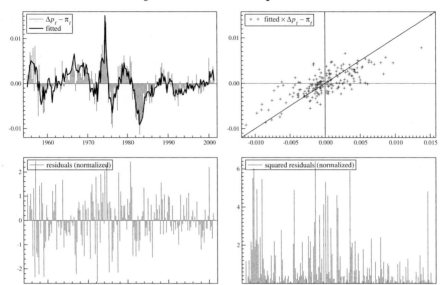

The long-run price Phillips curve implied by (2.22) is given by:

$$\Delta p - \pi = \underset{(0.0016)}{0.00634} + \underset{(0.0608)}{0.286}(\Delta w - \pi) - \underset{(0.0305)}{0.064}(\Delta y - \Delta l^d) - \underset{(0.00795)}{0.0393}\, U^c$$
$$+ \underset{(0.00366)}{0.0135}\, I(1974:3) \tag{2.23}$$

With respect to the theoretical price Phillips curve

$$\hat{p} = \beta_{p_1}(\bar{U}^c - U^c) + \beta_{p_2}(u - u_o) + \kappa_p(\hat{w} - n_x) + (1 - \kappa_p)\pi$$

we therefore obtain the quantitative expression

$$\hat{p} = 0.006 - 0.039\, U^c + 0.286\hat{w} + 0.714\pi$$

where we ignore the dummy and the productivity term in the long-run Phillips curve.[15] We notice that the wage share and labor productivity do again play no role in this specification of the money-wage Phillips curve. The result that demand pressure matters more in the labor market than in the goods market is

---

[15] From the perspective of the theoretical equation just shown this gives by calculating the mean of U^c the values $\bar{U}^c = 0.18, n_x = 0.004$.

in line with what is observed in Carlin and Soskice (1990, Section 18.3.1), and the result that firms are (slightly) more short-sighted than workers may be due to the smaller importance firms attach to past observations of wage inflation.

3.4. System results

So far we have modeled the wage and price dynamics of the system by analyzing one equation at a time. In the following we check for the simultaneity of the innovations to the price and wage inflation equations. The efficiency of a single-equation model reduction approach as applied in the previous subsection depends on the absence of instantaneous causality between $\Delta p_t - \pi_t$ and $\Delta w_t - \pi_t$ (see Krolzig, 2003). This requires the diagonality of the variance–covariance matrix Σ when the two Phillips curves are collected to the system

$$z_t = \sum_{j=1}^{5} A_j z_{t-j} + Bq_t + \varepsilon_t \tag{2.24}$$

which represents $z_t = (\Delta p_t - \pi_t, \Delta w_t - \pi_t)'$ as a fifth-order vector autoregressive (VAR) process with the vector of the exogenous variables $q_t = (1, U_{t-1}^c, U_{t-1}^l, \Delta y_{t-1} - \Delta l_{t-1}^d, I(1974{:}3))'$ and the null-restrictions found by *PcGets* being imposed. Also, ε_t is a vector white noise process with $E[\varepsilon_t \varepsilon_t'] = \Sigma$.

Estimating the system by FIML using PcGive10 (see Hendry and Doornik, 2001) gives almost identical parameter estimates (not reported here) and a log-likelihood of the system of 1589.34. The correlation of structural residuals in the $\Delta w - \pi$ and $\Delta p - \pi$ equation is just 0.00467, which is clearly insignificant.[16] Further support for the empirical Phillips curves (2.20) and (2.22) comes from a likelihood ratio (LR) test of the over-identifying restrictions imposed by *PcGets*. With $\chi^2(44) = 46.793[0.3585]$, we can accept the reduction. The presence of instantaneous noncausality justifies the model reduction procedure employed here, which was based on applying *PcGets* to each single equation in a turn.

The infinite-order vector moving average representation of the system corresponding to the system in (2.24) is given by

$$z_t = \sum_{j=0}^{\infty} \Psi_j Bq_{t-j} + \sum_{j=0}^{\infty} \Psi_j \varepsilon_{t-j} \tag{2.25}$$

where $\Psi(L) = A(L)^{-1}$ and L the lag operator. By accumulating all effects, $z = A(1)^{-1} Bq$, we get the results in Table 2.3.

---

[16] Note that under the null hypothesis, the FIML estimator of the system is given by OLS. So we can easily construct an LR test of the hypothesis $\Sigma_{12} = \Sigma_{21} = 0$. As the log-likelihood of the system under the restriction is 1587.51. Thus the LR test of the restriction can be accepted with $\chi^2(1) = 3.6554[0.0559]$.

Table 2.3.   Static long run solution

	Constant	U^c	U^l	$\Delta y - \Delta l^d$	I(1974:3)
$\Delta w - \pi$	0.0189	−0.0113	−0.2093	−0.0184	+0.0039
	(0.1109)	(0.0090)	(0.0300)	(0.0028)	(0.0011)
$\Delta p - \pi$	0.0118	−0.0426	−0.0600	−0.0693	+0.0146
	(0.0680)	(0.0340)	(0.0228)	(0.0105)	(0.0040)
$\Delta w - \Delta p$	0.0071	+0.0313	−0.1493	+0.0509	−0.0107

Note: Derived from the FIML estimates of the system in (2.24).

Note here that all signs are again as expected, but that the estimated parameters are now certain compositions of the β, κ terms and are in line with the values of these parameters reported earlier. Taking into account all dynamic effects of U^l and U^c on wage and price inflation, real wage growth reacts stronger on the under-utilization of the factor labor U^l than of the factor capital U^c.

3.5. Are there adverse Rose effects?

The wage Phillips curve in (2.20) and the price Phillips curve in (2.22) can be solved for the two endogenous variables $\hat{w}$ and $\hat{p}$. The resulting reduced form representation of these equations is similar to Equations (2.8) and (2.9), but for wages and prices now simplified due to the eliminated Blanchard–Katz-type error correction terms (i.e., $\beta_{w_2} = \beta_{p_2} = 0$):

$$\hat{w} - \pi = \kappa[\beta_{w_1}(\bar{U}^l - U^l) + \kappa_w \beta_{p_1}(\bar{U}^c - U^c)] \tag{2.26}$$

$$\hat{p} - \pi = \kappa[\beta_{p_1}(\bar{U}^c - U^c) + \kappa_p \beta_{w_1}(\bar{U}^l - U^l)] \tag{2.27}$$

with $\kappa = (1 - \kappa_{w_1}\kappa_{p_1})^{-1}$.

For the US economy, we found that wages reacted stronger to demand pressure than prices ($\beta_{w_1} > \beta_{p_1}$), that β_{w_2}, β_{p_2} and wage share influences as demand pressure corrections could be ignored (as assumed in Section 2) and that wage-earners are roughly equally short-sighted as firms ($\kappa_w \approx \kappa_p$). Furthermore, using the FIML estimates of the static long run solution of system $\hat{w} - \pi, \hat{p} - \pi$ reported in Table 2.3, we have the following empirical equivalents of (2.26) and (2.27):

$$\hat{w} - \pi \approx 0.019 - 0.209 U^l - 0.011 U^c \tag{2.28}$$

$$\hat{p} - \pi \approx 0.012 - 0.060 U^l - 0.043 U^c \tag{2.29}$$

where we abstract from the dummy and productivity term.

These calculations imply with respect to the critical condition (α) derived in Section 2,

$$\alpha = (1 - \kappa_p)\beta_{w_1}k_o - (1 - \kappa_w)\beta_{p_1}/y^p \approx 0.714 \cdot 0.209 - 0.734 \cdot 0.043 \approx 0.118 > 0$$

if we assume that $k = K/(xL)$ and $1/y^p = K/Y^p$ are ratios of roughly similar size, which is likely since full employment output should be not too different from full-capacity output at the steady state.

Hence, the Rose effect will be of adverse nature if the side-condition $i < c$ is met. For the US, this condition has been investigated in Flaschel *et al.*, 2002a in a somewhat different framework (see Flaschel *et al.*, 2002a , for the European evidence). Their estimated investment parameter i is 0.136, which should be definitely lower than the marginal propensity to consume out of wages.[17] Thus the real wage or Rose effect is likely to be adverse. In addition to what is known for the real rate of interest rate channel and the Mundell effect, increasing wage flexibility might add further instability to the economy. Advocating more wage flexibility may thus not be as unproblematic as it is generally believed.

Given the indication that the US wage–price spiral is characterized by adverse Rose effects, the question arises which mechanisms stabilized the US economy over the post-war period by taming this adverse real wage feedback mechanism. Some aspects of this issue will be theoretically investigated in the remainder of the paper. But a thorough analysis from a global point of view must be left for future theoretical and empirical research on core nonlinearities possibly characterizing the evolution of market economies.

The results obtained show that (as long as goods demand depends positively on the wage share) the wage–price spiral in its estimated form is unstable as the critical condition (α) creates a positive feedback of the wage share on its rate of change. We stress again that the innovations for obtaining such a result are the use of two measures of demand pressure and the distinction between temporary and permanent cost pressure changes (in a cross-over fashion) for the wage and price Phillips curves employed in this paper.

4. Wage flexibility, instability and an extended interest rate rule

In Section 2, we found that a sufficient wage flexibility supports economic stability. The imposed assumption $c < i$ ensured that the effective demand and thus output are decreased by a rising wage share; thus deviations from the steady-state equilibrium, are corrected by the normal reaction of the real wage to activity changes. In contrast, sufficiently flexible price levels (for given wage flexibility) result in an adverse reaction of the wage share, since a rising wage share stimulate further increases via output contraction and deflation.

---

[17] In the context of our model, one might want to estimate the effective demand function $y = [(n + g - i(r_o - \pi)]/[(1 - u)(1 - i) + (1 - c)u]$. In view of the local approach chosen, it would in fact suffice to estimate a linear approximation of the form $y = a_0 + a_1 u + a_2(r - \pi)$, where $\text{sign}(a_1) = \text{sign}(c - i)$ and $a_2 < 0$ holds. However, in preliminary econometric investigations, we found a_1 being statistically insignificant so that no conclusions could be drawn regarding the sign of $c - i$.

Motivated by the estimation results presented in the preceding section, we now consider the situation where $c > i$ and $\alpha > 0$ holds true with respect to the critical Rose condition (α). The violation of the critical condition implies that $\hat{u}$ depends positively on y. In connection with $c > i$, i.e., $y_u > 0$ it generates a positive feedback from the wage share u onto its rate of change $\hat{u}$. Thus sufficiently strong wage flexibility (relative to price flexibility) is now destabilizing. This is the adverse type of Rose effect.

4.1. Instability due to an unmatched Rose effect

Here we consider the simplified wage–price dynamics (2.14)–(2.16) under the assumption $i < c$ instead of (A.1). If, in the now considered situation, monetary policy is still inactive (A.4a), the Rose effect and the Mundell effect are both destabilizing the private sector of the economy:

Proposition 4. (Private sector instability). *Assume $i < c$, i.e., $y_u > 0$, i.e., an economy that is now wage-led, $\alpha > 0$ and $\kappa_p < 1$. Then, under the assumptions (A.2)–(A.4a) introduced earlier, the interior steady-state solution of the dynamics (2.14)–(2.16) is essentially repelling (exhibits at least one positive root).*

Let us consider again to what extent the interest rate policy (A.4b) can stabilize the economy and in particular enforce the inflationary target $\bar{\pi}$. We state here without proof that rule (A.4b) can stabilize the previously considered situation if the adjustment speed of wages with respect to demand pressure in the labor market is sufficiently low. However, this stability gets lost if wage flexibility is made sufficiently large as is asserted by the following proposition, where we assume $\kappa_p = 0$ for the sake of simplicity.

Proposition 5. (Instability by an adverse Rose effect). *We assume (in the case $i < c$) an attracting steady-state situation due to the working of the monetary policy rule (A.4b). Then: increasing the parameter β_{w_1} that characterizes wage adjustment speed will eventually lead to instability of the steady state by way of a Hopf bifurcation (if the parameters κ_p, i and β_r are jointly chosen sufficiently small). There is no reswitching to stability possible, once stability has been lost in this way.*

Note that the proposition does not claim that there is a wage adjustment speed, which implies instability for any parameter value β_r in the interest rate policy rule. It is also worth noting that the instability result is less clear-cut when, for example, $\kappa_p > 0$ is considered.Furthermore, increasing the adjustment speed β_r may reduce the dynamic instability in the case $\kappa_p = 0$ (as the trace of the Jacobian is made less positive thereby). In the next subsection we will however make use of another stabilizing feature that we so far neglected in the considered dynamics due to assumption (A.2): the Blanchard and Katz (1999) error correction term $\beta_{w_2}(u - u_o)$ in the money-wage Phillips curve.

4.2. Stability from Blanchard–Katz type 'error correction'

We now analyze dynamics under the assumption $\beta_{w_2} > 0$. Thus money wages react to deviations of the wage share from its steady-state value. In this situation the following proposition holds true:

Proposition 6. (Blanchard–Katz wage share correction). *Assume $i < c$, i.e., $y_u > 0$, $\alpha > 0$ and $\kappa_p < 1$. Then, under the interest rate policy rule (A.4b), a sufficiently large error correction parameter β_{w_2} implies an attracting steady state for any given adjustment speed $\beta_\pi > 0$ and all price flexibility parameters $\beta_{p_1} > 0$. This stability is established by way of a Hopf bifurcation, which in a unique way separates unstable from stable steady-state solutions.*

We thus have the result that the Blanchard–Katz error correction term if sufficiently strong overcomes the destabilizing forces of the adverse Rose effect in Proposition 5.

Blanchard and Katz (1999) find that the error correction term is higher in European countries than in the US, where it is also in our estimates insignificant. So the empirical size of the parameter β_{w_2} may be too small to achieve the stability result of Proposition 6. Therefore, we will again disregard the error correction term in the money-wage Phillips curve (A.2) in the following, and instead focus on the role of monetary policy in stabilizing the wage–price spiral.

4.3. Stability from an augmented Taylor rule

The question arises whether monetary policy can be of help to avoid the problematic features of the adverse Rose effect. Assume now that interest rates are determined by an augmented Taylor rule of the form,

$$r = \rho_o + \pi + \beta_{r_1}(\pi - \bar{\pi}) + \beta_{r_2}(u - u_o), \quad \beta_{r_1}, \beta_{r_2} > 0 \tag{2.30}$$

where the monetary authority responds to rising wage shares by interest rate increases in order to cool down the economy, counter-balancing the initial increase in the wage share.

The static equilibrium condition is now given the

$$y = \frac{n + g - i(\rho_o + \beta_{r_1}(\pi - \bar{\pi}) + \beta_{r_2}(u - u_o))}{(1 - i)(1 - u) + (1 - c)u}$$

Thus the augmented Taylor rule (2.30) gives rise to a negative dependence of output y on the inflationary climate π as well as the wage share u.

We now consider the implications for the stability of the steady state:

Proposition 7. (Wage-gap augmented Taylor rule). *Assume $i < c$, $\alpha > 0$ and $\kappa_p < 1$. Then: a sufficiently large wage-share correction parameter β_{r_2} in the augmented Taylor rule (2.30) implies an attracting steady state for any given adjustment speed $\beta_\pi > 0$ and all price flexibility parameters $\beta_{p_1} > 0$. This stability is established by* *way of a Hopf bifurcation which in a unique way separates unstable from stable steady-state solutions.*

Thus, convergence to the balanced growth path of private sector of the considered economy is generated by a modified Taylor rule that is augmented by a term that transmits increases in the wage share to increases in the nominal rate of interest. To our knowledge such an interest rate policy rule that gives income policy a role to play in the adjustment of interest rates by the central bank has not yet been considered in the literature. This is due to the general neglect of adverse real wage or Rose effects which induce an inflationary spiral independently from the one generated by the real rate of interest or Mundell effect, though both of these mechanisms derive from the fact that real magnitudes always allow for two interacting channels by their very definition, wages versus prices in the case of Rose effects and nominal interest versus expected inflation in the case of Mundell effects.

5. Conclusions

In context of the 'Goldilocks economy' of the late 1990s, Gordon (1998) stressed the need for explaining the contrast between decelerating prices and accelerating wages as well as the much stronger fall of the rate of unemployment than the rise of the rate of capital utilization. The coincidence of the two events is exactly what our approach to the wage–price spiral would predict: wage inflation is driven by demand and cost pressures on the labor market and price inflation is formed by the corresponding pressures on the goods markets.

Based on the two Phillips curves, we investigated two important macrodynamic feedback chains in a simple growth framework: (i) the conventional destabilizing Mundell effect and (ii) the less conventional Rose effect, which has been fairly neglected in the literature on demand and supply driven macrodynamics. We showed that the Mundell effect can be tamed by a standard Taylor rule. In contrast, the Rose effect can assume four different types depending on wage and price flexibilities, short-sightedness of workers and firms with respect to their cost-pressure measures and marginal propensities to consume c and invest i in particular (where we argued for the inequality $i < c$, i.e., a wage-led situation). Table 2.4 summarizes these four cases in a compact way:

Empirical estimates for the US economy then suggested the presence of adverse Rose effects: the wage level is more flexible than the price level with respect to demand pressure (and workers roughly equally short-sighted as firms with respect to cost pressure). We showed that this particular Rose effect can cause macroeconomic instabilities that cannot be tamed by a conventional Taylor rule. But the paper also demonstrated means by which adverse real interest rate and real wage rate effects may be modified or dominated in such a way that convergence back to the interior steady state is again achieved. We

Table 2.4.   Four scenarios for the real wage channel

Critical α-Condition	Profit-Led Regime	Wage-Led Regime
$\alpha < 0$	Unstable	Stable
$\alpha > 0$	Stable	Unstable

proved that stability can be reestablished by (i) an error-correction term in the money-wage Phillips curve (as in Blanchard and Katz, 1999),[18] working with sufficient strength, or (ii) a modified Taylor rule with monetary policy monitoring the labor share (or real unit labor costs) and reacting in response to changes in the income distribution.

In this paper, we showed that adverse Rose effects are of empirical importance, and indicated ways of how to deal with them by wage or interest rate policies. In future research, we intend to discuss the role of Rose effects for high and low growth phases separately, taken account of the observation that money wages may be more rigid in the latter phases than in the former ones (see Hoogenveen and Kuipers, 2000, for a recent empirical confirmation of such differences and Flaschel *et al.*, 2002b, for its application to a 6D Keynesian macrodynamics). The existence of a 'kink' in the money-wage Phillips curve should in fact increase the estimated) wage flexibility parameter further (in the case where the kink is not in operation). Furthermore, the robustness of the empirical results should be investigated (say, by analyzing the wage–price spiral in other OECD countries). Finally, more elaborate models have to be considered to understand the feedback mechanisms from a broader perspective (see Flaschel *et al.* (2001) for first attempts of the dynamic AS-AD variety).[19]

Acknowledgment

We wish to thank Reiner Franke for helpful comments on this paper.

---

[18] The related error correction in the price Phillips curve should allow for the same conclusion, but has been left aside here due to space limitations.

[19] Concerning the validity of Okun's law and the degree of correlation of labor and capital under-utilization we should then also distinguish between the unemployment rate on the external labor market and the under- or over-employment of the employed, which may in particular explain the difference in volatility of the under-utilization of labor and capital. This, however, would introduce two further parameters to the model, the impact of employment within firms on money-wage inflation and the speed with which the labor force of firms is adjusted to the observed under or over utilization of labor within firms. Here again, significant differences may be expected regarding the situation in the United States and Europe.

References

Ball, L. and R. Mofitt (2001), "Productivity growth and the Phillips curve", Working Paper 8241, NBER, Cambridge, MA.

Blanchard, O. and S. Fisher (1999), *Lectures on Macroeconomics*, Cambridge, MA: MIT Press.

Blanchard, O. and X. Katz (1999), "Wage dynamics: reconciling theory and evidence", *American Economic Review Papers and Proceedings*, Vol. 89, pp. 69–74.

Calvo, G.A. (1983), "Staggered prices in a utility-maximizing framework", *Journal of Monetary Economics*, Vol. 12, pp. 383–398.

Carlin, W. and D. Soskice (1990), *Macroeconomics and the Wage Bargain*, Oxford: Oxford University Press.

Chiarella, C. and P. Flaschel (2000), *The Dynamics of Keynesian Monetary Growth: Macrofoundations*, Cambridge: Cambridge University Press.

Clarida, R.D., J. Gali and M. Gertler (1999), "The science of monetary policy: a New Keynesian Perspective", *Journal of Economic Literature*, Vol. 37, pp. 1161–1707.

Clarida, R. D., J. Gali and M. Gertler (2000), "Monetary policy rules and macroeconomic stability: evidence and some theory", *The Quarterly Journal of Economics*, Vol. 115, pp. 147–180.

Fair, R. (2000), "Testing the NAIRU model for the United States", *The Review of Economics and Statistics*, Vol. 82, pp. 64–71.

Flaschel, P., G. Gong and W. Semmler (2001), "A Keynesian macroeconometric framework for the analysis of monetary policy rules", *Journal of Economic Behaviour and Organization*, Vol. 46, pp. 101–136.

Flaschel, P., G. Gong and W. Semmler (2002a), "A macroeconometric study on monetary policy rules: Germany and the EMU", *Jahrbuch für Wirtschaftswissenschaften*, Vol. 53, pp. 21–27.

Flaschel, P., G. Gong and W. Semmler (2002b), "Nonlinear Phillips curves and Monetary policy in a Keynesian macroeconometric model", Mimeo: Bielefeld University, Bielefeld.

Franke, R. (2001), "Three wage–price macro models and their calibration", Technical report, Bielefeld University, Center for Empirical Macroeconomics, Bielefeld, http://www.wiwi.uni-bielefeld.de/semmler/cem/wp.htm#2001.

Gali, J., M. Gertler, D. Lopez-Salido (2001), "European inflation dynamics", *European Economic Review*, Vol. 45, pp.1237–1270.

Gordon, R.J. (1997), "The time-varying Nairu and its implications for economic policy", *Journal of Economic Perspectives*, Vol. 11, pp. 11–32.

Gordon, R.J. (1998), "Foundations of the Goldilocks economy: supply shocks and the time-varying NAIRU", *Brookings Papers on Economic Activity*, Vol. 2, pp. 297–333.

Groth, C. (1993), "Some unfamiliar dynamics of a familiar macro model", *Journal of Economics*, Vol. 58, pp. 293–305.

Hendry, D.F. (1995), *Dynamic Econometrics*, Oxford: Oxford University Press.

Hendry, D.F. and J.A. Doornik (2001), *Empirical Econometric Modelling using PcGive: Volume I*, 3rd edition, London: Timberlake Consultants Press.

Hendry, D.F. and H.-M. Krolzig (2001), *Automatic Econometric Model Selection with PcGets*, London: Timberlake Consultants Press.

Hoogenveen, V. and S. Kuipers (2000), "The long-run effects of low inflation rates", *Banca Nazionale del Lavoro Quarterly Review*, Vol. 214, pp. 267–285.

Krolzig, H.-M. (2003), "General-to-specific model selection procedures for structural vector autoregressions", Vol. 65, pp. 769–801.

Laxton, D., D. Rose and D. Tambakis (1999), "The US Phillips-curve: the case for asymmetry", *Journal of Economic Dynamics and Control*, Vol. 23, pp. 1459–1485.

Lorenz, H.-W. (1993), *Nonlinear Dynamical Economics and Chaotic Motion*, 2nd edition, Heidelberg: Springer.

Mankiw, N.G. (2001), "The inexorable and mysterious tradeoff between inflation and unemployment", *Economic Journal* (forthcoming).

Mankiw, N.G. and R. Reis (2002), "Sticky information versus price. A proposal to replace the New Keynesian Phillips curve", *Quarterly Journal of Economics*, Vol. 117, pp. 1295–1328.

McCallum, B. (1997), "Comment", *NBER Macroeconomics Annual*, Vol. 12, pp. 355–359.

Phillips, A.W. (1958), "The relation between unemployment and the rate of change of money wage rates in the United Kingdom, 1861–1957", *Economica*, Vol. 25, pp. 283–299.

Plasmans, J., H. Meersman, A. van Poeck and B. Merlevede (1999). "Generosity of the unemployment benefit system and wage flexibility in EMU: time varying evidence in five countries", Mimeo.

Romer, D. (1996), *Advanced Macroeconomics*, New York: McGraw-Hill.

Romer, D. (2000), "Keynesian Macroeconomics without the LM curve", Working Paper 7461, NBER, Cambridge, MA.

Rose, H. (1967), "On the non-linear theory of the employment cycle", *Review of Economic Studies*, Vol. 34, pp. 153–173.

Rose, H. (1990), *Macroeconomic Dynamics. A Marshallian Synthesis*, Cambridge, MA: Basil Blackwell.

Sargent, T. (1987), *Macroeconomic Theory*, 2nd edition, New York: Academic Press.

Scarth, W. (1996), *Macroeconomics. An Introduction into Advanced Methods*, Toronto: Dryden.

Taylor, J. (1980), "Aggregate dynamics and staggered contracts", *Journal of Political Economy*, Vol. 88, pp. 1–24.

Taylor, J. (1993), "Discretion versus policy in practice", *Carnegie-Rochester Conference Series on Public Policy*, Vol. 39, pp. 195–214.

Taylor, J. (1999a), *Monetary Policy Rules*, Chicogo: University of Chicago Press.

Taylor, J. (1999b), "Staggered wage and price setting in macroeconomics", in: J. Taylor and M. Woodford, editors, *Handbook of Macroeconomics*, Amsterdam: North-Holland, chapter 15.

Tobin, J. (1975), "Keynesian models of recession and depression", *American Economic Review*, Vol. 65, pp. 195–202.

Tobin, J. (1993), "Price flexibility and output stability. An old-Keynesian view", *Journal of Economic Perspectives*, Vol. 7, pp. 45–65.

Wiggins, S. (1993), *Introduction to Applied Nonlinear Dynamical Systems and Chaos*, Heidelberg: Springer.

A. Appendix

A.1. The sectoral budget equations of the model

For reasons of completeness, we here briefly present the budget equations of our four types of economic agents (see Sargent, 1987, Chapter 1, for a closely related presentation of such budget equations, there for the sectors of the conventional AS-AD growth model). Consider the following scenario for the allocation of labor, goods and assets:

$$cupY + \dot{B}^d = upY + \bar{r}B \text{ (workers: consumption out of wage income and}$$
$$\text{saving deposits)}$$

$$p_b\dot{B}^d + p_e\dot{E}^d = B + (1 - u)pY \text{ (asset-holders: bond and equity holdings)}$$

$$pI = p_e\dot{E} \text{ (firms: equity financed investment)}$$

$$\bar{r}B + B + pG = \dot{B} + p_b\dot{B} \text{ (government: debt financed consumption)}$$

where $g = G/K$ =const. In these budget equations we use a fixed interest rate $\bar{r}$ for the saving deposits of workers and use – besides equities – perpetuities (with price $p_b = 1/r$) for the characterization of the financial assets held by asset-holders. Owing to this choice, and due to the fact that investment was assumed to depend on the long-term expected real rate of interest, we had to specify the Taylor rule in terms of r in the body of the paper. These assumptions allow to avoid the treatment of the term structure of interest rate that would make the model considerably more difficult and thus the analysis of Mundell or Rose effects more advanced, but also less transparent. For our purposes the above scenario is however fully adequate and very simple to implement.

Furthermore, we denote in these equations the amount of saving deposits of workers by B (and assume a fixed interest rate $\bar{r}$ on these saving deposits). Outstanding bonds (consols or perpetuities) are denoted by B and have as their price the usual expression $p_b = 1/r$. We finally use p_e for the price of shares or equities E. These equations are only presented for consistency reasons here and they immediately imply

$$p(Y - C - I - G) = (\dot{B}^d - \dot{B}) + p_b(\dot{B}^d - \dot{B}) + p_e(\dot{E}^d - \dot{E}) = 0$$

We have assumed goods–market equilibrium in this paper and assume in addition that all saving deposits of workers are channeled into the government sector ($\dot{B}^d = \dot{B}$). We thus can also assume equilibrium in asset market flows via a perfect substitute assumption (which determines p_e, while p_b is determined by an appropriate interest rate policy rule in this paper). Note that firms are purely equity financed and pay out all profits as dividends to the sector of asset holders. Note also that long-term bonds per unit of capital $b = B/(pK)$ will follow the law of motion

$$\dot{b} = r(b + g - s_w uy) - (\hat{p} + \hat{K})b$$

which – when considered in isolation (all other variables kept at their steady-state values) – implies a stable evolution of such government debt b toward a steady-state value for this ratio if $r^o - \hat{p}_o = \rho_o < n$ holds true. Since fiscal policy is not our concern in this paper we only briefly remark that this is the case for government expenditure per unit of capital that is chosen sufficiently small:

$$g < \frac{nu_o(1 - c)}{1 - u_o}$$

Similarly, we have for the evolution of savings per unit of capital $b = B/(pK)$ the law of motion

$$\dot{b} = s_w uy + (\bar{r} - (\hat{p} + \hat{K}))b$$

which – when considered in isolation – implies convergence to some finite steady-state value if $\bar{r} < \hat{p}_o + n$ holds true. Again, since the government budget restraint is not our concern in this paper, we have ignored this aspect of our model of wage–price and growth dynamics.

A.2. Wage dynamics: theoretical foundation

This subsection builds on the paper by Blanchard and Katz (1999) and briefly summarizes their theoretical motivation of a money-wage Phillips curve which is closely related to our dynamic equation (2.1).[20] Blanchard and Katz assume – following the suggestions of standard models of wage setting – that real wage expectations of workers, $\omega^e = w_t - p_t^e$, are basically determined by the reservation wage, $\bar{\omega}_t$, current labor productivity, $y_t - l_t^d$, and the rate of unemployment, U_t^l:

$$\omega_t^e = \theta \bar{\omega}_t + (1 - \theta)(y_t - l_t^d) - \beta_w U_t^l$$

---

[20] In this section, lower case letters (including w and p) indicate logarithms.

Expected real wages are thus a Cobb–Douglas average of the reservation wage and output per worker, but are departing from this normal level of expectations by the state of the demand pressure on the labor market. The reservation wage in turn is determined as a Cobb–Douglas average of past real wages, $\omega_{t-1} = w_{t-1} - p_{t-1}$, and current labor productivity, augmented by a factor $a < 0$:

$$\bar{\omega}_t = a + \lambda \omega_{t-1} + (1 - \lambda)(y_t - l_t^d)$$

Inserting the second into the first equation results in

$$\omega_t^e = \theta a + \theta \lambda \omega_{t-1} + (1 - \theta \lambda)(y_t - l_t^d) - \beta_w U_t^l$$

which gives after some rearrangements

$$\Delta w_t = p_t^e - p_{t-1} + \theta a - (1 - \theta \lambda)[(w_{t-1} - p_{t-1}) - (y_t - l_t^d)] - \beta_w U_t^l$$
$$= \Delta p_t^e + \theta a - (1 - \theta \lambda)u_{t-1} + (1 - \theta \lambda)(\Delta y_t - \Delta l_t^d) - \beta_w U_t^l$$

where Δp_t^e denotes the expected rate of inflation, u_{t-1} the past (log) wage share and $\Delta y_t - \Delta l_t^d$ the current growth rate of labor productivity. This is the growth law for nominal wages that flows from the theoretical models referred to in Blanchard and Katz (1999, p. 70).

In this paper, we proposed to operationalize this theoretical approach to money-wage inflation by replacing the short-run cost push term Δp_t^e by the weighted average $\kappa_w \Delta p_t^e + (1 - \kappa_w)\pi_t$, where Δp_t^e is determined by myopic perfect foresight. Thus, temporary changes in the correctly anticipated rate of inflation do not have full impact on temporary wage inflation, which is also driven by lagged inflation rates via the inflationary climate variable π_t. Adding inertia to the theory of wage inflation introduced a distinction between the temporary and persistent cost effects to this equation. Furthermore we have that $\Delta y_t - \Delta l_t^d = n_x$ due to the assumed fixed proportions technology. Altogether, we end up with an equation for wage inflation of the type presented in Section 2.1, though now with a specific interpretation of the model's parameters from the perspective of efficiency wage or bargaining models.[21]

---

[21] Note that the parameter in front of u_{t-1} cannot be interpreted as a speed of adjustment coefficient. Note furthermore that Blanchard and Katz (1999) assume that, in the steady state, the wage share is determined by the firms' markup $u = -\mu$ (both in logs) to be discussed in the next subsection. Therefore the NAIRU can be determined endogenously on the labor market by $\bar{U}^l = \beta_w^{-1}[\theta a - (1 - \theta \lambda)\bar{\mu} - \theta \lambda(\Delta y_t - \Delta l_t^d)]$. The NAIRU of their model therefore depends on both labor and goods market characteristics in contrast to the NAIRU levels for labor and capital employed in our approach.

A.3. Price dynamics: theoretical foundation

We here follow again Blanchard and Katz (1999, IV), see also Carlin and Soskice (1990, Chapter 18), and start from the assumption of normal cost pricing, here under the additional assumption of our paper of fixed proportions in production and Harrod neutral technological change. We therefore consider as rule for normal prices

$$p_t = \mu_t + w_t + l_t^d - y_t, \qquad \text{i.e., } \Delta p_t = \Delta \mu_t + \Delta w_t - n_x$$

where μ_t represents a markup on the unit wage costs of firms and where again myopic perfect foresight, here with respect to wage setting is assumed. We assume furthermore that the markup is variable and responding to the demand pressure in the market for goods $\bar{U}^c - U_t^c$, depending in addition negatively on the current level of the markup μ_t in its deviation from the normal level $\bar{\mu}$. Firms therefore depart from their normal cost pricing rule according to the state of demand on the market for goods, and this the stronger the lower the level of the currently prevailing markup has been (markup smoothing). For sake of concreteness let us here assume that the following behavioral relationship holds:

$$\Delta \mu_t = \beta_p(\bar{U}^c - U_{t-1}^c) + \gamma(\bar{\mu} - \mu_{t-1})$$

where $\gamma > 0$. Inserted into the formula for price inflation this in sum gives:

$$\Delta p_t = \beta_p(\bar{U}^c - U_{t-1}^c) + \gamma(\bar{\mu} - \mu_{t-1}) + (\Delta w_t - n_x)$$

In terms of the logged wage share $u_t = -\mu_t$ we get

$$\Delta p_t = \beta_p(\bar{U}^c - U_{t-1}^c) + \gamma(u_{t-1} - \bar{u}) + (\Delta w_t - n_x)$$

As in the preceding subsection of the paper, we again add persistence the cost pressure term $\Delta w_t - n_x$ now in the price Phillips curve in the form of the inflationary climate expression π and thereby obtain in sum the Equation (2.2) of Section 2.1.

A.4. Routh–Hurwitz stability conditions and Hopf bifurcations

We consider the matrix of partial derivatives at the steady state of the 3D dynamical systems of this paper in (u, k, π), the so-called Jacobian J, in detail represented by:

$$J = \begin{pmatrix} J_{11} & J_{12} & J_{13} \\ J_{21} & J_{22} & J_{23} \\ J_{31} & J_{32} & J_{33} \end{pmatrix}$$

We define the principal minors of order 2 of this matrix by the following three determinants:

$$J_1 = \begin{vmatrix} J_{22} & J_{23} \\ J_{32} & J_{33} \end{vmatrix}, \qquad J_2 = \begin{vmatrix} J_{11} & J_{13} \\ J_{31} & J_{33} \end{vmatrix}, \qquad J_3 = \begin{vmatrix} J_{11} & J_{12} \\ J_{21} & J_{22} \end{vmatrix}$$

We furthermore denote by a_1 the negative of the trace of the Jacobian $-\text{trace} J$, by a_2 the sum of the above three principal minors, and by a_3 the negative of the determinant $|J|$ of the Jacobian J. We note that the coefficients $a_i, i = 1, 2, 3$ are the coefficients of the characteristic polynomial of the matrix J.

The Routh–Hurwitz conditions (see Lorenz, 1993) then state that the eigenvalues of the matrix J all have negative real parts if and only if

$$a_i > 0, i = 1, 2, 3 \quad \text{and} \quad a_1 a_2 - a_3 > 0$$

These conditions therefore exactly characterize the case where local asymptotic stability of the considered steady state is given.

Supercritical Hopf bifurcations (the birth of a stable limit cycle) or subcritical Hopf bifurcations (the death of an unstable limit cycle) occur (if asymptotic stability prevailed below this parameter value) when the following conditions hold simultaneously for an increase of a parameter β of the model (see Wiggins, 1993, Chapter 3):

$$a_3(\beta) > 0, (a_1 a_2 - a_3)(\beta) = 0, (a_1 a_2 - a_3)'(\beta) > 0$$

We note here that the dynamics considered below indeed generally fulfill the condition $a_3 > 0$ and also $J_2 = 0$, the latter up to Proposition 6 and due to the proportionality that exists between the laws of motion (2.14) and (2.16) with respect to the state variables u and π.

A.5. Proofs of propositions

In the following we present the mathematical proofs of the Propositions 2–7 of the paper. The proofs involve the stability analysis of the 3D dynamics in (2.14) to (2.16) under certain parametric assumptions and different monetary regimes and are based on the Routh–Hurwitz conditions just considered.

Proof of Proposition 2. Choosing β_{p_1} or β_π sufficiently large will make the trace of J, the Jacobian of the dynamics (2.14)–(2.16) at the steady state, unambiguously positive and thus definitely lead to local instability.

Yet, even if β_{p_1} and β_π are sufficiently small, we get by appropriate row operations in the considered determinant the following sequence of result for the sign of det J:

$$|J| \hat{=} \begin{vmatrix} 0 & + & 0 \\ - & 0 & + \\ - & 0 & + \end{vmatrix} \hat{=} -(+) \begin{vmatrix} - & + \\ - & + \end{vmatrix} \hat{=} \begin{vmatrix} -y_0 & +1 \\ y_u & y_\pi \end{vmatrix}$$

$$= y_0 \begin{vmatrix} -1 & +1 \\ \frac{c-i}{(1-u)(1-i)+(1-c)u} & \frac{i}{(1-u)(1-i)+(1-c)u} \end{vmatrix}$$

$$= \frac{y_0}{(1-u)(1-i)+(1-c)u} \begin{vmatrix} -1 & +1 \\ c-i & i \end{vmatrix} = \frac{cy_0}{(1-u)(1-i)+(1-c)u} > 0$$

One of the necessary and sufficient Routh–Hurwitz conditions for local asymptotic stability is therefore always violated, independently of the sizes of the considered speeds of adjustment. ■

Proof of Proposition 3. Inserting the interest rule in (A.4b) into the $y(u, \pi)$ and $i(\rho - (r - \pi))$ functions gives rise to the functional dependencies

$$y = y(u, \pi) = \frac{n + g - i[\rho_o + \beta_r(\pi - \bar{\pi})]}{(1-u)(1-i)+(1-c)u}, \quad y_u < 0, y_\pi < 0$$

$$i = i(\rho - (r - \pi)) = i(u, \pi), \quad i_u < 0, i_\pi < 0.$$

The signs in the considered Jacobian are therefore here given by

$$J = \begin{pmatrix} - & + & - \\ - & 0 & - \\ - & + & - \end{pmatrix}$$

if β_{p_1} is chosen sufficiently small (and thus dominated by wage flexibility β_{w_1}). We thus then have trace $J < 0$ ($a_1 = -$ trace $J > 0$) and

$$J_3 = \begin{vmatrix} - & + \\ - & 0 \end{vmatrix} > 0, \quad J_1 = \begin{vmatrix} 0 & - \\ + & - \end{vmatrix} > 0, \text{ i.e.,}$$

$a_2 = J_1 + J_2 + J_3 > 0$ for β_{p_1} sufficiently small. Next, we get for $|J|$ with respect to signs:

$$|J| \hat{=} \begin{vmatrix} 0 & + & 0 \\ - & 0 & - \\ - & 0 & - \end{vmatrix} \hat{=} -(+) \begin{vmatrix} - & - \\ - & - \end{vmatrix} \hat{=} \begin{vmatrix} -y_0 & -\beta_r \\ y_u & y_\pi \end{vmatrix} = - \begin{vmatrix} -y_0 & -\beta_r \\ \frac{c-i}{N}y_o & \frac{-i\beta_r}{N} \end{vmatrix}$$

$$= -\beta_r(y_o/N) \begin{vmatrix} -1 & -1 \\ c-i & -i \end{vmatrix} = -\beta_r \frac{y_o}{N} c < 0$$

since $N = (1-u)(1-i) + (1-c)u > 0$ at the steady state. Therefore: $a_1, a_2, a_3 = -|J|$ are all positive.

It remains to be shown that also $a_1 a_2 - a_3 > 0$ can be fulfilled. Here it suffices to observe that a_1, a_2 stay positive when $\beta_{p_1} = 0$ is assumed, while a_3 becomes zero then. Therefore $a_1 a_2 - a_3 > 0$ for all adjustment parameters β_{p_1} chosen sufficiently small. These qualitative results hold independently of the size of β_π and β_r (with an adjusting size of β_{p_1}, however). ∎

Note in addition that the trace of J is given by

$$\kappa \beta_{p_1} / y^p [(1 - \kappa_w)(i - c)y - \beta_\pi \beta_r i] / ((1 - i)(1 - u) + (1 - c)u)$$

as far as its dependence on the parameter β_{p_1} is concerned. Choosing β_π or β_r, for given β_{p_1}, sufficiently small will make the trace of J positive and thus make the steady state of the considered dynamics locally unstable.

Proof of Proposition 4. With $r \equiv r_o$, we have for the Jacobian J of the dynamics at the steady state:

$$J = \begin{pmatrix} + & + & + \\ - & 0 & + \\ + & + & + \end{pmatrix}$$

and thus in particular trace $J > 0$ and

$$|J| \hat{=} \begin{vmatrix} 0 & + & 0 \\ - & 0 & + \\ + & 0 & + \end{vmatrix} = -(+) \begin{vmatrix} - & + \\ + & + \end{vmatrix} > 0$$

Thus there is at least one positive real root, which establishes the local instability of the investigated interior steady-state solution. ∎

Proof of Proposition 5. For the considered parameter constellations, the Jacobian J is given by

$$J = \begin{pmatrix} + & + & - \\ - & 0 & - \\ + & + & - \end{pmatrix}$$

This Jacobian first of all implies

$$|J| \hat{=} \begin{vmatrix} 0 & + & 0 \\ - & 0 & - \\ + & 0 & - \end{vmatrix} = -(+) \begin{vmatrix} - & - \\ + & - \end{vmatrix} < 0$$

and thus for the Routh–Hurwitz condition $a_3 = -|J| > 0$ as necessary condition for local asymptotic stability. We assert here without detailed proof that local stability will indeed prevail if β_{w_1} is chosen sufficiently close to zero, since $|J|$ will be close to zero then too and since the Routh–Hurwitz coefficients a_1 and a_2 are both positive and bounded away from zero. Wages that react sluggishly with respect to demand pressure therefore produce local stability in the case $c > i$.

This is indeed achieved, for example, by the assumption $\kappa_p = 0$. Obviously, trace of J is then an increasing linear function of the speed parameter β_{w_1} in the considered situation, since this parameter is then only present in J_{11} and not in J_{33}. This proves the first part of the assertion, if note is taken of the fact that $|J|$ does not change its sign. Eigenvalues therefore cannot pass through zero (and the speed condition for them is also easily verified). The second part follows from the fact that $a_1 a_2 - a_3$ becomes zero before trace $J = -a_1$ passes through zero, but cannot become positive again before this trace has become zero (since $a_1 a_2 - a_3$ is a quadratic function of the parameter β_{w_1} with a positive parameter before the quadratic term and since this function is negative at the value β_{w_1} where trace J has become zero). ∎

Proof of Proposition 6. The signs in the Jacobian of the dynamics at the steady state are given by

$$
J = \begin{pmatrix} - & + & - \\ - & 0 & - \\ - & + & - \end{pmatrix}
$$

if β_{w_2} is chosen sufficiently large (and thus dominating the wage flexibility β_{w_1} term). We thus have trace $J < 0$ ($a_1 = -\text{trace} J > 0$) and

$$
J_3 = \begin{vmatrix} - & + \\ - & 0 \end{vmatrix} > 0, \quad J_1 = \begin{vmatrix} 0 & - \\ + & - \end{vmatrix} > 0, \quad \text{sign} J_2 = \text{sign} \begin{vmatrix} - & - \\ + & - \end{vmatrix} > 0, \text{ i.e.,}
$$

$a_2 = J_1 + J_2 + J_3 > 0$, in particular due to the fact that the $\beta_{w_i}, i = 1, 2$-expressions can be removed from the second row of J_2 without altering the size of this determinant.

Next, we get for $|J|$ with respect to signs:

$$
|J| \doteq \begin{vmatrix} - & + & - \\ - & 0 & - \\ + & 0 & - \end{vmatrix} \doteq -(+) \begin{vmatrix} - & - \\ + & - \end{vmatrix} < 0
$$

since the $\beta_{w_i}, i = 1, 2$-expressions can again be removed now from the third row of $|J|$ without altering the size of this determinant.

Therefore: a_1, a_2 and $a_3 = -|J|$ are all positive as demanded by the Routh–Hurwitz conditions for local asymptotic stability. There remains to be shown that also $a_1 a_2 - a_3 > 0$ can be fulfilled. In the present situation this, however, is an easy task, since – as just shown – $|J|$ does not depend on the parameter β_{w_2}, while $a_1 a_2$ depends positively on it (in the usual quadratic way). Finally, the statement on the Hopf bifurcation can be proved in a similar way as the one in Proposition 5. ∎

Proof of Proposition 7. Inserting the Taylor rule

$$
r = \rho_o + \pi + \beta_{r_1}(\pi - \bar{\pi}) + \beta_{r_2}(u - u_o), \quad \beta_{r_1}, \beta_{r_2} > 0
$$

into the effective demand equation

$$y = \frac{n + g - i(r_o - \pi)}{(1 - u)(1 - i) + (1 - c)u}$$

adds the term

$$\tilde{y} = -\frac{i\beta_{r_2}(u - u_o)}{(1 - u)(1 - i) + (1 - c)u}$$

to our former calculations – in the place of the β_{w_2} term now. This term gives rise to the following additional partial derivative

$$\tilde{y}_u = -\frac{i\beta_{r_2}}{(1 - u_o)(1 - i) + (1 - c)u_o}$$

at the steady state of the economy. This addition can be exploited as the β_{w_2} expression in the previous subsection used there to prove Proposition 7.   ∎

CHAPTER 3

Three Wage-Price Macro Models and Their Calibration

Reiner Franke[*]

Abstract

Within a business cycle context, three alternative theories of inflation are combined with an extended money wage Phillips curve and adjustments of inflationary expectations. The first approach, almost directly, amounts to countercyclical motions of the price level; the second utilizes an extended price Phillips curve; the third module formalizes adjustments of a variable markup on unit labour costs. On the basis of stylized oscillations of capacity utilization as the only exogenous variable, the paper studies the model-generated time paths of, in particular, the real wage and the price level. For all three model variants, the parameters can be set such that the cyclical properties come close to what is empirically observed. In a general comparison, the variable markup approach may be said to have a slight edge over the other two models.

Keywords: wage-price dynamics, Phillips curve, inflation theory, variable markup rate, calibration

JEL classifications: E12, E24, E25, E32

1. Introduction

Directly or indirectly, wage-price dynamics play a central role in all macroeconomic theories of the business cycle. The present paper is concerned

[*]Corresponding author. Institute for Monetary Economics, Technical University, Vienna, Austria

CONTRIBUTIONS TO ECONOMIC ANALYSIS
VOLUME 277   ISSN: 0573-8555
DOI:10.1016/S0573-8555(05)77003-6

with nonmarket clearing approaches to this issue, where labour and capital may be under- or overutilized and the economic variables respond with partial adjustments. Three (deterministic) submodels are put forward, with a view that they may be integrated into a broader framework of cyclical disequilibrium dynamics. The models themselves, however, as any theory, impose almost no restrictions. To have content, quantitative restrictions have to be added, that is, numerical specifications of the adjustment parameters have to be examined. Moreover, a complete macrodynamic model of which such a wage-price submodel forms part is most likely to become so complex that a purely mathematical treatment would not carry very far. A numerical analysis has therefore to be undertaken anyway.

Accordingly, after discussing the theoretical significance of the three submodels, the paper is also devoted to their calibration in a business cycle context. The aim of calibrating a model economy is to conduct (computer) experiments in which its properties are derived and compared to those of an actual economy. In this respect, calibration procedures can be understood as a more elaborate version of the standard back-of-the-envelope calculations that theorists perform to judge the validity of a model. The underlying notion is that every model is known to be false. A model is not a null hypothesis to be tested, it is rather an improper or simplified approximation of the true data-generating process of the actual data. Hence, a calibrator is not interested in verifying whether the model is true (the answer is already known from the outset), but in identifying which aspects of the data a false model can replicate.[1]

Our investigation of how well the wage-price models match the data follows the usual practice. We select a set of stylized facts of the business cycle, simulate each model on the computer, and assess the corresponding cyclical properties of the resulting time series in a more or less informal way. Since a (false) model is chosen on the basis of the questions it allows to ask, and not on its being realistic or being able to best mimic the data, we share the point of view that rough reproduction of simple statistics is all that is needed to evaluate the implications of a model.[2] In sum, our philosophy of setting the numerical parameters is similar to that of the real business cycle school, though the methods will be different in detail.

As it turns out, the three model variants give rise to a hierarchical structure in the calibration process. Some variables which are exogenous in one model-building block are endogenous within another module at a higher level. Thus, the parameters need not all be chosen simultaneously, but fall into several

---

[1] See also the introductory discussion in Canova and Ortega (2000, pp. 400–403).

[2] As Summers (1991, p. 145) has expressed his scepticism about decisive formal econometric tests of hypotheses, "the empirical facts of which we are most confident and which provide the most secure basis for theory are those that require the least sophisticated statistical analysis to perceive."

subsets that can be successively determined. This handy feature makes the search for suitable parameters and the kind of compromises one has to accept more intelligible. On the other hand, the calibration hierarchies are different for each model, even with respect to those parameters that are common to all three models.

The endogenous variables whose cyclical behaviour is to be contrasted with the empirical data are labour productivity, the employment rate, the real wage rate, the wage share and (derived from the rates of inflation) the price level. Detrending of the variables is, of course, presupposed. Besides procyclical motions of productivity and employment, we, in particular, seek to obtain a basically procyclical real wage and a countercyclical price (CCP) level. A second aspect of the business cycle that has to be taken into account is the amplitude of the fluctuations, i.e., the standard deviation of the endogenous variables.

The models are driven by the motions of capacity utilization, which is the only exogenous variable. Since random shocks are neglected in the formulation of the models, these motions may well be of a regular and strictly periodic nature. Specifically, the simulation experiments underlying the calibration can be most conveniently organized if it is assumed that utilization oscillates like a sine wave. This perhaps somewhat unusual device is more carefully defended later in the paper. Nevertheless, at the end of our study we will also have to check whether the previous results of a base scenario are seriously affected if the exogenous sine wave is replaced with the more noisy time path of the empirical counterpart of the utilization variable.

At the theoretical level, the models have four building blocks in common: two simplified functional relationships concerning fixed investment (which will only have a minor bearing on the employment rate) and procyclical labour productivity; an extended nominal wage Phillips curve; and adjustments of a so-called inflation climate that enters the Phillips curve. On this basis, we advance three inflation modules. In the first one, changes in the rate of price inflation are postulated in such a way that a CCP level results almost directly by construction. The second module invokes a price Phillips curve (PPC), which is likewise somewhat more encompassing than the standard textbook versions. The third approach takes up a Kaleckian idea of a variable markup (VMK) on unit labour costs (ULCs) whose adjustments have a certain countercyclical element. Without going into further details, it can generally be said that, despite the conceptual as well as formal differences between the wage-price models thus defined, all three variants are similarly suited for calibration; though this does not rule out other reasons that the VMK approach may be preferred to CCP and PPC.

The remainder of the paper is organized as follows. Section 2 expounds the stylized facts of the business cycle that will be our guidelines. The building blocks around the nominal wage dynamics that are common to all three models are presented in Section 3. Subsequently, Section 4 introduces the three alternative inflation modules. It also works out the different levels at which the parameters can be determined in the calibration procedure. Section 5 provides an extensive discussion of the cyclical properties of the models and our strategy to arrive at a base scenario for each model. Employing these scenarios, Section 6 gives an evaluation of the three model variants. Lastly, the stylized sine wave of capacity utilization is here dropped and the numerical simulation is re-run with empirical values of that variable. Section 7 concludes. An appendix makes explicit some details about the construction of the empirical data we use.

2. Stylized facts

Besides an unobservable inflation climate and capacity utilization, u, which serves as a measure of the business cycle, the wage-price models to be set up concentrate on five endogenous macroeconomic variables. These are the employment rate, e, labour productivity, z, the (productivity-deflated) real wage rate, ω, the wage share, v and the price level, p. To see what a calibration should be aiming at, we first examine the cyclical features of their empirical proxies. (Source and construction of the empirical time series are described in the appendix.)

In modelling production, under- and overutilization of productive capacity is allowed for. The notion of capacity utilization rests on an output–capital ratio y^n that would prevail under 'normal' conditions. With respect to a given stock of fixed capital, K, productive capacity is correspondingly defined as $Y^n = y^n K$. Y being total output and y the output–capital ratio, capacity utilization is given by $u = Y/Y^n = y/y^n$. Against this theoretical background, we may take the motions of the output–capital ratio in the firm sector (nonfinancial corporate business) as the empirical counterpart of the fluctuations of u.

In the models' production technology, y^n is treated as a constant. In reality, there are some variations in y at lower than the business-cycle frequencies. We therefore detrend the empirical series of y and, treating the 'normal' output–capital ratio as variable over time, set $y^n = y^n_t$ equal to the trend value of y at time t. In this way, the model's deviations from normal utilization, $u - 1$, can be identified with the empirical trend deviations $(y_t - y^n_t)/y^n_t$.

To correct for the low frequency variation of y, the Hodrick–Prescott (HP) filter is adopted. Choosing a smoothing parameter $\lambda = 1600$ for the quarterly data and looking at the resulting time-series plot, one may feel that the trend line nestles too closely against the actual time path of y. This phenomenon is not too surprising since the HP 1600 filter amounts to defining the business cycle by those fluctuations in the time series that have periodicity of less than eight years (cf. King and Rebelo, 1999, p. 934), whereas the US economy experienced two trough-to-trough cycles that exceed this period.[3] Other filters, such as HP with values of $\lambda = 6400$ or higher, or a segmented linear trend, correspond better to what one may draw freehand as an intuitive trend line in a diagram. However, the cyclical pattern of the trend deviations is in all cases very similar, only the amplitudes are somewhat larger. Because in the literature the HP filter employs $\lambda = 1600$ with almost no exception, we may just as well follow this conventional practice. The trend deviations of the output–capital series thus obtained, or of capacity utilization $u - 1$, for that matter, are exhibited in the top panel of Figure 3.1.

The HP 1600 filter is also applied to the other empirical series we are interested in. The fact that the trend deviations of these cyclical components might likewise appear somewhat narrow need not be of great concern to us. It will serve our purpose to express their standard deviations in terms of the standard deviation of u.

Let us begin by considering labour productivity. This variable will have to be taken into account since in the modelling framework it connects, on the one hand, the employment rate with utilization and, on the other hand, the real wage rate with the wage share. Labour productivity has since long been counted a procyclical variable. May it suffice to mention that Okun (1980, pp. 821f) lists it among his stylized facts of the business cycle. Procyclical variations of z can to some degree also be recognized in the second panel in Figure 3.1, perhaps with a slight lead before u. The cross-correlation coefficients quantifying the comovements of z with u are given in Table 3.1, whose sample period 1961–1991 covers four major trough-to-trough cycles. Reckoning in a lead of z between one and three quarters, these statistics indicate a stronger relationship between z and u than one might possibly infer from a visual inspection of the time series alone.[4]

---

[3] According to the NBER reference data, one is from February 1961 to November 1970, the other from November 1982 to March 1991. In recent times, the band-pass (BP) filter developed by Baxter and King (1995) has gained in popularity. On the basis of spectral analysis, this procedure is mathematically more precise about what constitutes a cyclical component. The BP(6,32) filter preserves fluctuations with periodicities between six quarters and eight years, and eliminates all other fluctuations, both the low frequency fluctuations that are associated with trend growth and the high frequencies associated with for instance measurement error. More exactly, with finite data sets the BP(6,32) filter approximates such an ideal filter. As it turns out, for the time series with relatively low noise (little high frequency variation) the outcome of the HP 1600 and the BP(6,32) filter is almost the same. For real national US output, this is exemplified in King and Rebelo (1999, p. 933, Figure. 1).

[4] Unfortunately, the statistics cannot be compared with the most recent comprehensive compilation of stylized business cycle facts by Stock and Watson (1999), since they employ real GDP as a measure of the business cycle. Over the sample period 1953–1996, they report a cross-correlation coefficient as large as $\rho(z_{t-k}, \mathrm{GDP}_t) = 0.72$ for a lead of $k = 2$. Curiously enough, we could not reproduce a similar number with the trend deviations of the GDP series taken from Ray Fair's database (see the appendix), which is due to the fact that (especially) over the subperiod 1975–1982 this series is quite different from the Citibase GDP series used by Stock and Watson (statistically, it shows less first-order autocorrelation).

Figure 3.1. Cyclical components of empirical series

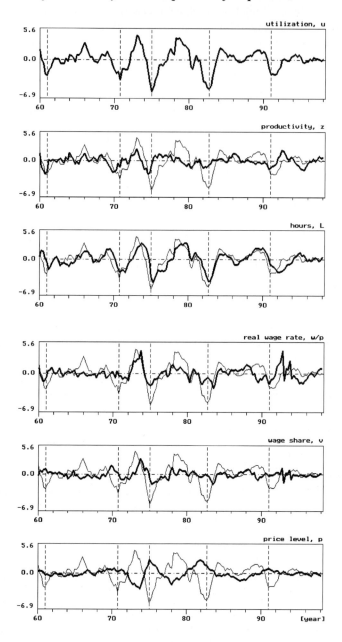

Note: Deviations from trend (HP 1600) in per cent. The thin line is the cyclical component of utilization.

To get information about the employment rate, we refer to total working hours, L. For simplicity, we directly interpret the trend line, $L^o = L^o_t$, as labour supply, i.e., as supply of normal working hours. In this view, the normal employment rate is given by $e = 1$, and the deviations from normal employment are proxied by $e_t - 1 = (L_t - L^o_t)/L^o_t \approx \ln(L_t - L^o_t)$, which is the series displayed in the third panel in Figure 3.1. The juxtaposition with utilization in the same panel makes clear that this employment rate is markedly procyclical. The third line in Table 3.1 details that it lags one or two quarters behind u.

The controversy surrounding the comovements of the real wage rate is usually summarized by saying that, if anything, it moves (weakly) procyclical, rather than countercyclical. Results about the cyclical properties of the real wage appear to be quite sensitive to precisely how it is constructed, depending on whether the numerator (w) includes various compensation items and on the index in the denominator (p). Since our modelling context is a one-good economy, we adopt the deflator of total output as our price level, so that w/p denotes the product real wage. On the other hand, we follow Ray Fair's procedure (see the appendix) and include a uniform 50% wage premium as a rough measure for overtime payment.

On the basis of this specification, Figure 3.1 (fourth panel) shows that the real wage rate is fairly close connected to the motions of capacity utilization, while quantitative evidence for its procyclicality is given in Table 3.1. Although this finding is in some contrast to what is reported in the literature, it should play an important role in the calibration later on.[5]

The variable that more directly describes the distribution of income between workers and capital owners is the wage share v. It is only rarely mentioned in the discussion of typical features of a business cycle. This might in part be due to the special difficulties that one encounters for this variable in separating the cyclical from some intermediate quasi-trend behaviour. The HP 1600 trend deviations depicted in the fifth panel in Figure 3.1 may therefore be taken with some care.

Accepting them as they are, we see another explanation for the infrequent reference to the wage share: it does not exhibit a distinctive and unique cyclical

---

[5] For example, King and Rebelo (1999, p. 938) obtain a contemporaneous correlation of compensation per hour with output of $\rho = 0.12$, and the coefficient for the correlation with GDP that is presented by Stock and Watson (1999, Table 3.2) is similarly low. As regards the present data, with no overtime payment in the wage rate the contemporaneous correlation is reduced to 0.34 (and no lagged coefficients are higher), even though the correlation of the trend deviations of the two real wage time series is as high as 0.93. On the other hand, considering the issue more carefully, Barsky *et al.* (1994) argue that real wage indexes may fail to capture changes in the composition of employment over the cycle. They conclude that real wages are procyclical if the composition is held constant.

Table 3.1. *Descriptive statistics for cyclical components of quarterly series, 1961:1–91:4*

Series x	σ_x/σ_u	Cross Correlations between u at Time t and x at Time						
		$t-3$	$t-2$	$t-1$	t	$t+1$	$t+2$	$t+3$
u	—	0.48	0.70	0.89	1.00	0.89	0.70	0.48
z	0.44	0.56	0.58	0.53	0.46	0.17	−0.06	−0.27
L	0.83	0.03	0.30	0.57	0.79	0.88	0.86	0.77
w/p	0.51	0.31	0.48	0.57	0.61	0.56	0.48	0.34
v	0.38	−0.21	−0.05	0.09	0.21	0.42	0.53	0.57
p	0.51	−0.59	−0.70	−0.73	−0.70	−0.62	−0.49	−0.32
gK	0.29	−0.06	0.20	0.48	0.72	0.84	0.86	0.80

Note: All series detrended by Hodrick–Prescott (with smoothing factor $\lambda = 1600$). Except for gK, the cyclical components are measured in per cent of the trend values. σ denotes their standard deviation: u is the output–capital ratio, z labour productivity, L total hours, w the nominal wage, p the output price level, v the wage share, and gK the capital growth rate.

pattern. Over the 1960s, v looks rather countercyclical, whereas from 1970 to 1990 it appears to be more or less procyclical. In fact over the 1960s, the highest (in modulus) correlation coefficient is negative, as large as $\rho(u_t, v_{t-1}) = -0.71$. Over the period 1970–1991, the maximal coefficient is positive; at a lag of three quarters it amounts to $\rho(u_t, v_{t+3}) = 0.67$. For this reason the cross correlations given in Table 3.1 over the full period 1961–1991 have to be cautiously interpreted. They do not summarize a general law of a systematic relationship between the business cycle and income distribution, but they reflect, in attenuated form, the relationship over a limited span of time. It will become clearer in the next section what is here involved. As indicated in the introduction, we will discuss three modules to represent price inflation. Time series of inflation rates are, however, relatively noisy and so cannot be easily related to the motions of utilization with its high persistence.[6] It is therefore more convenient to study the variations of the price level directly. While prices were formerly treated as procyclical, there seems now to be general consensus that their cyclical component moves countercyclical (see, for example, Cooley and Ohanian, 1991; Backus and Kehoe, 1992; Fiorito and Kollintzas, 1994). With respect to the price index for total output, this phenomenon is plainly visible in the bottom panel of Figure 3.1. According to Table 3.1, the inverse relationship between p and u is the strongest at a lead of the price level by one quarter. Given the

---

[6] Quarterly inflation rates have first-order serial correlation in the region of 0.35, which may be compared to the AR(1) coefficients for the trend deviations of u and p, which are 0.89 and 0.92, respectively.

Table 3.2. Desirable features of macrodynamic oscillations

Variable x	σ_x/σ_u	Lag x
dev z	0.40	0.00
dev e	0.75	0.00–0.75
dev ω	0.45–0.50	−0.50–0.50
dev v	0.30–0.40	—
−dev p	0.45–0.50	−0.75–0.25

Note: 'dev' is the percentage deviations from trend or steady-state values, e the employment rate and ω the (productivity-deflated) real wage rate. The lags are measured in years.

tightness of the relationship, CCPs are a challenge for any theory of inflation within a business cycle context.[7]

Lastly, Table 3.1 includes the growth rate of fixed capital, whose cyclical properties will be considered further below.

On the basis of the statistics in Table 3.1, we summarize the cyclical features that one may wish a small (deterministic) macrodynamic model to generate – at least insofar as it exhibits smooth and regular oscillations. They are listed in Table 3.2, which leaves some play in the numbers since a small model cannot be reasonably expected to match all the empirical statistics accurately. Moreover, when we state a zero lag for productivity z, then this is already due to the simplifying modelling assumption on the production technology in the next section.

The reason for fixing the standard deviation of z somewhat lower than the coefficient 0.44 given in Table 3.1 is the apparently lower amplitude of z in the recent past. In fact, over the sample period 1975–1991, the ratio σ_z/σ_u falls to 0.33 (and the relationship with utilization becomes weaker). The reduction of σ_z/σ_u should carry over to the variations of employment, hence the proportionately lower value of σ_e/σ_u. We also should not be too definitive about the variation of the wage share, because the precise empirical construction of this variable and the outcome of the specific detrending mechanism may not be overly robust against alternative procedures. By the same token, it would not be appropriate to commit oneself to a particular phase shift of v. This is all the more true if the lead in labour productivity is neglected (the relationship between

---

[7] A discussion of the issue of CCPs should make clear what in (structural and descriptive) economic theory the trend line is supposed to reflect: (a) the evolution of prices on a deterministic long-run equilibrium path around which the actual economy is continuously fluctuating or (b) the time path of an expected price level. From the latter point of view, Smant (1998, p. 159) argues that other procedures than HP detrending should be adopted and, doing this, concludes that the so specified (unexpected) price movements are clearly procyclical. By contrast, our theoretical background is notion (a).

the wage share and productivity is made explicit in Equation (3.5)). Given that $\sigma_v/\sigma_u = 0.31$ over the subperiod 1975–1991, we content ourselves with proposing the range $0.30 - 0.40$ for that ratio and leave the issue of desirable lags of v open.[8]

3. The common nominal wage dynamics

The nominal wage dynamics, which will be common for the three wage-price models here considered, is basically represented by a wage Phillips curve. It goes beyond the standard versions in that it includes the employment rate e as well as the wage share v. As is shortly made explicit, both variables are connected with capacity utilization u through average labour productivity $z = Y/L$. While we wish to account for the procyclicality of z, for a small macrodynamic model to be analytically tractable this should be done in a simplified way. We therefore neglect the lead of z in the comovements with u and postulate a direct positive effect of u on the percentage deviations of z from its trend value z^o.[9] Like the functional specifications to follow, we assume linearity in this relationship

$$z/z^o = f_z(u) := 1 + \beta_{zu}(u - 1) \tag{3.1}$$

β_{zu} and all other β-coefficients are nonnegative (in fact mostly positive) constants.

To deal with dynamic relationships, it is convenient to work in continuous time (where for a dynamic variable $x = x(t)$, $\dot{x}$ is its time derivative, $\hat{x}$ its growth rate; $\dot{x} = dx/dt$, $\hat{x} = \dot{x}/x$). Trend productivity is assumed to grow at an exogenous constant rate g_z

$$\hat{z}^o = g_z \tag{3.2}$$

and the growth rate of actual labour productivity derives from (3.1) as

$$\hat{z} = g_z + \beta_{zu}\dot{u}/f_z(u) \tag{3.3}$$

Trend productivity also serves to deflate real wages, or to express them in efficiency units. We correspondingly define

$$\omega = w/pz^o \tag{3.4}$$

For short, ω itself may henceforth be referred to as the real wage rate. Obviously, if w/p continuously grows at g_z, the rate of technical progress, ω remains fixed over time. Since $v = wL/pY = (w/pz^o)(z^oL/Y) = (w/pz^o)(z^o/z)$,

---

[8] The ratios $\sigma_{w/p}/\sigma_u$ and σ_p/σ_u are more stable. For the same subperiod 1975–1991, they amount to 0.46 and 0.50, respectively.

[9] Leaving aside (suitably scaled and autocorrelated) random shocks to the technology, an immediate explanation of the comovements of z and u may be overhead labour and labour hoarding.

the wage share and the real wage rate are linked together by

$$v = \omega/f_z(u) \tag{3.5}$$

To express the employment rate by variables which in a full model would constitute some of the dynamic state variables, we decompose it as $e = L/L^s = z^o(L/Y)(Y/Y^n)(Y^n/K)(K/z^oL^s)$, where L^s is the labour supply (which in the previous section was proxied by the trend values of working hours, L^o). As indicated before, productive capacity is given by $Y^n = y^n K$ with y^n a fixed technological coefficient, and utilization is $u = Y/Y^n$. Hence, if we denote capital per head in efficiency units by k^s,

$$k^s = K/z^o L^s \tag{3.6}$$

the employment rate can be written as

$$e = y^n u k^s / f_z(u) \tag{3.7}$$

Assuming a constant growth rate, g_ℓ, for the labour supply,

$$\hat{L}^s = g_\ell \tag{3.8}$$

the motions of k^s are described by the differential equation

$$\dot{k}^s = k^s(\hat{K} - g_z - g_\ell) \tag{3.9}$$

We can thus turn to the adjustments of the nominal wage rate w, for which we adopt the device of a Phillips curve. As already remarked, besides the usual positive effect of the employment rate on the wage changes, we include the wage share as another variable that might possibly exert some influence. A straightforward idea is that the parties in the wage bargaining process also have an eye on the general distribution of total income. At relatively low values of the wage share, workers seek to catch up to what is considered a normal, or 'fair', level, and this is to some degree taken up in the bargaining. By the same token, workers are somewhat restrained in their wage claims if v is presently above normal. Accordingly, if normal income distribution is (unanimously) characterized by a fixed value v^o, the deviations of v from v^o may have a negative impact on $\hat{w}$. It will be part of the calibration study to find out whether this additional mechanism must be active or whether it could be dispensed with, if the models are to be consistent with the stylized facts.

The feedback of e and v on $\hat{w}$ is the theoretical core of the present Phillips curve. Apart from that, the changes in the nominal wage rate are measured against the changes in prices and labour productivity. Regarding inflation, we allow for an influence of current inflation, $\hat{p}$, as well as a general "inflation climate", which is designated π; regarding labour productivity, we allow for the growth of actual productivity, $\hat{z}$, as well as trend productivity, $\hat{z}^o = g_z$. Taken together, our extended wage Phillips curve reads

$$\hat{w} = [\kappa_{wz}\hat{z} + (1 - \kappa_{wz})\hat{z}^o] + [\kappa_{wp}\hat{p} + (1 - \kappa_{wp})\pi] + f_w(e, v; \beta_{we}, \beta_{wv}) \qquad (3.10)$$

$$f_w = f_w(e, v; \beta_{we}, \beta_{wv}) := \beta_{we}(e - 1) - \beta_{wv}(v - v^o)/v^o \qquad (3.11)$$

where κ_{wz} and κ_{wp} are two weighting parameters between 0 and 1. To ease the exposition later on, the f_w function makes explicit reference to the reaction coefficients, too. Similarly as with $\beta_{wv} = 0$, theoretical reasons or the need to simplify may require $\kappa_{wz} = 0$ (to avoid Equation (3.3)). Again, numerical simulations in a broader modelling context will have to reveal the cyclical implications when the 'degrees of freedom' in setting the parameters are thus constrained.

Equations (3.10) and (3.11) can also be given another and somewhat richer theoretical underpinning. Blanchard and Katz (1999) specify a wage setting model in which the tighter the labour market, the higher the level(!) of the real wage, given the workers' reservation wage. They go on to interpret the latter as depending on labour productivity and lagged wages. If we rescale their unemployment rate U such that $U = 0$ in a steady state and $U = 1 - e$ with respect to the present employment rate, further invoke v^o as the wage share that would prevail on a steady-state growth path, and write $\tilde{x}$ for $\ln x$, then Equation (3.6) in Blanchard and Katz (1999, p. 5) can be rearranged such that it reads (maintaining their coefficients)

$$\tilde{w}_t - \tilde{w}_{t-1} = [\mu a - \mu\lambda\Delta\tilde{z}_t^o - (1 - \mu\lambda)\tilde{v}^o] + (1 - \mu\lambda)\Delta\tilde{z}_t + \mu\lambda\Delta\tilde{z}_t^o$$
$$+ (\tilde{p}_t^e - p_{t-1}) + \beta(e_t - 1) - (1 - \mu\lambda)(\tilde{w}_{t-1} - \tilde{p}_{t-1} - \tilde{z}_{t-1} - \tilde{v}^o)$$

Here the intercept in square brackets on the right-hand side can be shown to vanish, $a, \beta > 0$, and $0 \leqslant \mu, \lambda \leqslant 1$. Note that $\tilde{w}_t - \tilde{p}_t - \tilde{z}_t$ equals $\tilde{v}_t$, the log of the wage share. Hence, the discrete-time counterpart of Equation (3.10) would be compatible with the wage theory expounded by Blanchard and Katz if: $\kappa_{wz} = 1 - \mu\lambda$; $\kappa_{wp} = 0$ and $\pi_t = \tilde{p}_t^e - p_{t-1}$ ($\tilde{p}_t^e$ is an expected price level to which the nominal wage rate is related in the original formulation of the wage equation, or 'wage curve'); $\beta_{we} = \beta$; $\beta_{wv} = 1 - \mu\lambda$; and $(1 - \mu\lambda)(\tilde{v}_{t-1} - \tilde{v}_t)$ is negligibly small.

Blanchard and Katz quote evidence from macroeconomic as well as from regional data that for the US the coefficient $1 - \mu\lambda$ is close to zero. In most European countries, by contrast, $\tilde{w}_{t-1} - \tilde{p}_{t-1} - \tilde{z}_{t-1}$, which in the regression equations is usually referred to as an error correction term, comes in with a significantly negative coefficient; on average, $1 - \mu\lambda$ is around 0.25.[10]

---

[10] Cf. also Plasmans *et al.* (1999, Section 3). It may, however, be asked for the sensitivity of these results with respect to the measure of 'expected inflation', $\tilde{p}_t^e - p_{t-1}$, which might be possibly quite different from our concept of the inflation climate π_t.

The law of governing the variations of the inflation climate π entering (3.10) will also be the same across the three inflation modules. We make it a mix of two simple mechanisms. One of them, adaptive expectations, often proves destabilizing if the speed of adjustment is high enough. The other rule, regressive expectations, constitutes a negative feedback. Introducing the weight $\kappa_{\pi p}$, π^o as a 'normal' value of inflation (or the steady-state value in a full model), and $\beta\pi$ as the general adjustment speed, we specify

$$\dot{\pi} = \beta\pi[\kappa_{\pi p}(\hat{p} - \pi) + (1 - \kappa_{\pi p})(\pi^o - \pi)] \qquad (3.12)$$

Though after the intellectual triumph of the rational expectations hypothesis, working with adaptive expectations has become something of a heresy, in a disequilibrium context there are a number of theoretical and empirical arguments that demonstrate that adaptive expectations make more sense than is usually attributed to them (see Flaschel *et al.* (1997), pp. 149–162, or more extensively, Franke, 1999). This is all the more true if π is not inflation expected for the next quarter, but if it is employed as a benchmark value in a bargaining process, alternatively to current inflation. Since, on the other hand, π should not be completely decoupled from the recent time path of inflation, it makes sense if π adjusts gradually in the direction of $\hat{p}$. The regressive mechanism in (3.12), by contrast, expresses a 'fundamentalist' view, in the sense that the public perceives a certain tendency of inflation to return to normal after some time.[11]

Taken on their own, both principles ($\kappa_{\pi p} = 1$ or 0) are of course rather mechanical. They are, however, easy to integrate into an existing macrodynamic framework and, in their combination of stabilizing and destabilizing forces, already allow for some flexibility in modelling the continuous revision of benchmark rates of inflation.

The time paths of $\pi(\cdot)$ from (3.12) will evidently lag behind $\hat{p}(\cdot)$. This, as such, is no reason to worry, it is even consistent with inflationary expectations themselves that are made in the real world. Here forecast errors are found to be very persistent and forecasts of inflation often appear to be biased (see, e.g., Evans and Wachtel, 1993, Figure. 1 on p. 477, and pp. 481ff).

It has been mentioned in the introduction that our investigations are based on exogenous oscillations of utilization, to which we will also closely link the capital growth rate. Once the time paths $u = u(t)$ and $\hat{K} = \hat{K}(t)$ are given, the time path of the employment rate is determined as well, via (3.9) and (3.7) – independently of the rest of the economy. The only parameter here involved is

---

[11] The general idea that an inflation expectations mechanism, which includes past observed rates of inflation only (rather than observed increases in the money supply), may contain an adaptive and a regressive element is not new and can, for example, already been found in Mussa (1975). The specific functional form of Equation (3.12) is borrowed from Groth (1988, p. 254). It has since then been repeatedly applied in modern, nonorthodox macroeconomic theory (see Chiarella *et al.*, 2000), p. 64 or Chiarella and Flaschel, 2000a, p. 131, 2000b, p. 938).

β_{zu} from the hypothesis on labour productivity in Equation (3.1). This constitutes the first level in the hierarchy of calibration steps. We summarize

Level 1: employment rate e (parameter β_{zu})

$$\dot{k}^s = k^s(\hat{K} - g_z - g_\ell) \tag{3.9}$$

$$e = y^n u k^s / [1 + \beta_{zu}(u - 1)] \tag{3.7}$$

The evolution of the real wage and the wage share is determined at lower-hierarchy levels. These, however, will differ from each other, depending on the particular inflation module applied.

4. Three alternative inflation modules

4.1. Inflation module CCP: countercyclical prices

In the first of the three submodels determining inflation and prices, we postulate countercyclical movements of the price level in an almost direct way. In macrodynamic models, there is of course no scope for detrending procedures. A CCP level can, however, be brought about by referring to the rate of inflation. To this end, it is not $\hat{p}$ that is to be linked to utilization, but its time rate of change, $d\hat{p}/dt$ (the second derivative of the level, so to speak). It is worth noting that this type of relation is a positive one. Since no other variable interferes, we have a second hierarchy level for determining inflation or the price level, for that matter, where only a reaction coefficient $\beta_p > 0$ enters:

CCP Level 2: price level p (parameter β_p)

$$d\hat{p}/dt = \beta_p(u - 1) \tag{3.13}$$

Incidentally, because (3.13) has the time path of utilization as its only input, it might also be considered a level-1 equation. We have assigned it the second level to be more in line with the discussion of the other two inflation modules.

Making $\hat{p}$ itself a dynamic state variable, an equation like (3.13) will also be analytically tractable in a small macro model. Equation (3.13) implies that the variations of $\hat{p}(\cdot)$ lag $u(\cdot)$ a quarter of a cycle (at least if the oscillations of utilization are sufficiently regular). From this pattern, one infers that the series of the induced price level moves indeed countercyclically. Owing to the simplicity of (3.13), there are no leads or lags in this relationship. So (3.13) cannot account for the finer details of Table 3.1 in the cross correlations between u and p. On the other hand, we will have no difficulty in setting the coefficient β_p such that the resulting standard deviation of the percentage deviations of $p(\cdot)$ from a HP 1600 trend line matches a desired ratio from Table 3.2.[12]

---

[12] A discrete-time version of (3.13), by the way, has been empirically tested with success by Gittings (1989).

Theoretically, (3.13) may be conceived as a behavioural equation. Being aware that they live in an inflationary environment, firms see some room for adjusting their current rate of price inflation upward if utilization is above normal, while they feel some pressure to revise it downward if they have excess capacity. If this point of view does not appear convincing, (3.13) can be regarded as a reduced-form expression for the price adjustments of firms. The inflation module would then be given the status of a semi-structural model-building block.

Given the motions $e(\cdot)$ at hierarchy level 1, and $\hat{p}(\cdot)$ at level 2, besides of course the oscillations of capacity utilization, one can next compute the time path of the inflation climate by solving the differential equation (3.12). Involved here are the two parameters $\beta\pi$ and $\kappa_{\pi p}$:

CCP Level 3: inflation climate π (parameters β_π and $\kappa_{\pi p}$)

$$\dot{\pi} = \beta\pi[\kappa_{\pi p}(\hat{p} - \pi) + (1 - \kappa_{\pi p})(\pi^o - \pi)] \tag{3.12}$$

Subsequently, the time paths of the real wage rate is obtained by differentiating (3.4) with respect to time, $\hat{\omega} = \hat{w} - \hat{p} - \hat{z}^o$, and using (3.10) together with (3.2), (3.3) and (3.5). This constitutes the fourth level:

CCP Level 4: real wage ω, wage share v (parameters κ_{wz}, κ_{wp}, β_{we} and β_{wv})

$$\dot{\omega} = \omega[\kappa_{wz}(\hat{z} - g_z) - (1 - \kappa_{wp})(\hat{p} - \pi) + f_w(e, v; \beta_{we}, \beta_{wv})] \tag{3.14}$$

$$v = \omega/f_z(u) \tag{3.5}$$

$$\hat{z} = g_z + \beta_{zu}\dot{u}/f_z(u) \tag{3.3}$$

As hinted at before, many models may not wish to include Equation (3.3) because the time derivative of u would cause too many complications.

4.2. Inflation module PPC: a price Phillips curve

Despite its – by construction – pleasant property of a CCP level, Equation (3.13) may not be reckoned fully satisfactory from a theoretical point of view, since it somewhat lacks in structure. An immediate alternative with its long tradition in economic theory is a Phillips curve governing the rate of price inflation. Besides its great flexibility, the concept of a PPC may in the present context be particularly appealing, because it puts nominal wage and price adjustments on an equal footing.[13]

---

[13] Another argument is that, more or less easy to recognize, PPCs are at the theoretical core of a variety of macroeconometric models; for this and the general flexibility of the Phillips curve concept, see the discussion in Chiarella *et al.* (2000, pp. 52ff).

The core of the PPC we put forward includes a demand-pull and a cost-push argument. We specify them by the adjustment function

$$f_p = f_p(u, v; \beta_{pu}, \beta_{pv}) := \beta_{pu}(u - 1) + \beta_{pv}[(1 + \mu^o)v - 1] \tag{3.15}$$

As our framework allows for under- and overutilization of capacity, u can also be seen as representing the pressure of demand. So, the term $\beta_{pu}(u - 1)$ signifies a demand-pull term. The other component, $\beta_{pv}[(1 + \mu^o)v - 1]$, is a cost-push term proper, by which we mean that it goes beyond taking the present inflationary situation into account (this aspect is considered in a moment). In detail, μ^o is devised as a target markup rate over ULC. Accordingly, prices tend to rise (more than what is captured by the other terms) if labour costs are so high that, at current prices, $p < (1 + \mu^o)wL/Y$, which is equivalent to $0 < (1 + \mu^o)wL/pY - 1 = (1 + \mu^o)v - 1$. For the numerical simulations, we will assume that the target markup is consistent with the normal level v^o of the wage share in Equation (3.11), i.e., $(1 + \mu^o)v^o = 1$.

Since including the wage share in a (price) Phillips curve is still somewhat unusual, it may be mentioned that a positive impact of v on $\hat{p}$ has nevertheless already a certain indirect empirical support. Thus, Brayton *et al.* (1999, pp. 22–27) find that adding the markup $\tilde{\mu}$ of prices over trend ULCs to the other explanatory variables is significant in all versions of their estimations. This is to say that when the price level is high relative to trend ULC, downward pressure is exerted on inflation. To relate this effect to our setting, observe that trend ULC are w/z^o and that the markup $\tilde{\mu}$ over this expression is given by the equation $p = (1 + \tilde{\mu})w/z^o$. Accordingly, p is high relative to trend ULC and impacts negatively on the rate of inflation if $\tilde{\mu}$ or, equivalently, $p/(w/z^o)$ is high. Using the relationship $p/(w/z^o) = 1/\omega = 1/vf_z(u)$ (the latter inequality by virtue of (3.5)), the empirical results are therefore seen to imply that a ceteris paribus increase in the wage share has a positive effect on $\hat{p}$, just as this is stated in Equation (3.15).

Let us then return to the present Phillips curve. Regarding the influence of the inflationary tendencies in the economy, firms employ as their benchmark a weighted average of wage inflation $\hat{w}$ and the inflation climate π. Wage inflation has to be corrected for technical progress. Here the same mix of the growth rates of actual and trend productivity is used as in Equation (3.10). The PPC thus reads

$$\hat{p} = \kappa_{pw}\{\hat{w} - [\kappa_{wz}\hat{z} + (1 - \kappa_{wz})\hat{z}^o]\} + (1 - \kappa_{pw})\pi + f_p(u, v; \beta_{pu}, \beta_{pv}) \tag{3.16}$$

(of course, $0 \leqslant \kappa_{pw} \leqslant 1$).

Since in (3.10) and (3.16), $\hat{w}$ and $\hat{p}$ are mutually dependent on each other, in the next step the two equations have to be solved for $\hat{w}$ and $\hat{p}$. This yields the following reduced-form expressions for wage and price inflation, where it is presupposed that the weights κ_{pw} and κ_{wp} are not both unity. Obviously, wage inflation depends on the core terms in the PPC, and price inflation on the core terms in the wage Phillips curve:

$$\hat{w} = \kappa_{wz}\hat{z} + (1 - \kappa_{wz})\hat{z}^o + \pi + \kappa[\kappa_{wp}f_p(u, v) + f_w(e, v)] \tag{3.17}$$

$$\hat{p} = \pi + \kappa[f_p(u, v) + \kappa_{pw}f_w(e, v)] \tag{3.18}$$

$$\kappa = 1/(1 - \kappa_{pw}\kappa_{wp}) \tag{3.19}$$

It is then seen that in the growth rate of the real wage, $\hat{\omega} = \hat{w} - \hat{p} - \hat{z}^o$, the inflation climate π cancels out. The income distribution dynamics is therefore determined at a higher level than in the CCP module. Its independence from inflationary expectations may be considered another attractive feature of the PPC approach. On the other hand, in general seven parameters are entering at this level:

PPC Level 2: real wage ω, wage share v (κ_{pw}, κ_{wp}, κ_{wz}, β_{pu}, β_{pv}, β_{we}, β_{wv})

$$\hat{\omega} = \omega\{\kappa_{wz}(\hat{z} - g_z) + \kappa[(1 - \kappa_{pw})f_w(e, v; \beta_{we}, \beta_{wv})$$
$$- (1 - \kappa_{wp})f_p(u, v; \beta_{pu}, \beta_{pv})]\} \tag{3.20}$$

$$v = \omega/f_z(u) \tag{3.5}$$

$$\hat{z} = g_z + \beta_{zu}\hat{u}/f_z(u) \tag{3.3}$$

$$\kappa = 1/(1 - \kappa_{pw}\kappa_{wp}) \tag{3.19}$$

Also, the relationship between $\hat{p}$ and π is different from that in the CCP module. While there the computation of the time path of $\pi(\cdot)$ requires the computation of the time path of $\hat{p}(\cdot)$, it is here the other way round. The time paths of $\omega(\cdot)$ and $v(\cdot)$ being computed at level 2, Equation (3.18) can be plugged in the dynamic equation (3.12) for the adjustments of π. Subsequently, the solution of $\pi(\cdot)$ can be used in (3.18) to get the time path of the inflation rate. Apart from the two parameters β_π, $\kappa_{\pi p}$, all parameters have already been set at level 2. We summarize these operations in one step:

PPC Level 3: price inflation $\hat{p}$, inflation climate π (parameters β_π and $\kappa_{\pi p}$)

$$\dot{\pi} = \beta_\pi[\kappa_{\pi p}(\hat{p} - \pi) + (1 - \kappa_{\pi p})(\pi^o - \pi)] \tag{3.12}$$

$$\hat{p} = \pi + \kappa[f_p(u, v) + \kappa_{pw}f_w(e, v)] \tag{3.18}$$

4.3. Inflation module VMK: a variable markup

The third approach seeks to translate a Kaleckian line of reasoning on a VMK into formal language, where the adjustments are basically of a countercyclical nature. The markup rate μ applies to ULCs and gives rise to the price level

$$p = (1 + \mu) wL/Y \tag{3.21}$$

μ is a dynamic variable that is assumed to respond negatively to utilization and its own level. It is convenient to use a growth rate formulation, so that we have

$$\dot\mu = (1 + \mu)f\mu(u, \mu; \beta_{\mu u}, \beta_{\mu\mu}) := (1 + \mu)[-\beta_{\mu u}(u - 1) - \beta_{\mu\mu}(\mu - \mu^o)/\mu^o] \quad (3.22)$$

The gradual adjustments of μ towards μ^o expresses the notion of a target markup. The central issue, however, is the negative impact of capacity utilization. Kalecki observes that in a recession overheads are increasing in relation to prime costs, and then goes on to argue: "there will necessarily follow a 'squeeze of profits', unless the ratio of proceeds to prime costs is permitted to rise. As a result, there may arise a tacit agreement among firms of an industry to 'protect' profits and consequently to increase prices in relation to prime costs" (Kalecki, 1943, p. 50). Another reason for the reluctance of firms to reduce prices is their fear to unchain cut-throat competition (Kalecki, 1939, p. 54), whereas the danger of new competitors will appear much lower in a recession. As for the opposite phase of the business cycle, Kalecki states that this "tendency for the degree of monopoly [which corresponds to the present markup rate μ] to rise in a slump ... is reversed in the boom" (1943, p. 51). An argument here may be to deter new entry into the industry.[14]

Equation (3.21) connects the markup factor with the wage share. Solving it for v, and subsequently solving (3.5) (which relates the wage share to the real wage) for ω, it turns out that the income distribution dynamics is already fully determined by the markup variations in (3.22). Remarkably, the wage Phillips curve has no role to play at that stage. Taken together, level 2 of the VMK model variant is described by

VMK Level 2: real wage ω, wage share v (parameters $\beta_{\mu u}$ and $\beta_{\mu\mu}$)

$$\dot\mu = (1 + \mu)f\mu(u, \mu; \beta_{\mu u}, \beta_{\mu\mu}) \quad (3.22)$$

$$v = 1/(1 + \mu) \quad (3.23)$$

$$\omega = f_z(u)/(1 + \mu) \quad (3.24)$$

The wage Phillips curve contributes to the price inflation dynamics. Similarly as before, the target wage share v^o in (3.11) should be supposed to be consistent with the target markup μ^o in (3.22), $v^o = 1/(1 + \mu^o)$. Writing (3.21) as $p = (1 + \mu)w/z$, the rate of inflation is obtained from logarithmic differentiation, $\hat p = \dot\mu/(1 + \mu) + \hat w - \hat z$. Plugging in (3.22), (3.10) and (3.2), and ruling out a unit

---

[14] See also the discussion in Steindl (1976, p. 17). Kalecki himself undertook an elementary empirical analysis, where the Polish and American time series he examined showed weak support of his theory (Kalecki, 1939, p. 71, 1943, p. 57). Without the target markup, Equation (3.22) has been introduced in macroeconomic theory by Lance Taylor (see, e.g., Taylor, 1989, p. 7). For a small macrodynamic model of the business cycle that integrates (3.22) see also Flaschel *et al.* (1997, Ch. 11).

weight κ_{wp} for current inflation in the wage Phillips curve, the motions of $\hat{p}$ and π are computed at level 3 as follows:

VMK Level 3: price inflation $\hat{p}$, inflation climate π $(\beta_\pi, \kappa_{\pi p}, \kappa_{wp}, \kappa_{wz}, \beta_{we}, \beta_{wv})$

$$\dot{\pi} = \beta_\pi [\kappa_{\pi p}(\hat{p} - \pi) + (1 - \kappa_{\pi p})(\pi^o - \pi)] \tag{3.12}$$

$$\hat{p} = \pi + \frac{1}{1 - \kappa_{wp}} \left[-(1 - \kappa_{wz})(\hat{z} - g_z) + f\mu(u, \mu) + f_w(e, v; \beta_{we}, \beta_{wv}) \right] \tag{3.25}$$

$$\hat{z} = g_z + \beta_{zu}\dot{u}/f_z(u) \tag{3.3}$$

Note that the resulting hierarchy is the same as in the PPC approach: ω and v are determined at level 2 and π and $\hat{p}$ at level 3. However, the number of parameters entering at these levels is very different: in the PPC approach, there are seven (additional) coefficients at level 2 and two at level 3; in the present VMK approach, level 2 is based on just two parameters, while six are required at level 3.

It is also worth mentioning that in a full macroeconomic model, certainly $\kappa_{wz} = 1$ would be desirable in (3.25). In contrast, the polar case $\kappa_{wz} = 0$ would be preferred in the other two modules; see Equations (3.14) and (3.20), respectively.

5. Calibration of the wage-price dynamics

5.1. The exogenous oscillations

As indicated by Table 3.2, among the endogenous variables in the three model variants, we are interested in the cyclical features of five variables: z, e, ω, v and p. Their time paths are fully determined by the variations of utilization u and the capital growth rate $\hat{K}$. The influence of u is apparent at various places. By virtue of (3.9), $\hat{K}$ governs the evolution of k^s, which in turn enters Equation (3.7) for e. For both u and $\hat{K}$, we will assume regular oscillations, which may take the convenient form of a sine wave.

Sine waves would be the outcome in a linear deterministic model, but such undampened and persistent oscillations will there only occur by a fluke. Self-sustained cyclical behaviour in a deterministic modelling framework will accordingly be typically nonlinear, so that even if the solution paths were quite regular, they would still be more or less distinct from a sine-wave motion. Unfortunately, we have no clue in what form these nonlinearities may be taken into account. Any proposal in this direction would have to introduce additional hypotheses, for which presently no solid indications exist. Note that the detrended empirical time series in Figure 3.1 do not seem to exhibit any systematic asymmetries, a visual impression which is largely confirmed by the literature.[15] At least the symmetry in the sine waves would therefore be no counter-argument.

It may, on the other hand, be argued that the exogenous variables be driven by a random process. An obvious problem with this device is that our modelling approach has not intended to mimic the random properties of the time series under study. As a consequence, the three model versions could not be evaluated statistically, unless they were augmented by some random variables (cf. Gregory and Smith, 1993, p. 716). Similar as with the nonlinearities just mentioned, however, there are no clear options for such stochastic extensions. Thus, a stochastic fluctuations method would here be no less arbitrary than the deterministic sine-wave method.[16]

There is also another point why random perturbations cannot be readily introduced into the present deterministic framework. It relates to the fact that the exogenous sine waves bring about (approximately) symmetrical oscillations of the endogenous variables around the steady-state values, provided the initial conditions are suitably chosen. This phenomenon is more important than it might seem at first sight, because it allows us to maintain π^o, v^o, μ^o as constant benchmark values in the adjustment functions (3.11), (3.12), (3.15) and (3.22). By contrast, in a stochastic setting there may easily arise asymmetric fluctuations in the medium term, especially if, realistically, the exogenous random process has a near-unit root. The asymmetry that over a longer-time horizon u, for example, would be more above than below unity would lead to systematic distortions in the adjustment mechanisms. The distortions may be even so strong that they prompt the question if the adjustment rules still continue to make economic sense.[17]

Our methodological standpoint, therefore, is that in lack of a superior alternative, sine-wave motions of the exogenous variables are a reasonable starting point to begin with. At the end of our investigations, we will nevertheless also have a first look at a special 'random' series of the exogenous

---

[15] A standard reference is DeLong and Summers (1986). For a more sophisticated appproach (see Razzak, 2001).

[16] To underline that stochastic simulations are no easy way out, we may quote from a short contribution to an econometric symposium: "most econometricians are so used to dealing with stochastic models that they are rarely aware of the limitations of this approach", a main point being that "all stochastic assumptions, such as assumptions on the stochastic structure of the noise terms, are not innocent at all, in particular if there is no a priori reasoning for their justification" (Deistler, 2001, p. 72). More specifically, regarding a random shock term in a PPC, which (especially in the context of monetary policy) may possibly have grave consequences for the properties of a stochastic model, McCallum (2001, pp. 5f) emphasizes that its existence and nature is an unresolved issue, even when it is only treated as white noise.

[17] To avoid dubious adjustments in these circumstances, the benchmark values might themselves be specified as (slowly) adjusting variables, similar as, for example, a time-varying NAIRU in empirical Phillips curve estimations. While this device may be appealing, it would add further components – and parameters – to the model.

variables: in selected parameter scenarios, we will replace the sine wave of utilization with the empirical trend deviations over the sample period underlying the stylized facts of Table 3.1.

After these introductory methodological remarks, we can turn to the numerical details of the sine-wave oscillations. As the US economy went through four cycles between 1961 and 1991, and another cycle seems to have expanded over roughly the last ten years, we base our investigations on a cycle period of eight years. For utilization, we furthermore assume an amplitude of ±4%, so that we have

$$u(t) = 1 + 0.04 \sin(\phi t), \quad \phi = 2\pi/8 \tag{3.26}$$

The amplitude amounts to a standard deviation of $u(\cdot)$ over a full cycle of 2.84%, while the corresponding empirical value is 2.05%. We opt for the higher amplitude because of our feeling expressed in Section 2, that the HP 1600 trend line of the empirical output–capital ratio absorbs too much medium frequency variation. The choice of the amplitude is, however, only for concreteness and has no consequences for setting the parameters since the amplitudes, or standard deviations, of the endogenous variables will always be related to that of utilization.

In contrast, it should be pointed out that for some variables the cycle period (i.e., the parameter ϕ) does matter. It obviously makes a difference for the amplitude whether, with respect to a fixed adjustment coefficient and thus similar rates of change per unit of time, a variable increases for 24 months or only for, say, 18 months.

Regarding the motions of the capital growth rate, we see in Table 3.1 that it lags utilization by one or two quarters. In economic theory, this delay is usually ascribed to an implementation lag, according to which investment decisions respond quite directly to utilization or similarly fluctuating variables, but it takes some time until the investment projects are completely carried out and the plant and equipment has been actually built up. For simplicity, most macro models neglect the implementation lag, so that utilization and the capital growth rate tend to move in line (though this will have to be an endogenous feature of any particular model). For this reason, we assume that $\hat{K}$ is perfectly synchronized with u. According to the ratio of the two standard deviations reported in Table 3.1, the amplitude of $\hat{K}$ is a fraction of 0.29 of the 4% in (3.26). Thus, denoting the level around which $\hat{K}$ oscillates by g^o,

$$\hat{K}(t) = g^o + 0.29\,[u(t) - 1] \tag{3.27}$$

g^o has the status of a long-run equilibrium growth rate. By a most elementary growth accounting identity, it is given by adding up the (constant) growth rate of labour supply, g_ℓ and the productivity trend rate of growth, g_z. Numerically, we specify

$$g_z = 0.02, \quad g_\ell = 0.01, \quad g^o = g_z + g_\ell \tag{3.28}$$

5.2. Productivity and employment

The highest level of our hierarchy, Equations (3.9) and (3.7), determines the evolution of the employment rate. The only parameter entering here is β_{zu}, which indicates the percentage increase in labour productivity when capacity utilization rises by 1%. Settling on β_{zu} is tantamount to settling on the ratio of the standard deviations σ_z and σ_u of the oscillations of the two variables. In laying out the desirable features of a model calibration in Table 3.2, we have already decided on a definite value in this respect. We therefore set

$$\beta_{zu} = 0.40 \qquad\qquad (3.29)$$

$e^o = 1$ is what in a full model would constitute the long-run equilibrium value of the employment rate. The corresponding level of capital per head is $(k^s)^o = e^o/y^n = 1/y^n$; cf. Equation (3.7).[18] By virtue of $g^o - g_z - g_\ell = 0$ from (3.28), the variations of k^s resulting from (3.9) are stationary, so that a suitable choice of the initial value of k^s at $t = 0$ can make the oscillations symmetrical around $(k^s)^o$. Owing to the nonlinearity in (3.7), the induced oscillations of the employment rate are only approximately symmetrical around e^o; the precise value of the time average of $e(\cdot)$ over a cycle is 0.9998.

As it turns out, the amplitude of the employment rate is lower than desired. The relative standard deviation is $\sigma_e/\sigma_u = 0.69$, while in Table 3.2 we aspired to a ratio 0.75. Regarding the second cyclical characteristic, the motions of e exhibit a lag of three quarters behind utilization; this is just at the upper end of the range given in Table 3.2.

There are three reasons why these statistics do not accurately match the target values put forward in Table 3.2: the hypothesis that labour productivity is directly a function of utilization; the neglect of any lead or lag in this relationship; and the assumption that the variations of the capital growth rate are strictly synchronous with u. For a wider perspective, let us relax the latter two assumptions for a moment and introduce a lead τ_z for productivity in Equation (3.1), and a lag τ_k for the capital growth rate in Equation (3.27):

$$z(t)/z^o(t) = 1 + \beta_{zu}[u(t + \tau_z) - 1] \qquad\qquad (3.1a)$$

$$\hat{K}(t) = g^o + 0.29[u(t - \tau_k) - 1] \qquad\qquad (3.27a)$$

These relationships, especially (3.1a), are by no means supposed to be a theoretical contribution, they only serve exploratory purposes.

In the light of the empirical cross correlations in Table 3.1, consider $\tau_z = 0.62$ and $\tau_k = 0.37$. Table 3.3 summarizes the impact of these modifications on the

---

[18] Concretely, we use $y^n = 0.70$, but this value does not affect the results in any way.

Table 3.3. **Cyclical properties of the employment rate**

τ_k	τ_z	σ_e/σ_u	Lag e
0.00	0.00	0.69	0.75
0.37	0.00	0.60	0.83
0.00	0.62	0.84	0.92
0.37	0.62	0.75	1.08

Note: τ_k and τ_z are the time delays in Equations (3.1a) and (3.27a). The lags are measured in years.

cyclical properties of employment in Equations (3.9) and (3.7).[19] It is thus seen that the lag τ_k in the capital growth rate reduces the amplitude in the oscillations of e, whereas the lead τ_z in productivity increases it appreciably. Combining the two effects, a standard deviation σ_e results that is just what we were aiming at. On the other hand, the lag of e seems to become unduly long in this way. The last row in Table 3.3 especially reveals the merits and demerits of the approach of Equation (3.1) to labour productivity.

In the remainder of the paper, we again disregard the time delays τ_k and τ_z and proceed to work with Equations (3.1) and (3.27) as convenient modelling simplifications. We accept the coefficient β_{zu} in (3.29) together with the three-quarter lag in employment and the standard deviation $\sigma_e/\sigma_u = 0.69$. Even if the latter ratio is considered too low, this is just a matter of scale and does not seriously affect the calibration of the other model components. Notice to this end that e only enters the wage Phillips curve in Equations (3.10) and (3.11). Since its influence there is linear, a possible downward bias in the variability of $e(\cdot)$ can be readily compensated by a correspondingly higher value of the coefficient β_{we} in the function f_w.[20]

5.3. The model with inflation module CCP

The CCP model variant has the advantage that, accepting a price level that moves strictly countercyclically, the amplitude of the price oscillations is directly determined by Equation (3.13) at the hierarchy level 2. By the same token, with the parameter β_p in this adjustment equation for the rate of inflation, one has full control over the standard deviation σ_p.

In detail, we solve (3.13) for the rate of inflation, which gives us a monthly series in the simulations (cf. footnote 20), reconstruct from it the time path of the

---

[19] In the simulations the differential equations are approximated by their discrete-time analogues with an adjustment period of one month. Correspondingly, the lags reported from Table 3.3 onwards can only be measured on a monthly basis.

[20] More precisely, the issue is the following. Suppose, for the sake of the argument, the Phillips curve (3.10) and (3.11) is a correct description of the nominal wage adjustments and the parameter β_{we} is correctly estimated. Then, within the present theoretical framework, we would increase this coefficient by a factor 0.75/0.69 to make good for the lower amplitude of the employment rate.

log of the price level, extract a quarterly series, detrend it by Hodrick–Prescott with $\lambda = 1600$ and interpolate these trend deviations to get the same number of monthly data points as we have available for $u(\cdot)$. It is the standard deviation of the thus resulting time series to which we refer and that we designate σ_p. By virtue of the smoothness of the time paths, interpolation is here no problem. Also, differences between the standard deviations of the monthly and the quarterly series are negligible.

It should be remarked that the HP 1600 trend is not a straight line, so that these trend deviations are different from the theoretically appropriate expressions $\ln p(t) - \ln p^o(t)$, where $\ln p^o(t) = \pi^o t + const.$ are the steady-state equilibrium prices that would rise at the constant equilibrium rate of inflation π^o. While, with the sine wave in (3.26), one can analytically work out that the ratio of the standard deviation of the time path $\ln p(t) - \ln p^o(t)$ to that of $u(t)$ is given by $\beta_p/\phi^2 = \beta_p 1.621$, the present ratio σ_p/σ_u, which is based on the HP 1600 filter, is smaller.[21] Numerically, the latter relationship comes out as $\sigma_p/\sigma_u \approx \beta_p 1.10$.

In calibrating the price level, we wish to obtain a ratio $\sigma_p/\sigma_u = 0.50$. This is accomplished by setting

$$\beta_p = 0.45 \tag{3.30}$$

In order to limit the number of free parameters, we take an a priori decision about the adjustments of the inflation climate π at CCP level 3. Given the benchmark character of π, which is *not* just expected inflation for the next quarter, the adjustments toward current inflation should not be too fast. Likewise, agents will not expect inflation to return to normal too quickly. We therefore choose a moderate size of the adjustment speed $\beta\pi$ in Equation (3.12). As for the role of adaptive and regressive expectations, let us assume equal weights. Correspondingly, if not otherwise stated, for the following investigations we posit

$$\beta\pi = 1.00, \quad \kappa_{\pi p} = 0.50 \tag{3.31}$$

Similar motions of π, by the way, can also be generated by quite different parameter combinations of $\beta\pi$ and $\kappa_{\pi p}$. A more ambitious study could proxy π by empirical inflation forecasts, the Livingston survey of professional forecasters or the Survey Research Center survey of individuals from a random population sample, for example, and try to obtain estimates of $\beta\pi$ and $\kappa_{\pi p}$ on this basis. The ensuing calibration of the model components could then proceed along the same lines as with Equation (3.31).

---

[21] The simulated log series of the price level may be viewed as arising from a first-order integrated process. On the other hand, it is well known that the HP filter is an optimal signal extractor for univariate time series x_t in an uncorrelated components model which implies that x_t would be an I(2) process. Hence, by construction, the HP filter removes too much as trend from the price series.

Employing (3.30) and (3.31), the problem now is whether the countercyclical motions of the price level are compatible with the cyclical properties of the real wage and the wage share at which we aimed in Table 3.2. At CCP level 4, there are still four parameters to achieve this goal: κ_{wp}, κ_{wz}, β_{we} and β_{wv}. After some explorations, we take a first step and lay a grid of 6825 points over this parameter space, run a simulation for each quadruple and after each simulation compute the statistics we are concerned with. For κ_{wp} and κ_{wz} the five values 0.00, 0.25, 0.50, 0.75 and 1.00 are considered; for β_{we}, 21 equally spaced values between 0.200 and 0.700 (stepsize 0.025); for β_{wv}, 13 equally spaced values between 0.000 and 1.500 (stepsize 0.125). The most important result of this grid search is a negative one, namely, not all desirable features can be simultaneously realized.

To see the nature of the hindrance, assign highest priority to the amplitude of the real wage rate, demanding $0.45 \leqslant \sigma\omega/\sigma_u \leqslant 0.50$. Generally it may then be said that if this range is met, either the lag of the real wage is too long, or the amplitude of the wage share is too low. A shorter lag of ω is accompanied by lower standard deviations σ_v, and higher values of σ_v are accompanied by longer lags of ω. To give a few examples, lag $\omega \leqslant 0.50$ admits no higher ratio σ_v/σ_u than 0.203 (over the entire grid, there are just three parameter combinations with lag $\omega = 0.50$ and $\sigma_v/\sigma_u \geqslant 0.200$). Increasing the delay, lag $\omega = 0.75$ admits no higher ratio σ_v/σ_u than 0.284 (there being just five parameter combinations with lag $\omega = 0.75$ and $\sigma_v/\sigma_u \geqslant 0.275$). Likewise, $\sigma_v/\sigma_u \geqslant 0.300$ requires lag $\omega \geqslant 0.83$ (with lag $\omega = 0.83$, there are three combinations entailing $\sigma_v/\sigma_u = 0.300, 0.300, 0.304$, respectively), while $\sigma_v/\sigma_u \geqslant 0.350$ even requires the real wage rate to lag utilization by at least one year.

Following these results, we have to lower our sights. To proceed with our work, we put up a set of 'second-best' criteria that the model should satisfy. They are collected in Table 3.4, where with respect to the employment rate the discussion in the previous subsection is already taken into account. Regarding the other endogenous variables, in comparison with the desired features in Table 3.2 we here admit a longer lag for the real wage, and a lower standard deviation for the wage share. Parameter combinations giving rise to the features in Table 3.4 may be called *admissible*.

Table 3.4.   *Second-best criteria for the macrodynamic oscillations*

Variable x	σ_x/σ_u	Lag x
dev z	0.40	0.00
dev e	0.69	0.75
dev ω	0.45–0.50	−0.50–0.75
dev v	0.25–0.40	—
−dev p	0.45–0.50	−0.75–0.25

Knowing that admissible parameter combinations exist, let us turn to some numerical details concerning the level-4 coefficients κ_{wp}, κ_{wz}, β_{we} and β_{wv}. Three questions are of particular interest: (1) Given that a positive weight κ_{wz} in Equation (3.14) would make the growth rate of actual labour productivity and, thus, the time derivative of utilization enter the model's reduced-form equations, which certainly will impede a mathematical analysis, do admissible combinations with $\kappa_{wz} = 0$ exist? (2) Since wage Phillips curves usually do not make reference to the wage share, do combinations with $\beta_{wv} = 0$ exist? (3) Are the values of the core coefficient of the wage Phillips curve, β_{we}, within a familiar range, say, $0.30 \leqslant \beta_{we} \leqslant 0.50$? Information about these points is illustrated in Figure 3.2.

The '+' symbol in Figure 3.2 records the (β_{we}, β_{wv}) component of admissible parameter combinations that are obtained from the grid search just mentioned. While the answer to question (3.3) is in the affirmative, the coefficient β_{wv} may be low, but is still bounded away from zero. Hence, for the condition $\beta_{wv} = 0$ to be fulfilled, the coefficients $\beta\pi$ and/or $\kappa_{\pi p}$ have to be chosen more skillfully. This issue is taken up shortly.

To deal with point (1), we fix $\kappa_{wz} = 0$ and set up a finer grid of the other three coefficients κ_{wp}, β_{we} and β_{wv}. On the basis of this battery of simulation runs, we can conclude that for all pairs (β_{we}, β_{wv}) in the dotted area in Figure 3.2 there is a value between 0 and 1 of the coefficient κ_{wp} such that the corresponding

Figure 3.2.   Admissible pairs (β_{we}, β_{wv}) under CCP

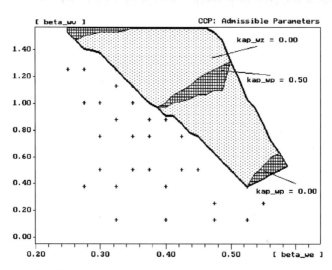

Note: Pairs (β_{we}, β_{wv}) in dotted area match second-best criteria of Table 3.4 for Equations (3.30), (3.31), $\kappa_{wz} = 0$, and some suitable $\kappa_{wp} \in [0, 1]$; pairs in the hatched area, in addition, are associated with $\kappa_{wp} = 0$, $\kappa_{wp} = 0.50$, $\kappa_{wp} \geqslant 0.95$ (as seen from below). '+' indicates (β_{we}, β_{wv}) meeting the criteria for some $\kappa_{wz} \in \{0.25, 0.50, 0.75, 1.00\}$ and $\kappa_{wp} \in \{0.00, 0.25, 0.50, 0.75, 1.00\}$ (coarse grid search).

Table 3.5. **Parameter variations in base scenario CCP**

β_{wv}	β_{we}	$\kappa_{\pi p}$	$\sigma\omega/\sigma_u$	Lag ω	σ_v/σ_u	Lag v
0.50	0.55	0.50	0.48	0.75	0.26	2.00
0.00	0.55	0.50	0.35	1.00	0.29	2.75
0.00	0.55	0.25	0.49	1.00	0.35	2.17
0.00	0.45	0.25	0.48	0.75	0.27	2.00
0.00	0.35	0.25	0.49	0.58	0.21	1.75

parameter combination satisfies the second-best criteria.[22] The subsets of the hatched areas indicate admissible pairs (β_{we}, β_{wv}) that, besides $\kappa_{wz} = 0$, are combined with $\kappa_{wp} = 0$ (the lower region), $\kappa_{wp} = 0.50$ (the middle region) or $\kappa_{wp} \in [0.95, 1.00]$ (the region in the north-west corner). Regarding the dynamic (3.14) that governs the motions of the real wage rate, note that as κ_{wp} increases from zero to unity, the influence of the gap between the current rate of inflation and the general inflation climate diminishes. Figure 3.2 shows a tendency that, going along with a moderate decline in the coefficient β_{we}, this is mainly made up by a considerable increase in β_{wv}.

we inquire into the existence of admissible parameter combinations with $\beta_{wv} = 0$, it is useful to set up a base scenario to which the outcomes of alternative parameters in this and the following sections can be compared. For theoretical reasons, we still want the employment rate to play a dominant role in the wage Phillips curve vis-à-vis the wage share. As will be more rigorously verified in a moment, this is achieved by pairs (β_{we}, β_{wv}) in the lower part of the dotted area in Figure 3.2, where $\kappa_{wp} = 0$. We therefore choose

Base Scenario CCP:

$$\beta_{zu} = 0.40, \quad \beta_p = 0.45, \quad \beta_\pi = 1.00, \quad \kappa_{\pi p} = 0.50$$
$$\kappa_{wp} = 0.00, \quad \kappa_{wz} = 0.00, \quad \beta_{we} = 0.55, \quad \beta_{wv} = 0.50$$

The first row in Table 3.5 reports the precise statistics that are generated by this reference set of coefficients. Beyond the previous discussion of their order of magnitude, the two-years lag in the wage share, which amounts to a quarter of the cycle, is worth pointing out. Similar lags of v are encountered for all other admissible parameter combinations. This type of comovements between measures of economic activity and income distribution is equally obtained in Goodwin's (1967) seminal growth cycle model and its various extensions. Hence,

---

[22] There may nonetheless exist other values of κ_{wp} and $\kappa_{wz} > 0$ for which the same pair (β_{we}, β_{wv}) establishes an admissible parameter combination.

the present framework is well compatible with this approach and could, indeed, provide a richer structure for its wage-price dynamics.

In order to compare the influence of the employment rate and the wage share in the wage Phillips curve, one has to take the amplitudes of these variables into account. Employing the standard deviations for this purpose, v can be said to be less influential than e if $\sigma_v \beta_{wv} < \sigma_e \beta_{we}$, that is, if $\beta_{wv} < \beta_{we} (\sigma_e/\sigma_u)/(\sigma_v/\sigma_u) = 0.55 \cdot 0.69/0.26 = 1.49$ (cf. the first row in Table 3.3 for σ_e/σ_u). It is thus established that the influence of the wage share is weaker by a factor of three. Incidentally, for a pair (β_{we}, β_{wv}) in the middle hatched region of Figure 3.2, the influence of e and v would be about equal.

The second row in Table 3.5 shows the consequences of a ceteris paribus drop of β_{wv} to zero, which has two unpleasant effects for the real wage: a decrease in the standard deviation and a longer lag.[23] The decrease in $\sigma\omega$ can be undone by giving regressive expectations in the adjustments of the inflation climate a greater weight, i.e., by reducing $\kappa_{\pi p}$ to 0.25. Subsequently, the lag of the real wage can be shortened by lowering the coefficient β_{we}. At the same time, this ceteris paribus change diminishes the (previously increasing) standard deviation of the wage share considerably, while under the given circumstances, perhaps somewhat surprisingly, the impact on $\sigma\omega$ is very weak. At $\beta_{we} = 0.45$, all second-best criteria are met again. A further reduction of β_{we} would be desirable insofar as the real wage becomes more procyclical. However, as we have observed above, this decreases σ_v too much.

There are additional examples of admissible parameter combinations with a vanishing coefficient β_{wv}. As in the exercise mentioned in Table 3.5, however, they always call for a specific conjunction of, especially, $\beta\pi$ and $\kappa_{\pi p}$. This is to say that the condition $\beta_{wv} = 0$, which relates to the wage Phillips curve, requires conditions to be met which have their place in another part of the model. In this sense, the assumption $\beta_{wv} = 0$ rests on rather shaky grounds and, in the present context with the CCP inflation module, may better be avoided.

5.4. The model with inflation module PPC

It has already been noted before that the inflation module with the PPC has the pleasant property that the real-wage dynamics is determined independently of the inflation climate π, at hierarchy level 2. On the other hand, this goes at the cost of seven parameters being involved. Macro models working with two Phillips curves usually concentrate on the utilization measures on the goods and labour markets and ignore a possible influence of the wage share (or a related variable), which in the present setting amounts to $\beta_{wv} = \beta_{pv} = 0$. If technical

---

[23] The adverse effects would be even more dramatic for admissible parameter combinations with a positive value of κ_{wp}.

progress is included, $\kappa_{wz} = 0$ is assumed as well. In this way, Equation (3.20) for the changes in the real wage becomes[24]

$$\dot\omega = \omega\kappa[(1 - \kappa_{pw})\beta_{we}(e - 1) - (1 - \kappa_{wp})\beta_{pu}(u - 1)] \tag{3.20a}$$

Since the employment rate is a nearly procyclical variable, it is immediately seen that the oscillations of the real wage will be shifted by about a quarter of a cycle; whether forward or backward depends on the relative magnitudes of $(1 - \kappa_{pw})$ β_{we} and $(1 - \kappa_{wp})\beta_{pu}$. It follows from this elementary observation that the approach of two standard Phillips curves is not compatible with the stylized fact of a procyclical real wage rate.

Taking it for granted that the two general Phillips curves (3.10), (3.11) and (3.15), (3.16) should not be prematurely simplified, we would nevertheless like to limit the variations of the seven parameters at PPC level 2. In addition, it should be possible to relate the investigations to our previous results. To this end, we begin the simulations with the wage Phillips curve parameters $\kappa_{wp}, \kappa_{wz}, \beta_{we}$ and β_{wv} from the CCP base scenario. There are thus only three parameters left for calibrating $\omega(\cdot)$ and $v(\cdot)$, namely, the PPC coefficients κ_{pw}, β_{pu} and β_{pv}. Regarding the price dynamics at PPC level 3, we also continue to fix the parameters $\beta\pi, \kappa_{\pi p}$ at the values assigned to them in the same scenario. The underlying belief is that, given the wage Phillips curve that has already turned out to be feasible, the PPC with its three coefficients have sufficient degrees of freedom to generate a satisfactory income distribution dynamics. It is furthermore hoped that then, with the likewise proven values of $\beta\pi$ and $\kappa_{\pi p}$, the implied price dynamics exhibits similar properties as before.

Figure 3.3 shows the outcome of a three-dimensional grid search across the parameters κ_{pw}, β_{pu} and β_{pv}. The diagram shows the set of pairs (β_{pu}, β_{pv}) for which at least one value of κ_{pw} exists such that these coefficients, together with the parameter values just mentioned, meet the six conditions for dev ω, dev v, dev p in the lower half of Table 3.4. For each pair (β_{pu}, β_{pv}) in the dotted area there is mostly a wider range of κ_{pw} with that property. The diagram also indicates the sets where the accompanying κ_{pw} can be 0.00 or 0.50, respectively. An insignificant subset of (β_{pu}, β_{pv}) has associated with it $\kappa_{pw} = 0.55$, which is the maximum value of all admissible κ_{pw} we find.

The most important feature to note in Figure 3.3 is that the coefficient β_{pu} may well vanish. Furthermore, even the highest admissible values of β_{pu} appear rather undersized. The influence of utilization in the PPC is in fact always markedly inferior to the wage share. That is, β_{pv} is always much larger than $\beta_{pu}/(\sigma_v/\sigma_u) \approx \beta_{pu}/0.26 > 0.18/0.26 = 0.69$ (which means $\sigma_u\beta_{pu} \ll \sigma_v\beta_{pv}$).

---

[24] For example, Equation (3.20a) is a constituting part of the models in Chiarella and Flaschel (2000a, pp. 182, 298, 2000b, p. 937), or Chiarella *et al.* (2000, p. 63).

Figure 3.3.   *Admissible pairs* (β_{pu}, β_{pv}) *under PPC*

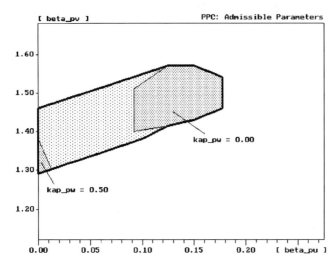

Note: Pairs (β_{we}, β_{wv}) in dotted area meet second-best criteria of Table 3.4 for some suitable value of $\kappa_{pw} \in [0, 1]$. The pairs in the closely dotted area are associated with $\kappa_{pw} = 0.00$ or $\kappa_{pw} = 0.50$, respectively. The values of the other parameters are taken over from the CCP- base scenario.

Actually, a Phillips curve with such a dominant influence of the wage share might no longer be considered a Phillips curve proper.

While the parameter combinations illustrated in Figure 3.3 meet the second-best criteria of Table 3.4, they also do no better than that. Thus, the shortest lag of the real wage is lag $\omega = 0.75$ years, and the maximum standard deviation of the wage share is $\sigma_v/\sigma_u = 0.283$. The oscillations of the price level are without exception strictly countercyclical, i.e., lag$(-$ dev $p) = 0$.

In deciding on a base scenario, we may therefore go anywhere in the dotted area in Figure 3.3. Let us choose a combination with a relatively high coefficient β_{pu}. So we arrive at

Base Scenario PPC:
$\beta_{\pi} = 1.00, \; \kappa_{\pi p} = 0.50$
$\beta_{zu} = 0.40, \; \kappa_{pw} = 0.00, \; \beta_{pu} = 0.15, \; \beta_{pv} = 1.50$
$\kappa_{wp} = 0.00, \; \kappa_{wz} = 0.00, \; \beta_{we} = 0.55, \; \beta_{wv} = 0.50$

The cyclical features of this scenario resemble very much those of the CCP base scenario. In detail, $\sigma\omega/\sigma_u = 0.47$, lag $\omega = 0.75$, $\sigma_v/\sigma_u = 0.26$, lag $v = 2.08$, $\sigma_p/\sigma_u = 0.48$ and lag$(-$ dev $p) = 0.00$.

In concluding the discussion of the PPC module, it may again be asked whether parameter combinations with $\beta_{wv} = 0$ in the wage Phillips curve are possible. We investigated this question by fixing $\beta_{wv} = 0$, $\kappa_{wz} = 0$ (besides

$\beta_{zu} = 0.40$, of course) and laying a 7-dimensional grid over the parameters $\beta_{pu}, \beta_{pv}, \kappa_{pw}, \beta_{we}, \kappa_{wp}, \beta_\pi$ and $\kappa_{\pi p}$. Invoking a random mechanism, 50,000 of these grid points were checked, with the result that not one parameter combination satisfied the second-best criteria. For example, if all criteria are fulfilled except for lag ω, then the minimal lag of the real wage is 0.83 years, which is realized by no more than three combinations. If, instead, we relax the condition on the standard deviation of the wage share, there are only four combinations with $\sigma_v/\sigma_u \geqslant 0.20$, where three of them rest on very slow adjustments of the inflation climate, $\beta\pi = 0.20$ or $\beta\pi = 0.40$.[25] The evaluation of the assumption $\beta_{wv} = 0$ in the wage Phillips curve is therefore similarly, if not even more, negative than for the wage-price dynamics under the CCP inflation module.

5.5. The model with inflation module VMK

At its highest hierarchy level, the VMK model variant has only two parameters, $\beta_{\mu u}$ and $\beta_{\mu\mu}$, to regulate the three statistics of the real wage dynamics: $\sigma\omega$, lag ω and σ_v. It is thus a nontrivial problem whether $\beta_{\mu u}$ and $\beta_{\mu\mu}$ are really capable of generating satisfactory cyclical properties in this respect.

After checking for an upper boundary of $\beta_{\mu u}$ and $\beta_{\mu\mu}$ beyond which there is no further scope for reasonable values of all three statistics, we set up a grid of 21 values of $\beta_{\mu u}$ that range from 0.050 to 0.350 (stepsize 0.015), and 21 values of $\beta_{\mu\mu}$ that range from 0.000 to 0.300 (likewise, stepsize 0.015). Among these 441 combinations, it turns out, there are four pairs that meet the second-best conditions. Three of them exhibit $\beta_{\mu u} = 0.200$, together with $\beta_{\mu\mu} = 0.000, 0.015$ and 0.030; the fourth one is not very much different with $\beta_{\mu u} = 0.215$ and $\beta_{\mu\mu} = 0.015$. The latter pair implies $\sigma_v/\sigma_u = 0.271$, for the remaining three the ratio σ_v/σ_u is between 0.253 and 0.258. One pair, $\beta_{\mu u} = 0.200$, $\beta_{\mu\mu} = 0.030$, entails a lag of the real wage of 0.67 years, while lag $\omega = 0.75$ in the other cases. Since this is the shortest lag that we have encountered so far for admissible parameter combinations, we accept the slightly lower standard deviation of the wage share with which it goes along, i.e., $\sigma_v/\sigma_u = 0.254$, and base the following investigations on

$$\beta_{\mu u} = 0.20, \quad \beta_{\mu\mu} = 0.03 \tag{3.32}$$

Shorter lags of the real wage are possible, but similarly as in the other modules, only at the price of higher values of $\sigma\omega$ and lower values of σ_v.

It should also be pointed out that, apart from the precise numerical implications, another reason for choosing a strictly positive coefficient $\beta_{\mu u}$ may arise in the context of a full macroeconomic model. Here, $\beta_{\mu\mu} > 0$ could help

---

[25] The fourth combination exhibits $\beta\pi = 1.00$. It also yields the 'best' combination, with $\sigma_v/\sigma_u = 0.247$. For completeness, the other coefficients are $\beta_{pu} = 0.05$, $\beta_{pv} = 1.80$, $\kappa_{pw} = 0.20$, $\beta_{we} = 0.45$, $\kappa_{wp} = 0.00$ and $\kappa_{\pi p} = 0.19$.

ensure uniqueness of a steady state position, which is reflected by a regular Jacobian matrix. Otherwise, if utilization appears, not only on the right-hand side of (3.22), but also in other reduced-form equations of the full dynamic system, the Jacobian might be singular.

As in the organization of the preceding simulations, we maintain the parameters $\beta\pi$, $\kappa_{\pi p}$ as stated in (3.31). An obvious question, then, is for the integration of the wage Phillips curve from the CCP and PPC base scenarios: will VMK, at level 3, yield similar cyclical statistics for the price level? The answer is, nearly so. The standard deviation amounts to $\sigma_p/\sigma_u = 0.50$, but there is a short lag of $-$ dev p of one quarter.

Even if this result is reckoned satisfactory, there are two coefficients in the Phillips curve that we would like to change. The first one is κ_{wz}, which is set to zero in the CCP and PPC scenarios. Referring to Equation (3.25), we recall that under VMK, $\kappa_{wz} = 1$ would be the preferred value in order to eliminate the growth rate $\hat{z}$ of actual productivity from the model. A direct ceteris paribus increase of κ_{wz} from zero to unity has, however, a drastic consequence for the price dynamics: while now $-$ dev p leads utilization by three quarters, which might still be agreeable, the standard deviation falls down to $\sigma_p/\sigma_u = 0.18$. This is another example of the strong influence that a weighting parameter may possibly have.

Much in line with the discussion of the CCP and PPC model, the second parameter which one perhaps would wish to determine a priori, i.e., fix at zero, is β_{wv}. Thus, set

$$\kappa_{wz} = 1.00, \quad \beta_{wv} = 0.00 \tag{3.33}$$

and let us see what the two remaining free parameters, β_{we} and κ_{wp}, can achieve. The outcome of a detailed grid search is shown in Figure 3.4. In the dotted area it depicts the pairs $(\beta_{we}, \kappa_{wp})$ that, given (3.29) and (3.31)–(3.33), imply $0.45 \leqslant \sigma_p/\sigma_u \leqslant 0.50$ and a lag of the price level (i.e., of $-$ dev p) between 0.25 and -0.50 years (the latter as indicated in the four subsets). The diagram, in particular, demonstrates that again the admissible slope coefficients β_{we} in the Phillips curve lie in a familiar range. Associated with suitable values of the weight parameter κ_{wp}, β_{we} may vary between 0.34 and 0.81. On the other hand, it is clear from (3.25) that κ_{wp} must be bounded away from unity. The precise upper bound in Figure 3.4 is $\kappa_{wp} = 0.63$.

In the light of the stylized facts in Table 3.1, we may, for setting up a base scenario, choose a pair $(\beta_{we}, \kappa_{wp})$ that entails a one-quarter lead of the countercyclical oscillations of the price level. In this way, we can even retain the previous slope coefficient β_{we}. In sum, we specify

Base Scenario VMK:

$\beta_\pi = 1.00$, $\kappa_{\pi p} = 0.50$

$\beta_{zu} = 0.40$, $\beta_{\mu u} = 0.20$, $\beta_{\mu\mu} = 0.03$

$\kappa_{wp} = 0.35$, $\kappa_{wz} = 1.00$, $\beta_{we} = 0.55$, $\beta_{wv} = 0.00$

Figure 3.4. **Admissible pairs $(\beta_{we}, \kappa_{wp})$ under VMK**

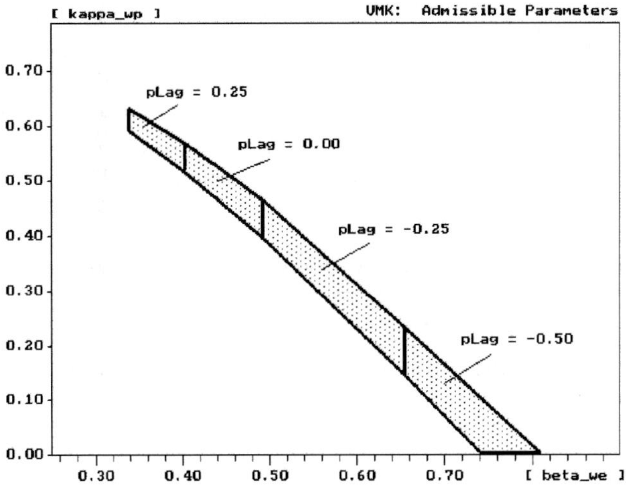

Note: Pairs $(\beta_{we}, \kappa_{wp})$ in dotted area meet second-best criteria of Table 3.4, given (3.29), (3.31)–(3.33). 'pLag' stands for lag($-$ dev p), in years.

6. Evaluation of the base scenarios

A main motive for undertaking the numerical simulations was to investigate whether the three wage-price submodels have sufficiently reasonable properties to be integrated into a broader modelling framework. A closely related question is which of the three versions may be best suited for this purpose. To ease the discussion of the topic, each model variant is represented by its base scenario. For convenience, the cyclical features produced by them are summarized in Table 3.6.

The table reiterates that all three submodels satisfy the second-best criteria established in Table 3.4, where, in particular, a certain lag of the real wage rate has to be accepted. Since also no model can do any better than that, the three are so far on an equal footing. In finer detail, one might perhaps say that VMK has a weak edge over CCP and PPC, insofar as it admits a slightly shorter lag of ω and a slight lead in the countercyclical motions of the price level. But given the still relatively simple structure of the modelling equations, this aspect should not be overrated.

Since the three submodels have the same functional specification of a wage Phillips curve underlying, one may ask for the compatibility of the inflation modules. That is, one may ask if one module can be exchanged for another while maintaining the coefficients of the wage Phillips curve (and, of course, β_{zu}, $\beta\pi$,

Table 3.6.   *Cyclical properties of the base scenarios*

	$\sigma\omega/\sigma_u$	Lag ω	σ_v/σ_u	Lag v	σ_p/σ_u	Lag $(-p)$
CCP	0.48	0.75	0.26	2.00	0.50	0.00
PPC	0.47	0.75	0.26	2.08	0.48	0.00
VMK	0.49	0.67	0.25	1.92	0.47	−0.25

Note: $x = $ dev ω, dev v, dev p indicates percentage deviations from steady state values (variables ω and v) or from HP trend (variable p). The statistics are computed over a full cycle.

Table 3.7.   *Synopsis of base scenario coefficients*

	β_{we}	β_{wv}	κ_{wp}	κ_{wz}	β_p	β_{pu}	β_{pv}	κ_{pw}	$\beta_{\mu u}$	$\beta_{\mu\mu}$	KC
CCP	0.55	0.50	0.00	0.00	0.45	—	—	—	—	—	4
PPC	0.55	0.50	0.00	0.00	—	0.15	1.50	0.00	—	—	6
VMK	0.55	0.00	0.35	1.00	—	—	—	—	0.20	0.03	4

Note: For all three model variants, the remaining parameters are given by Equations (3.29) and (3.31). KC is the number of 'key coefficients' (see text).

$\kappa_{\pi p}$). As it can be once again seen from the synopsis of the adjustment coefficients in Table 3.7, this is certainly true for the CCP and PPC base scenarios.

Thus, a decision between CCP and PPC would have to be made on other grounds. One argument supporting CCP is that this inflation module involves only one further parameter, vis-à-vis three for PPC. On the other hand, the approach of a PPC has theoretical content, while one may tend to view the CCP equation as a reduced-form representation of a price adjustment process that is not fully made explicit.

Regarding the third inflation module, it has already been pointed out in Section 5.5 that the wage Phillips curve with the CCP- and PPC-base scenario coefficients, when employed in the VMK model, leads to results that are only slightly inferior. Given suitably chosen numerical values of β_p, of $(\beta_{pu}, \beta_{pv}, \kappa_{pw})$, or $(\beta_{\mu u}, \beta_{\mu\mu})$, respectively, it can therefore be noted that the three inflation modules are indeed well compatible; in the sense that combining them with the same (suitably chosen) wage Phillips curve gives rise to very similar cyclical features. This is a remarkable conclusion since theoretically as well as formally, the three modules are quite distinct.

Two reasons have, however, been mentioned why in the VMK model we would prefer alternative coefficients for the wage Phillips curve. The first reason concerns the weighting coefficient κ_{wz} and its consequences for the analytical tractability of the model. Under CCP and PPC, the growth rate of labour productivity, $\hat{z}$, would show up in the dynamic equations unless $\kappa_{wz} = 0$ (cf. Equations (3.14) and (3.20)); under VMK, $\hat{z}$ would feed back on the dynamics unless $\kappa_{wz} = 1$ (cf. Equation (3.25)). Second, adopting this value $\kappa_{wz} = 1$ in the VMK model, it was found that a coefficient $\beta_{wv} = 0$ becomes admissible, whereas under CCP and PPC, this is only the case for very special combinations of $\beta\pi$ and $\kappa_{\pi p}$. Hence, if one wishes to work with a familiar wage Philips curve in which possible effects from the wage share are excluded, $\beta_{wv} = 0$ in the base scenario is a strong point in favour of VMK.

The VMK approach also fares well if one considers the number of 'key coefficients' in Table 3.7. By this we mean the number of coefficients here examined that cannot be a priori set equal to their desirable polar values, such as this is possible with $\kappa_{wz} = 0$ for CCP and PPC, or $\kappa_{wz} = 1$ and $\beta_{wv} = 0$ for VMK. Thus, there remain four key coefficients for CCP ($\beta_{we}, \beta_{wv}, \kappa_{wp}, \beta_p$), six for PPC ($\beta_{we}, \beta_{wv}, \kappa_{wp}, \beta_{pu}, \beta_{pv}, \kappa_{pw}$) for PPC and four for VMK ($\beta_{we}, \kappa_{wp}, \beta_{\mu\mu}, \beta_{\mu\mu}$). If the pure number of coefficients is the only concern, it might even be argued that VMK requires no more than three key coefficients, since putting $\beta_{\mu\mu} = 0$ would not violate the second-best criteria.[26]

Regarding a possible integration of CCP, PPC or VMK in a more encompassing macrodynamic model, we can summarize the brief discussion as follows. Either version may be employed if additional aspects come into play. A PPC, for example, may be chosen because it allows one to study various feedback effects in a familiar framework. Similarly, a theoretical interest in the Kaleckian elements of oligopolistic price setting may be a forceful argument for VMK. Or the CCP specification, despite its parsimony, may be discarded since it has less theoretical content than PPC and VMK. By contrast, if there is no other decisive argument in favour of one version, then the VMK model variant appears most attractive to us.

To conclude our calibration study, we return to the issue of the exogenous fluctuations of utilization. Though one might be rather content with the above cyclical features, the base scenario parameters would earn more confidence if this outcome would not deteriorate too much when the regular sine waves of u are replaced with the empirical observations of this variable.

Let us to this end concentrate on the VMK model (the results for CCP and PPC would make no great difference). In detail, we took the quarterly data on u (1961:1–91:4), which is depicted in Figure 3.1, and interpolated it to get a monthly series. As before, the simulation itself was run for the monthly discrete-time analogues of the model. Referring to the percentage deviations from their steady state values (or from the HP 1600 trend values, as far as the price level is concerned), it remained to compute the same statistics as in Table 3.1 for the empirical variables (again on a quarterly basis). The results are reported in Table 3.8.

---

[26] Recall the argument that $\beta_{\mu\mu} > 0$ could be needed in order to obtain a unique steady state within a full model.

Table 3.8. **Statistics obtained from VMK-base scenario under empirical utilization series**

Series x	σ_x/σ_u	Cross Correlations between u at Time t and x at Time						
		$t-3$	$t-2$	$t-1$	t	$t+1$	$t+2$	$t+3$
u	—	0.48	0.70	0.89	1.00	0.89	0.70	0.48
e	0.66	0.18	0.45	0.70	0.90	0.91	0.83	0.70
ω	0.45	0.19	0.45	0.70	0.90	0.91	0.84	0.71
v	0.19	−0.55	−0.39	−0.19	0.06	0.30	0.50	0.65
p	0.32	−0.71	−0.83	−0.89	−0.87	−0.78	−0.64	−0.47

Note: Quaterly series of percentage deviations from steady state values (u, e, ω, v) or from HP trend (p). Same sample period of u as in Table 3.1.

The cyclical statistics evince a positive and a negative facet. Owing to the deterministic modelling framework, the relationship between utilization and the other variables is, of course, closer than observed in reality. Apart from that, however, the profile of the cross-correlation coefficients is not so much different from Table 3.1. In particular, the lags that we have obtained in the sine-wave setting for the employment rate and the real wage have almost disappeared. As in Table 3.1, the negative-trend deviations of the price level lead utilization by one quarter, if we take the maximal correlation as an indicator of this feature. Even the wage share comes out nicely as qualitatively it exhibits the same pattern of correlation coefficients.

A negative point is that some of the standard deviations of the variables bear less resemblance to Table 3.1 and also to Table 3.6. As for as the employment rate, σ_e/σ_u is the same order of magnitude as in the sine-wave experiment (cf. Table 3.3, first row), but lower than in Table 3.1. The kind of this shortcoming has already been discussed in Section 5.2. While $\sigma\omega$ is only slightly smaller than in Table 3.6, σ_v and especially σ_p deviate more severely from what we have been aiming at. The latter standard deviation has a certain downward bias because of the end-of-period effects in the HP-filtering procedure of the price level,[27] but this is clearly not sufficient to explain the 'fall' from $\sigma_p/\sigma_u = 0.47$ in Table 3.6 to $\sigma_p/\sigma_u = 0.32$ in Table 3.8.

A hint on this discrepancy may be the observation that in the simulated time series from the 1970s until the beginning of the 1980s, the turning points have a lower amplitude than in Figure 3.1. At those times, the economy went through two trough-to-trough cycles over a period of 12 years, and it has already been indicated in Section 5.1 that the duration of the cycles may have a bearing on the standard deviations. To check this possible effect, we re-run the sine-wave

---

[27] In Table 3.1, HP was performed over 1953:1–98:2, while the price series here computed is confined to the sample period 1961:1–91:4.

simulation of the VMK model with a period of six years. The standard deviations here obtained come remarkably close to the ratios in Table 3.8: $\sigma_e/\sigma_u = 0.66$, $\sigma\omega/\sigma_u = 0.46$, $\sigma_v/\sigma_u = 0.19$ and $\sigma_p/\sigma_u = 0.35$. Also the lags in e and ω are shorter than in Table 3.6, both being reduced to five months.

On the other hand, back to the empirical utilization series, one can try out other numerical parameters for a better match of the standard deviations. Changing two parameters will do. A suitable increase of $\beta_{\mu u}$ and κ_{wp} yields the results displayed in Table 3.9 (note that the employment rate is not affected by this variation). The standard deviations of (briefly expressed) ω, v and p reach almost perfectly the values of Table 3.6, while only mildly modifying the cross-correlation coefficients. The coefficients of the wage share have not even changed, although the pattern of the real wage has somewhat shifted (and differs now more from the cross correlations of e than in Table 3.8).

A visual impression of what the VMK model may achieve and where it fails may be gained from Figure 3.5, which contrasts the simulated with the empirical data. Besides, the time series that are obtained with the original base values of $\beta_{\mu u}$ and κ_{wp} do not look much different. Figure 3.5 shows that still the simulated series have difficulties in tracing out the turning points of the actual series in 1973 and 1974. If, on the other hand, we are willing to discount for this feature and also take the elementary nature of the model into account, the cyclical properties of the base scenario or of this 'enhanced' scenario can be deemed rather satisfactory.

Of course, an exact match of the simulated time series would be unduly restrictive since the historical moments have sampling variability and so can differ from the model's population moments – even if the model happened to be true. As a matter of fact, the significance of a good match of the simulated and empirical sample moments is an unsettled issue. Given that a model cannot be expected to exactly duplicate reality, we can distinguish between a model variable, denote it by x_t^m, and its empirical counterpart, x_t^e, with error $\varepsilon_t = x_t^e - x_t^m$. To compare the standard deviations of x^m and x^e, i.e., their variances, the identity $\mathrm{var}(x^e) = \mathrm{var}(x^m) + 2\,\mathrm{cov}(x^m, \varepsilon) + \mathrm{var}(\varepsilon)$ has to be taken into account. As a consequence, if the difference between $\mathrm{var}(x^m)$ and $\mathrm{var}(x^e)$ is viewed as a statement about $\mathrm{var}(\varepsilon)$, as it mostly is, this would require $\mathrm{cov}(x^m, \varepsilon) = 0$ to be fulfilled, which amounts to making an assumption that a priori is not really obvious. But if one allows for potential correlation between x^m and ε, it might even be possible that $\mathrm{var}(x^m) = \mathrm{var}(x^e)$ despite large errors ε_t. The interpretation of a comparison between, say, Tables 3.9 and 3.1 is thus a deep methodological problem, which certainly goes beyond the scope of this paper.[28]

---

[28] The problem is hinted at in Kim and Pagan (1995, p. 371). The authors conclude, "the method of stylized facts really fails to come to grips with what is the fundamental problem in evaluating all small models, namely the assumptions that need to be made about the nature of the errors ζ_t," (ζ_t corresponds to ε_t in our notation). On pages 378ff, Kim and Pagan elaborate more on the problems connected with the fact that generally the errors ζ_t cannot be recovered.

Table 3.9.   Same experiment as in Table 3.8, with $\beta_{\mu\mu} = 0.27$ **and** $\kappa_{wp} = 0.60$

		Cross Correlations between u at Time t and x at Time						
Series x	σ_x/σ_u	$t-3$	$t-2$	$t-1$	t	$t+1$	$t+2$	$t+3$
ω	0.49	0.10	0.36	0.62	0.84	0.89	0.85	0.75
v	0.26	−0.55	−0.39	−0.19	0.06	0.30	0.50	0.65
p	0.47	−0.52	−0.68	−0.80	−0.85	−0.84	−0.77	−0.66

Figure 3.5.   Time series of experiment in Table 3.9

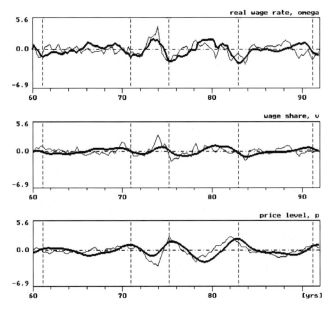

Note: Bold (thin) lines are the simulated (empirical) data.

7. Conclusion

The paper has put forward three submodels of (deterministic) wage-price dynamics which, in future work, may be integrated into a more encompassing macro model. The models have in common a positive functional relationship between capacity utilization and labour productivity; a positive relationship between capacity utilization and the capital growth rate; an adjustment mechanism for a so-called inflation climate; and a nominal wage Phillips curve. Regarding the three alternative model components determining inflation and the price level, the first one postulates a relationship between utilization and changes in the rate of inflation which almost directly implies a CCP level. The second approach advances a PPC. The third module formalizes adjustments of a VMK rate on ULCs that bear a certain countercyclical element. On the basis of stylized sine-wave oscillations for utilization as the only exogenous variable, it has been the main goal to find plausible numerical parameter values for each model variant such that the endogenous variables exhibit cyclical properties comparable to those that have been previously established as stylized facts for the corresponding (detrended) empirical time series.

The most important cyclical features we sought to reproduce are a procyclical real wage rate, a CCP level and the order of magnitude of their standard deviations. Accounting for the latter two characteristics, it turned out that all three models generate a lag of the real wage that is somewhat larger than desired. The main reason for this shortcoming seems to be the simplified modelling of labour productivity. However, once we are willing to accept the lag in a set of 'second-best' criteria of the cyclical statistics, each model can be calibrated in a satisfactory way.

The models include several coefficients that weight the influence of certain benchmark terms, such as, for example, the influence of actual inflation versus the inflation climate in the wage Phillips curve. These parameters appear quite innocuous at the theoretical level. It is a side result of the numerical analysis that they nevertheless have a strong impact on the cyclical features of the endogenous variables, so that they, too, must be carefully considered in the calibration procedure. In addition, this finding suggests that the weighting coefficients may also have a nonnegligible bearing on the stability properties of a full macrodynamic system.

Adopting suitable parameters, the three inflation modules are well compatible. That is, given the wage Phillips curve and the other common model components, one inflation module can be exchanged for another without affecting the cyclical properties too much. This is remarkable since theoretically and in their consequences for the model structure, the three modules are quite disparate.

In finer detail, however, we set up three base scenarios, one for each model variant, where the wage Phillips curve combined with VMK has different parameters from the curve in the CCP and PPC context. One reason for this are different polar values that, desirably, a weighting parameter should attain in order to eliminate the analytically rather inconvenient influence of the growth rate of actual productivity from the model. Another reason concerns the core of the wage Phillips curve, in the general version of which we allowed for a negative feedback of the wage share. Though being relatively weaker than the influence of the employment rate, the effect must be significant in the both the CCP and PPC model. Besides, the PPC, too, must incorporate a (positive) feedback of the wage share (which even dominates capacity utilization). In the VMK model variant, on the other hand, it is possible to dispense with the wage share effect and so to employ a traditional wage Phillips curve. If there are no other arguments, then this theoretical and analytical simplification could be a crucial point for a model builder to choose the VMK inflation module.

The base scenarios rely on parameters governing the adjustments of the inflation climate π which, to limit the degrees of freedom, were fixed freehand at a priori plausible values. Comparing the implied time path of this unobservable variable with survey data, perhaps even proxying π with such data, alternative coefficients might be preferred in this respect. We suspect that the base scenarios need not much be changed then, but in any case the calibration could be redone along the same lines as discussed in this paper.

Finally, we replaced the exogenous sine-wave motions of capacity utilization with the corresponding empirical time series. It is an encouraging feature of the base scenarios, and of the modelling approach altogether, that the qualitative cyclical behaviour of the endogenous variables was not seriously destroyed. On the contrary, we even obtained slight improvements concerning the lags of the employment rate and the real wage. The main shortcoming was that the standard deviation of the price level became too low, a phenomenon that could be explained by the duration of the most volatile cycles involved. Concentrating on the VMK model variant, a moderate change of two parameter values was sufficient to raise the standard deviation up to the desired level without the other statistics being essentially affected. On the whole, we may conclude that the wage-price submodels here presented are a useful workhorse in the (non-orthodox) modelling of small macrodynamic systems.

References

Barsky, R., J. Parker and G. Solon (1994), "Measuring the cyclicality of real wages: how important is the composition bias?", *Quarterly Journal of Economics*, Vol. 109, pp. 1–25.

Backus, D.K. and P.J. Kehoe (1992), "International evidence on the historical properties of business cycles", *American Economic Review*, Vol. 82, pp. 864–888.

Baxter, M. and R.G. King (1995), "Measuring business cycles: approximate band-pass filters for economic time series", NBER Working Paper 5022.

Blanchard, O. and L. Katz (1999), "Wage dynamics: reconciling theory and evidence", NBER Working Paper 6924.

Brayton, F., J.M. Roberts and J.C. Williams (1999), "What's happened to the Phillips curve?", *Finance and Economics Discussion Series*, 1999–49, Board of Governors of the Federal Reserve System.

Canova, F. and E. Ortega (2000), "Testing calibrated general equilibrium models", pp. 400–436 in R. Mariano, T. Schvermann and M.Weeks, editors, *Simulation-based Inference in Econometrics*, Cambridge: Cambridge University Press.

Chiarella, C. and P. Flaschel (2000a), *The dinamics of Keynesian Monetary Growth: Macro Foundations*, Cambridge: Cambridge University Press.

Chiarella, C. and P. Flaschel (2000b), "High order disequilibrium growth dynamics: theoretical aspects and numerical features", *Journal of Economic Dynamics and control*, Vol. 24, pp. 935–963.

Chiarella, C., P. Flaschel, G. Groh and W. Semmler (2000), *Disequilibrium, Growth and Labor Market Dynamics*, Berlin: Springer.

Cooley, T.F. and L.E. Ohanian (1991), "The cyclical behavior of prices", *Journal of Monetary Economics*, Vol. 28, pp. 25–60.

DeLong, J.B. and L.H. Summers (1986), "Are business cycles symmetrical?", pp. 166–179 in R. Gordon, editor, *American Business Cycles: Continuity and Change*, Chicago: University of Chicago Press.

Deistler, M. (2001), "Comments on the contributions by C.W.J. Granger and J.J. Heckman", *Journal of Econometrics*, Vol. 100, pp. 71–72.

Evans, M. and P. Wachtel (1993), "Inflation regimes and the sources of inflation uncertainty", *Journal of Money, Credit, and Banking*, Vol. 25, pp. 475–511.

Fiorito, R. and T. Kollintzas (1994), "Stylized facts of business cycles in the G7 from a real business cycle perspective", *European Economic Review*, Vol. 38, pp. 235–269.

Flaschel, P., R. Franke and W. Semmler (1997), *Nonlinear Macrodynamics: Instability Fluctuations and Growth in Monetary Economies*, Cambridge, MA: MIT Press.

Franke, R. (1999), "A reappraisal of adaptive expectations", *Political Economy*, Vol. 4, pp. 5–29.

Gittings, T.A. (1989), "Capacity utilization and inflation", *Economic Perspectives*, Vol. 13(3), pp. 2–9.

Goodwin, R.M. (1967), "A growth cycle", in C.H. Feinstein, editor, *Socialism, Capitalism and Economic Growth*, Cambridge: Cambridge University Press. Revised version pp. 442–449 in E.K. Hunt and J.G. Schwarz, editors (1972), *A Critique of Economic Theory*, Harmondsworth: Penguin.

Gregory, A.W. and G.W. Smith (1993), "Statistical aspects of calibration in macroeconomics", pp. 703–719 in G.S. Maddala, C.R. Rao and H.D. Vinod, editors, *Handbook of Statistics*, Vol. 11, Amsterdam: Elsevier.

Groth, C. (1988), IS-LM dynamics and the hypothesis of adaptive-forwardlooking expectations, pp. 251–266 in P. Flaschel and M. Krüger, editors, *Recent Approaches to Economic Dynamics*, Frankfurt a.M.: Peter Lang.

Kalecki, M. (1939), "Money and real wages", pp. 40–71 reprint of the Polish booklet in M. Kalecki, *Studies in the Theory of Business Cycles*, Warsaw and Oxford: Polish Scientific Publishers and Basil Blackwell (1966).

Kalecki, M. (1943), "Costs and prices", pp. 43–61 final version printed in M. Kalecki, *Selected Essays on the Dynamics of the Capitalist Economy 1933–1972*, Cambridge: Cambridge University Press (1971).

Kim, K. and A.R. Pagan (1995), The econometric analysis of calibrated macroeconomic models, pp. 356–390 in M.H. Pesaran and M.R. Wickens, editors, *Handbook of Applied Econometrics in Macroeconomics*, Oxford: Blackwell.

King, R.G. and S.T. Rebelo (1999), "Resuscitating real business cycles", pp. 927–1007 in J.B. Taylor and M. Woodford, editors, *Handbook of Macroeconomics*, Vol. 1B, Amsterdam: Elsevier.

McCallum, B.T. (2001), "Should monetary policy respond strongly to output gaps?", NBER Working Paper No. W8226.

Mussa, M. (1975), "Adaptive and regressive expectations in a rational model of the inflationary process", *Journal of Monetary Economics*, Vol. 1, pp. 423–442.

Okun, A.M. (1980), "Rational-expectations-with-misperceptions as a theory of the business cycle", *Journal of Money, Credit, and Banking*, Vol. 12, pp. 817–825.

Plasmans, J., H. Meersman, A. Van Poeck and B. Merlevede (1999), "Generosity of the unemployment benefit system and wage flexibility in EMU: time-varying evidence in five countries", *Mimeo*, UFSIA, Department of Economics, University of Antwerp.

Razzak, W.A. (2001), "Business cycle asymmetries: international evidence", *Review of Economic Dynamics*, Vol. 4, pp. 230–243.

Smant, D.J.C. (1998), "Modelling trends, expectations and the cyclical behaviour of prices", *Economic Modelling*, Vol. 15, pp. 151–161.

Steindl, J. (1976), *Maturity and Stagnation in American Capitalism*, Reprint of the 1952 edition with a new introduction, New York: Monthly Review Press.

Stock, J.H. and M.W. Watson (1999), "Business cycle fluctuations in US macroeconomic time series", pp. 3–63 in J.B. Taylor and M. Woodford, editors, *Handbook of Macroeconomics*, Vol. 1A, Amsterdam: Elsevier.

Summers, L.H. (1991), "The scientific illusion in empirical macroeconomics", *Scandinavian Journal of Economics*, Vol. 93, pp. 129–148.

Taylor, L. (1989), *Stabilization and Growth in Developing Countries: A Structuralist Approach*, Chur: Harwood Academic Publishers.

Appendix: The empirical time series

The time series examined in Table 3.1 are constructed from the data that are made available by Ray Fair on his homepage (http://fairmodel.econ.yale.edu), with a description being given in Appendix A of the US Model Workbook. Taking over Fair's abbreviations, the following time series of his database are involved. They all refer to the firm sector, i.e., nonfinancial corporate business.

HN	average number of nonovertime hours paid per job
HO	average number of overtime hours paid per job
JF	number of jobs
KK	real capital stock
PF	output price index

SIFG	employer social insurance contributions paid to US government
SIFS	employer social insurance contributions paid to state and local governments
WF	average hourly earnings excluding overtime of workers (but including supplements to wages and salaries except employer contributions for social insurance).
Y	real output

The variables in Table 3.1 are then specified as follows. For Fair's assumption of a 50% wage premium for overtime hours, see, e.g., his specification of disposable income of households (YD in Equation (115), Table A.3, The Equations of the US Model).

$y = Y/KK$ (output–capital ratio)

$L = JF \times (HN + HO)$ (total hours)

$e = L/\text{trend-}L$ (employment rate)

$z = Y/[JF \times (HN + HO)]$ (labour productivity)

$w = WF \times (HN + 1.5 \times HO)/(HN + HO)$ (nominal wage rate)

$p = PF$ (price level)

$v = [WF \times (HN + 1.5 \times HO) \times JF + SIFG + SIFS]/[Y \times PF]$ (wage share)

CHAPTER 4

The Decomposition of the Inflation–Unemployment Relationship by Time Scale Using Wavelets

Marco Gallegati, Mauro Gallegati, James B. Ramsey and Willi Semmler

Abstract

In this paper we apply the wavelets methodology to the analysis of the Phillips curve for the US between 1957 and 2004. We decompose core CPI inflation and unemployment rate into different time scale components using the non-decimated discrete wavelet transform and then analyse the relationships among these variables at different time scales. According to our results the long-run Phillips curve is not vertical, as the nonparametric additive model provides evidence, at the lowest time scale, of a nonlinear (generally positive) relationship between inflation and unemployment, with unemployment lagging inflation by more than 4 years. As regards the trade-off at all other scales, we find that the relationship is linear and, even when it is statistically significant, is of borderline significance. Finally, the scatterplots provide evidence, at a detail level, of the so-called "Phillips loops", loops that are particularly evident at business cycle scales.

Keywords: Phillips curve, wavelets, time-scale decomposition, nonparametric regression model

JEL classifications: C22, E31

1. Introduction

Since the seminal contributions by Phillips (1958), Lipsey (1960) and Samuelson and Solow (1960) the notion of "Phillips curve" has been used to denote the existence of an empirical regularity between unemployment and inflation. The conventional approach employed in testing empirical Phillips curve models tries

CONTRIBUTIONS TO ECONOMIC ANALYSIS
VOLUME 277   ISSN: 0573-8555
DOI:10.1016/S0573-8555(05)77004-8

to document the existence of a stable statistical (downward sloping) relationship between the level of unemployment and the level (or the change) of inflation, the so-called inflation–unemployment short-term *trade-off* (see Phelps, 1968; Friedman, 1968). The empirical evidence available indicates that the shape of the unemployment–inflation relationship has been far from being stable over the past 40 years as, according to some recent studies, the price Phillips curve has shifted *out* in the 1970s (the stagflation period), *back* in the 1980s (Stock and Watson, 1999) and, finally, *inward* in the 1990s (Staiger *et al.*, 2001). But if the instability of this relationship may be hardly considered a surprise, about the reasons and the factors that cause the trade-off to shifts (inflation expectations, supply shocks, demographic factors, productivity fluctuations, labor market institutions, and so on) there is, by contrast, less consensus and the question is still open to debate.

A potential shortcoming of conventional empirical analyses of the Phillips curve may concern the lack of distinction between trend and cycle movements in the relationship between inflation and unemployment. Although not prevalent, a different methodology has been suggested in the literature in order to avoid such shortcomings of the traditional approach (see Vercelli, 1977; Stock and Watson, 1999, for example). Vercelli (1977) shows that, when trend and cycle movements are separated, the cyclical movements in the empirical relationship between inflation and unemployment originally described by Phillips (1958) and Lipsey (1960), that is the so-called "Phillips loops", may emerge clearly. Also, Stock and Watson (1999, p. 21) show that "while there is no stable relationship between the levels of inflation and unemployment, there is a clear and remarkably stable negative relation between the *cyclical components* of these series". Finally, Staiger *et al.* (2001) find that price Phillips curve coefficients become stable when the unemployment rate is specified as deviation from its univariate trend, and that "explanations of movements of wages, prices and unemployment,..., must focus on understanding the univariate trends in the unemployment rate and in productivity growth and, perhaps, the relation between the two".

The two markets involved in the unemployment-inflation relationship, i.e. labour and goods market, provide an example of markets in which the agents involved, firms and workers/unions (consumers), interact at different time horizons and operate on several time scales at once. In this way the relationships among labour and goods market variables, i.e. wages, prices and unemployment, may well vary across time scales. Thus, if we recognise that time scale matters in economics, we would expect that many periods more than just two, i.e. the short and the long run, could be the relevant time scale in the analysis of economic decisions. In such a context, a useful analytical tool may be wavelet analysis. Wavelets are particular types of functions $f(x)$ that are localised both in time and frequency domain and used to decompose a function $f(x)$ (i.e. a signal, a surface, a series, etc.) in more elementary functions which include information about the same $f(x)$. The main advantage of wavelet analysis is its ability to decompose macroeconomic time series and data in general, into their time scale components. Several applications of wavelet analysis in economics and finance have been recently provided by Ramsey and Lampart (1998a,b), Ramsey (2002), Kim and In (2003) and Crivellini *et al.* (2005) among others, but no attempts have been made to apply this methodology to the analysis of price and labour market variables.

In this paper, instead of analysing the average relationships between prices and unemployment as it is standard in the analysis of the Phillips curve, we use wavelet time scales decomposition analysis to examine the relationships among prices and unemployment at each time scale separately. In this way we can analyse both the long-term relationship between inflation and unemployment and the shape of the inflation–unemployment *trade-off* at different time horizons. In recent years many studies have challenged the notion of a vertical long-run inflation–unemployment *trade-off* and questioned the linearity of the Phillips curve, an issue explored by Phillips (1958) himself. In particular, both theoretical studies have been developed that specify models generating a non-vertical long-run Phillips curve (Akerlof *et al.*, 1996, 2000; Holden, 2001) and empirical studies finding evidence of a long-run relationship between inflation and unemployment (King and Watson, 1994; Fair, 2000; Lundborg and Sacklen, 2001; Wyplosz, 2001). Other studies have explored the issue of the nonlinearity of the Phillips curve surveying models of nonlinearity of the Phillips curve (Dupasquier and Ricketts, 1998) and looking at the possible shape of the Phillips curve, i.e. convex (Clark *et al.*, 1996; Bean, 1997) concave (Stiglitz, 1997; Eisner, 1997) or convex-concave (Filardo, 1998). Thus, after extraction of the different time scale components, we investigate the shape of the relationship between inflation and unemployment by applying nonparametric estimation techniques to explore nonlinearities in the unemployment-inflation relationship at different time scales.

The remainder of this paper is organised as follows. The main properties of the wavelets and the analytical differences to other filtering methods are dealt with in Section 2. In Section 3, we first decompose the unemployment and inflation time series into a low-frequency base scale and six higher-frequency scale levels, then analyse these scales individually. In Section 4, we explore the shape of the relationship between inflation and unemployment at different time scales through nonparametric regression analysis of the Phillips curve and Section 5 concludes the paper.

2. Methodology and data

The series were filtered with a discrete wavelet transform that is a relatively new (at least for economists) statistical tool that, roughly speaking, decomposes a given series in orthogonal components, as in the Fourier approach, but according to scale (time components) instead of frequencies. The comparison with the Fourier analysis is useful first because wavelets use a similar strategy: find some orthogonal objects (wavelets functions instead of sines and cosines) and use them to decompose the series. Second, since Fourier analysis is a common tool in economics, it may be useful in understanding the methodology and also in the interpretation of results. Saying that, we have to stress the main difference between the two tools. Wavelets analysis does not need stationary assumption in order to decompose the series. This is because the Fourier approach decomposes in frequency space that may be interpreted as events of time-period T (where T is the number of observations). Put differently, spectral decomposition methods perform a global analysis whereas, on the other hand, wavelets methods act locally in time and so do not need stationary cyclical components. Recently, to relax the stationary frequencies assumption a windowing Fourier decomposition has been developed that essentially uses, for frequencies estimation, a time-period M (the window) event less than the number of observations T. The problem with this approach is the right choice of the window and, more importantly, its constancy over time.

Coming back to wavelets and going into some mathematical detail we may note that there are two basic wavelet functions: the father wavelet and the mother wavelet. The formal definition of the father wavelets is the function

$$\Phi_{J,k} = 2^{-\frac{J}{2}}\Phi\left(\frac{t - 2^J k}{2^J}\right) \tag{4.1}$$

defined as non-zero over a finite time length support that corresponds to given mother wavelets

$$\Psi_{J,k} = 2^{-\frac{J}{2}}\Psi\left(\frac{t - 2^J k}{2^J}\right) \tag{4.2}$$

with $j = 1, \ldots, J$ in a J-level wavelets decomposition. The former integrates to 1 and reconstructs the longest time-scale component of the series (trend), while the latter integrates to 0 (similarly to sine and cosine) and is used to describe all deviations from trend. The mother wavelets, as said above, play a role similar to sines and cosines in the Fourier decomposition. They are compressed or dilated, in time domain, to generate cycles fitting actual data.

To compute the decomposition we need to calculate wavelet coefficients at all scales representing the projections of the time series onto the basis generated by the chosen family of wavelets, that is

$$d_{j,k} = \int f(t)\Psi_{j,k}$$

$$s_{J,k} = \int f(t)\Phi_{J,k}$$

where the coefficients $d_{j,k}$ and $s_{J,k}$ are the wavelet transform coefficients representing, respectively, the projection onto mother and father wavelets.

The wavelet representation of the signal or function $f(t)$ in $L^2(R)$ can be given by

$$f(t) = \sum_k s_{J,k} \Phi_{J,k}(t) + \sum_k d_{J,k} \Psi_{J,k}(t) + \cdots$$
$$+ \sum_k d_{j,k} \Psi_{j,k}(t) + \cdots + \sum_k d_{1,k} \Psi_{1,k}(t) \qquad (4.3)$$

where J is the number of multiresolution components or scales, and k ranges from 1 to the number of coefficients in the specified components. The multiresolution decomposition of the original signal $f(t)$ is given by the following expression

$$f(t) = S_J + D_J + D_{J-1} + \cdots + D_j + \cdots + D_1 \qquad (4.4)$$

where $S_J = \sum_k s_{J,k} \Phi_{J,k}(t)$ and $D_j = \sum_k d_{J,k} \Psi_{J,k}(t)$ with $j = 1, \ldots, J$.

The sequence of terms $S_J, D_J, \ldots D_j, \ldots, D_1$ in (4.4) represents a set of signal components that provide representations of the signal at different resolution levels 1 to J, and the detail signals D_j provide the increments at each individual scale or resolution level.

Many economic and financial time series are nonstationary and, moreover, exhibit changing frequencies over time. Much of the usefulness of wavelet analysis has to do with its flexibility in handling a variety of nonstationary signals. Indeed, as wavelets are constructed over finite intervals of time and are not necessarily homogeneous over time, they are localised in both time and scale. Thus, two interesting features of wavelet time-scale decomposition for economic variables will be that (i) since the base scale includes any nonstationary components, the data need not be detrended or differenced, and (ii) the nonparametric nature of wavelets takes care of potential nonlinear relationships without losing detail (Schleicher, 2002).

3. Time scale decomposition of inflation and unemployment

We decompose the aggregate monthly series of core CPI inflation and total unemployment rate for the US between 1957:1 and 2004:10 into their time-scale components using the *non-decimated discrete wavelet transform* which is a non-orthogonal variant of the classical discrete wavelet transform.[1] The *non-decimated discrete wavelet transform*, unlike the orthogonal discrete wavelet

---

[1] The data are taken from the Bureau of Labor Statistics of the U.S. Department of Labor and are US monthly, seasonally adjusted data from 1957:1 to 2004:10. We use the Civilian Unemployment Rate percent, series ID: UNRATE, for the unemployment rate u, and the 12 months change of the Consumer Price Index for all urban consumers (All Items Less Food & Energy), Index 1982–84 = 100, series ID: CPILFESL, for the inflation rate π.

transform, is translation invariant, as shifts in the signal do not change the pattern of coefficients. After the application of the translation invariant wavelet transform we obtain three groups of scales: (i) the resolution of "trend" at the longest possible scale available for these data, namely 128 months, i.e. S6; (ii) a second group of signals from D6 to D4, from 64 to 16 months, that involves intermediate scales; and (iii) a third group of signals corresponding to the finest scales from D3 to D1, i.e. from 8 to 2 months. Figures 4.1 and 4.2 show the time series plots of the raw time series, in the top left panel, and of the components obtained from the time-scale decomposition, from S6 in the top right panel to D1 in the bottom right panel, for core CPI inflation and unemployment rate, respectively.

The long-scale smooth components of the signals shown in Figure 4.3 represent an estimate of the univariate long-run trends of core CPI inflation and

Figure 4.1.   *Time-scale decomposition of core CPI inflation*

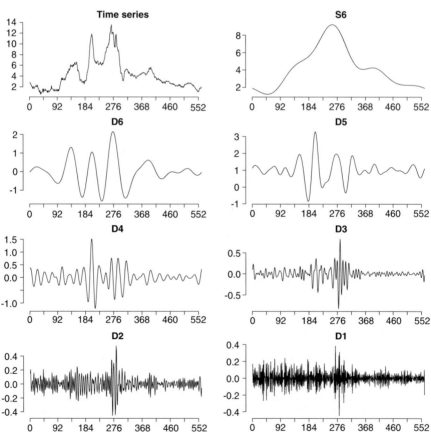

Figure 4.2.   Time-scale decomposition of unemployment rate

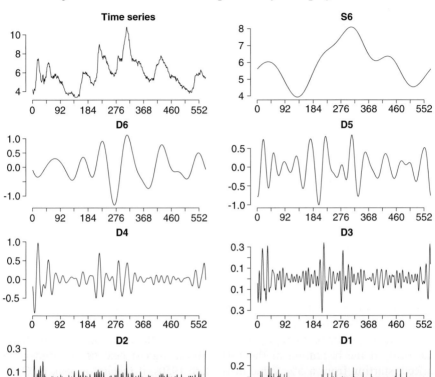

total unemployment rate.[2] Over the last 45 years, the main features of the two long-run trend components of unemployment and inflation have been that (i) both univariate trend components change over time, and (ii) the two smoothed series have a broadly similar hump-shaped path. As regards the time-varying behavior of the estimated trend component of the rate of inflation we may note that starting from 2% in the late 1950s, it trended up from the beginning of the 1960s until the 1980s, reaching a peak value of about 10% at the beginning of the 1980s; finally, over the last two decades, inflation has significantly declined

---

[2] There are other methods for estimating long-run trends in macroeconomic data, as the Hodrick–Prescott (1989) filter or the Baxter–King (1995) band-pass filter.

Figure 4.3.   *Long-run univariate trends of inflation and unemployment*

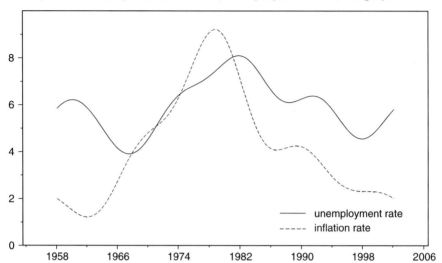

until 2% at the end of the 1990s but since then it has started increasing gradually (at the end-of-sample the value of long-run inflation is about 3%). The univariate trend rate of unemployment shows a double-hump shaped path, with a first peak at the beginning of the 1960s and a highest peak in the mid-1980s. Indeed, starting from a 5% value in the late 1950s, it reaches a peak at 6% in 1960 and falls to a 4% value in the mid-1960s. Since then it increased throughout the 1970s up to a peak of 8% in 1983, and finally declined slowly over the last two decades to a 4.5% value in 2000. From 2000 the long-run rate of unemployment starts increasing reaching a value of about 5% at the end of 2004.[3]

A visual inspection of long-run components of the two series suggests that, with the exception of the period corresponding to the first hump-shaped path of unemployment there is a linkage between the long-run trend components of inflation and unemployment rates. In particular, two aspects seem to emerge: a positive long-run relationship, at least since the end of the 1960s, and a lead–lag relationship where long-run inflation seems to lead the long-run rate

---

[3] The univariate trend of unemployment is very similar to the TV-NAIRU estimates obtained by Staiger *et al.* (2001) and Ball and Mankiw (2002) using different specification and estimation methodologies and, according to Cogley and Sargent (2001), may be interpreted as an estimate of the natural rate of unemployment. Indeed, as over a long-interval average inflation should equal actual inflation, the unemployment rate cannot deviate from the natural rate in the long run.

Figure 4.4. **Cross-correlation coefficients of the long-run components of inflation and unemployment**

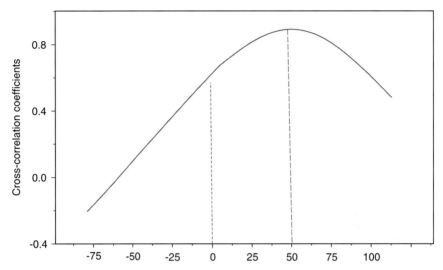

of unemployment by some years. A commonly used measure to analyse lead–lag relationships among variables is correlation analysis.[4] Figure 4.4 plots the correlation coefficients (measured on the y-axis) between the long-run components of inflation and unemployment for different leads and lags (measured on the x-axis).[5] The results of the cross-correlation analysis at lag 0 indicate that the long-run components of inflation and unemployment display a significant positive contemporaneous correlation. Moreover, on the basis of maximum lead–lag cross-correlation coefficients, a leading–lagging relationship emerges where unemployment tends to lag inflation by about 4 years.

The lead–lag relationship between two variables may also be analyzed using a causality test such as the Granger Causality test (Granger (1969)). The results from the pairwise Granger causality test between core CPI inflation and unemployment rate for the longest scale S6, i.e. the trend resolution level, are shown in Table 4.1. The null hypothesis for each F-test is that the added coefficients of unemployment rate (core CPI inflation) are zero in an AR

---

[4] For example, cross-country correlations have been widely used to obtain static estimates of the linkages in output movements across countries (among the others Backus and Kehoe, 1992; Christodoulakis *et al.*, 1995; Comin and Gertler, 2003).

[5] The value at 0 in Figure 4.4 gives the contemporaneous correlation coefficients between inflation and unemployment, while the values on the left (right) refer to the number of periods by which unemployment lead (lag) inflation.

Table 4.1.   *Granger causality test between the long-run components of*
unemployment rate and core CPI inflation (4 lags)

Null hypothesis	*F*-statistic	Probability
Unemployment rate does not GC core inflation	2.19601	0.06820
Core inflation does not GC unemployment rate	46.8032	7.4E−34

representation of core CPI inflation (unemployment rate) and thus that lagged values of unemployment rate (core CPI inflation) do not reduce the variance of core CPI inflation (unemployment rate) forecasts. The results of the joint *F*-tests indicate that we cannot reject the hypothesis that unemployment rate does not Granger cause core CPI inflation, but we do reject the hypothesis that core CPI inflation does not Granger cause unemployment rate. Thus, it appears that core CPI inflation Granger causes unemployment rate,[6] a result which is consistent with the findings obtained using cross-correlation analysis.

4. Time scale nonparametric analysis of the Phillips curve

In Figures 4.5 and 4.6 the scatterplots between core CPI inflation and unemployment rate at different time scales are displayed (together with a smooth regression function estimated from an additive nonparametric regression model of inflation on unemployment). The scatterplots at different time scales display very different features. In particular, while at the trend resolution level, S6, there is evidence of a long-run relationship between unemployment and inflation, at other time scales the scatterplots seem to draw what are known in the literature as *Phillips loops* (or *Phillips circles*) and that are quite evident at business cycle scales. The analysis of univariate trends in Figure 4.5 suggests a piecewise linear relationship characterised by periods of positive and negative trade-off between the univariate trends of the unemployment rate and core CPI inflation, which alternate over time. In particular, two periods are discernable: a period of increasing trend inflation from the late 1960s through the 1970s, and a period of declining trend inflation over the last two decades. From the early 1960s the "gravity centre" shifts towards east in concordance with the standard

---

[6] It is important to remember that the statement "*x* Granger causes *y*" has been interpreted as an indication of precedence and not as an indication of a cause–effect relationship.

Figure 4.5. **Scatterplot and nonparametric fitted function of the long-run inflation and unemployment trade-off**

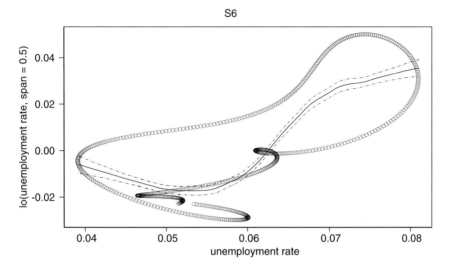

Phillips curve short-term trade-off.[7] At the end of the 1960s, however, the trade-off disappears as the univariate trends of inflation, first, and unemployment, then, begin to grow with the "gravity centre" shifting first towards west and then, after the first oil shock of 1973, toward north-west. By the beginning of the 1980s the trend of price inflation begins to reverse, and the "gravity centre" firstly shifts towards south, and, later, towards south-east, as during this period of falling trend inflation the univariate trend of unemployment declined too.

Traditionally, empirical estimates of the relationship between inflation and unemployment have assumed a linear framework, at least approximately, and, thus, imply a constant slope of the Phillips relation. Most of the recent studies

---

[7] The dynamic relationship between the level of price inflation and unemployment rate may be decomposed in a trend and a cyclical component, in which the first describes the movement of translation of the "gravity centre" and the latter the movements of rotation of the representative point around the "gravity centre" (Vercelli, 1977). In this way the movement of translation will depict the way the long-run relationships between the level of price inflation and unemployment rate may shift over time following the structural transformations of the labor market and the economy. On the other side, the movement of rotation may describe some clockwise or counterclockwise loops or circles, which are called "Phillips loops" or "Phillips circles" in the literature, according to the feed-back interactions between the accumulation process and the functional distribution of income (Vercelli, 1977).

Figure 4.6. Scatterplots and nonparametric fitted functions for the [D6] to [D1] scales

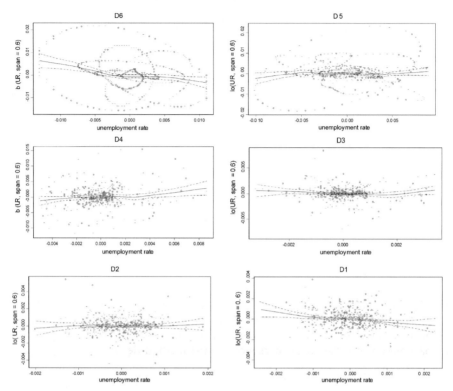

on the Phillips curve have analysed two main topics,[8] the shape and the assumption of linearity of the short- and long-run Phillips curves since they have important implications for the conduct of monetary policy, as "the optimal monetary policy reaction function changes with the shapes of the Phillips curve" (Semmler and Zhang, 2003, p. 13), and for the output cost of fighting inflation (Filardo, 1998). In particular, many recent theoretical and empirical contributions have found evidence of a nonlinear and/or non-vertical long-run Phillips curve (King and Watson, 1994; Akerlof *et al.*, 2000; Fair, 2000; Lundborg and Sacklen, 2001; Wyplosz, 2001; Graham and Snower (2002), among the others).

In what follows we apply a methodology that allows us to explore issues related to the shape and nonlinearity of the Phillips curve without making any *a priori* explicit or implicit assumption about the shape of the relationship between

---

[8] Another main topic is represented by the estimates of time-varying NAIRUs (see Staiger *et al.*, 2001; Semmler and Zhang, 2003 among the others).

inflation and unemployment, that is nonparametric regression. Indeed, nonparametric regressions can capture the shape of a relationship between variables without a prejudgment of the issue as they estimate the regression function $f(.)$ linking the dependent to the independent variables directly, without providing any parameters estimate.[9] There are several approaches available to estimate nonparametric regression models, [10] and most of these methods assume that the nonlinear functions of the independent variables to be estimated by the procedures are *smooth* continuous functions. One such model is the *generalised additive regression model* (GAMs),[11]

$$y_i = \alpha + \sum_{j=1}^{k} f_j(x_{ij}) + \varepsilon_i \tag{4.5}$$

where the functions $f_j(.)$ are *smooth* regression functions to be estimated from the data, and the estimates of $f_j(x_{ij})$ for every value of x_{ij}, written as $\hat{f}_j(x_{ij})$, are obtained by using a fitting algorithm known as *backfitting*.[12] Such a model allows us to gain more flexibility, as it replaces the linearity assumption with some univariate smooth functions in a nonparametric setting, but it retains the additivity assumption. Moreover, an important advantage of GAMs is the possibility to evaluate the statistical significance of the smooth nonparametric components. Two smoothing functions are available to estimate these partial-regression functions $f_j(.)$, that is spline and locally weighted regression smoothers. Both smoothers have similar fits with the same equivalent number of parameters, but the local regression (*loess*) method developed by Cleveland (1979) provides robust fitting when there are outliers in the data, support multiple dependent variables and computes confidence limits for predictions when the error distribution is symmetric, but not necessarily normal. In the *loess* method the regression function is evaluated at each particular value of the independent variable, x_i, using a local neighbourhood of each point and the fitted values are connected in a nonparametric regression curve. In fitting such a local regression, a fixed proportion of the data is included in each given local neighbourhood, called the *span* of the local regression smoother (or the

---

[9] The traditional nonlinear regression model introduces nonlinear functions of dependent variables using a limited range of transformed variables to the model (quadratic terms, cubic terms or piecewise constant function). An example of a methodology testing for nonlinearity without imposing any *a priori* assumption about the shape of the relationship is the smooth transition regression used in Eliasson (2001).

[10] See Fox (2000a,b) for a discussion on nonparametric regression methods.

[11] GAMs were introduced by Hastie and Tibshirani (1986) and are described in detail in Hastie and Tibshirani (1990).

[12] A full description of how the algorithm works in GAMs is available in Hastie and Tibshirani (1990).

smoothing parameter), and the data points are weighted by a smooth function whose weights decrease as the distance from the centre of the window increases.

In order to explore the issues about the shape and nonlinearity of the Phillips curve we estimate, for each time-scale component, a simple additive model of inflation on unemployment (and an intercept),

$$\pi_i = \alpha + lo(u_i) + \varepsilon_i \tag{4.6}$$

where π_i is the core CPI inflation rate, u_i the unemployment rate and $lo(.)$ is the locally weighted regression smoother (*loess*). The solid lines in Figures 4.5 and 4.6 show the nonparametric estimate of the regression function evaluated at the longest scale, S6, and at all the other scales, respectively, using a span $= 1/2$.[13] These smooth plots are drawn by connecting the points in plots of the fitted values for each function against its regressor, while the dashed lines above and below the smooth curves are constructed, at each of the fitted values, by adding and subtracting two pointwise standard errors.[14] Thus, the plot of u versus $\hat{l}o(u)$ will reveal the nature of the estimated relationship between the independent (unemployment) and the dependent variable (inflation), other things in the model being constant. The nonparametric fitted function estimating the relationship between the long-term time-scale components of unemployment and inflation is represented in Figure 4.5. According to the shape of the fitted smooth function the relationship of inflation to unemployment appears to be nonlinear. With regard to the shape of the nonlinear long-run Phillips curve, we may note that it is first downward sloping, and then upward sloping with its shape shifting from convex to concave. Thus, nonparametric regression provides evidence of a nonlinear long-run unemployment inflation trade-off.[15] Moreover, since the mid-1960s a long-run positive relationship seems to emerge between prices andunemployment.[16] Examples of models that imply that long-run unemployment increases with long-run inflation (not necessarily monotonously) are represented by Barro and Gordon's (1983) and Akerlof *et al.* 's models, where the positive long-run relationship depends on the time-consistency problem and the "sand effect" hypothesis, respectively.

---

[13] We use different smoothing parameters in estimating Equation (4.6), but our main findings do not show excess sensitivity to the choice of the span in the *loess* function within what appear to be reasonable ranges of smoothness.

[14] Under additional assumptions of no bias these upper and lower curves can be viewed as approximately 95% pointwise confidence intervals bands.

[15] Different theoretical hypotheses consistent with a nonlinear shape of the (short-run) Phillips curve, i.e. convex, concave or convex–concave, have been examined, for example, in Dupasquier and Ricketts (1998) and in Filardo (1998).

[16] Such a result is not a new one in the empirical analysis of the long-run Phillips curve (see Ireland, 1999; Wyplosz, 2001). Even Friedman (1977) presents some temptative empirical evidence in favour of a positively sloped Phillips curve in his nobel lecture.

Table 4.2.   Degrees of freedom and F-values for nonparametric effects
$$\pi_i = \alpha + lo(u_i) + \varepsilon_i$$

Time Scale	Nonpar. d.f.	Nonpar. χ^2	$P(\chi^2)$
S6	2.6	139.7	0.000
D6	3.8	2.18	0.073
D5	3.3	3.62	0.011
D4	4.7	1.03	0.395
D3	4.4	2.30	0.051
D2	3.9	0.60	0.662
D1	3.9	0.97	0.418

Figure 4.6 shows the shapes of the nonparametric fitted functions estimating the relationship between unemployment and inflation at different time scales. In this case the nonparametric fitted functions provide evidence of a linear relationship between inflation and unemployment at all scales. Moreover, a flat downward sloped relationship emerges only at the longest, D6, and shortest, D1, scales, while at the other scales there seems to be no relationship at all.

Finally, in order to evaluate the statistical significance of the nonparametric fitted functions estimated from the additive regression model in Equation (4.6) at different time-scale components we report the results of a type of score test in Table 4.2. The column headed "*Nonpar. d.f.*" contains the nonparametric degrees of freedom used up by the fit. They are related to the complexity of the nonparametric fitted curve, as the more complex the curve, the higher the penalty for complexity and the more the degrees of freedom lost (there are no exact degrees of freedom as, due to the nonparametric nature of GAMs, no parameters estimate are obtained). The column headed "*Nonpar. χ^2*" contains an approximate χ^2-statistic (see Bowman and Azzalini, 1997, p. 163) and represents a type of score test to evaluate the nonlinear contribution of each nonparametric term in the additive regression model through the p-values reported in the last column. The p-values of the approximate χ^2-statistic indicate a large importance of the nonparametrically fitted relationship between unemployment and inflation only at the trend level, S6. Some importance of the nonparametric fitted regression function emerges even at other scales, with values of borderline significance at the D6 and D3 scales, and well below the usual significance boundary level at the D5 time scale. In contrast, at the other scales, i.e. D4, D2 and D1, the nonparametric effect of unemployment to inflation appears to be nonsignificant.

Thus, the results obtained in this section indicate that time-scale decomposition may be very informative and allow for some interesting theoretical developments. Indeed, nonparametric analysis of the Phillips curve using a time-scale decomposition approach provides evidence of a nonlinear and highly significant long-run relationship between inflation and unemployment, with such relationship being generally positive (except at the beginning of the sample) and inflation leading unemployment by more than 4 years. In contrast, at the intermediate and finest scales, the short-run relationships are generally linear and even when they are statistically significant, their signficance level is definitely low when compared to the long-run one.

5. *Conclusion*

In this paper we analyse the relationships between inflation and unemployment using the wavelet analysis. Using the *non-decimated discrete wavelet transform* we decompose the original series in their time-scale components and analyse the unemployment–inflation relationship at different times scales. Specifically, the main features emerging from the nonparametric regression analysis of the Phillips curve at different scales are the following:

- the long-run Phillips curve is not vertical, as there is evidence of a long-run relationship between inflation and unemployment that is generally positive and significant;
- the long-run unemployment rate is a nonlinear function of long-run inflation, while at all the other scales there is no evidence of any nonlinearity in the inflation and unemployment relationship; and
- at business cycle scales, i.e. from D6 to D4, there is evidence of the so-called "Phillips loops."

These results confirm that time-scale decomposition may provide new insights to the analysis of economic relationships as both the nature and the strength of the relationships between variables may vary across time scales. A key issue now is how robust are these empirical results by sub period and for different countries. A result that has been obtained in other works (Ramsey and Lampart, 1998a,b) indicates that wavelet decompositions are far more stable in their results than any other macro, not decomposed, regression results. As a matter of fact, as unemployment and inflation data alone may be too limiting for a comprehensive analysis of the dynamic relationship of the inflation–unemployment trade-off, future analysis should include not only wages, but productivity data also.

Acknowledgment

We thank the participants at the XIIth Annual Meeting of the Society for Nonlinear Dynamics and Econometrics, Federal Reserve Bank of Atlanta, 10–13 March 2004, Atlanta and especially Buz Brock for suggestions and comments. We have also benefited from discussions with Domenico Delli Gatti. The usual *caveats* applies.

References

Akerlof, G.A., W.T. Dickens and G.L. Perry (1996), "The macroeconomics of low inflation", *Brookings Paper on Economic Activity*, Vol. 1, pp. 1–59.

Akerlof, G.A., W.T. Dickens and G.L. Perry (2000), "Near-rational wage and price setting and the long run Phillips curve", *Brookings Paper on Economic Activity*, Vol. 1, pp. 1–44.

Backus, D.K. and P.J. Kehoe (1992), "International evidence on the historical properties of business cycles", *American Economic Review*, Vol. 82, pp. 864–888.

Ball, L. and N.G. Mankiw (2002), "The NAIRU in theory and practice", NBER Working Paper, No. 8940.

Barro, R.J. and D.B. Gordon (1983), "A positive theory of monetary policy in a natural rate model", *Journal of Political Economy*, Vol. 91, pp. 589–610.

Baxter, M. and R.G. King (1995), "Measuring business cycles: approximate band-pass filters for economic time series", NBER Working Paper, No. 5022.

Bean, C. (1997), "The convex Phillips curve and macroeconomic policymaking under uncertainty", Manuscript, London School of Economics.

Bowman, A.W. and A. Azzalini (1997), *Applied Smoothing Techniques for Data Analysis*, Oxford: Clarendon Press.

Christodoulakis, N., S.P. Dimelis and T. Kollintzas (1995), "Comparisons of business cycles in the EC: idiosyncracies and regularities", *Economica*, Vol. 62, pp. 1–27.

Clark, P.B., D.M. Laxton and D.E. Rose (1996), "Asymmetry in the U.S. output–inflation nexus: issues and evidence", *IMF Staff Papers*, Vol. 43, pp. 216–250.

Cleveland, W.S. (1979), "Robust locally-weighted regression and scatterplot smoothing", *Journal of the American Statistical Association*, Vol. 74, pp. 829–836.

Cogley, T. and T.J. Sargent (2001), "Evolving post World War II U.S. inflation dynamics", *NBER Macroeconomics Annual*, Vol. 16, pp. 331–373.

Comin, D. and M. Gertler (2003), "Medium term business cycle", NBER Working Paper, No. 10003.

Crivellini, M., G. Marco, G. Mauro and A. Palestrini (2005), "Output fluctuations in G7 countries: a time-scale decomposition analysis", in: Monographs of official statistics, Papers and Proceedings of the 4th Eurostat Colloquium on modern tools for business cycle analysis, European Commission, Brussels, Belgium.

Dupasquier, C. and N. Ricketts (1998), "Non-linearities in the output–inflation relationship: some empirical results for Canada", *Bank of Canada Working Paper*, No. 98-14.

Eisner, R. (1997), "New view of the NAIRU", in: P. Davidson and J.A. Kregel, editors, *Improving the Global Economy: Keynesian and the Growth in Output and Employment*, Cheltenham, UK and Lyme, U.S.: Edward Elgar Publishing.

Eliasson, A.C. (2001), "Is the short-run Phillips curve nonlinear? Empirical evidence for Australia, Sweden and the United States", *Sverige Riksbank Working Paper Series*, No. 124.

Fair, R. (2000), "Testing the NAIRU model for the United States", *Review of Economic and Statistics*, Vol. 82, pp. 64–71.

Filardo, A.J. (1998), "New evidence on the output cost of fighting inflation", *Economic Review*, Federal Reserve Bank of Kansas City, Third Quarter, pp. 33–61.

Fox, J. (2000a), *Nonparametric Simple Regression: Smoothing Scatterplots*, thousand Oaks, CA: Sage.

Fox, J. (2000b), *Multiple and Generalized Nonparametric Regression*, Thousand Oaks, CA: Sage.

Friedman, M. (1968), "The role of monetary policy", *American Economic Review*, Vol. 58, pp. 1–17.

Friedman, M. (1977), "Inflation and unemployment", *Journal of Political Economy*, Vol. 85, pp. 451–472.

Graham, L. and D.J. Snower (2002), "Return of the long-run Phillips curve", *CEPR Discussion Paper*, No. 3691.

Granger, C.W. (1969), "Investigating casual relations by econometric models and cross-spectral methods", *Econometrica*, Vol. 37, pp. 424–438.

Hastie, T. and R. Tibshirani (1986), "Generalized additive models", *Statistical Science*, Vol. 1, pp. 297–318.

Hastie, T. and R. Tibshirani (1990), *Generalized Additive Models*, London: Chapman & Hall.

Holden, S. (2001), "Monetary policy and nominal rigidities under low inflation", Mimeo.

Ireland, P.N. (1999), "Does the time-consistency problem explain the behavior of inflation in the United States?", *Journal of Monetary Economics*, Vol. 44, pp. 279–291.

Kim, S. and F.H. In (2003), "The relationship between financial variables and real economic activity: evidence from spectral and wavelet analyses", *Studies in Nonlinear Dynamics and Econometrics*, Vol. 7(4), Article 4.

King, R.G. and M.W. Watson (1994), "The postwar U.S. Phillips curve: a revisionist econometric history", *Carnegie-Rochester Conference on Public Policy*, Vol. 41, pp. 157–219.

Lipsey, R.G. (1960), "The relation between unemployment and the rate of change of money wage rates in the United Kingdom 1862–1957: a further analysis", *Economica*, Vol. 27, pp. 456–487.

Lundborg, P. and H. Sacklen (2001), "Is there a long run unemployment-inflation trade-off in Sweden", *FIEF Working Paper Series*, No. 173.

Phelps, E. (1968), "Money-wage dynamics and labor market equilibrium", *Journal of Political Economy*, Vol. 76, pp. 678–711.

Phillips, A.W. (1958), "The relation between unemployment and the rate of change of money wage rates in the United Kingdom 1861–1957", *Economica*, Vol. 27, pp. 283–299.

Ramsey, J.B. (2002), "Wavelets in economics and finance: past and future", *C.V. Starr Center for Applied Economics*, No. 2002-02.

Ramsey, J.B. and C. Lampart (1998a), "The decomposition of economic relationship by time scale using wavelets: money and income", *Macro economic Dynamics*, Vol. 2, pp. 49–71.

Ramsey, J.B. and C. Lampart (1998b), "The decomposition of economic relationship by time scale using wavelets: expenditure and income", *Studies in Nonlinear Dynamics and Econometrics*, Vol. 3(4), pp. 23–42.

Samuelson, P.A. and R.M. Solow (1960), "Analytics of anti-inflation policy", *American Economic Review*, Vol. 50, pp. 177–194.

Schleicher, C. (2002), "An introduction to wavelets for economists", *Bank of Canada Working Paper*, No. 02-3.

Semmler, W. and W. Zhang (2003), "Monetary policy with nonlinear Phillips curve and endogenous NAIRU", *Center for Empirical Macroeconomics*, Working Paper, No. 55.

Staiger, D., J.H. Stock and M.W. Watson (2001), "Prices, wages and the U.S. NAIRU in the 1990s", *NBER Working Paper Series*, No. 8320.

Stiglitz, J. (1997), "Reflections on the natural rate", *Journal of Economic Perspectives*, Vol. 11, pp. 3–10.

Stock, J.H. and M.W. Watson (1999), "Business cycle fluctuations in U.S. macroeconomic time series", pp. 3–64 in: J. Taylor and M. Woodford, editors, *Handbook of Macroeconomics*, Vol. IA, Amsterdam, New York and Oxford: Elsevier Science, North-Holland.

Vercelli, A. (1977), "The Phillips dilemma: a new suggested approach", *Economic Notes*, No. 1, pp. 14–73.

Wyplosz, C. (2001), "Do we know how low inflation should be", *CEPR Discussion Paper*, No. 2722.

CHAPTER 5

New Keynesian Theory and the New Phillips Curves: A Competing Approach

Peter Flaschel and Ekkehart Schlicht

Abstract

This paper demonstrates that there is an alternative to the current New Keynesian approach of staggered wage–price setting with competing theoretical and empirical features. Our Keynesian formulation of a wage–price spiral distinguishes between a wage and price Phillips Curve, of the type considered in Blanchard and Katz (1999), but each with their own measure of demand pressure and both augmented by hybrid expectation formation. We use neoclassical dating of forward-looking perfect expectations and the concept of an inflationary climate to model the backward-looking component in expectation formation. The theoretical implications of our wage–price spiral differ radically from those of the New Keynesian formulation and permit inferences about stability properties of the implied real wage dynamics. Empirically, our wage and price Phillips curves perform quite well when estimated by ordinary least squares. The paper then estimates these two curves also with time-varying parameters in order to investigate which of their parameters have changed significantly over time. It is found that the Blanchard–Katz error correction term – which was found to be irrelevant for the U.S. economy as compared to Europe by these two authors – is significant also for the U.S. economy, though its significance has decreased over time.

Keywords: wage and price Phillips curves, time-varying adjustment speeds, normal or adverse real wage adjustments, (in) stability

JEL classifications: E24, E31, E32, J30

CONTRIBUTIONS TO ECONOMIC ANALYSIS
VOLUME 277   ISSN: 0573-8555
DOI:10.1016/S0573-8555(05)77005-X

1. Introduction

In this paper we reconsider the wage–price spiral from a Keynesian perspective. We construct distinct demand pressure indicators for the labor market and the market for commodities, and incorporate the error correction term proposed by Blanchard and Katz (1999). We assume as cost-pressure items perfectly foreseen price and wage inflation rates and an inflationary climate expression that captures inflation persistence. The proposed specification avoids logical inconsistencies of the old neoclassical synthesis concerning perfectly flexible prices combined with gradual wage adjustment and the marginal productivity theory of real wages, see Chiarella *et al.* (2003, Ch. 1) for details. Furthermore, the structural equations of this wage–price spiral are formally similar to the log-linear approximation of the New Keynesian purely forward-looking staggered wage and price setting, yet do not exhibit the empirical shortcomings in the wage–price dynamics encountered there, and the extreme instability implications (along with the rational expectations solutions they give rise to).

The mature Keynesian wage–price spiral to be estimated in this paper has been investigated and calibrated by Chiarella *et al.* (2005) and estimated by Chen *et al.* (2004b) as part of a full Keynesian DAS–DAD dynamics for the U.S. economy. This type of wage–price spiral was first estimated in isolation in Flaschel and Krolzig (2004). Calibrating the wage–price spiral entails the disadvantage that the calibrated fixed parameters tend to exaggerate their numerical values, while econometric estimation by single or system estimates tends to produce longer waves than are actually observed, since the parameters that are obtained are averages over the entire estimation period. Yet, we know that important magnitudes of the Keynesian theory of the business cycle, the marginal propensity to consume, the marginal efficiency of investment and liquidity preference, are varying over the business cycle in a patterned fashion. These variations may in important ways affect the shape of the cycle. This raises the question whether similar observations can be made regarding the wage–price spiral, the influence of demand pressure, cost pressure, and the Blanchard and Katz error correction term. We use a variable coefficient estimation procedure in order to approach this issue.

The paper is organized as follows. In Section 2, we start from the current New Keynesian approach to wage–price dynamics and show that a simple reformulation in its forward-looking terms, coupled with our concept of an underlying inflationary climate, provides us with a wage–price spiral (and its microfoundations) that engenders quite different theoretical and empirical implications. In Section 3, we discuss this wage–price spiral with respect to the implied real wage dynamics in four possible scenarios of normal or adverse real wage adjustments. In Section 4, we derive reduced-form representations of this wage–price spiral and the critical α-condition for stability of the implied real wage channel. Section 5 presents ordinary least squares (OLS) estimates of our structural wage and price Phillips curves (PCs). The time-paths of the corresponding time-varying coefficients are presented in Section 6. Section 7 concludes.

2. New Keynesian Phillips curves and beyond

In this section we consider briefly the modern analog to the old neoclassical synthesis (in its Keynesian format), the New Keynesian approach to macro-dynamics, in its advanced form, where both staggered price setting and staggered wage setting are assumed. We here follow Woodford (2003, p. 225) in his formulation of staggered wages and prices, which also imply a derived law of motion for real wages, but do not yet include New Keynesian IS-dynamics and the Taylor interest rate policy rule here. We shall only briefly look at this extended New Keynesian approach in order to compare the New Keynesian wage–price dynamics with ours. It will turn out – somewhat surprisingly, and from a formal perspective – that the approaches differ only in their handling of inflationary expectations, where we use hybrid expectations formation, neoclassical dating of expectations, cross-over cost-push linkages (coupled with two measures of demand pressure, a labor market stock and a goods market flow measure) right from the start, see Chiarella and Flaschel (1996) for an early formulation of such a Keynesian approach to the wage–price spiral.

Woodford (2003, p. 225) suggests the following two log-linear equations for the description of the joint evolution of staggered wages and staggered prices as representations of the New Phillips Curves (NPCs) of the New Keynesian approach. In these equations we denote by w, p the wage and the price level, by Y output (with normal output set equal to one) and by ω the real wage w/p (with steady-state wages also set equal to one):[1]

$$\Delta \ln w_t \overset{NWPC}{=} \beta E_t(\Delta \ln w_{t+1}) + \beta_{wy} \ln Y_t - \beta_{w\omega} \ln \omega_t$$

$$\Delta \ln p_t \overset{NPPC}{=} \beta E_t(\Delta \ln p_{t+1}) + \beta_{py} \ln Y_t + \beta_{p\omega} \ln \omega_t$$

where all parameters shown are assumed to be positive. Our first aim is to derive the continuous time analog to these equations describing the New Wage Phillips Curve (NWPC) and the New Price Phillips Curve (NPPC), and to show on this basis how this extended model is to be solved from the New Keynesian perspective and the rational expectations methodology.

In a deterministic setting, the above translates into

$$\Delta \ln w_{t+1} = \frac{1}{\beta}[\Delta \ln w_t - \beta_{wy} \ln Y_t + \beta_{w\omega} \ln \omega_t]$$

$$\Delta \ln p_{t+1} = \frac{1}{\beta}[\Delta \ln p_t - \beta_{py} \ln Y_t - \beta_{p\omega} \ln \omega_t]$$

---

[1] Δ the backward difference operator.

If we assume (in all of the following and without loss in generality) that the parameter β is not only close to one, but equal to one, this yields:

$$\Delta \ln w_{t+1} - \Delta \ln w_t = -\beta_{wy} \ln Y_t + \beta_{w\omega} \ln \omega_t$$

$$\Delta \ln p_{t+1} - \Delta \ln p_t = -\beta_{py} \ln Y_t - \beta_{p\omega} \ln \omega_t$$

Denoting by π^w the rate of wage inflation and by π^p the rate of price inflation, these equations can be recast into continuous time (with $\ln Y = y$ and $\theta = \ln \omega$):[2]

$$\dot{\pi}^w \overset{NWPC}{=} -\beta_{wy} y + \beta_{w\omega}\theta, \quad \pi^w = \hat{w} = \frac{\dot{w}}{w} \tag{5.1}$$

$$\dot{\pi}^p \overset{NPPC}{=} -\beta_{py} y - \beta_{p\omega}\theta, \quad \pi^p = \hat{p} = \frac{\dot{p}}{p} \tag{5.2}$$

$$\dot{\theta} \overset{RWPC}{=} \pi^w - \pi^p = (\beta_{py} - \beta_{wy})y + (\beta_{p\omega} + \beta_{w\omega})\theta \tag{5.3}$$

This reformulation of the originally given wage and price PCs shows that there has occurred a complete sign reversal on the right-hand side of the NWPC and the NPPC as compared to the initially given situation in combination with the use of rates of changes of inflation rates on the left-hand sides of the NWPC and the NPPC now. The continuous-time equations for the NWPC and the NPPC also imply – as shown in (5.1) – a law of motion for the log of real wages, and thus a three-dimensional system which is coupled with a forward-looking law of motion for (the log of) output and a kind of Taylor interest rate policy rule. In the case of a conventional Taylor rule this implies four laws of motion with four forward-looking variables. Searching for a zone of determinacy of the dynamics (appropriate parameter values that make the steady state the only bounded solution of the dynamics to which the economy then immediately returns after isolated shocks of any type) thus demands to establish conditions such that all roots of the Jacobian have positive real parts. We do not go into a discussion of the full dynamics here,[3] but restrict our discussion to the New Keynesian wage–price dynamics and its comparison to the Keynesian wage-spiral investigated in this paper.

There are a variety of critical arguments raised in the literature against the NPCs of the baseline model of Keynesian macrodynamics and its extensions, see in particular Mankiw (2001) and recently Eller and Gordon (2003) for particular strong statements on the NPPC.[4] These and other criticisms also apply to the

---

[2] Note that the period length of the discrete time case is 1 here and thus need not be displayed explicitly, a situation that is changed when period lengths h different from 1 are considered. In this case, the parameters on the right-hand side of the discrete time formulation will depend linearly on h.

[3] See Chen *et al.* (2004a) in this regard.

[4] With respect to this NPC it is stated in Mankiw (2001): "Although the new Keynesian Phillips curves has many virtues, it also has one striking vice: It is completely at odd with the facts."

above extended wage and price dynamics. In view of these and other critiques, as well as in view of the approach established in Chiarella and Flaschel (2000) and by further work along these lines, see in particular Chiarella *et al.* (2005), we here propose the following modifications to the above New Keynesian wage–price dynamics, which will remove the questionable feature of a sign reversal of the role of output and wage gaps, as caused by the fact that future values of the considered state variables are used on the right-hand side of their determining equations, which implies that the time rates of change of these variables depend on output and wage gaps with a reversed sign in front of them. These sign reversals are at the root of the problem when the empirical relevance of such NPCs is investigated.

We tackle the issue by using the following expectations augmented wage and price PCs, which describe a wage–price spiral. The letter 'M = Mature' in front of these wage and price PCs denotes its traditional orientation (in particular from the point of view of Keynesian structural macroeconometric model building), certainly in a matured form from the perspective of AS–AD macrotheoretic model building.[5]

$$\Delta \ln w_{t+1} \overset{MWPC}{=} \kappa_w \Delta \ln p_{t+1} + (1 - \kappa_w)\pi_t^c + \beta_{we}(e - \bar{e}) - \beta_{w\omega} \ln \omega_t$$

$$\Delta \ln p_{t+1} \overset{MPPC}{=} \kappa_p \Delta \ln w_{t+1} + (1 - \kappa_p)\pi_t^c + \beta_{pu}(u - \bar{u}) + \beta_{p\omega} \ln \omega_t$$

We have modified the New Keynesian approach to wage and price dynamics here with respect to the terms relating to expectations, in order to obtain a wage–price spiral. We first assume that expectation formation is of a crossover type, with perfectly foreseen price inflation in the wage PC of workers and perfectly foreseen wage inflation in the price PC of firms. Furthermore, we use a neoclassical dating in the considered PCs, which means that – as in the reduced-form PC often considered – we have the same dating for the expected and the actual wage and price inflation rates on both sides of the PCs. Finally, following Chiarella and Flaschel (1996), we assume expectation formation to be of a hybrid type, where a certain weight is given to current (perfectly foreseen) inflation rates (κ_w, κ_p) and the counterweight attached to a concept which we call the inflationary climate π^c that is surrounding the currently evolving wage–price spiral. We thus assume that workers as well as firms pay some attention to whether the current situation is embedded in a high- or low-inflation regime.

These relatively straightforward modifications of the expectational part of the New Keynesian approach to expectations formation will imply radically different solutions and stability features of the matured Keynesian approach to wage and price dynamics. There is, in particular, no need to single out the steady state as the only relevant situation for economic analysis in the deterministic

---

[5] To simplify the presentation we have assumed here again that the steady-state value of the real wage has the value 1.

setup (considered here and above) when goods market dynamics and interest rates rules are added to the model. Concerning microfoundations for the assumed wage–price spiral we note here that the wage PC can be microfounded as in Blanchard and Katz (1999), using standard labor market theories. If hybrid expectations formation is added to the Blanchard and Katz approach, this would give rise to similar results (with the employment rate gap $e - \bar{e}$ in the place of the logarithm of the output gap). We thus obtain from Blanchard and Katz (1999), in particular, a foundation for the fact that is indeed the log of the real wage or the wage share that should appear on the right-hand side of the wage PC (due to their theoretical starting point, given by an expected real wage behavioral relationship). We will call the $\ln \omega$ expressions in the MWPC (and the MPPC) Blanchard and Katz error corrections terms in the following. Concerning the price PC a similar procedure can be applied, based on desired markups of firms and implied expected real wages (now with the rate of capacity utilization gap $u–\bar{u}$ in the place of the employment rate gap).[6] Along these lines, we obtain an economic motivation for including the log-real wage (or wage share) with a negative sign into the MWPC and with a positive sign into the MPPC, without any need for log-linear approximations. We furthermore use the employment gap $e - \bar{e}$ (a stock measure) and the capacity utilization gap $u - \bar{u}$ (a flow measure) in these two PCs, respectively, in the place of a single measure (the log of the output gap y), in order to distinguish between the demand forces that drive wages and those that drive prices.

We conclude that this model of a wage–price spiral is an interesting alternative to the – theoretically rarely investigated and empirically questionable – New Keynesian form of wage–price dynamics. This wage–price spiral, when implanted into a somewhat conventional Keynesian macrodynamical model, will produce stability results as they are expected from a Keynesian theory of the business cycle, with much closer resemblance to what is stated in Keynes' (1936) 'Notes on the trade cycle' than is the case for the New Keynesian theory of business fluctuations which – when there are cycles at all – is entirely based on the Frisch paradigm. In the present paper, however, we will study the wage–price spiral in its own right and will do so primarily from an empirical perspective.

3. The wage–price spiral: Pro- or anti-cyclical real wage dynamics?

In order to obtain a PC structure that can easily be compared to the New Keynesian wage–price dynamics (5.1)–(5.3), we reformulate our PCs in deterministic terms in a continuous time setting. Transferred to continuous time we get from our discrete time MWPC, MPPC curves as a representation of

---

[6] See also Chiarella *et al.* (2005) for an alternative motivation of the MWPC and the MPPC.

the wage–price spiral the following structural form, making again use of our two separate measures of demand pressure in the labor and the goods market $e - \bar{e}$ ($= \bar{U} - U$ in terms of unemployment), the excess labor demand on the external labor market, and $u - \bar{u}$, denoting excess demand on the market for goods in terms of utilized capacity u.

$$\hat{w} = \frac{\dot{w}}{w} = \beta_{we}(e - \bar{e}) - \beta_{w\omega}\theta + \kappa_w\hat{p} + (1 - \kappa_w)\pi^c$$

$$\hat{p} = \frac{\dot{p}}{p} = \beta_{pu}(u - \bar{u}) + \beta_{p\omega}\theta + \kappa_p\hat{w} + (1 - \kappa_p)\pi^c$$

$$\dot{\theta} = \hat{w} - \hat{p}$$

Note here again the striking similarity with the New Keynesian wage and price dynamics, with the exception of our different treatment of expectations concerning wage and price inflation. Note also that the proper determination of the real wage dynamics requires some mathematical manipulations, since wage and price inflation rates appear on both sides of the equations.

It may be the case that the internal rate of employment – as different from the external rate – drives money wage inflation. In this case, the measure $u - \bar{u}$ may be included in the MWPC as a measure of the utilization rate of the labor force within firms. This rate may be used as a proxy for the hours worked within firms and thus may add insider effects into the wage–price spiral considered here. Note also that we have used linear specifications. Nonlinear approaches to the wage–price spiral are considered in Flaschel *et al.* (2004a) and Chen and Flaschel (2004).

In the following theoretical and empirical investigation of this wage–price spiral, we will still ignore this possible extension and will restrict attention to capacity utilization rates e, u for the labor and the goods market in their deviation from the corresponding NAIRU type rates $\bar{e}, \bar{u}$. This simplification of wage and price PCs represents in our view the minimum structure required for non-reduced-form investigations of wage and price dynamics, which therefore should only be simplified further – for example on the reduced-form levels it implies – if there are definite and empirically motivated reasons to do so.[7] Even in this case, all parameters of the structural wage and price PCs will show up in their reduced-form representations, however, which cannot be interpreted in terms of labor market phenomena or goods market character-istics alone. In macrotheoretic models, the above type of wage and price PCs (disregarding our inflationary climate expression π^c however) have played a

---

[7] A study of derivative or insider influences (and also integral ones) in their comparative explanatory power of wage and price inflation is provided in Flaschel *et al.* (2004b), where it is basically found that the traditional proportional measure of demand pressure items seems to be the most relevant one.

significant role in the rationing approaches of the 1970s and 1980s, see in particular Hénin and Michel (1982) in this regard. Yet, up to work of Rose (1967, 1990), it remained fairly unnoticed that having specific formulations and measures of demand and cost pressure on both the labor market and the market for goods would in sum imply that either wage or price flexibility must always be destabilizing, depending on marginal propensities to consume and to invest with respect to changes in the real wage, i.e., depending on whether the goods market is profit-led or wage-led.

The following two figures attempt to illustrate this assertion for the case of falling prices and wages, i.e., for periods of depression and deflationary wage–price spirals. Their implications are understood most easily for inflationary periods (inflationary wage–price spirals) where wage and price adjustment processes may be more pronounced than in phases of economic recession or depression. We have – broadly speaking – normal real wage reaction patterns (leading to converging real wage adjustments and thus economic stability from this partial point of view), if investment is more responsive to real wage changes than consumption and if wages are more flexible with respect to demand pressure on their market than prices with respect to their measure of demand pressure, the rate of underutilization of the capital stock (with additional assumptions concerning the forward-looking component in the cost-pressure items as will be shown later on).

In this case, aggregate demand depends negatively on the real wage (which is called a profit-led regime in the Postkeynesian literature) and real wages tend to fall in the depression (thereby reviving economic activity via corresponding aggregate demand changes), since the numerator in real wages is reacting more strongly than the denominator. The opposite occurs, of course, if it happens – in the considered aggregate demand situation – that wages are less flexible than prices with respect to demand pressure, which is not unlikely in cases of a severe depression. In such cases, it would be desirable to have consumption responding more strongly stronger to real wage changes than investment, since the implied real wage increases would then revive the economy. There is a fourth case – in the latter demand situation – where wages are more flexible than prices, where again an adverse real wage adjustment would take place leading the economy via falling real wages into deeper and deeper depression.

Figure 5.1 below provides an illustration of just two types of the wage–price spiral, to be supplemented by two further cases in a complete representation of possible outcomes of the wage–price spiral (in the case of deflation). The arrows immediately suggest that the exact form of the wage–price spiral is to be determined by empirical investigations and depends on the short-sightedness of workers and firms with respect to their cost-pressure terms, and the current rate of price and wage inflation, respectively. We note that the Blanchard and Katz error-correction terms in the wage and price PCs may modify these results significantly if they become sufficiently strong (which is however not supported by the data, see our estimates below).

Figure 5.1. Normal vs. adverse real wage effects in a deflationary environment

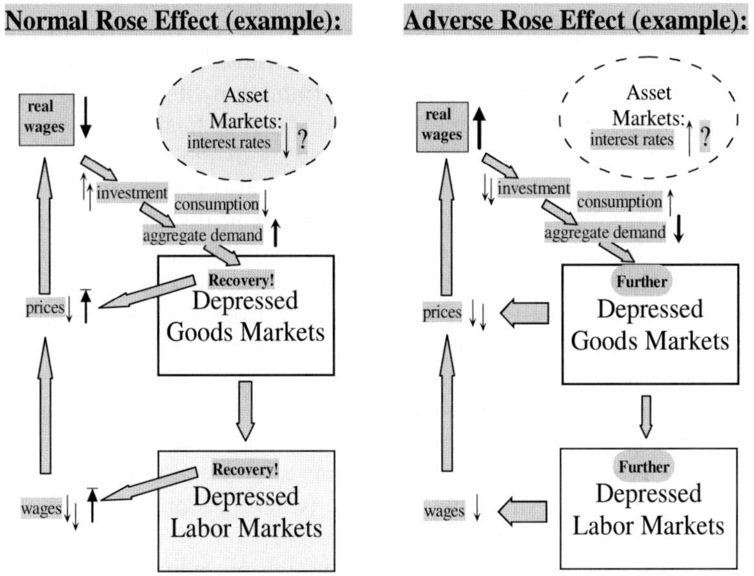

We conclude that wage and price PCs which pay sufficient attention to demand as well as cost-pressure indicators on both the market for labor and the market for goods may give rise to interesting dynamic phenomena regarding real wage adjustments. This deserves closer inspection, both theoretically and empirically. The present paper aims to discuss possible theoretical and empirical outcomes in a single-equation format and to assess the development in the U.S. economy after World War II in a time-varying parameter setup. We find evidence for a procyclical behavior of real wages in the sense that real wage growth depends positively on economic activity. The question whether aggregate demand is profit- or wage-led will be left unsettled however.

4. Reduced-form wage and price Phillips curves and the critical α-condition

We have emphasized the importance of using two separate PCs for wage and price dynamics, instead of one single equation. There exists a long, mainly non-mainstream, tradition to combine two such curves in economic theorizing, in particular in the growth cycle literature. We have already referred to this tradition in the previous section. There is an earlier article by Solow and Stiglitz (1968) where symmetrically formulated wage and price PCs are used, both with demand pressure and cost-pressure terms, to investigate medium-run dynamics where regime switching can occur. There is the related macroeconomic literature of non-Walrasian type, Malinvaud (1980), Hénin and Michel (1982), Picard

(1983), Benassy (1986, 1993) and others, where such PCs have often been used in conjunction with both labor and goods market disequilibrium, see Malinvaud (1980) for a typical example. Rowthorn (1980) makes use of a dynamic price PC coupled with a static wage PC in order to show how the conflict over income distribution allows for an endogenous determination of the NAIRU rate of capacity utilization of both labor and capital. There is finally the seminal work by Rose (1967), see also Rose (1990), where PCs of the type discussed above were first introduced. The two PCs approach has also been used extensively in Chiarella and Flaschel (2000) in a series of hierarchically structured models of monetary growth and in the present form in Chiarella *et al.* (2005).

Let us now derive reduced-form expressions from the wage and price PCs of the preceding section, one for the real part of an overall dynamics (in terms of the real wage) and the other for the nominal part of a complete dynamics (in terms of the price inflation rate), where both reduced-form dynamics are now driven by mixtures of excess demand expressions on the market for goods and for labor solely, and – in the case of the price inflation rate – by the inflationary climate with a unity coefficient. This latter fact shows that our approach is also applicable to situations of steady growth (where productivity growth may additionally be taken into account).

Note first that the wage and price PCs of the preceding section are of the general form

$$\hat{w} = \beta_{w's}(\cdot) + \kappa_w \hat{p} + (1 - \kappa_w)\pi^c$$
$$\hat{p} = \beta_{p's}(\cdot) + \kappa_p \hat{w} + (1 - \kappa_p)\pi^c$$

where the expressions $\beta_{w's}, \beta_{p's}$ for the labor and the goods market symbolize excess demand influences as well as those stemming from income distribution. Appropriately re-arranged, these equations are just two linear equations in the unknowns $\hat{w} - \pi^c$, $\hat{p} - \pi^c$, the deviations of wage and price inflation from the inflationary climate currently prevailing. They can be uniquely solved for $\hat{w} - \pi^c$, $\hat{p} - \pi^c$, when the weights applied to current inflation rates, $\kappa_w, \kappa_p \in [0, 1]$, fulfill the side condition $\kappa_w \kappa_p < 1$. This gives rise to the following reduced-form expressions for wage and price inflation, detrended by our concept of the inflationary climate into which current inflation is embedded:

$$\hat{w} - \pi^c = \frac{1}{1 - \kappa_w \kappa_p}[\beta_{w's}(\cdot) + \kappa_w \beta_{p's}(\cdot)]$$

$$\hat{p} - \pi^c = \frac{1}{1 - \kappa_w \kappa_p}[\beta_{p's}(\cdot) + \kappa_p \beta_{w's}(\cdot)]$$

All right-hand side variables act positively on the deviation of wage as well as price inflation from the inflationary climate variable π^c. Integrating our two PCs approach in this way across markets thus implies that two qualitatively different measures for demand pressure in the markets for labor as well as for goods have to be used both for money wage and price-level inflation for describing their deviation here from the prevailing inflation climate, formally seen in the usual way of an expectations augmented PC of the literature, see Laxton *et al.* (2000) for a typical example (where in addition only one measure of demand pressure, on the labor market, is again considered).

In more explicit terms we thus obtain the following reduced-form equations for wage inflation price inflation and real wage dynamics (where the second equation has been deducted from the first one). Note that the real wage PC represents a linear relationship, since the Blanchard and Katz error correction terms are derived in terms of logs and since $\hat{\omega} = \dot{\theta}$ holds true. Comparing the reduced-form representation of our wage–price spiral with the New Keynesian wage–price dynamics shows significant differences between these two approaches to supply-side dynamics despite the formal similarities we have noted. We have now laws of motion for wages and prices and not for inflation *per se*. Furthermore, no sign reversals in the role played by utilization gaps and real wage gaps occur. Note that we normalize steady-state capacity utilization rates to unity for reasons of notational simplicity.

$$\hat{w} = \frac{1}{1 - \kappa_w \kappa_p}[\beta_{we}(e - 1) - \beta_{w\omega}\theta + \kappa_w(\beta_{pu}(u - 1) + \beta_{p\omega}\theta)] + \pi^c \tag{5.4}$$

$$\hat{p} = \frac{1}{1 - \kappa_w \kappa_p}[\beta_{pu}(u - 1) + \beta_{p\omega}\theta + \kappa_p(\beta_{we}(e - 1) - \beta_{w\omega}\theta)] + \pi^c \tag{5.5}$$

$$\dot{\theta} = \frac{1}{1 - \kappa_w \kappa_p}[(1 - \kappa_p)(\beta_{we}(e - 1) - \beta_{w\omega}\theta) - (1 - \kappa_w)(\beta_{pu}(u - 1) + \beta_{w\omega}\theta)]$$

$$\tag{5.6}$$

We thus conclude that a mature Keynesian approach to the wage–price spiral, along lines established in Blanchard and Katz (1999), and from a different perspective in Chiarella *et al.* (2005), has quite interesting implications for reduced-form representations of wage *and* price PCs and the real wage dynamics, that – despite formal similarities with the New Keynesian approach – altogether differ sharply from the implications of the New Keynesian approach, see Chiarella *et al.* (2005) for further details.

Assuming in addition a relationship between the rate of employment e and the rate of capacity utilization u of an Okun's law type, i.e.

$$e = u^b, \quad b > 0, \quad \text{i.e.,} \quad \hat{e} = b\hat{u} \quad (e_u = bu^{b-1})$$

entails the following condition for the establishment of a positive association of the growth rate of real wages with economic activity (close to the normal working of the economy):

$$\alpha = [(1 - \kappa_p)\beta_{we}b - (1 - \kappa_w)\beta_{pu}]\frac{\partial u}{\partial \omega}$$

$$- [(1 - \kappa_p)\beta_{w\omega} + (1 - \kappa_w)\beta_{p\omega}] \begin{array}{c} < \\ \\ > \end{array} 0 \iff \begin{array}{l} \text{normal} \\ \text{RWE} \\ \text{adverse} \end{array}$$

This "critical α-condition", separating normal from adverse real wage effects establishes one positive and three negative influences of economic activity and real wages on the rate of real wage growth, and in particular a stabilizing dependence of real wage growth on its level. This holds if β_{pu} dominates β_{we} and if aggregate demand is profit-led (depending negatively on the real wage). If however economic activity depends positively on the real wage, we obtain a positive feedback of the real wage on its rate of growth if $\alpha > 0$ holds true. The situation $\alpha < 0$ by contrast will again imply a stabilizing effect of real wages on real wage growth in a wage-led aggregate demand regime. The conventional literature on the PCs generally focuses on the above-reduced form for price inflation (5.5). This holds in the special case where only the labor market matters and price inflation is passively trailing wage inflation. This provides a very partial representation of the wage–price spiral as compared to the view developed here, and it ignores the resulting effects on income distribution (real wages) completely. Note finally that if $\alpha > 0$ holds true, we must be in a wage-led regime in order to get a procyclical movement of real wages as it is typically found in the data, see Chiarella *et al.* (2005, Ch. 5) and our empirical findings below.

Conventional AS–AD growth dynamics thus draws a rather one-sided picture by recognizing the stabilizing Keynes-effect and (sometimes) of the destabilizing Mundell-effect. Both are working through the (expected) real-rate of interest channel on investment and consumption behavior. This neglects completely the other real-rate feedback mechanism: the real wage adjustment process which comes into being when consumption (positively) and investment (negatively) depend on the real wage and when wage and price dynamics are distinguished. Furthermore, it is known (see, for example, Chiarella and Flaschel, 2000) that the real rate of interest channel becomes destabilizing when the interest rate sensitivity of money demand is chosen sufficiently high combined with an adaptive revision of inflationary expectations that works sufficiently fast. In this case the Mundell effect dominates and creates an accelerating inflationary spiral, and thus an unstable nominal adjustment mechanism through the real rate of interest channel. In the case of the real wage channel – or the Rose effect, as it was named in Chiarella and Flaschel (2000) – the situation is even more complicated and thus also more interesting, since there are now four possible configurations, two of which provide a stable partial scenario and the other two an unstable one. It is obvious that empirical analysis is to determine which type of real wage effect predominates in a particular country at a particular time.

5. The MWPC and MPPC for the U.S. Economy: OLS estimates

So far we have argued from the theoretical perspective that PC approaches to the description of labor and goods market behavior are better modeled as a two-dimensional dynamic system (distinguishing between a wage PC and a price PC) instead of a single-labor market-oriented price PC. In this section we are going to provide empirical answers to the issues raised in the last two sections. We first present four different simple OLS estimates with constant parameters of both the wage and the price PCs in order to provide a baseline scenario to which the case of time-varying parameters – to be provided in the next section – can be usefully compared. We provide below some single equation OLS estimates for the wage and the price PCs on the basis of the linear curves as they were discussed above.[8]

In our estimates we disregard at first the steady-state condition imposed on the cost-pressure terms in our theoretical model and estimate the wage and price PCs with the terms $a_3\hat{w} + a_4\pi^c, b_3\hat{p} + b_4\pi^c$. Apart from current wage and price inflation $\hat{w}, \hat{p}$ we employ a moving average type of inflationary climate expression π^c, simply defined as the arithmetic mean of price inflation rates over the past 12 quarters. We use the U.S. data as described in Appendix 2, for the time range 1954:2–2000:3 and estimate the two linear curves

$$\hat{w} = a_0 + a_1 e(-1) - a_2\theta(-1) + a_3\hat{p} + a_4\pi^c + a_5\hat{y} \tag{5.7}$$

$$\hat{p} = b_0 + b_1 u(-1) + b_2\theta(-1) + b_3\hat{w} + b_4\pi^c - b_5\hat{y} \tag{5.8}$$

where $\hat{y}$ is the growth rate of labor productivity, here added, since it improves our estimates. (Removing it does not invalidate the estimated sizes of the parameter values.) We use a one-quarter delay for capacity utilization rates and the log of real wages, θ, and will also use the log of average real unit wage costs $(\tilde{\theta}(-1))$ as an alternative measure for the Blanchard–Katz error correction terms in the wage and the price PCs. Since real wages exhibit a pronounced upward trend and unit wage costs a pronounced downward trend in the U.S. economy over the period under consideration, we have detrended both series by way of the bandpass filter. The above two PCs are shown with the expected signs, and the growth rate of labor productivity influencing wage inflation positively and price inflation negatively. In a steady state, these coefficients are equal to one in the wage PC and $\kappa_p\hat{y}$ in the price PC, due to our definition of the inflationary climate expression π^c. Finally, for notational simplicity we have carried out a slight change in notation by using coefficients a and b in (5.7) and (5.8) instead of the $\beta's$ and $\kappa's$. This avoids double indexing and makes the model more readable, as now a-coefficients relate to the wage PCs while b-coefficients occur in the price PCs.

Equations (5.7) and (5.8) are estimated in two different forms, here exemplified for the wage PC only:

$$\hat{w} = a_0 + a_1 e(-1) - a_2\theta(-1) + a_3\hat{p} + a_4\pi^c + a_5\hat{y} \tag{5.9}$$

$$\hat{w} - \pi^c = \tilde{a}_0 + \tilde{a}_1 e(-1) - \tilde{a}_2\theta(-1) + \tilde{a}_3(\hat{p} - \pi^c) + \tilde{a}_5\hat{y} \tag{5.10}$$

---

[8] System estimates with by and large the same result are provided in Chen and Flaschel (2004) and Chen *et al.* (2004b), in the latter work by also including a dynamic IS-curve, Okun's law and a Taylor interest rate policy rule into the chosen system approach.

where the second equation differs from the first by imposing the condition $a_3 + a_4$ on the first equation. In (5.10) wage and price inflation are expressed in terms of their deviation from the inflationary climate π^c.

The estimation results for the four possible forms of the wage PC are provided in Table 5.1 (with the tables to the right obeying the discussed steady-state restriction). Data sources for the estimation are reported in Appendix 2.[9]

All four estimates shown suggest that the adjustment speed of wages in response to demand pressure β_{we} takes a value of around 0.15. Estimates for a_3 corresponding to the term κ_w in (5.9) represent the short-sightedness of wage earners with respect to the respective cost-pressure variable, price inflation, where a value of approximately 0.48 results. Wage adjustment with respect to demand pressure in the labor market is thus fairly strong (in particular in comparison to the respective price adjustment term, see below) and wage earners are fairly short-sighted, giving nearly 1/2 as weight to the present evolution of price inflation. The growth rate of labor productivity does not play a significant role in the evolution of wage inflation, though. (From a theoretical and steady-state perspective it should have the weight 1 in the place of approximately 0.18.)

It is remarkable that the Blanchard and Katz error correction term in the wage PC is approximately -0.13 and thus of significant size in contrast to what Blanchard and Katz (1999, p. 71) have suggested:

> "It has been known for some time that there is a striking difference between the empirical wage–unemployment relations in the United States and Europe. The difference, which might appear at first to be rather esoteric, is the presence of an error correction term in the European but not in the U.S. wage equation."

Our findings do not support such a conclusion, although our estimates for the U.S. differ from what Blanchard and Katz have suggested for Europe. Our estimates for the U.S. are half the size of what Blanchard and Katz (1999, p. 71) suggest for Europe (0.25). This difference can be attributed to our use of an inflationary climate expression in the wage PC, which is missing in the wage PC of Blanchard and Katz. Note also that their approach implies that the coefficients for the wage gap and the growth rate of productivity should be the same, and the latter is to be much smaller than 1, which is approximately the case in our estimates. Note finally that we have extended the Blanchard and Katz approach to the price PC as well, where the error correction term should be positive,[10] which is also confirmed unambiguously by our estimates.

---

[9] Here, the obtained results can be usefully compared with those obtained in Flaschel and Krolzig (2004), see also Ch. 5 in the present volume.

[10] See, however, Flaschel and Krolzig (2004) for an estimate that does not support the findings of the present paper, due to a different estimation procedure and a different measure for real unit wage costs.

Table 5.1. OLS estimates for the MWPC (1954:2–2000:3)

Variable	Estimate	t-value	Estimate	t-value
	Dependent variable: $\hat{w}$		Dependent variable: $\hat{w} - \pi^c$	
const	−0.1569	−5.1610	−0.1376	−5.6454
$e(-1)$	0.1696	5.3234	0.1498	5.7883
$\theta(-1)$	−0.1435	2.8033	−0.1446	−2.8245
$\hat{p}$	0.4853	4.2553	0.5130	4.6178
π^c	0.5921	3.9858	0.4870	implied
$\hat{y}$	0.1635	4.3610	0.1562	4.2361
R^2	0.6111		0.4318	
$\bar{R}^2$	0.6003		0.4192	
RSS	0.0043		0.0043	
DW	1.6793		1.6744	
const	−0.1614	−5.4243	−0.1356	−5.6309
$e(-1)$	0.1739	5.5731	0.1476	5.7624
$\tilde{\theta}(-1)$	−0.1049	−3.5532	−0.1008	−3.4196
$\hat{p}$	0.4603	4.1885	0.4945	4.5911
π^c	0.6453	4.4914	0.5055	implied
$\hat{y}$	0.2221	5.7979	0.2169	5.6003
R^2	0.6207		0.4141	
$\bar{R}^2$	0.6102		0.4022	
RSS	0.0042		0.0040	
DW	1.7788		1.9582	

In sum we find for the labor market – in contrast to Fair (2000) – that demand pressure matters on the labor market, and – in contrast to Blanchard and Katz (1999) – that error correction in this market is sizeable in the U.S. economy, and thus not specific to Europe. Wage earners do not only use present information to formulate their wage claims, but rely on the inflationary climate into which current goods price inflation is embedded. There is thus considerable persistence of price inflation with respect to formation of wage inflation in the wage PC (and even more in the price PC, as shown below).

In Table 5.2 we show similar calculations for the price PC and obtain that demand pressure, now on the market for goods, matters for price inflation, yet compared to wage inflation to a much smaller degree, with β_{pu} being approximately 0.03 – again opposite to findings in Fair (2000). This can partly (but not totally) be explained by the fact that the volatility of the capacity utilization rate on the goods market is much higher than on the labor market (where over- and undertime of the employed workforce is ignored). In addition, inertia with respect to wage pressure in the price PC is much larger than in the wage PC, since current wage inflation only gets the proximate weight 0.25 in its comparison with the inflationary climate expression π^c. Labor productivity matters in the price PC more than in the wage PC (since it is there weighted with κ_p rather than with a coefficient of unity). The analog to the Blanchard and Katz

Table 5.2.   OLS estimates for the MPPC (1954:2–2000:3)

Variable	Estimate	t-value	Estimate	t-value
	Dependent variable: $\hat{p}$		Dependent variable: $\hat{p} - \pi^c$	
const	−0.0310	−6.5037	−0.0288	−6.5093
$u(-1)$	0.0368	6.4177	0.0346	6.3301
$\theta(-1)$	0.1272	4.1489	0.1294	−4.2221
$\hat{w}$	0.2050	4.9433	0.1294	−4.8860
π^c	0.8432	15.2178	0.7973	implied
$\hat{y}$	−0.0522	−2.1491	−0.0579	−2.4266
R^2	0.8245		0.4845	
$\bar{R}^2$	0.8196		0.4731	
RSS	0.0026		0.0026	
DW	1.3652		1.3507	
const	−0.0380	−8.0950	−0.0358	−8.1802
$u(-1)$	0.0455	8.0761	0.0435	8.0402
$\tilde{\theta}(-1)$	0.1005	5.5130	0.1017	5.5774
$\hat{w}$	0.1925	4.8371	0.1901	4.7734
π^c	0.8541	16.0458	0.8099	implied
$\hat{y}$	−0.0946	−3.9705	−0.1007	−4.3157
R^2	0.8358		0.5180	
$\bar{R}^2$	0.8309		0.5073	
RSS	0.0025		0.0025	
DW	1.4684		1.4518	

error correction term in their wage PC is also significantly involved in the price inflation dynamics, there approximately with a value of 0.1.

We thus obtain the result that wages are more flexible than prices with respect to demand pressure on their respective markets, that wage earners are more short-sighted than firms with respect to the cost-pressure items they are facing and that wage share error correction matters in both the wage and the price PCs for the U.S. economy. It is also to be emphasized that all sign restrictions imposed by our approach to the wage–price spiral have been confirmed by our estimation and this with good statistical characteristics, in particular with respect to the standard errors involved in our estimates. This is remarkable, since it implies that the complete sign reversal suggested by the New Keynesian approach to staggered wage and price setting and their specific type of forward-looking behavior (Section 2) is not at all confirmed by our approach to wage–price dynamics. It appears furthermore that the use of unit cost instead of the real wage is preferable. Ignoring the growth rate of labor productivity in both the wage and the price PCs, finally, would not produce much change, though it clearly plays a role in the wage PC as derived in Blanchard and Katz (1999), though with a coefficient that is below unity, in contrast to what is concluded from a straightforward steady-state point of view as employed above.

Taken together, the above parameter estimates imply for the critical condition for real wage adjustments

$$\alpha = [(1 - \kappa_p)\beta_{we}b - (1 - \kappa_w)\beta_{pu}]\frac{\partial u}{\partial \omega}$$

$$- [(1 - \kappa_p)\beta_{w\omega} - (1 - \kappa_w)\beta_{p\omega}] \begin{array}{c} < \\ > \end{array} 0 \iff \begin{array}{c} \text{normal} \\ \text{RWE} \\ \text{adverse} \end{array}$$

the following result (where $e'(u) = b$):

$$\alpha = [0.056b - 0.016]\frac{\partial u}{\partial \omega} - 0.150\left\{\begin{array}{c} < \\ > \end{array}\right\}0 \iff \left\{\begin{array}{c} \text{normal} \\ \text{adverse} \end{array}\right\}\text{RWE}$$

In Chen *et al.* (2004b) we have estimated the parameters for Okun's law as $b = 0.2$ and $\frac{\partial u}{\partial \omega} = -0.7$ i.e., we found that the U.S. economy has been profit-led to a significant degree. Basically due to this latter result, it is obvious that the critical condition is likely to be negative during the time under discussion, as the only positive term is resulting from $(1 - \kappa_w)\beta_{pu} \sim 0.02$. Even in the case $b = 0$ and $\frac{\partial u}{\partial \omega} = -1$ we would therefore then get a negative value, due to the considerable parameter sizes we have found for the Blanchard and Katz error correction terms and due to the low adjustment speed of prices with respect to demand pressure on the market for goods. Of course, the α-condition is composed of various estimated parameters and thus cannot be judged from such average calculations alone. Nevertheless, the tentative result here is that the real wage feedback channel $(1 - \kappa_p)\beta_{we}b - (1 - \kappa_w)\beta_{pu}\frac{\partial u}{\partial \omega}$ may be a weak one and may be dominated by the direct impact of real wage changes on their rate of growth, which is given by: $(1 - \kappa_p)\beta_{w\omega} - (1 - \kappa_w)\beta_{p\omega}$. Be that as it may, the most general implication of the estimated results is that income distribution matters in the dynamic adjustments of the economy, a result that is not easily found in mainstream macrodynamical literature which normally restricts attention to the real rate of interest channel and not at all the real wage channel investigated in this paper. Yet, consideration of this real wage channel should be an important issue when the question of why real wages tend to be procyclical is approached.

The findings of this paper supports orthodox views of the labor market, though in a more complicated scenario than is generally used to justify such views, namely that real wage changes are self-correcting (from the viewpoint of a partial feedback chain in the set of all Keynesian feedback mechanisms). In addition to the information on the parameters and their sizes that drive the wage–price spiral, we conclude that this wage–price spiral contributes to economic stability, at least as long as the economy is profit-led in its aggregate demand formation. This stabilizing role of profit-led economies can however get lost in situations where (downward) wage rigidity obtains and the employment rate reacts more flexibly to demand pressure, and where the Blanchard and Katz terms become weak, through changes in the inflation regime that prevail in long-lasting economic depressions. Periods of low inflation, emphasized in current analyses, may differ in this regard. This is a topic that is to be addressed in future research by extending the results we obtain in the next section on our mature wage and price PCs, which still seem to support the views of the present section also for low-inflation regimes, and this even in a framework of time-varying parameters, at least as far as the U.S. economy is concerned.

6. Estimating the MWPC and the MPPC with time-varying parameters

We now present some time-varying estimates corresponding to the eight OLS estimates in the preceding section, both for the wage and the price PCs, and with either real wage error correction terms or real unit wage costs error correction terms as well as with cost-push weights κ in restricted and unrestricted form. Each of the coefficients encountered in the corresponding OLS estimates is now allowed to vary over time, and its time-path is estimated. The estimation procedure is briefly described in an Appendix to this paper. In each single estimation we show the six parameters of the unrestricted case and the five of the case where the parameters in front of the cost-push terms have to sum (are restricted) to unity at each point in time. The parameter sets in the unrestricted case are summarized in (Table 5.3).

Figure 5.2 (which corresponds to the first table given above) shows significant parameter variations only for the parameters in front of (the log of) the real wage and current wage inflation. With respect to the latter term we see that the influence of current wage inflation decreases significantly over time, partly explained by the observation that the economy has moved from a high-inflation regime to a low one, though the peaks and the troughs in these two regimes are not really visible in Figure 5.2(c). In contrast, the inflationary climate seems to exercise a constant influence on wage inflation. With respect to the error correction term discussed by Blanchard and Katz (1999) we see in Figure 5.2(b) that it has been very important in the U.S. economy before 1990 but dwindled to the fairly low values in the 1990s that have been suggested by Blanchard and Katz (1999) for Europe. In any case, the error correction is, in our estimates, also fairly relevant for the U.S. economy, a fact that may be due to our inclusion of an inflationary climate expression in addition to the use of only current price

Table 5.3. The parameter scenarios to be estimated

Wage PC (six figures)

β_{we}, $\beta_{w\omega}$ the impact of the employment rate e and of log real wage θ
κ_w, "$1 - \kappa_w$" the cost-pressure weights
$\hat{y}$, *const* the influence of labor productivity and the intercept

Price PC (six figures)

β_{pu}, $\beta_{p\omega}$ the impact of capacity utilization u and of log real wage θ
κ_p, "$1 - \kappa_p$" the cost-pressure weights
$\hat{y}$, *const* the influence of labor productivity and the intercept

Figure 5.2. Unrestricted wage PC

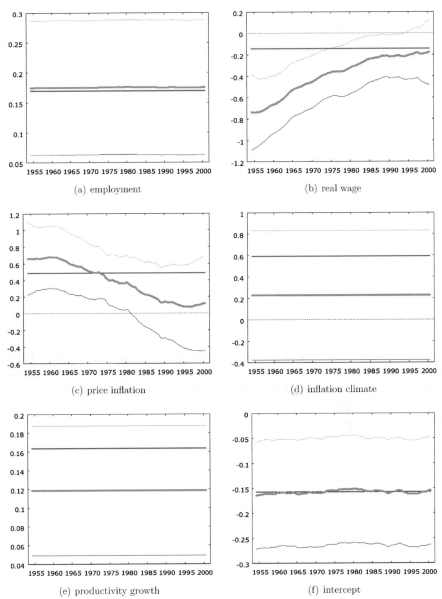

(a) employment

(b) real wage

(c) price inflation

(d) inflation climate

(e) productivity growth

(f) intercept

Note: In Figures 5.2–5.9, the variable coefficient estimates for the wage PC are represented by the thick line and the 95% confidence limits are given by the thin lines. The horizontal line gives the corresponding OLS estimates. (a) Employment (b) Real wage (c) Price inflation (d) Inflation climate (e) Productivity growth (f) Intercept.

inflation in the wage PC. The remaining figures show that the OLS estimates are close to the time-varying parameters in the case of the demand pressure term as well as the intercept, while they differ significantly with respect to the influence of the inflationary climate as well as productivity growth. Despite these differences, our findings are that demand pressure in the labor market matters for wage inflation (in contrast to what is observed in Fair, 2000) and that the inflation climate is of more importance than current wage inflation for the dynamics of money wages, while the influence of labor productivity is weak. This is in line with the weight in the Blanchard and Katz' (1999, p. 70) wage PC.

The situation considered in Figure 5.2 is by and large confirmed in Figure 5.3 where the unity condition is imposed on the κ-terms. The weight of current price inflation in the explanation of wage inflation now even drops slightly below zero in the low-inflation regime and the Blanchard and Katz error correction term becomes even less important in the 1990s as compared to the case depicted in Figure 5.2. The adjustment coefficient with respect to demand pressure in the labor market exhibits some fluctuations. There are also changes with respect to the productivity term and the intercept, but less pronounced.

An astonishing change takes place when the log of real wages in Figure 5.2 is replaced by the log of real unit wage costs in Figure 5.4. In this latter case there is practically no difference between the OLS estimation with constant parameters and the one where parameters are allowed to vary over time. Error correction then stays constant over time at a value below -0.1 and thus remains of importance compared to Blanchard and Katz (1999) findings in this matter. This also holds in the case where the sum of the $\kappa's$ is restricted to 1. Here the weight of current inflation abates as the economy moves into the low-inflation regime. Our overall conclusion is that the measurement of the error correction term may be of decisive importance in evaluating the case of time-varying parameters, while the restriction of the sum of the $\kappa's$ to unity is to be considered more as an additional source of information for a steady-state analysis of the model (Figure 5.5).

Turning now to the price PC (Figures 5.6–5.9) we note that the working of the analog to the Blanchard/Katz error correction term in the wage PC is similar for the restricted and the unrestricted cases with a downward trend in the case of the real wage and a pronounced peak and trough in the case of real unit wage costs. In all four situations the similarities between the different cases are considerable. The variability in the term that measures price flexibility with respect to demand pressure is generally modest, but more pronounced than in the case of wage inflation and it departs to a significant degree from those measured by the OLS estimates. In the case of unrestricted cost-pressure terms, we have strong volatility in the κ_p term to a certain degree in the restricted case (completely in the case of unit cost-error correction). Again we consider the productivity term and the intercept as being of secondary interest.

We conclude from these estimates that the consideration of time-varying parameters is an important issue in evaluating macroeconomic theory

Figure 5.3. *Restricted Wage PC*

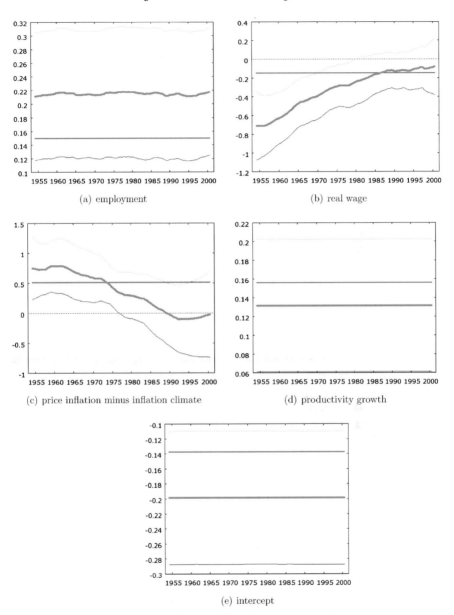

(a) employment

(b) real wage

(c) price inflation minus inflation climate

(d) productivity growth

(e) intercept

Note: In Figures 5.2–5.9, the variable coefficient estimates for the wage PC are represented by the thick line and the 95% confidence limits are given by the thin lines. The horizontal line gives the corresponding OLS estimates. (a) Employment (b) Real wage (c) Price inflation minus inflation climate (d) Productivity growth (e) Intercept.

Figure 5.4.   *Unrestricted Wage PC*

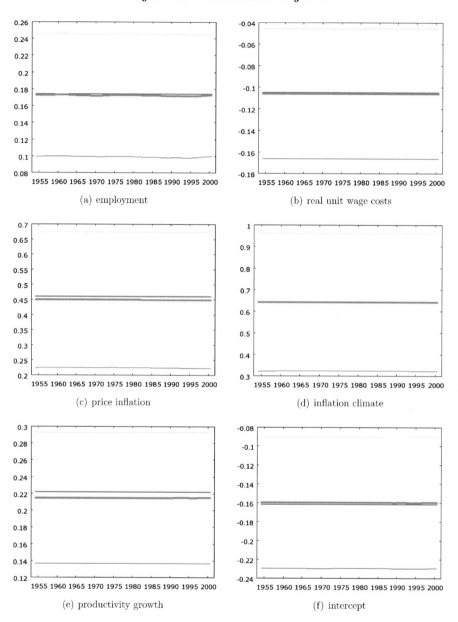

(a) employment

(b) real unit wage costs

(c) price inflation

(d) inflation climate

(e) productivity growth

(f) intercept

Note: In Figures 5.2–5.9, the variable coefficient estimates for the wage PC are represented by the thick line and the 95% confidence limits are given by the thin lines. The horizontal line gives the corresponding OLS estimates. (a) Employment (b) Real unit wage costs (c) Price inflation (d) Inflation climate (e) Productivity growth (f) Intercept.

Figure 5.5. *Restricted Wage PC*

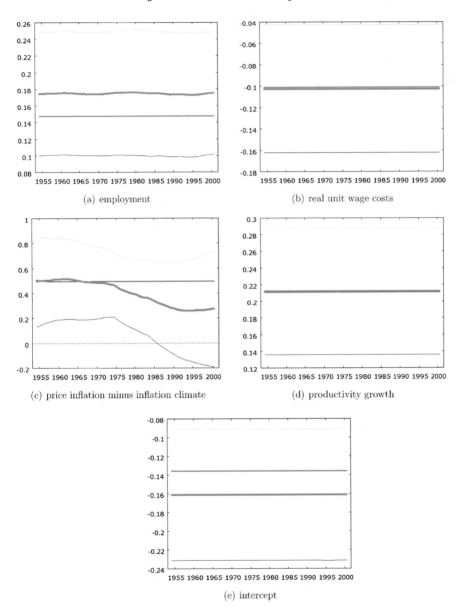

(a) employment

(b) real unit wage costs

(c) price inflation minus inflation climate

(d) productivity growth

(e) intercept

Note: In Figures 5.2–5.9, the variable coefficient estimates for the wage PC are represented by the thick line and the 95% confidence limits are given by the thin lines. The horizontal line gives the corresponding OLS estimates. (a) Employment (b) Real unit wage costs (c) Price inflation minus inflation climate (d) Productivity growth (e) Intercept.

Figure 5.6.   Nominal price PC

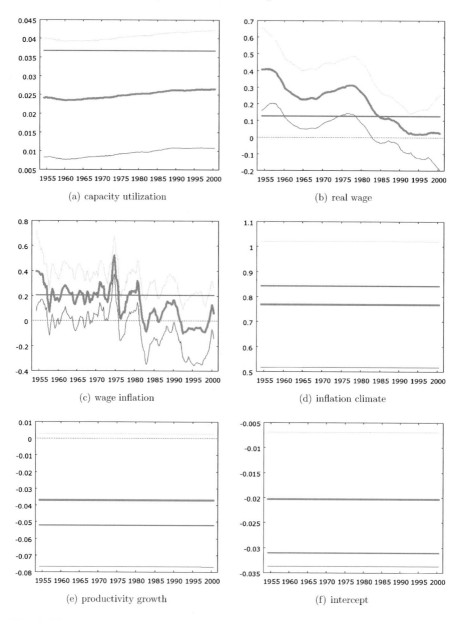

(a) capacity utilization

(b) real wage

(c) wage inflation

(d) inflation climate

(e) productivity growth

(f) intercept

Note: In Figures 5.2–5.9, the variable coefficient estimates for the wage PC are represented by the thick line and the 95% confidence limits are given by the thin lines. The horizontal line gives the corresponding OLS estimates. (a) Capacity utilization (b) Real wage (c) Wage inflation (d) Inflation climate (e) Productivity growth (f) Intercept.

Figure 5.7. *Restricted price PC*

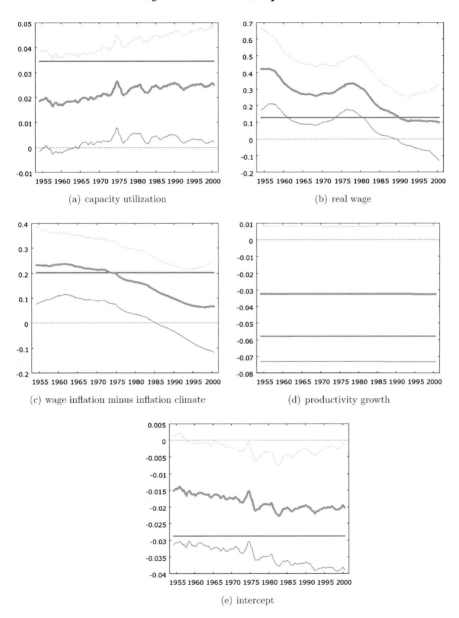

(a) capacity utilization

(b) real wage

(c) wage inflation minus inflation climate

(d) productivity growth

(e) intercept

Note: In Figures 5.2–5.9, the variable coefficient estimates for the wage PC are represented by the thick line and the 95% confidence limits are given by the thin lines. The horizontal line gives the corresponding OLS estimates. (a) Capacity utilization (b) Real wage (c) Wage inflation minus inflation climate (d) Productivity growth (e) Intercept.

Peter Flaschel and Ekkehart Schlicht

Figure 5.8.   Price PC

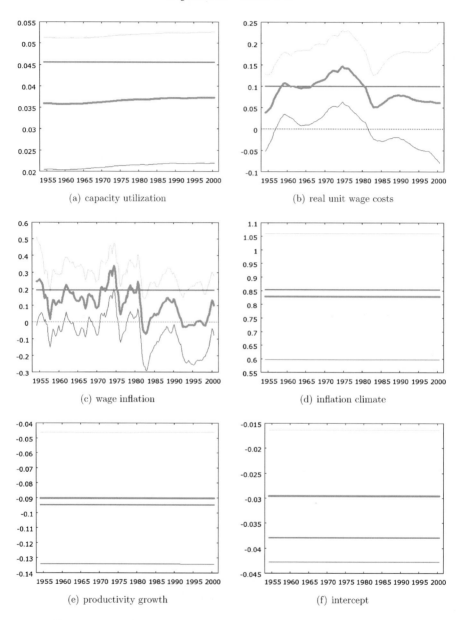

(a) capacity utilization

(b) real unit wage costs

(c) wage inflation

(d) inflation climate

(e) productivity growth

(f) intercept

Note: In Figures 5.2–5.9, the variable coefficient estimates for the wage PC are represented by the thick line and the 95% confidence limits are given by the thin lines. The horizontal line gives the corresponding OLS estimates. (a) Capacity utilization (b) Real unit wage costs (c) Wage inflation (d) Inflation climate (e) Productivity growth (f) Intercept.

Figure 5.9. *Restricted price PC*

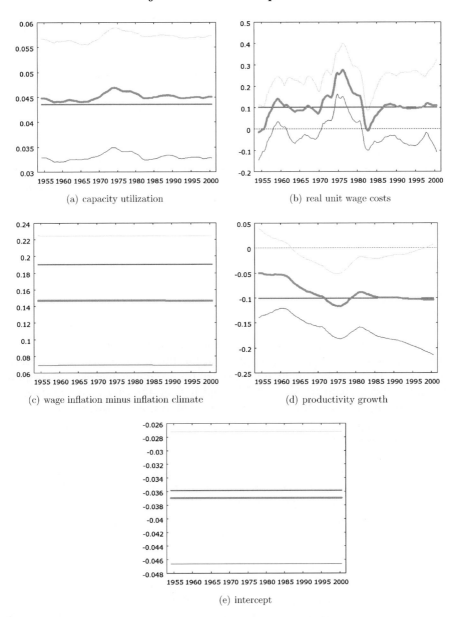

(a) capacity utilization

(b) real unit wage costs

(c) wage inflation minus inflation climate

(d) productivity growth

(e) intercept

Note: In Figures 5.2–5.9, the variable coefficient estimates for the wage PC are represented by the thick line and the 95% confidence limits are given by the thin lines. The horizontal line gives the corresponding OLS estimates. (a) Capacity utilization (b) Real unit wage costs (c) Wage inflation minus inflation climate (d) Productivity growth (e) Intercept.

empirically. In the case of liquidity preference, there are clear statements already in Keynes' (1936, Ch. 22) on how this parameter can be expected to vary over the business cycle, in particular as a leading indicator in the case of downturns. In the wage–price spiral – the subject of this paper – it is not so obvious what we should expect, as so many parameters are involved. The finding that demand pressure on the market for labor and for goods matters only with fairly constant speeds of adjustment is surely a bit surprising, but may be due to the fact that institutional changes do not matter much in this context. By contrast, these changes generally matter quite a lot with respect to the Blanchard and Katz (1999) error correction term and its price inflation analog. In view of the discussion conducted in this paper this is not too surprising. This can also be stated with respect to the influence of the measures of current cost pressure both in the wage and the price PCs, since we have two clearly distinguishable phases in the evolution of inflation after World War II. In the unrestricted cost-pressure cases, the inflation climate is influencing wage and price inflation with a constant parameter value, which is not implausible due to the averaging nature given to the concept in this paper. In the restricted case, however, the variability in the current cost-pressure term is enforced onto this concept as well, which is again an argument against the importance of such a restriction. According to Blanchard and Katz (1999) the influence of labor productivity on wage inflation should be weak in the U.S. economy. This has been confirmed in our OLS estimates of the considered wage–price spiral. The observed lack of variability in the corresponding parameter may be a bit astonishing in view of what has been stated on the real wage and unit cost terms, but this is not of central interest in this paper. The intercept finally is not needed for a stability analysis with respect to the feedback channels of the model and it is in any case a composition of various parameters and thus of no particular interest in the present context.

7. Conclusions and outlook

This paper suggests an alternative to the current New Keynesian formulation of wage price dynamics. On the purely formal level, this alternative looks very similar to the New Keynesian approach, but entails quite different theoretical implications and avoids empirical failures entailed by the purely forward-looking New Keynesian formulation of the wage–price mechanism. There is no longer any need for an application of the jump variable methodology of the rational expectations school and its consideration of determinacy issues when solving such dynamics in a purely forward-looking way. Instead, we have only predetermined variables in our wage–price spiral which may be subject to centripetal or centrifugal forces, and which must therefore be bounded in the latter case by way of behavioral nonlinearities in the place of purely mathematical boundedness assumptions and the consideration of uniqueness.

We have discussed the implied real wage channel of our model in Section 3 and reduced-form expressions for nominal wage and price dynamics in Section 4, and have combined this with an analytical expression for the dynamics of the real wage rate. This gave rise to a critical α-condition for stability of these dynamics. Turning to estimation, we found a significant role of demand pressure primarily in the labor market and also (as in the market for goods) a significant role for the Blanchard and Katz (1999) error correction term. Furthermore, the inflationary climate expression was always influencing the wage–price spiral in a pronounced way, while labor productivity – in line with the theoretical derivation of its role in Blanchard and Katz (1999) – was less important than could be expected from a straightforward steady-state analysis. In such a steady-state approach the wage price spiral of Section 3 would read:

$$\hat{w} = \frac{\dot{w}}{w} = \beta_{we}(e - \bar{e}) - \beta_{w\omega}\theta + \kappa_w\hat{p} + (1 - \kappa_w)\pi^c + \hat{y}$$

$$\hat{p} = \frac{\dot{p}}{p} = \beta_{pu}(u - \bar{u}) + \beta_{p\omega}\theta + \kappa_p(\hat{w} - \hat{y}) + (1 - \kappa_p)\pi^c$$

This is confirmed by our price PC, but the coefficient of unity in the wage PC is not. In line with the derivation of the wage PC in Blanchard and Katz (1999), we therefore get a feedback from the parameter in front of labor productivity to the steady-state values of the employment rate e and/or the wage rate of wage share $\theta, \tilde{\theta}$. We have set the NAIRU as given and would therefrom obtain a steady-state value for the wage rate from the wage PC, while Blanchard and Katz fix the wage share through simple markup pricing and thus obtain an endogenous expression for the NAIRU rate of employment.

Such steady-state considerations however were not of central interest here, but the quite different topic of the time variability of the parameters that characterize demand pressure influences, cost-pressure influences including the role of the inflationary climate expression, error correction terms, the role of labor productivity growth and the intercept. Our findings are that variability in parameter values is primarily observed for the employed error correction terms and short-run cost-pressure items, while for the climate measure, labor productivity and the intercept a constant parameter value was generally observed. The same holds true for the demand pressure terms (not so obviously for the price PC however), which is astonishing in the light of the debates on increasing labor market flexibility. The changes in the role of the error correction parameter reflect institutional changes and point into the direction of Blanchard and Katz's (1999) observation of their unimportance for the U.S. economy. In our variable parameter estimates this holds true for recent periods but not before the 1980s. The 1960s and even more the 1970s may be characterized as a high-inflation regimes where broadly speaking and short-term cost pressure mattered, but this effect vanished in the low-inflation regime thereafter. Of course, these broad statements appear only in somewhat mixed form in all of our estimates, but may be useful in characterizing the tendencies exhibited in our Figures 5.2–5.6.

These tendencies suggest that demand pressure terms – as compared to the error correction terms – became more relevant in our critical α-condition for the stability of the real wage channel, with the wage adjustment speed being significantly larger than the price adjustment speed in this respect. This however does not immediately imply that the real wage channel has become more unstable in the low-inflation regime, since the weights κ_w, κ_p have also changed and more importantly, since the Okun term b that relates the growth rate of the employment rate with the growth rate of capacity utilization may have decreased significantly. The time variability of this latter parameter and a proper formulation of Okun's law must however remain a matter for future research. Similarly, the estimation of a full macrodynamic model as formulated and estimated in Chen *et al.* (2004b) must also be left for future investigation.

References

Benassy, J.-P. (1986), *Macroeconomics. An Introduction to the Non-Walrasian Approach*, New York: Academic Press.

Benassy, J.-P. (1993), "Nonclearing markets: microeconomic concepts and macroeconomic applications", *Journal of Economic Literature*, Vol. XXXI, pp. 732–761.

Blanchard, O.J. and L. Katz (1999), "Wage dynamics: reconciling theory and evidence," NBER working paper 6924.

Chen, P. and P. Flaschel (2004), "Testing the dynamics of wages and prices for the U.S. economy," Discussion paper, Center for Empirical Macroeconomics, Bielefeld University.

Chen, P., C. Chiarella, P. Flaschel and H. Hung (2004a), "*Keynesian DAS DAD dynamics. Estimated convergence, stability analysis and the emergence of complex dynamics*", UTS Sydney: School of Finance and Economics.

Chen, P., C. Chiarella, P. Flaschel and H. Hung (2004b), "*Keynesian dynamics and the wage price. Estimating and analyzing a baseline disequilibrium approach*, UTS Sydney: School of Finance and Economics.

Chiarella, C. and P. Flaschel (1996), "Real and monetary cycles in models of Keynes Wicksell type", *Journal of Economic Behavior and Organization*, Vol. 30, pp. 327–351.

Chiarella, C. and P. Flaschel (2000), *The Dynamics of Keynesian Monetary Growth: Macro Foundations*, Cambridge, UK: Cambridge University Press.

Chiarella, C., P. Flaschel and R. Franke (2005), *Foundations for a Disequilibrium Theory of the Business Cycle. Qualitative Analysis and Quantitative Assessment*, Cambridge, UK: Cambridge University Press, to appear.

Eller, J.W. and R.T. Gordon (2003), "Nesting the New Keynesian Phillips Curve within the Mainstream Model of U.S. Inflation Dynamics," Paper presented at CEPR conference, The Phillips Curve Revisited, June, Berlin.

Fair, R. (2000), "Testing the NAIRU model for the United States", *The Review of Economics and Statistics*, Vol. 82, pp. 64–71.

Flaschel, P., G. Kauermann and W. Semmler (2004a), "Testing wage and price Phillips curves for the United States", Discussion Paper, Center for Empirical Macroeconomics, Bielefeld University.

Flaschel, P., G. Kauermann and W. Semmler (2004), *Phillips Curves, Phillips Loops and Wage Curves. A Model Selection Approach*, Mimeo: Bielefeld University.

Flaschel, P. and H.-M. Krolzig (2004), Wage and price Phillips curves. An empirical analysis of destabilizing wage–price spirals, Discussion paper, Oxford, Oxford University.

Hénin, P.-Y. and P. Michel (1982), *Croissance et Accumulation en Deséquilibre*, Paris: Economica.

Keynes, J.M. (1936), *The General Theory of Employment Interest and Money*, New York: Macmillan.

Laxton, D., D. Rose and D. Tambakis (2000), "The U.S. Phillips-curve: the case for asymmetry", *Journal of Economic Dynamics and Control*, Vol. 23, pp. 1459–1485.

Malinvaud, E. (1980), *Profitability and Unemployment*, Cambridge: Cambridge University Press.

Mankiw, N.-G. (2001), "The inexorable and mysterious tradeoff between inflation and unemployment", *Economic Journal*, Vol. 111, pp. 45–61.

Picard, P. (1983), "Inflation and growth in a disequilibrium macroeconomic model", *Journal of Economic Theory*, Vol. 30, pp. 266–295.

Rose, H. (1967), "On the non-linear theory of the employment cycle", *Review of Economic Studies*, Vol. 34, pp. 153–173.

Rose, H. (1990), *Macroeconomic Dynamics. A Marshallian Synthesis*, Cambridge, MA: Basil Blackwell.

Rowthorn, B. (1980), *Capitalism Conflict and Inflation*, London: Lawrence and Wishart.

Schlicht, E. (1989), "Variance estimation in a random coefficients model", Paper presented at the Econometric Society European Meeting Munich. Online at http://www.lrz.de/~ekkehart.

Schlicht, E. (2005), "VC – a program for estimating time-varying coefficients", Online at http://epub.ub.uni-muenchen.de.

Solow, R. and J. Stiglitz (1968), "Output, employment and wages in the short-run", *Quarterly Journal of Economics*, Vol. 82, pp. 537–560.

Woodford, M. (2003), *Interest and Prices*, Princeton: Princeton University Press.

Appendix: Variable coefficients estimation

The estimation of time-varying coefficients is performed by a method proposed by Schlicht (1989) and implemented in Schlicht (2005). It estimates the time-varying coefficients $a'_t = (a_{1,t}, a_{2,t}, \ldots, a_{n,t})$ of the regression

$$y_t = a'_t \cdot x_t + u_t \tag{5.11}$$

with y_t and x_t denoting the observations at time $t = 1, 2, \ldots, T$. The disturbances u_t are assumed *i.i.d.* normally distributed with mean 0 and variance σ^2. The coefficients are assumed to be generated by a random walk

$$a_{i,t} = a_{i,t-1} + v_{i,t}, \quad t = 2, 3, \ldots, T; \quad i = 1, 2, \ldots, n \qquad (5.12)$$

with disturbances $v_{i,t}$ *i.i.d.* normally distributed with means 0 and variances σ_i^2. The program estimates the variances $\sigma^2, \sigma_1^2, \sigma_2^2, \ldots, \sigma_n^2$ by a moments estimator that coincides with the corresponding maximum-likelihood estimator in large samples, and it estimates the expectations of the coefficients $a_1, a_2, \ldots, a_T$ along with their standard deviations and confidence bands. The averages $\bar{a}_i = \frac{1}{T} \sum_t a_{i,t}$ of the time-varying coefficients are Aitken estimators of the corresponding linear regression.

Data sources

The data for the estimation are taken from the Federal Reserve Bank of St. Louis (see http://www.stls.frb.org/fred). The data are quarterly, seasonally adjusted and are all available from 1948:1 to 2001:2. Except for the unemployment rates of the factors labor, $U^l = 1 - e$, and capital, $U^c = 1 - u$, the log of the series are used (see Table below).[11]

Variable	Transformation	Mnemonic	Description of the untransformed series
$U = 1 - e$	UNRATE/100	UNRATE	Unemployment rate
u	1-CUMFG/100	CUMFG	Capacity utilization: Manufacturing, percent of capacity
$\ln w$	log(COMPNFB)	COMPNFB	Nonfarm business sector: Compensation per hour, 1992 = 100
$\ln p$	log(GNPDEF)	GNPDEF	Gross national product: Implicit price deflator, 1992 = 100
$\ln y$	log(OPHNFB)	OPHNFB	Nonfarm business sector: Output per hour of all persons, 1992 = 100
$\tilde{\theta} = \ln w - \ln p - \ln y$	$\log(\frac{\text{COMPRNFB}}{\text{OPHNFB}})$	COMPRNFB	Nonfarm business sector: Real compensation per hour, 1992 = 100
$\theta = \ln w - \ln p$	log(COMPRNFB)	COMPRNFB	Nonfarm business sector: Real compensation per hour, 1992 = 100

---

[11] The series for $\tilde{\theta}$ have been bandpass filtered to eliminate their obvious trend terms.

For reasons of simplicity as well as empirical reasons, we measure the inflationary climate surrounding the current working of the wage–price spiral, see Sections 2–4, by an unweighted 12-month moving average:

$$\pi_t^c = \frac{1}{12} \sum_{j=1}^{12} \Delta p_{t-j}$$

This moving average provides a simple approximation of the theoretical adaptive expectations mechanism, which defines the inflation climate as an infinite weighted moving average of the past inflation rates with exponentially declining weights. The assumption here is that economic agents apply a certain window (three years) to past observations, without significantly discounting their observations.

PART II
DYNAMIC AD-AS ANALYSIS: QUALITATIVE FEATURES, NUMERICS AND ESTIMATION

CHAPTER 6

Keynesian Theory and the AD–AS Framework: A Reconsideration

Amitava Krishna Dutt and Peter Skott

Abstract

Contrary to what has been argued by a number of critics, the aggregate demand–aggregate supply (AD–AS) framework is both internally consistent and in conformity with Keynes's own analysis. Moreover, the eclectic approach to behavioral foundations allows models in this tradition to take into account aggregation problems as well as evidence from behavioral economics. Unencumbered by the straightjacket of optimizing microfoundations, the approach can provide a useful starting point for the analysis of dynamic macroeconomic interactions. In developing this analysis, the AD–AS approach can draw on insights from the post-Keynesian, neo-Marxian and structuralist traditions, as well as from the burgeoning literature on behavioral economics.

Keywords: AD–AS, Keynes, New Keynesian theory, microeconomic foundations

JEL classifications: E12, O11, B22, B41, B50

1. Introduction

Several turn-of-the-century assessments of the state of macroeconomics regard the discipline as healthy. There may have been fierce debates and controversies, but these debates mainly served to highlight deficiencies of existing models and to stimulate the creation of new improved hybrid models. The history of macroeconomics, according to Blanchard (2000, p. 1375) is "one of a surprisingly steady accumulation of knowledge", and "progress in macroeconomics may well be the success story of twentieth century economics". Woodford's (1999) assessment gives slightly more weight to the disagreements and revolutions in the second half of the twentieth century. But Woodford also sees convergence, and he concludes that "modern macroeconomic models are intertemporal general equilibrium models derived from the same foundations of optimizing behavior on the part of households and firms as are employed in other branches of economics" (p. 31).

We disagree with these assessments. In our view, a large part of what has happened in macroeconomics since the late 1960s has been a wasteful detour. A generation of macroeconomists has grown up learning tools that may be sophisticated, but the usefulness of these tools is questionable. Moreover, a great deal of damage may be, and has been, done when the tools are applied to real-world situations.

In this paper we shall argue that, for all their limitations, the simple models of the old Keynesian school using the aggregate demand–aggregate supply (AD–AS) framework provide a better starting point for serious analysis than more recent models in the New Keynesian (NK) or real business cycle (RBC) traditions, which have come to dominate modern macroeconomics. The obsession with optimization and microeconomic foundations has meant that a promising Keynesian research program has been largely abandoned. Our preferred version of this program builds on the old Keynesian models, but extends and modifies them to accommodate insights from the post-Keynesian, neo-Marxian and structuralist traditions.

The main emphasis in this paper is on the usefulness and shortcomings of the basic AD–AS framework, and on how the framework may be developed and improved. Section 2 outlines a standard version of the AD–AS model and shows that it can be given a logically consistent Marshallian interpretation. It also shows that the model does not, as claimed by some critics, suffer from internal logical contradictions. Section 3 discusses some alleged shortcomings of the model. Section 4 considers the NK alternative, focusing on two main issues: microeconomic foundations and the treatment of stability. Section 5 introduces post-Keynesian and other arguments for the relevance of aggregate demand, not just in the short run but also, as an influence on real outcomes, in the medium and the long run. Section 6, finally, ends with a few concluding remarks.

2. The AD–AS framework

Following Keynes, the AD–AS approach visualizes the economy as a whole, that is, the theory is 'general' rather than 'partial'.[1] Keynes's (1936/1973)

---

[1] According to the preface to the French edition of the GT, written three years after the English publication, Keynes (1936/1973, p. xxxii) explains:

"I have called my theory a general theory. I mean by this that I am chiefly concerned with the behavior of the economic system as a whole, -with aggregate incomes, aggregate profits, aggregate output, aggregate employment, aggregate investment, aggregate saving rather than with the incomes, profits, output, employment, investment and saving of particular industries, firms and individuals. And I argue that important mistakes have been made through extending to the system as a whole conclusions which have been arrived at in respect of a part of it taken in isolation".

derivation of a fix-wage general equilibrium in chapters 1–18 of *The General Theory of Employment, Interest and Money* (*GT*) was an enormous intellectual achievement, and the one stressed by both Blanchard and Woodford in their accounts of the Keynesian revolution. The AD–AS framework gives a reasonable representation of the analytical skeleton behind this fix-wage general equilibrium. The strength of the AD–AS apparatus is precisely the explicit attempt to integrate the analysis of goods, labor and financial markets.

The AD–AS framework divides the economy into two parts – the 'demand side' and the 'supply side' – and examines their interaction using accounting identities, equilibrium conditions and behavioral and institutional equations. The 'demand side' typically examines factors relating to the demand for goods and the demand and supply of assets. The 'supply side' typically examines factors relating to output and pricing decisions of producers, and factor markets. The framework ensures that neither demand nor supply-side factors are overlooked in the analysis and that macroeconomic outcomes depend on the interaction between the different markets. The particular partitioning into 'aggregate demand' and 'aggregate supply' along with the choice of terminology may provide the pedagogic advantage of making macroeconomic analysis possible in terms of the same tools as the simplest microeconomic model of the market. But this advantage comes at a high price. The aggregate demand and supply curves embody complex interactions and are clearly not the same as the microeconomic curves, which take a partial view of the economy. The analogy therefore is spurious, and forgetting this has led to a great deal of confusion in the literature, as briefly discussed later.

The basic AD–AS model is well-known, of course, but to ease the exposition it is helpful to state a simple version of it explicitly. There are two equilibrium conditions:

$$Y = C + I + G \qquad\qquad (6.1)$$

$$\frac{M}{P} = L \qquad\qquad (6.2)$$

where, in standard notation, Y is the real output, C, I and G, are real consumption, investment and government expenditure, respectively, M the supply of money, P the price level and L the real demand for money. The six behavioral or institutional equations are as follows:

$$C = C(Y) \qquad\qquad (6.3)$$

$$I = I(r) \qquad\qquad (6.4)$$

$$L = L(Y, r) \qquad\qquad (6.5)$$

$$Y = F(N) \qquad\qquad (6.6)$$

$$\frac{W}{P^e} = F'(N) \qquad\qquad (6.7)$$

$$W = W_0 \qquad\qquad (6.8)$$

where $0 < C' < 1, I' < 0, L_1 > 0, L_2 < 0, F' > 0$ and $F'' < N$, and r is the rate of interest, N the level of employment, W the money wage and P^e the price expected by firms. Equations (6.3)–(6.6) are standard consumption, investment, money demand and production functions. Since C, I and L are used to denote desired amounts in Equations (6.3)–(6.5), Equations (6.1) and (6.2) are equilibrium conditions (rather than accounting identities) showing that output is equal to the demand for it and that the money supply in real terms is equal to the demand. Behind these equilibrium conditions lie dynamic adjustment processes with excess demand for goods leading to an increase in P and excess demand for money leading to an increase in r.[2] Equation (6.7) is the profit maximizing condition of firms that are assumed to be price takers in perfectly competitive markets; since there is a production lag and firms make production plans prior to knowing what price they will receive for their goods, the price that is relevant for their production decision is the expected price. The levels of M, G and W are given exogenously. To stress that this is the case for the money wage, Equation (6.8) states that the money wage is given at the exogenous level W_0.

Our interpretation of the model is Marshallian and we examine the behavior of the economy in two different 'runs'. The expected price and the level of output are given in the 'market' (or 'ultra-short') run. In the 'short' run, expected price changes in response to its deviations from the actual price, and this change is accompanied by changes in the level of production; in a short-run equilibrium expectations are being met and the expected and the actual price coincide.

In the market run, given P^e, and given W from Equation (6.8), N is determined by Equation (6.7), and Y by Equation (6.6). For this level of Y, substitution of Equations (6.3) and (6.4) into (6.1) yields a value of r which satisfies that equation, irrespective of the price level. The IS curve in Figure 6.1, which shows equilibrium in the goods market in (P, r)-space, is vertical at this level of r.[3] The vertical arrows show the direction of price adjustments when the economy is out of goods market equilibrium. Also for the given level of Y, substitution of Equation (6.5) into Equation (6.2) yields a positive LM relation between P and r, which represents money-(and assets) market equilibrium. The horizontal arrows show the direction of interest adjustments when the economy is out of money-market equilibrium. The intersection of the IS and LM curves gives the market-run equilibrium values of P and r. The equilibrium value of r is determined by the position of the vertical IS curve, and the LM curve determines the value of P. With off-equilibrium dynamics

---

[2] The dynamics can be explicitly formalized by the equations $dP/dt = \beta_G[C + I + G - Y]$, $dr/dt = \beta_A[L - (M/P)]$, where t denotes time and $\beta_i > 0$ are speed of adjustment parameters for the goods and asset markets.

[3] If we introduce real balance effects that make C (and, possibly, I) depend positively on M/P, the IS curve would be negatively sloped rather than vertical. We abstract from this complication here, but refer to it later.

Figure 6.1. *The basic adjustment process of the Keynesian system*

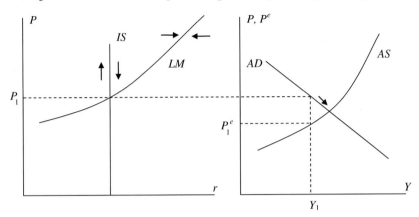

given by the equations in footnote 2, it is readily seen that the market-run equilibrium is stable for a given Y.

In the short run, P^e is allowed to change in response to unfulfilled expectations. When P^e changes to a new level, firms adjust their employment and output levels. This adjustment is captured by the AS curve, which shows the profit-maximizing level of output produced by the firms for a given P^e. When Y changes, the IS and LM curves shift in (r, P)-space and determine a new market-run equilibrium of r and P. The level of P which clears goods and money markets for each level of Y is shown along the AD curve. A higher level of Y increases the level of saving, so that goods market equilibrium requires an increase in investment, a fall in r and hence a leftward shift of the IS curve. A higher level of Y increases the real demand for money, so that money market equilibrium requires a fall in P (or an increase in r), so that the LM curve shifts to the right in (r, P)-space. Consequently, a higher Y implies a lower P for market-run equilibrium, explaining the negative slope of the AD curve.

The short-run dynamics shown in Figure 6.1 can be described as follows. Starting from an initial level of expected price, P_1^e, output is determined at Y_1 (as shown by the AS curve) and price at P_1 (as shown by the AD curve). Since $P_1 > P_1^e$, if firms revise their price expectations adaptively, P^e rises, making Y expand along the AS curve and the market-run equilibrium move along the AD curve (representing shifts in the IS and LM curve) as shown by the arrow. This adjustment will continue till the economy arrives at the short-run equilibrium at the intersection of the AD and AS curves, where $P = P^e$.[4]

---

[4] The stability of short-run equilibrium can be verified by representing the dynamics of expected price by the equation: $dP^e/dt = \beta_E \, [P - P^e]$, where $\beta_E > 0$ is the speed of expectations adjustment parameter.

Amitava Krishna Dutt and Peter Skott

Three comments about this model are in order. First, the Marshallian interpretation of the model finds a great deal of exegetical support in Keynes's own work and in the writings of many Keynesians. Clower (1989), for instance, notes the Marshallian aspects of Keynes's *GT*, although not as precisely as done in our model (see Dutt, 1992a).

Second, the Marshallian interpretation is important for the internal consistency of the economic argument. It has been argued by Barro (1994), Fields and Hart (1990), Colander (1995) and Bhaduri *et al.* (1999) that the AD–AS model embodies two mutually-contradictory approaches to pricing and production by firms. According to this criticism, the AD curve is based on IS and LM curves, but the analysis assumes that firms fix the price (having the ability to do so) and that equilibrium levels of r and Y are determined from Equations (6.1) and (6.2), using (6.3)–(6.5). The story told is that firms fix their price and adjust their output in response to changes in demand conditions. The AS curve, on the other hand, assumes price-taking behavior on the part of firms operating in purely competitive markets with demand constraints, producing to maximize profits given, the money wage and the production function. While some textbook versions of the AD–AS model do suffer from this inconsistency, our Marshallian model is free of it. The equations of the model are similar to those of the standard textbook version,[5] but in our interpretation the AD and AS curves both embody profit maximization and price-taking behavior: the AD curve in our interpretation shows equilibrium price for a given level of output and not, as the standard AD curve, the equilibrium value of Y for different levels of P.[6]

Third, the model can easily be recast using Keynes's own 'AD–AS diagram' with employment and the value of output (price times quantity) on the axes (he did not actually draw this diagram in *GT*, but described it in words in chapter 3).[7] Keynes's Aggregate Supply function is given by $W_0 F(N)/F'(N)$ and is derived from Equations (6.6)–(6.8): its curve shows the expected value of output at each level of employment consistent with profit maximizing behavior. The AD function is derived from Equations (6.1)–(6.6), and its curve shows the actual equilibrium proceeds (PY) for any given level of N. The level of N determines Y from Equation (6.6), and given this Y, P is determined as shown in the IS–LM diagram of Figure 6.1, which determines the equilibrium level of PY. The value of aggregate demand at the intersection between the supply and demand curves defines "the effective demand" (*GT*, p. 25).

---

[5] For a discussion of the history of the AD–AS model, including that of its emergence and spread in macroeconomic textbooks, see Dutt (2002).

[6] See Dutt and Skott (1996) for further discussion of the internal-consistency criticisms.

[7] He probably used this type of diagram, rather than that in (P, Y) space, because aggregate price level and real output were not in common use in his day, while value of output and total employment, involving fewer aggregation problems, were.

By construction expectations are being met at the point of effective demand. In chapter 5 of *GT,* however, Keynes discusses the formation and revision of short-period expectations, showing how firms produce a certain level of output with a certain level of employment, given short period expectations, and then adjust these expectations if they are not fulfilled. Though he does not explicitly analyze this process, we can do so by using the expected proceeds curve, given by $P^e Y = P^e F(N)$, for a given P^e from Equation (6.6): it shows what firms expect the value of output to be for a given price expectation. The intersection of this curve with the curve for the Aggregate Supply function determines the market-run equilibrium level of employment, since it satisfies Equation (6.7). For the market-run equilibrium employment level, one can read off actual proceeds from the Aggregate Demand function. If actual proceeds are different from expected proceeds, P^e will change, shifting the expected proceeds curve, till the economy arrives at short-run equilibrium at the intersection of all three curves.[8] For most of the *GT,* however, Keynes confines attention to short-run equilibrium in which actual and expected price are equal, thereby concealing the Marshallian adjustment process because it was not central to his demonstration of the possibility of unemployment short-run equilibrium.[9]

3. Shortcomings

An AD–AS model of the type just described has many well-known weaknesses and limitations, of which three are relevant for our purposes.

The criticisms that have received the most attention concern the alleged lack of microeconomic foundations of the model. NKs (along with new classical economists and RBC theorists), who have been vocal in this criticism, wish to supplant the model with models based on explicit optimization. We shall take up

---

[8] Keynes's AD function does not actually use the simultaneous equations approach to solving P, focusing only on goods market equilibrium without taking into account asset markets explicitly. An alternative formulation of the model, which focuses only on the goods market, but allows consumption demand to respond to price changes due to either the real balance effect or distribution shifts, can easily be developed. See Dutt (1987) for a version in which changes in price affect the value of output through changes in income distribution between wages and profits.

[9] The *Treatise on Money* had concentrated on the Marshallian ultra-short run (or market-run) equilibrium:

"My so-called 'fundamental equations' were an instantaneous picture taken on the assumption of a given output. They attempted to show how, assuming the given output, forces could develop which involved a profit-disequilibrium, and thus required a change in the level of output. But the dynamic development, as distinct from the instantaneous picture, was left incomplete and extremely confused (Keynes, 1936/1973, p. xxii".

Skott (1989a, 1989b) develops a model of cyclical growth using the Marshallian (or Keynes-of-the-Treatise) ultra-short-run equilibrium as the basic building block; see also Skott (1983) for a discussion of this Marshallian approach and the relation between the *Treatise on Money* and the *GT*.

the issue of optimizing microfoundations in Section 4 where we discuss the NK approach. But the behavioral approach of the AD–AS model has also been criticized from another angle. Many post-Keynesian economists, but also some impeccably mainstream old Keynesians, have suggested that the model is too mechanical and does not take into account uncertainty and expectations in a serious manner.[10] It is beyond the scope of the present paper to address this important issue in any detail, but, in our view, 'mechanical' mathematical formalization can be extremely useful. This formalization needs to be supplemented by verbal descriptions and empirical analysis, and less formal discussions of possible outcomes may also come into play if the relations determining the evolution of the system are not capable of being formalized in a precise manner. Even this informal discussion, however, will often benefit from using more formal analyses as points of reference and by suggesting where and how the results of the models may need to be modified.

A second set of criticisms claims that the AD–AS model omits many important features of reality and that some of its implications are not consistent with empirical observation. Assumptions of imperfect competition, for instance, should replace perfect competition, and the money supply should not be treated as an exogenous variable in an economy with modern monetary institutions.[11] The consumption function should also take into account income distributional effects on consumption, increases in aggregate demand should provide a direct stimulus to investment and the distinction between nominal and real rates of interest may be critical (not least for the reactions of aggregate demand to changes in money wages and the stability of full employment). These (and other) modifications may complicate the model and affect some of its properties, but in principle their introduction is quite straightforward and the resulting model can still be depicted with AD and AS curves (see, for instance, Dutt and Skott, 1996). The modifications, moreover, help to address some of the empirical criticisms of the AD–AS model. The simple model, for instance, predicts a counter-cyclical movement of the real wage. This implication, which finds little support in the data (as noted early on by Dunlop, 1938; Tarshis, 1939), no longer holds in versions of the model that include imperfect competition (perhaps with markup pricing à la Kalecki, 1971) and some combination of non-diminishing returns to labor and/or a counter-cyclical pattern in the markup.

A third set of problems with the AD–AS model concerns the unsatisfactory treatment of dynamics. There is a lack of integration between the analysis of

---

[10] For a review of post-Keynesian contributions, see Dutt and Amadeo (1990). For more mainstream discussions, see Hicks (1980–81), Tobin (1975) and Meltzer (1988).

[11] See, for instance, Moore (1988). NKs have also abandoned the exogenous-money assumption, but rather than stressing the nature of monetary institutions, they focus on the specific policy rule adopted by the Central Bank in the US and elsewhere (e.g. Romer, 2000; Woodford, 2003).

the short-run and more long-term issues, and even when it comes to the treatment of the short run, the analysis often relies on unstated or questionable assumptions concerning the process leading to a short-run Keynesian equilibrium. Our own presentation above is quite explicit in its assumptions (footnotes 2 and 4) but, perhaps unrealistically, it presumes that the adjustment to market-run equilibrium is 'very fast' relative to the adjustments of price expectations. The adjustment to market-run equilibrium could therefore be based on given price expectations, and in the analysis of adjustments to short-run equilibrium it could be assumed that there is a continuous market equilibrium during the adjustment process.[12]

The shortcomings of simple AD–AS models with respect to dynamics may be a legacy of Keynes's own focus on short-run equilibria in *GT*. The assumption of fulfilled expectations facilitated the presentation of the fix-wage general equilibrium.[13] Unfortunately, it makes it hard to discuss the stability issues, and from today's perspective – having before us a well-developed theory of general equilibrium – the truly revolutionary and provocative message of the *GT* concerns the destabilizing effects of money wage flexibility, rather than the existence of a fix-wage equilibrium with unemployment.

The AD–AS model does not address the stability issue – it takes the money wage as given – but can serve as a starting point. The model can be easily extended in a way which makes it have the implications presented in the typical textbook: (i) that unemployment can exist in the model because the money wage is exogenously fixed; (ii) that if one allows the money wage to fall in response to the existence of unemployment, the AS curve, given by $P = F'(F^{-1}(Y))/W$ is shifted downward; and that (iii) this leads to an expansion of output and employment along the negatively sloped AD curve and moves the economy to the 'natural rate of unemployment' (corresponding to the absence of Keynesian involuntary unemployment). The mechanism behind this adjustment is the 'Keynes effect' by which a reduction in wage and price

---

[12] In the context of our simple specification, however, it is easy to prove that local stability carries over to the case where P, P^e and r are all treated as state variables, with their dynamics shown by the equations in footnotes 2 and 4.

[13] In a set of lecture notes from 1937, Keynes argues as follows:
"When one is dealing with aggregates, aggregate effective demand at time A has no corresponding aggregate income at time B. All one can compare is the expected and actual income resulting to an entrepreneur from a particular decision. Actual investment may differ through unintended stock changes, price changes, alteration of decision. The difference, if any, is due to a mistake in the short-period expectation and the importance of the difference lies in the fact that this difference will be one of the relevant factors in determining subsequent effective demand.
I began, as I have said, by regarding this difference as important. But eventually I felt it to be of secondary importance, emphasis on it obscuring the real argument. For the theory of effective demand is substantially the same if we assume that short-period expectations are always fulfilled (Keynes, 1973, p. 181)".

increases the real supply of money, lowers the interest rate and increases investment and aggregate demand. This effect can be supplemented by the real balance effect by which the rise in real balances directly stimulates the aggregate demand for goods.

This standard analysis is at odds with Keynes's own argument in *GT* where, in chapter 19, he insisted that involuntary unemployment would not be eliminated by increased wage flexibility. Falling money wages will influence the economy in a number of ways but, on balance, are unlikely to stimulate output.[14] Keynes's analysis of the effects of changes in money wages may have been sketchy, but the logic behind potential instability is impeccable. The real balance effect was overlooked by Keynes, but has been found to be empirically insignificant, and the expansionary effects of a decline in money wages due to the Keynes effect may be more than offset by the adverse influences of debt deflation, distributional shifts and expectations of continuing reductions of wages and prices. 'Old Keynesians' have been aware of these stability problems (see Tobin, 1975), and post-Keynesians have stressed additional problems arising from the role of uncertainty, the financial situation of firms and the effects of an endogenous money supply.

These complicating factors can be addressed by an informal discussion of the diverse effects of money wage changes, using the AD–AS model as the starting point. This is basically what Keynes did in chapter 19 of *GT*. The analysis and the destabilizing effects can be illustrated using the AD–AS diagram (see Dutt and Amadeo, 1990). For instance, debt deflation problems can make the AD curve upward-sloping and, in addition, money wage reductions can shift the AD curve to the left (because of a higher propensity to consume out of wage income than non-wage income), both of which prevent the economy from converging to the 'natural' level of output. The analysis can be made more precise by incorporating specific effects into more general Keynesian models in order to formally examine the stability question, as done by Chiarella and Flaschel (2000), among others. Their analysis demonstrates that the Keynesian models can generate very complex dynamics and that local instability is a likely outcome for plausible specifications.

4. The New Keynesian detour

The NK approach can be characterized as one which attempts to derive Keynesian conclusions with respect to the existence of unemployment equilibrium and/or the effectiveness of aggregate demand policy, while using a standard neoclassical methodology.

---

[14] Hicks (1974) used the term Keynes's 'wage theorem' to denote the benchmark result that variations in money wages have no net effects on real output and employment in a closed economy'.

Unemployment equilibrium can be explained in terms of the optimizing behavior of agents in models that depart from Walrasian perfect competition by introducing perceived demand curves for imperfectly competitive firms, asymmetric information, efficiency wages, credit rationing and the like.[15] Some of these models are very insightful, but they largely fail to address the issue of involuntary unemployment in Keynes's sense. Keynes explicitly defined 'voluntary unemployment' to include all frictional and structural unemployment, that is, to include unemployment caused by minimum wage legislation and excessive union wage demands, for instance. By extension, Keynes's notion of voluntary unemployment also includes structural unemployment generated by the various departures from perfect competition that have been invoked by NK. Structural unemployment of this kind may be theoretically interesting and empirically significant, but it is not the kind of unemployment addressed by Keynes. His involuntary unemployment is defined in terms of inadequate aggregate demand and the failure of the market mechanism to ensure the adjustment of aggregate demand to the level of aggregate supply associated with a structurally determined (minimum) rate of unemployment. It is the deviation from a structural unemployment rate that makes demand policy desirable.

In NK models, the effectiveness of aggregate demand policy is confined to the short run and derives from nominal wage and price rigidities. Some of the early NK models were of the spanner-in-the-works variety, which merely introduced nominal wage and price rigidities into new classical or RBC models with rational expectations. But the NK methodology requires that such rigidities be based on optimizing behavior: "rather than postulating that prices and wages respond mechanically to some measure of market disequilibrium, they are set optimally, that is, so as to best serve the interests of the parties assumed to set them, according to the information available at the time" (Woodford, 2003, p. 7). Thus, prices and wages are set in a forward-looking manner, expectations are assumed to be rational and preferences are regarded as structural and invariant to changes in policy.

Our comments on the NK approach focus on two issues: the obsession with microeconomic foundations based on explicit optimization, and the treatment of stability issues. The two issues are related since the obsession with optimization stands in the way of serious stability analysis.

4.1. *Optimization*

Optimization, in our view, can sometimes be very useful as a simple way of describing goal-oriented behavior (indeed, both our simple AD–AS model and

---

[15] Some contributions are adventurous enough to depart from optimization to invoke 'near' rationality! (see Akerlof and Yellen, 1987).

Keynes's own analysis included the assumption of profit maximizing firms). But insisting on optimization can also result in problems. The problems with the optimization approach are largely well-known and a brief summary of some of the main points will suffice.

The cognitive limitations and bounded rationality of all real-world decision makers have been stressed by many authors, most notably perhaps by Simon, and a more recent literature has documented the existence of systematic departures from optimizing behavior (see Kahneman, 2000; Camerer *et al.*, 2004). From this perspective the NK demand for optimizing microeconomic foundations is remarkable primarily because of the highly restrictive form that it takes.[16]

Aggregation represents another problem for the optimizing approach. To obtain definite results, macroeconomics theories have to engage in aggregation. Thus, there can be no attempt at full disaggregation in the agent space, as in Arrow–Debreu models of general equilibrium, and it is well-known that even if all individual agents were fully rational and maximized well-behaved utility functions subject to standard constraints, the aggregate variables do not behave as if determined by an optimizing representative agent (see, for instance, Kirman, 1992). Aggregation problems therefore imply that the use of an optimizing representative agent in NK models has little to recommend itself.

The existence of social norms and conventions provides a further reason to eschew the mechanical application of optimization methods based on exogenously given and constant preferences. The role of relative wages and norms of fairness in Keynes's *GT* analysis of wage formation presents an example of this perspective. The existence of norms and conventions may be a source of 'conditional stability' in Keynesian models of uncertainty (Crotty, 1994), but norms and conventions also change over time, both endogenously and as a result of exogenous shocks. We shall return to these issues in Section 5 below.

A more subtle danger of the optimization approach is that it may predispose the analysis to slide from individual 'rationality' to systemic 'rationality'. Some economists may view optimization as simply an organizing principle (see footnote 16), but countless examples suggest that an optimization approach may

---

[16] It can be argued that problems related to information gathering and computational ability need not undermine the neoclassical optimizing hypothesis, because this hypothesis does not assume rationality in an empirical sense (whatever that means), but simply uses the organizing framework of analyzing behavior in terms of the optimization of *some* objective function subject to *some* constraints (see Boland, 1981). This argument, however, suggests that there is no overriding justification for insisting on the use of the optimizing approach (for instance, based on some notion of the rationality of economic agents), and that a non-optimizing approach need not be inferior to the neoclassical one.

generate (sometimes unconsciously) a slippery slope in which individual optimization eventually leads to social optimality. Sargent (1993), for instance, is able to assume bounded rationality and yet produce, eventually, his unique, new classical equilibrium. As a second example, many of the problems caused by efficiency wage considerations can be 'solved' when credit markets function efficiently (again, with clever institutions). A history of how a focus on individual optimization in neoclassical economics inexorably, albeit tortuously, has led to presumptions of social optimality awaits an author, if one does not exist already.

A serious problem, finally, arises from the bounded rationality of the theorist. Carrying the straightjacket of optimization – especially in its dynamic versions – reduces the ability of the theory to incorporate many important aspects of reality in a tractable manner, and therefore encourages the theorist to ignore them. One may insist on treating all agents in a model as fully optimizing, but there is a cost to meeting this demand. Simplifications then need to be made in other areas in order to keep the model tractable; the number of distinct agents, for instance, may have to be kept very small and the nature of the interaction between the agents very simple.

All useful models, of course, represent drastically stylized pictures of a complex reality. The art of model building consists in choosing appropriate simplifying assumptions, and in our view the insistence on fully optimizing behavior represents a suboptimal 'corner solution' to the modeling problem: the gains from explicit optimization are often minimal and the costs of the required simplifications in other areas high. Thus, over the last 30 years, macroeconomists have struggled to solve problems of intertemporal optimization. These optimization problems grossly simplify real-world decision problems, and the astounding implicit presumption has been that agents in the real world solve (or act as if they had solved) these much more complex problems. The neglect of the aggregation problem and the use of representative agents in models that purport to provide microeconomic foundations only serve to make the picture even more bizarre. In fact, the contemporary approach with its sophisticated and perfectly rational representative agents would seem to embody a good example of how not to use mathematics: mathematical models arguably are useful primarily because they allow a clear analysis of complex interactions between agents, each of whom may follow relatively simple (but possibly changing) behavioral rules.

4.2. Stability and rational expectations

NK models may include non-clearing labor markets and allow for real effects of aggregate demand policy. But it is assumed that, in the absence of shocks, the economy converges to an equilibrium position, and cyclical fluctuations are generated by introducing stochastic shocks into models with a stable equilibrium solution. If only prices and wages were flexible, there would be no Keynesian problems of effective demand.

The stability concerns that were at the center of Keynes's message have been largely forgotten.[17] Is there an NK answer to these stability concerns? Not really. Stability is simply assumed in NK models. The models typically involve saddlepoints and jump variables, and the presumption of stability is used to pin down the outcome in the short run. Agents have rational expectations, and the jump variables seek out the stable saddlepath. Thus, to the extent that there is an answer, it comes from the NK focus on microfoundations and rational expectations, and from the implicit rejection of the old Keynesian analysis because of its alleged deficiencies in these areas.

Rational expectations have been used before Muth and Lucas, although without using that name. Keynes's own *GT* approach of assuming that short-period expectations are fulfilled is an example of rational expectations in the sense of perfect foresight, and Harrod's (1939) warranted growth path also represents a rational expectations path. But the extension of rational expectations to all models – and not just steady growth paths or Robinsonian mythical ages – lacks both theoretical and empirical foundations. We confine our attention to a few observations about theory.

The theoretical argument relies on the claim that the systematic deviations characterizing other specifications would lead to changes in expectation formation. This claim has some force and, indeed, changing expectations may be an important source of instability (as suggested by the role of 'animal spirits' in Keynesian analysis). But the claim does not justify a focus on rational expectations. It has been notoriously difficult to get convergence to rational expectations even in simple models of rational learning, and the real-world learning process takes place within a complex overall environment and one that is subject to constant and profound technical and institutional change (Frydman and Phelps, 1983). These changes in the environment may lead to shifts in expectations; indeed, some institutional or structural change is often invoked to justify expectations that would otherwise seem unreasonable, viz. the appeal to a 'new economy' during the stock market boom of the 1990s. However, structural

---

[17] The Japanese stagnation in the 1990s may have alerted the profession to some stability issues, and the 'liquidity trap' has made a comeback (e.g. Krugman, 1998). The liquidity trap arises because of an inability of monetary policy to reduce interest rates, that is, to change intertemporal prices. It seems to have escaped attention, however, that the liquidity trap and the problem of intertemporal prices are indicative of the general stability problem. Money wage reductions fail to solve the unemployment problem because "[a]ccording to Keynes' diagnosis, it is fundamentally the *intertemporal relative values* observed or implicit in the actual vector that are 'wrong,'" and, "*although the most eye-catching symptom of maladjustment is the great excess supply in the labor markets, ... the burden of adjustment should not be thrown on this market*" (Leijonhufvud, 1968, pp. 336 and 338; italics in original).

and institutional changes of this kind count against rational expectations since the learning processes underlying the claims in favor of rational expectations fare better in a stable environment.[18]

It should be noted, finally, that a dismissal of stability concerns cannot be justified by reference to Walrasian general equilibrium theory. In fact, the realization that stability had not and probably could not be established under reasonable assumptions may have been a critical factor behind the virtual abandonment in microeconomics of all research on Walrasian general equilibrium theory (Kirman, 1989; Katzner, 2004).[19]

The use of individual optimization therefore does not imply that one can ignore stability issues, and in fact not all contributions that can be called NK have ignored these issues. A notable exception is the work of Hahn and Solow (1995), who develop an overlapping-generations model and introduce real money balances using a variant of the Clower constraint to show that wage-price flexibility can result in macroeconomic instability. They also show that wage and price sluggishness as explained by standard NK techniques can be stabilizing but also prevent the economy from attaining full employment. However, unlike many of the other elegant theoretical contributions of these authors, the model becomes extremely unwieldy, primarily due to its optimizing assumptions (despite the artificial way money is introduced) and they have to resort to simulation techniques to examine the behavior of the economy.

5. Post-Keynesian, structuralist and neo-Marxian alternatives

The AD–AS tradition – including the recent work on 'integrated Keynesian disequilibrium dynamics' by Chiarella and Flaschel and their associates – rightly stresses the need to consider dynamic interactions across markets, and it is justifiably critical of optimization methodology. But theories in the AD–AS tradition need to be developed not just in terms of more advanced mathematical analysis of the dynamic interactions but also in terms of a renewed attention to the behavioral assumptions and their implications for the specification of the various equations.

---

[18] The learning argument is particularly vulnerable with respect to some of the key variables of macroeconomic interest – saving for retirement, for instance, or educational choices (investment in human capital) – where essentially each agent makes only a single decision. Parental background and experience may be a critical influence on these choices but for backward rather than forward looking reasons.

[19] Joan Robinson's criticism of tatonnement-based stability should have provided additional impetus for this shift, but her criticism was not widely understood (e.g. Robinson, 1962, pp. 23–29; Skott, 2005b).

The behavioral foundations, of course, have not been neglected in the Keynesian literature, as is evident from even a cursory look at Keynes's own analysis or the efforts of many old Keynesians. Nonetheless, some of the presumptions of the AD–AS tradition seem questionable from a heterodox perspective. A post-Keynesian approach questions the limited role of aggregate demand in determining medium- and long-run growth patterns in AD–AS models; a neo-Marxian approach suggests a greater focus on income distribution and its interaction with the rate of accumulation and the movements in the 'reserve army of labor'; a structuralist approach (see Taylor, 1991, 2004) emphasizes the need to examine how the structural and institutional characteristics of economies determine their dynamics.

It is beyond the scope of this paper to discuss the behavioral alternatives in any detail. We shall confine ourselves to a couple of examples of what we have in mind. The examples concern assumptions that affect the role of aggregate demand in the medium and long run, and we shall focus on medium- and long-run steady states rather than the stability of these steady states.

5.1. The medium run: fairness and the 'natural rate of unemployment'

The existence of a 'natural rate of unemployment' has been a mainstay of NK models, and the extensions of the AD–AS models by Chiarella and Flaschel (2000) share this feature; the natural rate of unemployment may not be asymptotically stable in their models, but cycles take place around a structurally determined long-run equilibrium (except for a brief sketch in their final chapter on the "road ahead"). The existence of a natural rate of unemployment implies that aggregate demand plays (almost) no role in the determination of the trend of output and the average long-run value of the unemployment rate. We find this aspect of the models questionable, both empirically and theoretically.

Money wages may be sticky partly because workers care about relative wages (as suggested by Keynes). This argument implies a rejection of a traditional view of preferences as defined over the agent's own consumption. Instead, a notion of fairness becomes central, and the behavioral literature has provided strong support for the role of 'fairness' in wage formation (see, for instance, Akerlof and Yellen, 1990; Bewley, 1998; Fehr and Gächter, 2000). The literature also shows that changes in nominal wages are relevant for the perceived fairness of the wage offer. The relevance of nominal changes implies a kind of 'money illusion'. As a result, there is no natural rate of unemployment. Instead, a downward sloping Phillips curve emerges, and demand policies may affect real output and employment in the medium and long run (Akerlof *et al.* (1996); Shafir *et al.* (1997)).

A more radical conclusion can be obtained if it is recognized that norms of fairness may change over time and that the prevailing wage norms are strongly influenced by the actual wage patterns in the past. Thus, according to

Kahneman *et al.* (1986, pp. 730–731) notions of fairness tend to adjust gradually to actual outcomes:[20]

> "the reference transaction provides a basis for fairness judgments because it is normal, not because it is just. Psychological studies of adaptation suggest that any stable state of affairs tends to become accepted eventually, at least in the sense that alternatives to it no longer readily come to mind. Terms of exchange that are initially seen as unfair may in time acquire the status of reference transaction. Thus, the gap between the behavior that people consider fair and the behavior that they expect in the market-place tends to be rather small".

Skott (1999, 2005a) shows that this conventional aspect of wage norms may lead to employment hysteresis, even in models that exclude money illusion of any kind.[21] If inflationary expectations are formed adaptively and adjustments in wage norms take a simple linear form, the models generate a downward-sloping Phillips curve. In general, however, aggregate demand policy will affect output in the medium run, but there will be no well-behaved Phillips relation, vertical or downward-sloping, betweenemployment and the inflation rate.

These examples illustrate how lessons from behavioral economics may cast doubt on the natural rate hypothesis.[22] Theoretical doubts might not carry a lot of weight if the empirical evidence was overwhelming, but this is not the case. Even strong supporters of the framework concede that the applicability of the theory may be limited. Thus, Gordon (1997, p. 28) concludes that

> "Within the postwar experience of the United States, the modest fluctuations in the NAIRU seem plausible in magnitude and timing. When applied to Europe or to the United States in the Great Depression, however, fluctuations in the NAIRU seem too large to be plausible and seem mainly to mimic movements in the actual unemployment rate".

From a Popperian perspective, Gordon's reading of the evidence must imply that the theory should be rejected.

---

[20] The conventional aspect of fairness is implicit in many discussions of these issues. Keynes (1930b), for instance, expressed his sympathy with the view that "there is a large arbitrary element in the relative rates of remuneration, and the factors of production get what they do, not because in any strict sense they precisely earn it, but because past events have led to these rates being customary and usual" (quoted from Keynes, 1981, p. 7). Marshall (1887) noted that fairness must be defined "with reference to the methods of industry, the habits of life and the character of the people" (p. 212). Fairness, he argues, requires that a worker

> "ought to be paid for his work at the usual rate for his trade and neighbourhood; so that he may live in that way to which he and his neighbours in his rank of life *have been accustomed* (p. 213; italics added)".

Similar views have been advocated by Hicks (1974) and Solow (1990).

[21] Here, we use the term hysteresis in a broad sense to include zero-root models, and not just models with 'remanence' (see Cross, 1988).

[22] Other theoretical and arguments against the natural rate hypothesis are discussed in, for instance, Cross (1988, 1995).

5.2. The long run: growth, accumulation and technological change

Models of the long run, which introduce capital accumulation, technological change and labor supply growth, are generally of two varieties.

By far, the more popular is the one in which aggregate demand disappears from the scene and aggregate supply determines growth. In fact, neoclassical growth theory following Solow (1956), and new growth theory, following Romer (1986) and others, abstracts entirely from the AD side, assuming perpetual full employment and investment being determined identically by saving. The debate between neoclassical and new growth theory revolves around whether or not the marginal product of the produced factor of production, capital, falls to zero as the capital–labor ratio rises indefinitely and, therefore, whether long-run growth is affected by the saving rate and other economic variables. The neglect of AD is usually not explicitly explained in these models, but it is implicitly assumed that wage and price flexibility will remove unemployment in the medium run or, failing that, that government aggregate demand policy will do the job. Thus, the long-run growth path is independent of AD factors.

A less popular variety, with roots in the Keynesian theories of Harrod (1939), Robinson (1962) and others, focuses on AD as determining growth. In these models, growth is determined by the interaction between aggregate demand and supply factors (including, for instance, firms' pricing decisions). Some work in this tradition has included the labor market explicitly and linked the long-run rate of growth of output to the growth of the labor supply in efficiency units (see, for instance, Kaldor, 1957; Skott, 1989a; Dutt, 1992b). Most models, however, do not impose the requirement that the unemployment rate be constant in the long run but simply assume that the labor supply does not constrain the rate of growth (see Marglin, 1984; Dutt, 1984; Taylor, 1991). These models have many interesting implications, including the possibility that a more equal distribution of income can increase the rate of growth and that technological change can have immiserizing effects. Their assumption of no labor constraints can be defended by pointing to the existence of large amounts of hidden unemployment in the primary and tertiary sectors in most countries, developed as well as less developed, until some time in the post World War II period. For the more recent period, however, the hidden-unemployment argument may not be persuasive, at least for advanced industrial countries. Most of the OECD economies arguably have become 'mature' in Kaldor's (1966) sense: they certainly have unemployment, both open and disguised, but it would be misleading to treat the labor supply to the modern sector as perfectly elastic and to disregard the labor constraints on the long-run rate of growth. Even under conditions of maturity, however, the rate of growth may be influenced by aggregate demand.

As argued in Section 5.1, the rate of employment cannot be taken as independent of the demand side, even in the medium run, and this dependence of employment on aggregate demand opens up ways in which demand may also influence the rate of growth in the long run.

One channel runs through migration. Even if a country has exhausted its domestic reserves of hidden unemployment, the possibility of immigration provides an international reserve army and, immigration laws permitting, the growth rate of the country need not be limited by its labor supply. Immigration laws respond to economic conditions (as evidenced, for instance, by the change in attitudes of European countries between the 1960s and the more recent period), and the employment rate can therefore have a significant effect on the rate of growth of the labor force.[23]

Induced technical progress represents a second possible channel. Labor shortages provide an incentive for firms to seek out new labor saving techniques, and this technology channel suggests that the rate of growth of the labor supply in efficiency units may be positively related to the employment rate. Both the employment and technology channels imply that insofar as aggregate demand policy influences the rate of employment, it also affects the long-run rate of growth (Flaschel and Skott, 2006).[24]

A more radical approach is pursued by Dutt (2006) who considers a range of models in which the rate of labor productivity growth responds to labor market conditions, with tight labor markets speeding up labor-saving technological change. One of the models makes the employment rate affect both changes in the 'autonomous' investment parameter (to capture the effects of unemployment and wage reductions on aggregate demand through the Keynes effect) and the rate of labor productivity growth. Since the same rate of employment makes investment and labor productivity growth stationary, the result is a zero root model in which a change in the level of autonomous demand (for instance, government expenditure) has a permanent effect on the long-run rate of growth. The economy converges to its long-run rate of growth, at which the economy grows with unemployment at its 'natural' rate, but the long-run rate of growth itself is affected by aggregate demand. AD and AS grow at the same rate, but the growth rate of the economy is not independent of factors determining AD.

6. Conclusion

We have argued in this paper that the older Keynesian tradition based on the AD–AS framework provides a more suitable and promising framework for building macroeconomics than the currently-dominant approach, including its NK variant. This is for a number of reasons.

---

[23] This channel may be reinforced by the effects of unemployment on changes in the labor force participation rate; women's participation rate and the average retirement age, for instance, may respond gradually to labor market conditions.

[24] Verdoorn's-law effects in which learning by doing generates a positive impact of the rate of growth of output on productivity growth imply an additional stimulus from faster immigration to productivity growth.

Contrary to what has been argued by a number of critics, first, the traditional AD–AS approach is internally consistent, at least in its Marshallian interpretation, as well as consistent with Keynes's own analysis.

Second, it has the strength of explicitly including the major markets and sectors of the economy and examining their interactions. In this sense it is a general, rather than a partial, theory. Walrasian general equilibrium theory may also be general in this sense, but is different in several ways, including the perspective on behavioral foundations.

Third, the AD–AS approach does not insist on optimizing microfoundations. The AD–AS model is not necessarily inconsistent with optimizing behavior, but the approach is eclectic. It starts with some basic and commonly-used accounting identities, adds rules of behavior of individuals or groups in specific institutional settings and examines their consequences for the performance and evolution of the system. The theorist must be prepared to explain and defend the choice of behavioral rules, but an appeal to optimization is neither necessary nor sufficient for a successful defense. This eclecticism, we have argued, is a strength, and the NK methodological position is flawed. NK macroeconomics has produced interesting insights, but the insistence on optimizing microfoundations means that these insights have come at the cost of neglecting a variety of important issues, including the analysis of stability.

Fourth, it is true that a great deal of analysis using the AD–AS framework is mechanical and fails to capture important aspects of reality, and its extensions to medium- and long-run issues typically ignore the role of aggregate demand. However, unencumbered by the straightjacket of optimizing microfoundations, the approach provides a useful starting point for the analysis of dynamic macroeconomic interactions. In developing this analysis, the approach can draw on insights from the post-Keynesian, neo-Marxian and structuralist traditions, as well as from the burgeoning literature on behavioral economics.

References

Akerlof, G.A. and J.L. Yellen (1987), "Rational models of irrational behavior", *American Economic Review*, May, pp. 137–142.

Akerlof, G.A. and J.L. Yellen (1990), "The fair wage-effort hypothesis and unemployment", *Quarterly Journal of Economics*, Vol. 105, pp. 254–283.

Akerlof, G.A., W.T. Dickens and G.L. Perry (1996), "The macroeconomics of low inflation", *Brookings Papers on Economic Activity*, Vol. 1996(1), pp. 1–59.

Barro, R.J. (1994), "The aggregate-supply/aggregate-demand model", *Eastern Economic Journal*, Winter, pp. 1–6.

Bewley, T. (1998), "Why not cut pay", *European Economic Review*, Vol. 42, pp. 459–490.

Bhaduri, A., K. Laski and M. Riese (1999), "Effective demand versus profit maximization in aggregate demand/supply analysis from a dynamic perspective", *Banca Nazionale del Lavoro Quarterly Review*, Vol. 52(210), pp. 281–293.

Blanchard, O. (2000), "What do we know about macroeconomics that Fisher and Wicksell did not?", *Quarterly Journal of Economics*, Vol. 115, pp. 1375–1409.

Boland, L.A. (1981), "On the futility of criticizing the neoclassical maximization hypothesis", *American Economic Review*, Vol. 71(5), December, pp. 1031–1036.

Camerer, C.F., G. Loewenstein and M. Rabin (2004), *Advances in Behavioral Economics*, Princeton: Princeton University Press.

Chiarella, C. and P. Flaschel (2000), *The Dynamics of Keynesian Monetary Growth*, Cambridge: Cambridge University Press.

Clower, R.W. (1989), "Keynes's *General Theory*: The Marshallian connection", in: D.A. Walker, editor, *Perspectives on the History of Economic Thought*, Vol. II, Aldershot: Edward Elgar.

Colander, D. (1995), "The stories we tell: a reconsideration of AS/AD analysis", *Journal of Economic Perspectives*, Summer, pp. 169–188.

Cross, R. (ed.) (1988), *Hysteresis and the Natural Rate Hypothesis*, Oxford: Blackwell.

Cross, R. (ed.) (1995), *The Natural Rate of Unemployment. Reflections on 25 Years of the Hypothesis*, Cambridge: Cambridge University Press.

Crotty, J. (1994), "Are Keynesian uncertainty and macrotheory compatible? Conventional decision making, institutional structures, and conditional stability in Keynesian macromodels", pp. 105–142 in: G. Dymski and R. Pollin, editors, *New Perspectives in Monetary Macroeconomics: Explorations in the Tradition of Hyman Minsky*, Ann Arbor: University of Michigan Press.

Dunlop, J.G. (1938), "The movement of real and money wage rates", *Economic Journal*, Vol. 48(191), pp. 413–434.

Dutt, A.K. (1984), "Stagnation, income distribution and monopoly power", *Cambridge Journal of Economics*, Vol. 8(1), March, pp. 25–40.

Dutt, A.K. (1987), "Keynes with a perfectly competitive goods market", *Australian Economic Paper*, Vol. 26, pp. 275–293.

Dutt, A.K. (1992a), "Keynes, market forms, and competition", in: B. Gerrard and J. Hillard, editors, *The Philosophy and Economics of J M Keynes*, Aldershot: Edward Elgar.

Dutt, A.K. (1992b), "Conflict inflation, distribution, cyclical accumulation and crises", *European Journal of Political Economy*, Vol. 8, pp. 579–597.

Dutt, A.K. (2002), "Aggregate demand and aggregate supply: a history", *History of Political Economy*, Summer, Vol. 34(2), pp. 321–363.

Dutt, A.K. (2006), "Aggregate demand, aggregate supply and economic growth", *International Review of Applied Economics*, forthcoming.

Dutt, A.K. and E.J. Amadeo (1990), *Keynes's Third Alternative? The Neo-Ricardian Keynesians and the Post Keynesians*, Aldershot: Edward Elgar.

Dutt, A.K. and P. Skott (1996), "Keynesian theory and the aggregate-supply/aggregate-demand framework: a defense", *Eastern Economic Journal*, Vol. 22(3), Summer, pp. 313–331.

Fehr, E. and S. Gächter (2000), "Fairness and retaliation: the economics of reciprocity", *Journal of Economic Perspectives*, Vol. 14, pp. 159–181.

Fields, T.W. and W.R. Hart (1990), "Some pitfalls in the conventional treatment of aggregate demand", *Southern Economic Journal*, Vol. 56(3), pp. 676–684.

Flaschel, P. and P. Skott (2006), "Steindlian models of growth and stagnation", *Metroeconomica*, forthcoming.

Frydman, R. and E.S. Phelps (eds.) (1983), *Individual Forecasting and Aggregate Outcomes: 'Rational Expectations' Examined*, Cambridge: Cambridge University Press.

Gordon, R.J. (1997), "The time-varying NAIRU and its implications for economic policy", *Journal of Economic Perspectives*, Vol. 11, pp. 11–32.

Hahn, F. and R.M. Solow (1995), *A Critical Essay on Modern Macroeconomic Theory*, Cambridge, MA: MIT Press.

Harrod, R.F. (1939), "An essay in dynamic theory", *Economic Journal*, Vol. 49, pp. 14–33.

Hicks, J. (1974), *"The Crisis in Keynesian Economics"*, Oxford: Blackwell.

Hicks, J. (1980–81), "IS–LM: an explanation", *Journal of Post Keynesian Economics*, Vol. 3, Winter, pp. 139–154.

Kahneman, D. (ed.) (2000), *Choices, Values and Frames*, Cambridge: Cambridge University Press.

Kahneman, D., J.L. Knetsch and R. Thaler (1986), "Fairness as a constraint on profit seeking: entitlements in the market", *American Economic Review*, Vol. 76, pp. 728–741.

Kaldor, N. (1957), "A model of economic growth", *Economic Journal*, Vol. 67, pp. 591–624.

Kaldor, N. (1966), *Causes of the Slow Rate of Economic Growth in the United Kingdom*, Cambridge: Cambridge University Press.

Kalecki, M. (1971), *Selected Essays on the Dynamics of the Capitalist Economy*, Cambridge: Cambridge University Press.

Katzner, D.W. (2004), "The current non-status of general equilibrium theory", University of Massachusetts Working Paper 2004-10.

Keynes, J.M. (1930a), *A Treatise on Money*, London and Basingstoke: Macmillan.

Keynes, J.M. (1930b), "The question of high wages", *The Political Quarterly*. Reprinted in *Collected Writings, vol. 20: Activities 1929–1931*, London and Basingstoke: Macmillan, 1981.

Keynes, J.M. (1936/1973), *The General Theory of Employment, Interest and Money*, London: Macmillan.

Keynes, J.M. (1973), *Collected Writings, vol. 14: The General Theory and After – Part II Defence and Development*, London and Basingstoke: Macmillan.

Keynes, J.M. (1981), in: D. Moggridge, editor, *The Collected Writing of John Maynard Keynes, Vol. XX, Activities 1929– 31: Rethinking Employment and Unemployment Policies*, London: Macmillan for the Royal Economic Society.

Kirman, A.P. (1989), "The intrinsic limits of modern economic theory: the emperor has no clothes", *Economic Journal*, Vol. 99, pp. 126–139.

Kirman, A.P. (1992), "Whom or what does the representative individual represent?", *Journal of Economic Perspectives*, Vol. 6, pp. 117–136.

Krugman, P.R. (1998), "It's baaack: Japan's slump and the return of the liquidity trap", Brookings Papers on Economic Activity, No. 2, pp. 137–187.

Leijonhufvud, A. (1968), *On Keynesian Economics and the Economics of Keynes*, Oxford: Oxford University Press.

Marglin, S.A. (1984), *Growth, Distribution and Prices*, Cambridge, MA: Harvard University Press.

Marshall, A. (1887), "A fair rate of wages", pp. 212–226 in: A.C. Pigou, editor, 1956, *Memorials of Alfred Marshall*, New York: Kelley & Millman, pp. 212–226.

Meltzer, A.H. (1988), *Keynes's Monetary Theory. A Different Interpretation*, Cambridge: Cambridge University Press.

Moore, B.J. (1988), *Horizontalists and Verticalists*, Cambridge: Cambridge University Press.

Robinson, J. (1962), *Essays in the Theory of Economic Growth*, London: Macmillan.

Romer, D. (2000), "Keynesian macroeconomics without the LM curve", *Journal of Economic Perspectives*, Vol. 14(2), Spring, pp. 149–169.

Romer, P.M. (1986), "Increasing returns and long-run growth", *Journal of Political Economy*, Vol. 94, pp. 1102–1137.

Sargent, T.J. (1993), *Bounded Rationality in Macroeconomics*, Oxford: Oxford University Press.

Shafir, E., P. Diamond and A. Tversky (1997), "Money illusion", *Quarterly Journal of Economics*, Vol. 112, pp. 341–374.

Skott, P. (1983), "An essay on Keynes and general equilibrium theory", *Thames Papers in Political Economy*, Summer, pp. 1–43.

Skott, P. (1989a), *Conflict and Effective Demand in Economic Growth* Cambridge: Cambridge University Press.

Skott, P. (1989b), "Effective demand, class struggle and cyclical growth", *International Economic Review*, Vol. 30. pp. 231–247.

Skott, P. (1999), "Wage formation and the (non-) existence of the NAIRU", *Economic Issues*, Vol. 4, pp. 77–92.

Skott, P. (2005a), "Fairness as a source of hysteresis in employment and relative wages", *Journal of Economic Behaviour and Organization*, Vol. 57, pp. 305–331.

Skott, P. (2005b), "Equilibrium, stability and economic growth", pp. 175–196 in: B. Gibson, editor, *Joan Robinson: A Centennial Celebration*, Northampton, MA: Edward Elgar.

Solow, R.M. (1956), "A contribution to the theory of economic growth", *Quarterly Journal of Economics*, Vol. 70, pp. 65–94.

Solow, R. (1990), *The Labor Market as a Social Institution*, Oxford: Blackwell.

Tarshis, L. (1939), "Changes in real and money wages", *Economic Journal*, Vol. 49(193), pp. 150–154.

Taylor, L. (1991), *Distribution, Growth and Inflation. Lectures in Structuralist Macroeconomics*, Cambridge, MA: MIT Press.

Taylor, L. (2004), *Reconstructing Macroeconomics*, Cambridge, MA: Harvard University Press.

Tobin, J. (1975), "Keynesian models of recession and depression", *American Economic Review*, Vol. 65, pp. 195–202.

Woodford, M. (1999), "Revolution and evolution in twentieth-century macroeconomics", Unpublished, Princeton: Princeton University.

Woodford, M. (2003), *Interest and Prices: Foundations of a Theory of Monetary Policy*, Princeton and Oxford: Princeton University Press.

CHAPTER 7

AD–AS and the Phillips Curve: A Baseline Disequilibrium Model

Toichiro Asada, Pu Chen, Carl Chiarella and Peter Flaschel

Abstract

We reformulate and extend the standard AD–AS growth model of the neoclassical synthesis (stage I) with its traditional microfoundations. The model retains an LM curve in the place of a Taylor interest rate rule, exhibits sticky wages as well as sticky prices, myopic perfect foresight of current inflation rates and adaptively formed medium-run expectations concerning the investment and the inflation climate in which the economy is operating. The resulting nonlinear five-dimensional (5D) model of labor and goods market disequilibrium dynamics avoids the striking anomalies of the standard AD–AS model of the neoclassical synthesis (stage I). It exhibits instead Keynesian feedback dynamics proper with, in particular, asymptotic stability of its unique interior steady state for low adjustment speeds and with cyclical loss of stability – by way of Hopf bifurcations – when some adjustment speeds are made sufficiently large, even leading to purely explosive dynamics soon thereafter. In this way, we obtain and analyze a baseline AD-D(isequilibrium) AS model with Keynesian feedback channels with a rich set of stability/instability features as sources of the business cycle. The outcomes of the model stand in stark contrast to those of the currently fashionable baseline model of the New Keynesian alternative (the neoclassical synthesis, stage II) that we suggest is more limited in scope.

Keywords: AD-DAS growth, wage and price Phillips curves, real interest effects, real wage effects, (in)stability, growth cycles

JEL classifications: E24, E31, E32

CONTRIBUTIONS TO ECONOMIC ANALYSIS
VOLUME 277   ISSN: 0573-8555
DOI:10.1016/S0573-8555(05)77007-3

1. Introduction

In this paper[1] we reformulate and extend the standard AD–AS growth dynamics
of the neoclassical synthesis (stage I) with its traditional microfoundations, as it
is for the example treated in detail in Sargent (1987, Chapter 5).[2] Our extension
does not yet replace the LM curve with a now standard Taylor rule, as is done in
the New Keynesian approaches.[3] The model exhibits sticky wages as well as
sticky prices, underutilized labor as well as capital, myopic perfect foresight of
currently evolving wage and price inflation rates and adaptively formed medium-
run expectations concerning the investment and inflation climate in which the
economy is operating. The resulting nonlinear five-dimensional (5D) dynamics
of labor and goods market disequilibrium (with a traditional LM treatment of
the financial part of the economy) avoids striking anomalies of the conventional
model of the neoclassical synthesis, stage I.[4] Instead, it exhibits Keynesian
feedback dynamics proper with, in particular, asymptotic stability of its unique
interior steady-state solution for low adjustment speeds of wages, prices and
expectations. The loss of stability occurs cyclically, by way of Hopf bifurcations,
when these adjustment speeds are made sufficiently large, leading eventually to
purely explosive dynamics.

Locally, we thus obtain and prove in detail – for a certain range of parameter
values – the existence of damped or persistent fluctuations in the rates of
capacity utilization of both labor and capital, and of wage and price inflation
rates accompanied by interest rate fluctuations that (due to the conventional
working of the Keynes effect) move in line with the goods price level. Our
modification and extension of traditional AD–AS growth dynamics, as
investigated from the orthodox point of view in Sargent (1987) (see also
Chiarella *et al.* (2005, Chapter 2)), thus provides us with a Keynesian theory of
the business cycle. This is so even in the case of myopic perfect foresight, where
the structure of the traditional approach dichotomizes into independent supply-
side real dynamics – that cannot be influenced by monetary policy – and
subsequently determined inflation dynamics that are purely explosive if the price
level is taken as a predetermined variable, turned then into an always convergent
process by an application of the jump-variable technique of the rational
expectations school (with unmotivated jumps in the money wage level however).

---

[1] The formulation of the model presented here was first proposed in Chiarella *et al.* (2003) in a short
response to the comments of Velupillai (2003) on our earlier work. Due to space limitations the
implication of the model could however not be investigated there.
[2] See also Chiarella *et al.* (2005, Chapter 2).
[3] How this can be done is sketched in Section 7 of this paper and elaborated in detail in Asada *et al.*
(2006); see also Chen *et al.* (2005a) and Chapter 8 in this volume.
[4] These anomalies include in particular saddle point dynamics that imply instability unless some
poorly motivated (and in fact inconsistent) jumps are imposed on certain variables, here on both the
price and the wage level (despite the use of a conventional money wage Phillips curve).

In our new type of Keynesian labor and goods market dynamics we, in contrast, can treat myopic perfect foresight of both firms and wage earners without any need for the methodology of the rational expectations approach to unstable saddlepoint dynamics.

The dynamic outcomes of this baseline AD-DAS model can be usefully contrasted with those of the currently fashionable microfounded baseline New Keynesian alternative (the neoclassical synthesis, stage II) that in our view is more limited in scope, at least as far as interacting Keynesian feedback mechanisms and thereby implied dynamic possibilities are concerned. This comparison reveals in particular that one does not always end up with the typical (in our view strange) dynamics of rational expectation models, owing to certain types of forward-looking behavior, if myopic perfect foresight is of cross-over type in the considered wage-price spiral, is based on a neoclassical dating of expectations, and is coupled with plausible backward looking behavior for the medium-run evolution of the economy. Furthermore, our dual Phillips curves approach to the wage-price spiral indeed performs quite well also from the empirical point of view,[5] and in particular does not give rise to the situation observed for the New (Keynesian) Phillips curve(s), found to be completely at odds with the facts in the literature.[6] In our approach, standard Keynesian feedback mechanisms have always been coupled with a wage-price spiral having a considerable degree of inertia,[7] with the result that these feedback mechanisms work in the large as is known from partial analysis, also in their interaction with the added wage and price level dynamics.

In Section 2 we briefly reconsider the fully integrated Keynesian AD–AS model of the neoclassical synthesis, stage I, and show that it gives rise to an implausible real/nominal dichotomy – with an appended nominal dynamics of purely explosive type – when operated under myopic perfect foresight with respect to the price inflation rate. Furthermore, money wage levels must then be allowed to jump just as the price level, despite the presence of a conventional money wage Phillips curve, in order to overcome the observed nominal instability by means of the rational expectations solution methodology (which indeed makes this solution procedure an inconsistent one in the chosen framework). We conclude from this that this model type is not suitable for a Keynesian approach to economic dynamics which should allow for myopic perfect foresight on inflation rates without much change in its structure under normal circumstances. In Section 3 we then briefly discuss the baseline New

---

[5] See Flaschel and Krolzig (2004), Flaschel *et al.* (2005), Chen and Flaschel (2004) and Chapter 8 in this volume.

[6] In this connection, see the statements made in this respect in Mankiw (2001) and also (with even more emphasis) the ones in Eller and Gordon (2003), whereas Gali *et al.* (2003) argue in favor of a hybrid form of the New Phillips curve in order to defend the New Phillips curve.

[7] See Chiarella and Flaschel (1996) for an early example.

Keynesian approach to economic dynamics and find there too, that it raises more questions than it helps to answer. This section is supplemented by some methodological considerations in Section 4. Section 5 proposes our new and nevertheless (matured) traditional approach to Keynesian dynamics, by taking note of the empirical facts that both labor and capital can be under or overutilized, that both wages and prices adjust only gradually and that there are certain climate expressions surrounding the current state of the economy which add sufficient inertia to the dynamics.

The resulting 5D model type is analyzed with respect to its stability features in Section 6 and is shown to give rise to local asymptotic stability when certain Keynesian feedback chains – to some extent well known to be destabilizing from a partial perspective – are made sufficiently weak, including a real wage adjustment mechanism that is not so well established in the literature. The somewhat informal stability analysis presented there is made rigorous in an appendix to this paper, where the calculation of the Routh–Hurwitz conditions for the relevant Jacobians is considered in great detail and where the occurrence of Hopf bifurcations (i.e., cyclical loss of stability) is also considered. In Section 7 we briefly sketch how the model's structure is changed when a Taylor interest rate policy rule is used in place of a given growth rate of the money supply. Section 8 concludes and provides an outlook on empirical and policy analyses of the model of this chapter that are undertaken in two companion chapters.

2. Neoclassical synthesis, stage I: 'rational expectations' supply side solutions?

In this section we briefly discuss the traditional AD–AS growth dynamics with prices set equal to marginal wage costs, and nominal wage inflation driven by an expectations-augmented Phillips curve. Introducing myopic perfect foresight (i.e., the assumption of no errors with respect to the short-run rate of price inflation) into such a Phillips curve alters the dynamics implied by the model in a radical way, in fact towards a globally stable (neo-) classical real-growth dynamics with real-wage rigidity and thus fluctuating rates of under- or overemployment. Furthermore, price level dynamics no longer feed back into these real dynamics and are now unstable in the large. The accepted approach in the literature is then to go on from myopic perfect foresight to 'rational expectations' and to construct a purely forward-looking solution (which incorporates the whole future of the economy) by way of the so-called jump-variable technique of Sargent and Wallace (1973). However, in our view, this does not represent a consistent solution to the dynamic results obtained in this model type under myopic perfect foresight, as we shall argue in this chapter.

The case of myopic perfect foresight in a dynamic AD–AS model of business fluctuations and growth has been considered in very detailed form in Sargent (1987, Chapter 5). The model of Sargent's (1987, Chapter 5) so-called Keynesian dynamics is given by a standard combination of AD based on IS-LM, and AS based on the condition that prices always equal marginal wage costs, plus finally an expectations-augmented money wage Phillips curve or WPC. The specific features that characterize this textbook treatment of AD–AS–WPC are that investment includes profitability considerations besides the real rate of interest, that there is not immediately a reduced-form PC employed in this dynamic analysis, and most importantly, that expectations are rational (i.e., of the myopic perfect foresight variety in the deterministic context). Consumption is based on current disposable income in the traditional way, the LM curve is of standard type and there is neoclassical smooth-factor substitution and the assumption that prices are set according to the marginal productivity principle and thus optimal from the viewpoint of the firm. These more or less standard ingredients give rise to the following set of equations that determine the statically endogenous variables: consumption, investment, government expenditure, output, interest, prices, taxes, the profit rate, employment and the rate of employment $C, I, G, Y, r, p, T, \rho, L^d, V^l$ and these feed into the dynamically endogenous variables: the capital stock, labor supply and the nominal wage level K, L, w, respectively, for which laws of motion are provided in the equations shown below. The equations are

$$C = c(Y + rB/p - \delta K - T) \tag{7.1}$$

$$I/K = i(\rho - (r - \pi)) + n, \quad \rho = \frac{Y - \delta K - \omega L^d}{K}, \quad \omega = \frac{w}{p} \tag{7.2}$$

$$G = gK, \quad g = \text{const.} \tag{7.3}$$

$$Y \overset{IS}{=} C + I + \delta K + G \tag{7.4}$$

$$M \overset{LM}{=} p(h_1 Y + h_2(r_0 - r)W) \tag{7.5}$$

$$Y = F(K, L^d) \tag{7.6}$$

$$p \overset{AS}{=} w/F_L(K, L^d) \tag{7.7}$$

$$\hat{w} \overset{PC}{=} \beta_w(V^l - \bar{V}^l) + \pi, \quad V^l = L^d/L \tag{7.8}$$

$$\pi \overset{MPF}{=} \hat{p} \tag{7.9}$$

$$\hat{K} = I/K \tag{7.10}$$

$$\hat{L} = n \ (= \hat{M} \text{ for analytical simplicity}) \tag{7.11}$$

We make the simplifying assumptions that all behavior is based on linear relationships in order to concentrate on the intrinsic nonlinearities of this type of AD–AS–WPC growth model. Furthermore, following Sargent (1987, Chapter 5), we assume that $t = (T - rB/p)/K$ is a given magnitude and thus, like real government expenditure per unit of capital, g, a parameter of the model. This excludes feedbacks from government bond accumulation and thus from the government budget equation on real economic activity. We thus concentrate on the working of the private sector with minimal interference from the side of fiscal policy, which is not an issue in this paper. The model is fully backed-up by budget equations as in Sargent (1987): pure equity financing of firms, money and bond financing of the government budget deficit and money, bond and equity accumulation in the sector of private households. There is flow consistency, since the new inflow of money and bonds is always accepted by private households. Finally, Walras' Law of Stocks and the perfect substitute assumption for government bonds and equities ensure that equity price dynamics remain implicit. The LM curve is thus the main representation of the financial part of the model, which is therefore still of a very simple type at this stage of its development.

The treatment of the resulting dynamics turns out to be not very difficult. In fact, Equations (7.8) and (7.9) imply a real-wage dynamics of the type

$$\hat{\omega} = \beta_w(l^d/l - \bar{V}^l), \quad l^d = L^d/K \quad l = L/K$$

From $\dot{K} = I = S = Y - \delta K - C - G$ and $\dot{L} = nL$ we furthermore get

$$\hat{l} = n - (y - \delta - c(y - \delta - t) - g) = n - (1 - c)y - (1 - c)\delta + ct - g$$

with $y = Y/K = F(1, l^d) = f(l^d)$.

Finally, by Equation (7.7) we obtain

$$\omega = f'(l^d)$$

i.e.,

$$l^d = (f')^{-1}(\omega) = h(\omega), \quad h' < 0$$

Hence, the real dynamics of the model can be represented by the following autonomous two-dimensional (2D) dynamical system:

$$\hat{\omega} = \beta_w(h(\omega)/l - \bar{V}^l)$$
$$\hat{l} = n - (1 - c)\delta - g + ct - (1 - c)f(h(\omega))$$

It is easy to show, see e.g., Flaschel (1993), that this system is well defined in the positive orthant of the phase space, has a unique interior steady state, which moreover is globally asymptotically stable in the considered domain. In fact, this is just a Solow, 1956 growth dynamics with a real-wage Phillips curve (real-wage rigidity) and thus classical under or overemployment dynamics if $\bar{V}^l < 1$. There may be a full-employment ceiling in this model type, but this is an issue of secondary importance here.

The unique interior steady state is given by

$$y_0 = \frac{1}{1 - c}[(1 - c)\delta + n + g - ct] = \frac{1}{1 - c}[n + g - t] + \delta + t$$
$$l_0^d = f^{-1}(y_0), \quad \omega_0 = f'(l_0^d), \quad l_0 = l_0^d/\bar{V}^l$$
$$m_0 = h_1 y_0, \quad \hat{p}_0 = 0, \quad r_0 = \rho_0 = f(l_0^d) - \delta - \omega_0 l_0^d$$

Keynes' (1936) approach is almost entirely absent in this type of analysis, which seems to be Keynesian in nature (AS–AD), but which – owing to the neglect of short-run errors in inflation forecasting – has become in fact of very (neo-) classical type. The marginal propensity of consume, the stabilizing element in Keynesian theory, is still present, but neither investment nor money demand plays a role in the real dynamics we have obtained from Equations (7.1)–(7.11). Volatile investment decisions and financial markets are thus simply irrelevant for the real dynamics of this AS–AD growth model when *myopic* perfect foresight on the current rate of price inflation is assumed. What, then, remains for the role of traditional Keynesian "troublemakers", the marginal efficiency of investment and liquidity preference schedule? The answer again is, in technical terms, a very simple one:

We have for given $\omega = \omega(t) = (w/p)(t)$ as implied by the real dynamics (owing to the $I = S$ assumption):

$$(1 - c)f(h(\omega)) - (1 - c)\delta + ct - g = i(f(l) - \delta - \omega h(\omega) - r + \hat{p}) + n$$

i.e.,

$$\hat{p} = \frac{1}{i}[(1 - c)f(h(\omega)) - (1 - c)\delta + ct - g - n] - (f(l) - \delta - \omega h(\omega)) + r$$
$$= g(\omega, l) + r$$

with an added reduced-form LM equation of the type

$$r = (h_1 f(h(\omega)) - m)/h_2 + r_0, \quad m = \frac{M}{pK}$$

The foregoing equations imply

$$\hat{m} = \hat{l}(\omega) - g(\omega, l) - r_0 + \frac{m - h_1 f(h(\omega))}{h_2}$$

as the non-autonomous[8] differential equation for the evolution of real-money balances, as the reduced-form representation of the nominal dynamics.[9] Owing to this feedback chain, $\hat{m}$ depends positively on the level of m and it seems as if the jump-variable technique needs to be implemented in order to tame such explosive nominal processes; see Flaschel (1993), Turnovsky (1995) and Flaschel *et al.* (1997) for details on this technique. Advocates of the jump-variable technique, therefore are led to conclude that investment efficiency and liquidity preference only play a role in appended purely nominal processes and this solely in a stabilizing way, though with initially accelerating phases in the case of anticipated monetary and other shocks. A truly neoclassical synthesis.

---

[8] Since the independent (ω, l) block will feed into the right-hand side as a time function.

[9] Note that we have $g(\omega, l) = -\rho_0$ in the steady state.

By contrast, we believe that Keynesian IS-LM growth dynamics proper (demand-driven growth and business fluctuations) must remain intact if (generally minor) errors in inflationary expectations are excluded from consideration in order to reduce the dimension and to simplify the analysis of the dynamical system to be considered. A correctly formulated Keynesian approach to economic dynamics and fluctuating growth should not give rise to such a strange dichotomized system with classical real and purely nominal IS-LM inflation dynamics, here in fact of the most basic jump-variable type, namely

$$\hat{m} = \frac{m - h_1 y_0}{h_2} \left[\hat{p} = -\frac{(M/K)_0 \frac{1}{p} - h_1 y_0}{h_2} \right]$$

if it is assumed for simplicity that the real part is already at its steady state. This dynamic equation is of the same kind as the one for the Cagan monetary model and can be treated with respect to its forward-looking solution in the same way, as it is discussed in detail, for example, in Turnovsky (1995, 3.3/4), i.e., the nominal dynamics assumed to hold under the jump-variable hypothesis in AD–AS–WPC is then of a very well-known type.

However, the basic fact that the AD–AS–WPC model under myopic perfect foresight is not a consistently formulated one and also not consistently solved arises from its *ad hoc* assumption that nominal wages here must jump with the price level $p(w = \omega p)$, since the real wage ω is now moving continuously in time according to the derived real-wage dynamics. The level of money wages is thus now capable of adjusting instantaneously, which is in contradiction to the assumption of only sluggishly adjusting nominal wages according to the assumed money wage PC.[10] Furthermore, a properly formulated Keynesian growth dynamics should – besides allowing for un- or overemployed labor – also allow for un- or overemployment of the capital stock, at least in certain episodes. Thus, the price level, like the wage level, should better and alternatively be assumed to adjust somewhat sluggishly; see also Barro (1994) in this regard. We will come back to this observation after the next section which is devoted to new developments in the area of Keynesian dynamics, the so-called New Keynesian approach of the macrodynamic literature.

The conclusion of this section is that the neoclassical synthesis, stage I, must be considered a failure on logical grounds and not a valid attempt "to formalize for students the relationships among the various hypotheses advanced in Milton Friedman's AEA presidential address (1968)", see Sargent (1987, p. 117).

---

[10] See Flaschel (1993) and Flaschel *et al.* (1997) for further investigations along these lines.

3. *Neoclassical synthesis, stage II: baseline New Keynesian macrodynamics*

The baseline New Keynesian macrodynamic model is based on market-clearing money wages and only gradually adjusting prices. In this choice of its baseline scenario it is therefore just the opposite case compared to the model of the old neoclassical synthesis we considered in the preceding section.

We here follow Walsh (2003, 11.1) in the discrete time formulation of the New Keynesian dynamics which consists of three components. Its demand side is represented by a loglinear approximation to the representative household's Euler conditions for optimal consumption, giving rise to an expectational IS curve, where therefore investment behavior of firms is not yet considered. Next, concerning its supply side, we have inflation adjustment occurring under the assumption of monopolistic competition, with individual firms adjusting prices in a staggered overlapping fashion. The third component, the monetary policy reaction function, is for the moment simply represented by an interest rate peg i_0 (at the steady state of the model). The first two components of the model thus are of the form (with steady-state values $\pi_0 = 0$, $Y_0 = \bar{Y} = 1$)

$$\ln Y_t \overset{IS}{=} E_t \ln Y_{t+1} - \alpha_{yi}(i_t - E_t \pi_{t+1} - i_0) + u_t$$

$$\pi_t \overset{PPC}{=} \beta E_t \pi_{t+1} + \beta_{py} \ln Y_t + \varepsilon_t, \quad \pi_t = (p_t - p_{t-1})/p_{t-1}$$

As in the neoclassical synthesis, stage I, the IS-curve depends on the expected real rate of interest (but not yet on the rate of profit of firms). Furthermore, because of labor market clearing money wages, a price Phillips curve relates the currently observed rate of price inflation to the one expected for the next period and a currently prevailing output gap.

We assume in these equations that the NAIRU output level is normalized to 1, and thus vanishes in a loglinear representation, and that the steady-state rate of interest i_0 is given such that the steady state is inflation free. The steady-state values of output and the inflation rate, Y_0, π_0 are thus simply given by $0, 0$. Note that the rate of inflation π_t is indexed in New Keynesian approaches by the endpoint of its reference period and thus defined by $\pi_t = (p_t - p_{t-1})/p_{t-1}$ in its relationship to the relevant price levels (which shows that the price level p_t is a statically endogenous variable at the point in time t and depending on the expected price level p_{t+1}).

In a deterministic framework these equations can be reformulated and rearranged as follows (using y_t now for $\ln Y_t$):

$$y_{t+1} \overset{IS}{=} y_t + \alpha_{yi}(i_t - \pi_{t+1} - i_0)$$

$$\pi_{t+1} \overset{PPC}{=} (1/\beta)(\pi_t - \beta_{py} y_t)$$

Inserting the second equation into the first then finally gives in terms of first differences

$$y_{t+1} - y_t \overset{IS}{=} \alpha_{yi}(i_t - i_0) - (\alpha_{yi}/\beta)(\pi_t - \beta_{py}y_t)$$

$$\pi_{t+1} - \pi_t \overset{PPC}{=} (1/\beta - 1)\pi_t - (\beta_{py}/\beta)y_t$$

We stress that we have obtained thereby – as reduced form of the original dynamics – a linear first-order system of difference equations that in principle can be solved in the conventional way by employing the so-called predetermined values for the two endogenous variables of the model. Yet, solving such systems by way of historically given initial conditions, and looking for behavioral nonlinearities that may bound the dynamics when it departs too much from the steady state, is not considered as a meaningful solution procedure by authors working in the presently given modeling framework.

We now replace the difference quotients shown in this equation system by differential quotients, assuming that the thereby obtained mathematical model mirrors the features of the difference system in an adequate way. The change in the model is therefore a purely mathematical one and should not be interpreted as if a limit economy has been formulated and the period length of the model has shrunk to zero. We then obtain the autonomous linear 2D dynamical continuous time system[11]

$$\dot{y} \overset{IS}{=} \alpha_{yi}(i_t - i_0) - (\alpha_{yi}/\beta)\pi + (\beta_{py}\alpha_{yi}/\beta)y$$

$$\dot{\pi} \overset{PPC}{=} (1/\beta - 1)\pi - (\beta_{py}/\beta)y$$

It is straightforward to show – still assuming $i_t = i_0$ for the time being – that the steady state of the dynamics, $y_0 = 0$, $\pi_0 = 0$, is a saddlepoint. This however implies that the solution to these dynamics is indeterminate from a New Keynesian perspective, since we have two forward-looking and thus non-predetermined variables in these IS-PC dynamics. Application of the jump variable technique to the two non-predetermined variables y, π thus would not provide us with a unique convergent solution path, if only the boundedness condition is imposed on the myopic perfect foresight solutions that this model allows for. In comparison to the main result in the preceding section we thus now have that the private sector when left to itself does not provide us with an unambiguous adjustment path to the steady state when some shock moves the economy out of its steady-state position.[12] Since the private sector of the economy thus does not provide us with a determinate reaction pattern outside

---

[11] See Fuhrer and Moore (1995) for a variety of models of New Keynesian type that are expressed and analyzed in continuous time.

[12] Note that we had an inconsistent solution in the case of the neoclassical synthesis, stage I, in the opposite case of gradually adjusting wages and completely flexible prices.

the steady state, we may ask whether the addition of a more or less active monetary policy, in the form of a Taylor interest rate policy rule for example, can make the dynamics determinate, implying in particular that such a policy is indeed indispensable for the proper operation of the economy.

To show that determinacy is possible if an interest rate policy rule is pursued by the central bank, we choose the rule considered in Walsh (2003, p. 247) which is of a classical Taylor-rule type

$$i_t = i_0 + \beta_{i\pi}\pi + \beta_{iy}y \tag{7.12}$$

Adding this rule preserves the steady state of the economy and gives rise to the dynamics

$$\dot{y} \stackrel{IS}{=} \alpha_{yi}(\beta_{i\pi}\pi + \beta_{iy}y) - (\alpha_{yi}/\beta)\pi + (\beta_{py}\alpha_{yi}/\beta)y \tag{7.13}$$

$$\dot{\pi} \stackrel{PPC}{=} (1/\beta - 1)\pi - (\beta_{py}/\beta)y \tag{7.14}$$

The Jacobian of these extended dynamics is given by

$$J = \begin{pmatrix} \alpha_{yi}(\beta_{iy} + \beta_{py}/\beta) & \alpha_{yi}(\beta_{i\pi} - 1/\beta) \\ -\beta_{py}/\beta & 1/\beta - 1 \end{pmatrix}$$

whose trace is always positive and determinant is given by

$$|J| = (\alpha_{yi}/\beta)[(1 - \beta)\beta_{iy} + \beta_{py}(\beta_{i\pi} - 1)]$$

This latter quantity is positive iff

$$|J| > 0 \Longleftrightarrow (1 - \beta)\beta_{iy} + \beta_{py}(\beta_{i\pi} - 1) > 0$$

and furthermore both eigenvalues must have positive real parts in this case. The result of this modification of the model therefore is that we can thereby enforce that the steady state becomes a source, either an unstable node or an unstable focus. In the language of New Keynesian economics and other related approaches this means that we have determinacy, since – as in the Sargent and Wallace case considered in the preceding section – we have a uniquely determined bounded response of the system to all occurring shocks. In the presently considered situation it always places the system back onto its steady-state position $y_0 = 0$, $\pi_0 = 0$, i_0.

The line separating determinacy from indeterminacy in the 2D space of the policy parameters is according to the above given by

$$\beta_{i\pi} = \frac{\beta - 1}{\beta_{py}}\beta_{iy} + 1$$

We thus get the characterization of the parameter space shown in Figure 7.1.

Figure 7.1. *Zones of determinate and indeterminate dynamics*

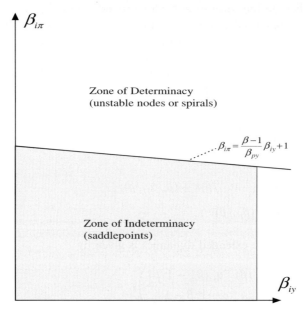

We briefly note here that continuous time determinacy must always imply discrete time determinacy, but that the converse need not hold. In the present baseline case however, we have in the case of indeterminacy in the continuous time case a negative determinant and thus a saddle. Going back to the discrete time version than adds a 1 to the two eigenvalues of the continuous time case. Since we have a positive determinant in the discrete time case, there follows that both eigenvalues must be positive then, but one of course smaller than, while the other is larger than one. This shows (in)determinacy is equivalently measured by the two approaches.

The Taylor principle for a sufficiently active monetary policy certainly applies if $\beta = 1$ holds, since $\beta_{i\pi}$ must be larger than one then in order to provide the necessary nominal anchor by way of monetary policy for the determinacy of the rational expectations solution. This type of active monetary policy can however be reduced in its strength if the output gap plays a role in the considered monetary policy ($\beta < 1$) in which case we can reduce the impact of the inflation gap somewhat according to the then negative slope of the line separating determinate and indeterminate dynamics (the regions blocked out from consideration as zones of indeterminacy).

We obtain the unambiguous result that policy is here indispensable for the working of the economy and that the dynamics of the private sector are moved from the indeterminacy region towards the determinacy region, and will indeed be pushed into the determinacy region for $\beta_{i\pi} > 1$. We here stress that the outcome that the private sector is not workable by itself is a general outcome in New Keynesian baseline approaches. Woodford (2003), Walsh (2003) and King (2000) provide a variety of further examples where an (active) Taylor-type rule, also with forward-looking behavior, is employed in order to get determinacy regions for the considered 2D dynamical system. For 2D New Keynesian baseline models we must therefore conclude that monetary policy can and must be used in order to get determinacy, but since there is no stable manifold as long as the dynamics remains deterministic and of dimension two, we get that neither unanticipated nor anticipated shocks can move the economy out of its steady-state position, as long as this position is not changed by the shocks under consideration. There is thus no inertia in these cases in the baseline New Keynesian approach to economic dynamics.

We observe however with respect to this application of the jump-variable technique that it is quite generally no longer based on an internal inconsistency with respect to the treatment of money wages and wage inflation. In such a framework wages are, on the one hand, perfectly flexible, and there is indeed, on the other hand, no need for a jump in nominal wage and price levels in this continuous time framework, since the rate of price inflation is now the state variable to which the jump-variable technique is applied (which allows the price level to remain a continuous variable in time). Furthermore, the model no longer dichotomizes into an independent dynamics for its real part and a dependent inflation rate dynamics. Instead, inflation is now interacting with the dynamics of the output level – up to unanticipated jumps in the inflation rate – though here in fact however only in the case where stochastic components are added to the model.

4. Some methodological considerations

The situations of unanticipated and anticipated shocks and their implications under the assumptions made by the jump-variable methodology have developed a long tradition in macrodynamics, so long a tradition that purely economic, and not only mathematical justifications for this type of approach are generally no longer given, (see Turnovsky, 1995, part II for an exception). Yet, authors working in the tradition of the present paper have expressed doubts on the economic meaningfulness of this jump-variable procedure on various occasions. These authors point to a variety of weaknesses in this contrived procedure to overcome the explosive forces of saddlepoint dynamics, or even purely explosive dynamics, in particular if such explosiveness is used to approach convergent solutions in the case of anticipated events, see Flaschel *et al.* (1997), Chiarella and Flaschel (2000) and Asada *et al.* (2003) in particular. We basically believe here that in a fully specified, then necessarily nonlinear model of economic dynamics, an analysis along the lines of the jump-variable technique represents not only an exceptional case with hyper-perfect foresight on the whole set of future possibilities of the economy, that in particular in the case of anticipated events cannot be learned, that is generally intractable from the mathematical point of view, and in a nonlinear world also not unambiguously motivated through certain boundedness conditions.

We acknowledge that the jump-variable technique of the Rational Expectations School is a rigorous approach to forward-looking behavior, often however restricted to loglinear approximations even of the baseline New Keynesian macromodel, with potentially very demanding calculational capabilities even in such simplified situations. Our aim in this chapter is to demonstrate that acceptable situations of myopic perfect foresight can be handled in general – also when (un)anticipated shocks are occurring – without employing non-predetermined variables in order to place the economy on some stable manifold (if it exists at all) in a unique fashion such that processes of accelerating instability can only occur when anticipated shocks are assumed to happen. Instead, local instability will be an integral part in the adjustment processes we consider, here however tamed not by imposing jumps on some non-predetermined variables that bypass instability, but by making use of certain nonlinearities in the behavior of economic agents when the economy departs too much from its steady-state position. In sum, we therefore find with respect to the dynamic situation we have sketched above, that it may provide a rigorous way out of certain instability scenarios, one that does not fail on logical grounds as the one considered in the preceding section, but nevertheless one with a variety of questionable features of theoretical (as well as empirical) content that demand other solution procedures with respect to the local instability features that often, but not always, come about in models with forward-looking behavior.

We are fairly skeptical as to whether the New PPC – in particular due to its slope – is really an improvement over traditional structural approaches which employ separate equations for wage and price dynamics. Such skepticism is also expressed in Mankiw (2001) where this New Phillips curve is characterized as being completely at odds with the facts. Eller and Gordon (2003) go even further and state that the NKPC approach is an empirical failure by every measure. Gali *et al.* (2003) by contrast defend this NKPC by now basing it on real marginal costs in the place of an output gap (which however can be shown to be strictly positively correlated, see the next section) and what they call a simple hybrid variant of the NKPC derived from Calvo's staggered price-setting framework. They find in such a framework 'that forward-looking behavior is highly important; the coefficient on expected future inflation is large and highly significant.'

Chiarella and Flaschel (1996, 2000) have considered hybrid approaches to wage and price Phillips curves in various analytical frameworks, the forward-looking component is however given by $\pi_t = p_{t+1} - p_t/p_t$ (also for wages) and not by π_{t+1}. Empirical work based on their formulation of the interacting wage-price dynamics (see the introduction to this paper) generally found coefficients significantly below 0.5 for the forward-looking components in wage and price inflation. Their approach will be introduced now into a Keynesian framework that allows for smooth factor substitution as the New Keynesian model and that also gives real marginal wage costs a role in the PPC, though one with a significant delay in its full impact on price level formation in the production sector. We believe that this approach provides an important alternative to the New Keynesian theory of the business cycle, that does not fail on empirical grounds, but indeed provides a structural extension of the mainstream model of the reduced form US inflation dynamics of Eller and Gordon (2003) with a great potential for further generalizations. Furthermore, this extension removes all logical inconsistencies of the neoclassical synthesis, stage I when embedded into it as we shall show in the next two sections.

We notice finally that hybrid approaches based on forward- *and* backward-looking behavior (comparable to the one in the following section), also coupled with staggered price and wage setting, have started to receive attention by researchers in the New Keynesian or mainstream area, see in particular Woodford (2003) from the theoretical perspective[13] and Rudebusch and Svensson (1999) with respect to a more traditional type of approach. Our modeling of sluggishly updated climate expressions for inflation as well as for excess profitability (to be introduced in the next section) takes such hybrid forms of expectations formation into account right from the very beginning, see Chiarella and Flaschel (1996), initially motivated by the attempt to avoid the anomalies of the neoclassical synthesis, stage I. A detailed theoretical and numerical comparison to the work of Rudebusch and Svensson (1999) and its detailed consideration of Taylor rules is provided in Chiarella *et al.* (2005, Chapter 8). Based on such observations we shall in the next section present an alternative approach to New Keynesian macrodynamics that may be characterized as being of traditional type still, but of a mature Keynesian one indeed (in any case not really as 'new').

This approach, as extension of the neoclassical synthesis, stage I, with now backward- and forward-looking elements in its wage-spiral (with a New Classical dating of the latter), allows for strong inertia in inflation dynamics, without assuming adaptive expectations for the prediction of future short-run rates of inflation. It includes investment (depending on excess profitability, and thus not only on the real rate of interest) and integrates growth, avoids loglinear approximations and their restriction to linear rational expectations solutions, exhibits wage and price dynamics right from the start, can exhibit local instability, but remains nevertheless determinate by the introduction of nonlinearities in economic behavior if the economy departs too much from its steady-state position, and above all, does not need at all the jump-variable technique in order to overcome certain indeterminacies in

---

[13] See Chiarella *et al.* (2005) for detailed presentations of these extended dynamics in a continuous time framework.

the purely local instability features of the interior steady-state position of the model.

Our approach therefore overcomes severe restrictions in the treatment of even the baseline New Keynesian model (still without staggered wages and hybrid expectations formation),[14] though it also requires some further extension, concerning its still traditional treatment of consumption and investment behavior and of course the detailed analysis of the type of policy reaction functions that are the central subject of the New Keynesian approach to macrodynamics, see Chiarella *et al.* (2005) for such extensions.

5. *Keynesian AD-D(isequilibrium)AS dynamics: an alternative baseline model*

We have already remarked that a Keynesian model of aggregate demand fluctuations should (independently of whether justification can be found in Keynes' General Theory) allow for under- (or over-)utilized labor as well as capital in order to be general enough from the descriptive point of view. As Barro (1994) for example observes IS-LM is (or should be) based on imperfectly flexible wages *and* prices and thus on the consideration of wage as well as price Phillips curves. This is precisely what we will do in the following, augmented by the observation that medium-run aspects count both in wage and price adjustment as well as in investment behavior, here still expressed in simple terms by the introduction of the concept of an inflation as well as an investment climate. These economic climate terms are based on past observation, while we have model-consistent expectations with respect to short-run wage and price inflation. The modification of the traditional AD–AS model of Section 2 that we shall introduce now thus treats expectations in a hybrid way, myopic perfect foresight on the current rates of wage and price inflation on the one hand and an

---

[14] The baseline New Keynesian model with staggered prices and wages and hybrid expectations, but no other extensions yet, reads in a continuous-time framework (with $\theta = \ln \omega$, $q = \hat{\pi}^p$ as auxiliary variables), see Chiarella *et al.* (2005, Chapter 1 for details):

$$\dot{y} \stackrel{IS}{=} \frac{1}{1 - \phi_y}[-\alpha_{yi}(i - \pi^p - \phi_p q - \beta_{py}y - \beta_{p\omega}\theta - i_0) + g] \tag{7.15}$$

$$\dot{\pi}^p \stackrel{PPC1}{=} q \tag{7.16}$$

$$\dot{q} \stackrel{PPC2}{=} -(1 - \phi_p)q - \beta_{py}y - \beta_{p\omega}\theta \tag{7.17}$$

$$\dot{\pi}^w \stackrel{WPC}{=} \phi_w q - \beta_{wy}y + \beta_{w\omega}\theta \tag{7.18}$$

$$\dot{\theta} \stackrel{RWPC}{=} \pi^w - \pi^p \tag{7.19}$$

and thus becomes already fairly involved even at this early stage of the investigation. We stress here however that the structural representation of New Keynesian wage-price dynamics differs basically from our own approach only in the dating and in the ordering of expectations in the forward-looking part of these dynamics, see Chen *et al.* (2005b) for details.

adaptive updating of economic climate expressions, with an exponential weighting scheme, on the other hand.

In light of the foregoing discussion, we assume here two Phillips curves or PCs in the place of only one. In this way we provide wage and price dynamics separately, both based on measures of demand pressure $V^l - \bar{V}^l$, $V^c - \bar{V}^c$, in the market for labor and for goods, respectively. We denote by V^l the rate of employment on the labor market and by $\bar{V}^l$ the NAIRU-level of this rate, and similarly by V^c the rate of capacity utilization of the capital stock and $\bar{V}^c$ the normal rate of capacity utilization of firms. These demand pressure influences on wage and price dynamics, or on the formation of wage and price inflation, $\hat{w}, \hat{p}$, are both augmented by a weighted average of cost-pressure terms based on forward-looking perfectly foreseen price and wage inflation rates, respectively, and a backward-looking measure of the prevailing inflationary climate, symbolized by π^m. Cost pressure perceived by workers is thus a weighted average of the currently evolving price inflation rate $\hat{p}$ and some longer-run concept of price inflation, π^m, based on past observations. Similarly, cost pressure perceived by firms is given by a weighted average of the currently evolving (perfectly foreseen) wage inflation rate $\hat{w}$ and again the measure of the inflationary climate in which the economy is operating. We thus arrive at the following two PCs for wage and price inflation, here formulated in a fairly symmetric way.

Structural form of the wage-price dynamics:

$$\hat{w} = \beta_w(V^l - \bar{V}^l) + \kappa_w \hat{p} + (1 - \kappa_w)\pi^m$$
$$\hat{p} = \beta_p(V^c - \bar{V}^c) + \kappa_p \hat{w} + (1 - \kappa_p)\pi^m$$

Inflationary expectations over the medium run, π^m, i.e., the *inflationary climate* in which current wage and price inflation is operating, may be adaptively following the actual rate of inflation (by use of some exponential weighting scheme), may be based on a rolling sample (with hump-shaped weighting schemes), or on other possibilities for updating expectations. For simplicity of exposition we shall here make use of the conventional adaptive expectations mechanism. Besides demand pressure we thus use (as cost pressure expressions) in the two PCs weighted averages of this economic climate and the (foreseen) relevant cost pressure term for wage setting and price setting. In this way we get two PCs with very analogous building blocks, which despite their traditional outlook turn out to have interesting and novel implications. These two PCs have been estimated for the US-economy in various ways in Flaschel and Krolzig (2004), Flaschel *et al.* (2005) and Chen and Flaschel (2004) and found to represent a significant improvement over single reduced-form price PCs, with wage flexibility being greater than price flexibility with respect to demand pressure in the market for goods and for labor, respectively. Such a finding is not possible in the conventional framework of a single reduced-form PC.

Note that for our current version, the inflationary climate variable does not matter for the *evolution of the real wage* $\omega = w/p$, the law of motion of which is given by

$$\hat{\omega} = \kappa[(1 - \kappa_p)\beta_w(V^l - \bar{V}^l) - (1 - \kappa_w)\beta_p(V^c - \bar{V}^c)], \quad \kappa = 1/(1 - \kappa_w\kappa_p)$$

This follows easily from the obviously equivalent representation of the above two PCs:

$$\hat{w} - \pi^m = \beta_w(V^l - \bar{V}^l) + \kappa_w(\hat{p} - \pi^m)$$
$$\hat{p} - \pi^m = \beta_p(V^c - \bar{V}^c) + \kappa_p(\hat{w} - \pi^m)$$

by solving for the variables $\hat{w} - \pi^m$ and $\hat{p} - \pi^m$. It also implies the two cross-markets or *reduced form PCs*

$$\hat{p} = \kappa[\beta_p(V^c - \bar{V}^c) + \kappa_p\beta_w(V^l - \bar{V}^l)] + \pi^m \tag{7.20}$$

$$\hat{w} = \kappa[\beta_w(V^l - \bar{V}^l) + \kappa_w\beta_p(V^c - \bar{V}^c)] + \pi^m \tag{7.21}$$

which represent *a considerable generalization of* the conventional view of a single-market price PC with only one measure of demand pressure, the one in the labor market. This traditional expectations-augmented PC formally resembles the above-reduced form $\hat{p}$-equation if Okun's Law holds in the sense of a strict positive correlation between $V^c - \bar{V}^c$, $V^c = Y/Y^p$ and $V^l - \bar{V}^l$, $V^l = L^d/L$, our measures of demand pressures on the market for goods and for labor. Yet, the coefficient in front of the traditional PC would even in this situation be a mixture of all of the βs and κs of the two originally given PCs and thus represent a synthesis of goods and labor market characteristics.

With respect to the investment climate we proceed similarly and assume that this climate is adaptively following the current risk premium $\varepsilon(= \rho - (r - \hat{p}))$, the excess of the actual profit rate over the actual real rate of interest (which is perfectly foreseen). This gives[15]

$$\dot{\varepsilon}^m = \beta_{\varepsilon^m}(\varepsilon - \varepsilon^m), \quad \varepsilon = \rho + \hat{p} - r$$

which is directly comparable to

$$\dot{\pi}^m = \beta_{\pi^m}(\pi - \pi^m), \quad \pi = \hat{p}$$

We believe that it is very natural to assume that economic climate expressions evolve sluggishly toward their observed short-run counterparts. It is however easily possible to introduce also forward-looking components into the updating of the climate expressions, for example, based on the p^* concept of central banks and related potential output calculations. The investment function of the model of this section is now given simply by $i(\varepsilon^m)$ in the place of $i(\varepsilon)$.

---

[15] In our response to Velupillai (2003), see Chiarella *et al.* (2003), we have used a slightly different expression for the updating of the investment climate, in this regard see the introductory observation in Section 6 below and the appendix to this paper.

We have now covered all modifications needed to overcome the extreme conclusions of the traditional AD–AS approach under myopic perfect foresight as they were sketched in Section 2. The model simply incorporates sluggish price adjustment besides sluggish wage adjustment and makes use of certain delays in the cost pressure terms of its wage and price PC and in its investment function. In the Sargent (1987) approach to Keynesian dynamics, the β_{ε^m}, β_{π^m}, β_p are all set equal to infinity and $\bar{V}^c$ set equal to one, which implies that only current inflation rates and excess profitabilities matter for the evolution of the economy and that prices are perfectly flexible, so that full capacity utilization, not only normal capacity utilization, is always achieved. This limit case has however little in common with the properties of the model of this section.

This brings us to one point that still needs definition and explanation, namely the concept of the rate of capacity utilization that we will be using in the presence of neoclassical smooth-factor substitution, but Keynesian over or underemployment of the capital stock. Actual use of productive capacity is of course defined in reference to actual output Y. As measure of potential output Y^p we associate with actual output Y the profit-maximizing output with respect to currently given wages and prices. Capacity utilization V^c is therefore measured relative to the profit maximizing output level and thus given by[16]

$$V^c = Y/Y^p$$

with

$$Y^p = F(K, L^p), \quad \omega = F_L(K, L^p)$$

where Y is determined from the IS-LM equilibrium block in the usual way. We have assumed in the price PC as normal rate of capacity utilization a rate that is less than one and thus assume in general that demand pressure leads to price inflation, before potential output has been reached, in line with what is assumed in the wage PC and demand pressure on the labor market. The idea behind this assumption is that there is imperfect competition on the market for goods so that firms raise prices before profits become zero at the margin.

Sargent (1987, Chapter 5) not only assumes myopic perfect foresight ($\beta_{\pi^m} = \infty$), but also always the perfect – but empirically questionable – establishment of the condition that the price level is given by marginal wage costs ($\beta_p = \infty$, $\bar{V}^c = 1$). This 'limit case' of the dynamic AD–AS model of this section does not represent a meaningful model, in particular since its dynamic properties are not at all closely related to situations of very fast adjustment of prices and climate expressions to currently correctly observed inflation rates and excess profitability.

There is still another motivation available for the imperfect price level adjustment we are assuming. For reasons of simplicity, we here consider the case

---

[16] In intensive form expressions the following gives rise to $V^c = y/y^p$ with $y^p = f((f')^{-1}(\omega))$ in terms of the notation we introduced in Section 2.

of a Cobb–Douglas production function, given by $Y = K^{\alpha}L^{1-\alpha}$. According to the above we have

$$p = w/F_L(K, L^p) = w/[(1 - \alpha)K^{\alpha}(L^p)^{-\alpha}]$$

which for given wages and prices defines potential employment. Similarly, we define competitive prices as the level of prices p_c such that

$$p_c = w/F_L(K, L^d) = w/[(1 - \alpha)K^{\alpha}(L^d)^{-\alpha}]$$

From these definitions we get the relationship

$$\frac{p}{p_c} = \frac{(1 - \alpha)K^{\alpha}(L^d)^{-\alpha}}{(1 - \alpha)K^{\alpha}(L^p)^{-\alpha}} = (L^p/L^d)^{\alpha}$$

Owing to this we obtain from the definitions of L^d, L^p and their implication $Y/Y^p = (L^d/L^p)^{1-\alpha}$ an expression that relates the above price ratio to the rate of capacity utilization as defined in this section:

$$\frac{p}{p_c} = \left(\frac{Y}{Y^p}\right)^{\frac{-\alpha}{1-\alpha}}$$

or

$$\frac{p_c}{p} = \left(\frac{Y}{Y^p}\right)^{\frac{\alpha}{1-\alpha}} = (V^c)^{\frac{\alpha}{1-\alpha}}$$

We thus get that (for $\bar{V}^c = 1$) upward adjustment of the rate of capacity utilization to full capacity utilization is positively correlated with downward adjustment of actual prices to their competitive value and vice versa. In particular in the special case $\alpha = 0.5$ we would get as reformulated price dynamics (see Equation 7.20 with $\bar{V}_c$ being replaced by $(p_c/p)_0$):

$$\hat{p} = \beta_p(p_c/p - (p_c/p)_0) + \kappa_p\hat{w} + (1 - \kappa_p)\pi^m$$

which resembles the New PC of the New Keynesian approach as far as the reflection of demand pressure forces by means of real marginal wage costs are concerned. Price inflation is thus increasing when competitive prices (and thus nominal marginal wage costs) are above the actual ones and decreasing otherwise (neglecting the cost-push terms for the moment). This shows that our understanding of the rate of capacity utilization in the framework of neoclassical smooth-factor substitution is related to demand pressure terms as used in New Keynesian approaches[17] and is thus further motivating its adoption. Actual

---

[17] See also Powell and Murphy (1997) for a closely related approach, applied there to an empirical study of the Australian economy. We would like to stress here that this property of our model represents an important further similarity with the New Keynesian approach, yet here in a form that gives substitution (with moderate substitution elasticity) no big role to play in overall dynamics.

prices will fall if they are above marginal wage costs to a sufficient degree. However, our approach suggests that actual prices start rising before marginal wage costs are in fact established, i.e. in particular, we have that actual prices are always higher than the competitive ones in the steady state.

We note that the steady state of the now considered Keynesian dynamics is the same as the one in the dynamics of Section 2 (with $\varepsilon_0^m = 0$, $V_0^c = \bar{V}^c$, $V_0^l = \bar{V}^l$, $y_0^p = y_0/V_0^c$, $l_0^p = f^{-1}(y_0^p)$ in addition). Furthermore, the dynamical equations considered above have of course to be augmented by the ones that have remained unchanged by the modifications just considered. The intensive form of all resulting static and dynamic equations is presented below, from which we then start the stability analysis of this baseline model in the next section. The modifications of the AD–AS model of Section 2 proposed in the present section imply that it no longer dichotomizes and there is no need here to apply the poorly motivated jump-variable technique. Instead, the steady state of the dynamics is locally asymptotically stable under conditions that are reasonable from a Keynesian perspective, loses its asymptotic stability by way of cycles (by way of so-called Hopf bifurcations) and becomes sooner or later globally unstable if (generally speaking) adjustment speeds become too high.

We no longer have state variables in the model that can be considered as being not predetermined, but in fact can reduce the dynamics to an autonomous system in the five predetermined state variables: the real wage, real balances per unit of capital, full employment labor intensity and the expressions for the inflation and the investment climate. When the model is subject to explosive forces, it requires extrinsic nonlinearities in economic behavior, assumed to come into effect far off the steady state, that bound the dynamics to an economically meaningful domain in the 5D state space. Chen *et al.* (2005a) provide details of such an approach and its numerical investigation.

Summing up we can state that we have arrived at a model type that is much more complex, but also much more convincing, that the labor market dynamics of the traditional AD–AS dynamics of the neoclassical synthesis, stage I. We now have five in the place of only three laws of motion, which incorporate myopic perfect foresight without any significant impact on the resulting Keynesian dynamics. We can handle factor utilization problems both for labor and capital without necessarily assuming a fixed proportions technology, i.e., we can treat AD–AS growth with neoclassical smooth-factor substitution. We have sluggish wage as well as price adjustment processes with cost pressure terms that are both forward and backward looking, and that allow for the distinction between temporary and permanent inflationary shocks. We have a unique interior steady-state solution of (one must stress) supply side type, generally surrounded by business fluctuations of Keynesian short-run as well as medium-run type. Our AD-DAS growth dynamics therefore exhibits a variety of features that are much more in line with a Keynesian understanding of the features of the trade cycle than is the case for the conventional modeling of AD–AS growth dynamics.

Taken together the model of this section consists of the following five laws of motion for real wages, real balances, the investment climate, labor intensity and the inflationary climate:

$$\hat{\omega} = \kappa[(1 - \kappa_p)\beta_w(l^d/l - \bar{V}^l) - (1 - \kappa_w)\beta_p(y/y^p - \bar{V}^c)] \tag{7.22}$$

$$\hat{m} = -\hat{p} - i\varepsilon^m \tag{7.23}$$

$$\dot{\varepsilon}^m = \beta_{\varepsilon^m}(\rho + \hat{p} - r - \varepsilon^m) \tag{7.24}$$

$$\hat{l} = -i\varepsilon^m \tag{7.25}$$

$$\dot{\pi}^m = \beta_{\pi^m}(\hat{p} - \pi^m) \tag{7.26}$$

with

$$\hat{p} = \kappa[\beta_p(y/y^p(\omega) - \bar{V}^c) + \kappa_p\beta_w(l^d/l - \bar{V}^l)] + \pi^m$$

We here already employ reduced-form expressions throughout and consider the dynamics of the real wage, ω, real balances per unit of capital, m, the investment climate ε^m, labor intensity, l and the inflationary climate, π^m on the basis of the simplifying assumptions that natural growth n determines also the trend growth term in the investment function as well as money supply growth. The above dynamical system is to be supplemented by the following static relationships for output, potential output and employment (all per unit of capital) and the rate of interest and the rate of profit:

$$y = \frac{1}{1 - c}[i\varepsilon^m + n + g - t] + \delta + t \tag{7.27}$$

$$y^p = f((f')^{-1}(\omega)), \quad F(1, L^p/K) = f(l^p) = y^p$$
$$F_L(1, L^p/K)) = f'(l^p) = \omega \tag{7.28}$$

$$l^d = f^{-1}(y) \tag{7.29}$$

$$r = r_0 + (h_1 y - m)/h_2 \tag{7.30}$$

$$\rho = y - \delta - \omega l^d \tag{7.31}$$

which have to be inserted into the right-hand sides in order to obtain an autonomous system of five differential equations that is nonlinear in a natural or intrinsic way. We note however that there are many items that reappear in various equations, or are similar to each other, implying that stability analysis can exploit a variety of linear dependencies in the calculation of the conditions for local asymptotic stability. This dynamical system will be investigated in the next section in somewhat informal terms and, with slight modifications, in a rigorous way in the appendix to this paper.

As the model is now formulated it exhibits – besides the well-known real rate of interest channel, giving rise to destabilizing Mundell-effects that are traditionally tamed by the application of the jump-variable technique – another real feedback channel, see Figure 7.2, which we have called the Rose real-wage effect (based on the work of Rose (1967)) in Chiarella and Flaschel (2000). This channel is completely absent from the considered New Keynesian approach and it is in a weak form present in the model of the neoclassical synthesis, stage I, due to the inclusion of the rate of profit into the considered investment function. The Rose effect only gives rise to a clearly distinguishable and significant feedback channel, however, if wage and price flexibilities are both finite and if aggregate demand depends on the income distribution between wages and profits. In the traditional AD–AS model of Section 2 it only gives rise to a directly stabilizing dependence of the growth rate of real wages on their level, while in our mature form of this AD–AS analysis it works through the interaction of the law of motion (7.20) for real wages, the investment climate and the IS-curve we have derived on this basis. The real marginal costs effect of the New Keynesian approach is here present in addition, in the denominator of the expression we are using for rate of capacity utilization, ($V^c = y/y^p$) and contributes to some extent to stability should the Rose effect by itself be destabilizing.

We thus have now two feedback channels interacting in our extended AD-DAS dynamics which in specific ways exhibit stabilizing as well as destabilizing features (Keynes vs. Mundell effects and normal vs. adverse Rose effects). A variety of further feedback channels of Keynesian macrodynamics is

Figure 7.2.   Rose effects: the real-wage channel of Keynesian macrodynamics

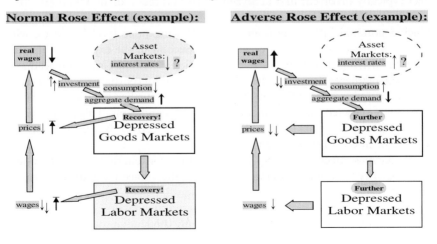

investigated in Chiarella *et al.* (2000). The careful analysis of these channels and the partial insights that can be related with them form the basis of the 5D stability analysis of the next section and the appendix to this paper. Such an analysis differs radically from the always convergent jump-variable analysis of the rational expectations school in models of the neoclassical synthesis, stage I and stage II and many other approaches to macrodynamics.

Figure 7.2 indicates that the real-wage channel will be stabilizing when investment reacts more strongly than consumption to real-wage changes (which is the case in our model type, since here consumption does not depend at all on the real-wage) if this is coupled with wages being more flexible than prices, in the sense that Equation (7.22) establishes a positive link between economic activity and induced real-wage changes. If this latter relationship becomes however a negative one, then a sufficient degree of price level flexibility will destabilize the economy, since shrinking economic activity due to real-wage increases will then induce further real-wage increases, due to a price level that is falling faster than the wage level in this state of depressed markets for goods and for labor. We stress here that the degree of forward-looking behavior in both the wage and the price level dynamics is also important here, since these weights also enter the crucial Equation (7.22) describing the dynamics of real wages for any given state of economic activity.

6. Feedback-guided stability analysis

In this section, we illustrate an important method to prove local asymptotic stability of the interior steady state of the considered dynamics, through partial motivations from the feedback chains that characterize our baseline model of Keynesian dynamics. Since the model is an extension of the standard AD–AS growth model we know from the literature that there is a real rate of interest effect typically involved, first analyzed by formal methods in Tobin (1975), see also Groth (1992). There is the stabilizing Keynes effect based on activity-reducing nominal interest rate increases following price level increases, which provides a check to further price increases. Second, if the expected real rate of interest is driving investment and consumption decisions (increases leading to decreased aggregate demand), there is the stimulating (partial) effect of increases in the expected rate of inflation that may lead to further inflation and further increases in expected inflation under appropriate conditions. This is the so-called Mundell effect that works opposite to the Keynes effect, but also through the real rate of interest rate channel as just seen.

The Keynes effect is stronger if the parameter h_2 characterizing the interest rate sensitivity of money demand becomes smaller, since the reduced-form LM equation reads

$$r = r_0 + (h_1 y - m)/h_2, \quad y = Y/K, \quad m = M/(pK)$$

The Mundell effect is stronger if the inflationary climate adjusts to the present level of price inflation faster, since we have

$$\dot{\pi}^m = \beta_{\pi^m}(\hat{p} - \pi^m) = \beta_{\pi^m}\kappa[\beta_p(V^c - \bar{V}^c) + \kappa_p\beta_w(V^l - \bar{V}^l)]$$

and since both rates of capacity utilization depend positively on the investment climate ε^m which in turn (see Equation 7.24) is driven by excess profitability $\varepsilon = \rho + \hat{p} - r$. Excess profitability in turn depends positively on the inflation rate and thus on the inflationary climate as the reduced-form price PC shows in particular.

There is – as we already know – a further potentially (at least partially) destabilizing feedback mechanism as the model is formulated. Excess profitability depends positively on the rate of return on capital ρ and thus negatively on the real-wage ω. We thus get – since consumption does not yet depend on the real wage – that real-wage increases depress economic activity (though with the delay that is caused by our concept of an investment climate transmitting excess profitability to investment behavior). From our reduced-form real-wage dynamics

$$\hat{\omega} = \kappa[(1 - \kappa_p)\beta_w(V^l - \bar{V}^l) - (1 - \kappa_w)\beta_p(V^c - \bar{V}^c)]$$

we thus obtain that price flexibility should be bad for economic stability due to the minus sign in front of the parameter β_p while the opposite should hold true for the parameter that characterizes wage flexibility. This is a situation already investigated in Rose (1967). It gives the reason for our statement that wage flexibility gives rise to normal, and price flexibility to adverse, Rose effects as far as real-wage adjustments are concerned. Besides real rate of interest effect, establishing opposing Keynes and Mundell effects, we thus have also another real adjustment process in the considered model where now wage and price flexibility are in opposition to each other, see Chiarella and Flaschel (2000) and Chiarella *et al.* (2000) for further discussion of these as well as other feedback mechanisms in Keynesian growth dynamics.

There is still another adjustment speed parameter in the model, the one (β_{ε^m}) that determines how fast the investment climate is updated in the light of current excess profitability. This parameter will play no decisive role in the stability investigations that follow, but will become important in the more detailed and rigorous stability analysis to be considered in the appendix to the paper. In the present stability analysis we will however focus on the role played by $h_2, \beta_w, \beta_p, \beta_{\pi^m}$ in order to provide one example of asymptotic stability of the interior steady-state position by appropriate choices of these parameter values, basically in line with the above feedback channels of partial Keynesian macrodynamics.

The above adds to the understanding of the dynamical system (7.22)–(7.26) whose stability properties are now to be investigated by means of varying adjustment speed parameters. With the feedback scenarios considered above in mind, we first observe that the inflationary climate can be frozen at its steady-state value, here $\pi_0^m = \hat{M} - n = 0$, if $\beta_{\pi^m} = 0$ is assumed. The system thereby becomes 4D and it can indeed be further reduced to 3D if in addition $\beta_w = 0$ is assumed, since this decouples the l-dynamics from the remaining dynamical system in ω, m and ε^m.

We intentionally will consider the stability of these 3D subdynamics – and its subsequent extensions – in informal terms here, leaving rigorous calculations of stability criteria to the appendix. In this way we hope to demonstrate to the reader how one can proceed from low to high-dimensional analysis in such stability investigations. This method has already been applied to various other often much more complicated dynamical systems, see Asada *et al.* (2003) for a variety of typical examples.

Proposition 1. *Assume that the parameters h_2, β_p are chosen sufficiently small and that the κ_w, κ_p parameters do not equal 1. Then the interior steady state of the reduced 3D dynamical system*

$$\hat{\omega} = -\kappa(1 - \kappa_w)\beta_p(y/y^p(\omega) - \bar{V}^c)$$
$$\hat{m} = -i\varepsilon^m - \kappa\beta_p(y/y^p(\omega) - \bar{V}^c)$$
$$\dot{\varepsilon}^m = \beta_{\varepsilon^m}(\rho + \kappa\beta_p(y/y^p(\omega) - \bar{V}^c) - r - \varepsilon^m)$$

is locally asymptotically stable.

Sketch of proof. Assuming h_2, β_p sufficiently small gives for the Jacobian J at the steady state the sign structure:

$$J = \begin{pmatrix} - & 0 & - \\ - & 0 & - \\ - & + & - \end{pmatrix}$$

Furthermore, the entries J_{23}, J_{33} can be made as large as desired by choosing h_2, the carrier of the Keynes effect, sufficiently small. This immediately implies that all principal minors of order 2 are then nonnegative (their sum a_2 is positive), while trace $J < 0$ follows directly ($= -a_1$). And for det $J = -a_3$ one easily gets by way of the linear dependencies present in the Jacobian of the considered 3D dynamics

$$0 > \det J > -J_{11}J_{23}J_{32}$$

which – taken together – implies that all coefficients a_1, a_2, a_3 of the Routh Hurwitz polynomial are positive and in addition fulfill $a_1 a_2 - a_3 > 0$. ∎

Proposition 2. *Assume in addition that the parameter β_w is now positive and chosen sufficiently small. Then the interior steady state of the implied 4D dynamical system (where the law of motion for l has now been incorporated)*

$$\hat{\omega} = \kappa[(1 - \kappa_p)\beta_w(l^d/l - \bar{V}^l) - (1 - \kappa_w)\beta_p(y/y^p - \bar{V}^c)]$$

$$\hat{m} = -i\varepsilon^m - \kappa[\beta_p(y/y^p - \bar{V}^c) + \kappa_p\beta_w(l^d/l - \bar{V}^l)]$$

$$\dot{\varepsilon}^m = \beta_{\varepsilon^m}(\rho + \kappa[\beta_p(y/y^p(\omega) - \bar{V}^c) + \kappa_p\beta_w(l^d/l - \bar{V}^l)], -r - \varepsilon^m)$$

$$\hat{l} = -i\varepsilon^m$$

is locally asymptotically stable.

Sketch of proof. Exploiting the many linear dependencies shown in the considered dynamical system one can easily reduce the right-hand side of the Jacobian of the dynamics at the steady state to

$$\hat{\omega} = (1 - \kappa_p)\beta_w(l^d/l - \bar{V}^l)$$

$$\hat{m} = -\beta_p(y/y^p(\omega) - \bar{V}^c)$$

$$\dot{\varepsilon}^m = \beta_{\varepsilon^m}(\rho - r - \varepsilon^m)$$

$$\hat{l} = -i\varepsilon^m$$

without any change in the sign of its determinant. Continuing in this way one can then even obtain

$$\hat{\omega} = (1 - \kappa_p)\beta_w(l_0^d/l - \bar{V}^l)$$

$$\hat{m} = -\beta_p(y_0/y^p(\omega) - \bar{V}^c)$$

$$\dot{\varepsilon}^m = -\beta_{\varepsilon^m}\frac{h_1 y_0 - m}{h_2}$$

$$\hat{l} = -i\varepsilon^m$$

again without change in the signs of the determinants to be calculated at each step. The sign of the determinant of the now corresponding Jacobian is however easily shown to be positive. The eigenvalue zero of the situation where the 4D system is considered for $\beta_w = 0$ thus must become negative if the change in β_w is sufficiently small, since the other three eigenvalues must then continue to have negative real parts. ∎

Proposition 3. *Assume in addition that the parameter β_{π^m} is now positive and chosen sufficiently small. Then the interior steady state of the full 5D dynamical system (where the differential equation for π^m is now included)*

$$\hat{\omega} = \kappa[(1 - \kappa_p)\beta_w(l^d/l - \bar{V}^l) - (1 - \kappa_w)\beta_p(y/y^p - \bar{V}^c)]$$

$$\hat{m} = -\pi^m - i\varepsilon^m - \kappa[\beta_p(y/y^p - \bar{V}^c) + \kappa_p\beta_w(l^d/l - \bar{V}^l)]$$

$$\dot{\varepsilon}^m = \beta_{\varepsilon^m}(\rho + \kappa[\beta_p(y/y^p(\omega) - \bar{V}^c) + \kappa_p\beta_w(l^d/l - \bar{V}^l)] + \pi^m - r - \varepsilon^m)$$

$$\hat{l} = -i\varepsilon^m$$

$$\dot{\pi}^m = \beta_{\pi^m}(\kappa[\beta_p(y/y^p(\omega) - \bar{V}^c) + \kappa_p\beta_w(l^d/l - \bar{V}^l)])$$

is locally asymptotically stable.

Sketch of proof. As for Proposition 2, by now simply making use of the rows corresponding to the laws of motion for l and m in order to reduce the row corresponding to the law of motion for π^m to the form $(0, 0, 0, 0, -)$, again without change in the sign of the determinants of the accompanying Jacobians. The fifth eigenvalue must therefore change from zero to a negative value if the parameter β_π is made positive (but not too large). ∎

We observe that the parameters β_p and β_{π^m} have been chosen such that adverse Rose and destabilizing Mundell effects are both weak and accompanied by a strongly stabilizing Keynes effect. Due to our reliance on the continuity of eigenvalues with respect to parameter changes we however had to specify in addition that also β_w should be sufficiently small. This is possibly not really necessary, since wage flexibility is stabilizing from the partial perspective. Note however that the size of the parameter ε^m is not at all restricted in the present approach to β-stability. The more detailed stability analysis in the appendix indicates that ε^m also affects stability.

We formulate as a *corollary* to Proposition 3 that, due to the always negative sign of the just considered 5D determinant, loss of stability can only occur by way of *Hopf bifurcations*, i.e., through the generation of cycles in the real-nominal interactions of the model. Since the model is in a natural way a nonlinear one, we know from the Hopf bifurcation theorem[18] that usually loss of stability will occur through the death of an unstable limit cycle or the birth of a stable one, when destabilizing parameters pass through their bifurcation values. Such loss of stability is here possible if prices become sufficiently flexible compared to wage flexibility, leading to an adverse type of real wage adjustment, or if the inflationary climate expression is updated sufficiently fast, i.e., if the system loses the inertia – we have built into it – to a sufficient degree. These are

---

[18] See the mathematical appendix in Asada *et al.* (2003) for details.

typical feedback structures of a properly formulated Keynesian dynamics that may give rise to local instability, directly in the case of subcritical Hopf bifurcations, and thus give rise to the need to add further *extrinsic or behavioral nonlinearities* to the model in order to bound the generated business fluctuations. Such issues are further considered in companion papers to the present one, there from the numerical as well as the empirical perspective, see Asada *et al.* (2006), Chen *et al.* (2005a) and Chen *et al.* (2005b).

We conclude from this section that our Keynesian dynamical system – with labor and capital both over or underutilized in the course of the generated business fluctuations – integrates important feedback channels based on partial perspectives into a consistent whole, with all behavioral and budget restrictions fully specified. We can have damped oscillations, persistent fluctuations or even explosive oscillations in such a framework. The latter case necessitates the introduction of certain behavioral nonlinearities in order to allow for viable business fluctuations. Moreover, a variety of well-known stabilizing or destabilizing feedback channels are still excluded from the present stage of the modeling of Keynesian macrodynamics, such as wealth effects in consumption or Fisher debt effects in investment behavior, all of which define the agenda for future extensions of this model type.

7. Blanchard–Katz error correction and Taylor policy rules

Flaschel and Schlicht, see Chapter 5 in this volume, compare the New Keynesian approach with the two PC approach of this paper in an extended format which we here briefly recapitulate and then include into our AD–AS dynamics together with a Taylor interest rate policy rule in the place of the LM-curve, in order to show how our matured Keynesian AD–AS dynamics is differentiated from the New Keynesian approach when this latter approach is extended to the treatment of two PCs (with both staggered price and wage setting). Referring to this chapter, we simplify the New Keynesian approach to wage-price dynamics slightly and obtain from it the two equations

$$d \ln w_t \overset{NWPC}{=} E_t(d \ln w_{t+1}) + \beta_{wy} \ln Y_t - \beta_{w\omega} \ln \omega_t$$

$$d \ln p_t \overset{NPPC}{=} E_t(d \ln p_{t+1}) + \beta_{py} \ln Y_t + \beta_{p\omega} \ln \omega_t$$

Current wage and price inflation here depend on expected future wage and price inflation, respectively, and in the usual way on the output gap, augmented by a negative (positive) dependence on the real wage gap in the case of the wage (price) PC. Assuming a deterministic framework and myopic perfect foresight allows to suppress the expectations operator.

In order to get from these two laws of motion the corresponding PCs of our matured, but traditional AD–AS dynamics, we simply have to use neoclassical dating of expectations of a crossover type, i.e., perfectly foreseen wage inflation in the price PC and perfectly foreseen price inflation in the wage PC, now coupled with hybrid expectations formation as in the AD-DAS model of the preceding sections. We furthermore replace the output gap in the NWPC by the employment rate gap and by the capacity utilization gap in the NPPC as in the matured Keynesian macrodynamics introduced in Section 5. Finally, we now also use real wage gaps in the MWPC and the MPPC, here based on microfoundations of Blanchard and Katz type, as in the paper by Flaschel and Krolzig in this volume. In this way, we arrive at the following general form of our M(atured)WPC and M(atured)PPC, formally discriminated from the New Keynesian case of both staggered wage and price setting solely by a different treatment of wage and price inflation expectations.

$$d\ln w_{t+1} \overset{MWPC}{=} \kappa_w d\ln p_{t+1} + (1 - \kappa_w)\pi_t^m + \beta_{wV^l}(V_t^l - \bar{V}^l) - \beta_{w\omega}(\ln \omega_t - \ln \omega_0)$$

$$d\ln p_{t+1} \overset{MPPC}{=} \kappa_p d\ln w_{t+1} + (1 - \kappa_p)\pi_t^m + \beta_{pV^c}(V_t^c - \bar{V}^c) + \beta_{p\omega}(\ln \omega_t - \ln \omega_0)$$

Note again that we employ two separate measures for the output gap now, in line with our matured Keynesian AD–AS macrodynamics, the employment gap and the capacity utilization gap, and that we represent the real wage gap with explicit reference to the steady-state real wage now. In continuous time these wage and price dynamics read

$$\hat{w} = \kappa_w \hat{p} + (1 - \kappa_w)\pi^m + \beta_{wV^l}(V^l - \bar{V}^l) - \beta_{w\omega}(\ln \omega - \ln \omega_0)$$

$$\hat{p} = \kappa_p \hat{w} + (1 - \kappa_p)\pi^m + \beta_{pV^c}(V^c - \bar{V}^c) + \beta_{p\omega}(\ln \omega - \ln \omega_0)$$

Reformulated as reduced-form expressions, these equations give rise to the following linear system of differential equations ($\theta = \ln \omega$):

$$\hat{w} = \frac{1}{1 - \kappa_w\kappa_p}[\beta_{wV^l}(V^l - \bar{V}^l) - \beta_{w\omega}(\theta - \theta_0) + \kappa_w(\beta_{pV^c}(V^c - \bar{V}^c)$$
$$+ \beta_{p\omega}(\theta - \theta_0))] + \pi^m$$

$$\hat{p} = \frac{1}{1 - \kappa_w\kappa_p}[\beta_{pV^c}(V^c - \bar{V}^c) + \beta_{p\omega}(\theta - \theta_0) + \kappa_p(\beta_{wV^l}(V^l - \bar{V}^l)$$
$$- \beta_{w\omega}(\theta - \theta_0))] + \pi^m$$

$$\dot{\theta} = \frac{1}{1 - \kappa_w\kappa_p}[(1 - \kappa_p)(\beta_{wV^l}(V^l - \bar{V}^l) - \beta_{w\omega}(\theta - \theta_0))$$
$$- (1 - \kappa_w)(\beta_{pV^c}(V^c - \bar{V}^c) + \beta_{w\omega}(\theta - \theta_0))]$$

As monetary policy we now in addition employ a Taylor interest rate rule, given by

$$r^* = (r_0 - \bar{\pi}) + \hat{p} + \alpha_p(\hat{p} - \bar{\pi}) + \alpha_{V^c}(V^c - \bar{V}^c) \qquad (7.32)$$

$$\dot{r} = \alpha_r(r^* - r) \qquad (7.33)$$

These equations describe the interest rate target r^* and the interest rate smoothing dynamics chosen by the central bank. The target rate of the central bank r^* is here made dependent on the steady-state real rate of interest, augmented by actual inflation back toward a specific nominal rate of interest, and is as usual dependent on the inflation gap with respect to the target inflation rate $\bar{\pi}$ and the capacity utilization gap (as measure of the output gap). With respect to this interest rate target, there is then interest rate smoothing with strength α_r. Inserting r^* and rearranging terms we get from this latter expression the following form of a Taylor rule

$$\dot{r} = -\gamma_r(r - r_0) + \gamma_p(\hat{p} - \bar{\pi}) + \gamma_{V^c}(V^c - \bar{V}^c)$$

where we have $\gamma_r = \alpha_r$, $\gamma_p = \alpha_r(1 + \alpha_p)$, i.e., $\alpha_p = \gamma_p/\alpha_r - 1$ and $\gamma_{V^c} = \alpha_r\alpha_{V^c}$.

Since the interest rate is temporarily fixed by the central bank, we must have an endogenous money supply now and get that the law of motion of the original model

$$\hat{m} = -\hat{p} - i\varepsilon^m$$

does no longer feed back into the rest of the dynamics.

Taken together the revised AD–AS model of this section consists of the following five laws of motion for the log of real wages, the nominal rate of interest, the investment climate, labor intensity and the inflationary climate:

$$\dot{\theta} = \frac{1}{1 - \kappa_w\kappa_p}[(1 - \kappa_p)(\beta_{wV^l}(V^l - \bar{V}^l) - \beta_{w\omega}(\theta - \theta_0))$$
$$- (1 - \kappa_w)(\beta_{pV^c}(V^c - \bar{V}^c) + \beta_{w\omega}(\theta - \theta_0))]$$
$$\dot{r} = -\gamma_r(r - r_0) + \gamma_p(\hat{p} - \bar{\pi}) + \gamma_{V^c}(V^c - \bar{V}^c)$$
$$\dot{\varepsilon}^m = \beta_{\varepsilon^m}(\varepsilon - \varepsilon^m)$$
$$\hat{l} = -i\varepsilon^m$$
$$\dot{\pi}^m = \beta_{\pi^m}(\hat{p} - \pi^m)$$

with

$$\hat{p} = \frac{1}{1 - \kappa_w\kappa_p}[\beta_{pV^c}(V^c - \bar{V}^c) + \beta_{p\omega}(\theta - \theta_0) + \kappa_p(\beta_{wV^l}(V^l - \bar{V}^l)$$
$$- \beta_{w\omega}(\theta - \theta_0))]$$

This dynamical system is to be supplemented by the following static relationships for output, potential output and employment (all per unit of capital), the rate of interest and the rate of profit:

$$y = \frac{1}{1-c}[i\varepsilon^m + n + g - t] + \delta + t$$

$$y^p = f((f')^{-1}(\exp\theta)), \quad F(1, L^p/K) = f(l^p) = y^p, \quad F_L(1, L^p/K)) = f'(l^p) = \omega$$

$$l^d = f^{-1}(y)$$

$$V^c = y/y^p, \quad V^l = l^d/l$$

$$\rho = y - \delta - \omega l^d, \quad \varepsilon = \rho - (r - \hat{p})$$

$$r_0 = \rho_0 + \bar{\pi}$$

which have to be inserted into the right-hand sides of the dynamics in order to obtain an autonomous system of five differential equations that is nonlinear in a natural or intrinsic way.

The interior steady-state solution of the above dynamics is given by

$$y_0 = \frac{1}{1-c}[n + g - t] + \delta + t$$

$$l_0^d = f^{-1}(y_0)$$

$$l_0 = l_0^d / \bar{V}^l$$

$$y_0^p = y_0 / \bar{V}^c$$

$$l_0^p = f^{-1}(y_0^p)$$

$$\omega_0 = f'(l_0^p), \quad \theta_0 = \ln \omega_0$$

$$\hat{p}_0 = \pi_0^m = \bar{\pi}$$

$$\rho_0 = f(l_0^d) - \delta - \omega_0 l_0^d$$

$$r_0 = \rho_0 + \hat{p}_0$$

$$\varepsilon_0 = \varepsilon_0^m = 0$$

Note that income distribution in the steady state is again determined by marginal productivity theory, since income distribution does not yet play a role in aggregate demand in the steady state.

Despite formal similarities in the building blocks of the New Keynesian AD–AS dynamics and the above-matured Keynesian AD–AS dynamics, the resulting reduced-form laws of motion, see footnote 8, have not much in common in their structure and nothing in common in their applied solution strategies. The New Keynesian model has four forward-looking variables and thus demands for its determinacy four unstable roots, while our approach only exhibits myopic perfect foresight of a crossover type and thus allows again, with respect to all its variables, for predeterminacy and for stability results as in the preceding section and in the mathematical appendix of this paper. We note in this regard again that there are many items that reappear in various equations, implying that stability analysis can exploit a variety of linear dependencies in the calculation of the conditions for local asymptotic stability. The dynamical system we have derived in this section is investigated in detail in an informal way (but also rigorously) in Asada *et al.* (2006).

8. *Conclusions*

We have considered in this paper an extension and modification of the traditional approach to AD–AS growth dynamics that allowed us to avoid the logical inconsistencies of the old neoclassical synthesis and also the empirically rejected two-times reversed feedback structure of the New Keynesian approach, the new neoclassical synthesis. The conventional wisdom in these two approaches avoids the stability problems of these model types by just assuming global asymptotic stability or boundedness (coupled with the search for determinacy) through the adoption of an appropriate set of non-predetermined variables and the application of the so-called jump-variable technique. This approach of the Rational Expectations School is however much more than just the consideration of *rational* expectations or even only myopic perfect foresight, but in fact the assumption of global perfect foresight on the future paths the economy may allow for, coupled with a solution technique that avoids all potential accelerating mechanisms of macrodynamic economic systems by assumption. In the present context, this approach would impose the condition that prices – and also nominal wages – (or inflation rates, in the New Keynesian approach) must be allowed to jump in a particular way in order to establish (by assumption) the stability of the dynamics under consideration (if determinacy is ensured).

By contrast, our alternative approach – which allows for somewhat gradual wage as well as price adjustment, on account of unbalanced labor as well as product markets, and also allows for certain economic climate expressions, representing the medium-run evolution of inflation and profitability differentials – completely bypasses such stability assumptions. Instead it shows in a very detailed way local asymptotic stability under certain parameter restrictions (very plausible from the perspective of partial Keynesian theorizing), cyclical loss of local stability towards persistent economic fluctuations when these assumptions are violated (if speeds of adjustment become sufficiently high) and even explosive fluctuations in the case of further increases of the crucial speeds of adjustment of the model. In the latter case extrinsic behavioral nonlinearities have to be introduced in order to tame the explosive dynamics in the spirit of the ones considered in Chiarella and Flaschell (2000, Chapters 6, 7) in the framework of models with both sluggish price and quantity adjustment (but not yet smooth factor substitution).

The analysis of this paper may be summarized as in Table 7.1.

Table 7.1. Four baseline approaches to macrodynamic theory

	Equilibrium Prices	Gradual Price Adjustment
Equilibrium wages	w, p NCS I: Classical AD–AS version	$w, \dot{p}$ New Keynesian model
Gradual wage adjustment	$\dot{w}, p$ NCS I: Keynesian AD–AS version	$\dot{w}, \dot{p}$ Mature Keynesian model

Note: (NCS = neoclassical synthesis).

We have four possibilities of combining perfect and gradual price and wage adjustment. The traditional classical case (not considered in this paper, but see Sargent (1987) for a detailed exposition) combines perfectly flexible prices with perfectly flexible wages and argues on this basis that full employment is then a compelling outcome. The old neoclassical synthesis, under Keynesian gradual wage adjustment, has been shown to be flawed by logical inconsistencies in Section 2 of this paper. In Section 3 we have considered the new neoclassical synthesis, in the form of the New Keynesian baseline model, and argued that it overcomes such logical inconsistencies at the expense of empirical implausible-ness however, which has forced this model type to introduce backward-looking expectations in addition (with in fact not so clear microfoundations). The baseline model of the old synthesis has gradual wage, but perfect price adjustment, while the baseline model of the new synthesis just makes the opposite assumptions. Our own approach, a matured kind of traditional Keynesian business cycle theory, by contrast, starts immediately with both gradual wage and price adjustment and backward- as well as forward-looking expectations, and it shows on this basis that a Keynesian theory of the business cycle is available which includes myopic perfect foresight, but no rational expectations solution methodologies, with only predetermined variables and the possibility for stability in the conventional sense of the word and persistent fluctuations if certain adjustment speeds pass certain critical values (possibly needing further behavioral nonlinearities later on).

It should be stressed that the stability features of our appropriately reformulated (matured) AD–AS Keynesian dynamics are based on specific (conventional) interactions of traditional Keynes and Mundell effects working through the real rate of interest channel (here present only in the employed investment function) with so-called Rose or real-wage effects, which in the present framework – from a partial perspective – work in such a way that increasing wage flexibility should be stabilizing and increasing price flexibility destabilizing, based on the assumption that aggregate demand here always depends negatively on the real wage (due to the assumed investment function) and also based on our extended types of PCs (for wages and prices). The interaction of these three effects (i.e., Keynes, Mundell, Rose effects coupled with our extended PCs) is what explains the obtained analytical stability results under the further not very demanding assumption of myopic perfect foresight and thus gives rise to a matured type of Keynesian business cycle theory (with short-run fluctuations in marginal propensities to consume, in investment efficiency and in the state of liquidity preference still missing). This approach to Keynesian macrodynamics is not at all plagued by the logical inconsistencies of the AD–AS dynamics of the old neoclassical synthesis and the empirical implausibility of the new neoclassical synthesis (as will be shown in companion paper to the present one, see in particular Chen *et al.* (2005b) and in this volume Chapter 8).

The model of this paper, with extrinsic nonlinearities added, will be numerically explored and – as stated – also estimated in Chen *et al.* (2005a) and Chen *et al.* (2005b), in order to analyze in greater depth and also with an empirical background the interaction of the various feedback channels. At that point we will then also make detailed use of Taylor interest rate policy rules in the place of the traditional LM curve so far employed in order to study the working of monetary policy in a modern institutional context. The discussion in Sections 3–5 and our work on related models (seeing Chiarella *et al.* (2005)) in this respect suggest that interest rate policy rules (even if suitably augmented) may not however – by themselves – be sufficient to tame the explosive dynamics in all relevant situations. We will then therefore also, and in fact primarily, make use of an important institutional nonlinearity, expressed in stylized form as a kinked money wage PC – representing downward money wage rigidity – and Blanchard and Katz-type (1999) error correction mechanisms in both the WPC and the PPC in order to make the dynamics viable and thus economically meaningful in the cases where the steady state is a repeller (and not surrounded by a limit cycle generated via the generation of a supercritical Hopf-bifurcation). Taking all this together, our general conclusion is that this framework not only overcomes the failures of the neoclassical syntheses, stage I and the very restrictive solution procedures of stage II, but also provides a coherent alternative to the now fashionable New Keynesian theory of the business cycle, the second attempt at a neoclassical synthesis, as it is sketched in Gali (2000) for example.

Summing up, our matured Keynesian dynamics are based on disequilibrium in the market for goods and for labor, on sluggish adjustment of prices as well as wages and on myopic perfect foresight interacting with certain economic climate expectations that evolve adaptively – creating the necessary inertia – with a rich array of dynamic outcomes that provide great potential for future general-izations. Some of these generalizations are considered in Chiarella *et al.* (2000), Asad *et al.* (2003) and Chiarella *et al.* (2005). Our approach, a disequilibrium approach to business cycle modeling, thereby provides a theoretical framework within which to consider the contributions of authors such as Zarnowitz (1999), who also stresses the dynamic interactions of many traditional macroeconomic building blocks and the feedback mechanisms they generate.

References

Asada, T., C. Chiarella, P. Flaschel and R. Franke (2003), *Open Economy Macrodynamics. An Integrated Disequilibrium Approach*, Heidelberg: Springer.

Asada, T., P. Chen, C. Chiarella and P. Flaschel (2006), "Keynesian dynamics and the wage-price spiral. A baseline disequilibrium model", *Journal of Macroeconomics*, Vol. 28, pp. 90–130.

Asada, T. and H. Yoshida (2003), "Coefficient criterion for four-dimensional Hopf-bifurcations: a complete mathematical characterization and applications to economic dynamics", *Chaos, Solitons & Fractals*, Vol. 15, pp. 525–536.

Barro, X. (1994), "The aggregate supply/aggregate demand model", *Eastern Economic Journal*, Vol. 20, pp. 1–6.

Blanchard, O. and X. Katz (1999), "Wage dynamics. Reconciling theory and evidence", *American Economic Review. Papers and Proceedings*, Vol. 89, pp. 69–74.

Chen, P., C. Chiarella, P. Flaschel and H. Hung (2005a), "Keynesian Disequilibrium Dynamics: estimated Convergence, roads to instability and the emergence of complex business fluctuations", in: H. Galler and C. Dreger, editors, *Advances in Macroeconometric Modeling*, Papers and Proceedings of the 5th IWH Workshop in Macroeconometrics. Baden-Baden: Nomos Verlagsgesellschaft, forthcoming.

Chen, P., C. Chiarella, P. Flaschel and W. Semmler (2005b), "Keynesian dynamics and the Phillips curve. An empirical analysis of a Baseline Disequilibrium Approach", Working paper: UTS Sydney, School of Finance and Economics.

Chen, P. and P. Flaschel (2004), "Testing the dynamics of wages and prices for the US economy", Working paper: Bielefeld, Center for Empirical Macroeconomics.

Chiarella, C. and P. Flaschel (1996), "Real and monetary cycles in models of Keynes–Wicksell type", *Journal of Economic Behavior and Organization*, Vol. 30, pp. 327–351.

Chiarella, C. and P. Flaschel (2000), *The Dynamics of Keynesian Monetary Growth: Macro Foundations*, Cambridge, UK: Cambridge University Press.

Chiarella, C., P. Flaschel and R. Franke (2005), *Foundations for a Disequilibrium Theory of the Business Cycle. Quantitative Analysis and Qualitative Assessment*, Cambridge, UK: Cambridge University Press.

Chiarella, C., P. Flaschel, R. Franke and W. Semmler (2002), "Stability analysis of a high-dimensional macrodynamic model of real-financial interaction", Working paper: Bielefeld University: Center for Empirical Macroeconomics.

Chiarella, C., P. Flaschel, G. Groh and W. Semmler (2000), *Disequilibrium, Growth and Labor Market Dynamics*, Heidelberg: Springer.

Chiarella, C., P. Flaschel, G. Groh and W. Semmler (2003), "AS–AD, KMG Growth and Beyond. A Reply to Velupillai", *Journal of Economics*, Vol. 78, pp. 96–104.

Eller, J.W. and R.J. Gordon (2003), "Nesting the New Keynesian Phillips Curve within the Mainstream Model of U.S. Inflation Dynamics", Paper presented at the CEPR Conference: The Phillips curve revisited, June 2003, Berlin.

Flaschel, P. (1993), *Macrodynamics. Income Distribution, Effective Demand and Cyclical Growth*, Bern: Peter Lang.

Flaschel, P., R. Franke and W. Semmler (1997), *Dynamic Macroeconomics: Instability, Fluctuations and Growth in Monetary Economies*, Cambridge, MA: The MIT Press.

Flaschel, P. and H.-M. Krolzig (2004), "Wage and price Phillips curves. An empirical analysis of destabilizing wage-price spirals", Oxford: Oxford University, Discussion paper (see also Chapter 2 in this volume).

Flaschel, P., G. Kauermann and W. Semmler (2005), "Testing wage and price Phillips curves for the United States", *Metroeconomica*, forthcoming.

Fuhrer, J.C. and G.R. Moore (1995), "Forward-looking behavior and the stability of a conventional monetary policy rule", *Journal of Money, Credit, and Banking*, Vol. 27, pp. 1060–1070.

Gali, J. (2000), "The return of the Phillips curve and other recent developments in business cycle theory", *Spanish Economic Review*, Vol. 2, pp. 1–10.

Gali, J., M. Gertler, and J.D. Lopez-Salido (2003), "Robustness of the Estimates of the Hybrid New Keynesian Phillips Curve", Paper presented at the CEPR Conference: The Phillips curve revisited. June 2003, Berlin.

Gandolfo, G. (1996), *Economic Dynamics*, Berlin: Springer.

Groth, C. (1992), "Some unfamiliar dynamics of a familiar macromodel", *Journal of Economics*, Vol. 58, pp. 293–305.

Keynes, J.M. (1936), *The General Theory of Employment, Interest and Money*, New York: Macmillan.

King, R.G. (2000), "The new IS-LM model: language, logic, and limits", *Economic Quarterly*, Federal Reserve Bank of Richmond, Vol. 86(3), pp. 45–103.

Liu, W.M. (1994), "Criterion of Hopf bifurcations without using eigenvalues", *Journal of Mathematical Analysis and Applications*, Vol. 182, pp. 250–256.

Mankiw, G. (2001), "The inexorable and mysterious tradeoff between inflation and unemployment", *Economic Journal*, Vol. 111, pp. 45–61.

Powell, A. and C. Murphy (1997), *Inside a Modern Macroeconometric Model. A Guide to the Murphy Model*, Heidelberg: Springer.

Rose, H. (1967), "On the non-linear theory of the employment cycle", *Review of Economic Studies*, Vol. 34, pp. 153–173.

Rudebusch, G.D. and L.E.O. Svensson (1999), "Policy rules for inflation targeting", pp. 203–246 in: J.B. Taylor, editor, *Monetary Policy Rules*, Chicago: Chicago University Press.

Sargent, T. (1987), *Macroeconomic Theory*, New York: Academic Press.

Sargent, T. and N. Wallace (1973), "The stability of models of money and growth with perfect foresight", *Econometrica*, Vol. 41, pp. 1043–1048.

Solow, R.M. (1956), "A contribution the theory of economic growth", *Quarterly Journal of Economics*, Vol. 70, pp. 65–94.

Tobin, J. (1975), "Keynesian models of recession and depression", *American Economic Review*, Vol. 65, pp. 195–202.

Turnovsky, S. (1995), *Methods of Macroeconomic Dynamics*, Cambridge, MA: The MIT Press.

Velupillai, K. (2003), "Book review", *Journal of Economics*, Vol. 78, pp. 326–332.

Walsh, C.E. (2003), *Monetary Theory and Policy*, Cambridge, MA: The MIT press.

Woodford, M. (2003), *Interest and Prices. Foundations of a Theory of Monetary Policy*, Princeton: Princeton University Press.

Yoshida, H. and T. Asada (2006), "Dynamic analysis of policy lag in a Keynes–Goodwin model: stability, instability, cycles and chaos", *Journal of Economic Behavior and Organization*, forthcoming.

Zarnowitz, V. (1999), "Theory and history behind business cycles: are the 1990s the onset of a golden age?", NBER Working Paper 7010, http://www.nber.org/papers/w7010.

Appendix

Rigorous stability analysis: the baseline case

The objective of this section is to consider, on the one hand, a modified version of the AD-DAS dynamics of Section 5 as it was proposed in Chiarella *et al.* (2003) in a reply to Velupillai (2003) and to demonstrate, on the other hand, in a very detailed and also new way propositions on asymptotic stability and Hopf bifurcations by a different approach to the use of the Routh–Hurwitz conditions for local asymptotic stability. We thereby provide another set of sufficient conditions for such stability which supplement the ones in Section 5. The result here will be that we now have to choose the parameters h_1, β_w, β_{π^m} sufficiently small and h_2 and β_{ε^m} in a certain middle range in order to get the stability propositions looked for. Astonishingly enough, a condition on the parameter β_p, characterizing price flexibility, can be completely avoided now.

The model of Section 5 is here changed, to the extent that we now employ for the formation of the investment climate the law of motion

$$\dot{\varepsilon}^m = \beta_{\varepsilon^m}(\rho + \hat{p} - r - \varepsilon_0^m)$$

in the place of

$$\dot{\varepsilon}^m = \beta_{\varepsilon^m}(\rho + \hat{p} - r - \varepsilon^m)$$

This however simply means that the weights with which past excess profitabilities are aggregated are now changed, as can be shown by way of integration of the two laws of motion, since

$$\varepsilon^m = \varepsilon(t_0)\mathrm{e}^{-\beta_{\varepsilon^m}(t-t_0)} + \beta_{\varepsilon^m}\int_{t_0}^{t}\mathrm{e}^{-\beta_{\varepsilon^m}(t-s)}\varepsilon(s)\,\mathrm{d}s$$

is now simply replaced by

$$\varepsilon^m = \beta_{\varepsilon^m} \int_{t_0}^t \varepsilon(s)\,\mathrm{d}s$$

Instead of an exponential weighting scheme we now use an unweighted aggregate of past observation as measure of the investment climate in which the economy is operating.

The model

In this section we analyze mathematically the five-dimensional macrodynamic model that is obtained from the structural equations of Section 4 (including the above modification of the model) and that has already been briefly investigated in Chiarella *et al.* (2003). This model is represented – in its initial format – by the following sets of algebraic and dynamic equations which appropriately transformed will provide us with an autonomous system of five interdependent differential equations. The local asymptotic stability properties of the model will be investigated in great detail in this section by making use of the fact that the various adjustment speeds of the considered model (in fact, β_w, β_p, β_{π^m}, β_{ε^m}) allow to reduce the dynamics to cases (only one is considered here) where the Routh–Hurwitz conditions can be considered and proved explicitly, while the higher dimensional cases are then treated by continuity arguments with respect to the eigenvalues of the full dynamics. This method of proof has been established in Chiarella and Flaschel (2000) and has since then been used in a variety of other cases, see for example Chiarella *et al.* (2002) for typical examples. We call this approach to the stability investigation of large(r) macrodynamical systems the β-stability method for obvious reasons. Note here also that this proof strategy generally gives rise to Hopf bifurcations when some β-adjustment speeds become so large that local stability gets lost, giving rise to persistent fluctuations in such situations.

The *static part* of the equations is represented as follows:

$$y = [i(\varepsilon^m) + g - t]/s + \delta + t = y(\varepsilon^m), \quad y_{\varepsilon^m} = i_{\varepsilon^m}/s > 0 \tag{7.34}$$

$$r = r_0 + (h_1 y - m)/h_2 = r_0 + (h_1 y(\varepsilon^m) - m)/h_2 = r(\varepsilon^m, m)$$
$$r_{\varepsilon^m} = h_1 y_{\varepsilon^m}/h_2 > 0, \quad r_m = -1/h_2 < 0 \tag{7.35}$$

$$\rho = y - \delta - \omega l^d(y) = y(\varepsilon^m) - \omega l^d(y(\varepsilon^m)) = \rho(\varepsilon^m, \omega), \quad l^d = f^{-1}(y) = l^d(y)$$
$$\rho_{\varepsilon^m} = (1 - \omega l_y^d) y_{\varepsilon^m} = \{1 - \omega/f'(l^d)\} y_{\varepsilon^m} > 0, \quad \rho\omega = -l^d < 0 \tag{7.36}$$

$$V^l = l^d/l = l^d(y)/l = l^d(y(\varepsilon^m))/l = V^l(\varepsilon^m, l)$$
$$V_{\varepsilon^m}^l = l_y^d y_{\varepsilon^m}/l > 0, \quad V_l^l = -l^d/l^2 < 0 \tag{7.37}$$

$$V^c = y/y^p(\omega) = y(\varepsilon^m)/y^p(\omega) = V^c(\varepsilon^m, \omega), \quad y^p(\omega)$$

given by solving

$$\omega = f'(l^p) \quad y^p = f(l^p) \quad V^c_{\varepsilon^m} = y_{\varepsilon^m}/y^p > 0, \quad V\omega^c = -yy\omega^p/(y^p)^2 > 0 \quad (7.38)$$

where $y_{\varepsilon^m} = y'(\varepsilon_m)$, $i_{\varepsilon^m} = i'(\varepsilon^m)$, $r_{\varepsilon^m} = \partial r/\partial\varepsilon^m$, $r_m = \partial r/\partial m$ etc. The meanings of the symbols are as follows:

$y = Y/K = $ actual gross output/capital ratio, $i = I/K = \dot{K}/K = $ rate of net investment (rate of capital accumulation), $g = G/K = $ government expenditure/capital ratio (fixed), $t = T/K = $ tax/capital ratio (fixed), $s = $ marginal propensity to save (fixed, $0 < s < 1$), $\delta = $ rate of capital depreciation (fixed, $0 \leqq \delta \leqq 1$), $Y = $ actual real gross output (real gross national income), $K = $ real-capital stock, $I = \dot{K} = $ real-net investment, $G = $ real government expenditure, $T = $ real tax, $\varepsilon^m = $ investment climate, $r = $ nominal rate of interest, $m = M/(pK) = $ real money balance per capital, $M = $ nominal money supply, $p = $ price level, $\rho = $ net rate of profit, $\omega = w/p = $ real-wage rate, $w = $ nominal wage rate, $l^d = L^d/K = $ employment/capital ratio, $L^d = $ labor employment, $l = L/K = $ full-employment labor intensity, $L = $ labor supply, $V^l = $ rate of employment, $y^p = $ full capacity gross output/capital ratio, $V^c = $ rate of capacity utilization.

We can derive Equation (7.35) as follows. We can express the equilibrium condition for money market as $m = h_1 y + h_2(r_0 - r)$, where the right-hand side is the linear real money demand function per capital stock ($h_1 > 0$, $h_2 > 0$, $r_0 > 0$). Solving this equation with respect to r, we have Equation (7.35).

It is assumed that output is demand-constrained, i.e., $l^d < l^p$, which means that $f'(l^d) > f'(l^p) = \omega$ because of the assumption of decreasing marginal productivity of labor, $f''(l) < 0$. This is the reason why we have $\rho_{\varepsilon^m} > 0$ in Equation (7.36). In this case, we also have $y^p_\omega = f'(l^p)/f''(l^d) < 0$, implying $V^c_\omega > 0$ in Equation (7.38). In the short run, ε^m, m, ω and l are given data. Correspondingly, y, r, ρ, V^l and V^c are determined by Equations (7.34)–(7.38).

The *dynamic part* of the equations is given as follows:

$$\hat{w} = \dot{w}/w = \beta_w(V^l - \bar{V}^l) + \kappa_w\hat{p} + (1 - \kappa_w)\pi^m, \quad \beta_w > 0, \quad 0 < \kappa_w < 1 \quad (7.39)$$

$$\hat{p} = \dot{p}/p = \beta_p(V^c - \bar{V}^c) + \kappa_p\hat{w} + (1 - \kappa_p)\pi^m, \quad \beta_p > 0, \quad 0 < \kappa_p < 1 \quad (7.40)$$

$$\dot{\pi}^m = \beta_{\pi^m}(\hat{p} - \pi^m), \quad \beta_{\pi^m} > 0 \quad (7.41)$$

$$\dot{\varepsilon}^m = \beta_{\varepsilon^m}\varepsilon, \quad \varepsilon = \rho - (r - \hat{p}), \quad \beta_{\varepsilon^m} > 0 \quad (7.42)$$

$$\hat{l} = \dot{l}/l = n - i(\varepsilon^m) \quad (7.43)$$

$$\hat{m} = \dot{m}/m = \hat{M} - \hat{p} - \hat{K} = \mu - \hat{p} - i(\varepsilon^m) \quad (7.44)$$

where π^m is the medium-term inflation climate, ε the current risk premium on investment, $n = \hat{L}$ is the rate of growth of labor supply (natural rate of growth) which is assumed to be constant and $\mu = \hat{M}$ is the rate of growth of nominal money supply which is assumed to be constant.

Five-dimensional dynamical system

The system in the previous section can be reduced to the following nonlinear five-dimensional system of differential equations.

$$
\begin{aligned}
\text{(i)}\quad \dot{\omega} &= \frac{\omega}{1 - \kappa_p \kappa_w}[(1 - \kappa_p)\beta_w\{V^l(\varepsilon^m, l) - \bar{V}^l\} \\
&\qquad -\beta_p(1 - \kappa_w)\{V^c(\varepsilon^m, \omega) - \bar{V}^c\}] \\
&\equiv F_1(\omega, l, \varepsilon^m) \\[4pt]
\text{(ii)}\quad \dot{l} &= l\{n - i(\varepsilon^m)\} \equiv F_2(l, \varepsilon^m) \\[4pt]
\text{(iii)}\quad \dot{m} &= m\left[\mu - \frac{\kappa_p \beta_w}{1 - \kappa_p \kappa_w}\{V^l(\varepsilon^m, l) - \bar{V}^l\}\right. \\
&\qquad \left. - \frac{\beta_p}{1 - \kappa_p \kappa_w}\{V^c(\varepsilon^m, \omega) - \bar{V}^c\} - \pi^m - i(\varepsilon^m)\right] \\
&\equiv F_3(\omega, l, m, \varepsilon^m, \pi^m) \\[4pt]
\text{(iv)}\quad \dot{\varepsilon}^m &= \beta_{\varepsilon^m}\left[\rho(\varepsilon^m, \omega) - r(\varepsilon^m, m) + \frac{\kappa_p \beta_w}{1 - \kappa_p \kappa_w}\{V^l(\varepsilon^m, l) - \bar{V}^l\}\right. \\
&\qquad \left. + \frac{\beta_p}{1 - \kappa_p \kappa_w}\{V^c(\varepsilon^m, \omega) - \bar{V}^c\} + \pi^m\right] \\
&\equiv \beta_{\varepsilon^m} G_4(\omega, l, m, \varepsilon^m, \pi^m) \equiv F_4(\omega, l, m, \varepsilon^m, \pi^m; \beta_{\varepsilon^m}) \\[4pt]
\text{(v)}\quad \dot{\pi}^m &= \beta_{\pi^m}\left[\frac{\kappa_p \beta_w}{1 - \kappa_p \kappa_w}\{V^l(\varepsilon^m, l) - \bar{V}^l\}\right. \\
&\qquad \left. + \frac{\beta_p}{1 - \kappa_p \kappa_w}\{V^c(\varepsilon^m, \omega) - \bar{V}^c\}\right] \\
&\equiv \beta_{\pi^m} G_5(\omega, l, \varepsilon^m) \equiv F_5(\omega, l, \varepsilon^m; \beta_{\pi^m})
\end{aligned}
\right\}(S_1)
$$

Next, let us consider how to derive these equations. First, we can rewrite Equations (7.39) and (7.40) in terms of the matrix notation as follows:

$$
\begin{bmatrix} 1 & -\kappa_w \\ -\kappa_p & 1 \end{bmatrix} \begin{bmatrix} \hat{w} \\ \hat{p} \end{bmatrix} = \begin{bmatrix} \beta_w(V^l - \bar{V}^l) + (1 - \kappa_w)\pi^m \\ \beta_p(V^c - \bar{V}^c) + (1 - \kappa_p)\pi^m \end{bmatrix} \tag{7.45}
$$

Solving this equation, we obtain the following reduced form of $\hat{w}$ and $\hat{p}$:

$$
\begin{aligned}
\hat{w} &= \begin{vmatrix} \beta_w(V^l - \bar{V}^l) + (1 - \kappa_w)\pi^m & -\kappa_w \\ \beta_p(V^c - \bar{V}^c) + (1 - \kappa_p)\pi^m & 1 \end{vmatrix} \Bigg/ \begin{vmatrix} 1 & -\kappa_w \\ -\kappa_p & 1 \end{vmatrix} \\
&= \frac{\beta_w}{1 - \kappa_p \kappa_w}(V^l - \bar{V}^l) + \frac{\beta_p \kappa_w}{1 - \kappa_p \kappa_w}(V^c - \bar{V}^c) + \pi^m
\end{aligned} \tag{7.46}
$$

$$\hat{p} = \begin{vmatrix} 1 & \beta_w(V^l - \bar{V}^l) + (1 - \kappa_w)\pi^w \\ -\kappa_p & \beta_p(V^c - \bar{V}^c) + (1 - \kappa_p)\pi^w \end{vmatrix} \bigg/ \begin{vmatrix} 1 & -\kappa_w \\ -\kappa_p & 1 \end{vmatrix}$$

$$= \frac{\kappa_p \beta_w}{1 - \kappa_p \kappa_w}(V^l - \bar{V}^l) + \frac{\beta_p}{1 - \kappa_p \kappa_w}(V^c - \bar{V}^c) + \pi^m \tag{7.47}$$

Substituting the Equations (7.46) and (7.47) into the equality $\hat{\omega} = \hat{w} - \hat{p}$, we obtain Equation (S_1)(i). Equation (S_1)(ii) follows from Equation (7.43). Substituting Equation (7.47) into the Equations (7.44), (7.42) and (7.41), we have Equation (S_1)(iii), (iv), and (v), respectively.

Long-run equilibrium solution

Next, let us investigate the properties of the stationary solution (long-run equilibrium solution) of the system (S_1) which satisfies $\hat{\omega} = \hat{l} = \dot{m} = \dot{\varepsilon}^m = \dot{\pi}^m = 0$. Substituting $\hat{\omega} = \dot{\pi}^m = 0$ into the Equations (S_1)(i) (v), we have the following system of equations:

$$\begin{bmatrix} (1 - \kappa_p)\beta_w & -\beta_p(1 - \kappa_w) \\ \kappa_p \beta_w & \beta_p \end{bmatrix} \begin{bmatrix} V^l - \bar{V}^l \\ V^c - \bar{V}^c \end{bmatrix} = \begin{bmatrix} 0 \\ 0 \end{bmatrix} \tag{7.48}$$

The solution of this system of equations becomes $V^l - \bar{V}^l = 0$ and $V^c - \bar{V}^c = 0$ because we have the following inequality:

$$\begin{vmatrix} (1 - \kappa_p)\beta_w & -\beta_p(1 - \kappa_w) \\ \kappa_p \beta_w & \beta_p \end{vmatrix} = (1 - \kappa_p)\beta_p \beta_w + \beta_p \kappa_p \beta_w(1 - \kappa_w) > 0 \tag{7.49}$$

Therefore, we can characterize the long-run equilibrium solution as follows:

$$\left.\begin{array}{llll} \text{(i)} & V^l(\varepsilon^m, l) & = & l^d(y(\varepsilon^m))/l = \bar{V}^l \\ \text{(ii)} & V^c(\varepsilon^m, \omega) & = & y(\varepsilon^m)/y^p(\omega) = \bar{V}^c \\ \text{(iii)} & i(\varepsilon^m) & = & n \\ \text{(iv)} & \pi^m & = & \mu - n \\ \text{(v)} & \rho(\varepsilon^m, \omega) & - & r(\varepsilon^m, m) + \mu - n = 0 \end{array}\right\} \tag{7.50}$$

We shall write the vector of the equilibrium values as $(\omega*, l*, m*, \varepsilon^m*, \pi^m*)$. π^m* is uniquely determined by Equation (7.50)(iv). Since $i_{\varepsilon^m} > 0$, ε^m* is uniquely determined by Equation (7.50)(iii) if it exists. We shall assume that $\varepsilon^m* > 0$ in fact exists. In this case, we obtain the unique $l* > 0$ substituting $\varepsilon^m = \varepsilon^m*$ into Equation (7.50)(i). We can also determine unique $\omega* > 0$ (if it exists) by substituting $\varepsilon^m = \varepsilon^m*$ into Equation (7.50)(ii), since $y_\omega^p < 0$. Finally, we can determine unique $m* > 0$ (if it exists) by substituting $\varepsilon^m = \varepsilon^m*$ and $\omega = \omega*$ into Equation (7.50)(v), since $r_m < 0$.

The above analysis reveals that *at most* one long-run equilibrium point exists. In other words, there is no possibility of the existence of the multiple equilibria. In the next section, we shall investigate the local stability/instability of the long-run equilibrium point of this 5D system by *assuming* that an economically meaningful long-run equilibrium point exists.

A five-dimensional analysis of local stability

We can write the Jacobian matrix of the system (S_1) which is evaluated *at the equilibrium point* as follows:

$$J_1 = \begin{bmatrix} F_{11} & F_{12} & 0 & F_{14} & 0 \\ 0 & 0 & 0 & F_{24} & 0 \\ F_{31} & F_{32} & 0 & F_{34} & F_{35} \\ \beta_{\varepsilon^m} G_{41} & \beta_{\varepsilon^m} G_{42} & \beta_{\varepsilon^m} G_{43} & \beta_{\varepsilon^m} G_{44} & \beta_{\varepsilon^m} \\ \beta_{\pi^m} G_{51} & \beta_{\pi^m} G_{52} & 0 & \beta_{\pi^m} G_{54} & 0 \end{bmatrix} \tag{7.51}$$

where $F_{11} = \partial F_1/\partial \omega = -\frac{\omega \beta_p(1-\kappa_w)}{1-\kappa_p \kappa_w} \underset{(+)}{V\omega^c} < 0$, $F_{12} = \partial F_1/\partial l = \frac{\omega(1-\kappa_p)\beta_w}{1-\kappa_p \kappa_w} \underset{(-)}{V_l^l} < 0$,

$F_{14} = \partial F_1/\partial \varepsilon^m = \frac{\omega}{1-\kappa_p \kappa_w}\{(1-\kappa_p)\beta_w \underset{(+)}{V_{\varepsilon^m}^l} - \beta_p(1-\kappa_w) \underset{(+)}{V_{\varepsilon^m}^c}\}$,

$F_{24} = \partial F_2/\partial \varepsilon^m = -l \underset{(+)}{i_{\varepsilon^m}} < 0$, $F_{31} = \partial F_3/\partial \omega = -\frac{m\beta_p}{1-\kappa_p \kappa_w} \underset{(+)}{V\omega^c} < 0$,

$F_{32} = \partial F_3/\partial l = -\frac{m\kappa_p \beta_w}{1-\kappa_p \kappa_w} \underset{(-)}{V_l^l} > 0$,

$F_{34} = \partial F_3/\partial \varepsilon^m = -\frac{m}{1-\kappa_p \kappa_w}(\kappa_p \beta_w \underset{(+)}{V_{\varepsilon^m}^l} + \beta_p \underset{(+)}{V_{\varepsilon^m}^c}) < 0$, $F_{35} = \partial F_3/\partial \pi^m = -m < 0$,

$G_{41} = \partial G_4/\partial \omega = \underset{(-)}{\rho_\omega} + \frac{\beta_p}{1-\kappa_p \kappa_w} \underset{(+)}{V\omega^c}$, $G_{42} = \partial G_4/\partial l = \frac{\kappa_p \beta_w}{1-\kappa_p \kappa_w} \underset{(-)}{V_l^l} < 0$,

$G_{43} = \partial G_4/\partial m = 1/h_2 > 0$,

$G_{44} = \partial G_4/\partial \varepsilon^m = \underset{(+)}{\rho_{\varepsilon^m}} - \underset{(+)}{(h_1 y_{\varepsilon^m}/h_2)} + \frac{1}{1-\kappa_p \kappa_w}(\kappa_p \beta_w \underset{(+)}{V_{\varepsilon^m}^l} + \beta_p \underset{(+)}{V_{\varepsilon^m}^c})$,

$G_{51} = \partial G_5/\partial \omega = \frac{\beta_p}{1-\kappa_p \kappa_w} \underset{(+)}{V\omega^c} > 0$, $G_{52} = \partial G_5/\partial l = \frac{\kappa_p \beta_w}{1-\kappa_p \kappa_w} \underset{(-)}{V_l^l} < 0$, and

$G_{54} = \partial G_5/\partial \varepsilon^m = \frac{1}{1-\kappa_p \kappa_w}(\kappa_p \beta_w \underset{(+)}{V_{\varepsilon^m}^l} + \beta_p \underset{(+)}{V_{\varepsilon^m}^c}) > 0$.

The sign pattern of the matrix J_1 becomes as follows:

$$sign\, J_1 = \begin{bmatrix} - & - & 0 & ? & 0 \\ 0 & 0 & 0 & - & 0 \\ - & + & 0 & - & - \\ ? & - & + & ? & + \\ + & - & 0 & + & 0 \end{bmatrix} \tag{7.52}$$

The characteristic equation of this system can be written as

$$\Gamma_1(\lambda) \equiv |\lambda I - J_1| = \lambda^5 + a_1\lambda^4 + a_2\lambda^3 + a_3\lambda^2 + a_4\lambda + a_5 = 0 \tag{7.53}$$

where each coefficient is given as follows:

$$a_1 = -\text{trace}\, J_1 = -\underset{(-)}{F_{11}} -\underset{(?)}{\beta_{\varepsilon^m}\, G_{44}} \equiv a_1(\beta_{\varepsilon^m}) \tag{7.54}$$

$a_2 = $ sum of all principal second-order minors of J_1

$$= \begin{vmatrix} F_{11} & F_{12} \\ 0 & 0 \end{vmatrix} + \begin{vmatrix} F_{11} & 0 \\ F_{31} & 0 \end{vmatrix} + \beta_{\varepsilon^m}\begin{vmatrix} F_{11} & F_{14} \\ G_{41} & G_{44} \end{vmatrix} + \beta_{\pi^m}\begin{vmatrix} F_{11} & 0 \\ G_{51} & 0 \end{vmatrix}$$

$$+ \begin{vmatrix} 0 & 0 \\ F_{32} & 0 \end{vmatrix} + \beta_{\varepsilon^m}\begin{vmatrix} 0 & F_{24} \\ G_{42} & G_{44} \end{vmatrix} + \beta_{\pi^m}\begin{vmatrix} 0 & 0 \\ G_{52} & 0 \end{vmatrix} + \beta_{\varepsilon^m}\begin{vmatrix} 0 & F_{34} \\ G_{43} & G_{44} \end{vmatrix}$$

$$+ \begin{vmatrix} 0 & F_{35} \\ 0 & 0 \end{vmatrix} + \beta_{\varepsilon^m}\beta_{\pi^m}\begin{vmatrix} G_{44} & 1 \\ G_{54} & 0 \end{vmatrix}$$

$$= \beta_{\varepsilon^m}(\underset{(+)}{-\beta_{\pi^m}\, G_{54}} + \underset{(-)}{F_{11}\, G_{44}} \underset{(?)}{} - \underset{(?)}{F_{14}\, G_{41}} \underset{(?)}{} - \underset{(-)}{F_{24}\, G_{42}} \underset{(-)}{} - \underset{(-)}{F_{34}\, G_{43}} \underset{(+)}{})$$

$$\equiv a_2(\beta_{\varepsilon^m}, \beta_{\pi^m}) \tag{7.55}$$

$a_3 = -($sum of all principal third-order minors of $J_1)$

$$= -\begin{vmatrix} F_{11} & F_{12} & 0 \\ 0 & 0 & 0 \\ F_{31} & F_{32} & 0 \end{vmatrix} - \beta_{\varepsilon^m}\begin{vmatrix} F_{11} & F_{12} & F_{14} \\ 0 & 0 & F_{24} \\ G_{41} & G_{42} & G_{44} \end{vmatrix} - \beta_{\pi^m}\begin{vmatrix} F_{11} & F_{12} & 0 \\ 0 & 0 & 0 \\ G_{51} & G_{52} & 0 \end{vmatrix}$$

$$- \beta_{\varepsilon^m}\begin{vmatrix} F_{11} & 0 & F_{14} \\ F_{31} & 0 & F_{34} \\ G_{41} & G_{43} & G_{44} \end{vmatrix} - \beta_{\pi^m}\begin{vmatrix} F_{11} & 0 & 0 \\ F_{31} & 0 & F_{35} \\ G_{51} & 0 & 0 \end{vmatrix} - \beta_{\varepsilon^m}\beta_{\pi^m}\begin{vmatrix} F_{11} & F_{14} & 0 \\ G_{41} & G_{44} & 1 \\ G_{51} & G_{54} & 0 \end{vmatrix}$$

$$- \beta_{\varepsilon^m}\begin{vmatrix} 0 & 0 & F_{24} \\ F_{32} & 0 & F_{34} \\ G_{42} & G_{43} & G_{44} \end{vmatrix} - \beta_{\pi^m}\begin{vmatrix} 0 & 0 & 0 \\ F_{32} & 0 & F_{35} \\ G_{52} & 0 & 0 \end{vmatrix} - \beta_{\varepsilon^m}\beta_{\pi^m}\begin{vmatrix} 0 & F_{24} & 0 \\ G_{42} & G_{44} & 1 \\ G_{52} & G_{54} & 0 \end{vmatrix}$$

$$- \beta_{\varepsilon^m}\beta_{\pi^m}\begin{vmatrix} 0 & F_{34} & F_{35} \\ G_{43} & G_{44} & 1 \\ 0 & G_{54} & 0 \end{vmatrix}$$

$$= \beta_{\varepsilon^m}\{\beta_{\pi^m}(\underset{(?)}{-F_{14}\, G_{51}} + \underset{(+)}{F_{11}\, G_{54}} \underset{(-)}{} - \underset{(+)}{F_{24}\, G_{52}} \underset{(-)}{} - \underset{(-)}{F_{35}\, G_{54}\, G_{43}}) - \underset{(-)}{F_{12}\, F_{24}\, G_{41}} \underset{(+)}{} \underset{(-)}{} \underset{(-)}{} \underset{(?)}{}$$

$$+ \underset{(-)}{F_{11}\, G_{42}\, F_{24}} \underset{(-)}{} \underset{(-)}{} - \underset{(?)}{F_{14}\, G_{43}\, F_{31}} \underset{(+)}{} \underset{(-)}{} + \underset{(-)}{F_{11}\, G_{43}\, F_{34}} \underset{(+)}{} \underset{(-)}{} - \underset{(-)}{F_{24}\, G_{43}\, F_{32}}\underset{(+)}{} \underset{(+)}{}\}$$

$$\equiv a_3(\beta_{\varepsilon^m}, \beta_{\pi^m}) \tag{7.56}$$

a_4 = sum of all principal fourth-order minors of J_1

$$= \beta_{\varepsilon^m}\beta_{\pi^m}\begin{vmatrix} 0 & 0 & F_{24} & 0 \\ F_{32} & 0 & F_{34} & F_{35} \\ G_{42} & G_{43} & G_{44} & 1 \\ G_{52} & 0 & G_{54} & 0 \end{vmatrix} + \beta_{\varepsilon^m}\beta_{\pi^m}\begin{vmatrix} F_{11} & 0 & F_{14} & 0 \\ F_{31} & 0 & F_{34} & F_{35} \\ G_{41} & G_{43} & G_{44} & 1 \\ G_{51} & 0 & G_{54} & 0 \end{vmatrix}$$

$$+ \beta_{\varepsilon^m}\beta_{\pi^m}\begin{vmatrix} F_{11} & F_{12} & F_{14} & 0 \\ 0 & 0 & F_{24} & 0 \\ G_{41} & G_{42} & G_{44} & 1 \\ G_{51} & G_{52} & G_{54} & 0 \end{vmatrix} + \beta_{\pi^m}\begin{vmatrix} F_{11} & F_{12} & 0 & 0 \\ 0 & 0 & 0 & 0 \\ F_{31} & F_{32} & 0 & F_{35} \\ G_{51} & G_{52} & 0 & 0 \end{vmatrix}$$

$$+ \beta_{\varepsilon^m}\begin{vmatrix} F_{11} & F_{12} & 0 & F_{14} \\ 0 & 0 & 0 & F_{24} \\ F_{31} & F_{32} & 0 & F_{34} \\ G_{41} & G_{42} & G_{43} & G_{44} \end{vmatrix}$$

$$= \beta_{\varepsilon^m}\left\{ \beta_{\pi^m}\left(F_{24}\begin{vmatrix} F_{32} & 0 & F_{35} \\ G_{42} & G_{43} & 1 \\ G_{52} & 0 & 0 \end{vmatrix} - G_{43}\begin{vmatrix} F_{11} & F_{14} & 0 \\ F_{31} & F_{34} & F_{35} \\ G_{51} & G_{54} & 0 \end{vmatrix} \right. \right.$$

$$\left. \left. - F_{24}\begin{vmatrix} F_{11} & F_{12} & 0 \\ G_{41} & G_{42} & 1 \\ G_{51} & G_{52} & 0 \end{vmatrix} \right) + F_{24}\begin{vmatrix} F_{11} & F_{12} & 0 \\ F_{31} & F_{32} & 0 \\ G_{41} & G_{42} & G_{43} \end{vmatrix} \right\}$$

$$= \beta_{\varepsilon^m}\{ \beta_{\pi^m}(\underset{(-)}{- F_{24}} \underset{(-)}{F_{35}} \underset{(+)}{G_{43}} \underset{(-)}{G_{52}} \underset{(+)}{- G_{43}} \underset{(?)}{F_{14}} \underset{(-)}{F_{35}} \underset{(+)}{G_{51}} + \underset{(+)}{G_{43}} \underset{(-)}{F_{11}} \underset{(+)}{G_{54}} \underset{(-)}{F_{35}} \underset{(-)}{- F_{24}} \underset{(-)}{F_{12}} \underset{(+)}{G_{51}}$$

$$+ \underset{(-)}{F_{24}} \underset{(-)}{F_{11}} \underset{(-)}{G_{52}}) + \underset{(-)}{F_{24}} \underset{(+)}{G_{43}}(\underset{(-)}{F_{11}} \underset{(+)}{F_{32}} \underset{(-)}{- F_{12}} \underset{(-)}{F_{31}})\}$$

$$\equiv a_4(\beta_{\varepsilon^m}, \beta_{\pi^m}) \tag{7.57}$$

$$a_5 = -\det J_1 = -\beta_{\varepsilon^m}\beta_{\pi^m}\begin{vmatrix} F_{11} & F_{12} & 0 & F_{14} & 0 \\ 0 & 0 & 0 & F_{24} & 0 \\ F_{31} & F_{32} & 0 & F_{34} & F_{35} \\ G_{41} & G_{42} & G_{43} & G_{44} & 1 \\ G_{51} & G_{52} & 0 & G_{54} & 0 \end{vmatrix}$$

$$= -\beta_{\varepsilon^m}\beta_{\pi^m}F_{24}\begin{vmatrix} F_{11} & F_{12} & 0 & 0 \\ F_{31} & F_{32} & 0 & F_{35} \\ G_{41} & G_{42} & G_{43} & 1 \\ G_{51} & G_{52} & 0 & 0 \end{vmatrix} = -\beta_{\varepsilon^m}\beta_{\pi^m}F_{24}G_{43}\begin{vmatrix} F_{11} & F_{12} & 0 \\ F_{31} & F_{32} & F_{35} \\ G_{51} & G_{52} & 0 \end{vmatrix}$$

$$= \beta_{\varepsilon^m} \beta_{\pi^m} F_{24} G_{43} F_{35}(- F_{12} G_{51} + F_{11} G_{52}) \equiv a_5(\beta_{\varepsilon^m}, \beta_{\pi^m}) > 0 \qquad (7.58)$$
$$ \underset{(-)\ (+)\ (-)}{} \quad \underset{(-)\ (+)}{} \quad \underset{(-)\ (-)}{}$$

Next, let us consider the conditions for local stability of the equilibrium point in this system. It is well known that the Routh–Hurwitz conditions for stable roots in this 5D system can be expressed as follows (cf. Gandolfo, 1996, Chapter 16):

$$(i) \quad \Delta_1 \equiv a_1 > 0$$

$$(ii) \quad \Delta_2 \equiv \begin{vmatrix} a_1 & a_3 \\ 1 & a_2 \end{vmatrix} = a_1 a_2 - a_3 > 0$$

$$(iii) \quad \Delta_3 \equiv \begin{vmatrix} a_1 & a_3 & a_5 \\ 1 & a_2 & a_4 \\ 0 & a_1 & a_3 \end{vmatrix}$$
$$= a_3 \Delta_2 + a_1(a_5 - a_1 a_4) = a_1 a_2 a_3 - a_1^2 a_4 - a_3^2 + a_1 a_5 > 0$$

$$(iv) \quad \Delta_4 \equiv \begin{vmatrix} a_1 & a_3 & a_5 & 0 \\ 1 & a_2 & a_4 & 0 \\ 0 & a_1 & a_3 & a_5 \\ 0 & 1 & a_2 & a_4 \end{vmatrix} = a_4 \Delta_3 - a_5 \begin{vmatrix} a_1 & a_3 & a_5 \\ 1 & a_2 & a_4 \\ 0 & 1 & a_2 \end{vmatrix}$$
$$= a_4 \Delta_3 + a_5(-a_1 a_2^2 - a_5 + a_2 a_3 + a_1 a_4)$$
$$= a_4 \Delta_3 + a_5(a_1 a_4 - a_5 - a_2 \Delta_2) > 0$$

$$(v) \quad \Delta_5 \equiv \begin{vmatrix} a_1 & a_3 & a_5 & 0 & 0 \\ 1 & a_2 & a_4 & 0 & 0 \\ 0 & a_1 & a_3 & a_5 & 0 \\ 0 & 1 & a_2 & a_4 & 0 \\ 0 & 0 & a_1 & a_3 & a_5 \end{vmatrix} = a_5 \Delta_4 > 0$$

$$\left. \phantom{\begin{matrix} 1 \\ 1 \\ 1 \\ 1 \\ 1 \\ 1 \\ 1 \\ 1 \\ 1 \end{matrix}} \right\} (7.59)$$

It is easy to see that two inequalities $a_1 > 0$ and $a_5 > 0$ are a set of *necessary* conditions for the local stability of this system. The condition $a_5 > 0$ is always satisfied because of Equation (7.58). However, a_1 depends on the value of the parameter β_{ε^m} because of Equation (7.54). Furthermore, we can see that G_{44} is an increasing function of the sensitivity of the money demand with respect to the nominal rate of interest (h_2), and we have $\lim_{h_2 \to 0} G_{44} = -\infty$, $\lim_{h_2 \to +\infty} G_{44} > 0$. The following proposition follows from this fact.

Proposition 4. *Suppose that h_2 is so large that $G_{44} > 0$. Then, the equilibrium point of the system (S_1) is locally unstable if the inequality*

$$\beta_{\varepsilon^m} > - F_{11} / G_{44} \qquad (7.60)$$
$$\underset{(-)}{} \quad \underset{(+)}{}$$

is satisfied.

Proof. If the inequality (7.60) is satisfied, we have $a_1 < 0$, which violates one of the Routh–Hurwitz conditions for stable roots. ∎

This proposition implies that the system becomes dynamically unstable if the values of the parameters h_2 and β_{ε^m} are sufficiently large. This proposition provides us a *sufficient* condition for local *instability*. On the other hand, the following proposition provides us an interesting set of *sufficient* conditions for the local *stability*.

Proposition 5. *Suppose that the following set of inequalities is satisfied at the parameter values $\beta_{\varepsilon^m} = \beta_{\varepsilon^m}^0 > 0$ and $\beta_{\pi^m} = 0$.*

$$a_1(\beta_{\varepsilon^m}^0) > 0, \qquad a_3(\beta_{\varepsilon^m}^0, 0) > 0,$$

$$a_1(\beta_{\varepsilon^m}^0) a_2(\beta_{\varepsilon^m}^0, 0) a_3(\beta_{\varepsilon^m}^0, 0) - a_1(\beta_{\varepsilon^m}^0)^2 a_4(\beta_{\varepsilon^m}^0, 0) - a_3(\beta_{\varepsilon^m}^0, 0)^2 > 0 \qquad (7.61)$$

Then, a set of inequalities (7.59)(i)–(v) is satisfied at $\beta_{\varepsilon^m} = \beta_{\varepsilon^m}^0$ for all sufficiently small $\beta_{\pi^m} > 0$.

Proof. We have the following relationships at $[\beta_{\varepsilon^m}, \beta_{\pi^m}] = [\beta_{\varepsilon^m}^0, 0]$ because $a_5(\beta_{\varepsilon^m}^0, 0) = 0$:

$$
\left.
\begin{aligned}
\text{(i)} \quad \Delta_1 &= a_1(\beta_{\varepsilon^m}^0) \\
\text{(ii)} \quad \Delta_2 &= a_1(\beta_{\varepsilon^m}^0) a_2(\beta_{\varepsilon^m}^0, 0) - a_3(\beta_{\varepsilon^m}^0, 0) \\
\text{(iii)} \quad \Delta_3 &= a_3(\beta_{\varepsilon^m}^0, 0) \Delta_2 - a_1(\beta_{\varepsilon^m}^0)^2 a_4(\beta_{\varepsilon^m}^0, 0) \\
&= a_1(\beta_{\varepsilon^m}^0) a_2(\beta_{\varepsilon^m}^0, 0) a_3(\beta_{\varepsilon^m}^0, 0) - a_1(\beta_{\varepsilon^m}^0)^2 a_4(\beta_{\varepsilon^m}^0, 0) \\
&\quad - a_3(\beta_{\varepsilon^m}^0, 0)^2 \\
\text{(iv)} \quad \Delta_4 &= a_4(\beta_{\varepsilon^m}^0, 0) \Delta_3
\end{aligned}
\right\} \qquad (7.62)
$$

We can easily see from these relationships that four conditions $\Delta_j > 0$ $(j = 1, 2, 3, 4)$ are satisfied at $[\beta_{\varepsilon^m}, \beta_{\pi^m}] = [\beta_{\varepsilon^m}^0, 0]$ if a set of inequalities (7.61) are satisfied, because we have $a_4(\beta_{\varepsilon^m}^0, 0) = \beta_{\varepsilon^m}^0 F_{24} G_{43}(F_{11} F_{32} - F_{12} F_{31}) > 0$. It is
$$\underset{(-)}{} \quad \underset{(+)}{} \quad \underset{(-)}{} \quad \underset{(+)}{} \quad \underset{(-)}{} \; \underset{(-)}{}$$

clear that four inequalities $\Delta_j > 0$ $(j = 1, 2, 3, 4)$ are also satisfied at $\beta_{\varepsilon^m} = \beta_{\varepsilon^m}^0$ for all sufficiently small $\beta_{\pi^m} > 0$, because each coefficient is the continuous function of the parameter β_{π^m}. The inequality $\Delta_5 > 0$ is also satisfied at $\beta_{\varepsilon^m} = \beta_{\varepsilon^m}^0$ for all sufficiently small $\beta_{\pi^m} > 0$, because we have $a_5(\beta_{\varepsilon^m}^0, \beta_{\pi^m}) > 0$ if $\beta_{\pi^m} > 0$. ∎

Proposition 5 implies that the equilibrium point of the system (S_1) is locally asymptotically stable at $\beta_{\varepsilon^m} = \beta_{\pi^m}^0 > 0$ for all sufficiently small $\beta_{\pi^m} > 0$ if a set of inequalities (7.61) is satisfied. In the next section, we shall show that these inequalities in fact correspond to the exact local stability conditions of a degenerated four-dimensional system.

Local stability and Hopf Bifurcations in a degenerated four-dimensional system, and implications for the 5D dynamics

It is easy to see that the characteristic equation (7.53) becomes as follows as $\beta_{\pi^m} \to 0$:

$$\lim_{\beta_{\pi^m} \to 0} \Gamma_1(\lambda) = \lim_{\beta_{\pi^m} \to 0} |\lambda I - J_1| = \lambda |\lambda I - J_2| = 0 \tag{7.63}$$

where J_2 is the following (4×4) submatrix of the (5×5) matrix J_1.

$$J_2 = \begin{bmatrix} F_{11} & F_{12} & 0 & F_{14} \\ 0 & 0 & 0 & F_{24} \\ F_{31} & F_{32} & 0 & F_{34} \\ \beta_{\varepsilon^m} G_{41} & \beta_{\varepsilon^m} G_{42} & \beta_{\varepsilon^m} G_{43} & \beta_{\varepsilon^m} G_{44} \end{bmatrix} \tag{7.64}$$

Equation (7.63) has a root $\lambda = 0$, and other four roots are determined by the following equation:

$$\Gamma_2(\lambda) \equiv |\lambda I - J_2| = \lambda^4 + b_1 \lambda^3 + b_2 \lambda^2 + b_3 \lambda + b_4 = 0 \tag{7.65}$$

where each coefficient becomes as follows:

$$b_1 = a_1(\beta_{\varepsilon^m}) = A - \beta_{\varepsilon^m} B \tag{7.66}$$

$$b_2 = a_2(\beta_{\varepsilon^m}, 0) = \beta_{\varepsilon^m} C \tag{7.67}$$

$$b_3 = a_3(\beta_{\varepsilon^m}, 0) = \beta_{\pi^m} D \tag{7.68}$$

$$b_4 = a_4(\beta_{\varepsilon^m}, 0) = \beta_{\varepsilon^m} E \tag{7.69}$$

In these expressions, A, B, C, D and E are constants which are given as follows:

$$A = -\underset{(-)}{F_{11}} = \frac{\omega \beta_p (1 - \kappa_w)}{1 - \kappa_p \kappa_w} \underset{(+)}{V \omega^c} > 0$$

$$B = \underset{(?)}{G_{44}} = \underset{(+)}{\rho_{\varepsilon^m}} - \underset{(+)}{(h_1\, y_{\varepsilon_m}/h_2)} + \frac{1}{1 - \kappa_p\kappa_w}(\underset{(+)}{\kappa_p\beta_w\, V^l_{\varepsilon^m}} + \underset{(+)}{\beta_p\, V^c_{\varepsilon^m}})$$

$$C = \underset{(-)}{F_{11}}\,\underset{(?)}{G_{44}} - \underset{(?)}{F_{14}}\,\underset{(?)}{G_{41}} - \underset{(-)}{F_{24}}\,\underset{(-)}{G_{42}} - \underset{(-)}{F_{34}}\,\underset{(+)}{G_{43}}$$

$$= -\frac{\omega\beta_p(1-\kappa_w)}{1-\kappa_p\kappa_w}\,\underset{(+)}{V\omega^c}\left\{\underset{(+)}{\rho_{\varepsilon^m}} - \underset{(+)}{(h_1\, y_{\varepsilon^m}/h_2)} + \frac{1}{1-\kappa_p\kappa_w}(\underset{(+)}{\kappa_p\beta_w\, V^l_{\varepsilon^m}} + \underset{(+)}{\beta_p\, V^c_{\varepsilon^m}})\right\}$$

$$-\frac{\omega}{1-\kappa_p\kappa_w}\{\underset{(+)}{(1-\kappa_p)\beta_w\, V^l_{\varepsilon^m}} - \underset{(+)}{\beta_p(1-\kappa_w)\, V^c_{\varepsilon^m}}\}\left(\underset{(-)}{\rho\omega} + \frac{\beta_p}{1-\kappa_p\kappa_w}\underset{(+)}{V\omega^c}\right)$$

$$+\frac{\kappa_p\beta_w}{1-\kappa_p\kappa_w}\,\underset{(-)}{V^l_l}\,\underset{(+)}{i_{\varepsilon^m}} + \frac{m}{1-\kappa_p\kappa_w}(\underset{(+)}{\kappa_p\beta_w\, V^l_{\varepsilon^m}} + \underset{(+)}{\beta_p\, V^c_{\varepsilon^m}})(1/h_2)$$

$$D = -\underset{(-)}{F_{12}}\,\underset{(-)}{F_{24}}\,\underset{(?)}{G_{41}} + \underset{(-)}{F_{11}}\,\underset{(-)}{G_{42}}\,\underset{(-)}{F_{24}} + \underset{(+)}{G_{43}}(\underset{(?)}{-F_{14}}\,\underset{(-)}{F_{31}} + \underset{(-)}{F_{11}}\,\underset{(-)}{F_{34}} - \underset{(-)}{F_{24}}\,\underset{(+)}{F_{32}})$$

$$= \frac{\beta_w}{1-\kappa_p\kappa_w}\left[\underset{(-)}{\omega(1-\kappa_p)}\,\underset{(+)}{V^l_l\, i_{\varepsilon^m}}\left(\underset{(-)}{\rho\omega} + \frac{\beta_p}{1-\kappa_p\kappa_w}\underset{(+)}{V\omega^c}\right)\right.$$

$$\left.+\frac{\omega\beta_p(1-\kappa_w)\kappa_p}{1-\kappa_p\kappa_w}\,\underset{(+)}{V\omega^c}\,\underset{(-)}{V^l_l}\,\underset{(+)}{i_{\varepsilon^m}}\right] + \frac{\beta_w}{1-\kappa_p\kappa_w}(1/h_2)m$$

$$\left[\frac{\omega\beta_p}{1-\kappa_p\kappa_w}\{(1-\kappa_p) + (1-\kappa_w)\kappa_p\}\,\underset{(+)}{V^l_{\varepsilon^m}}\,\underset{(+)}{V\omega^c} - \underset{(+)}{\kappa_p l\, i_{\varepsilon^m}}\,\underset{(-)}{V^l_l}\right]$$

$$\equiv \frac{\beta_w}{1-\kappa_p\kappa_w}H$$

$$E = \underset{(-)}{F_{24}}\,\underset{(+)}{G_{43}}(\underset{(-)}{F_{11}}\,\underset{(+)}{F_{32}} - \underset{(-)}{F_{12}}\,\underset{(-)}{F_{31}})$$

$$= \frac{m\omega\beta_p\beta_w}{(1-\kappa_p\kappa_w)^2}(1/h_2)l\,\underset{(+)}{i_{\varepsilon^m}}\{-\underset{(+)}{(1-\kappa_w)\kappa_p\, V^c_{\varepsilon^m}\, V^l_l} - \underset{(-)}{(1-\kappa_p)\, V^l_l}\,\underset{(+)}{V\omega^c}\} > 0 \qquad (7.70)$$

In fact, Equation (7.65) is identical to the characteristic equation of a degenerated four-dimensional system, which we can construct by freezing the inflation climate π^m at the equilibrium level $\mu - n$ in the system (S_1) (i)–(iv). For simplicity, we shall call this degenerated four-dimensional system as the system (S_2).

We can express the Routh–Hurwitz conditions for stable roots in this four-dimensional system as follows (*cf.* Gandolfo, 1996, Chapter 16):

(i) $\Phi_1 \equiv b_1 > 0$

(ii) $\Phi_2 \equiv \begin{vmatrix} b_1 & b_3 \\ 1 & b_2 \end{vmatrix} = b_1 b_2 - b_3 > 0$

(iii) $\Phi_3 \equiv \begin{vmatrix} b_1 & b_3 & 0 \\ 1 & b_2 & b_4 \\ 0 & b_1 & b_3 \end{vmatrix} = b_3 \Phi_2 - b_1^2 b_4 = b_1 b_2 b_3 - b_1^2 b_4 - b_3^2 > 0$

(iv) $\Phi_4 \equiv \begin{vmatrix} b_1 & b_3 & 0 & 0 \\ 1 & b_2 & b_4 & 0 \\ 0 & b_1 & b_3 & 0 \\ 0 & 1 & b_2 & b_4 \end{vmatrix} = b_4 \Phi_3 > 0$

A set of inequalities (i)–(iv) is equivalent to the following set of conditions:

$$b_1 > 0, \ \ b_3 > 0, \ \ b_4 > 0, \ \ \ \Phi_3 \equiv b_1 b_2 b_3 - b_1^2 b_4 - b_3^2 > 0 \tag{7.71}$$

Remark 1. A set of inequalities (7.71) automatically implies the inequality $b_2 > 0$.

By the way, the inequality $b_4 > 0$ is always satisfied for all $\beta_{g^m} > 0$. Therefore, the exact local stability conditions of the system (S_2) can be reduced to the following three inequalities as far as $\beta_{g^m} > 0$:

$$b_1 > 0, \ \ \ b_3 > 0, \ \ \ \Phi_3 > 0 \tag{7.72}$$

It is important to note that a set of inequalities (7.72) is exactly the same as a set of conditions (7.61). Now, we can easily obtain the following proposition.

Proposition 6. *The equilibrium point of the system (S_2) is locally unstable for all $\beta_{g^m} > 0$ if either of the inequalities $C < 0$ or $D < 0$ is satisfied.*

Proof. If $C < 0$, we have $b_2 < 0$ for all $\beta_{g^m} > 0$, which violates one of the Routh–Hurwitz conditions for stable roots. If $D < 0$, we have $b_3 < 0$ for all $\beta_{g^m} > 0$, which also violates one of the conditions for stable roots. ∎

This proposition implies that *both* of the inequalities $C > 0$ and $D > 0$ are *necessary* conditions for the local stability of the system (S_2). We can see from Equation (7.70) that these conditions are satisfied if the value of the parameter h_2 (sensitivity of the money demand with respect to the changes of the nominal rate of interest) is sufficiently *small*.

By the way, we have the following relationships from Equation (7.70) ($A > 0$ is independent of the changes of the parameter β_w).

$$B(0) \equiv \lim_{\beta_w \to 0} B = \underset{(+)}{\rho_{\varepsilon^m}} - \underset{(+)}{(h_1 \, y_{\varepsilon^m} / h_2)} + \frac{\beta_p}{1 - \kappa_p \kappa_w} \underset{(+)}{V^c_{\varepsilon^m}} \tag{7.73}$$

$$C(0) \equiv \lim_{\beta_w \to 0} C = \frac{\beta_p}{1 - \kappa_p \kappa_w} \left[\omega(1 - \kappa_w) \left\{ -\underset{(+)}{\rho_{\varepsilon^m}} + \underset{(+)}{(h_1 \, y_{\varepsilon^m} / h_2)} - \frac{\beta_p}{1 - \kappa_p \kappa_w} \underset{(+)}{V^c_{\varepsilon^m}} \right. \right.$$

$$\left. \left. + \underset{(+)}{V^c_{\varepsilon^m}} \left(\underset{(-)}{\rho \omega} + \frac{\beta_p}{1 - \kappa_p \kappa_w} \underset{(+)}{V \omega^c} \right) \right\} + m \underset{(+)}{V^c_{\varepsilon^m}}(1/h_2) \right] \tag{7.74}$$

We shall study the local stability of the equilibrium point of the four-dimensional system (S_2) under the following assumption.

Assumption 1. $B(0) > 0$, $C(0) > 0$, and $H > 0$. The condition $B(0) > 0$ implies that

$$1/h_2 < \left(\underset{(+)}{\rho_{\varepsilon^m}} + \frac{\beta_p}{1 - \kappa_p \kappa_w} \underset{(+)}{V^c_{\varepsilon^m}} \right) / \underset{(+)}{(h_1 \, y_{\varepsilon^m})} \equiv Q \tag{7.75}$$

This means that the value of the parameter h_2 is not too small. The conditions $C(0) > 0$ and $H > 0$ imply the following two inequalities:

$$1/h_2 > \beta_p \left\{ \omega(1 - \kappa_w) \left(\underset{(+)}{\rho_{\varepsilon^m}} + \frac{\beta_p}{1 - \kappa_p \kappa_w} \underset{(+)}{V^c_{\varepsilon^m}} \right) \right.$$

$$\left. + \underset{(+)}{V^c_{\varepsilon^m}} \left(-\underset{(-)}{\rho \omega} - \frac{\beta_w}{1 - \kappa_p \kappa_w} \underset{(+)}{V \omega^c} \right) \right\} / \{ \omega(1 - \kappa_w) \underset{(+)}{h_1 \, y_{\varepsilon^m}} + m \underset{(+)}{V^c_{\varepsilon^m}} \} \equiv T \tag{7.76}$$

$$1/h_2 > \left\{ -\omega(1 - \kappa_p) \underset{(-)}{V^l_l} \underset{(+)}{l_{i_{\varepsilon^m}}} \left(\underset{(-)}{\rho \omega} + \frac{\beta_p}{1 - \kappa_p \kappa_w} \underset{(+)}{V \omega^c} \right) \right.$$

$$\left. - \frac{\omega \beta_p(1 - \kappa_w)\kappa_p}{1 - \kappa_p \kappa_w} \underset{(+)}{V \omega^c} \underset{(-)}{V^l_l} \underset{(+)}{l_{i_{\varepsilon^m}}} \right\} / \frac{m \omega \beta_p}{1 - \kappa_p \kappa_w}$$

$$\{(1 - \kappa_p) + (1 - \kappa_w)\kappa_p\} \underset{(+)}{V^l_{\varepsilon^m}} \underset{(+)}{V \omega^c} - m \kappa_p \underset{(+)}{l_{i_{\varepsilon^m}}} \underset{(-)}{V^l_l} \} \equiv W \tag{7.77}$$

These two inequalities mean that the value of the parameter h_2 is not too large. That is to say, Assumption 1 is equivalent to the following set of inequalities:

$$\max[T, W] < 1/h_2 < Q \tag{7.78}$$

This set of inequalities is meaningless unless

$$\max[T, W] < Q \tag{7.79}$$

The inequality (7.79) will in fact be satisfied if the value of the parameter h_1 (sensitivity of the money demand with respect to the changes of the real income) is sufficiently small, since we have $\lim_{h_1 \to 0} Q = +\infty$, $\lim_{h_1 \to 0} T < +\infty$, and $W < +\infty$. The small h_1 means the mild slope of the LM curve (see Equation (7.35)). To sum up, Assumption 1 will in fact be satisfied if h_1 is relatively small and h_2 is at the intermediate level.

Under Assumption 1, we have

$$B > 0, \quad C > 0 \quad \text{and} \quad D > 0 \tag{7.80}$$

for all sufficiently small $\beta_w > 0$. In this case, we can simplify a set of local stability conditions as follows:

$$0 < \beta_{\varepsilon^m} < A/B, \quad \Phi_3 > 0 \tag{7.81}$$

We can write the function Φ_3 as follows:

$$
\begin{aligned}
\Phi_3(\beta_{\varepsilon^m}) &= (A - \beta_{\varepsilon^m} B)\beta_{\varepsilon^m}^2 CD - (A - \beta_{\varepsilon^m} B)^2 \beta_{\varepsilon^m} E - \beta_{\varepsilon^m}^2 D^2 \\
&= -B(CD + BE)\beta_{\varepsilon^m}^3 + \{(AC - D)D + 2ABE\}\beta_{\varepsilon^m}^2 \\
&\quad - A^2 E \beta_{\varepsilon^m}
\end{aligned}
\tag{7.82}
$$

Suppose that $\beta_w > 0$ is so small that a set of inequalities (7.81) is satisfied. Since $\Phi_3(0) = 0$ and $\Phi_3'(0) = -A^2 E < 0$, we have $\Phi_3 < 0$ for all sufficient small $\beta_{\varepsilon^m} > 0$. This observation implies that the equilibrium point of this system becomes locally unstable for all sufficient small $\beta_{\varepsilon^m} > 0$. On the other hand, we already know that the system becomes unstable for all $\beta_{\varepsilon^m} > A/B$. Therefore, we have the instability result for very small as well as very large β_{ε^m}. If $\beta_{\varepsilon^m} = 0$, the investment climate does not move, i.e., $\varepsilon^m = \varepsilon^m(0)$ for all time. In this case the movement of l is governed by the equation $\dot{l} = l\{n - i(\varepsilon^m(0))\}$, so that l continues to increase or continues to decrease unless $n = i(\varepsilon^m(0))$. Obviously, this means instability, and this property applies also for sufficiently small $\beta_{\varepsilon^m} > 0$. On the other hand, the instability of the system in case of the large adjustment parameter can be interpreted as an 'overshooting' phenomenon. Next, let us investigate whether the stable region exists at the intermediate range of the adjustment parameter values or not.

The equation $\Phi_3(\beta_{\varepsilon^m}) = 0$ has the following three roots:

$$
\left.
\begin{aligned}
&\text{(i)} \quad \beta_{\varepsilon^m}^0 = 0 \\[2mm]
&\text{(ii)} \quad \beta_{\varepsilon^m}^1 = \frac{\{(AC-D)D+2ABE\} - \sqrt{\{(AC-D)D+2ABE\}^2 - 4B(CD+BE)A^2E}}{2B(CD+BE)} \\[2mm]
&\qquad\quad = \frac{\{(AC-D)D+2ABE\} - D\sqrt{(AC-D)^2 - 4ABE}}{2B(CD+BE)} \\[2mm]
&\text{(iii)} \quad \beta_{\varepsilon^m}^2 = \frac{\{(AC-D)D+2ABE\} + D\sqrt{(AC-D)^2 - 4ABE}}{2B(CD+BE)}
\end{aligned}
\right\}
\tag{7.83}
$$

An interval with $\Phi_3 > 0$ exists in the region $\beta_{\varepsilon m} \in (0, +\infty)$ *if and only if* $\beta^1_{\varepsilon m}$ and $\beta^2_{\varepsilon m}$ are real roots such that $0 < \beta^1_{\varepsilon m} < \beta^2_{\varepsilon m}$. We can prove that in fact that is the case if the value of the parameter $\beta_w > 0$ is sufficiently small under Assumption 1.

We can easily see that the following properties are satisfied:

$$D(0) \equiv \lim_{\beta_w \to 0} D = 0 \tag{7.84}$$

$$E(0) \equiv \lim_{\beta_w \to 0} E = 0 \tag{7.85}$$

$$\lim_{\beta_w \to 0} (AC - D) = AC(0) > 0 \tag{7.86}$$

In this case, $\beta^1_{\varepsilon m}$ and $\beta^2_{\varepsilon m}$ in Equation (7.83) become the real roots such that $0 < \beta^1_{\varepsilon m} < \beta^2_{\varepsilon m}$ for sufficient small $\beta_w > 0$, because of the inequality (7.86) and the fact that $\lim_{\beta_w \to 0}(ABE) = 0$. This situation is illustrated in Figure 7.3.

Furthermore, we can show that

$$A/B - \beta^2_{\varepsilon m} = \frac{D\{(AC - D) - \sqrt{(AC - D)^2 - 4ABE}\}}{2B(CD + BE)} \tag{7.87}$$

which becomes positive for sufficiently small $\beta_w > 0$.

We can obtain the following important proposition from the above observations.

Figure 7.3. **The parameter Φ_3 as a function of $\beta_{\varepsilon m}$**

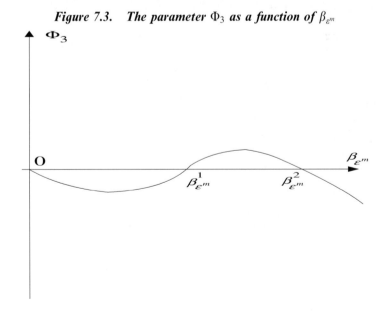

Proposition 7. *Suppose that $\beta_w > 0$ is sufficiently small. Then, under Assumption 1, there exist the parameter values $\beta_{g^m}^1$ and $\beta_{g^m}^2$ such that $0 < \beta_{g^m}^1 < \beta_{g^m}^2$ which satisfy the following properties*:

(i) The equilibrium point of the degenerated four-dimensional system (S_2) is locally asymptotically stable for all $\beta_{g^m} \in (\beta_{g^m}^1, \beta_{g^m}^2)$, and it is locally unstable for all $\beta_{g^m} \in (0, \beta_{g^m}^1) \cup (\beta_{g^m}^2, +\infty)$.

(ii) The equilibrium point of the original five-dimensional system (S_1) is locally asymptotically stable for all sufficiently small $\beta_{\pi^m} > 0$ if $\beta_{g^m} \in (\beta_{g^m}^1, \beta_{g^m}^2)$.

(iii) The equilibrium point of the original five-dimensional system (S_1) is locally unstable for all sufficiently small $\beta_{\pi^m} > 0$ if $\beta_{g^m} \in (0, \beta_{g^m}^1) \cup (\beta_{g^m}^2, +\infty)$.

Proof. (i) We already know from the above observations that there exist the parameter values $\beta_{g^m}^1$ and $\beta_{g^m}^2$ such that $0 < \beta_{g^m}^1 < \beta_{g^m}^2$ with the following properties if the relevant assumptions are satisfied. For all $\beta_{g^m} \in (\beta_{g^m}^1, \beta_{g^m}^2)$, we have both of $\Phi_3 > 0$ and $0 < \beta_{g^m} < A/B$, so that all of the Routh–Hurwitz conditions for stable roots of the system (S_2) are satisfied. For all $\beta_{g^m} \in (0, \beta_{g^m}^1) \cup (\beta_{g^m}^2, +\infty)$, we have $\Phi_3 < 0$, so that at least one of the Routh–Hurwitz conditions of the system (S_2) is violated.

(ii) If $\beta_{g^m} \in (\beta_{g^m}^1, \beta_{g^m}^2)$, all of the inequalities (7.61) are satisfied, so that we can apply the result of Proposition 5.

(iii) If $\beta_{g^m} \in (0, \beta_{g^m}^1) \cup (\beta_{g^m}^2, +\infty)$, the characteristic Equation (7.63) has at least one root with positive real part. In this case, the characteristic Equation (7.53) also has at least one root with positive real part for all sufficiently small $\beta_{\pi^m} > 0$ by continuity.

By the way, at the points $\beta_{g^m} = \beta_{g^m}^1$ and $\beta_{g^m} = \beta_{g^m}^2$, we have the following properties:

$$b_1 > 0, \quad b_3 > 0, \quad b_4 > 0, \quad \Phi_3 = 0, \quad \Phi'(\beta_{g^m}) \neq 0 \qquad (7.88)$$

This means that at these points the 'simple' Hopf bifurcations occur in the 4D system (S_2) (as for the mathematical proof, see Liu (1994), Yoshida and Asada (2006), or Asada and Yoshida (2003)). The 'simple' Hopf bifurcation is the particular type of the Hopf bifurcation at which all the characteristic roots *except* a pair of purely imaginary ones have negative real parts. In other words, at these points the characteristic equation (7.65) has a pair of purely imaginary roots and two roots with negative real parts.

Furthermore, we can observe that there is no other Hopf bifurcation point in this system because of the following reason. Asada and Yoshida (2003) proved that both of the conditions $b_4 \neq 0$ and $\Phi_3 = 0$ are *necessary* conditions for the occurrence of the Hopf bifurcation, whether it is simple or non-simple, in the four-dimensional system. The point $\beta_{g^m} = 0$ is the only other point which satisfies $\Phi = 0$, but at that point we have $b_4 = 0$. Therefore, the point $\beta_{g^m} = 0$ is *not* the Hopf bifurcation point. These analyses lead us to the following final important proposition, which establishes the existence of the cyclical fluctuation in both the degenerated system and the original system.

Proposition 8. (i) *There exist some non-constant periodic solutions of the degenerated four-dimensional system* (S_2) *at some parameter values* $\beta_{g^m} > 0$ *which are sufficiently close to* $\beta_{g^m}^i$ $(i = 1, 2)$ *which are defined in Proposition 7.*

(ii) *At the parameter values* $\beta_{g^m} > 0$ *which are sufficiently close to* $\beta_{g^m}^i (i = 1, 2)$ *which are defined in Proposition 7, the characteristic equation* (7.53) *of the original five-dimensional system* (S_1) *has a pair of complex roots for all sufficiently small* $\beta_{\pi^m} > 0$.

Proposition 8 (ii) follows from the continuity of the characteristic roots with respect to the changes of the coefficients of the characteristic equation. This proposition establishes the existence of the cyclical fluctuation in the original five-dimensional nonlinear dynamical system (S_1).

Remark 2. If we can find a parameter value $\beta_{g^m} = \beta_{g^m} * > 0$ at which all of the conditions $\Delta_j > 0$ $(j = 1, 2, 3)$, $\Delta_4 = 0$, $\Delta_4'(\beta_{g^m}) \neq 0$ are satisfied, we can establish the existence of a (simple) Hopf bifurcation in the original 5D system (cf. Liu (1994)). In this case, we can establish the existence of the closed orbit in the original five-dimensional system. (In fact, we also need another condition $a_5 > 0$, but this condition is always satisfied in this model.) However, the existence of the closed orbit (existence of a pair of purely imaginary roots) is not necessary for the existence of the cyclical fluctuation. Rather, the existence of a pair of complex roots is enough for the existence of the cyclical movement.

CHAPTER 8

Keynesian Macrodynamics and the Phillips Curve: An Estimated Model for the U.S. Economy

Pu Chen*, Carl Chiarella, Peter Flaschel and Willi Semmler

Abstract

This paper formulates and empirically estimates a baseline disequilibrium AS–AD model with time series data for the U.S. economy. The model exhibits a Phillips curve, a dynamic IS curve and a Taylor interest rate rule. It is based on sticky wages and prices, perfect foresight of current inflation rates and adaptive expectations concerning the inflation climate in which the economy operates. A version of Okun's law links capacity utilization to employment. The resulting nonlinear 5D model of real market dynamics overcomes anomalies of the old Neoclassical synthesis and also the rational expectations methodology of the new Neoclassical synthesis. It resembles New Keynesian macroeconomics but permits nonclearing of markets. It exhibits typical Keynesian feedback structures with asymptotic stability (instability) of its steady state for low (high) adjustment speeds. Estimates of the model, for quarterly time series data of the U.S. economy 1965.1–2001.1, are provided and used to study the stability features of the U.S. economy with respect to its various feedback channels. It is found in particular that goods market dynamics are profit-led, and that the dynamics are strongly convergent around the steady state, if monetary policy is sufficiently active; however this feature is lost if the inflationary climate variable or the price inflation rate adjust sufficiently fast. The stabilizing effects of more active interest rate feedback rules or downward wage rigidity are also studied, as well as the economy's behavior due to faster adjustments. It is found that monetary policy should allow for sufficient steady-state inflation in order to avoid stability problems in areas of the phase space where wages are not flexible in a downward direction.

*Corresponding author.

CONTRIBUTIONS TO ECONOMIC ANALYSIS
VOLUME 277   ISSN: 0573-8555
DOI:10.1016/S0573-8555(05)77008-5

Keywords: AS–AD disequilibrium, wage and price Phillips curves, Okun's law, (in-)stability, persistent fluctuations, monetary policy

JEL Classifications: E24, E31, E32

1. Introduction

This paper formulates and estimates a Keynesian macroeconomic model for the U.S. economy. It builds, as do recent New Keynesian macrodynamic models, on gradual wage and price adjustments, furthermore it employs two Phillips curves, in order to relate factor utilization rates and wage and price dynamics, and includes a dynamic IS curve and a Taylor interest rate rule. It resembles the New Keynesian macromodels in that it includes elements of forward-looking behavior, but it permits nonclearing markets, underutilized labor and capital stock and a mix of myopic perfect foresight and adaptively formed medium run expectations concerning an inflation climate of the economy. In order to link output to employment the paper will make use of a dynamic form of Okun's law. Although our model is akin to the traditional AS–AD model, the resulting nonlinear 5D model of nonclearing labor and goods market avoids the anomalies of the conventional AS–AD model.

Our approach exhibits similarities but also difference to New Keynesian macroeconomics. We use the same formal structure for the variables that drive wage and price inflation rates (utilizations rates and real wages), but with microfoundations that are, for example, based on the Blanchard and Katz (1999) reconciliation of wage Phillips curves (wage PCs) and current labor market theories. The basic difference in the wage–price module is that we augment this structure by hybrid expectations formation where the forward-looking part is based on a neoclassical type of dating and where expectations are of cross-over type – we have price inflation expectations in the wage PC and wage inflation expectations in the price Phillips curve (price PC). Our formulation of the wage–price dynamics permits therefore an interesting comparison to New Keynesian work that allows for both staggered price and wage setting. Concerning the IS curve we make use of a law of motion for the rate of capacity utilization of firms that depends on the level of capacity utilization (the dynamic multiplier), the real rate of interest and finally on the real wage and thus on income distribution. New Keynesian authors often use a purely forward-looking IS curve (with only the real rate of interest effect) and a Phillips curve which has been criticized from the empirical point of view; see in particular Fuhrer and Rudebusch (2004) and Eller and Gordon (2003). Since we distinguish between the rate of employment of the labor force and that of the capital stock, namely the rate of capacity utilization, we employ some form of Okun's law to relate capacity utilization to employment.

The present paper intends to provide empirical evidence on a baseline model of a Keynesian disequilibrium AS–AD (DAS–DAD) variety. It presents the feedback structures of this (semi-)reduced form of a macromodel and its stability implications, first on a general level and then on the level of the sign and size restrictions obtained from empirical estimates of the five laws of motion of the dynamics. These estimates, undertaken for the U.S. economy for quarterly data 1965.1–2001.1 also allow us to discuss asymptotic stability for the estimated parameter sizes and to determine stability boundaries.

The remainder of the paper is organized as follows. Section 2 considers the New Keynesian macrodynamic model with staggered wage and price setting in a deterministic and continuous time framework. Section 3 then presents our formulation of a baseline Keynesian DAS–DAD growth dynamics model that is suitable for empirical estimation. Section 4 considers the feedback chains of the reformulated model and derives cases of local asymptotic stability and of loss of stability by way of Hopf bifurcations. In Section 5, we then estimate the model to find out sign and size restrictions for its behavioral equations and we study which type of feedback mechanisms may apply to the U.S. economy after World War II. Section 6 investigates in detail the stability properties of the estimated model. Section 7 analyzes the stability problems that occur when there is a floor to money wage deflation and the role of monetary policy in such a case. Section 8 discusses related literature and Section 9 concludes.

2. New Keynesian macrodynamics

In this section, we consider briefly the modern analog to the old neoclassical synthesis, namely the New Keynesian approach to macrodynamics in its advanced form, where both staggered price setting and staggered wage setting are assumed. We here follow Woodford (2003, p. 225) in his formulation of staggered wages and prices, where their joint evolution is coupled with the usual forward-looking output dynamics, and in addition coupled with a derived law of motion for real wages. Here we shall only briefly look at this extended approach and leave to later sections of the paper a consideration of the similarities and differences between these New Keynesian dynamics and our own approach.

Woodford (2003, p. 225) basically makes use of the following two loglinear equations for describing the joint evolution of wages and prices (d the backward oriented difference operator[1]).

$$d \ln w_t \overset{WPC}{=} \beta E_t(d \ln w_{t+1}) + \beta_{wy} \ln Y_t - \beta_{w\omega} \ln \omega_t$$

$$d \ln p_t \overset{PPC}{=} \beta E_t(d \ln p_{t+1}) + \beta_{py} \ln Y_t + \beta_{p\omega} \ln \omega_t$$

where all parameters are assumed to be positive. Our first aim here is to derive the continuous time analog to these two equations (and the other equations of

---

[1] We make use of this convention throughout this paper and thus have to write $r_{t-1} - dp_t$ for the real rate of interest.

the full model) and to show on this basis how this extended model is solved in the spirit of the rational expectations school.

In a deterministic setting we obtain from the above

$$d \ln w_{t+1} \stackrel{WPC}{=} \frac{1}{\beta}[d \ln w_t - \beta_{wy} \ln Y_t + \beta_{w\omega} \ln \omega_t]$$

$$d \ln p_{t+1} \stackrel{PPC}{=} \frac{1}{\beta}[d \ln p_t - \beta_{py} \ln Y_t - \beta_{p\omega} \ln \omega_t]$$

If we assume (as we do in all of the following and without much loss in generality) that the parameter β is not only close to 1, but in fact set equal to 1, then the last two equations can be expressed as

$$d \ln w_{t+1} - d \ln w_t \stackrel{WPC}{=} -\beta_{wy} \ln Y_t + \beta_{w\omega} \ln \omega_t$$

$$d \ln p_{t+1} - d \ln p_t \stackrel{PPC}{=} -\beta_{py} \ln Y_t - \beta_{p\omega} \ln \omega_t$$

Denoting by π^w the rate of wage inflation and by π^p the rate of price inflation (both indexed by the end of the corresponding period) we then obtain the continuous time dynamics (with $\ln Y = y$ and $\theta = \ln \omega$):

$$\dot{\pi}^w \stackrel{WPC}{=} -\beta_{wy}y + \beta_{w\omega}\theta$$

$$\dot{\pi}^p \stackrel{PPC}{=} -\beta_{py}y - \beta_{p\omega}\theta$$

From the output dynamics of the New Keynesian approach, namely

$$y_t = y_{t+1} - \alpha_{yi}(i_t - \pi^p_{t+1} - i_0), \quad \text{i.e.,} \quad y_{t+1} - y_t = \alpha_{yi}(i_t - \pi^p_{t+1} - i_0)$$

we obtain the continuous time reduced-form law of motion

$$\dot{y} \stackrel{IS}{=} \alpha_{yi}[(\beta_{i\pi} - 1)\pi^p + (\beta_{iy} + \beta_{py})y + \beta_{p\omega}\theta)]$$

where we have already inserted an interest rate policy rule in order to (hopefully) obtain determinacy as in the New Keynesian baseline model, which is known to be indeterminate for the case of an interest rate peg. Here we have chosen the simple Taylor interest rate policy rule

$$i = i_t = i_o + \beta_{i\pi}\pi + \beta_{iy}y$$

see Walsh (2003, p. 247), which is of a classical Taylor rule type (though without interest rate smoothing yet).

There remains finally the law of motion for real wages to be determined, which setting $\theta = \ln \omega$ simply reads

$$\dot{\theta} = \pi^w - \pi^p$$

We thus get from this extended New Keynesian model an autonomous linear dynamical system, in the variables π^w, π^p, y and θ. The, in general, uniquely determined steady state of the dynamics is given by $(0.0, 0, i_o)$. From the definition of θ we see that the model exhibits four forward-looking variables, in direct generalization of the baseline New Keynesian model with only staggered price setting. Searching for a zone of determinacy of the dynamics (appropriate parameter values that make the steady state the only bounded solution of the dynamics to which the economy then immediately returns after isolated shocks of any type) thus requires establishing conditions under which all roots of the Jacobian have positive real parts.

The Jacobian of the four dimensional (4D) dynamical system under consideration reads

$$J = \begin{pmatrix} 0 & 0 & -\beta_{wy} & \beta_{w\omega} \\ 0 & 0 & -\beta_{py} & -\beta_{p\omega} \\ 0 & \alpha_{yi}(\beta_{i\pi} - 1) & \alpha_{yi}(\beta_{iy} + \beta_{py}) & \alpha_{yi}\beta_{p\omega} \\ 1 & -1 & 0 & 0 \end{pmatrix}$$

For the determinant of this Jacobian we calculate

$$-|J| = (\beta_{wy}\beta_{p\omega} + \beta_{py}\beta_{w\omega})\alpha_{yi}(\beta_{i\pi} - 1) \gtreqless 0 \text{ iff } \beta_{i\pi} \gtreqless 1$$

We thus get that an active monetary policy of the conventional type (with $\beta_{i\pi} > 1$) is – compared to the baseline New Keynesian model – no longer appropriate to ensure determinacy (for which a positive determinant of J is a necessary condition). One can show in addition, (see Chen *et al.*, 2006), via the minors of order 3 of the Jacobian J, that the same holds true for a passive monetary policy rule, i.e., the model in this form must be blocked out from consideration. There consequently arises the necessity to specify an extended or modified active Taylor interest rate policy rule from which one can then obtain determinacy for the resulting dynamics, i.e., the steady state as the only bounded solution and therefore, according to the logic of the rational expectations approach, the only realized situation in this deterministic setup. This would then generalize the New Keynesian baseline model with only staggered prices, which is known to be indeterminate in the case of an interest rate peg or a passive monetary policy rule, but which exhibits determinacy for a conventional Taylor rule with $\beta_{i\pi} > 1$.

We briefly observe here that when the discrete time dynamics makes use of a system matrix J the system matrix of the continuous time analog is given by $J - I$, I the identity matrix. The eigenvalues of the discrete time case are thus all shifted to the left by 1 in the continuous time analog. In the case of the considered dynamics this means that determinacy in the continuous time case implies determinacy in the discrete time case, but the same does not at all hold for indeterminacy in the place of determinacy. The discrete time case therefore can be determinate, though the continuous time case has been shown to be indeterminate, for example, simply because the stable roots of the continuous time case are situated to the left of -1. In this example, a very stable root in the continuous system may cause strong overshooting divergence in the discrete situation and thus turn stable roots into unstable ones. We would consider the occurrence of such a situation as resulting from over-synchronization in the considered market structure, since theoretical discrete time systems are then allowed only to react in the discrete point in time $t, t+1, \ldots$ Depending on the period length that is underlying the model this can mean (in the case of one quarter) that shopping can only be done every three months which – if implemented by law on an actual economy – would make it probably a very unstable one. Discrete time modeling is important in empirical analysis due to data availability, but should not be implemented as a theoretical model, unless it can be checked that it is not in stark contradiction compared to the case where all difference quotients are replaced by differential quotients. There are processes in agriculture and biology where discrete time analysis is reasonable by itself, but this statement does not carry over to the macrolevel of industrialized economies, where staggered price and wage setting is not restricted to four points in time within a year, and where therefore an assumption of this type can give rise to instability results simply due to over-synchronization and a lack of smoothness, aspects that are very questionable from a macroeconomic point of view. We conclude that the lack of determinacy in continuous time is also a problem for the discrete time analog that should not be overcome by making the period length so large that stable processes are in fact turned into unstable ones.

There are a variety of critical arguments raised in the literature against the New Phillips curve (NPC) of the baseline model of Keynesian macrodynamics; see in particular Mankiw (2001) and recently Eller and Gordon (2003) for particularly strong statements.[2] These and other criticisms in our view will also apply to the above extended wage and price dynamics. In order to overcome these and other critiques we here propose some modifications to the above presentation of the wage–price dynamics which will remove from it completely the questionable feature of a sign reversal for the role of output and wage gaps. This sign reversal is caused by the fact that future values of the considered state values are used on the right hand side of their determining equations, which implies that the time rates of change of these variables depend on output and wage gaps with a reversed sign in front on them. These sign reversals are at the root of the problem when the empirical relevance of such NPCs is investigated. We instead will make use of the following expectations augmented wage and price PCs:

$$d \ln w_{t+1} \overset{WPC}{=} \kappa_w d \ln p_{t+1} + (1 - \kappa_w)\pi_t^m + \beta_{wy} \ln Y_t - \beta_{w\omega} \ln \omega_t]$$

$$d \ln p_{t+1} \overset{PPC}{=} \kappa_p d \ln w_{t+1} + (1 - \kappa_p)\pi_t^m + \beta_{py} \ln Y_t + \beta_{p\omega} \ln \omega_t]$$

We have modified the New Keynesian approach to wage and price dynamics here only with respect to the terms that concern expectations, in order to generate the potential for a wage–price spiral. We first assume that expectations formation is of

[2] With respect to the NPC it is stated in Mankiw (2001): "Although the new Keynesian Phillips curves has many virtues, it also has one striking vice: It is completely at odd with the facts."

a crossover type, with perfectly foreseen price inflation in the wage PC of workers and perfectly foreseen wage inflation in the price PC of firms. Furthermore, we make use in this regard of a neoclassical dating in the considered PCs, which means that – as is usually the case in the reduced-form PC – we have the same dating for expectations and actual wage and price formation on both sides of the PCs. Finally, following Chiarella and Flaschel (1996), we assume expectations formation to be of a hybrid type, where a certain weight is given to current (perfectly foreseen) inflation rates and the counterweight attached to a concept that we have dubbed the inflationary climate π^m that is surrounding the currently evolving wage–price spiral. We thus assume that workers as well as firms to a certain degree pay attention to whether the current situation is embedded in a high inflation regime or in a low inflation one.

These relatively straightforward modifications of the New Keynesian approach to expectations formation will imply for the dynamics of what we call a matured traditional Keynesian approach – to be completed in the next section – radically different solutions and stability features, with in particular no need to single out the steady state as the only relevant situation for economic analysis in the deterministic setup here considered. Concerning microfoundations for the assumed wage–price spiral we here only note that the wage PC can be microfounded as in Blanchard and Katz (1999), using standard labor market theories, giving rise to nearly exactly the form shown above (with the unemployment gap in the place of the logarithm of the output gap) if hybrid expectations formation is in addition embedded into their approach. Concerning the price PC a similar procedure may be applied based on desired markups of firms. Along these lines one in particular gets an economic motivation for the inclusion of – indeed the logarithm of – the real wage (or wage share) with negative sign into the wage PC and with positive sign into the price PC, without any need for loglinear approximations. We furthermore use the (un-)employment gap and the capacity utilization gap in these two PCs, respectively, in the place of a single measure (the log of the output gap). We conclude that the above wage–price spiral is an interesting alternative to the – theoretically rarely discussed and empirically questionable – New Keynesian form of wage–price dynamics. This wage–price spiral will be embedded into a complete Keynesian approach in the next section, exhibiting a dynamic IS equation as in Rudebusch and Svensson (1999), but now also including real wage effects and thus a role for income distribution, exhibiting furthermore Okun's law as the link from goods to labor markets, and exhibiting of course the classical type of a Taylor interest rate policy rule in the place of an LM curve.

3. Keynesian disequilibrium dynamics: Empirical reformulation of a baseline model

In this section, we reformulate the theoretical disequilibrium model of AS–AD growth of Asada *et al.* (2006) in order to obtain a somewhat simplified version that is more suitable for empirical estimation and for the study of the role of contemporary interest rate policy rules. We dispense with the LM curve of the original approach and replace it here by a Taylor-type policy rule. In addition, we use dynamic IS as well as employment equations in the place of the originally static ones, where with respect to the former the dependence of consumption and investment on income distribution now only appears in an aggregated format. We use Blanchard and Katz (1999) error-correction terms both in the wage and the price PC and thus give income distribution a role to play in wage as well as in price dynamics. Finally, we will again have inflationary inertia in a world of myopic perfect foresight through the inclusion of a medium-run variable, the inflationary climate in which the economy is operating, and its role for the wage–price dynamics of the considered economy.

We start from the observation that a Keynesian model of aggregate demand fluctuations should (independently of whether justification can be found for this in Keynes' General Theory) allow for under- (or over-)utilized labor *as well as* capital in order to be general enough from the descriptive point of view. As Barro (1994) for example observes, IS–LM is (or should be) based on imperfectly flexible wages and prices and thus on the consideration of wage as well price PCs. This is precisely what we will do in the following, augmented by the observation that also medium-run aspects count both in wage and price adjustments, here formulated in simple terms by the introduction of the concept of an inflation climate. We have moreover model-consistent expectations with respect to short-run wage and price inflation. The modification of the traditional AS–AD model that we shall consider thus treats – as already described in the preceding section – expectations in a hybrid way, with crossover myopic perfect foresight of the currently evolving rates of wage and price inflation on the one hand and an adaptive updating of an inflation climate expression with exponential or any other weighting schemes on the other hand.

We consequently assume, see also the preceding section, two PCs in the place of only one. In this way, we can discuss wage and price dynamics separately from each other, in their structural forms, now indeed both based on their own measure of demand pressure, namely $V^l - \bar{V}^l$, $V^c - \bar{V}^c$, in the market for labor and for goods, respectively. We here denote by V^l the rate of employment on the labor market and by $\bar{V}^l$ the NAIRU level of this rate, and similarly by V^c the rate of capacity utilization of the capital stock and $\bar{V}^c$ the normal rate of capacity utilization of firms. These demand pressure influences on wage and price dynamics, or on the formation of wage and price inflation rates; $\hat{w}$, $\hat{p}$, are both augmented by a weighted average of corresponding cost-pressure terms, based on forward-looking myopic perfect foresight $\hat{p}$, $\hat{w}$, respectively, and a backward-looking measure of the prevailing inflationary climate, symbolized by π^m.

We thereby arrive at the following two PCs for wage and price inflation, which in this core version of Keynesian AS–AD dynamics are – from a qualitative perspective – formulated in a fairly symmetric way.[3] We stress that we include forward-looking behavior here, without the need for an application of the jump variable technique of the rational expectations school in general and the New Keynesian approach in particular as will be shown in the next section.[4] The structural form of the wage–price dynamics:

$$\hat{w} = \beta_{w_1}(V^l - \bar{V}^l) - \beta_{w_2}(\ln \omega - \ln \omega_o) + \kappa_w \hat{p} + (1 - \kappa_w)\pi^m \tag{8.1}$$

$$\hat{p} = \beta_{p_1}(V^c - \bar{V}^c) + \beta_{p_2}(\ln \omega - \ln \omega_o) + \kappa_p \hat{w} + (1 - \kappa_p)\pi^m \tag{8.2}$$

Somewhat simplified versions of these two PCs have been estimated for the U.S. economy in various ways in Flaschel and Krolzig (2004), Flaschel *et al.* (2004) and Chen and Flaschel (2004), and have been found to represent a significant improvement over the conventional single reduced-form PC. A particular finding was that wage flexibility was greater than price flexibility with respect to their demand pressure measure in the market for goods and for labor,[5] respectively, and workers were more short-sighted than firms with respect to their cost pressure terms. Note that such a finding is not possible in the conventional framework of a single reduced-form PC. Inflationary expectations over the medium run, π^m, i.e., the inflationary climate in which current inflation is operating, may be adaptively following the actual rate of inflation (by use of some linear or exponential weighting scheme), may be based on a rolling sample (with hump-shaped weighting schemes), or on other possibilities for updating expectations. For simplicity of the exposition we shall make use of the conventional adaptive expectations mechanism in the theoretical part of this paper, namely

$$\dot{\pi}^m = \beta_{\pi^m}(\hat{p} - \pi^m) \tag{8.3}$$

Note that for our current version of the wage–price spiral, the inflationary climate variable does not matter for the evolution of the real wage $\omega = w/p$, the law of motion of which is given by (with $\kappa = 1/(1 - \kappa_w\kappa_p)$)

$$\hat{\omega} = \kappa[(1 - \kappa_p)(\beta_{w_1}(V^l - \bar{V}^l) - \beta_{w_2}(\ln \omega - \ln \omega_o)) - (1 - \kappa_w)(\beta_{p_1}(V^c - \bar{V}^c)$$
$$+ \beta_{p_2}(\ln \omega - \ln \omega_o))]$$

This follows easily from the following obviously equivalent representation of the

---

[3] With respect to empirical estimation one could also add the role of labor productivity growth. But this will not be done here in order to concentrate on the cycle component of the model, caused by changing income distribution in a world of stable goods market and interest rate dynamics. With respect to the distinction between real wages and unit wage costs we shall therefore detrend the corresponding time series such that the following types of PCs can still be applied.

[4] For a detailed comparison with the New Keynesian alternative to our model type see Chiarella *et al.* (2005).

[5] For lack of better terms we associate the degree of wage and price flexibility with the size of the parameters β_{w_1}, β_{p_1}, though of course the extent of these flexibilities will also depend on the size of the fluctuations of the excess demands in the market for labor and for goods, respectively.

above two PCs:

$$\hat{w} - \pi^m = \beta_{w_1}(V^l - \bar{V}^l) - \beta_{w_2}(\ln \omega - \ln \omega_o) + \kappa_w(\hat{p} - \pi^m)$$

$$\hat{p} - \pi^m = \beta_{p_1}(V^c - \bar{V}^c) + \beta_{p_2}(\ln \omega - \ln \omega_o)) + \kappa_p(\hat{w} - \pi^m)$$

by solving for the variables $\hat{w} - \pi^m$ and $\hat{p} - \pi^m$. It also implies the following two across-markets or *reduced-form PCs*:

$$\hat{p} = \kappa[\beta_{p_1}(V^c - \bar{V}^c) + \beta_{p_2}(\ln \omega - \ln \omega_o) + \kappa_p(\beta_{w_1}(V^l - \bar{V}^l)$$
$$- \beta_{w_2}(\ln \omega - \ln \omega_o))] + \pi^m$$

$$\hat{w} = \kappa[\beta_{w_1}(V^l - \bar{V}^l) - \beta_{w_2}(\ln \omega - \ln \omega_o)) + \kappa_w(\beta_{p_1}(V^c - \bar{V}^c)$$
$$+ \beta_{p_2}(\ln \omega - \ln \omega_o))] + \pi^m$$

which represent a considerable generalization of the conventional view of a single-market price PC with only one measure of demand pressure, the one in the labor market.

The remaining laws of motion of the private sector of the model are as follows:

$$\hat{V}^c = -\alpha_{V^c}(V^c - \bar{V}^c) \pm \alpha\omega(\ln \omega - \ln \omega_o) - \alpha_r((r - \hat{p}) - (r_o - \bar{\pi})) \tag{8.4}$$

$$\hat{V}^l = \alpha_{V_1^l}(V^c - \bar{V}^c) + \alpha_{V_2^l}\hat{V}^c \tag{8.5}$$

The first law of motion is of the type of a dynamic IS equation (see also Rudebusch and Svensson (1999) in this regard) here represented by the growth rate of the capacity utilization rate of firms. It has three important characteristics: (i) it reflects the dependence of output changes on aggregate income and thus on the rate of capacity utilization by assuming a negative, i.e., stable dynamic multiplier relationship in this respect, (ii) it shows the joint dependence of consumption and investment on the real wage (which in the aggregate may in principle allows for positive or negative signs before the parameter $\alpha\omega$, depending on whether consumption or investment is more responsive to real wage changes), and (iii) it shows finally the negative influence of the real rate of interest on the evolution of economic activity. Note here that we have generalized this law of motion in comparison to the one in the original baseline model of Asada *et al.* (2006), since we now allow for the possibility that also consumption, not only investment, depends on income distribution as measured by the real wage. We note that we also use $\ln \omega$ in the dynamic multiplier equation, since this variable will be used later on to estimate this equation.

In the second law of motion, for the rate of employment, we assume that the employment policy of firms follows – in the form of a generalized Okun law – the rate of capacity utilization (and the thereby implied rate of over- or underemployment of the employed workforce) partly with a lag (measured by $1/\beta_{V_1^l}$), and partly without a lag (through a positive parameter $\alpha_{V_2^l}$).

Employment is thus assumed to adjust to the level of current activity in somewhat delayed form which is a reasonable assumption from the empirical point of view. The second term, $\alpha_{V_2^l} \hat{V}^c$, is added to take account of the possibility that Okun's law may hold in level form rather than in the form of a law of motion, since this latter dependence can be shown to be equivalent to the use of a term $(V^c/\bar{V}^c)^{\alpha_{V_2^l}}$ when integrated, i.e., the form of Okun's law in which this law was originally specified by Okun (1970) himself.

The above two laws of motion therefore reformulate in a dynamic form the static IS curve (and the employment this curve implies) that was used in Asada *et al.* (2006). They only reflect implicitly the assumed dependence of the rate of capacity utilization on the real wage, due to on smooth factor substitution in production (and the measurement of the potential output this implies in Asada *et al.* (2006)), which constitutes another positive influence of the real wage on the rate of capacity utilization and its rate of change. This simplification helps to avoid the estimation of separate equations for consumption and investment, C, I, respectively and for potential output Y^p.

Finally, we no longer need to employ here a law of motion for real balances as was still the case in Asada *et al.* (2006). Money supply is now accommodating to the interest rate policy pursued by the Central Bank and thus does not feedback into the core laws of motion of the model. As interest rate policy we assume the following classical type of Taylor rule:

$$r^* = (r_o - \bar{\pi}) + \hat{p} + \alpha_p(\hat{p} - \bar{\pi}) + \alpha_{V^c}(V^c - \bar{V}^c) \tag{8.6}$$

$$\dot{r} = \alpha_r(r^* - r) \tag{8.7}$$

The target rate of the Central Bank r^* is here made dependent on the steady-state real rate of interest augmented by actual inflation back to a nominal rate, and is as usually dependent on the inflation gap and the capacity utilization gap (as measure of the output gap). With respect to this target there is then interest rate smoothing with strength α_r. Inserting r^* and rearranging terms we get from this expression the following form of a Taylor rule:

$$\dot{r} = -\gamma_r(r - r_o) + \gamma_p(\hat{p} - \bar{\pi}) + \gamma_{V^c}(V^c - \bar{V}^c) \tag{8.8}$$

where we have $\gamma_r = \alpha_r, \gamma_p = \alpha_r(1 + \alpha_p)$, i.e., $\alpha_p = \gamma_p/\alpha_r - 1$ and $\gamma_{V^c} = \alpha_r\alpha_{V^c}$.

We thus allow now for interest rate smoothing in this rule in contrast to Section 2. Furthermore, the actual (perfectly foreseen) rate of inflation $\hat{p}$ is used to measure the inflation gap with respect to the inflation target $\bar{\pi}$ of the Central Bank. Note finally that we could have included (but have not done this here yet) a new kind of gap into the above Taylor rule, the real wage gap, since we have in our model a dependence of aggregate demand on income distribution and the real wage. The state of income distribution matters for the dynamics of our model and thus should also play a role in the decisions of the Central Bank. All of the employed gaps are measured relative to the steady state of the model, in order to allow for an interest rate policy that is consistent with it.

We note that the steady state of the dynamics, due to its specific formulation, can be supplied exogenously. For reasons of notational simplicity we choose $V_o^c = \bar{V}^c = 1$, $V_o^l = \bar{V}^l = 1$, $\omega_o = 1$, $\pi_o^m = \bar{\pi} = 0.005$, $r_o = 0.02$ in the later estimation of the model by means of quarterly U.S. data. As the model is formulated now it exhibits five gaps, to be closed in the steady state and has five laws of motion, which when set equal to zero, exactly imply this result, since the determinant of the Jacobian of the dynamics is shown to be always nonzero in the next section of the paper. Note finally that the model becomes a linear one when utilization gaps are approximated by logs of utilization rates.

The steady state of the dynamics is locally asymptotically stable under certain sluggishness conditions that are reasonable from a Keynesian perspective, loses its asymptotic stability cyclically (by way of so-called Hopf bifurcations) if the system becomes too flexible, and becomes sooner or later globally unstable if (generally speaking) adjustment speeds become too high, as we shall show below. If the model is subject to explosive forces, it requires extrinsic nonlinearities in economic behavior – like downward money wage rigidity – to manifest themselves at least far off the steady state in order to bound the dynamics to an economically meaningful domain in the considered 5D state space. Chen *et al.* (2006) provide a variety of numerical studies for such an approach with extrinsically motivated nonlinearities and thus undertake its detailed numerical investigation. In sum, therefore, our dynamic AS–AD growth model here and there will exhibit a variety of features that are much more in line with a Keynesian understanding of the characteristics of the trade cycle than is the case for the conventional modeling of AS–AD growth dynamics or its radical reformulation by the New Keynesians (where – if nondeterminacy can be avoided by the choice of an appropriate Taylor rule – only the steady-state position is a meaningful solution in the related setup we considered in the preceding section).

Taken together the model of this section consists of the following five laws of motion (with the derived reduced-form expressions as far as the wage–price spiral is concerned and with reduced-form expressions by assumption concerning the goods and the labor market dynamics):[6]

$$\hat{V}^c \overset{Dyn.IS}{=} -\alpha_{V^c}(V^c - \bar{V}^c) \pm \alpha\omega(\ln\omega - \ln\omega_o) - \alpha_r((r - \hat{p}) - (r_o - \bar{\pi})) \tag{8.9}$$

$$\hat{V}^l \overset{O.Law}{=} \beta_{V_1^l}(V^c - \bar{V}^c) + \beta_{V_2^l}\hat{V}^c \tag{8.10}$$

$$\dot{r} \overset{T.Rule}{=} -\gamma_r(r - r_o) + \gamma_p(\hat{p} - \bar{\pi}) + \gamma_{V^c}(V^c - \bar{V}^c) \tag{8.11}$$

---

[6] As the model is formulated we have no real anchor for the steady-state rate of interest (via investment behavior and the rate of profit it implies in the steady state) and thus have to assume here that it is the monetary authority that enforces a certain steady-state values for the nominal rate of interest.

$$\hat{\omega} \stackrel{RWPC}{=} \theta = \kappa[(1 - \kappa_p)(\beta_{w_1}(V^l - \bar{V}^l) - \beta_{w_2}(\ln \omega - \ln \omega_o))$$
$$- (1 - \kappa_w)(\beta_{p_1}(V^c - \bar{V}^c) + \beta_{p_2}(\ln \omega - \ln \omega_o))], \quad \theta = \ln \omega \quad (8.12)$$

$$\dot{\pi}^m \stackrel{I.Climate}{=} \beta_{\pi^m}(\hat{p} - \pi^m) \quad \text{or} \quad (8.13)$$

$$\pi^m(t) = \pi^m(t_o)e^{-\beta_{\pi^m}(t-t_o)} + \beta_{\pi^m} \int_{t_o}^t e^{\beta_{\pi^m}(t-s)}\hat{p}(s)\,ds$$

The above equations represent, in comparison to the baseline model of New Keynesian macroeconomics, the IS goods market dynamics (8.9), here augmented by Okun's law as link between the goods and the labor market (8.10), and of course the Taylor rule (8.11), and a law of motion (8.12) for the real wage $\hat{\omega} = \pi^w - \pi^p$ that makes use of the same explaining variables as the New Keynesian one considered in Section 2 (but with inflation rates in the place of their time rates of change and with no accompanying sign reversal concerning the influence of output and wage gaps), and finally the law of motion (8.13) that describes the updating of the inflationary climate expression.[7] We have to make use in addition of the following reduced-form expression for the price inflation rate or the price PC, our law of motion for the price level p in the place of the New Keynesian law of motion for the price inflation rate π^p:

$$\hat{p} = \kappa[\beta_{p_1}(V^c - \bar{V}^c) + \beta_{p_2}(\ln \omega - \ln \omega_o)$$
$$+ \kappa_p(\beta_{w_1}(V^l - \bar{V}^l) - \beta_{w_2}(\ln \omega - \ln \omega_o))] + \pi^m \quad (8.14)$$

which has to be inserted into the above laws of motion in various places in order to get an autonomous nonlinear system of differential equations in the state variables: capacity utilization V^c, the rate of employment V^l, the nominal rate of interest r, the real wage rate ω, and the inflationary climate expression π^m. We stress that one can consider Equation (8.14) as a sixth law of motion of the considered dynamics which however – when added – leads a system determinant which is zero and which therefore allows for zero-root hysteresis for certain variables of the model (in fact in the price level if the target rate of inflation of the Central Bank is zero and if interest rate smoothing is present in the Taylor rule). We have written the laws of motion in an order that first presents the dynamic equations also present in the baseline New Keynesian model of inflation dynamics, and then our formulation of the dynamics of income distribution and of the inflationary climate in which the economy is operating.

With respect to the empirically motivated restructuring of the original theoretical framework, the model is as pragmatic as the approach employed by

---

[7] In correspondence to the Blanchard and Katz error-correction terms in our wage and price PC, here we also make use of the log of the real wage in the law of motion which describes goods market dynamics, partly due also to our later estimation of the model.

Rudebusch and Svensson (1999). By and large we believe that it represents a working alternative to the New Keynesian approach, in particular when the current critique of the latter approach is taken into account. It overcomes the weaknesses and the logical inconsistencies of the old Neoclassical synthesis, see Asada et al. (2006), and it does so in a minimal way from a mature, but still traditionally oriented Keynesian perspective (and is thus not really 'New'). It preserves the problematic stability features of the real rate of interest channel, where the stabilizing Keynes effect or the interest rate policy of the Central Bank is interacting with the destabilizing, expectations-driven Mundell effect. It preserves the real wage effect of the old Neoclassical synthesis, where – due to an unambiguously negative dependence of aggregate demand on the real wage – we had that price flexibility was destabilizing, while wage flexibility was not. This real wage channel is not really discussed in the New Keynesian approach, due to the specific form of wage–price dynamics there considered, see the preceding section, and it is summarized in Figure 8.1 for the situation where investment dominates consumption with respect to real wage changes. In the opposite case, the situations considered in this figure will be reversed with respect to their stability implications.

The feedback channels just discussed will be the focus of interest in the now following stability analysis of our D (isequilibrium) AS–D (isequilibrium) AD dynamics. We have employed reduced-form expressions in the above system of differential equations whenever possible. We have thereby obtained a dynamical system in five state variables that is in a natural or intrinsic way nonlinear (due to its reliance on growth rate formulations). We note that there are many items that reappear in various equations, or are similar to each other, implying that stability analysis can exploit a variety of linear dependencies in the calculation of the conditions for local asymptotic stability. This dynamical system will be investigated in the next section in somewhat informal terms with respect to some stability assertions to which it gives rise. A rigorous proof of local asymptotic stability and its loss by way of Hopf bifurcations can be found in Asada et al. (2006), for the original baseline model. For the present model variant we supply a more detailed stability proofs in Chen et al. (2006), where also more detailed numerical simulations of the model are provided.

4. 5D Feedback-guided stability analysis

In this section, we illustrate an important method to prove local asymptotic stability of the interior steady state of the dynamical system (8.9)–(8.13) (with Equation (8.14) inserted wherever needed) through partial considerations from the feedback chains that characterize this empirically oriented baseline model of Keynesian dynamics. Since the model is an extension of the standard AS–AD growth model, we know from the literature that there is a real rate of interest effect typically involved, first analyzed by formal methods in Tobin (1975) (see also Groth, 1992). Instead of the stabilizing Keynes effect, based on

Figure 8.1. The Rose effects: the real wage channel of Keynesian macrodynamics

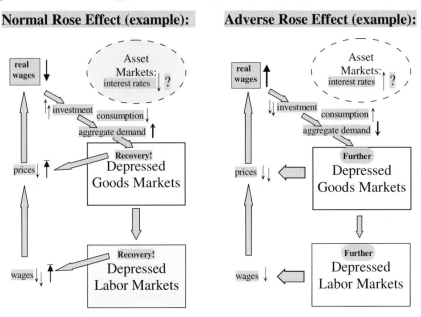

activity-reducing nominal interest rate increases following price level increases, we have here however a direct steering of economic activity by the interest rate policy of the Central Bank. Since the (correctly anticipated) short-run real rate of interest is driving investment and consumption decisions (increases leading to decreased aggregate demand), there is furthermore the activity stimulating (partial) effect of increases in the rate of inflation (as part of the real rate of interest channel) that may lead to accelerating inflation under appropriate conditions. This is the so-called Mundell effect that normally works in opposition to the Keynes effect, but through the same real rate of interest channel as this latter effect. Owing to our use of a Taylor rule in the place of the conventional LM curve, the Keynes effect is here implemented in a more direct way toward a stabilization of the economy (coupling nominal interest rates directly with the rate of price inflation) and it is supposed to work more strongly if larger is the choice of the parameters γ_p, γ_{V^c}. The Mundell effect by contrast is stronger if the inflationary climate adjusts to the present level of price inflation faster, since we have a positive influence of this climate variable both on price as well as on wage inflation and from there on rates of employment of both capital and labor.

There is a further important potentially (at least partially) destabilizing feedback mechanism as the model is formulated. Excess profitability depends positively on the rate of return on capital and thus negatively on the real wage ω. We thus get – since consumption may also depend (positively) on the real wage – that real wage increases can depress or stimulate economic activity depending on whether investment or consumption is dominating the outcome of real wage increases (we here neglect the stabilizing role of the additional Blanchard and Katz-type error-correction mechanisms). In the first case, we get from the reduced-form real wage dynamics

$$\hat{\omega} = \kappa[(1 - \kappa_p)\beta_{w_1}(V^l - \bar{V}^l) - (1 - \kappa_w)\beta_{p_1}(V^c - \bar{V}^c)]$$

that price flexibility should be bad for economic stability, due to the minus sign in front of the parameter β_p, while the opposite should hold true for the parameter that characterizes wage flexibility. This is a situation that was already investigated in Rose (1967). It gives the reason for our statement that wage flexibility gives rise to normal, and price flexibility to adverse, Rose effects as far as real wage adjustments are concerned (if it is assumed – as in our theoretical baseline model – that only investment depends on the real wage). Besides real rate of interest effects, establishing opposing Keynes- and Mundell effects, we thus have also another real adjustment process in the considered model where now wage and price flexibility are in opposition to each other, see Chiarella and Flaschel (2000) and Chiarella *et al.* (2000) for further discussion of these as well as of other feedback mechanisms of such Keynesian growth dynamics. We observe again that our theoretical DAS–AD growth dynamics in Asada *et al.* (2006) – due to their origin in the baseline model of the Neoclassical Synthesis, stage I – allows for negative influence of real wage changes on aggregate demand solely, and thus only for cases of destabilizing wage level flexibility, but not price level flexibility. In the empirical estimation of the model (8.9)–(8.13), we will indeed find that this case seems to be the one that characterizes our empirically and broader oriented dynamics (8.9)–(8.13).

The foregoing discussion enhances our understanding of the feedback mechanisms of the dynamical system (8.9)–(8.13) whose stability properties will now be investigated by means of varying adjustment speed parameters appropriately. With the feedback scenarios considered above in mind, we first observe that the inflationary climate can be frozen at its steady-state value, $\pi_o^m = \bar{\pi}$, if $\beta_{\pi^m} = 0$ is assumed. The system thereby becomes 4D and it can indeed be further reduced to 3D if in addition $\alpha\omega = 0$, $\beta_{w_2} = 0$, $\beta_{p_2} = 0$ is assumed, since this decouples the ω-dynamics from the remaining system dynamics V^c, V^l, r. We will consider the stability of these 3D subdynamics – and its subsequent extensions – in informal terms only here, reserving rigorous calculations to the alternative scenarios provided in Chen *et al.* (2006). We nevertheless hope to be able to demonstrate to the reader how one can indeed proceed systematically from low- to high-dimensional analysis in such stability investigations from the perspective of the partial feedback channels implicitly contained in the considered 5D dynamics. This method has been already applied successfully to various other, often more complicated, dynamical systems; see Asada *et al.* (2003) for a variety of typical examples.

Before we start with our stability investigations we establish the fact that for the dynamical system (8.7)–(8.11) loss of stability can in general only occur by way of Hopf bifurcations, since the following proposition can be shown to hold true under mild – empirically plausible – parameter restrictions.

Proposition 1. *Assume that the parameter γ_r is chosen sufficiently small and that the parameters β_{w_2}, β_{p_2}, κ_p fulfill $\beta_{p_2} > \beta_{w_2}\kappa_p$. Then the 5D determinant of the Jacobian of the dynamics at the interior steady state is always negative in sign.*

Proof (*sketch*). We have for the sign structure in the Jacobian under the given assumptions the following situation to start with (we here assume as limiting situation $\gamma_r = 0$ and have already simplified the law of motion for V^l by means of the one for V^c through row operations that are irrelevant for the size of the determinant to be calculated):

$$J = \begin{pmatrix} \pm & + & - & \pm & + \\ + & 0 & 0 & 0 & 0 \\ + & + & 0 & + & + \\ - & + & 0 & - & 0 \\ + & + & 0 & + & 0 \end{pmatrix}$$

We note that the ambiguous sign in the entry J_{11} in the above matrix is due to the fact that the real rate of interest is a decreasing function of the inflation rate which in turn depends positively on current rates of capacity utilization.

Using the second row and the last row in their dependence on the partial derivatives of $\hat{p}$ we can reduce this Jacobian to

$$J = \begin{pmatrix} 0 & 0 & - & \pm & + \\ + & 0 & 0 & 0 & 0 \\ 0 & 0 & 0 & 0 & + \\ 0 & + & 0 & - & 0 \\ 0 & + & 0 & + & 0 \end{pmatrix}$$

without change in the sign of its determinant. In the same way we can now use the third row to get another matrix without any change in the sign of the corresponding determinants:

$$J = \begin{pmatrix} 0 & 0 & - & \pm & 0 \\ + & 0 & 0 & 0 & 0 \\ 0 & 0 & 0 & 0 & + \\ 0 & + & 0 & - & 0 \\ 0 & + & 0 & + & 0 \end{pmatrix}$$

The last two columns can under the observed circumstances be further reduced to

$$
J = \begin{pmatrix}
0 & 0 & - & \pm & 0 \\
+ & 0 & 0 & 0 & 0 \\
0 & 0 & 0 & 0 & + \\
0 & + & 0 & 0 & 0 \\
0 & 0 & 0 & + & 0
\end{pmatrix}
$$

which finally gives

$$
J = \begin{pmatrix}
0 & 0 & - & 0 & 0 \\
+ & 0 & 0 & 0 & 0 \\
0 & 0 & 0 & 0 & + \\
0 & + & 0 & 0 & 0 \\
0 & 0 & 0 & + & 0
\end{pmatrix}
$$

This matrix is easily shown to exhibit a negative determinant which proves the
proposition, also for all values of γ_r which are chosen sufficiently small. ∎

Proposition 2. *Assume that the parameters β_{w_2}, β_{p_2}, $\alpha\omega$ and β_{π^m} are all set equal to
zero. This decouples the dynamics of V^c, V^l, r from the rest of the system. Assume
furthermore that the partial derivative of the first law of motion (8.7) depends
negatively on V^c, i.e., $\alpha_{V^c} > \alpha_r \kappa \beta_{p_1}$, so that the dynamic multiplier process,
characterized by α_{V^c}, dominates this law of motion with respect to the overall
impact of the rate of capacity utilization V^c. Then the interior steady state of the
implied 3D dynamical system*

$$
\hat{V}^c = -\alpha_{V^c}(V^c - \bar{V}^c) - \alpha_r((r - \hat{p}) - (r_o - \bar{\pi})) \tag{8.15}
$$

$$
\hat{V}^l = \beta_{V_1^l}(V^c - \bar{V}^c) \tag{8.16}
$$

$$
\dot{r} = -\gamma_r(r - r_o) + \gamma_p(\hat{p} - \bar{\pi}) + \gamma_{V^c}(V^c - \bar{V}^c) \tag{8.17}
$$

*is locally asymptotically stable if the interest rate smoothing parameter γ_r and the
employment adjustment parameter β_{V^l} are chosen sufficiently small in addition.*

Proof (*sketch*). In the considered situation we have for the Jacobian of these
reduced dynamics at the steady state

$$
J = \begin{pmatrix}
- & + & - \\
+ & 0 & 0 \\
+ & + & -
\end{pmatrix}
$$

The determinant of this Jacobian is obviously negative if the parameter γ_r is
chosen sufficiently small. Similarly, the sum of the minors of order 2: a_2, will be
positive if β_{V^l} is chosen sufficiently small. The validity of the full set of

Routh–Hurwitz conditions then easily follows, since trace $J = -a_1$ is obviously negative and since det J is part of the expressions that characterize the product $a_1 a_2$. ■

Proposition 3. *Assume now that the parameter $\alpha\omega$ is negative, but chosen sufficiently small, while the error-correction parameters β_{w_2}, β_{p_2} are still kept at zero. Then the interior steady state of the resulting 4D dynamical system (where the state variable ω is now included)*

$$\hat{V}^c = -\alpha_{V^c}(V^c - \bar{V}^c) - \alpha\omega(\ln\omega - \ln\omega_o) - \alpha_r((r - \hat{p}) - (r_o - \bar{\pi})) \tag{8.18}$$

$$\hat{V}^l = \beta_{V_1^l}(V^c - \bar{V}^c) \tag{8.19}$$

$$\dot{r} = -\gamma_r(r - r_o) + \gamma_p(\hat{p} - \bar{\pi}) + \gamma_{V^c}(V^c - \bar{V}^c) \tag{8.20}$$

$$\hat{\omega} = \kappa[(1 - \kappa_p)\beta_{w_1}(V^l - \bar{V}^l) - (1 - \kappa_w)\beta_{p_1}(V^c - \bar{V}^c) \tag{8.21}$$

is locally asymptotically stable.

Proof (*sketch*). It suffices to show in the considered situation that the determinant of the resulting Jacobian at the steady state is positive, since small variations of the parameter $\alpha\omega$ must then move the zero eigenvalue of the case $\alpha\omega = 0$ into the negative domain, while leaving the real parts of the other eigenvalues – shown to be negative in the preceding proposition – negative. The determinant of the Jacobian to be considered here – already slightly simplified – is characterized by

$$J = \begin{pmatrix} 0 & + & - & - \\ + & 0 & 0 & 0 \\ 0 & + & - & 0 \\ 0 & + & 0 & 0 \end{pmatrix}$$

This can be further simplified to

$$J = \begin{pmatrix} 0 & 0 & 0 & - \\ + & 0 & 0 & 0 \\ 0 & 0 & - & 0 \\ 0 & + & 0 & 0 \end{pmatrix}$$

without change in the sign of the corresponding determinant which proves the proposition. ■

We note that this proposition also holds where $\beta_{p_2} > \beta_{w_2}\kappa_p$ holds true as long as the thereby resulting real wage effect is weaker than the one originating from $\alpha\omega$. Finally – and in sum – we can also state that the full 5D dynamics must also exhibit a locally stable steady state if β_{π^m} is made positive, but chosen sufficiently small, since we have already shown that the full 5D dynamics exhibits a negative determinant of its Jacobian at the steady state under the stated conditions.

Increasing β_{π^m} from zero to a small positive value therefore must move the corresponding zero eigenvalue into the negative domain of the plane of complex numbers.

Summing up, we can state that a weak Mundell effect, the neglect of Blanchard–Katz error-correction terms, a negative dependence of aggregate demand on real wages, coupled with nominal wage and also to some extent price level inertia (in order to allow for dynamic multiplier stability), a sluggish adjustment of the rate of employment toward actual capacity utilization and a Taylor rule that stresses inflation targeting therefore are here (for example) the basic ingredients that allow for the proof of local asymptotic stability of the interior steady state of the dynamics (8.9)–(8.13). We expect however that indeed a variety of other and also more general situations of convergent dynamics can be found, but have to leave this here for future research and numerical simulations of the model. Instead we now attempt to estimate the signs and also the sizes of the parameters of the model in order to gain insight into the question to what extent for example the U.S. economy after World War II supports one of the real wage effects considered in Figure 8.1 and also the possibility of overall asymptotic stability for such an economy, despite a destabilizing Mundell effect in the real interest rate channel. Owing to Proposition 1 we know that the dynamics will generally only lose asymptotic stability in a cyclical fashion (by way of a Hopf bifurcation) and will indeed do so if the parameter β_{π^m} is chosen sufficiently large. We thus arrive at a radically different outcome for the dynamics implied by our mature traditional Keynesian approach as compared to the New Keynesian dynamics. The question that naturally arises here is whether the economy can be assumed to be in the convergent regime of its alternative dynamical possibilities. This of course can only be decided by an empirical estimation of its various parameters which is the subject of the next section.

5. *Estimating the model*

We now provide some estimates for the signs and sizes of the parameters of the model of this paper and will do so – with respect to the wage–price spiral – on the level of its structural form (where it has not yet been reduced to the dynamics of real wages, see Equation (8.14)). The further aim of these estimates is of course to determine whether the equivalent autonomous reduced-form 5D dynamics we considered in the preceding section – obtained when Equation (8.14) is inserted into (8.9)–(8.13) – exhibits asymptotic stability of (convergence to) its interior steady-state position. We proceed in three steps in this matter, first by estimating an unrestricted VAR approach for the core variables of the model, secondly by comparing its results with a linear structural VAR model that is a linear approximation of the (weakly) nonlinear model of the theoretical part of the paper and finally by estimating and evaluating this latter approach in comparison to the result achieved in step 2. The central aim of these estimations is to determine the signs and sizes of the entries in the Jacobian matrix of the considered dynamics, which indeed will allow us later on to formulate certain specific (in)stability propositions on the in fact, then 4D dynamics implied by our estimates of Okun's law.

In their theoretical form these dynamics exhibit the following sign structure in their Jacobian, calculated at its interior steady state:

$$
J = \begin{pmatrix}
\pm & + & - & \pm & + \\
\pm & + & - & \pm & + \\
+ & + & - & \pm & + \\
- & + & 0 & - & 0 \\
+ & + & 0 & \pm & 0
\end{pmatrix}
$$

There are therefore still a variety of ambiguous effects embedded in the general theoretical form of the dynamics, due to the Mundell effect and the Rose effect in the dynamics of the goods-market and the opposing Blanchard–Katz error-correction terms in the reduced-form price PC.

In Section 4, we have then considered certain special cases of the general model which allowed for the derivation of asymptotic stability of the steady state and its loss of stability by way of Hopf bifurcations if certain speed parameters become sufficiently large. In the present section, we now provide empirical estimates for the laws of motion (8.9)–(8.13) of our disequilibrium AS–AD model, by means of the structural form of the wage and price PC, coupled with the dynamic multiplier equation, Okun's law and the interest rate policy rule. These estimates, on the one hand, serve the purpose of confirming the parameter signs we have specified in the initial theory-guided formulation of the model and to determine the sizes of these parameters in addition. On the other hand, we have three different situations where we cannot specify the parameter signs on purely theoretical grounds and where we therefore aim at obtaining these signs from the empirical estimates of the equations whenever this happens.

There is first of all, see Equation (8.9), the ambiguous influence of real wages on (the dynamics of) the rate of capacity utilization, which should be a negative one if investment is more responsive than consumption to real wage changes and a positive one in the opposite case. There is secondly, with an immediate impact effect if the rates of capacity utilization for capital and labor are perfectly synchronized, the fact that real wages rise with economic activity through money wage changes on the labor market, while they fall with it through price level changes on the goods market, see Equation (8.11). Finally, we have in the reduced-form equation for price inflation a further ambiguous effect of real wage increases, which lower $\hat{p}$ through their effect on wage inflation, while speeding up $\hat{p}$ through their effect on price inflation, effects which work into opposite directions in the reduced-form price PC (8.14). Mundell-type, Rose-type and Blanchard–Katz error-correction feedback channels therefore make the dynamics indeterminate on the general level.

In all of these three cases empirical analysis will now indeed provide us with definite answers as to which ones of these opposing forces will be the dominant ones. Furthermore, we shall also see that the Blanchard and Katz (1999) error-correction terms do play a role in the U.S. economy, in contrast to what has been found out by these authors for the money wage PC in the U.S. However, we will not attempt to estimate the parameter β_{π^m} that characterizes the evolution of the inflationary climate in our economy. Instead, we will use moving averages with linearly declining weights for its representation, which allows us to bypass the estimation of the law of motion (8.13). We consider this as the simplest approach to the treatment of our climate expression (comparable with recent New Keynesian treatments of hybrid expectation formation), which should later on be replaced by more sophisticated ones, for example one that makes use of the Livingston index for inflationary expectations as in Laxton *et al.* (2000), which in our view mirrors some adaptive mechanism in the adjustment of inflationary expectations.

We take an encompassing approach to conduct our estimates. The structural laws of motion of our economy (see Section 3) have been formulated in an intrinsically nonlinear way (due to certain growth rate formulations). We note that single equation estimates have suggested the use of only $\alpha_{V_1^l}$ in the equation that describes the dynamics of the employment rate. In the wage–price spiral we use – in line with Blanchard and Katz's theoretical derivation (1999) – the log of unit wage costs, removing their significant downward trend in the employed data (see Figure 8.2) appropriately. Note here again that we use the log of the unit wage costs in the dynamic multiplier equations as well.

We conduct our estimates in conjunction with time-invariant estimates of all the parameters of our model. This in particular implies that Keynes' (1936) explanation of the trade cycle, which employed systematic changes in the propensity to consume, the marginal efficiency of investment and liquidity preference over the course of the cycle, find no application here and that – due the use of detrended measures for income distribution changes and unit wage costs – also the role of technical change is downplayed to a significant degree, in line with its neglect in the theoretical equations of the model presented in Section 3. As a result we expect to obtain from our estimates long-phased economic fluctuations, but not yet long waves, since important fluctuations in aggregate demand (based on time-varying parameters) are still ignored and since the dynamics is then driven primarily by slowly changing income distribution, indeed a slow process in the overall evolution of the U.S. economy after World War II.

To show that such an understanding of the model is a suitable description of (some of) the dynamics of the observed data, we first fit a corresponding 6D VAR model to the data to uncover the dynamics in the six independent variables there employed. We then identify a linear structural model that parsimoniously encompasses the employed VAR. Finally, we contrast our nonlinear structural model, i.e., the laws of motion (8.1)–(8.5) in structural form (and the Taylor rule),

Figure 8.2. **The fundamental data of the model (*uc* bandpass-filtered)**

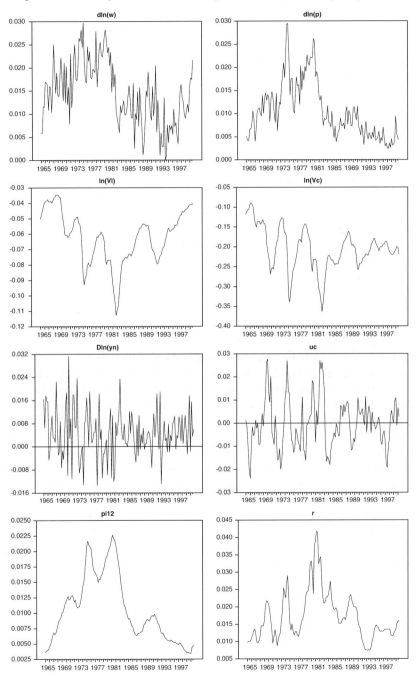

with the linear structural VAR model and show through a J test[8] that the nonlinear model is indeed preferred by the data. In this way we show that our (weakly) nonlinear structural model represents a proper description of the data.

The relevant variables for the following investigation are the wage inflation rate, the price inflation rate, the rates of utilization of labor and of capital, the nominal interest rate, the log of average unit wage cost,[9] to be denoted in the following by: $d \ln w_t$, $d \ln p_t$, V_t^l, V_t^c, r_t and uc_t, where uc_t is the cycle component of the log of the time series for the unit real wage cost, filtered by the bandpass filter.[10]

5.1. Data description

The empirical data of the corresponding time series are taken from the Federal Reserve Bank of St. Louis data set (see http:/www.stls.frb.org/fred). The data are quarterly, seasonally adjusted and concern the period from 1965:1 to 2001:2. Except for the unemployment rates of the factors labor, U^l, and capital, U^c (and of course the interest rate and the derived inflation climate) the log of the series are used in Table 8.1 (note however that the intermediate estimation step of a linear structural VAR makes use of the logs of both utilization rates however, see also their representation in Figure 8.2).

We now use $\ln w_t$ and $\ln p_t$, i.e., logarithms, in the place of the original level magnitudes. Their first differences $d \ln w_t$, $d \ln p_t$ thus give the current rate of wage and price inflation (backwardly dated). We use π_t^{12} in this section to denote specifically a moving average of price inflation rates with linearly decreasing weights over the past 12 quarters, interpreted as a particularly simple measure for the inflationary climate expression of our model, and we denote by V^l, $V^c(U^l, U^c)$ the rates of (under-)utilization of labor and the capital stock.

There is a pronounced downward trend in part of the employment rate series (over the 1970s and part of the 1980s) and in the wage share (normalized to 0 in 1996). The latter trend is not the topic of this chapter which concentrates on the cyclical implications of change in income distribution. Wage inflation shows three trend reversals, while the inflation climate representation clearly show two periods of low inflation regimes and in between a high inflation regime.

We expect that the six independent time series for wages, prices, capacity utilization rates, the growth rate of labor productivity and the interest rate

---

[8] See Davidson and Mackinnon (1993) for details.
[9] Or alternatively the real wage which does not modify the obtained results in significant ways.
[10] For details on the bandpass filter see Baxter and King (1995, 1999).

Table 8.1. Data used for the empirical investigation

Variable	Transformation	Mnemonic	Description of the Untransformed Series
$U^l = 1 - V^l$	UNRATE/100	UNRATE	Unemployment rate
$U^c = 1 - V^c$	1-CUMFG/100	CUMFG	Capacity utilization: manufacturing, percent of capacity
$\ln w$	ln(COMPNFB)	COMPNFB	Nonfarm business sector: compensation per hour, 1992 = 100
$\ln p$	ln(GDPDEF)	GDPDEF	Gross domestic product: implicit price deflator, 1996 = 100
$\ln yn = \ln y - \ln l^d$	ln(OPHNFB)	OPHNFB	Nonfarm business sector; output per hour of all persons, 1992 = 100
uc	$\ln\left(\frac{COMPRNFB}{OPHNFB}\right)$	COMPRNFB	Nonfarm business sector: real compensation per output unit, 1992 = 100
$d \ln yn$	$d \ln(OPHNFB)$	OPHNFB	Growth rate of labor productivity
r	FEDFUNDS	FEDFUNDS	Federal funds rate

(federal funds rate) are stationary. The graphs of the series for wage and price inflation, capacity utilization rates, $d \ln w_t$, $d \ln p_t$, $\ln V_t^l$, $\ln V_t^c$ seem to confirm our expectation. In addition, we carry out the DF unit-root test for each series. The test results are shown in Table 8.2.

The applied unit root test confirms our expectations with the exception of V^l and r. Although the test cannot reject the null of a unit root, there is no reason to expect the rate of unemployment and the federal funds rate to be unit root processes. Indeed we expect that they are constrained in certain limited ranges, say from zero to 0.3. Because of the lower power of the DF test, this test result should only provide hints that the rate of unemployment and the federal funds rate exhibit strong autocorrelations, respectively.

5.2. Estimation of the unrestricted VAR

Given the assumption of stationarity, we can construct a VAR model for the six variables of the structural model to mimic their DGP (data generating process of these six variables) by linearizing our given structural model in a straightforward way.

Table 8.2.   Summary of DF-test results

Variable	Sample	Critical Value	Test Statistic
$d \ln w$	1965:01 to 2000:04	-3.41000	-3.74323
$d \ln p$	1965:01 to 2000:04	-3.41000	-3.52360
$\ln V^l$	1965:01 to 2000:04	-2.86000	-2.17961
$\ln V^c$	1965:01 to 2000:04	-3.41000	-3.92688
r	1965:01 to 2000:04	-2.86000	-2.67530

$$
\begin{pmatrix} d \ln w_t \\ d \ln p_t \\ \ln V^l_t \\ \ln V^c_t \\ r_t \\ uc_t \end{pmatrix} = \begin{pmatrix} c_1 \\ c_2 \\ c_3 \\ c_4 \\ c_5 \\ c_6 \end{pmatrix} + \begin{pmatrix} b_1 \\ b_2 \\ b_3 \\ b_4 \\ b_5 \\ b_6 \end{pmatrix} d74 + \sum_{k=1}^{P} \begin{pmatrix} a_{11k} & a_{12k} & a_{13k} & a_{14k} & a_{15k} & a_{16k} \\ a_{21k} & a_{22k} & a_{23k} & a_{24k} & a_{25k} & a_{26k} \\ a_{31k} & a_{32k} & a_{33k} & a_{34k} & a_{35k} & a_{36k} \\ a_{41k} & a_{42k} & a_{43k} & a_{44k} & a_{45k} & a_{46k} \\ a_{51k} & a_{52k} & a_{53k} & a_{54k} & a_{55k} & a_{56k} \\ a_{61k} & a_{62k} & a_{63k} & a_{64k} & a_{65k} & a_{66k} \end{pmatrix}
$$

$$
\times \begin{pmatrix} d \ln w_{t-k} \\ d \ln p_{t-k} \\ \ln V^l_{t-k} \\ \ln V^c_{t-k} \\ r_{t-k} \\ uc_{t-k} \end{pmatrix} + \begin{pmatrix} e_{1t} \\ e_{2t} \\ e_{3t} \\ e_{4t} \\ e_{5t} \end{pmatrix} \tag{8.22}
$$

To determine the lag length of the VAR we apply sequential likelihood tests. We start with a lag length of 24, at which the residuals can be taken as white noise process. The sequence likelihood ratio test procedure gives a lag length of 11. The test results are listed below.

- $H_0 : P = 20$ vs. $H_1 : P = 24$
  $\chi^2(144) = 147.13$ with significance level 0.91
- $H_0 : P = 16$ vs. $H_1 : P = 20$
  $\chi^2(144) = 148.92$ with significance level 0.41
- $H_0 : P = 12$ vs. $H_1 : P = 16$
  $\chi^2(36) = 118.13$ with significance level 0.94
- $H_0 : P = 11$ vs. $H_1 : P = 12$
  $\chi^2(36) = 42.94$ with significance level 0.19
- $H_0 : P = 10$ vs. $H_1 : P = 11$
  $\chi^2(36) = 51.30518$ with significance level 0.04

According to these test results we use a VAR(12) model to represent a general model that should be a good approximation of the DGP. Because the variable

uc_t is treated as exogenous in the structural form (8.1)–(8.8) of the dynamical system, we factorize the VAR(12) process into a conditional process of $d \ln w_t$, $d \ln p_t$, $\ln V_t^l$, $\ln V_t^c$, r_t given uc_t and the lagged variables, and the marginal process of uc_t given the lagged variables.

$$
\begin{pmatrix} d \ln w_t \\ d \ln p_t \\ \ln V_t^l \\ \ln V_t^c \\ r_t \end{pmatrix} = \begin{pmatrix} c_1^* \\ c_2^* \\ c_3^* \\ c_4^* \\ c_5^* \end{pmatrix} + \begin{pmatrix} b_1^* \\ b_2^* \\ b_3^* \\ b_4^* \\ b_5^* \end{pmatrix} d74 + \begin{pmatrix} a_1 \\ a_2 \\ a_3 \\ a_4 \\ a_5 \end{pmatrix} uc_t
$$

$$
+ \sum_{k=1}^{P} \begin{pmatrix} a_{11k}^* & a_{12k}^* & a_{13k}^* & a_{14k}^* & a_{15k}^* & a_{16k}^* \\ a_{21k}^* & a_{22k}^* & a_{23k}^* & a_{24k}^* & a_{25k}^* & a_{26k}^* \\ a_{31k}^* & a_{32k}^* & a_{33k}^* & a_{34k}^* & a_{35k}^* & a_{36k}^* \\ a_{41k}^* & a_{42k}^* & a_{43k}^* & a_{44k}^* & a_{45k}^* & a_{46k}^* \\ a_{51k}^* & a_{52k}^* & a_{53k}^* & a_{54k}^* & a_{55k}^* & a_{56k}^* \end{pmatrix} \begin{pmatrix} d \ln w_{t-k} \\ d \ln p_{t-k} \\ \ln V_{t-k}^l \\ \ln V_{t-k}^c \\ r_{t-k} \\ uc_{t-k} \end{pmatrix}
$$

$$
+ \begin{pmatrix} e_{1t}^* \\ e_{2t}^* \\ e_{3t}^* \\ e_{4t}^* \\ e_{5t}^* \end{pmatrix} \tag{8.23}
$$

$$
uc_t = c_6 + \sum_{k=1}^{P} \begin{pmatrix} a_{61k} & a_{62k} & a_{63k} & a_{64k} & a_{65k} & a_{66k} \end{pmatrix} \begin{pmatrix} d \ln w_{t-k} \\ d \ln p_{t-k} \\ \ln V_{t-k}^l \\ \ln V_{t-k}^c \\ r_{t-k} \\ uc_{t-k} \end{pmatrix} + e_{6t} \tag{8.24}
$$

We now examine whether uc_t can be taken as an "exogenous" variable. The partial system (8.23) is exactly identified. Hence the variable uc_t is weakly exogenous for the parameters in the partial system.[11] For the strong exogeneity of uc_t, we test whether $d \ln w_t$, $d \ln p_t$, $\ln V_t^l$, $\ln V_t^c$, r_t Granger cause uc_t. The test

---

[11] For a detailed discussion of this procedure, see Chen (2003).

is carried out by testing the hypothesis: $H_0 : a_{ijk} = 0$, $(i = 6; j = 1,2,3,4,5;$ $k = 1,2, \ldots ,12)$ in (8.24) based on the likelihood ratio

• $\chi^2(60) = 57.714092$ with significance level 0.55972955

The result of the test uc_t is strongly exogenous with respect to the parameters in (8.23). Hence, we can investigate the partial system (8.23) taking uc_t as exogenous.

5.3. Estimation of the structural model

As discussed in Section 3, the law of motion for the real wage rate, Equation (8.12), represents a reduced-form expression of the two structural equations for $d \ln w_t$ and $d \ln p_t$. Noting again that the inflation climate variable is defined in the estimated model as a linearly declining function of past price inflation rates, the dynamics of the system (8.1)–(8.8) can be rewritten in linearized form as shown in the following equations:[12]

$$d \ln w_t = \beta_{w_1} \ln V^l_{t-1} - \beta_{w_2} uc_{t-1} + \kappa_w d \ln p_t + (1 - \kappa_w)\pi^{12}_t + c_1 + e_{1t} \qquad (8.25)$$

$$d \ln p_t = \beta_{p_1} \ln V^c_{t-1} + \beta_{p_2} uc_{t-1} + \kappa_p d \ln w_t + (1 - \kappa_p)\pi^{12}_t + c_2 + e_{2t} \qquad (8.26)$$

$$d \ln V^l_t = \alpha_{V^l_2} d \ln V^l_t + e_{3t} \qquad (8.27)$$

$$d \ln V^c_t = -\alpha_{V^c} \ln V^c_{t-1} - \alpha_r(r_{t-1} - d \ln p_t) - \alpha_\omega uc_{t-1} + c_4 + e_{4t} \qquad (8.28)$$

$$dr_t = -\gamma_r r_{t-1} + \gamma_p d \ln p_t + \gamma_{V^c} \ln V^c_{t-1} + c_5 + e_{5t} \qquad (8.29)$$

Obviously, the model (8.25)–(8.29) is nested in the VAR(12) of (8.23). Therefore, we can use (8.23) to evaluate the empirical relevance of the model (8.25)–(8.29). First we test whether the parameter restrictions on (8.23) implied by (8.25)–(8.29) are valid.

The linearized structural model (8.25)–(8.29) puts 349 restrictions on the unconstrained VAR(12) of the system (8.23). Applying likelihood ratio methods we can test the validity of these restrictions. For the period from 1965:1 to 2001:2 we cannot reject the null of these restrictions. The test result is the following:

• $\chi^2(349) = 361.716689$ with significance level 0.34902017

Obviously, the specification (8.25)–(8.29) is a valid one for the data set from 1965:1 to 2001:2. This result shows strong empirical relevance for the laws of motions as described in (8.1)–(8.8) as a model for the U.S. economy from 1965:1 to 2001:2. It is worthwhile to note that altogether 349 restrictions are implied

---

[12] Note here that the difference operator d is to be interpreted as backward in orientation and that the nominal rate of interest is dated at the beginning of the relevant period. The linearly declining moving average π^{12}_t in turn concerns the past 12 price inflation rates.

through the structural form of the system (8.1)–(8.8) on the VAR(12) model. A p-value of 0.349 thus means that (8.1)–(8.8) is a much more parsimonious presentation of the DGP than VAR(12), and henceforth a much more efficient model to describe the economic dynamics for this period.

To get a result that is easier to interpret from the economic perspective, we transform the model (8.25)–(8.29) back to its originally nonlinear form (8.1)–(8.8).[13]

$$d \ln w_t = \beta_{w_1} V^l_{t-1} - \beta_{w_2} uc_{t-1} + \kappa_w d \ln p_t + (1 - \kappa_w)\pi_t^{12} + c_1 + e_{1t} \qquad (8.30)$$

$$d \ln p_t = \beta_{p_1} V^c_{t-1} + \beta_{p_2} uc_{t-1} + \kappa_p d \ln w_t + (1 - \kappa_p)\pi_t^{12} + c_2 + e_{2t} \qquad (8.31)$$

$$d \ln V^l_t = \alpha_{V^l_2} d \ln V^c_t + e_{3t} \qquad (8.32)$$

$$d \ln V^c_t = -\alpha_{V^c} V^c_{t-1} - \alpha_u uc_{t-1} - \alpha_r(r_{t-1} - d \ln p_t) + c_4 + e_{4t} \qquad (8.33)$$

$$dr_t = -\gamma_r r_{t-1} + \gamma_p d \ln p_t + \gamma_{V^c} V^c_{t-1} + c_5 + e_{5t} \qquad (8.34)$$

This model therefore differs from the model (8.25)–(8.29) by referring now again to the explanatory variables V^c and V^l instead of $\ln V^c$ and $\ln V^l$ which were necessary to construct a linear VAR(12) system. We compare on this basis the model (8.30)–(8.34) with the model (8.25)–(8.29) in a non-nested testing framework. Applying the J test to such a nonlinear estimation procedure, we get significant evidence that the model (8.30)–(8.34) is to be preferred to the model (8.25)–(8.29).

Model	J test
H_1: Model of (8.25)–(8.29) is true	$t_\alpha = 4.611$
H_2: Model of (8.30)–(8.34) is true	$t_\phi = -0.928$

We have already omitted in the following summaries of our model estimates the insignificant parameters in the displayed quantitative representation of the semi-structural model and also the stochastic terms. By putting furthermore the NAIRU expressions and all other expressions that are here still assumed as constant into overall constant terms, we therefore finally obtain the following (approximate) two-stage least squares estimation results (with t-statistics in parenthesis):

$$d \ln w_t = \begin{array}{cccccc} 0.13 V^l_{t-1} & -0.07 uc_{t-1} & +0.49 d \ln p_t & +0.51\pi_t^{12} & -0.12 \\ (3.95) & (-1.94) & (2.61) & (2.61) & (-3.82) \end{array}$$

$$d \ln p_t = \begin{array}{cccccc} 0.04 V^c_{t-1} & +0.05 uc_{t-1} & +0.18 d \ln w_t & +0.82\pi_t^{12} & -0.04 \\ (2.32) & (2.52) & (2.32) & (2.32) & (-6.34) \end{array}$$

---

[13] Note that $dr_t = -\gamma_r r_{t-1} + \gamma_p d \ln p_t + \gamma_{V^c} V^c_{t-1} + c_5 + e_{5t}$ can also be represented by $r_t = (1 - \gamma_r) r_{t-1} + \cdots$ in the equations to be estimated below.

$$d \ln V_t^l = \frac{0.18 d \ln V_t^c}{(14.62)}$$

$$d \ln V_t^c = \frac{-0.14 V_{t-1}^c}{(-5.21)} \quad \frac{-0.94(r_{t-1} \quad -d \ln p_t)}{(-4.72)} \quad \frac{-0.54 uc_{t-1}}{(-4.84)} \quad \frac{+0.12}{(5.41)}$$

$$dr_t = \frac{-0.08 r_{t-1}}{(24.82)} \quad \frac{+0.06 d \ln p_t}{(1.2)} \quad \frac{+0.01 V_{t-1}^c}{(2.46)} \quad \frac{-0.01}{(-2.19)}$$

We thus here get that Blanchard and Katz error-correction terms matter in particular in the labor market, that the adjustment speed of wages is larger than the one for prices with respect to their corresponding demand pressures and that wage earners are more short-sighted than firms with respect to the influence of the inflationary climate expression. Okun's law which relates the growth rate of employment with the growth rate of capacity utilization is below a 1:5 relationship and thus in fact represents a fairly weak relationship. There is a strong influence of the real rate of interest on the growth rate of capacity utilization in the error correcting dynamic multiplier equation and also a significant role for income distribution in this equation. Since this role is based on a negative sign we have the result that the economy is profit-led, i.e., investment behavior (which is assumed to depend negatively on real unit wage costs) dominates the outcome of a change in income distribution. With respect to the interest rate policy we finally obtain a sluggish form of interest rate smoothing, based on a passive policy rule (with a coefficient 0.06/0.08 in front of the inflation gap).

Next, we compare the preceding situation with the case where the climate expression π^m is based on a 24 quarter horizon in the place of the 12 quarter horizon we have employed so far.[14]

$$d \ln w_t = 0.12 V_{t-1}^l - 0.06 uc_{t-1} + 0.71 d \ln p_t + 0.29 \pi_t^{24} - 0.10$$
$$d \ln p_t = 0.04 V_{t-1}^c + 0.09 uc_{t-1} + 0.38 d \ln w_t + 0.62 \pi_t^{24} - 0.03$$
$$d \ln V_t^l = 0.18 d \ln V_t^c$$
$$d \ln V_t^c = -0.14 V_{t-1}^c - 0.94(r_{t-1} - d \ln p_t) - 0.54 uc_{t-1} + 0.12$$
$$dr_t = -0.09 r_{t-1} + 0.07 d \ln p_t + 0.01 V_{t-1}^c - 0.01$$

---

[14] Details on the estimation of the subsequently reported results are provided in an appendix of the working paper version of this paper.

We see that the application of a time horizon of 24 quarters for the formation of the inflationary climate variable does not alter the qualitative properties of the dynamics significantly as compared to the case of a moving average with linearly declining weights over 12 quarters only (which approximately corresponds to a value of $\beta_{\pi^m} = 0.15$ in an adaptive expectations mechanism as used for the theoretical version of the model in Section 3). Even choosing only a six quarter horizon for our linearly declining weights preserves the qualitative features of our estimated model and also by and large the stability properties of the dynamics as we shall see later on, though inflationary expectations over the medium run are then updated with a speed comparable to the ones used for the price PC in hybrid New Keynesian approaches:

$$d \ln w_t = 0.12 V^l_{t-1} - 0.08 uc_{t-1} + 0.27 d \ln p_t + 0.73 \pi^6_t - 0.11$$
$$d \ln p_t = 0.03 V^c_{t-1} + 0.02 uc_{t-1} + 0.10 d \ln w_t + 0.90 \pi^6_t - 0.03$$
$$d \ln V^l_t = 0.18 d \ln V^c_t$$
$$d \ln V^c_t = -0.14 V^c_{t-1} - 0.94(r_{t-1} - d \ln p_t) - 0.54 uc_{t-1} + 0.12$$
$$dr_t = -0.08 r_{t-1} + 0.06 d \ln p_t + 0.01 V^c_{t-1} - 0.01$$

We thereby arrive at the general qualitative result that wages are more flexible than prices with respect to their corresponding measures of demand pressure and that wage earners are more short-sighted than firms with respect to the weight they put on their current (perfectly foreseen) measure of cost pressure as compared to the inflationary climate that surrounds this situation. Blanchard and Katz (1999) type error-correction mechanisms play a role both in the wage PC and also in the price PC for the U.S. economy and have the sign that is predicted by theory, in contrast to what is found out by these two authors themselves. We have the validity of Okun's law with an elasticity coefficient of less than 20 percent and have the correct signs for the dynamic multiplier process as well as with respect to the influence of changing real rate of interests on economic activity. Finally, the impact of income distribution on the change in capacity utilization is always a negative one and thus of an orthodox type, meaning that rising average unit wage costs will decrease economic activity, and will therefore imply at least from a partial perspective that increasing wage flexibility is stabilizing, while increasing price flexibility (again with respect to its measure of demand pressure) is not.

We conclude from the above that it should be legitimate to use the system estimate with π^{12} as inflation climate term for the further evaluation of the dynamic properties of our theoretical model of Section 3, in order to see what more can be obtained as compared to the theoretical results of Section 4 when empirically supported parameter signs and sizes are (approximately) taken into account. As a further support for this parameter approximation we finally also report single equation estimates for our 5D system in order to get a feeling for the intervals in which the parameter values may sensibly assume to lie:[15]

$$d \ln w_t = 0.19 V^l_{t-1} - 0.07 uc_{t-1} + 0.16 d \ln p_t + 0.84 \pi^{12}_t - 0.17$$

$$d \ln p_t = 0.05 V^c_{t-1} + 0.05 uc_{t-1} + 0.09 d \ln w_t + 0.91 \pi^{12}_t - 0.04$$

$$d \ln V^l_t = 0.16 d \ln V^c_t$$

$$d \ln V^c_t = -0.14 V^c_{t-1} - 0.93(r_{t-1} - d \ln p_t) - 0.54 uc_{t-1} + 0.12$$

$$dr_t = -0.10 r_{t-1} + 0.10 d \ln p_t + 0.01 V^c_{t-1} - 0.01$$

Again parameter sizes are changed to a certain degree. We do not expect however that this changes the stability properties of the dynamics in a qualitative sense and we will check this in the following section from the theoretical as well as numerical perspective.

The above by and large similar representation of the sizes of the parameter values of our dynamics thus reveal various interesting assertions on the relative importance of demand pressure influences as well as cost pressure effects in the wage–price spiral of the U.S. economy. The Blanchard and Katz error-correction terms have the correct signs and are of relevance in general. Okun's law holds as a level relationship between the capacity utilization rate and the rate of employment, basically of the form $V^l / \bar{V}^l = (V^c / \bar{V}^c)^b$ with an elasticity parameter b of about 18 percent. The dynamic IS equation shows from the partial perspective stabilizing role of the multiplier process and a significant dependence of the rate of change of capacity utilization on the current real rate of interest. There is a significant and negative effect of real unit wage costs (we conjecture: since investment dominates consumption) on this growth rate of capacity utilization, which in this aggregated form suggests that the economy is profit-led as far as aggregate goods demand is concerned, i.e., real wage cost increases significantly decrease economy activity.

Finally, for the Taylor interest rate policy rule, we get the result that interest rate smoothing takes place around the 10 percent level, and that monetary policy is to be considered as somewhat passive $(\gamma_p / (1 - \gamma_r) < 1)$ in such an environment as far as the inflation gap is concerned, and that there is only a weak direct influence of the output gap on the rate of change of the nominal rate of interest. It may therefore be expected that instability can be an outcome of the theoretical model when simulated with these estimated parameter values. Finally, we note that it is not really possible to recover the steady-state rate of interest from the constant in the above estimated Taylor rules in a statistically significant way, since the expression implied for this rate by our formulation of the Taylor rule

---

[15] Details on the *t*-statistics of the subsequently reported results can be found in the appendix of the working paper version of the paper.

would be

$$r_o = (const + \gamma_p \bar{\pi} + \gamma_{V^c})/\gamma_r$$

which does not determine this rate with any reliable statistical confidence. This also holds for the other constants that we have assumed as given in our formulation of Keynesian DAS–DAD dynamics.

In sum, the system estimates of this section provide us with a result that confirms theoretical sign restrictions. They moreover provide definite answers with respect to the role of income distribution in the considered disequilibrium AS–AD or DAS–DAD dynamics, confirming in particular the orthodox point of view that economic activity is likely to depend negatively on real unit wage costs. We have also a negative real wage effect in the dynamics of income distribution, in the sense that the growth rate of real wages, see our reduced-form real wage dynamics in Section 3, depends – through Blanchard and Katz error-correction terms – negatively on the real wage. Its dependence on economic activity levels however is somewhat ambiguous, but in any case small. Real wages therefore only weakly increase with increases in the rate of capacity utilization which in turn however depends in an unambiguous way negatively on the real wage, implying in sum that the Rose (1967) real wage channel is present, but may not dominate the dynamic outcomes.

Finally, the estimated adjustment speed of the price level is so small that the dynamic multiplier effect dominates the overall outcome of changes in capacity utilization on the growth rate of this utilization rate, which therefore establishes a further stabilizing mechanism in the reduced form of our multiplier equation. The model and its estimates thus by and large confirm the conventional Keynesian view on the working of the economy and thus provide in sum a result very much in line with the traditional ways of reasonings from a Keynesian perspective. There is one important qualification however, as we will show in the next sections, namely that downward money wage flexibility can be good for economic stability, in line with Rose's (1967) model of the employment cycle, but in opposition to what Keynes (1936) stated on the role of downwardly rigid money wages. Yet, the role of income distribution in aggregate demand and wage vs. price flexibility was not really a topic in the General Theory, which therefore did not comment on the possibility that wage declines may lead the economy out of a depression via a channel different from the conventional Keynes effect.

6. Stability analysis of the estimated model

In the preceding section, we have provided definite answers with respect to the type of real wage effect present in the data of the U.S. economy after World War II, concerning the dependence of aggregate demand on the real wage, the degrees of wage and price flexibilities and the degree of forward-looking behavior in the wage and price PC. The resulting combination of effects and the estimated sizes of the parameters (in particular the relative degree of wage vs. price flexibility) suggest that their particular type of interaction is favorable for stability, at least if monetary policy is sufficiently active.

We start the stability analysis of the semi-structural theoretical model with estimated parameters from the following reference situation (the system estimate where the inflationary climate is measured as by the 12 quarter moving average):

$$d \ln w_t = 0.13 V_{t-1}^l - 0.07 uc_{t-1} + 0.49 d \ln p_t + 0.51 \pi_t^{12} - 0.12$$

$$d \ln p_t = 0.04 V_{t-1}^c + 0.05 uc_{t-1} + 0.18 d \ln w_t + 0.82 \pi_t^{12} - 0.04$$

$$d \ln V_t^l = 0.18 d \ln V_t^c$$

$$d \ln V_t^c = -0.14 V_{t-1}^c - 0.94(r_{t-1} - d \ln p_t) - 0.54 uc_{t-1} + 0.12$$

$$dr_t = -0.08 r_{t-1} + 0.06 d \ln p_t + 0.01 V_{t-1}^c - 0.01$$

We consider first the 3D core situation obtained by totally ignoring adjustments in the inflationary climate term, by setting $\pi^m = \bar{\pi}$ in the theoretical model, and by interpreting the estimated law of motion for V^l in level terms, i.e., by moving from the equation $\hat{V}^l = b \hat{V}^c$ to the equation $V^l = \bar{V}^l (V^c / \bar{V}^c)^b$, with $b = 0.18$ (and $\bar{V}^l = \bar{V}^c = 1$ for reasons of simplicity and without much loss of generality). On the basis of our estimated parameter values we furthermore have that the expression $\beta_{p_1} - \kappa_p \beta_{w_1}$ is approximately zero (slightly positive), i.e., the weak influence of the state variable ω in the reduced-form price PC will not be of relevance in the following reduced form of the dynamics (which however is not of decisive importance for the following stability analysis). Finally, the critical condition for normal or adverse Rose effects

$$\alpha = (1 - \kappa_p)\beta_{w_1} b - (1 - \kappa_w)\beta_{p_1} \approx 0$$

is also – due to the measured size of the parameter b – close to zero (which is of importance for stability analysis, see the matrix J below). Rose real-wage effects are thus not very strong in the estimated form of the model, at least from this partial point of view, despite a significant negative dependence of capacity utilization on real unit wage costs (the wage share).

Under these assumptions, the laws of motion (8.9)–(8.13) – with the reduced-form price PC inserted again – can be reduced to the following qualitative form (where the undetermined signs of a_1, b_1, c_1 do not matter for the following stability analysis and are assumed to be sufficiently close to 0):

$$\hat{V}^c = a_1 - a_2 V^c - a_3 r - a_4 \ln \omega \tag{8.35}$$

$$\dot{r} = b_1 + b_2 V^c - b_3 r \pm b_4 \ln \omega \tag{8.36}$$

$$\hat{\omega} = c_1 \pm c_2 V^c - c_4 \ln \omega \tag{8.37}$$

since the dependence of $\hat{p}$ on V^c is a weak one, to be multiplied by 0.17 in comparison with the direct impact of V^c on its rate of growth, and thus does not modify the sign measured for the direct influence of this variable on the growth rate of the capacity utilization rate significantly. Note with respect to this qualitative characterization of the remaining 3D dynamics that the various influences of the same variable in the same equation have been aggregated always into a single expression, the sign of which has been obtained from the quantitative estimates shown above. We thus have to take note here in particular of the fact that the reduced-form expression for the price inflation rate has been inserted into the first two laws of motion for the capacity utilization dynamics and the interest rate dynamics, which have been rearranged on this basis so that the influence of the variables V^c and ω appears at most only once, though both terms appear via two different channels in these laws of motion, one direct channel and one via the price inflation rate.

The result of our estimates of this equation is that the latter channel is not changing the signs of the direct effects of capacity utilization (via the dynamic multiplier) and the real wage (via the aggregate effect of consumption and investment behavior). We note again that the parameter c_2 may be uncertain in sign, but will in any case be close to zero, while the sign of b_4 does not matter in the following. A similar treatment applies to the law of motion for the nominal rate of interest, where price inflation is again broken down into its constituent parts (in its reduced-form expression) and where the influence of V^l in this expression is again replaced by V^c through Okun's law. Finally, the law of motion for real wages themselves is obtained from the two estimated structural laws of motion for wage and price inflation in the way shown in Section 3. We have stated the very weak, but possibly the positive influence of capacity utilization on the growth rate of real wages, since the wage PC slightly dominates the outcome here and an unambiguously negative influence of real wages on their rate of growth due to the signs of the Blanchard and Katz error-correction terms in the wage and the price dynamics.

On this basis, we arrive – if we set the considered small magnitudes equal to zero – at the following sign structure for the Jacobian at the interior steady state of the above reduced model for the state variables V^c, r, ω:

$$
J = \begin{pmatrix} - & - & - \\ + & - & 0 \\ 0 & 0 & - \end{pmatrix}
$$

We therefrom immediately get that the steady state of these 3D dynamics is asymptotically stable, since the trace is negative, the sum a_2 of principal minors of order two is always positive, and since the determinant of the whole matrix is negative. The coefficients k_i, $i = 1, 2, 3$ of the Routh–Hurwitz polynomial of this matrix are therefore all positive as demanded by the Routh–Hurwitz stability conditions. The remaining stability condition is

$$
k_1 k_2 - k_3 = (-\text{trace } J)k_2 + \det J > 0
$$

With respect to this condition we immediately see that the determinant of the Jacobian J, given by

$$J_{33}(J_{11}J_{22} - J_{12}J_{21})$$

is dominated by the terms that appear in $k_1 k_2$, i.e., this Routh–Hurwitz condition is also of correct sign as far as the establishment of local asymptotic stability is concerned. The weak and may be ambiguous real wage effect or Rose effect that is included in the working of the dynamics of the private sector thus does not work against the stability of the steady state of the considered dynamics. Ignoring the Mundell effect by assuming $\beta_{\pi^m} = 0$ therefore allows for an unambiguous stability result, basically due to the stable interaction of the dynamic multiplier with the Taylor interest rate policy rule, augmented by real wage dynamics that in itself is stable due to the estimated signs (and sizes) of the Blanchard error-correction terms, where the estimated negative dependence of the change in economic activity on the real wage is welcome from an orthodox point of view, but does not really matter for the stability features of the model. The neglectance of the Mundell effect therefore leaves us with a situation that is close in spirit to the standard textbook consi-derations of Keynesian macrodynamics. Making the β_{π^m} slightly positive does not overthrow the above stability assertion, since the determinant of the 4D case is positive in the considered situation, see also Chen *et al.* (2006), where it is also shown in detail, that a significant increase of this parameter must lead to local instability in a cyclical fashion via a so-called Hopf bifurcation (if $\gamma_r < \gamma_p$).

Figure 8.3 shows simulations of the estimated dynamics where indeed the parameter β_{π^m} is now no longer zero, but set equal to $0.075, 0.15$ in correspondence to the measures π^{12}, π^6 of the inflationary climate used in our estimates (these values arise approximately when we estimate β_{π^m} by means of these moving averages). We use a large real wage shock (increase by 10 percent) to investigate the response of the dynamics (with respect to capacity utilization) to such a shock. The resulting impulse responses are unstable ones in the case of the estimated policy parameter $\gamma_p = 0.6$ as shown in the two graphs on the left hand side of Figure 8.3. This is due to the fact that the estimated passive Taylor rule allows for a positive real eigenvalue that leads to divergence when the dominant root of the estimated situation has run its course and brought the dynamics sufficiently close to the steady state. Increasing the parameter γ_p toward 0.8 (a Taylor rule right at the border toward an active one) or even to 0.12 (where α_p assumes a standard value of 0.5) moves the positive real eigenvalue into the negative half plane of the plane of complex numbers and thus makes the dynamics produce trajectories that converge back to the steady state as shown in Figure 8.3 on its left hand side. On its right hand side we show in the top figure how the positive real eigenvalue (the maximum of the real parts of the eigenvalues of the dynamics) varies with the parameter γ_p. We clearly see

Figure 8.3. Responses to real wage shocks in the range of estimated parameter values

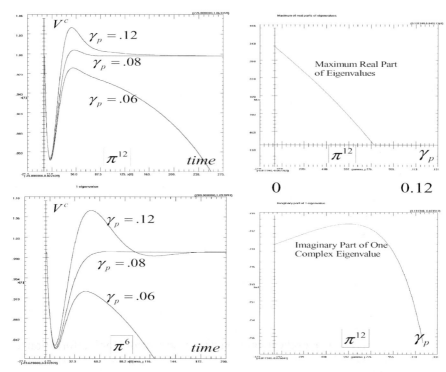

that instability is reduced and finally removed as this policy parameter is increased.[16]

More active monetary policy leading to stability is a result that holds for all measures of the inflation climate as shown for the case π^6 in Figure 8.3. Bottom-right, we finally show in this figure that there are complex roots involved in the considered situation (there for the case π^{12}). Adjustment to the steady state is therefore of a cyclical nature, though only weakly cyclical as shown in this figure. In sum, we therefore get that active Taylor rules as estimated for the past two decades (but not for our larger estimation period) will bring stability to the dynamics, since the dominant root then enforces convergence to the steady state without any counteracting force close to the steady state. In the considered range for the parameter β_{π^m} the overall responses of the dynamics are then by and large of the shown type, i.e., the system has strong, though somewhat cyclical stability

---

[16] Note that – due to the estimated form of Okun's law – one eigenvalue of the 5D dynamics must always be zero.

properties over this whole range, if monetary policy is made somewhat more active than estimated, independent of the particular combination of the speed of adjustment of the inflationary climate and the set of other parameter values we have estimated in the preceding section. The impulse-response situation shown in Figure 8.3 is the expected one. The same holds true for the response of V^l, $\hat{w}$, $\hat{p}$, r, which all decrease in the contractive phase shown in Figure 8.3.

We again note that the system is subject to zero root hysteresis, since the laws of motion for V^l, V^c are here linearly dependent (since α_{V^l}, has been estimated as being zero), i.e., it need not converge back to the initially given steady-state value of the rate of capacity utilization which was assumed to be 1. Note also that the parameter estimates are based on quarterly data, i.e., the plots in Figure 8.3 correspond to 25 years and thus show a long period of adjustment, due to the fact that all parameters have been assumed as time-invariant, so that only the slow process of changing income distribution and its implications for Keynesian aggregate demand is thus driving the economy here.

Next we test in Figure 8.4 the stability properties of the model if one of its parameters is varied in size. We there plot the maximum value of the real parts of the eigenvalues against specific parameter changes shown on the horizontal axis in each case. We by and large find (also for parameter variations that are not shown) that all partial feedback chains (including the working of the Blanchard and Katz error-correction terms) translate themselves into corresponding 'normal' eigenvalue reaction patterns for the full 5D dynamics.

With respect to the wage flexibility parameter β_{w_1} we see in Figure 8.4 top-left that its increase helps to reduce the instability of the system with respect to the estimated parameter set, but is not able by itself to enforce convergence. The same holds true for the other adjustment parameters in the wage and the price PCs. Top-right we then determine the range of values for the parameter γ_r where local asymptotic stability is indeed established and find that this is approximately true for the interval $(0.1, 0.6)$, while large parameters values imply a switch back to local instability. Interest rate smoothing of a certain degree therefore can enforce convergence back to the steady state. We thus now change the estimated parameter set in this respect and assume for the parameter γ_r the value 0.4 in the remainder of Figure 8.4.

The two plots in the middle of Figure 8.4 then show that too low wage flexibility and too high price flexibility will destabilize the dynamics again. This is what we expect from the real wage effect in a profit-led economy, due to what has been said on normal and adverse Rose effects. Furthermore, concerning the Mundell effect, we indeed also find that an adjustment of the inflationary climate expression that is too fast induces local asymptotic instability and is therefore destabilizing (see Figure 8.4, bottom-left). Finally, bottom-right we see that a Taylor interest rate policy rule that is too passive with respect to the inflation gap will also endanger the stability we have created by increasing the speed of interest rate smoothing. Such eigenvalue diagrams therefore nicely confirm what is known from partial reasoning on Keynesian macrodynamic feedback chains.

Figure 8.4. Eigenvalue diagrams for varying parameter sizes

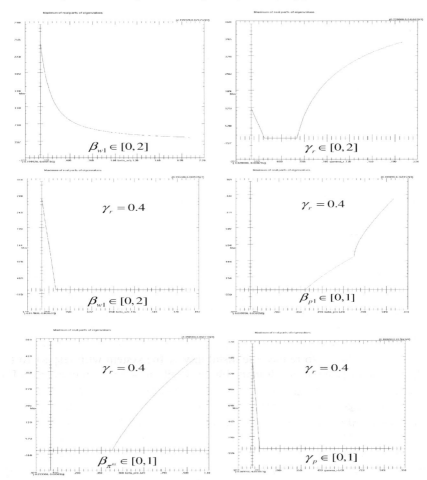

Note here that increasing price flexibility is also destabilizing via the Mundell effect, since the growth rate $\hat{V}^c$ of economic activity can thereby be made to depend positively on its level (via the real rate of interest channel, see Equation (8.14)), leading to an unstable augmented dynamic multiplier process in the trace of J under such circumstances. Moreover, such increasing price flexibility will give rise to a negative dependence of the growth rate of the real wage on economic activity (whose rate of change in turn depends negatively on the real wage) and thus leads to further sign changes in the Jacobian J. Increasing price flexibility is therefore bad for the stability of the considered dynamics from at least two perspectives.

Let us return now to our analytical stability considerations again. The destabilizing role of price flexibility is enhanced if we add to the above stability analysis for the 3D Jacobian law of motion for the inflationary climate surrounding the current evolution of price inflation. Under this extension we go back to a 4D dynamical system, the Jacobian J of which is obtained by augmenting the previous one in its sign structure in the following way (see again Equation (8.14)):

$$J = \begin{pmatrix} - & - & - & + \\ + & - & 0 & + \\ 0 & 0 & - & 0 \\ + & 0 & 0 & 0 \end{pmatrix}$$

As the positive entries J_{14}, J_{41} show, there is now a new destabilizing feedback chain included, leading from increases in economic activity to increases in inflation and climate inflation and from there back to increases in economic activity, again through the real rate of interest channel (where the inflationary climate is involved due to the expression that characterizes our reduced-form price PC). This destabilizing, augmented Mundell effect must become dominant sooner or later (even under the estimated simplified feedback structure) as the adjustment speed of the climate expression β_{π^m} is increased. This is obvious from the fact that the only term in the Routh–Hurwitz coefficient a_2 that depends on the parameter β_{π^m} exhibits a negative sign, which implies that a sufficiently high β_{π^m} will make the coefficient a_2 negative eventually. The Blanchard and Katz error-correction terms in the fourth row of J, obtained from the reduced-form price PC, that are (only as further terms) associated with the speed parameter β_{π^m}, are of no help here, since they do not appear in combination with the parameter β_{π^m} in the sum of principal minors of order 2. In this sum the parameter β_{π^m} thus only enters once and with a negative sign implying that this sum can be made negative (leading to instability) if this parameter is chosen sufficiently large. This stands in some contrast to the estimation results where the defined inflation climate term has been varied significantly without finding a considerable degree of instability.

Assuming – as a mild additional assumption – that interest rate smoothing is sufficiently weak furthermore allows for the conclusion that the 4D determinant of the above Jacobian exhibits a positive sign throughout. We thus in sum get that the local asymptotic stability of the steady state of the 3D case extends to the 4D case for sufficiently small parameters $\beta_{\pi^m} > 0$, since the eigenvalue that was zero in the case $\beta_{\pi^m} = 0$ must become negative due to the positive sign of the 4D determinant (since the other three eigenvalues must have negative real parts for small β_{π^m}). Loss of stability can only occur through a change in the sign of the Routh–Hurwitz coefficient k_2, which can occur only once by way of a Hopf bifurcation where the system loses its local stability through the local death of an unstable limit cycle or the local birth of a stable limit cycle. This result is due to the destabilizing Mundell effect of a faster adjustment of the inflationary climate into which the economy is embedded, which in the present dynamical system works through the elements J_{14}, J_{41} in the Jacobian J of the dynamics and thus through the positive dependence of economic activity on the inflationary climate expression and the positive dependence of this climate expression on the level of economic activity.

To sum up, we have established that the 4D dynamics will be convergent for sufficiently small speeds of adjustments β_{π^m}, and for a monetary policy that is sufficiently active, while they will be divergent for parameters β_{π^m} chosen sufficiently large. The Mundell effect thus works as expected from a partial perspective. There will a unique Hopf bifurcation point $\beta_{\pi^m}^H$ in between (for γ_r sufficiently small), where the system loses asymptotic stability in a cyclical fashion. Yet sooner or later purely explosive behavior will indeed be established (as can be checked by numerical simulations), where there is no longer room for persistent economic fluctuations in the real and the nominal magnitudes of the economy.

In such a situation global behavioral nonlinearities must be taken into account in order to limit the dynamics to domains in the mathematical phase space that are of economic relevance. Compared to the New Keynesian approach briefly considered in Section 2 of this paper we thus have that – despite many similarities in the wage–price block of our dynamics – we have completely different implications for the resulting dynamics which – for active interest rate policy rules – are convergent (and thus determined from the historical perspective) when estimated empirically (with structural PCs that are not at all odds with the facts) and which – should loss of stability occur via a faster adjustments of the inflationary climate expression – must be bounded by appropriate changes in economic behavior far off the steady state and not just by mathematical assumption as in the New Keynesian case. Furthermore, we have employed in our model type a dynamic IS relationship in the spirit of Rudebusch and Svensson's (1999) approach, also confirmed in its backward orientation by a recent article of Fuhrer and Rudebusch (2004). One may therefore state that the results achieved in this and the preceding section can provide an alternative of mature, but traditional Keynesian type that does not lead to the radical – and not very Keynesian – New Keynesian conclusion that the deterministic part of the model is completely trivial and the dynamics but a consequence of the addition of appropriate exogenous stochastic processes.

7. Instability, global boundedness and monetary policy

Next we will express some conjectures concerning other scenarios. Based on the estimated range of parameter values, and for an active monetary policy rule, the preceding section has shown that the model then exhibits strong convergence properties, with only mild fluctuations around the steady state in the case of small shocks, but with a long downturn and a long-lasting adjustment in the case of strong shocks (as in the case of Figure 8.3, where a 10 percent increase in real wages shocks the economy). Nevertheless, the economy reacts in a fairly stable way to such a large shock and thus seems to have the characteristics of a strong shock absorber. Figure 8.3 however is based on estimated linear PCs, i.e., in particular, on wage adjustment that is as flexible in an upward as well as in a downward direction. It is however much more plausible that wages behave differently in a high and in a low inflation regime, see Chen and Flaschel (2004) for a study of the wage PC along these lines which confirms this common sense statement. Following Filardo (1998) we here go even one step further and indeed assume a three regime scenario as shown in Figure 8.5 where we make use of his Figure 8.4 and for illustrative purposes of the parameter sizes shown there[17] (though there they refer to output gaps on the horizontal axis, inflation surprises on the vertical axis and a standard reduced-form PC relating these two magnitudes).

Figure 8.5 suggests that the wage PC of the present model is only in effect if there holds simultaneously that wage inflation is above a certain floor f – here (following Filardo) shown to be negative[18] – and the employment rate is still above a certain floor $\underline{V}^l$, where wage inflation starts to become (downwardly) flexible again. In this latter area (where wage inflation according to the original linear curve is below f and the employment rate below $\underline{V}^l$), we assume as form for the resulting wage-inflation curve the following simplification and modification of the original one:

$$\hat{w} = \beta_{w_1}(V^l - \underline{V}^l) + \kappa_w \hat{p} + (1 - \kappa_w)\pi^m$$

i.e., we do not consider the Blanchard and Katz error-correction term to be in operation then any more. In sum, we therefore assume a normal operation of the economy if both lower floors are not yet reached, constant wage inflation if only the floor f has been reached and further falling wage inflation or deflation rates (as far as demand pressure is concerned) if both floors have been passed. Downward wage inflation or wage deflation rigidity thus does not exist for all states of a depressed economy, but can give way to its further downward adjustment in severe states of depression in actual economies.[19]

In Figure 8.6, we consider a situation as depicted in Figure 8.3, i.e., the working of a wage PC as it was already formulated in Rose (1967) and again contractive real wage shocks.[20] Top-left we plot the rate of capacity utilization

---

[17] Here adjusted to quarterly data.

[18] By contrast, this floor is claimed and measured to be positive for six European countries in Hoogenveen and Kuipers (2000).

[19] An example for this situation is given by the German economy, at least since 2003.

[20] The parameters of the plot are the estimated one with the exception of $\beta_{\pi^m} = 0.4$, $\gamma_p = 0.12$. The first parameter has therefore been increased in order to get local instability of the steady state and the policy parameter has been increased in order to tame the resulting instability to a certain degree. Moreover, we have assumed in this plot that the steady-state value of V^l coincides with the value where wages become downwardly flexible again, i.e., we here only switch of the Blanchard and Katz error-correction term in the downward direction, but have added a floor $f = 0.0004$ to wage inflation for employment rates above the steady-state level ($\bar{V}^c = 0.9$ now). This combination of wage regimes indeed tames the explosive dynamics and gives rise to a limit cycle attractor instead as is shown below.

Figure 8.5.   Three possible regimes for wage inflation

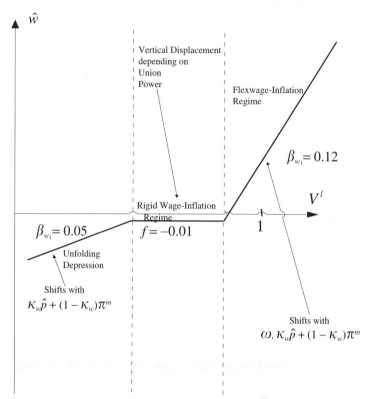

against the nominal rate of interest and obtain that the economy now adjusts to a fairly simple persistent fluctuation in this projection of the 5D phase space with an overshooting interest rate adjustment, since, for example, the interest rate keeps on rising though economic activity has started to fall already for quite a while. There is a strict positive correlation between the rates of utilization of capital and labor, i.e., all assertions made with respect to one utilization rate also hold for the other one. The reason for this overshooting reaction of interest rate policy is that this policy closely follows the inflation gap and not the utilization gap, here represented with respect to the inflation climate term in Figure 8.6, top-right. This figure also shows that deflation is indeed occurring in the course of one cycle, though only weakly in a brief subperiod of it.

As already indicated there is also overshooting involved in the phase plot between the rate of employment and the inflation climate (Figure 8.6, bottom-left), i.e., the model clearly generates periods of stagflation and also periods where disinflation is coupled with a rising employment rate. This pattern is well-known from empirical investigations. Less close to such investigations, see Flaschel and Groh (1995) for example, is the pattern that is shown bottom-right

Figure 8.6.   Rose–Filardo-type wage PCs and the emergence of persistent business fluctuations

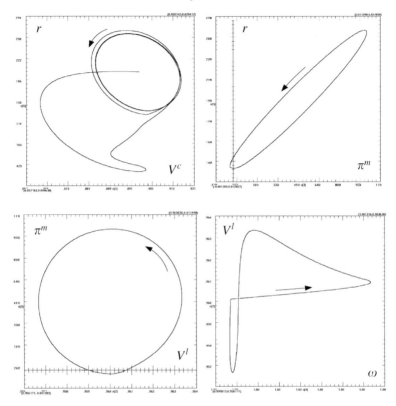

in Figure 8.6, i.e., a phase plot between the real wage and the rate of employment which according to the Goodwin (1967) model of a growth cycle should be also an overshooting one with a clockwise orientation which in Figure 8.6 is only partly visible in fact. Taken together, we however have the general result that a locally unstable steady state can be tamed toward the generation of a persistent fluctuation around it if wages become sufficiently flexible far off the steady state (both in an upward as well as in a downward direction).

We next show that the corridor $(\underline{V}^l, \bar{V}^l)$ where the second regime in Figure 8.5 applies may be of decisive importance for the resulting dynamics. Small changes in the size of this interval can have significant effects on the observed volatility of the resulting trajectories as Figure 8.7 exemplifies. In Figure 8.7, we lower the value of $\underline{V}^l$ from 0.96 to 0.959, 0.585, 0.958, 0.9575 and see that the limit cycle is becoming larger and is approached in more and more complicated ways. In the case 0.575 we finally get a quite different limit cycle with lower r, V^c

Figure 8.7. **Changes in the regime where rigid wage inflation or deflation prevails**

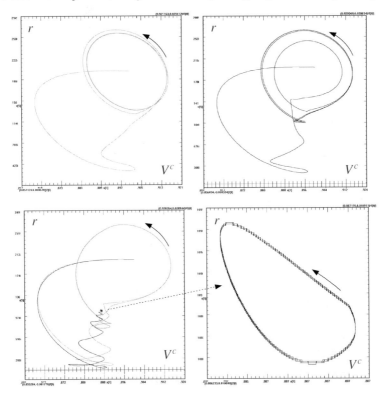

on average and only a small amplitude which is shown in enlarged form in Figure 8.7, bottom-right.

Finally, increasing the opposing forces β_{π^m} and γ_p even further to 1.4 and 0.6, respectively, and assuming now $\underline{V}^l = 0.94 < \bar{V}^l = 1$, i.e., a large range where there is a floor to money wages (and adjusting the interest rate such that it does not become negative along the trajectories that are shown) provides as with a (somewhat extreme) scenario where even complex dynamics are generated from the mathematical point of view (not directly from the economic point of view) as is shown in Figure 8.8.

Turning now to the effects of monetary policy we first show in Figure 8.9 the situation where the economy is strongly convergent to the steady state in the case of the active monetary policy underlying Figure 8.3. Adding a global floor to this situation radically changes the situation and implies economic collapse once this floor is reached, since real wages are then rising due to falling prices. This situation is again shown to be prevented if wages become flexible again (in a downward direction) at 92 percent of employment. Monetary policy that is then

Figure 8.8.   Depressed complex dynamics with long deflationary episodes

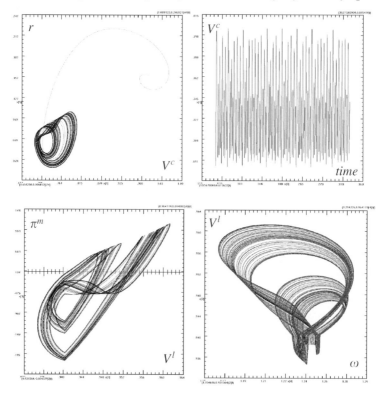

assumed more active either with respect to the utilization gap or the inflation gap can however prevent both situations from occurring, when it implies – as shown – that the floor to money wages can be avoided to come into operation thereby.

The question arises as to whether monetary policy works better the stronger is its reaction with respect to the inflation gap, i.e., the larger the parameter γ_p becomes. From an applied perspectives it is not to be expected that this is to be the case in reality, since active monetary policy is surely limited by some cautious bounds from above. In this 5D dynamical system with its still simple trajectories, it may, however be a theoretical possibility, though we have already presented a counterexample to a general proposition of this kind in Figure 8.4. Figure 8.10 now exemplifies this again by means of phase plots, i.e., of projections of the full dynamics into the V^c, r plane. We see in this figure, top-left with respect to our estimated parameter set (but with $\beta_{\pi^m} = 0/4$ now again), that a more active monetary policy ($0.12 \rightarrow 0.15$) enlarges the generated limit cycle (see Figure 8.6) and thus makes the economy more volatile. By contrast (see Figure 8.10, top-right), a lower value of $\gamma_p = 0.10$ as compared to Figure 8.6, makes the dynamics

Figure 8.9.   The existence of floors and more active monetary policy rules

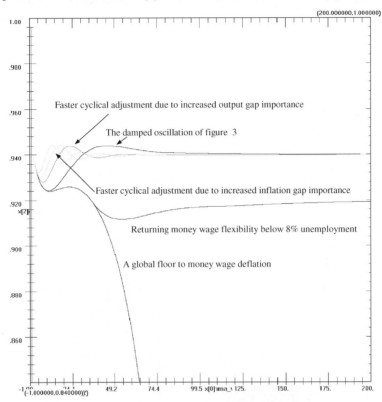

in fact convergent with smaller cycles when the transient behavior is excluded, but with a longer transient than in the case of Figure 8.10, top-left. This longer transient behavior can be made of an extreme type – with severely underutilized capital along the depressed transient cycles – when the policy reaction to the inflation gap is further reduced (to 0.092), see Figure 8.10, bottom-right and -left. The degree of activeness of monetary policy matters therefore a lot for the business fluctuations that are generated and this in a way with clear benchmark for the appropriate choice of the parameter γ_p.

In Figure 8.11, finally, we vary the parameter $\bar{\pi}$ that characterizes the inflation target of the Central Bank. A first implication of such variations is shown in the plot, top-left, where we show the limit cycle of Figure 8.6 once again, now together with two trajectories that are based on the assumptions $f = \bar{\pi} = 0.0004$ and $f = \bar{\pi} = 0.0004 > \pi = 0.0002$ concerning the temporary floor in money wages and the inflation target of the Central Bank. In the first case, the limit cycle disappears completely and we get instead convergence to the steady state, though with a long transient again. In the second case of an even more

Figure 8.10.   Corridor problems for active monetary policy rules

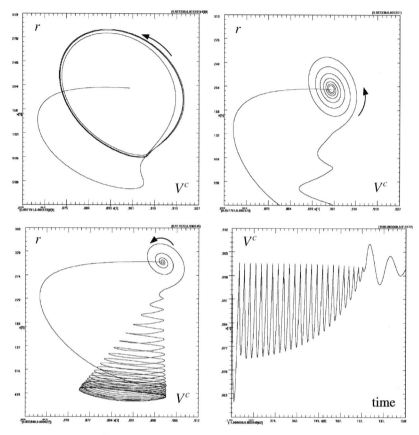

restrictive monetary policy we no longer get complete convergence back to the steady state, but instead convergence to a small limit cycle below this steady state, shown in enlarged form in Figure 8.11, top-right. Lowering $\bar{\pi}$ even further (to zero) gives the same result, but with a slightly more depressed limit cycle now, see Figure 8.11, bottom-left. In Figure 8.11, bottom-right, finally, we compare an inflation target of 0.05 with a deflation target of the Central Bank of -0.002 (both not topical themes in monetary policy). In the first case, the persistent fluctuation of the initial situation gets lost and is changed into a business fluctuation with increasing amplitude, that is the economy becomes an unstable one. In the second case we now get in a pronounced way a stable, but depressed limit cycle below the NAIRU levels for the rates of capacity utilization.

We conclude from these few simulation exercises on other scenarios in the neighborhood of our estimated Keynesian disequilibrium dynamics that one might observe a variety of interesting scenarios when certain kinks in money

Figure 8.11. **Tight and loose inflation targets**

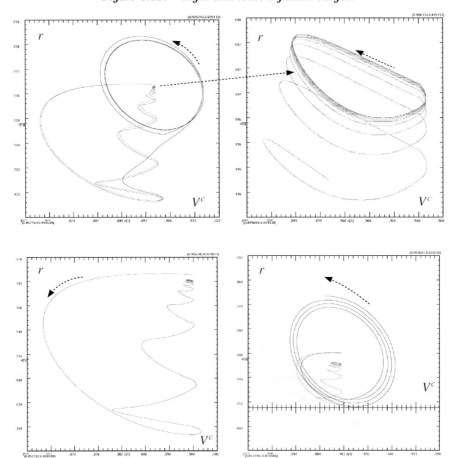

wage behavior and changes in the adjustment speed of our inflationary climate expression are taken into account. These changes furthermore show that further investigations of such behavioral nonlinearities are needed; see Chen and Flaschel (2004) and Flaschel *et al.* (2004) for some attempts into this direction for the U.S. economy.

8. *Related literature*

In this section we will compare some technical aspects of various recent macrodynamic models. An important technical aspect of the model of this paper is that it exhibits Keynesian feedback dynamics in particular with asymptotic stability of its unique interior steady-state solution for low adjustment speeds of wages, prices and expectations. The loss of stability occurs cyclically, generally by way of Hopf bifurcations, when some of these adjustment speeds are made sufficiently large, even leading eventually to purely explosive dynamics sooner or later. This latter fact – if it occurs – implies the need to look for appropriate extrinsic (behavioral) nonlinearities that can bound the dynamics in an economically meaningful domain, such as (some) downward rigidity of wages and prices and the like, if the economy departs too much from its steady-state position. Our procedure for making explosive dynamics bounded and thus viable stands in stark contrast to the New Keynesian approach to macro-dynamics where on a similar level of formalization total instability is desirable and achieved by the choice of an appropriate Taylor policy rule. The economy is then made a bounded one simply by assumption (and is thus always sitting in the steady state if exogenously given stochastic processes are removed from the dynamics). The model of this paper can usefully be compared (on the formal level) to the New Keynesian one with staggered wage and price dynamics. Yet, it is radically different from this approach with respect to implications, since we are not forced into a framework with four forward-looking variables where we would have to look for four unstable roots in order to get the conclusion that the variables are at their steady-state values (assuming boundedness as part of the solution procedure) as long as only isolated shocks occur. The dynamics are thus driven as far as business cycle implications are concerned solely by the exogenous stochastic processes that are added to its deterministic core. We have forward-looking behavior (with neoclassical dating) and will find asymptotic stability in the traditional sense of the word over certain ranges in the parameter space. In the case of local instability we look for behavioral nonlinearities that allow the dynamics to remain bounded in an economically meaningful range, in the place of an imposition of such boundedness on admissible solution curves and a quest for determinacy.

We, by contrast, therefore obtain and can prove – from the purely theoretical perspective – based on empirically still unrestricted sizes of the considered adjustment speeds of wages, prices, and quantities, the existence of damped, persistent or explosive fluctuations in the real and the nominal part of the dynamics, in the rates of capacity utilization of both labor and capital, and of wage and price inflation rates. These effects here induce interest rate adjustments by the monetary authority through the attempt to stabilize the observed output and price level fluctuations. We thus obtain a Keynesian theory of an income distribution driven cycle, including a modern approach to monetary policy in such a context. This even holds in the case of myopic perfect foresight, where the structure of the old Neoclassical synthesis radically dichotomizes into independent supply-side real-wage and growth dynamics – that cannot be influenced by monetary policy – and subsequently determined inflation dynamics that are purely explosive if the price level is taken as a predetermined variable, a situation that forces conventional approaches to these dichotomizing dynamics to assume convergence by an inconsistent application of the jump-variable technique;[21] see Asada *et al.* (2006) for details. In our new matured type of Keynesian labor and goods market dynamics we, however can treat myopic perfect foresight of both firms and wage earners without the need to adopt this 'rational expectations' solution methodology in the context of an unstable saddlepoint dynamics, be it of old or new Keynesian type.

From the global perspective, if our theoretical model loses asymptotic stability for higher adjustment speeds, in the present framework specifically of prices and our inflationary climate expression, purely explosive behavior is the generally observed outcome, as it can be demonstrated by means of numerical simulations. The considered, so far only intrinsically nonlinear, model type therefore cannot be considered as being completely specified under such circumstances, since some mechanism is then required to bound the fluctuations to economically viable regions. Downward money wage rigidity was the mechanism we have often used for this purpose and which we try here, however with limited success, in contrast to its successful application in the numerical investigations of the underlying theoretical model in Asada *et al.* (2006).

The here estimated somewhat simplified feedback structure of their theoretical model, now indeed no longer (in general) supports the view (of Keynes and others) that downward money wage rigidity will stabilize the economy (as was shown in the structurally more elaborated theoretical paper). Instead, this downward rigidity may now even cause economic breakdown when applied to situations that were strongly stable (convergent to the steady state) without it. This is due to our estimation of the dynamics of capacity utilization rates where we find, on the one hand, besides the usual negative dependence on the real rate of interest, a strong negative dependence on the real wage and thus on income distribution. On the other hand, we find in the wage–price block of the model the sign restrictions of New Keynesian wage and price inflation equations (but do not have their sign reversals in their reduced-form expressions later on, due to our different handling of forward-looking expectations and the inclusion of backward-looking ones). As far as the money wage PC is concerned we also confirm the form specified in Blanchard and Katz (1999) and find a similar general form to hold for the price inflation PC. These estimated curves then by and large suggest that real wage changes depend at best slightly positively on economic activity, and that this effect becomes more pronounced the more strongly nominal wages react to the employment gap on the market for labor. In sum, we therefore find that the growth rate of real wages depends negatively on its level, with this stabilizing feedback chain being stronger the more flexibly do nominal wages react to labor market imbalances in the upward as well as in the downward direction. Complete downward wage rigidity may

---

[21] Since the nominal wage is transformed into a nonpredetermined variable, there, despite the initial assumption of only gradually adjusting money wages.

therefore become a problem, and this already in situations where the economy is producing fairly damped cycles (due to an interest rate policy rule that is sufficiently active), if – for instance – the monetary authority is using too low an inflation target.

In the numerical simulations of the estimated model we indeed then found that the reestablishment of money wage flexibility in severely depressed regions of the phase space (however coupled with some midrange downward wage rigidity) can avoid this breakdown, however at the costs of persistent economic fluctuations, to some extent below the normal operating level of the economy. In the present framework (of a profit-led goods demand regime, where real wage increases lead to a decrease in economic activity), downward money wage flexibility is therefore good for economic stability. The opposite conclusion however holds with respect to price flexibility.

The dynamic outcomes of this baseline disequilibrium AS–AD or DAS–DAD model can be usefully contrasted with those of the currently fashionable New Keynesian alternative (the new Neoclassical Synthesis), which in our view is more limited in scope, at least as far as the treatment of interacting Keynesian feedback mechanisms and the thereby implied dynamic possibilities are concerned. A detailed comparison with this New Keynesian approach is provided in Chiarella *et al.* (2005, Ch. 1). This comparison reveals in particular that one does not really need the typical (in our view strange) dynamics of rational expectation models, based on the specification of certain forward-looking variables, if such forward-looking behavior is coupled with backward-looking behavior for the medium-run evolution of the economy (and neoclassical dating in the forward-looking part) and if certain nonlinearities in economic behavior make the obtained dynamics bounded far off the steady state. In our approach, standard Keynesian feedback mechanisms are coupled with a wage–price spiral having – besides partial forward-looking behavior – a considerable degree of inertia, with the result that these feedback mechanisms by and large work as expected (as known from partial analysis), in their interaction with the added wage and price level dynamics.

9. Conclusions and outlook

We have considered in this paper a significant extension and modification of the traditional approach to AS–AD growth dynamics, primarily by way of an appropriate reformulation of the wage–price block of the model, which allows us to avoid the dynamical inconsistencies of the traditional Neoclassical Synthesis. It also allows us to overcome the empirical weaknesses and theoretical indeterminacy problems of the New Keynesian approach that arise from the existence of only purely forward-looking behavior in baseline models of staggered price and wage setting. Conventional wisdom, based on the rational expectations approach, in such situations avoids the latter indeterminacy problems by appropriate extensions of the baseline model that enforce its total instability (the existence of only unstable roots), with the result that the steady state represents the only bounded trajectory in the deterministic core of the model (to which the economy must then by construction immediately return when hit by a demand, supply or policy shock).

By contrast, our alternative approach – which allows for sluggish wage as well as price adjustment and also for certain economic climate variables, representing the medium-run evolution of inflation – completely bypasses the purely formal imposition of such boundedness assumptions. Instead it allows us to demonstrate in a detailed way, guided by the intuition behind important macroeconomic feedback channels, local asymptotic stability under certain plausible assumptions (indeed very plausible from the perspective of Keynesian feedback channels), cyclical loss of stability when these assumptions are violated (if speeds of adjustment become sufficiently high), and even explosive fluctuations in the case of further increases of the crucial speeds of adjustment of the model. In the latter case further behavioral nonlinearities have to be introduced in order to tame the explosive dynamics, for example, as in Chiarella and Flaschel (2000, Chs. 6, 7), where a kinked PC (downward wage rigidity) is employed to achieve global boundedness.

The stability features of these – in our view properly reformulated – Keynesian dynamics are based on specific interactions of traditional Keynes- and Mundell effects or real rate of interest effects with real-wage effects. In the present framework – for our estimated parameters – these effects simply imply that increasing price flexibility will be destabilizing but increasing wage flexibility might be stabilizing. On the other hand, if monetary policy responds sufficiently strongly to the output or inflation gap there can be less wage flexibility to obtain boundedness of fluctuations. This is based on the empirical fact that aggregate demand here depends negatively on the real wage and on the extended types of PCs we have employed in our new approach to traditional Keynesian growth dynamics. The interaction of these three effects is what explains the obtained stability results under the (in this case not very important) assumption of myopic perfect foresight, on wage as well as price inflation, and thus gives rise to a traditional type of Keynesian business cycle theory, not at all plagued by the anomalies of the textbook AS–AD dynamics.[22]

Our model provides an array of stability results, which however are narrowed down to damped oscillations when the model is estimated with data for the U.S. economy after World War II (and monetary policy is made somewhat more active in the theoretical model than in the estimated one). Yet, also in the strongly convergent case, there can arise stability problems if the linear wage PC is modified to allow for some downward money wage rigidities. In such a case, prices may fall faster than wages in a depression, leading to real wage increases

---

[22] See Chiarella *et al.* (2005) for a detailed treatment and critique of this textbook approach.

and thus to further reductions in economic activity. We have shown in this regard how the reestablishment of downward movement may be avoided leading then to a persistent business fluctuations of more or less irregular type and thus back to a further array of interesting stability scenarios. As we have shown monetary policy can avoid such downward movements and preserve damped oscillatory behavior, primarily through the adoption of a target rate of inflation that is chosen appropriately, and in case of the establishment of persistent fluctuations of the above type, reduce such fluctuations by a controlled activation of its response to output gaps or a choice of its response to inflation gaps in a certain corridor, as was shown by way of numerical examples. Therefore, no simple answer can be given to the question into which direction monetary policy should be changed in order to make the economy less and indeed not more volatile.[23]

Taking all this together, our general conclusion is that the framework proposed here does not only overcome the anomalies of the Neoclassical Synthesis, Stage I, but also provides a coherent alternative to its second stage, the New Keynesian theory of the business cycle, as for example sketched in Gali (2000). Our alternative to this approach to macrodynamics is based on disequilibrium in the market for goods and labor, on sluggish adjustment of prices as well as wages and on myopic perfect foresight interacting with a certain economic climate expression. The rich array of dynamic outcomes of our model provide great potential for further generalizations. Some of these generalizations have already been considered in Chiarella *et al.* (2000) and Chiarella *et al.* (2005). Our overall approach, which may be called a disequilibrium approach to business cycle modeling of mature Keynesian type, thus provides a theoretical framework within which to consider the contributions of authors such as Zarnowitz (1999), who also stresses the dynamic interaction of many traditional macroeconomic building blocks.

---

[23] The model of the current paper is further explored numerically in a companion paper (see Chen *et al.*, (2006)), in order to analyze in greater depth, the interaction of the various feedback channels present in the considered dynamics. There use is made of LM curves as well as Taylor interest rate policy rules, kinked PCs and Blanchard and Katz error-correction mechanisms in order to investigate in detail the various ways by which locally unstable dynamics can be made bounded and thus viable. The question then is which assumption on private behavior and fiscal and monetary policy – once viability is achieved – can reduce the volatility of the resulting persistent fluctuations. Our work on related models suggests that interest rate policy rules may not be sufficient to tame the explosive dynamics in all conceivable cases, or even make them convergent. But when viability is achieved – for example by downward wage rigidity – we can then investigate parameter corridors where monetary policy can indeed reduce the endogenously generated fluctuations of this approach to Keynesian business fluctuations.

References

Asada, T., P. Chen, C. Chiarella and P. Flaschel (2006), *"Keynesian Dynamics and the Wage–Price Spiral. A Baseline Disequilibrium Model"*, Journal of Macroeconomics, Vol. 28, 90–130.

Asada, T., C. Chiarella, P. Flaschel and R. Franke (2003), *Open Economy Macrodynamics. An Integrated Disequilibrium Approach*, Heidelberg: Springer.

Barro, R. (1994), "The aggregate supply/aggregate demand model", *Eastern Economic Journal*, Vol. 20, pp. 1–6.

Baxter, M. and R. King (1995), "Measuring business cycles: approximate band-pass filters for economic time series", NBER Working Paper, No. 5022.

Baxter, M. and R. King (1999), "Measuring business cycles: approximate band-pass filters for economic time series", *The Review of Economics and Statistics*, Vol. 81(4), pp. 575–593.

Blanchard, O.J. and L. Katz (1999), "Wage dynamics: reconciling theory and evidence", *American Economic Review Papers and Proceedings*, Vol. 89(2), pp. 69–74.

Chen, P. (2003), "Weak exogeneity in simultaneous equations systems", Discussion Paper No. 502, University of Bielefeld.

Chen, P., C. Chiarella, P. Flaschel and H. Hung (2006), "Keynesian disequilibrium dynamics. Estimated convergence, roads to instability and the emergence of complex business fluctuations", Working paper, School of Finance and Economics, UTS.

Chen, P. and P. Flaschel (2004), "Testing the dynamics of wages and prices for the US economy", Working paper, Bielefeld: Center for Empirical Macroeconomics.

Chiarella, C. and P. Flaschel (1996), "Real and monetary cycles in models of Keynes–Wicksell type", *Journal of Economic Behavior and Organization*, Vol. 30, pp. 327–351.

Chiarella, C. and P. Flaschel (2000), *The Dynamics of Keynesian Monetary Growth: Macro Foundations*, Cambridge, UK: Cambridge University Press.

Chiarella, C., P. Flaschel and R. Franke (2005), *Foundations for a Disequilibrium Theory of the Business Cycle. Qualitative Analysis and Quantitative Assessment*, Cambridge, UK: Cambridge University Press.

Chiarella, C., P. Flaschel, G. Groh and W. Semmler (2000), *Disequilibrium, Growth and Labor Market Dynamics*, Heidelberg: Springer.

Davidson, R. and J. Mackinnon (1993), *Estimation and Inference in Econometrics*, New York: Oxford University Press.

Eller, J.W. and R.J. Gordon (2003), "Nesting the New Keynesian Phillips curve within the mainstream model of U.S. inflation dynamics", Paper presented at the CEPR conference: The Phillips curve revisited, June 2003, Berlin.

Filardo, A. (1998), "New Evidence on the output cost of fighting inflation", *Economic Review*. Federal Bank of Kansas City, Vol. 83, pp. 33–61.

Flaschel, P. and G. Groh (1995), "The classical growth cycle: reformulation, simulation and some facts", *Economic Notes*, Vol. 24, pp. 293–326.

Flaschel, P., G. Kauermann and W. Semmler (2004), "Testing wage and price Phillips curves for the United States", Discussion Paper, Center for Empirical Macroeconomics, Bielefeld University.

Flaschel, P. and H.-M. Krolzig (2004), "Wage and price Phillips curves. An empirical analysis of destabilizing wage–price spirals", Discussion paper, Oxford University, Oxford.

Fuhrer, J.C. and G.D. Rudebusch (2004), "Estimating the Euler equation for output", *Journal of Monetary Economics*, Vol. 51, 1133 ff.

Gali, J. (2000), "The return of the Phillips curve and other recent developments in business cycle theory", *Spanish Economic Review*, Vol. 2, pp. 1–10.

Groth, C. (1992), "Some unfamiliar dynamics of a familiar macromodel", *Journal of Economics*, Vol. 58, pp. 293–305.

Hoogenveen, V.C. and S.K. Kuipers (2000), "The long-run effects of low inflation rates", *Banca Nazionale del Lavoro Quarterly Review*, Vol. 53, pp. 267–286.

Keynes, J.M. (1936), *The General Theory of Employment, Interest and Money*, New York: Macmillan.

Laxton, D., D. Rose and D. Tambakis (2000), "The U.S. Phillips-curve: the case for asymmetry", *Journal of Economic Dynamics and Control*, Vol. 23, pp. 1459–1485.

Mankiw, G. (2001), "The inexorable and mysterious tradeoff between inflation and unemployment", *Economic Journal*, Vol. 111, pp. 45–61.

Okun, A.M. (1970), *The Political Economy of Prosperity*, Washington, DC: The Brookings Institution.

Rose, H. (1967), "On the non-linear theory of the employment cycle", *Review of Economic Studies*, Vol. 34, pp. 153–173.

Rudebusch, G.D. and L.E.O. Svensson (1999), "Policy rules for inflation targeting", in: J.B. Talor, editor, *Monetary Policy Rules*, Chicago: Chicago University Press.

Tobin, J. (1975), "Keynesian models of recession and depression", *American Economic Review*, Vol. 65, pp. 195–202.

Walsh, C.E. (2003), *Monetary Theory and Policy*, Cambridge, MA: The MIT Press.

Woodford, M. (2003), *Interest and Prices*, Princeton: Princeton University Press.

Zarnowitz, V. (1999), "Theory and history behind business cycles: are the 1990s the onset of a golden age?" NBER Working paper 7010, http://www.nber.org/papers/w7010.

CHAPTER 9

Advanced Keynes–Metzler–Goodwin Macro Modeling: A Calibration Study

Reiner Franke*

Abstract

The paper puts forward a deterministic macrodynamic model of the business cycle that allows for sluggish price and quantity adjustments in response to disequilibrium on product and labour markets. Based on regular oscillations of two exogenous variables, 14 reaction coefficients are determined in such a way that the cyclical patterns of the endogenous variables are broadly compatible with stylized facts. This calibration procedure is organized in a hierarchical structure, so that subsets of the parameters can be established step by step. In a second stage, the previous findings are checked with empirical fluctuations of the exogenous variables. Thirdly, the latter are endogenized and the corresponding additional parameters are chosen. The resulting dynamic system, which in its reduced form is of dimension six, generates persistent cyclical behaviour with similar time series properties of the variables as obtained before.

Keywords: calibration, business cycle theory, disequilibrium adjustments, wage–price dynamics, aggregate demand

JEL classifications: E12, E24, E25, E32

1. Introduction

The paper takes up a deterministic macrodynamic modelling framework from the literature as it has been recently expounded by Chiarella and Flaschel (2000, Chapter 6), Chiarella *et al.* (2000, Chapters 3 and 4), or Flaschel *et al.* (2001).

---

*Corresponding author. Institute for Monetary Economics, Technical University, Vienna, Austria.

CONTRIBUTIONS TO ECONOMIC ANALYSIS
VOLUME 277   ISSN: 0573-8555
DOI:10.1016/S0573-8555(05)77009-7

Allowing for disequilibrium on the product and labour markets, which gives rise to sluggish price and quantity adjustments, the approach incorporates elements of economic theory that are, in particular, connected with the names of Keynes, Metzler and Goodwin. Briefly, Keynesian elements are encountered in the treatment of aggregate demand (besides an LM-sector), Metzler has stimulated the modelling of production and inventory investment decisions, and Goodwinian ideas are reflected in the income distribution dynamics. Although each modelling block is quite simple, the model in its entirety is already of dimension six. It is thus still possible to carry out a mathematical analysis that delivers meaningful conditions for local stability (see Köper, 2000), but an investigation of the global dynamics of the system has to rely on computer simulations. This, in turn, raises the problem of setting the numerical parameters, especially the reaction coefficients. After all, even without the investment function there are 14 parameters to be determined.

One approach to numerical parameter setting is, of course, econometric estimation. Using single equation or subsystem estimations, it was employed in Flaschel *et al.* (2001). This study, however, cannot yet deemed to have settled the issue since the presentation is not always transparent and, more seriously, not all coefficients appear credible.[1] Supplementarily to this kind of work, we therefore choose an alternative approach. That is, referring to a business cycle context we seek to calibrate the model.

A few words may be in order to clarify the concept of calibration as we understand it here. The aim of calibrating a model economy is to conduct (computer) experiments in which its properties are derived and compared to those of an actual economy. In this respect calibration procedures can be viewed as a more elaborate version of the standard back-of-the-envelope calculations that theorists perform to judge the validity of a model. The underlying notion is that every model is known to be false. A model is not a null hypothesis to be tested, it is rather an improper or simplified approximation of the true data-generating process of the actual data. Hence, a calibrator is not interested in verifying whether the model is true (the answer is already known from the outset), but in identifying which aspects of the data a false model can replicate.[2]

Our investigation of how well the model-generated trajectories match the data follows the usual practice. We select a set of stylized facts of the business cycle, simulate the model on the computer, and assess the corresponding cyclical properties of the resulting time series in a more or less informal way. Since a (false) model is chosen on the basis of the questions it allows to ask, and not on its being realistic or being able to best mimic the data, we share the point of view

---

[1] For example, in the working paper version (October 2000) the time unit underlying the fluctuations in the time series diagrams is not made explicit; the stock adjustment speed is implausibly low; or a discussion of the cyclical implications for the real wage dynamics is missing.

[2] See also the introductory discussion in Canova and Ortega (2000, pp. 400–403).

that rough reproduction of simple statistics for comovements and variability is all that is needed to evaluate the implications of a model.[3] In sum, our philosophy of setting the numerical parameters is similar to that of the real business cycle school, though the methods will be different in detail.

It turns out that the model gives rise to a hierarchical structure in the calibration process. Some variables which are exogenous in one model-building block are endogenous within another module at a higher level. Thus, the parameters need not all be chosen simultaneously, but fall into several subsets that can be successively determined. This handy feature makes the search for suitable parameters and the kind of compromises one has to accept more intelligible.

The evaluation of the numerical parameters takes place at three stages. Most of the work is done at the first stage. Here we suppose exogenous motions of two exogenous variables that drive the rest of the model. These are capacity utilization and, synchronously with it, the capital growth rate. Since random shocks are neglected in our framework, the exogenous motions may well be of a regular and strictly periodic nature, most conveniently specified as sine waves. This perhaps somewhat unusual approach can be viewed as a heuristic device. It is more carefully defended later in the paper.

Tying ourselves down to a base scenario, it is then checked at a second stage whether the previous results are seriously affected if the exogenous sine waves are replaced with the more noisy time paths of the empirical counterpart of the utilization variable and the thus induced capital growth rate.

The decisive test to which the numerical parameters are put is, however, stage three. Here we endogenize capacity utilization and propose an investment function. Setting the parameters thus newly introduced, the model is now fully endogenous and we can study the properties of the time series it generates. The calibration will have passed this test if the model produces persistent cyclical behaviour with similar features as found before.

The remainder of the paper is organized as follows. Section 2 expounds the stylized facts of the business cycle that will be used as guidelines. Section 3 presents the model at calibration levels 1–3, which determine the wage-price dynamics. Section 4 turns to the interest rate and then to demand and the quantity adjustments on the goods market, with the parameters to be set at levels 4–6. The main calibration is undertaken in Section 5. It puts forward the numerical coefficients and discusses their cyclical implications, as well as the kind of compromises we make, at stage one and two of the analysis. The complete endogenous model, stage three, is examined in Section 6. Section 7 concludes. An appendix makes explicit the details concerning the construction of the empirical time series we are referring to. It also contains a list of notation.

---

[3] As Summers (1991, p. 145) has expressed his scepticism about decisive formal econometric tests of hypotheses, "the empirical facts of which we are most confident and which provide the most secure basis for theory are those that require the least sophisticated statistical analysis to perceive."

2. Stylized facts

Our measure of the business cycle is capacity utilization u. As we use it, this notion rests on an output–capital ratio y^n that would prevail under 'normal' conditions. With respect to a given stock of fixed capital K, productive capacity is correspondingly defined as $Y^n = y^n K$. Y being total output and y the output–capital ratio, capacity utilization is thus given by $u = Y/Y^n = y/y^n$. Against this theoretical background, the motions of the output–capital ratio in the firm sector (nonfinancial corporate business) may be taken as the empirical counterpart of the fluctuations of u.

In the models' production technology, y^n is treated as a constant. In reality, however, there are some variations in y at lower than the business cycle frequencies. To filter out the cyclical component of this as well as the other variables below, we employ the concept of a deterministic trend.[4] Regarding y, this means that we treat the 'normal' output–capital ratio as variable over time and set $y^n = y_t^n$ equal to the trend value of y at time t. In this way, the model's deviations from normal utilization, $u - 1$, can be identified with the empirical trend deviations $(y_t - y_t^n)/y_t^n$.

Specifically, the Hodrick–Prescott (HP) filter is adopted for detrending. Choosing a smoothing parameter $\lambda = 1600$ for the quarterly data of the output–capital ratio and looking at the resulting time series plot, one may feel that the trend line nestles too closely against the actual time path of y. This phenomenon is not too surprising since the HP 1600 filter amounts to defining the business cycle by those fluctuations in the time series that have periodicity of less than eight years (cf. King and Rebelo, 1999, p. 934), whereas the US post-war economy experienced two trough-to-trough cycles that exceed this period.[5]

---

[4] Beginning with Nelson and Plosser (1982), it was argued that the trends in macroeconomic time series were stochastic, so that much of the variation that had been considered business cycles would actually be permanent shifts in trend. While this stochastic view of the world soon became predominant, the pendulum has in the meantime swung back from that consensus. Thus, from recent research on this issue it can be concluded "that at the very least there is considerable uncertainty regarding the nature of the trend in many macroeconomic time series, and that, in particular, assuming a fairly stable trend growth path for real output – perhaps even a linear deterministic trend – may not be a bad approximation" (Diebold and Rudebusch, 2001, p. 8; this short paper is a slightly revised version of the introductory chapter of their book on business cycles from Diebold and Rudebusch (1999)).

[5] According to the NBER reference data, one is from February 1961 to November 1970, the other from November 1982 to March 1991. In recent times, the band-pass (BP) filter developed by Baxter and King (1995) has gained in popularity. On the basis of spectral analysis, this procedure is mathematically more precise about what constitutes a cyclical component. The BP(6,32) filter preserves fluctuations with periodicities between six quarters and eight years, and eliminates all other fluctuations, both the low frequency fluctuations that are associated with trend growth and the high frequencies associated with, for instance, measurement error. More exactly, with finite data sets the BP(6,32) filter approximates such an ideal filter. As it turns out, for the time series with relatively low noise (little high-frequency variation) the outcome of the HP 1600 and the BP(6,32) filter is almost the same. For real national US output, this is exemplified in King and Rebelo (1999, p. 933, Figure 9.1).

Other filters, such as HP with values of $\lambda = 6400$ or higher, or a segmented linear trend, correspond better to what one may draw freehand as an intuitive trend line in a diagram. However, the cyclical pattern of the trend deviations is in all cases very similar, only the amplitudes are somewhat larger. Because in the literature the HP filter is based on $\lambda = 1600$ with almost no exception, we may just as well follow this conventional practice. The trend deviations of the output–capital series thus obtained, or likewise of capacity utilization $u - 1$, are exhibited in the top panel of Figure 9.1.

The HP 1600 filter is also applied to the other empirical series we are studying. Similarly as with the output–capital ratio, the trend deviations of these cyclical components might appear somewhat narrow, too. This phenomenon, however, need not be of great concern to us, as it will serve our purpose to express the standard deviations of these variables in terms of the standard deviation of u.

In the calibration procedure, we are concerned with the cyclical behaviour of nine endogenous variables. Regarding the wage–price dynamics, these are the employment rate e, labour productivity z, the (productivity-deflated) real wage rate ω, the wage share v and the price level, p. In addition, with respect to the goods and money markets our interest attaches to excess demand ξ (in relative terms, $\xi = (Y^d - Y)/Y$, where Y^d are real sales), to the consumption ratio C/Y, the inventory ratio $n = N/K$ (N the stock of inventories) and the bond rate of interest i. The empirical counterparts of these variables are depicted as the bold lines in Figures 9.1 and 9.2. For a first assessment of their cyclical properties and the size of their variation, the thin lines reproduce the reference series of capacity utilization. Source and construction of the empirical data are described in the appendix.

Note that in Figure 9.1 the cyclical components are measured in per cent of the trend values, that is, a variable x_t with trend values x_t^o is represented as $100(x_t - x_t^o)/x_t^o$. By contrast, the trend deviations of the variables in Figure 9.2, which are already themselves expressed in percentage points, are just the differences $x_t - x_t^o$ between the original values and the trend values. Relative excess demand ξ is plotted directly. Here the reference line is not the zero level but is drawn at -0.657%, which is the time average of the series. It is explained in the theoretical part that on average ξ should indeed be slightly less than zero because a small fraction of production is excepted from being sold on the market and put to inventories to keep them growing with the rest of economy.

The first endogenous variable, labour productivity z, has to be dealt with since in the modelling framework it connects, on the one hand, the employment rate with utilization and, on the other hand, the real wage rate with the wage share. Labour productivity has since long been counted a procyclical variable. May it suffice to mention that Okun (1980, pp. 821f) lists it among his stylized facts of the business cycle. Procyclical variations of z can to some degree also be recognized in the second panel in Figure 9.1, perhaps

Figure 9.1.   Cyclical components of empirical series 1

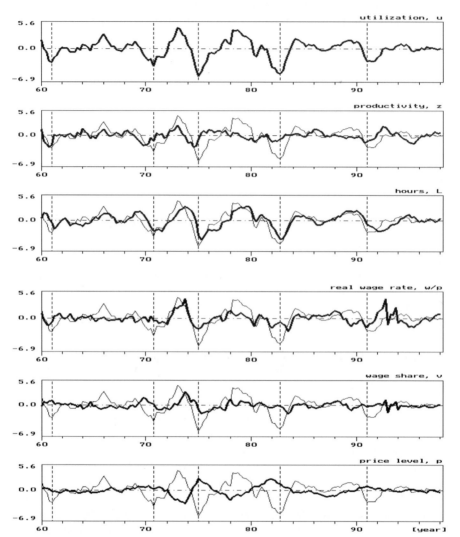

Note: Variables measured in per cent of their trend values (HP 1600). The thin line is the cyclical component of utilization.

with a slight lead before u. The cross-correlation coefficients quantifying the comovements of z with u are given in Table 9.1, whose sample period 1961–1991 covers four major trough-to-trough cycles. Reckoning in a lead of z between one and three quarters, these statistics indicate a stronger relationship

Figure 9.2. Cyclical components of empirical series 2

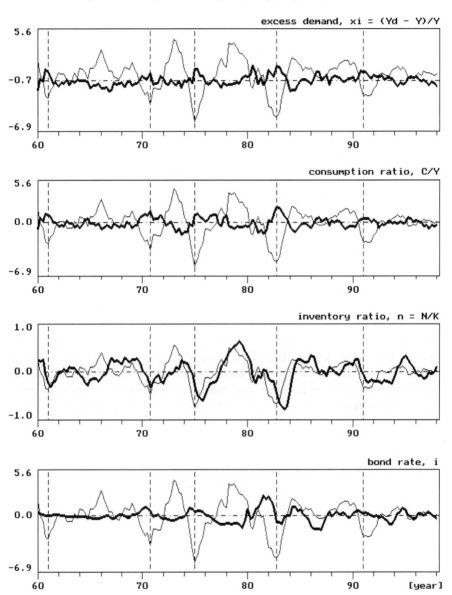

Note: Except for the top panel, differences between variables and their trend values (HP 1600), both measured in percentage points. The thin line is the cyclical component of utilization (in the third panel it is scaled down by the standard deviation of *n*).

**Table 9.1. Descriptive statistics for cyclical components of quarterly series,
1961:1–91:4**

| Series x | σ_x/σ_u | Cross Correlations between u at Time t and x at Time | | | | | | |
		$t-3$	$t-2$	$t-1$	t	$t+1$	$t+2$	$t+3$
u	–	0.48	0.70	0.89	1.00	0.89	0.70	0.48
z	0.44	0.56	0.58	0.53	0.46	0.17	−0.06	−0.27
L	0.83	0.03	0.30	0.57	0.79	0.88	0.86	0.77
w/p	0.51	0.31	0.48	0.57	0.61	0.56	0.48	0.34
v	0.38	−0.21	−0.05	0.09	0.21	0.42	0.53	0.57
p	0.51	−0.59	−0.70	−0.73	−0.70	−0.62	−0.49	−0.32
ξ	0.32	−0.29	−0.39	−0.49	−0.62	−0.52	−0.35	−0.17
C/Y	0.35	0.07	−0.17	−0.43	−0.68	−0.69	−0.62	−0.51
n	0.13	0.01	0.17	0.36	0.59	0.74	0.81	0.79
i	0.36	−0.59	−0.59	−0.50	−0.37	−0.27	−0.18	−0.09
g_k	0.29	−0.06	0.20	0.48	0.72	0.84	0.86	0.80

Note: All series detrended by Hodrick–Prescott (with smoothing factor $\lambda = 1600$). g_k is the capital growth rate, notation of the other variables as in Figures 9.1 and 9.2. σ designates the standard deviation.

between z and u than one might possibly infer from a visual inspection of the time series alone.[6]

To get information about the employment rate, we refer to total working hours L. For simplicity, we directly interpret the trend line, $L^o = L^o_t$, as labour supply, i.e., as supply of normal working hours. In this view, the normal employment rate is given by $e = 1$, and the deviations from normal employment are proxied by $e_t - 1 = (L_t - L^o_t)/L^o_t \approx \ln(L_t - L^o_t)$, which is the series displayed in the third panel in Figure 9.1. The juxtaposition with utilization in the same panel makes clear that this employment rate is markedly procyclical. The third line in Table 9.1 details that it lags one or two quarters behind u.

The controversy surrounding the comovements of the real wage rate is usually summarized by saying that, if anything, it moves (weakly) procyclical, rather than countercyclical. Results about the cyclical properties of the real wage appear to be quite sensitive to precisely how it is constructed, depending on the

---

[6] Unfortunately, the statistics cannot be compared with the most recent comprehensive compilation of stylized business cycle facts by Stock and Watson (1999), since they employ real GDP as a measure of the business cycle. Over the sample period 1953–1996, they report a cross-correlation coefficient as large as $\rho(z_{t-k}, \text{GDP}_t) = 0.72$ for a lead of $k = 2$. Curiously enough, we could not reproduce a similar number with the trend deviations of the GDP series taken from Ray Fair's database (see the appendix), which is due to the fact that (especially) over the subperiod 1975–1982 this series is quite different from the Citibase GDP series used by Stock and Watson (statistically, it shows less first-order autocorrelation).

particular index in the denominator (p) and on whether the numerator (w) includes various compensation items. Since our modelling context is a one-good economy, we adopt the deflator of total output as our price level, so that w/p denotes the product real wage. On the other hand, we follow Ray Fair's procedure (see the appendix) and include a uniform 50% wage premium as a rough measure for overtime payment.

On the basis of this specification, Figure 9.1 (fourth panel) shows that the real wage rate is fairly closely connected to the motions of capacity utilization, while quantitative evidence for its procyclicality is given in Table 9.1. Although this finding is in some contrast to what is reported in the literature, it should play an important role in the calibration later on.[7]

The variable that more directly describes the distribution of income between workers and capital owners is the wage share v. It is only rarely mentioned in the discussion of typical features of a business cycle. This might in part also be due to the special difficulties that one encounters for this variable in separating a cyclical component from some intermediate quasi-trend behaviour. The HP 1600 trend deviations depicted in the fifth panel in Figure 9.1 may therefore be taken with some care.

Accepting them as they are, we here see another explanation for the infrequent reference to the wage share: it does not exhibit a distinctive and unique cyclical pattern. Over the 1960s, v looks rather countercyclical, whereas from 1970 to 1990 it appears to be more or less procyclical. In fact, over the 1960s the highest (in modulus) correlation coefficient is negative, as large as $\rho(u_t, v_{t-1}) = -0.71$. Over the period 1970–1991 the maximal coefficient is positive; at a lag of three quarters it amounts to $\rho(u_t, v_{t+3}) = 0.67$. For this reason, the cross-correlations given in Table 9.1 over the full period 1961–1991 have to be cautiously interpreted. They do not summarize a general law of a systematic relationship between the business cycle and income distribution, they rather sort of average out these different relationships.

As far as price inflation is concerned, it has to be noted that time series of inflation rates are relatively noisy and so cannot be easily related to the motions of utilization with its high persistence.[8] It is therefore more convenient to study

---

[7] For example, King and Rebelo (1999, p. 938) obtain a contemporaneous correlation of compensation per hour with output of $\rho = 0.12$, and the coefficient for the correlation with GDP that is presented by Stock and Watson (1999, Table 9.2) is similarly low. As regards the present data, with no overtime payment in the wage rate the contemporaneous correlation is reduced to 0.34 (and no lagged coefficients are higher), even though the correlation of the trend deviations of the two real wage time series is as high as 0.93. On the other hand, considering the issue more carefully, Barsky *et al.* (1994) argue that real wage indexes may fail to capture changes in the composition of employment over the cycle. They conclude that real wages are procyclical if the composition is held constant.

[8] Quarterly inflation rates have first-order serial correlation in the region of 0.35, which may be compared to the AR(1) coefficients for the trend deviations of u and p, which are 0.89 and 0.92, respectively.

the variations of the price level directly. While prices were formerly treated as procyclical, there seems now to be general consensus that their cyclical component behaves countercyclically (see, for example, Cooley and Ohanian, 1991; Backus and Kehoe, 1992; Fiorito and Kollintzas, 1994). With respect to the price index for total output, this phenomenon is plainly visible in the bottom panel of Figure 9.1. According to Table 9.1, the inverse relationship between p and u is strongest at a lead of the price level by one quarter. Given the tightness of the relationship, countercyclical prices are a challenge for any theory of inflation within a business cycle context.[9]

The next set of variables are related to the goods market. The crucial point is that we here allow for disequilibrium, which is buffered by inventories. It is well known that in low-dimensional versions of the Metzlerian modelling approach used below, inventory investment can possibly be strongly destabilizing through an accelerator mechanism. Because the motions of inventories and their feedbacks on the rest of the economy are determined by the variations of excess demand, it is important to have a representation of this latter variable with reliable cyclical properties. The top panel of Figure 9.2 shows that relative excess demand $\xi = (Y^d - Y)/Y$ behaves in fact quite systematically. That is, ξ displays a fairly consistent countercyclical pattern, though at a much lower amplitude than utilization. This is numerically confirmed in Table 9.1.

Given that in other model variants some components of aggregate demand could be more flexible than they presently are, we may also study consumption on its own. Referring to the consumption ratio C/Y, it is seen that this series exhibits similar properties as ξ.

The state variable in the model that keeps track of the evolution of inventories is the inventory ratio $n = N/K$. The third panel in Figure 9.2 indicates that the motions of the capital stock and excess demand give rise to a markedly procyclical behaviour of this ratio, with a short lag of two or three quarters. The variation of n is, however, quite small (note the different scale of n in Figure 9.2).

The final endogenous variable is the bond rate i in the bottom panel of Figure 9.2. Since the modelling of the financial sector and monetary policy will remain at a very elementary level, we should be content with meeting only some crude qualitative features of this variable.

---

[9] A discussion of the issue of countercyclical prices should make clear what in (structural and descriptive) economic theory the trend line is supposed to reflect: (a) the evolution of prices on a deterministic long-run equilibrium path around which the actual economy is continuously fluctuating, or (b) the time path of an expected price level. From the latter point of view, Smant (1998) argues that other procedures than HP detrending should be adopted and, doing this, concludes that the so specified (unexpected) price movements are clearly procyclical (p. 159). By contrast, our theoretical background is notion (a).

Table 9.1 concludes the review of our business cycle variables with the growth rate of fixed capital g_k. It will be the second exogenous variable in the calibration study, whose cyclical properties will be considered further below.

On the basis of the statistics in Table 9.1, we summarize the cyclical features that one may ideally wish a small (deterministic) macrodynamic model to generate – at least insofar as it exhibits smooth and regular oscillations. Leaving some small play in the numbers, they are listed in Table 9.2. It should be added that when it states a zero lag for productivity z, then this is already due to the simplifying modelling assumption on the production technology in the next section.

A direct implication of the specification of technology will be that, independently of the rest of the model, any standard deviation of z can be achieved. The reason for fixing σ_z somewhat lower than the coefficient 0.44 given in Table 9.1 is the apparently lower amplitude of z in the recent past. In fact, over the sample period 1975–1991, the ratio σ_z/σ_u falls to 0.33 (and the relationship with utilization becomes weaker). The reduction of σ_z/σ_u should carry over to the variations of employment, hence the proportionately lower value of σ_e/σ_u.

We should not be too definitive about the variation of the wage share, either, because the precise empirical construction of this variable and the outcome of the specific detrending mechanism may not be overly robust against alternative procedures. By the same token, it would not be appropriate to commit oneself to a particular phase shift of v. This is all the more true when the lead in labour productivity is neglected (the relationship between the wage share and productivity is made explicit in Equation (9.4) below). Given that $\sigma_v/\sigma_u = 0.31$ over the subperiod 1975–1991, we content ourselves with

Table 9.2. *Desirable features of macrodynamic oscillations*

Variable x	σ_x/σ_u	Lag x
dev z	0.40	0.00
dev e	0.75	0.00–0.75
dev ω	0.45–0.50	−0.50–0.50
dev v	0.30–0.40	—
−dev p	0.45–0.50	−0.75–0.25
−ξ	0.28–0.35	−0.50–0.50
−C/Y	0.30–0.40	−0.25–0.75
n	0.10–0.15	0.00–0.75
i	0.30–0.40	—

Note: 'dev' means deviations from trend or steady-state values in per cent. e is the employment rate, ω the (productivity-deflated) real wage rate. The lags are measured in years.

proposing the range 0.30–0.40 for that ratio and leave the issue of desirable lags of v open.[10]

The desired statistics of the remaining four endogenous variables are straightforward. Our reduced ambitions regarding the cyclical pattern of the bond rate have already been mentioned.

3. Wage–price dynamics

Wage and price adjustments are represented by two Phillips curves. Besides the standard arguments, which are the employment rate e for the wage Phillips curve and capacity utilization u for the price Phillips curve, both curves will also include the wage share v as an additional factor. As is shortly made explicit, e as well as v are connected with capacity utilization through average labour productivity $z = Y/L$. The evolution of z has therefore to be dealt with first.

While we wish to account for the procyclicality of productivity, for a small macrodynamic model to be analytically tractable this should be done in a simplified way. To this end we neglect the lead of z in the comovements with u and postulate a direct positive effect of u on the percentage deviations of z from its trend value z^o.[11] Like the functional specifications to follow, we assume linearity in this relationship,

$$z/z^o = f_z(u) := 1 + \beta_{zu}(u - 1) \tag{9.1}$$

β_{zu} and all other β-coefficients later on are positive constants.

Trend productivity is assumed to grow at an exogenous constant rate g_z. To deal with dynamic relationships, it is convenient to work in continuous time (where for a dynamic variable $x = x(t)$, $\dot{x}$ is its time derivative and $\hat{x}$ its growth rate; $\dot{x} = dx/dt$, $\hat{x} = \dot{x}/x$). Thus,

$$\hat{z}^o = g_z \tag{9.2}$$

Trend productivity also serves to deflate real wages, or to express them in efficiency units. We correspondingly define

$$\omega = w/pz^o \tag{9.3}$$

For short, ω itself may henceforth be referred to as the real wage rate. Obviously, if w/p grows steadily at the rate of technical progress, ω remains fixed over time. Since $v = wL/pY = (w/pz^o)(z^oL/Y) = (w/pz^o)(z^o/z)$, the wage share and the real wage rate are linked together by

$$v = \omega/f_z(u) \tag{9.4}$$

---

[10] The ratios $\sigma_{w/p}/\sigma_u$ and σ_p/σ_u are more stable. For the same subperiod 1975–1991, they amount to 0.46 and 0.50, respectively.

[11] Leaving aside (suitably scaled and autocorrelated) random shocks to the technology, an immediate explanation of the comovements of z and u may be overhead labour and labour hoarding.

To express the employment rate by variables which in a full model would constitute some of the dynamic state variables, we decompose it as $e = L/L^s = z^o(L/Y)(Y/Y^n)(Y^n/K)(K/z^oL^s)$, where L^s is the labour supply (which in the previous section was proxied by the trend values of working hours, L^o). As indicated before, productive capacity is given by $Y^n = y^n K$ with y^n a fixed technological coefficient, and utilization is $u = Y/Y^n$. Hence, if capital per head in efficiency units is denoted by k^s,

$$k^s = K/z^oL^s \tag{9.5}$$

the employment rate can be written as

$$e = y^n u k^s / f_z(u) \tag{9.6}$$

Assuming a constant growth rate g_ℓ for the labour supply,

$$\hat{L}^s = g_\ell \tag{9.7}$$

and denoting the (variable) capital growth rate by g_k, the motions of k^s are described by the differential equation

$$\dot{k}^s = k^s(g_k - g_z - g_\ell) \tag{9.8}$$

It has been mentioned in the introduction that our investigations are based on exogenous oscillations of utilization together with the capital growth rate. Once the time paths $u = u(t)$ and $g_k = g_k(t)$ are given, the time path of the employment rate is determined as well, via (9.8) and (9.6) – independently of the rest of the economy. The only parameter here involved is β_{zu} from the hypothesis on labour productivity in Equation (9.1). This constitutes the first level in the hierarchy of calibration steps. In sum:

Level 1: employment rate e (parameter β_{zu})

$$\dot{k}^s = k^s(g_k - g_z - g_\ell) \tag{9.8}$$

$$e = y^n u k^s / [1 + \beta_{zu}(u - 1)] \tag{9.6}$$

We can thus turn to the Phillips curve mechanism for the nominal wage rate w, where our approach is more flexible than the standard formulations. The main point is that we augment the usual positive feedback from the employment rate by a negative feedback from the wage share, an effect that will turn out to be essential in the calibration of the real wage dynamics. The theoretical content of this extension is discussed in Franke (2001).[12] Apart from that, the changes in w

---

[12] It may directly be argued that at relatively low levels of the wage share, workers seek to catch up to what is considered a normal, or 'fair', level, and that this is to some degree taken up in a wage bargaining process. More rigorously, the negative wage share effect can also be derived from the wage setting model by Blanchard and Katz (1999, p. 6), which makes reference to the workers' reservation wage and interpret it as depending on labour productivity and lagged wages.

are measured against the changes in prices and trend labour productivity, which brings us to a second point. Regarding benchmark inflation here invoked, workers may be conceded to have full knowledge of the short-term evolution of prices. This makes clear that myopic perfect foresight is no problem at all for Keynesian macroeconomics. Besides current inflation $\hat{p}$, the wage bargaining process may refer to expectations about inflation that are related to the medium term. Our notion is that the latter represent a general inflation climate, designated π. Combining these elements we have

$$\hat{w} = \hat{z}^o + \kappa_{wp}\hat{p} + (1 - \kappa_{wp})\pi + f_w(e, v) \tag{9.9}$$

$$f_w = f_w(e, v) := \beta_{we}(e - 1) - \beta_{wv}(v - v^o)/v^o \tag{9.10}$$

where the abbreviation f_w will simplify the presentation below, κ_{wp} is a parameter between 0 and 1 that weighs $\hat{p}$ and π, unity is the normal rate of employment, and v^o serves as a reference value for the wage share.

As for the price adjustments, price Phillips curves are a flexible concept which is at the theoretical core of a variety of macroeconometric models.[13] We employ the following version:

$$\hat{p} = \kappa_{pw}(\hat{w} - \hat{z}^o) + (1 - \kappa_{pw})\pi + f_p(u, v) \tag{9.11}$$

$$f_p = f_p(u, v) := \beta_{pu}(u - 1) + \beta_{pv}[(1 + \mu^o)v - 1] \tag{9.12}$$

The parameter κ_{pw} ($0 \leqslant \kappa_{pw} \leqslant 1$) weighs the influence of current wage inflation (corrected for technical progress) and the inflation climate, which provides a benchmark. As utilization u reflects the pressure of demand, the term $\beta_{pu}(u - 1)$ signifies a demand-pull term. The last component, $\beta_{pv}[(1 + \mu^o)v - 1]$, can be viewed as a cost-push term proper, which goes beyond taking the present inflationary situation into account. Devising μ^o as a target markup rate, we mean by this that prices tend to rise by more than what is captured by the other terms if labour costs are so high that, at current prices, $p < (1 + \mu^o)wL/Y$, which is equivalent to $0 < (1 + \mu^o)wL/pY - 1 = (1 + \mu^o)v - 1$. For reasons of consistency it is assumed that the target markup is compatible with the normal level v^o of the wage share in (9.10), i.e., $(1 + \mu^o)v^o = 1$.[14]

Since in (9.9) and (9.11), current wage and price inflation $\hat{w}$ and $\hat{p}$ are mutually dependant on each other, in the next step the two equations have to be solved for $\hat{w}$ and $\hat{p}$. This presupposes that the weights κ_{pw} and κ_{wp} are not both unity. Obviously, in the resulting reduced-form expressions for $\hat{w}$ and $\hat{p}$, wage

---

[13] For an elaboration of this point see Chiarella *et al.* (2000, pp. 52ff).
[14] Empirical support for a positive impact of v on $\hat{p}$ can be inferred from Brayton *et al.* (1999, pp. 22–27). This is more clearly explained in Franke (2001).

inflation also depends on the core terms in the price Phillips curve, and price inflation on the core terms in the wage Phillips curve. In detail,

$$\hat{w} = \hat{z}^o + \pi + \kappa[\kappa_{wp} f_p(u, v) + f_w(e, v)] \tag{9.13}$$

$$\hat{p} = \pi + \kappa[f_p(u, v) + \kappa_{pw} f_w(e, v)] \tag{9.14}$$

$$\kappa = 1/(1 - \kappa_{pw} \kappa_{wp}) \tag{9.15}$$

It is then seen that in the growth rate of the real wage, $\hat{\omega} = \hat{w} - \hat{p} - \hat{z}^o$, not only trend productivity growth but also the inflation climate π cancels out. This independence of the income distribution dynamics from inflationary expectations may be considered a particularly attractive feature of the approach with two Phillips curves. On the other hand, as emphasized by the notation of the functional expressions f_p and f_w, six new parameters are entering at this level:

Level 2: real wage ω, wage share v ($\kappa_{pw}, \kappa_{wp}, \beta_{pu}, \beta_{pv}, \beta_{we}, \beta_{wv}$)

$$\dot{\omega} = \omega\kappa[(1 - \kappa_{pw})f_w(e, v; \beta_{we}, \beta_{wv}) - (1 - \kappa_{wp})f_p(u, v; \beta_{pu}, \beta_{pv})] \tag{9.16}$$

$$v = \omega/f_z(u) \tag{9.4}$$

$$\kappa = 1/(1 - \kappa_{pw} \kappa_{wp}) \tag{9.15}$$

The inflation climate does have a bearing on the rate of inflation. The law governing the variations of π is specified as a mix of two simple mechanisms. One of them, adaptive expectations, often proves destabilizing if the speed of adjustment is high enough. The other rule, regressive expectations, constitutes a negative feedback. Introducing the weight $\kappa_{\pi p}$ and adopting π^o as a 'normal' value of inflation (or the steady-state value in a full model), and β_π as the general adjustment speed, we posit

$$\dot{\pi} = \beta_\pi[\kappa_{\pi p}(\hat{p} - \pi) + (1 - \kappa_{\pi p})(\pi^o - \pi)] \tag{9.17}$$

Although after the intellectual triumph of the rational expectations hypothesis, working with adaptive expectations has become something of a heresy, in a disequilibrium context there are a number of theoretical and empirical arguments which demonstrate that adaptive expectations make more sense than is usually attributed to them (see Flaschel *et al.*, 1997, pp. 149–162; or more extensively, Franke, 1999). This is all the more true if π is not inflation expected for the next quarter, but if it represents a general climate that is employed as a benchmark value in wage and price decisions, complementarily to current inflation. Contenting ourselves with univariate mechanisms, it thus makes sense if π is assumed to adjust gradually in the direction of $\hat{p}$. The regressive mechanism in (9.17), by contrast, expresses a 'fundamentalist' view, in the sense that the public perceives a certain tendency of inflation to return to normal after some time.[15]

Taken on their own, both principles ($\kappa_{\pi p} = 1$ or $\kappa_{\pi p} = 0$) are of course rather mechanical. They are, however, easy to integrate into an existing macrodynamic framework and, in their combination of stabilizing and destabilizing forces, already allow for some flexibility in modelling the continuous revision of benchmark rates of inflation.

The time paths of $\pi(\cdot)$ from (9.17) will evidently lag behind actual inflation $\hat{p}(\cdot)$. This, as such, is no reason for concern; it is even consistent with inflationary expectations themselves that are made in the real world. Here forecast errors are found to be very persistent, and forecasts of inflation often appear to be biased (see, e.g., Evans and Wachtel, 1993, Figure 9.1 on p. 477, and pp. 481ff).

The time paths of $e(\cdot)$ and $v(\cdot)$ being computed at levels 1 and 2, Equation (9.14) with $f_p = f_p(u, v)$ and $f_w = f_w(e, v)$ for $\hat{p}$ can be plugged in the dynamic Equation (9.17) for the adjustments of π. The solution of $\pi(\cdot)$ here computed can also be used in (9.14) to record the time path of the inflation rate itself. Apart from the two parameters β_π, $\kappa_{\pi p}$, all parameters have already been set before. We review these operations in one step at calibration level 3:

Level 3: price inflation $\hat{p}$, inflation climate π (parameters β_π, $\kappa_{\pi p}$)

$$\dot{\pi} = \beta_\pi[\kappa_{\pi p}(\hat{p} - \pi) + (1 - \kappa_{\pi p})(\pi^o - \pi)] \tag{9.17}$$

$$\hat{p} = \pi + \kappa[f_p(u, v) + \kappa_{pw}f_w(e, v)] \tag{9.14}$$

4. Supply and demand on goods and money markets

4.1. The money market

Financial markets are treated at a textbook level. Only two assets are relevant: money and government bonds.[16] Given the money supply M, the bond rate of interest i is determined by a quasi-linear LM equation,

$$M = pY(\beta_{mo} - \beta_{mi}i) \tag{9.18}$$

---

[15] The general idea that an inflation expectations mechanism, which includes past observed rates of inflation only (rather than observed increases in the money supply), may contain an adaptive and a regressive element is not new and can, for example, already been found in Mussa (1975). The specific functional form of Equation (9.17) is borrowed from Groth (1988, p. 254).

[16] For reasons of consistency, equities may be present to finance fixed investment of firms. Their price, however, remains in the background.

In intensive form with output–capital ratio $y = Y/K = (Y/Y^n)(Y^n/K)$ and real balances normalized by the capital stock, $m = M/pK$, Equation (11.17) is readily solved as

$$i = (\beta_{mo} - m/y)/\beta_{mi} \tag{9.19}$$

$$y = uy^n \tag{9.20}$$

The responsiveness of money demand is best measured by the interest elasticity $\eta_{m,i}$, which may be conceived as a positive number. Referring to an equilibrium position with output–capital ratio $y^o = y^n$, a real balances ratio m^o and bond rate i^o, the elasticity is defined as $\eta_{m,i} = (\partial M/\partial i)(i/M) = \beta_{mi}i^o/(\beta_{mo} - \beta_{mi}i^o)$ $= \beta_{mi}i^o/(m^o/y^n)$. Hence, if for the calibration we choose a value of the interest elasticity, the two coefficients β_{mo} and β_{mi} are computed as

$$\beta_{mi} = \eta_{m,i}m^o/y^n i^o \tag{9.21}$$

$$\beta_{mo} = \beta_{mi}i^o + m^o/y^n \tag{9.22}$$

To concentrate on the properties inherent in the private sector, monetary policy is supposed to be completely neutral. Correspondingly, the money supply grows at a constant growth rate g_m,[17]

$$\hat{M} = g_m \tag{9.23}$$

By logarithmic differentiation of $m = M/pK$, real balances therefore evolve according to the differential equation

$$\dot{m} = m(g_m - \hat{p} - g_k) \tag{9.24}$$

Since $g_k(\cdot)$ is exogenous and the time path of $\hat{p}(\cdot)$ is obtained at level 3 of the calibration, no further parameter is needed to determine the solution of (9.24). On this basis, we can then study the implications of different values of the interest elasticity $\eta_{m,i}$ for the motions of the interest rate i. To summarize

Level 4: interest rate i (parameter $\eta_{m,i}$)

$$\dot{m} = m(g_m - \hat{p} - g_k) \tag{9.24}$$

---

[17] A monetary policy rule, most prominently in the form of a Taylor-like rule for setting the rate of interest, may – and should – be introduced into the model in a next step of research.

$$i = (\beta_{mo} - m/y)/\beta_{mi} \tag{9.19}$$

$$y = uy^n \tag{9.20}$$

$$\beta_{mi} = \eta_{m,i}m^o/y^n i^o \tag{9.21}$$

$$\beta_{mo} = \beta_{mi}i^o + m^o/y^n \tag{9.22}$$

4.2. Excess demand for goods

In modelling disequilibrium on the goods market, it is assumed that demand for final goods is always realized. This demand is satisfied from current production and the existing stocks of inventories, while any excess of production over sales replenishes inventories. The thus implied motions of inventories are discussed below. Let us first consider aggregate demand Y^d, which is made up of consumption C, net investment in fixed capital I, replacement investment δK (δ the constant rate of depreciation), and real government spending G,

$$Y^d = C + I + \delta K + G \tag{9.25}$$

Among the components of demand that are presently treated as endogenous, the most important feedback effects are contained in consumption demand of private households. Here we differentiate between workers and asset owners, or more precisely, between consumption financed out of wage income and consumption financed out of rental income. As for the former, it is assumed for simplicity that disposable wage income is exclusively spent on consumption. With respect to a tax rate τ_w and hours worked L, this component of (nominal) consumption expenditures is given by $(1 - \tau_w)wL$.

Next, let B be variable-interest bonds outstanding, whose price is fixed at unity. Disposable income of asset owners consists of interest payments iB plus dividends from firms, minus taxes pT^c. A fraction s_c of this income is saved, the remainder is consumed. Regarding dividends, firms are supposed to pay out all net earnings to the shareholders, where the earnings concept may be based on expected sales, Y^e. Another assumption is that equities are the only external source of financing fixed investment, so that firms incur no interest on debt. Hence dividends are given by $pY^e - wL - \delta pK$, and (nominal) consumption spending out of total rental income is $(1 - s_c)(pY^e - wL - \delta pK + iB - pT^c)$.

In addition to consumption out of wage and rental income, we identify consumption by that part of the population who do not earn income from economic activities, like people living on welfare or unemployment benefits, or retired people drawing on a pension. Since these expenditures are not too closely linked to the business cycle, they may be assumed to grow with the capital stock

pK, as governed by a coefficient $c_p > 0$.[18] We expect this type of consumption to help account for the observed countercyclical consumption ratio C/Y.

Collecting the terms of the three consumption components, total consumption expenditures sum up to

$$pC = c_p pK + (1 - \tau_w)wL + (1 - s_c)(pY^e - wL - \delta pK + iB - pT^c) \qquad (9.26)$$

Fiscal policy, too, should presently play a neutral role, with minimal feedbacks on the private sector. This most conveniently means that taxes T^c, which are conceived as net of real interest receipts, and government spending G are postulated to remain in a fixed proportion to the capital stock:

$$G = \gamma K \qquad (9.27)$$

$$T^c = \theta_c K + iB/p \qquad (9.28)$$

On this basis aggregate demand, normalized by the capital stock, is now fully determined. Defining the constant term a_y,

$$a_y := c_p + \gamma + s_c \delta - (1 - s_c)\theta_c \qquad (9.29)$$

dividing (9.25) by K, using (11.7)–(11.10), and denoting $y^e = Y^e/K$, $y^d = Y^d/K$, we arrive at

$$y^d = (1 - s_c)y^e + (s_c - \tau_w)vy + g_k + a_y \qquad (9.30)$$

The parameters entering (9.29) and (11.29), however, cannot all be freely chosen. We shall later directly set the equilibrium values g^o for the real growth rate, v^o for the wage share, and $y^o = y^n$ for the output–capital ratio. When discussing the production decisions of firms in the next subsection, it will also be shown that equilibrium demand $(y^d)^o$ is slightly less than output y^o. We here anticipate that the two are connected through g^o and another parameter β_{ny}, which is related to inventories: $(y^d)^o = y^n/(1 + \beta_{ny}g^o)$ (cf. Equations (9.36) and (9.44) below). β_{ny} will be equally determined in advance, as will be the parameters δ, γ and θ_c in (9.29). Considering (11.29) in the steady state with $y^e = y^d$ and solving this equation for a_y, we have therefore only two 'free' parameters left on which this magnitude depends, namely, the tax rate on wages τ_w and the propensity s_c to save out of rental income. In explicit terms, a_y and subsequently c_p result like

$$a_y = a_y(s_c, \tau_w) = s_c y^n/(1 + \beta_{ny}g^o) - (s_c - \tau_w)v^o y^n - g^o \qquad (9.31)$$

$$c_p = c_p(s_c, \tau_w) = a_y(s_c, \tau_w) - \gamma - s_c \delta + (1 - s_c)\theta_c \qquad (9.32)$$

---

[18] $c_p pK$ can be thought of as being financed by taxes. In a full model, this expression would also have to show up in the government budget restraint, which lends $c_p pK$ the same formal status as government expenditures. A part of the tax collections could be conceived of as payments into a pension fund, which are directly passed on to retired people. Admittedly, this interpretation neglects the fact that pension funds accumulate financial assets and actively operate on the financial markets, which might be an issue for a more elaborated financial sector.

As we are concerned with the motions of relative excess demand $\xi = (Y^d - Y)/Y$, it remains to put

$$\xi = y^d/y - 1 \tag{9.33}$$

Especially in models where the rigid rule (9.27) for government expenditures is relaxed, one might also be interested in the cyclical pattern of the consumption ratio C/Y. Using (11.7) and (11.10), it is given by

$$C/Y = (s_c - \tau_w)v + [(1 - s_c)y^e + c_p - (1 - s_c)(\delta + \theta_c)]/y \tag{9.34}$$

4.3. Production and inventory decisions

The modelling of stock management and production of firms follows the production-smoothing/buffer-stock approach, which was initiated by Metzler (1941). Although in recent times, its economic significance has been questioned (cf. the survey article by Blinder and Maccini, 1991), it was demonstrated in Franke (1996) that it can be made compatible with the main stylized facts of the inventory cycle.

The approach distinguishes between actual and desired changes in inventories, which are denoted by N. The actual change is just the difference between production Y and sales $=$ demand Y^d,

$$\dot{N} = Y - Y^d \tag{9.35}$$

Desired inventory changes are based on a ratio β_{ny} of inventories over expected sales. Correspondingly, the desired level N^d of inventories is given by

$$N^d = \beta_{ny} Y^e \tag{9.36}$$

N^d generally differs from N, and firms seek to close this gap gradually with speed β_{nn}. That is, if everything else remained fixed, the stock of inventories would reach its target level in $1/\beta_{nn}$ years. In addition, firms have to account for the overall growth of the economy, for which they employ the long-run equilibrium growth rate g^o. The desired change in inventories, designated I_N^d, thus reads

$$I_N^d = g^o N^d + \beta_{nn}(N^d - N) \tag{9.37}$$

Equation (9.37) is the basis of the so-called production-smoothing model; see, e.g., Blinder and Maccini (1991, p. 81).

Production of firms takes care of these desired inventory changes. Otherwise, of course, firms produce to meet expected demand,

$$Y = Y^e + I_N^d \tag{9.38}$$

Equation (9.38) represents the buffer-stock aspect. In fact, by inserting (9.38) into (9.35), which yields $\dot{N} = I_N^d + (Y^e - Y^d)$, it is seen that sales surprises are completely buffered by inventories.

In specifying the formation of sales expectations, we assume adaptive expectations as a straightforward device. Invoking growth similarly as in (9.37), they take the form[19]

$$\dot{Y}^e = g^o Y^e + \beta_y (Y^d - Y^e) \tag{9.39}$$

The time rate of change of the expected sales ratio $y^e = Y^e/K$ is then obtained from $\hat{y}^e = \hat{Y}^e - \hat{K} = g^o + \beta_y[(Y^d - Y^e)/K](K/Y^e) - g_k$. The implied evolution of inventories, equally studied in the intensive form of the inventory ratio $n = N/K$, derives from (9.35) and $\hat{n} = \hat{N} - \hat{K} = (\dot{N}/K)(K/N) - g_k = [(Y - Y^d)/K]/n - g_k$.

On the whole, the goods market dynamics is represented by the following set of equations. Although they require no more input variables (computed at a higher level) than the motions of the rate of interest at level 4, we assign them level 5. Not only would other numbering conventions be more cumbersome, later extensions of the present model might also include the interest rate as another argument in private consumption. We recall that, in particular, the parameters y^n, δ, γ, θ_c and β_{ny} will be determined in advance of the cyclical calibration, so that at this level we only deal with the savings propensity s_c, the tax rate on wages τ_w, and the adjustment speed of the adaptive sales expectations β_y.

Level 5: excess demand ξ, consumption ratio C/Y, inventory ratio n (parameters s_c, τ_w and β_y)

$$\xi = y^d/y - 1 \tag{9.33}$$

$$C/Y = (s_c - \tau_w)v + [(1 - s_c)y^e + c_p - (1 - s_c)(\delta + \theta_c)]/y \tag{9.34}$$

$$y^d = (1 - s_c)y^e + (s_c - \tau_w)vy + g_k + a_y \tag{9.30}$$

$$\dot{y}^e = (g^o - g_k)y^e + \beta_y(y^d - y^e) \tag{9.40}$$

$$\dot{n} = y - y^d - ng_k \tag{9.41}$$

$$a_y = a_y(s_c, \tau_w) = s_c y^n/(1 + \beta_{ny}g^o) - (s_c - \tau_w)v^o y^n - g^o \tag{9.31}$$

$$c_p = c_p(s_c, \tau_w) = a_y(s_c, \tau_w) - \gamma - s_c\delta + (1 - s_c)\theta_c \tag{9.32}$$

---

[19] As an alternative to the usual interpretation of partial adjustments of expected sales Y^e towards realized sales Y^d, (9.39) can also be viewed as an approximation to the results of (univariate) extrapolative forecasts on the basis of a rolling sample period. If the latter has length T, the speed of adjustment β_y is related to T by $\beta_y = 4/T$ (Franke, 1992). Such extrapolative predictions are in the same spirit as the simple extrapolative forecasts that Irvine (1981, p. 635) reports to be common practice in real-world retailer forecasting.

4.4. Endogenous utilization

It may have been noted that one behavioural parameter has not yet been made use of, namely, the stock-adjustment speed β_{nn} from Equation (9.37). Even more important, the previous subsection has put forward a theory of production that so far has not been fully exploited. The point is that the output level in (9.38) implies an endogenous determination of the rate of utilization. So we face the following situation: the exogenous variations of utilization u and the capital growth rate g_k give rise to variations in income distribution (and inflation), which in turn determine aggregate demand, which in turn determines sales expectations and the motions of inventories, from which then firms derive their production decisions and, thus, the utilization of their present productive capacity.

Denoting the endogenously determined value of utilization by u^{endo}, the crucial problem is how such an endogenous time path of $u^{endo}(\cdot)$ compares to the exogenous time path $u(\cdot)$ from which it has been ultimately generated. Ideally, we would like the two trajectories $u^{endo}(\cdot)$ and $u(\cdot)$ to coincide. That is, we are looking for a set of parameters that not only produce acceptable cyclical patterns for the variables already discussed, but which also imply that the underlying motions of utilization exhibit a fixed-point property. It goes without saying that we will be content if the time paths of $u^{endo}(\cdot)$ and $u(\cdot)$ are close, while too large discrepancies between the two would clearly be dubious.

In detail, using (9.38), (9.37) and (9.36), u^{endo} is determined from $Y = Y^e + I_N^d = Y^e + (g^o + \beta_{nn})\beta_{ny} Y^e - \beta_{nn}N$. Division by K gives the endogenous output–capital ratio y^{endo} as a function of y^e and n,

$$y^{endo} = f_y(y^e, n) := [1 + (g^o + \beta_{nn})\beta_{ny}]y^e - \beta_{nn}n \tag{9.42}$$

where now also the abovementioned parameter β_{nn} comes in. β_{nn} can therefore be set at level 6 of the calibration procedure.

Level 6: endogenous utilization u^{endo} (parameter β_{nn})

$$u^{endo} = f_y(y^e, n)/y^n \tag{9.43}$$

$$f_y(y^e, n) = [1 + (g^o + \beta_{nn})\beta_{ny}]y^e - \beta_{nn}n \tag{9.41}$$

At the end of the section, we may provide the argument determining the steady-state value of y^d, which entered the coefficient a_y in (9.31) above. In the same step, the equilibrium value for the inventory ratio n can be derived. Note first that $\dot{y}^e = 0$ and $g_k = g^o$ in (9.40) gives $y^d = y^e$ in the steady state. Then, putting $y = f_y(y^e, n)$ and, in Equation (9.41), $\dot{n} = 0$, we obtain $0 = y - y^d - ng_k = [1 + (g^o + \beta_{nn})\beta_{ny}]y^e - \beta_{nn}n - y^e - ng^o = (g^o + \beta_{nn})\beta_{ny}y^e - (g^o + \beta_{nn})n$; hence $n = \beta_{ny}y^e$. Inserting this in $y = f_y(y^e, n)$ leads to $y = (1 + \beta_{ny}g^o)y^e$. In sum,

$$(y^d)^o = (y^e)^o = y^n/(1 + \beta_{ny}g^o) \tag{9.44}$$

$$n^o = \beta_{ny}y^n/(1 + \beta_{ny}g^o) \tag{9.45}$$

5. Calibration of the model

5.1. The exogenous oscillations

As indicated in Table 9.2, on the whole we are interested in the cyclical behaviour of nine endogenous variables. In the calibration procedure itself, two variables will be exogenous: utilization u and the capital growth rate g_k. Once their time paths are given, the motions of the endogenous variables follow, successively, from the equations summarized under 'level 1' to 'level 6'. To this end, we assume regular oscillations of u and g_k. For convenience, they may take the form of sine waves.

Sine waves would be the outcome in a linear deterministic model, but such undampened and persistent oscillations will there only occur by a fluke. Self-sustained cyclical behaviour in a deterministic modelling framework will accordingly be typically nonlinear, so that even if the solution paths were quite regular, they would still be more or less distinct from a sine wave motion. Unfortunately, we have no clue in what form the endogenous oscillations are affected by these nonlinearities. Any proposal in this direction would have to introduce additional hypotheses, for which presently no solid indications exist. Note that the empirical time series in Figures 9.1 and 9.2 do not seem to exhibit any systematic asymmetries over the single trough-to-trough cycles, a visual impression which is largely confirmed by the literature.[20] So at least this symmetry in the sine waves could be well accepted. It may, on the other hand, be argued that the exogenous variables be driven by a random process. An obvious problem with this device is that our approach has not intended to mimic the random properties of the time series under study. The model could therefore not be evaluated by statistical methods, unless it were augmented by some random variables (cf. Gregory and Smith, 1993, p. 716). Similar as with the nonlinearities just mentioned, however, there are no clear options for such stochastic extensions. Hence, exogenous stochastic fluctuations would here be no less arbitrary than the deterministic sine waves.[21]

There is also another point why random perturbations cannot be readily introduced into the present deterministic framework. It relates to the fact that

---

[20] A standard reference is DeLong and Summers (1986). For a more sophisticated approach (see Razzak, 2001).

[21] To underline that stochastic simulations are no easy way out, we may quote from a short contribution to an econometric symposium: "Most econometricians are so used to dealing with stochastic models that they are rarely aware of the limitations of this approach", a main point being that "all stochastic assumptions, such as assumptions on the stochastic structure of the noise terms, are not innocent at all, in particular if there is no a priori reasoning for their justification" (Deistler, 2001, p. 72). More specifically, regarding a random shock term in a price Phillips curve, which (especially in the context of monetary policy) may possibly have grave consequences for the properties of a stochastic model, McCallum (2001, pp. 5f) emphasizes that its existence and nature is an unresolved issue, even when it is only treated as white noise.

the sine waves generate (approximately) symmetrical deviations of the endogenous variables from their steady-state values, provided the initial levels are suitably chosen. This phenomenon is more important than it might seem at first sight, because it allows us to maintain $v^o, 1, \mu^o, \pi^o$ as constant benchmark values in the adjustment functions (9.10), (9.12) and (9.17). By contrast, in a stochastic setting there may easily arise asymmetric fluctuations in the medium term, especially if, realistically, the exogenous random process has a near-unit root. The asymmetry that over a longer-time horizon utilization, for example, would be more above than below unity would lead to systematic distortions in the adjustment mechanisms. The distortions may be even so strong that they prompt the question if the adjustment rules still continue to make economic sense.[22]

Our methodological standpoint is that sine wave motions of the exogenous variables are a reasonable starting point to begin with. We will, however, not stop there. After deciding on a combination of reasonable parameter values, we will replace the sine waves with a special 'random' series of the exogenous variables, that is, with the empirical trend deviations. In this second step, we will have to check if the basic properties of the endogenous variables are at least qualitatively preserved.

The ensuing third step is the decisive one. Here utilization as well as the capital growth rate are endogenized, which, in particular, means we still have to set up an investment function. Once starting values of the dynamic-state variables are given, the evolution of the economy will then be completely determined. Satisfactory cyclical patterns of the variables generated within the full (deterministic) model will be the final proof for the proposed parameter scenario. In this perspective, the initial sine wave experiments are a heuristic device to find, step by step, or one calibration level after the other, promising numerical values for the many parameters in the model.

After these introductory methodological remarks, we can turn to the numerical details of the sine-wave oscillations. As the US economy went through four cycles between 1961 and 1991, and another cycle seems to have expanded over roughly the last 10 years, we base our investigations on a cycle period of eight years. For utilization, we furthermore assume an amplitude of $\pm 4\%$, so that we have

$$u(t) = 1 + 0.04 \sin(2\pi t/8) \tag{9.46}$$

The amplitude amounts to a standard deviation of $u(\cdot)$ over the eight-year cycle of 2.84%, while the corresponding empirical value is 2.05%. We opt for the

---

[22] To avoid dubious adjustments in these circumstances, the benchmark values might themselves be specified as (slowly) adjusting variables, similar as, for example, a time-varying NAIRU in empirical Phillips curve estimations. While this device may be appealing, it would add further components – and parameters – to the model.

higher amplitude because of our feeling articulated in Section 2 that the HP 1600 trend line of the empirical output–capital ratio absorbs too much medium frequency variation. The choice of the amplitude is, however, only for concreteness and has no consequences for setting the parameters, since the standard deviations of the endogenous variables will always be expressed in terms of utilization.

In contrast, it should be pointed out that for some variables the duration of the cycle does matter. It obviously makes a difference for the amplitude whether, with respect to a fixed adjustment coefficient and thus similar rates of change per unit of time, a variable increases for 24 months or only for, say, 18 months.

Regarding the motions of the capital growth rate, we see in Table 9.1 that it lags utilization by one or two quarters. In economic theory, this delay is usually ascribed to an implementation lag, according to which investment decisions might respond quite directly to utilization or similarly fluctuating variables, but it takes some time until the investment projects are completely carried out and the plant and equipment has actually been built up. For simplicity, most macro models neglect the implementation lag, so that utilization and the capital growth rate tend to move in line (although this will have to be an endogenous feature of any particular model). For this reason, we assume that g_k is perfectly synchronized with u. According to the ratio of the two standard deviations reported in Table 9.1, the amplitude of g_k is a fraction of 0.29 of the 4% in (9.46). Thus,

$$g_k(t) = g^o + 0.29[u(t) - 1] \qquad (9.47)$$

where g^o is the long-run equilibrium growth rate introduced into Equations (9.37) and (9.39) in Section 4.3. By a most elementary growth-accounting identity, g^o is given by adding up the (constant) growth rates of labour supply g_ℓ and trend productivity g_z. As 3% is the order of magnitude of the average growth rate of real output over the period 1960–1998, we specify

$$g_z = 0.02, \quad g_\ell = 0.01, \quad g^o = g_z + g_\ell = 0.03 \qquad (9.48)$$

5.2. Steady-state values and other constant relationships

Before beginning with the calibration of the adjustment parameters of level 1 to level 6, a number of more 'technical' coefficients have to be set, which presumably have a lesser bearing on the dynamics. These are the steady-state ratios and certain coefficients in the demand relationships. (Incidentally, they do not enter the calibration until level 4.) Continuing to denote steady-state values by a superscript 'o', our numerical choice is as follows:

$$y^n = 0.70, \quad v^o = 70\%, \quad \mu^o = 0.429, \quad \delta = 9.5\%$$

$$(k^s)^o = 1.429, \quad \pi^o = 3\%, \quad i^o = 7\%, \quad m^o = 0.140$$

$$\gamma = 0.077, \quad \theta_c = 0.025, \quad \beta_{ny} = 0.220, \quad n^o = 0.153 \qquad (9.49)$$

To check the data we use the package of empirical time series of the US economy that is provided by Ray C. Fair on his home page (see the appendix), which is particularly helpful since it also contains a capital stock series of the nonfinancial firm sector. As concerns the output–capital ratio, the ratio of the empirical real magnitudes, Y/K, is in the region of 0.90. The price ratio p_y/p_k of the output and capital goods is, however, systematically different from unity. It varies around 0.75 until the early-1980s and then steadily increases up to around 1 at the end of the 1990s. Correspondingly, the nominal output–capital ratio, $p_y Y/p_k K$, first varies around 0.65 and then steadily increases up to 0.90. On the grounds that in a two- or multi-sectoral context the relevant ratio would be $p_y Y/p_k K$, we prefer to make reference to the nominal magnitudes and choose an equilibrium value $y^o = y^n = 0.70$, which is slightly higher than 0.65.

When employer social security contribution is included in the definition of the wage share, $v = wL/pY \approx 0.70$ results as the time average between 1952 and 1998. Insofar as wages are a cost on the part of firms, entering the definition of profits, this is an obvious convention. Insofar as, implicitly, these receipts from social insurances are included in the theoretical model, they are taxed at the same rate as wages and the rest is likewise fully spent on consumption. Taking v^o for granted, the target markup rate μ^o derives from the consistency condition $(1 + \mu^o)v^o = 1$.

The physical depreciation rate of the capital stock given by Fair is lower than the value of δ here proposed. However, what Fair calls (nominal) 'capital consumption' in his identity for profits in the firm sector, yields a higher ratio when related to the nominal capital stock $p_k K$. In this way, we decide on $\delta = 9.5\%$. Note that the implied equilibrium (gross) rate of return on real capital is $(1 - v^o)y^o - \delta = 11.5\%$, which does not appear too unreasonable.

In the second row of (9.49), the equilibrium value of k^s is inferred from (9.6). With $e^o = 1$, the solution of this equation for k^s is $(k^s)^o = e^o/y^n = 1.42857$.

Setting the equilibrium values of inflation and the bond rate takes into account that over the period 1960–1998, the real rate of interest is nearly 4% on average. The real balances ratio m is based on a value of 0.20 for M/pY, which is roughly the time average of M1 to nominal output in the last 20 years, when this ratio was relatively stable (as compared to the steady decline until the end of the 1970s). It remains to calculate $m = M/pK = (M/pY)(pY/pK)$, i.e., $m^o = 0.20y^n$. In a similar manner, the government spending coefficient γ is decomposed as $\gamma = G/K = (G/Y)(Y/K)$. Here we take for G/Y the average ratio of nominal government demand to nominal output between 1960 and 1998, which amounts to 0.11 (though the ratio varies considerably over different subperiods).

To get an idea of the order of magnitude of the tax parameter θ_c, view taxes on rental income net of interest receipts, $pT^c - iB = \theta_c pK$ from (11.10), as a fraction τ_c of the profit flow $pY - wL - \delta pK$. Dividing the equation $\tau_c(pY - wL - \delta pK) = \theta_c pK$ by pK allows us to express θ_c as $\theta_c = \tau_c[(1 - v^o)y^n - \delta]$. Setting $\tau_c = 0.20$ yields 0.023 for θ_c, and $\tau_c = 0.25$ increases this value up to 0.02875. Against this background we settle for the value given in (9.49).

Regarding the ratio β_{ny} of desired inventories to expected sales in (9.36), we have the steady state relationship $Y/Y^d = 1 + \beta_{ny}g^o$ from (9.44). On the other hand, in commenting on Figure 9.2 the time average of $\xi = (Y^d - Y)/Y$ was reported to be $\bar{\xi} = -0.657\%$. Rearranging these terms as $Y/Y^d = 1/(1 + \bar{\xi})$, we may equate $1 + \beta_{ny}g^o$ to $1/(1 + \bar{\xi})$, which solving for β_{ny} gives $\beta_{ny} = -\bar{\xi}/(1 + \bar{\xi})g^o = 0.220$. The steady-state value of the inventory ratio n^o is then directly computed from (9.45).

5.3. Calibration of the wage–price dynamics

The calibration of the wage–price dynamics, levels 1–3, can be taken over from one of the wage–price modules investigated in Franke (2001). We briefly report the results relevant for the present model, which emerged as a compromise of different issues. Parameters and cyclical statistics are given in the running text in the course of discussion. For better display, they are collected in an extra compilation in Section 5.6.

We begin with the desired standard deviation, $\sigma_{\text{dev}\,z}/\sigma_u = 0.40$, of the trend deviations of labour productivity in Table 9.2. It is achieved by setting $\beta_{zu} = 0.40$. The induced amplitude of the employment rate is then, however, lower than desired: $\sigma_e/\sigma_u = 0.69$ rather than 0.75. With three quarters, the lag of e is at the upper end of the range given in Table 9.2.

Subsequently, a battery of simulation runs led to the following choice of the six parameters at level 2: $\kappa_{pw} = \kappa_{wp} = 0$, $\beta_{pu} = 0.15$, $\beta_{pv} = 1.50$, $\beta_{we} = 0.55$ and $\beta_{wv} = 0.50$. In this way, the desired standard deviation of the real wage can be met, $\sigma_{\text{dev}\,\omega}/\sigma_u = 0.47$, while the lag is somewhat longer than we aspired to, lag $\omega = 0.75$. With $\sigma_{\text{dev}\,v}/\sigma_u = 0.26$, the oscillations of the wage share are (necessarily, as it turns out) lower than in Table 9.2. They are shifted by about a quarter of a cycle with respect to utilization, lag $v = 2.08$. It is worth pointing out that this type of comovements between measures of economic activity and income distribution is equally obtained in Goodwin's (1967) seminal growth cycle model and its various extensions. Hence the present framework is well compatible with Goodwin's basic approach and could, indeed, provide a richer underpinning of its income distribution dynamics.

The coefficients at level 3 were set freehand at $\beta_\pi = 1.00$, $\kappa_{\pi p} = 0.50$. This choice proves to be justified by the good cyclical pattern of the price level, which is precisely countercyclical, lag$(-\text{dev}\,p) = 0$, and displays a variability of $\sigma_{\text{dev}\,p}/\sigma_u = 0.48$.

The many simulation experiments undertaken in Franke (2001) showed that any improvement in the characteristics of one of the variables here discussed goes at the expense of some other variable(s). These trade-offs were judged worse than what has already been achieved. It was, in particular, worked out that a considerable influence of the wage share in the price as well as in the wage Phillips curve is indispensable for approximately procyclical real wages. As an aside, one might ask whether the present price Phillips curve with its dominant influence of the wage share, through the cost push/target markup argument in Equation (9.12), could still be reckoned a Phillips curve proper.

5.4. Interest rate oscillations

On the basis of the price level dynamics obtained above, we can now turn to the interest rate elasticity $\eta_{m,i}$ at level 4. Given the equilibrium rates of growth, $g^o = 3\%$, and inflation, $\pi^o = 3\%$, the constant growth rate of the money supply in the real balances Equation (9.24) has, of course, to be fixed at $g_m = 6\%$. The time path of $m = M/pK$ is then fully determined, and with a suitable initial value, this ratio oscillates around the steady-state value m^o. Setting the parameters β_{mi} and β_{mo} of the money demand function as done in Equations (9.21) and (9.22) ensures that the bond rate, which is calculated in (9.19), likewise oscillates around its equilibrium value $i^o = 7\%$.[23]

Inspection of Equation (9.19) shows that the cyclical pattern of the interest rate is independent of the interest elasticity, as $\eta_{m,i}$ only affects the coefficients β_{mo} and β_{mi}, but not the time path of m/y. Since $m(\cdot)$ shortly leads $y(\cdot)$ and the sign of the time derivative of i is given by the expression $m\dot{y} - y\dot{m}$, it follows that i still increases when y is already on the downturn (di/dt being still positive when $\dot{y}$ is already negative but so small that $|m\dot{y}| < -y\dot{m}$). Numerically, it turns out that the bond rate peaks 1.17 years after u or y, respectively. In this way the bond rate and utilization display less negative correlation than the empirical coefficients in Table 9.1, but at least the lag is sizeable. In fact, taking into account the extreme simplicity of the financial sector as well as the chosen specification of neutral monetary policy, this result may even be considered rather acceptable. That is, while a more elaborate financial sector is certainly an important task for future modelling, for the time being the LM specification together with the constant money growth rate does not do too much harm.

As the only effect of the interest elasticity is on the amplitude of the bond rate oscillations, $\eta_{m,i}$ may be set at any level desired. Table 9.3 reports the outcome in terms of the relative standard deviation σ_i/σ_u.

A familiar order of magnitude of the elasticity is perhaps $\eta_{m,i} = 0.20$. However, this brings about a fairly low variation of the bond rate. On the other hand, to achieve a standard deviation in the empirical range of $\sigma_i/\sigma_u = 0.36$ of Table 9.1, $\eta_{m,i}$ has to be reduced as much as $\eta_{m,i} = 0.10$ or 0.08. The reason for this phenomenon is, of course, the relatively low variation in the real balances ratio M/pK, which is due to the constant growth rate of M. Incidentally, it may be noted that empirically in the pre-Volcker period the bond rate showed much

---

[23] To be precise, the time average of the inflation rate $\hat{p}$ over a cycle is (very) slightly less than π^o. There is hence a slight upward trend in the time path of m, and a slight downward trend in the time path of the bond rate. It takes, however, more than 30 years for this effect to become directly visible in the time series diagrams.

Table 9.3. Standard deviation (σ_i) of the bond rate at calibration level 4

$\eta_{m,i}$	0.08	0.10	0.12	0.14	0.16	0.20
σ_i/σ_u	0.38	0.30	0.25	0.21	0.19	0.15

less variation. For example, over the period 1961–1975 (which excludes the soaring levels in the second half of the 1970s up to more than 14% at the beginning of the 1980s), we measure $\sigma_i/\sigma_u = 0.19$.

As $\eta_{m,i} = 0.10$ or 0.08 appears unusually small, a value between 0.10 and 0.20 may be chosen. Concretely, in the fully endogenous model in the next section it will be useful to employ $\eta_{m,i} = 0.14$.

5.5. Goods market dynamics

Because of the limited compatibility that our still relatively simple modelling framework exhibits with empirical data on the income flows of groups like 'workers' and 'rentiers', we have some freedom in choosing the numerical values for the latters' savings propensity s_c and the tax rate on wages τ_w. In particular, the presence of the term $c_p p K$ in the consumption function (11.7) allows us to set these parameters somewhat higher than is perhaps usually suggested. The range of a priori admissible values is nevertheless bounded. So we consider $s_c = 0.60, 0.80, 1.00$ for the savings propensity and $\tau_w = 0.30, 0.35$ for the tax rate. A finer subdivision is not necessary.

Before, it should be briefly checked how these values affect the coefficients a_y and c_p in (9.31) and (9.32). This is, however, no problem. a_y and c_p remain within a reasonable range and do not vary too much with changes in s_c and τ_w. Thus, with $\tau_w = 0.35$, a_y increase from 0.265 to 0.347 as s_c rises from 0.60 to 1.00, while c_p increases from 0.141 to 0.175. The effect is similar when $\tau_w = 0.30$ is underlying, only that the values are slightly lower.

Since the cyclical characteristics of the variables turn out to change in a monotonic and regular way, it also suffices to report the results for just two selected values of the adjustment speed β_y of sales expectations: $\beta_y = 4.0$ and 8.0. As discussed in Section 4.3, the three parameters s_c, τ_w, β_y constitute level 5 in the calibration hierarchy and determine the time paths of excess demand ξ, the consumption ratio C/Y, and the inventory ratio n.

Setting subsequently the stock adjustment speed β_{nn} at level 6 has some influence on the endogenous utilization variable u^{endo}. One may, however, be prepared that once the time paths of $u(\cdot)$ and also $y^e(\cdot)$ have been determined at level 5, the chances of suitable and meaningful variations of β_{nn} controlling for the cyclical features of $u^{endo}(\cdot)$ are restricted. For this reason, we set a value of β_{nn} simultaneously with s_c, τ_w, β_y and have then also a look at the characteristics of $u^{endo}(\cdot)$. Concretely, β_{nn} is fixed at 3.0. After dealing with these simulation runs, β_{nn} is changed and we examine if the previous results can thus be improved.

Our final choice of the four parameters s_c, τ_w, β_y, β_{nn} can be discussed on the basis of the results given in Table 9.4. With respect to $\tau_w = 0.35$, $\beta_y = 8$, $\beta_{nn} = 3$ underlying, it shows the consequences of variations of the savings propensity s_c. An increase in s_c raises the standard deviation of the consumption ratio C/Y and relative excess demand ξ. The increase is, however, not sufficient to reach the desired levels of Table 9.2, the gap being larger for excess demand than for consumption. This deficiency cannot be essentially reduced with other values of τ_w and β_y. If we are to maintain the model's otherwise convenient specifications of aggregate demand, then the variability of C/Y and ξ has to be accepted to be confined to the order of magnitude of Table 9.4.

Both the consumption ratio and excess demand display a certain tendency for countercyclical movements, though this feature is weaker for excess demand. It is a bit surprising that despite the imperfections of excess demand, the cyclical features of the inventory ratio $n = N/K$ are within the desired range. This gives us some hope that in the fully endogenous model later on, the implications of the simplifying assumptions on aggregate demand are not too injurious to the inventory dynamics and its repercussion effects.

Regarding the variations of the savings propensity, higher values of s_c are favourable for the countercyclicality of C/Y and ξ and, weakly so, also for their amplitudes. s_c is, of course, bounded from above by unity. Since $s_c = 1$ appears too extreme, we may settle for $s_c = 0.80$. An additional argument for this value is that the associated oscillations, under $\beta_{nn} = 3$, of endogenous utilization u^{endo} are rather promising. The standard deviation of $u^{endo}(\cdot)$ is not too different from the standard deviation of the exogenous sine wave $u(\cdot)$, and the two series are almost synchronous. Note that the more desirable features of C/Y and ξ that can be brought about by increasing s_c go at the expense of a lower amplitude of $u^{endo}(\cdot)$.

As a preliminary conclusion it can thus be stated that, given $\tau_w = 0.35$, $\beta_y = 8$, $\beta_{nn} = 3$, setting $s_c = 0.80$ is a good compromise between the conflicting goals regarding C/Y and ξ on the one hand, and u^{endo} on the other. The value is also economically meaningful.

Taking this for granted, we can now ask for the effects of changing the numerical values of the underlying three parameters. A lower value of the tax rate, $\tau_w = 0.30$, slightly reduces the standard deviation of C/Y and ξ as well as

Table 9.4.   *Cyclical features of variables at calibration levels 5 and 6*

	C/Y		ξ		n		u^{endo}	
s_c	$\tilde{\sigma}$	lag	$\tilde{\sigma}$	lag	$\tilde{\sigma}$	lag	$\tilde{\sigma}$	lag
0.60	0.22	3.25	0.14	2.50	0.12	0.00	1.04	0.50
0.80	0.26	3.42	0.16	2.92	0.12	0.42	0.95	0.25
1.00	0.28	3.50	0.17	3.08	0.12	0.67	0.91	0.08

Note: Besides the parameters set at levels 1–3, $\tau_w = 0.35$, $\beta_y = 8$, $\beta_{nn} = 3$ are underlying. $\tilde{\sigma}$ is the standard deviation of the respective variable in relation to σ_u. The cycle period is 8 years.

their lags. The latter carries over to lag n. The amplitude of $u^{\text{endo}}(\cdot)$ is higher, a little above 1, but the lag is longer, lag $u^{\text{endo}} = 0.50$. On the whole, $\tau_w = 0.30$ may be reckoned slightly inferior to $\tau_w = 0.35$, whereas $\tau_w = 0.40$ not only seems too high a value to us but also reduces the standard deviation of $u^{\text{endo}}(\cdot)$ by too much.

A slower adjustment speed of expected sales, $\beta_y = 4$, results in a small increase in the amplitudes of C/Y, ξ, n and affects the lags of these variables only marginally. These improvements are, however, more than outweighed by the strong decrease in the standard deviation of $u^{\text{endo}}(\cdot)$, whose ratio to σ_u falls down to 0.77 (the lag becomes half a year). The original value $\beta_y = 8$ is therefore better maintained.

As pointed out before, changes in the stock adjustment speed β_{nn} have a bearing on $u^{\text{endo}}(\cdot)$ alone. While the impact on the lags of endogenous utilization turn out to be negligible, a reduction of β_{nn} lowers the standard deviation of $u^{\text{endo}}(\cdot)$, a phenomenon which could also be analytically inferred from the function $f_y = f_y(y^e, n)$ in (9.42). Numerically, $\tilde{\sigma}$, the ratio to σ_u, decreases to 0.90 if $\beta_{nn} = 1$. On the other hand, $\beta_{nn} = 5$ raises it to 1. For the moment being, we may nevertheless keep to $\beta_{nn} = 3$ for two reasons. This adjustment speed amounts to $1/3$ years $= 4$ months within which firms in (9.37) seek to close the gap between actual and desired inventories. By contrast, a lag of $1/5$ years $= 2.4$ months might already appear a bit short. Second, at least in low-dimensional models of the inventory cycle, β_{nn} proves to be destabilizing (cf. Franke, 1996). It is to be feared for the endogenous model that the centrifugal forces evoked by $\beta_{nn} = 5$ are unpleasantly strong.

5.6. Summary of calibration results

For a better overview of what has been done and achieved, we collect the numerical parameter values, 14 in number, in an extra box and then, in Table 9.5, list the statistics of the cyclical features to which they give rise.

We repeat that it could not have been our goal to obtain a perfect match of the cyclical statistics of the empirical series. And even if we came close to full success in this respect, we would not yet know what it would be worth since admittedly the exogenous sine-wave motions of utilization u are very stylized indeed. The results in Table 9.5 and the way we arrived at them being more of a heuristic value, we will have to see how the present set of numerical parameters performs under different conditions.

This brings us to the second test to which the parameters are subjected, where the regular sine waves of u are replaced with the empirical observations of this variable. To this end, we take the quarterly data on u (1960:1–91:4) depicted in Figure 9.1 and interpolate it to get a monthly series. As before, the simulation itself is run for the monthly discrete-time analogues of the model. Figure 9.3 selects six endogenous variables computed in this experiment (i.e., their deviations from the steady-state values) and contrasts them with their empirical

Table 9.5. Cyclical statistics of variables under exogenous sine wave oscillations of utilization

Synopsis of numerical parameters

Level 1:	$\beta_{zu} = 0.40$		
Level 2:	$\beta_{pu} = 0.15$	$\beta_{pv} = 1.50$	$\kappa_{pw} = 0.00$
	$\beta_{we} = 0.55$	$\beta_{wv} = 0.50$	$\kappa_{wp} = 0.00$
Level 3:	$\beta_{\pi} = 1.00$	$\kappa_{\pi p} = 0.50$	
Level 4:	$\eta_{m,i} = 0.14$		
Level 5:	$s_c = 0.80$	$\tau_w = 0.35$	$\beta_y = 8.00$
Level 6:	$\beta_{nn} = 3.00$		

Variable x	σ_x/σ_u	Lag x
dev z	0.40	0.00
e	0.69	0.75
dev ω	0.47	0.75
dev v	0.26	2.08
$-$dev p	0.48	0.00
i	0.21	1.17
ξ	0.16	2.92
C/Y	0.26	3.42
n	0.12	0.42
u^{endo}	0.95	0.25

counterparts. The most remarkable result is that the simulated series follow the essential movements of the empirical variables. This finding supports the parameter choice.

Regarding the wage–price dynamics in the first three panels of Figure 9.3, one notes that in the first half of the 1970s the turning points of the real wage, the wage share as well as the price level have a lower amplitude than in reality. This phenomenon can be attributed to the shorter cycle over that period, so that here, with the same adjustment speeds (in, especially, the two Phillips curves), the variables do not have enough time to reach the empirical peak or trough values.

This bias does not apply to the two demand variables ξ and C/Y. Over the whole sample period of Figure 9.3, their standard deviation is also somewhat higher than in Table 9.5; for ξ the ratio to σ_u increases to 0.20 and for C/Y it increases to 0.30. Hence the assumptions on the components of aggregate demand are not too bad a simplification. Lastly, the slight upward trend in the inventory series, which precisely is depicted as $100(n - n^o)$, is due to the fact that the capital growth rate from (9.47) is not perfectly tuned to the other growth components that make themselves felt in the ratio N/K.[24]

---

[24] This distorting effect is even stronger in the real balances ratio $m = M/pK$ and, thus, in the simulated time series of the rate of interest.

Figure 9.3. Endogenous variables under empirical fluctuations of *u*

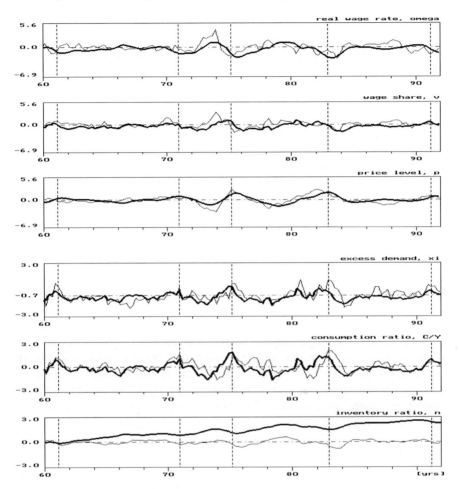

Note: Bold lines are simulated time series and thin lines are the empirical counterparts.

On the basis of these results it might now be argued that, maintaining the empirical data for the fluctuations of *u*, one should try further variations of some of the parameters in order to achieve better cyclical statistics in this framework. The significance of a good match of the empirical statistics is, however, an unsettled issue. The problem is that the historical moments have sampling variability and so can differ from the model's population moments – even if the model happened to be true. More specifically, given that a model cannot be expected to exactly duplicate reality, we can distinguish between a model variable, denote it by x_t^m, and its empirical counterpart x_t^e, the error being

$\varepsilon_t = x_t^e - x_t^m$. To compare the standard deviations of x^m and x^e, i.e. their variances, the identity $\text{var}(x^e) = \text{var}(x^m) + 2\,\text{cov}(x^m, \varepsilon) + \text{var}(\varepsilon)$ has to be taken into account. As a consequence, if the difference between $\text{var}(x^m)$ and $\text{var}(x^e)$ is viewed as a statement about $\text{var}(\varepsilon)$, as it mostly is, this would require $\text{cov}(x^m, \varepsilon) \approx 0$ to be fulfilled, which amounts to making an assumption that a priori is not really obvious. But if one allows for potential correlation between x^m and ε, it might even be possible that $\text{var}(x^m) = \text{var}(x^e)$ despite large errors ε_t. The problem here indicated is certainly beyond the scope of this paper.[25]

6. The fully endogenous model and its dynamics

The modelling equations so far provided can already be viewed as constituting a fully endogenous macrodynamic model if the exogenous motions of utilization are dropped and $u = u^{\text{endo}}$ is obtained from (9.43). Equation (9.47) for the capital growth rate g_k would then have the status of an investment function. In this respect, however, we want to be more flexible, both on the grounds of greater conceptual richness as it is common in modern Keynesian-oriented modelling, and in order to gain some control over the stability of the system. We therefore bring another variable into play.

Two motives for investment in fixed capital are considered. First, for reasons not explicitly taken into account in the model formulation, firms not only seek to avoid excess capacity but also desire no permanent overutilization of productive capacity. Hence investment increases with utilization u. The second motive refers to the profitability of firms. We may measure it by the rate $r := (pY - wL -\delta pK)/pK = (1 - v)uy^n - \delta$. Since investment is exclusively financed by equities, this profit rate is seen in relation to the yields from holding bonds, which is the alternative of financial investment that shareholders have, with the real (ex-post) interest rate $i - \pi$ as the relevant rate of return. In sum, besides utilization, fixed investment is additionally a positive function of the differential returns q, defined as $q := r - (i - \pi)$, or

$$q = (1 - v)uy^n - \delta - (i - \pi) \tag{9.50}$$

Our methodological approach to persistent cyclical behaviour in this paper is a deterministic one. We do not, however, wish to rely on a Hopf bifurcation.[26] Within a vicinity of the steady-state position, the dynamics may rather be more

---

[25] The problem is hinted in Kim and Pagan (1995, p. 371). The authors conclude, "the method of stylized facts really fails to come to grips with what is the fundamental problem in evaluating all small models, namely the assumptions that need to be made about the nature of the errors ζ_t," (ζ_t corresponds to ε_t in our notation). On 378ff, Kim and Pagan elaborate more on the problems connected with the fact that generally the errors ζ_t cannot be recovered.

[26] One reason is that, a priori, we can by no means be sure that the periodic orbits of the Hopf bifurcation are attractive. But even then, meaningful cyclical trajectories would only exist over a very small range of parameter values.

or less destabilizing. Though there are a number of intrinsic nonlinearities in the model, they are only weak and 'dominated' by the many linear specifications in the behavioural functions. It thus turns out that the destabilizing forces are also globally operative. This means we have to build in some additional, extrinsic nonlinearities, which take effect in the outer regions of the state space and prevent the dynamics from totally diverging. For our present purpose, we can content ourselves with just one such nonlinearity, which we introduce into the investment function.

A simple idea will prove sufficient. Suppose utilization is steadily rising in an expansionary phase. The corresponding positive influence on the flow of investment may be reinforced or curbed by the differential returns q. If, however, utilization has become relatively high, firms will not expect the economy to grow at the same speed for too long. If moreover q is relatively low in that stage, so that this influence on investment is already negative, then the positive utilization motive may be further weakened. That is, we assume that under these circumstances the negative effect from q is stronger than it otherwise is at lower levels of capacity utilization. With signs reversed, the same type of mechanism applies when the economy is on the downturn. Introducing two positive reaction coefficients β_{Iu} and β_{Iq} and referring for simplicity directly to the growth rate g^o and the differential returns q^o in a long-run equilibrium, we specify this concept for g_k, the capital growth rate, as follows:

$$g_k = g_k(u, q) = g^o + \beta_{Iu}(u - 1) + \alpha(u, q)\beta_{Iq}(q - q^o) \tag{9.51}$$

where with respect to given values d_1 and d_2, $0 < d_1 < d_2$, the flexibility function $\alpha = \alpha(u, q)$ is defined as[27]

$$\alpha = \alpha(u, q)$$

$$= \begin{cases} 1 + [u - (1 + d_1)]/(d_2 - d_1) & \text{if } u \geqslant 1 + d_1 \text{ and } q \leqslant q^o \\ 1 + [(1 - d_1) - u]/(d_2 - d_1) & \text{if } u \leqslant 1 - d_1 \text{ and } q \geqslant q^o \\ 1 & \text{else} \end{cases} \tag{9.52}$$

Evidently, for this mechanism to work it is required that the q-series peaks considerably before utilization, a property we have already checked in the sine-wave experiments. Being essentially dependant on the relative amplitude of the bond rate and the rate of inflation, the mechanism cannot necessarily be expected to be effective under different circumstances. In this sense, (9.52) represents only a minimal nonlinearity to tame the centrifugal forces in the economy.

---

[27] It may be noted that though the function α is not continuous in q, the multiplicative term $\alpha(q - q^o)$ in g_k is.

On the whole, we have now a self-contained differential equations system of dimension six. The state variables are $k^s = K/z^o L^s$, capital per head (measured in efficiency units); $\omega = w/pz^o$, the real wage rate (deflated by trend labour productivity); π, the inflation climate; $m = M/pK$, the real balances ratio; $y^e = Y^e/K$, the expected sales ratio; and $n = N/K$, the inventory ratio (where clearly the term 'ratio' refers to the stock of fixed capital). Collecting the equations of the laws of motions as they were presented at calibration levels 1–6, the system reads

$$\dot{k}^s = k^s(g_k - g_z - g_\ell) \tag{9.8}$$

$$\dot{\omega} = \omega\kappa[(1 - \kappa_{pw})f_w(e, v) - (1 - \kappa_{wp})f_p(u, v)] \tag{9.16}$$

$$\dot{\pi} = \beta\pi[\kappa_{\pi p}(\hat{p} - \pi) + (1 - \kappa_{\pi p})(\pi^o - \pi)] \tag{9.17}$$

$$\dot{m} = m(g_m - \hat{p} - g_k) \tag{9.24}$$

$$\dot{y}^e = (g^o - g_k)y^e + \beta_y(y^d - y^e) \tag{9.40}$$

$$\dot{n} = y - y^d - ng_k \tag{9.41}$$

To see that actually no more than these six dynamic variables are involved, note that κ is defined in (11.34) and $g_k = g_k(u, q)$ is determined in (9.51) and (9.52), $u = f_y(y^e, n)/y^n$ is determined in (9.43), $q = q(u, v, i, \pi)$ in (9.50), $v = v(u, \omega)$ in (9.4), $e = e(u, k^s)$ in (9.6), $\hat{p} = \hat{p}(u, e, v, \pi)$ in (9.14), $i = i(m, y)$ in (9.19), $y = uy^n$ in (9.20), $y^d = y^d(y^e, v, y, g_k)$ in (11.29).

To simulate this economy on the computer, it remains to set the investment parameters in (9.51) and (9.52). We choose

$$\beta_{Iu} = 0.260 \quad \beta_{Iq} = 0.115 \quad d_1 = 0.020 \quad d_2 = 0.070 \tag{9.53}$$

It seems that the influence of q on g_k tends to stabilize the system, while u gives rise to a positive feedback effect and so destabilizes it. The relatively high choice of the coefficient β_{Iu} vis-à-vis β_{Iq} renders the steady state unstable. The values of d_1 and d_2, on the other hand, make the nonlinearity in g_k sufficiently effective to keep the economy within realistic bounds. The system will therefore be characterized by persistent cyclical behaviour. The precise level of β_{Iu} is essential for the period of the fluctuations thus obtained.

All parameters being given, the endogenous model can now be numerically simulated. To set the system in motion, we start out from a steady-state growth path and disturb it by a strong temporary shock. We do this by raising the growth rate of the money supply over one year from 6% up to 8%. Afterwards it is set back to its original level, from when on the economy is left to its own.

The short fall of the bond rate induced by the monetary impulse initiates an expansion, but after the economy has reached its peak, the economy steers into a severe recession four years after the suspension of the shock. That is, this negative deviation of u from normal is significantly larger than the previous positive deviation. With the recovery then setting in, the economy begins to move in an oscillatory fashion, such that the peak and trough values of the variables tend to level off. Some 15 or 20 years after the shock, the oscillations become quite regular. After a while, the trajectories are even almost periodic. We illustrate this phenomenon by the four phase diagrams in Figure 9.4.[28]

The first diagram in Figure 9.4 plots the wage share against utilization as the measure of economic activity (the '+' symbol indicates the steady-state values of the variables). The picture is much the same as the income distribution dynamics in a Goodwin (1967) growth cycle model. The upper-right panel displays the pairs of inflation and utilization as they evolve over time. What results is not a Phillips curve relationship, but the so-called Phillips loops. The real wage rate, too, forms no firm functional relationship with utilization. We rather observe a similar looping behaviour, though the shape of the loop is somewhat different from the previous two variables.

While the loops in these first three panels are fairly symmetric, the panel in the lower-right corner shows an example of a variable, namely the rate of interest, with less regularity. It indicates that the lag of the bond rate with respect to u is larger in the upper than in the lower turning point.

Having established the basically cyclical behaviour of the economy, we may turn to the time series characteristics of the trajectories. An introductory visual impression is given in Figure 9.5. Note first of all the period of the oscillations, which precisely is 8.33 years.

The top panel of Figure 9.5 shows utilization u as the central time series of the business cycle. It is contrasted with a sine wave motion – the dotted line – that has the same period and amplitude. The middle panel displays the capital growth rate g_k in a likewise fashion. It is thus seen that the endogenous dynamics allows u and g_k move almost synchronously. Moreover, at least at first sight both series do not differ very much from a sine wave. Hence, we may point out that the approach of specifying the exogenous variables as sine waves in the calibration procedure has not been too inappropriate after all. Besides, the amplitude of u is also of the same order of magnitude as in the calibration experiments.

At a closer look, the differences between u and the sine wave are greater in the expansion than in the contraction, and similarly so for g_k. The reason is that a contraction takes a bit longer: the time from peak to trough is 4.33 years, while the trough-to-peak period is 4.00 years. More consequential for the dynamic properties of the system is the fact that the peak and trough values are not exactly symmetric. Figure 9.5 demonstrates, and Table 9.6 makes it numerically

---

[28] Intuitively, with the steady state being unstable and only one essential nonlinearity, the resulting limit cycles should be unique. A more careful investigation of this issue is here, however, left aside.

Figure 9.4.   Selected phase diagrams of the calibrated endogenous model

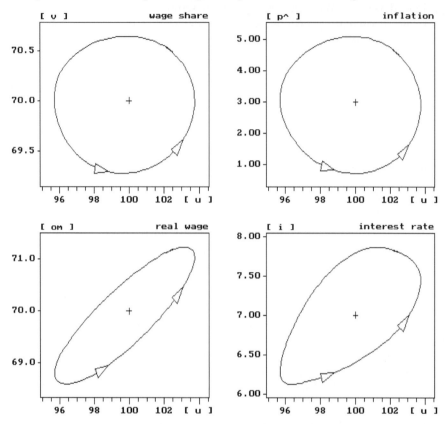

precise, that for u as well as for g_k, the lower turning points deviate slightly more from the steady-state values than the upper turning points. Given the linear specification of the behavioural functions and the strictly symmetric nonlinearity in the investment function, this asymmetry is somewhat surprising. In the end, it must originate with the intrinsic nonlinearities in the model, however weak they are. More directly it can be seen as being brought about by the asymmetric timing of the turning points of the q series documented in Table 9.6 (which can be traced back to the interest rate; see below) and its impact on investment.

The table states in addition that the capital growth rate has a short lead of one month with respect to utilization (a lag would have been 'preferable'). Comparing the peak and trough values of u with the coefficients d_1 and d_2 in (9.53) makes clear that the nonlinearity in (9.51), (9.52) does indeed take effect (observe the long lead of q in Table 9.6). The particular choice of the two parameters accomplishes that the standard deviation of g_k relative to that of u is about the same as for the empirical series in Table 9.1.

Figure 9.5.   Selected time series of the calibrated endogenous model

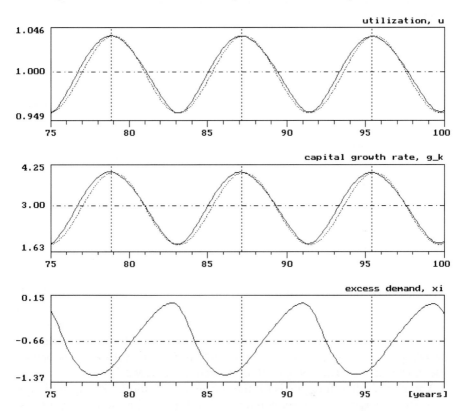

Note: Dotted lines are synchronous sine wave motions fitted in.

Similarly as the phase diagram in Figure 9.4 has it already indicated for the bond rate, excess demand ξ is a second variable whose upper and lower turning points have different lags with respect to u. The peak in ξ moves quite close to the trough in u, whereas more time elapses from the trough in ξ until u reaches its peak. The lags given in Table 9.6 can also be read as saying that $-\xi$ leads utilization by 0.42 years in the trough, and by 1.08 years in the peak. Excess demand has thus become more countercyclical than in the sine-wave simulations (cf. Table 9.5), where ξ also showed no apparent differences in its behaviour around the upper and lower turning points.

If we take the sine waves of u and g_k as a reference scenario, then the high sensitivity of the cyclical features of the excess demand variable to the relatively minor changes in the time series of u and g_k can be explained by the very definition of ξ, which involves a *ratio* of two variables, y^d and y. Thus, $\xi = y^d/y - 1$ can be quite 'self-willed', although y is practically the same as u itself

Table 9.6.   Cyclical statistics of the calibrated endogenous model

Variable x	x^o	In peak	In trough	σ_x/σ_u	Lag (peak)	Lag (trough)
u	100.00	+ 3.73	−4.32	—	—	—
g_k	3.00	+ 1.02	−1.16	0.27	−0.08	−0.08
e	100.00	+ 2.59	−2.97	0.70	0.75	0.42
ω	70.00	+ 1.23	−1.40	0.47	0.75	0.58
v	70.00	+ 0.64	−0.73	0.25	2.25	1.75
$-\text{dev}\,p$	0.00	+ 1.90	−2.04	0.50	0.08	0.08
$\hat{p}$	3.00	+ 2.08	−2.28	0.56	2.25	1.92
π	3.00	+ 0.87	−0.91	0.23	3.08	2.75
m	14.00	+ 0.44	−0.46	0.82	−0.58	−0.58
i	7.00	+ 0.85	−0.88	0.22	1.67	0.58
q	7.50	+ 0.51	−0.52	0.13	−3.17	−2.33
ξ	−0.66	+ 0.67	−0.58	0.16	3.83	2.92
C/Y	70.48	+ 1.11	−0.92	0.25	3.83	3.33
n	15.30	+ 0.40	−0.47	0.11	0.83	0.83

Note: All variables are multiplied by 100. x^o denotes the steady-state value of variable x, $-\text{dev}\,p$ is the deviation of the price level from its HP 1600 trend in per cent. The standard deviations of ω, v and m are divided by the respective steady-state values.

and y^d lags y by only one month in the peak as well as in the trough (the peaks and troughs are, however, 0.023 and 0.026 above and below $(y^d)^o = 0.695$). On the other hand, the implications of excess demand for the inventory ratio n, via the *difference* between y^d and y in (9.41) for $\dot{n}$, are restricted to asymmetric peak and trough values of n. Their timing is again symmetric, with the lags being a little longer than in Table 9.5, or than desired in Table 9.2.

A similar result as for ξ holds for the consumption ratio C/Y (which likewise has somewhat improved in its countercyclicality) and for the rate of interest, where the differences in the lags at peak and trough times are even greater. The latter effect is equally remarkable as it was for ξ, since i depends on the ratio m/y according to (9.19), but m displays no asymmetry at all in the timing of its turning points. The irregularity in the cyclical pattern of the bond rate is also mainly responsible for a similar phenomenon in the abovementioned differential returns $q = r - (i - \pi)$, though it is shifted in time. Interestingly, the mean value of the lags 1.67 and 0.58 of the bond rate is nearly the same as its lag of 1.17 years in the sine wave scenario, which generated fairly symmetrical motions of i.

The inflation rate, too, exhibits different lags of its turning points. They are, however, completely washed out in the integrated series of the price level, which is almost perfectly countercyclical. Besides, the difference in the peak and trough lags of $\hat{p}$ is the same as for the inflation climate π, even though, as Equation (9.14) and the standard deviations of $\hat{p}$ and π show, the inflation rate is predominantly influenced by the price Phillips curve term $f_p = f_p(u, v)$ (the term $f_w = f_w(e, v)$ does not feed back on $\hat{p}$ because of $\kappa_{pw} = 0$).

All the asymmetries that have been pointed out have no effect on the amplitude of the variables. The standard deviations in Table 9.6 are therefore practically the same as they resulted from the sine wave calibration in Table 9.5. This is another aspect corroborating this methodological approach.

7. Conclusion

The paper has put forward a complete deterministic macro model of the business cycle that takes up elements which may be connected with, in particular, the names of Keynes, Metzler and Goodwin. The aim of the paper was a calibration of the model. This procedure was organized in a hierarchical structure, so that the numerical coefficients need not all be determined simultaneously but could be chosen step by step. Given stylized oscillations of two exogenous variables, capacity utilization and the capital growth rate, each step gave rise to motions of some endogenous variables. Their cyclical pattern could then be compared to the behaviour of their empirical counterparts.

The calibration analysis has ended up with numerical values of, on the whole, 14 parameters. Subsequently, the hitherto exogenous variables were endogenized, which added another four parameters in the investment function thus introduced. They were set such that the steady-state position of the fully endogenous model became unstable, while a suitable nonlinearity in the investment function prevented the system from totally diverging. Hence, the model produces persistent cyclical behaviour, actually in the form of a limit cycle.

The main characteristics of the model's time series, their variability and comovements, may be judged to be by and large satisfactory. Specifically, this concerns more or less procyclical movements of the capital growth rate, the employment rate, the (productivity deflated) real wage and the inventory ratio (relative to the capital stock), as well as countercyclicality in the price level, relative excess demand and the consumption ratio (the latter two relative to total output). Of course, the cyclical statistics are not always perfect. Within the present modelling framework a single statistic could also hardly be improved any further without seriously affecting another one. In a brief summary, we may nevertheless claim that the results we arrived at can stand comparison with the properties generated by the competitive equilibrium models of the real business cycle school.

To keep a curb on the system's centrifugal forces, it was sufficient to introduce just one extrinsic nonlinearity in the investment function. The efficiency of this mechanism is, however, rather sensitive to the choice of the two investment reaction intensities β_{Iu} and β_{Iq}, and possibly also to changes in other parameters (especially those that have a direct bearing on the motions of the differential returns q). Extensions of the model may therefore in the first instance include additional nonlinearities in other parts of the models, which can contribute to a better containment of the instabilities at the outer boundaries of the state space. On the basis of further exploratory simulations we feel that fixed investment is still the most important, from a constructivist point of view even indispensable, point of intervention for a global stabilization. Nevertheless, future investigations of the dynamics should systematically study what other mechanisms can support the present nonlinear investment schedule.

A conceptual weakness of the model is the financial sector. On the one hand, markets for other, nonsubstitutable financial assets need to be introduced, such that they play a more active role than is admitted by the textbook LM sector. Our interest in this respect lies in equities and bank loans to firms. A good candidate of a financial sector that besides money and bonds takes these assets into account is the temporary equilibrium approach by Franke and Semmler (1999), which should be relatively easy to integrate into the present framework. On the other hand, in addition to equities, fixed investment of firms may also be financed by retained earnings and, as just mentioned, bank loans. This will allow firms' reactions to strong disequilibria to be more flexible as it is presently the case. Regarding global stabilization, supplementary and more robust nonlinearities in the investment function may thus arise in quite a natural way.

References

Backus, D.K. and P.J. Kehoe (1992), "International evidence on the historical properties of business cycles", *American Economic Review*, Vol. 82, pp. 864–888.

Barsky, R., J. Parker and G. Solon (1994), "Measuring the cyclicality of real wages: how important is the composition bias?", *Quarterly Journal of Economics*, Vol. 109, pp. 1–25.

Baxter, M. and R.G. King (1995), "Measuring business cycles: approximate band-pass filters for economic time series", NBER Working Paper 5022.

Blanchard, O. and L. Katz (1999), "Wage dynamics: reconciling theory and evidence", NBER Working Paper 6924.

Blinder, A.S. and L.J. Maccini (1991), "Taking stock: a critical assessment of recent research on inventories", *Journal of Economic Perspectives*, Vol. 5, pp. 73–96.

Brayton, F., J.M. Roberts and J.C. Williams (1999), "What's happened to the Phillips curve?", *Finance and Economics Discussion Series*, 1999–49, Board of Governors of the Federal Reserve System.

Canova, F. and E. Ortega (2000), "Testing calibrated general equilibrium models", pp. 400–436 in: R. Mariano, T. Schvermann and M. Weeks, editors, *Simulation-based Inference in Econometrics*, Cambridge: Cambridge University Press.

Chiarella, C. and P. Flaschel (2000), *The Dynamics of Keynesian Monetary Growth: Macro Foundations*, Cambridge: Cambridge University Press.

Chiarella, C., P. Flaschel, G. Groh and W. Semmler (2000), *Disequilibrium, Growth and Labor Market Dynamics*, Berlin: Springer.

Cooley, T.F. and L.E. Ohanian (1991), "The cyclical behavior of prices", *Journal of Monetary Economics*, Vol. 28, pp. 25–60.

Deistler, M. (2001), "Comments on the contributions by C.W.J. Granger and J.J. Heckman", *Journal of Econometrics*, Vol. 100, pp. 71–72.

DeLong, J.B. and L.H. Summers (1986), "Are business cycles symmetrical?", pp. 166–179 in: R. Gordon, editor, *American Business Cycles: Continuity and Change*, Chicago: University of Chicago Press.

Diebold, F.X. and G.D. Rudebusch (1999), *Business Cycles: Durations, Dynamics, and Forecasting*, New Jersey: University Presses of California, Columbia and Princeton.

Diebold, F.X. and G.D. Rudebusch (2001), "Five questions about business cycles, Federal Reserve Bank of San Francisco", *Economic Review*, pp. 1–15.

Evans, M. and P. Wachtel (1993), "Inflation regimes and the sources of inflation uncertainty", *Journal of Money, Credit, and Banking*, Vol. 25, pp. 475–511.

Fiorito, R. and T. Kollintzas (1994), "Stylized facts of business cycles in the G7 from a real business cycle perspective", *European Economic Review*, Vol. 38, pp. 235–269.

Flaschel, P., R. Franke and W. Semmler (1997), *Nonlinear Macrodynamics: Instability, Fluctuations and Growth in Monetary Economies*, Cambridge, MA: MIT Press.

Flaschel, P., G. Gong and W. Semmler (2001), "A Keynesian macroeconometric framework for the analysis of monetary policy rules", *Journal of Economic Behavior and Organization*, Vol. 25, 101–113.

Franke, R. (1992), "A note on the relationship between adaptive expectations and extrapolative regression forecasts", *mimeo*, University of Bielefeld, Department of Economics.

Franke, R. (1996), "A Metzlerian model of inventory growth cycles", *Structural Change and Economic Dynamics*, Vol. 7, pp. 243–262.

Franke, R. (1999), "A reappraisal of adaptive expectations", *Political Economy*, Vol. 4, pp. 5–29.

Franke, R. (2001), "Three wage-price macro models and their calibration", *mimeo*, University of Bielefeld, Center for Empirical Macroeconomics (http://www.wiwi.uni-bielefeld.de/~semmler/cem/wp.htm#2001).

Franke, R. and W. Semmler (1999), "Bond rate, loan rate and Tobin's q in a temporary equilibrium model of the financial sector", *Metroeconomica*, Vol. 50, pp. 351–385.

Goodwin, R.M. (1967), "A growth cycle", in C.H. Feinstein, editor, *Socialism, Capitalism and Economic Growth*, Cambridge: Cambridge University Press. Revised version pp. 442–449 in: E.K. Hunt and J.G. Schwarz, editors, (1972), *A Critique of Economic Theory*, Harmondsworth: Penguin.

Gregory, A.W. and G.W. Smith (1993), "Statistical aspects of calibration in macroeconomics", pp. 703–719 in: G.S. Maddala *et al.*, editors, *Handbook of Statistics*, Vol. 11, Amsterdam: Elsevier.

Groth, C. (1988), "IS-LM dynamics and the hypothesis of adaptive-forward-looking expectations", pp. 251–266 in: P. Flaschel and M. Krüger, editors, *Recent Approaches to Economic Dynamics*, Frankfurt a.M.: Peter Lang.

Irvine, F.O. Jr. (1981), "Retail inventory investment and the cost of capital", *American Economic Review*, Vol. 71, pp. 633–648.

Kim, K. and A.R. Pagan (1995), "The econometric analysis of calibrated macroeconomic models", pp. 356–390 in: M.H. Pesaran and M.R. Wickens, editors, *Handbook of Applied Econometrics in Macroeconomics*, Oxford: Blackwell.

King, R.G. and S.T. Rebelo (1999), "Resuscitating real business cycles", pp. 927–1007 in: J.B. Taylor and M. Woodford, editors, *Handbook of Macroeconomics*, Vol. 1B, Amsterdam: Elsevier.

Köper, C. (2000), "Stability analysis of an extended KMG growth dynamics", University of Bielefeld, Department of Economics, Discussion Paper No. 464.

McCallum, B.T. (2001), "Should monetary policy respond strongly to output gaps?", NBER Working Paper No. W8226.

Metzler, L.A. (1941), "The nature and stability of inventory cycles", *Review of Economic Statistics*, Vol. 23, pp. 113–129.

Mussa, M. (1975), "Adaptive and regressive expectations in a rational model of the inflationary process", *Journal of Monetary Economics*, Vol. 1, pp. 423–442.

Nelson, C.R. and C.I. Plosser (1982), "Trends and random walks in macroeconomic time series: some evidence and implications", *Journal of Monetary Economics*, Vol. 10, pp. 139–162.

Okun, A.M. (1980), "Rational-expectations-with-misperceptions as a theory of the business cycle", *Journal of Money, Credit, and Banking*, Vol. 12, pp. 817–825.

Razzak, W.A. (2001), "Business cycle asymmetries: international evidence", *Review of Economic Dynamics*, Vol. 4, pp. 230–243.

Smant, D.J.C. (1998), "Modelling trends, expectations and the cyclical behaviour of prices", *Economic Modelling*, Vol. 15, pp. 151–161.

Stock, J.H. and Watson, M.W. (1999), "Business cycle fluctuations in US macroeconomic time series", pp. 3–63 in: J.B. Taylor and M. Woodford, editors, *Handbook of Macroeconomics*, Vol. 1A, Amsterdam: Elsevier.

Summers, L.H. (1991), "The scientific illusion in empirical macroeconomics", *Scandinavian Journal of Economics*, Vol. 93, pp. 129–148.

Appendix: The empirical time series

The time series examined in Table 9.1 are constructed from the data that are made available by Ray Fair on his homepage (`http://fairmodel.econ. yale.edu`), with a description being given in Appendix A of the US Model Workbook. Taking over Fair's abbreviations, the following time series of his database are involved. They all refer to the firm sector, i.e., nonfinancial corporate business.

CD	real consumption expenditures for durable goods
CD	real consumption expenditures for nondurable goods
CD	real consumption expenditures for services
HN	average number of nonovertime hours paid per job
HO	average number of overtime hours paid per job
JF	number of jobs
KK	real capital stock
PF	output price index
RB	bond rate (percentage points)
SIFG	employer social insurance contributions paid to US government
SIFS	employer social insurance contributions paid to state and local governments
V	real stock of inventories
WF	average hourly earnings excluding overtime of workers (but including supplements to wages and salaries except employer contributions for social insurance).
X	real sales
Y	real output

The variables in Table 9.1 are then specified as follows. For Fair's assumption of a 50% wage premium for overtime hours, see, e.g., his specification of disposable income of households (YD in Equation (115), Table A.3, The Equations of the US Model).

$$y = Y/\text{KK} \quad \text{(output–capital ratio)}$$

$$L = \text{JF} \times (\text{HN} + \text{HO}) \quad \text{(total hours)}$$

$$e = L/\text{trend-}L \quad \text{(employment rate)}$$

$$z = Y/[\text{JF} \times (\text{HN} + \text{HO})] \quad \text{(labour productivity)}$$

$$w = \text{WF} \times (\text{HN} + 1.5 \times \text{HO})/(\text{HN} + \text{HO}) \quad \text{(nominal wage rate)}$$

$$p = \text{PF} \quad \text{(price level)}$$

$$v = [\text{WF} \times (\text{HN} + 1.5 \times \text{HO}) \times \text{JF} + \text{SIFG} + \text{SIFS}]/[Y \times \text{PF}] \quad \text{(wage share)}$$

$$\xi = 100 \times (X - Y)/Y \quad \text{(relative excess demand)}$$

$$C/Y = 100 \times (\text{CD} + \text{CN} + \text{CS})/Y \quad \text{(consumption ratio)}$$

$$n = V/\text{KK} \quad \text{(inventory–capital ratio)}$$

$$i = \text{RB} \quad \text{(nominal interest rate)}$$

In the theoretical part, we have in addition (L^s denoting the labour supply and y^n the normal output–capital ratio)

$e = L/L^s$ (employment rate)

$g_k = \dot{K}/K$ (capital growth rate)

$m = M/pK$ (real balances normalized by K)

$u = y/y^n$ (capacity utilization)

$y^d = Y^d/K$ (aggregate demand normalized by K)

$y^e = Y^e/K$ (expected output–capital ratio)

$\omega = (w/p)/z$ (real wage rate, deflated by productivity)

PART III
MODELS OF REAL-FINANCIAL MARKET INTERACTIONS AND CAPITAL ACCUMULATION

CHAPTER 10

A Stochastic Model of Real-Financial Interaction with Boundedly Rational Heterogeneous Agents

Carl Chiarella, Peter Flaschel, Xue-Zhong He and Hing Hung

Abstract

We reformulate and extend the Blanchard model of output dynamics, the stock market and interest rates that incorporates equities and bonds into traditional Keynesian IS–LM analysis. As investment demand now depends on Tobin's average q in the place of the real rate of interest, the share price dynamics feedback into the real sector. Our model allows imperfect asset substitutability, and contains boundedly rational heterogenous agents who make imperfect forecasts of capital gains and whose expectations are state-of-the market dependent. These elements introduce an underlying nonlinear dynamic feedback mechanism between the real and financial sectors that allows for bursts of optimism and pessimism. Furthermore, we introduce some stochastic elements into the model and use numerical simulations to study the interaction of the nonlinear and stochastic elements, focusing in particular on the propensity of the model to generate stock market booms and crashes.

Keywords: real-financial interaction, market reaction coefficient, bounded rationality heterogenous agents, non-linear stochastic models, stock market booms and crashes

1. Introduction

"History can be thought of as society's memory. If it is fuzzy or inaccurate we may be condemned to relive it. There does seem to be a danger that the application of some recent developments in economics, such as extreme versions of the rational expectations approach, are in danger of depriving us of manias, panics, crashes, and even modest booms and slumps. This may not be helpful in terms of society's memory. But perhaps a certain amount of this is

CONTRIBUTIONS TO ECONOMIC ANALYSIS
VOLUME 277   ISSN: 0573-8555
DOI:10.1016/S0573-8555(05)77010-3

a matter of semantics or of emphasis. Those who argue that it is rational to buy when prices are rising if the expectation is that prices will keep rising sound entirely reasonable. Those who say it is folly are surely simply shifting the emphasis to the fact that we do not know when the terminal condition, that is the change in fashion or whatever, will come. To describe all of these episodes as rational surely stretches the definition of rationality to an unhelpful extent."

—— F. Capie, Early Asset Bubbles, in White (1990)"

The above quotation is taken from an article by one of the discussants in White (1990) on two essays giving a current perspective on contemporary accounts of two of the most famous examples of financial mania, panic and subsequent crash – the tulip mania of the 17th century and the South Sea bubble of the 18th century. It serves to emphasize the point that standard macroeconomic models leave little place for extreme market movements, except as the result of some exogenous stochastic process.

Moods of extreme optimism and then pessimism, long periods of deviation by even supposedly well-informed agents from anything remotely resembling valuation of expected return on securities based on economic fundamentals seem to be a permanent feature of financial markets, at least from a perspective of almost four centuries. Yet one would search in vain in modern finance and economics texts for any discussion of the effect of such factors on the financial sector of the economy. Rather there one finds an economy populated with rational agents who seem to have full knowledge (at least in the sense of probability distributions) of the laws driving the economic system they inhabit and who perform a very precise decision calculus to optimally trade-off risk and return. The perturbations that one observes in such markets are supposedly due solely to exogenous semi-martingale processes. These agents are too rational to allow themselves to experience bouts of optimism or pessimism, or to be influenced by what they perceive other agents to be doing. There is usually an implied assumption that if (somehow) all external noise impacts were to cease, the economy would be stable to its steady state.

Perhaps the only economist to write seriously about such "irrational" behaviour is Kindleberger (1978). The concept of boundedly rational agents was developed by Simon (1997) over a number of years; however it is really only in the last decade or so that researchers have started to look seriously at stock market models involving heterogeneity of agents, positive feedback (leading to self-reinforcement of trends up and down), herding behaviour and critical points (when extreme optimism changes to pessimism of vice versa).

For empirical evidence of these phenomena we can cite Sornette and Zhou (2002), and there is certainly no shortage of theoretical models: Day and Huang (1990), Chiarella (1992), Lux (1995), Lux (1997), Lux and Marchesi (1999), Brock and Hommes (1997) and Andresen (1991).

The motivation for this paper arises from the observation that little has been done to incorporate features such as heterogeneity, positive feedback and switching from optimism to pessimism into standard macroeconomic models.

Here we take the well-known Blanchard (1981) model of real-financial interaction and incorporate into its structure fundamentalists and chartists as well as a mechanism that allows a switch from optimism to pessimism (and vice versa). We allow for background extrinsic noise (in fact Wiener process noise) in the stock market that may be interpreted either as noise trading or as the incessant arrival of market news.

In fact, we modify the original Blanchard model in a number of ways. In order to give a more prominent role to the impact of the share market on the real sector of the economy, we change Blanchard's investment demand to depend on Tobin's average q in the place of the real rate of interest. In this way the share price dynamics feedback into the real sector, thereby creating one of the key links of the real-financial interaction. The conventional LM schedule or money market equilibrium of this approach, in turn provides the channel back from real to financial markets. The Blanchard model is also enriched by allowing for imperfect asset substitution and less-than perfect foresight. Furthermore we introduce a state-of-market dependent reaction function in the way agents react to disequilibria in the stock market. We know from the work of Chiarella *et al.* (2004) that these extensions to the Blanchard model can generate regimes of stock market upswings and downswings. Here we add to that earlier work by allowing for heterogeneity of agents by introducing two groups – rational fundamentalists and trend chasing chartists. Initially we hold these groups fixed, subsequently we allow them to evolve as a function of the evolution of the stock market dynamics à la Brock and Hommes (1997). We show that in a deterministic setting these mechanisms can generate a locally unstable equilibrium that is stable to some fluctuating attractor. We then add noise to the model and consider, by use of simulation analysis, how the model in its locally unstable regime can generate more stock market booms and crashes than in the stable regime. We study, in particular, how the severity of the booms and crashes are affected by various reaction parameters of the two groups.

The plan of the paper is as follows: In Section 2 we outline the real and financial sector of the model, in particular the imperfect substitutability between stocks and bonds. In Section 3 we discuss the role of the two groups of agents, rational fundamentalists and trend chasing chartists, how they form their expectations and how their optimism or pessimism about the short run evolution of the stock market feed into the stock market dynamics. Section 4 studies the deterministic skeleton of the model when all external noise sources are absent. We analyze the steady state and determine how local stability turns to instability as certain key parameters affecting expectations and the mood of optimism/pessimism are varied. We also study in this section the global dynamics in situations when the steady state becomes locally unstable. Section 5 studies the stochastic version of the model. We use Monte-Carlo simulation to obtain the distributions of booms and busts and how these are affected by the expectation and mood parameters. Section 6 concludes.

2. The model

In this section we introduce the notation and set out the static and dynamic economic relationships that define the macroeconomy with real-financial interaction that will be the object of our study. Note that we use extensive form variables[1] (and thus not logarithms of money and the price level as in Blanchard (1981)) throughout and that the money demand function, though here completely linear, represents a generalisation of the form that was used by Blanchard (1981). For simplicity, Tobin's q is only used (in average form) in the investment functions, which is based on the assumption of fixed proportions in production. This assumption allows us to make more transparent the dynamic structure of the model by simplifying some of the algebraic relationships between the endogenous variables and also reducing by one the number of laws of motion. In subsequent developments of the model one would need to gauge the impact of smooth factor substitution.

First consider the static relations that describe a simple aggregate demand function Y^d (Equation (10.1)) depending on output (via consumption) and Tobin's average q (via investment). The demand for real balances (Equation (10.2)) is a traditional one depending positively on output and negatively on the short-term interest rate. Equation (10.3) is a standard equation for money market equilibrium. Finally, we have an obvious equation for real profits (Equation (10.4)), which depend on economic activity Y solely. Thus we have

$$Y^d = C + c(Y - \delta K - T) + I + i(q - 1) + \delta K + G, \quad c \in (0, 1) \tag{10.1}$$

$$m^d = M^d/p = kY + h_1 - h_2 r \tag{10.2}$$

$$m = m^d \tag{10.3}$$

$$\Pi = (1 - u)Y - \delta K \tag{10.4}$$

The dynamic variables are output, share and bond prices. Output adjustment is based on the simple textbook dynamic multiplier story as indicated in Equation (10.5). Blanchard assumes that short-term bonds, long-term bonds and shares are perfect substitutes, and there is myopic perfect foresight on capital gains. Thus, Equations (10.6) and (10.7) indicate that the dividend rate of return on equities and the interest rate of return on long-term bonds are both to be augmented by a corresponding expression for capital gains when comparing their full return with the return on short-term fixed price bonds.

---

[1] The variables and parameters of the model are listed in the appendix.

Thus we write

$$\dot{Y} = \beta_y(Y^d - Y) \tag{10.5}$$

$$r = \frac{p\Pi + \dot{p}_e E}{p_e E} = \frac{p\Pi}{p_e E} + \hat{p}_e = \frac{\Pi/K}{q} + \hat{q} \quad (K, E, p = \text{const!}) \tag{10.6}$$

$$r = \frac{B + \dot{p}_b B}{p_b B} = \hat{p}_b + \frac{1}{p_b} \tag{10.7}$$

The stock market reacts to the expected return differential $(\pi/K/q + z - r)$, where z is the market's expectation of the capital gain $\hat{q}(= \hat{p}_e)$. For share price dynamics we consider the stochastic differential equation

$$dq = \beta_q\left(\frac{\Pi/K}{q} + z - r\right)q\,dt + \sigma_q q\,dW$$
$$= \beta_q \varepsilon q\,dt + \sigma_q q\,dW \tag{10.8}$$

with

$$\varepsilon = \frac{\Pi/K}{q} + z - r \tag{10.9}$$

Here $W(t)$ is a Wiener process and σ_q the standard deviation of the stock market return. This extension assumes (Equation (10.8)) that there is imperfect substitution between shares and short-term bonds, and that share prices p^e (as reflected by Tobin's q) react with less than infinite speed (β_q) to ε, the differential between expected equity returns (dividend return plus expected capital gains) and the short-term rate of interest. The Wiener increments dW can be interpreted as noise trading (Black, 1986) or as random fluctuations in the stock market brought about by the incessant arrival of "news".

Our assumption of a standard fixed proportions technology with only labour as variable input, and with capital depreciation, gives for real profits (Π) and rate of profit (ρ) the expressions

$$\Pi = Y - \delta K - (w/p)L^d \quad (L^d = Y/x, x = \text{const.})$$
$$= Y(1 - w/(px)) - \delta K$$
$$= Y(1 - u) - \delta K \quad (u = w/(px) = \text{const.}) \tag{10.10}$$

$$\rho = \Pi/K = (1 - u)Y/K - \delta \tag{10.11}$$

where u denotes the (given) wage share. Thus substituting (10.10) into (10.9), we have

$$\varepsilon = \frac{(1 - u)Y/K - \delta}{q} + z - r \tag{10.12}$$

The inverted money market equilibrium from Equations (10.2) and (10.3) reads[2]

$$r = \frac{kY + h_1 - m}{h_2}, \quad m = M/p \tag{10.13}$$

and we use this relation to determine r in Equation (10.12).

Note that we are assuming a background of a stationary economy in which the capital stock is not growing and no new shares are issued. Furthermore, the assumption of constant nominal and real money stock will result in no inflation and so in steady state there is no increase in the equity price.

In discrete time Equations (10.5) and (10.8) may be written as

$$Y_{t+\Delta t} = Y_t + \beta_y \Delta t(-(1-c)Y_t + i(q_t - 1) + A) \tag{10.14}$$

$$q_{t+\Delta t} = q_t + \beta_q \varepsilon_t q_t \Delta t + \sigma_q q_t \sqrt{\Delta t} \tilde{\xi}_t \tag{10.15}$$

where Δt is the length of the "trading day". Let N be the trading frequency per year, then $\Delta t = 1/N$. Typically, $N = 1, 12, 52, 250$ for a trading frequency of year, month, week and day, respectively. Note also that $\tilde{\xi}_t \sim N(0, 1)$ and that $A = C + I + G - cT + (1-c)\delta K$.

We interpret z_t as the expected share market capital gain/loss over the next time interval i.e.

$$z_t = \mathbb{E}_t \left[\frac{q_{t+\Delta t} - q_t}{\Delta t q_t} \right]$$

where $\mathbb{E}_t$ denotes expectations formed at time t for quantities at $t + \Delta t$.

In order to close the model we need to specify how z_t is formed; this we do in the next section.

3. Heterogenous expectations

We assume that there are two groups of agents in the market, rational fundamentalists who are able to form model-consistent expectations and trend-chasing chartists. The market's expectation is a combination of fundamentalist (z_t^f) and chartist (z_t^c) expectations where n_t^f and n_t^c, respectively denote the fraction of fundamentalists and chartists in the economy. Each group of agents uses their expectation of $\hat{q}_t$ to form an estimate of the expected return differential between stocks and bonds, i.e. they form

$$\varepsilon_t^c = \frac{(1-u)Y_t/K - \delta}{q_t} + z_t^c - r_t \tag{10.16}$$

---

[2] This should be contrasted with Blanchard's (10.2), which uses the logarithm of m in place of our m.

and

$$\varepsilon_t^f = \frac{(1-u)Y_t/K - \delta}{q_t} + z_t^f - r_t \tag{10.17}$$

If we assume that each group reacts to its expected return differential with its own speed of adjustment (β_q^f and β_q^c, respectively), then Equation (10.15) would be modified to read

$$q_{t+\Delta t} = q_t + (n_t^f \beta_q^f \varepsilon_t^f + n_t^c \beta_q^c \varepsilon_t^c) q_t \Delta t + \sigma_q q_t \sqrt{\Delta t} \tilde{\xi}_t \tag{10.18}$$

Consider first the chartists who are of the classical trend-chasing kind and so form expectations according to[3]

$$z_t^c = (1 - \beta_{z_c}) z_{t-\Delta t}^c + \beta_{z_c} \left(\frac{q_t - q_{t-\Delta t}}{\Delta t q_{t-\Delta t}} \right) \quad (0 \leqslant \beta_{z_c} \leqslant 1/\Delta t) \tag{10.19}$$

The fundamentalists are assumed to form expectations using traditional rational expectations (it is also assumed that they know the chartists react according to Equation (10.19)), thus from (10.18) they form

$$z_t^f = \mathbb{E}_t^f \left[\frac{q_{t+\Delta t} - q_t}{\Delta t q_t} \right] = n_t^f \beta_q^f \varepsilon_t^f + n_t^c \beta_q^c \varepsilon_t^c \tag{10.20}$$

which may be solved for z_t^f to yield

$$z_t^f = \frac{(n_t^f \beta_q^f + n_t^c \beta_q^c) \left(\frac{(1-u)Y_t/K - \delta}{q_t} - r_t \right) + n_t^c \beta_q^c z_t^c}{1 - n_t^f \beta_q^f} \tag{10.21}$$

provided $1 - n_t^f \beta_q^f \neq 0$.[4] We furthermore assume that both the groups view their reaction coefficients β_q and β_q^s as depending on the state of the market, in particular as a function of the most recently observed return differential $\varepsilon_{t-\Delta t}$ between equity and the short-term rate of interest. When market conditions are such that ε is close to its steady state ε_0, the reaction coefficients are rather high so that the agents react strongly to the expected return differential. However, the high reaction coefficients (coupled with a high β_{z_c} on the part of chartists) cause the steady state to be locally unstable and lead to a rise (or fall) in the stock market and hence a rise or fall in the expected return differential. Both groups

---

[3] Note that β_{z_c} may be interpreted as a speed of adjustment, and hence $1/\beta_{z_c}$ as the mean time delay in adjusting expectations. We thus must impose the restriction $1/\beta_{z_c} \geqslant \Delta t$ otherwise the chartists would be revising expectations more frequently than they are receiving information on the evolution of the quantity about which they form expectations.

[4] Note that during the simulations reported below it does occasionally happen that $1 - n_t^f \beta_q^f = 0$. Such points have been removed from the bifurcation diagrams.

will initially follow this general movement in the stock market; however as it proceeds further and further they are conscious that the economy is moving ever further from its perceived steady state and they start to react more cautiously to the return differential. This cautiousness is reflected in an eventual lowering of the value of the reaction coefficients β_q, to a value sufficiently low that causes a turnaround in the dynamics that once again become stable towards the steady state. Eventually, the β_q return to former high levels and the possibility of another upward (or downward) stock market movement is established. The behaviour of β_q as a function of the difference in ε from its steady-state value ε_0 is illustrated in Figure 10.1. We have drawn this function somewhat skewed to the right to indicate greater (less) caution when the share market is below (above) its steady-state value. Each group would have their own particular values of β_q^+, β_q^-, ε^- and ε^+, therefore allowing for differing degrees of optimism/ pessimism between each group.

So far we have not discussed how the proportions n_t^f and n_t^c are formed. In this study we shall make two assumptions. First, we shall assume the proportions are constant and analyze the dynamic properties of the model as these proportions are changed. Second, we shall assume that they change as a function of realised returns of each group (assumed known to all market participants) according to the Brock and Hommes (1997) mechanism. Under this assumption we would have

$$n_t^i = N_t^i/Z_t \quad (i \in \{c,f\}) \tag{10.22}$$

where

$$N_t^i = \exp\{-\lambda[(\varepsilon_{t-1} - \varepsilon_{t-1}^i)^2 + \kappa^i]\} \quad (\lambda > 0) \tag{10.23}$$

and

$$Z_t = N_t^c + N_t^f \tag{10.24}$$

Figure 10.1. The behaviour of the reaction coefficient β_q

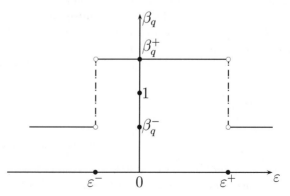

The quantities κ^c and κ^f represent the costs incurred by each group in forming expectations. Typically we would expect $\kappa^f > \kappa^c$, reflecting the fact that fundamentalists incur greater costs in learning about the fundamentals driving the economy.

It turns out to be convenient to keep track of the proportions of fundamentalists and chartists in terms of the single quantity n_t defined via

$$n_t^f = (1 + n_t)/2, \quad \text{and} \quad n_t^c = (1 - n_t)/2$$

where $-1 \leqslant n_t \leqslant 1$.

The laws of motion of the economy are given by Equations (10.14), (10.18), (10.19) and (10.21) in the case of fixed proportions of agents, or in the case of variable proportions the laws for n_t^c and n_t^f; Equations (10.22)–(10.24) also need to be appended.

The original Blanchard model is recovered by taking $\sigma_q = 0$ in Equation (10.8) and setting $\beta_q^f = \beta_q^c = \infty$ in Equation (10.18), which then collapses to the arbitrage condition $(\pi/K)/q = r - z$, and setting $n_t^c = 0$, $n_t^f = 1$ in Equation (10.20) so that only rational fundamentalists are present in the market.

4. Analysis of the deterministic skeleton

In this section we analyze the dynamics of the underlying deterministic model, i.e. when $\sigma_q = 0$.

4.1. The steady state

Proposition 1. *Assume*

$$\frac{1+n}{2} \beta_q^f \neq 1, \quad \frac{1+n}{2} \beta_q^f + \frac{1-n}{2} \beta_q^c \neq 0, 1$$

The steady state of the dynamical system (10.14), (10.18), (10.19) *and* (10.21) *(the case of fixed proportions) is characterized by*

$$\bar{Y} = \frac{A + i(\bar{q} - 1)}{1 - c} \quad \text{(IS curve)} \tag{10.25}$$

$$(1 - u)\frac{\bar{Y}}{K} = \delta + \bar{q}\,\frac{k\bar{Y} + h_1 - m}{h_2} \quad \text{(LM curve)} \tag{10.26}$$

$$\bar{z}^c = 0 \tag{10.27}$$

The steady-state value of the interest rate is given by

$$\bar{r} = \frac{k\bar{Y} + h_1 - m}{h_2}$$

In the case of variable proportions (when Equations (10.22)–(10.24) *are appended to the dynamics), the steady-state values of* $\bar{Y}$, $\bar{q}$ *and* $\bar{z}_c$ *remain the same. In addition, the steady-state values of the population proportions are given by*

$$\bar{n}_i = \frac{e^{\kappa_i}}{e^{\kappa_c} + e^{\kappa_f}}, \quad i \in (c, f) \tag{10.28}$$

Proof. For convenience write (10.14), (10.18) and (10.19) as

$$Y_{t+\Delta t} \equiv F_1(Y_t, q_t, z_t^c)$$

$$q_{t+\Delta t} \equiv F_2(Y_t, q_t, z_t^c)$$

$$z_t^c \equiv F_3(Y_t, q_t, z_t^c)$$

where

$$F_1(Y, q, z^c) = Y + \beta_y \Delta t [-(1-c)Y - i(q-1) + A]$$

$$F_2(Y, q, z^c) = q + q\Delta t \, G(Y, q, z^c)$$

$$F_3(Y, q, z^c) = (1 - \Delta t \beta_{z_c}) z^c + \Delta t \beta_{z_c} G(Y, q, z^c)$$

with

$$G(Y, q, z^c) = \frac{1}{1 - n_t^f \beta_q^f} \left\{ n_t^c \beta_q^c z_t^c + (n_t^f \beta_q^f + n_t^c \beta_q^c) \left(\frac{(1-u)Y_t/K - \delta}{q_t} - r_t \right) \right\}$$

and we recall that

$$r_t = \frac{kY_t + h_1 - m}{h_2}. \tag{10.29}$$

Let $E(\bar{Y}, \bar{q}, \bar{z}^c)$ denote the steady state. Then it follows from $\bar{Y} = F_1(\bar{Y}, \bar{q}, \bar{z}^c)$ that

$$\bar{Y} = \frac{i(\bar{q} - 1) + A}{1 - c},$$

which is the IS curve. From $\bar{q} = F_2(\bar{Y}, \bar{q}, \bar{z}^c)$, we have

$$G(\bar{Y}, \bar{q}, \bar{z}^c) = 0 \tag{10.30}$$

from which

$$\frac{1}{1 - \frac{1+n}{2}\beta_q^f} \left\{ \frac{1-n}{2} \beta_q^c \bar{z}^c + \frac{(1+n)\beta_q^f + (1-n)\beta_q^c}{2} \right.$$
$$\left. \times \left(\frac{(1-u)\bar{Y}/K - \delta}{\bar{q}} - \frac{k\bar{Y} + h_1 - m}{h_2} \right) \right\} = 0 \tag{10.31}$$

It follows from $\bar{z}^c = F_3(\bar{Y}, \bar{q}, \bar{z}^c)$ and (10.30) and (10.31) that

$$G(\bar{Y}, \bar{q}, \bar{z}^c) = \bar{z}^c = 0 \tag{10.32}$$

It then follows from (10.31) and (10.32) that

$$\frac{(1-u)\bar{Y}}{K} - \delta - \bar{q}\,\frac{k\bar{Y} + h_1 - m}{h_2} = 0 \tag{10.33}$$

from which the LM curve (10.26) follows. The steady-state value for r follows directly from (10.29). Equations (10.21), (10.32) and (10.33) imply that

$$\bar{z}^f = 0 \tag{10.34}$$

Next we note that (10.16), (10.17), (10.26), (10.32) and (10.34) imply that

$$\bar{\varepsilon}^c = \bar{\varepsilon}^f = 0 \tag{10.35}$$

Substituting (10.35) into (10.23) yields (10.28). ∎

We refer the reader to Chiarella *et al.* (2004) for a detailed discussion of the characterization of the steady states in the real sector.[5] For reasons discussed there we follow Blanchard and consider the steady state at which the slope (as measured by $d\bar{q}/d\bar{y}$) of the IS curve is steeper than the slope of the LM curve.

4.2. Local stability analysis

Defining

$$B^f = \frac{1+n}{2}\,\beta_q^f, \quad B^c = \frac{1-n}{2}\,\beta_q^c, \quad B = B^f + B^c \quad \text{(assume } B \neq 1\text{)}$$

the Jacobian of the dynamical system (10.14), (10.18), (10.19) and (10.21) at the steady state may be written as

$$J = \begin{pmatrix} 1 - (1-c)\Delta t\beta_y & i\Delta t\beta_y & 0 \\[2ex] \dfrac{B}{1-B^f}\left(\dfrac{1-u}{K} - \dfrac{k\bar{q}}{h_2}\right)\Delta t & 1 - \dfrac{B\bar{r}}{1-B^f}\Delta t & \dfrac{B^c\bar{q}}{1-B^f}\Delta t \\[2ex] \dfrac{B}{1-B^f}\left(\dfrac{1-u}{K} - \dfrac{k\bar{q}}{h_2}\right)\Delta t\beta_{z_c}\bar{q} & -\dfrac{B\bar{r}}{1-B^f}\dfrac{\beta_{z_c}}{\bar{q}}\Delta t & 1 - \left(\dfrac{1-B}{1-B^f}\right)\beta_{z_c}\Delta t \end{pmatrix}$$

so that the characteristic equation may be written as

$$\Gamma(\lambda) \equiv \lambda^3 + p_1\lambda^2 + p_2\lambda + p_3 = 0 \tag{10.36}$$

---

[5] These authors consider a model without fundamentalists and chartists. However, the steady state of the real sector is the same as that here.

where

$$p_1 = \text{trace}(J)$$

$$p_2 = \text{sum of the principal minors of } J$$

$$p_3 = \det(J)$$

Proposition 2. *The roots of the characteristic Equation (10.36) lie within the unit circle (and hence the dynamical system (10.14), (10.18), (10.19) and (10.21) is locally asymptotically stable) if and only if $\Delta_i > 0$ ($i = 1, 2, 3$) and $p_2 < 3$, where*

$$\Delta_1 = 1 + p_1 + p_2 + p_3$$

$$\Delta_2 = 1 - p_1 + p_2 - p_3$$

$$\Delta_3 = 1 - p_2 + p_3(p_1 - p_3)$$

Furthermore

(i) *If $\Delta_1 = 0$, two eigenvalues lie in the unit circle and the third satisfies $\lambda = 1$; this case corresponds to a saddle-node bifurcation.*
(ii) *If $\Delta_2 = 0$, two eigenvalues lie in the unit circle and the third satisfies $\lambda = -1$; this case corresponds to a flip bifurcation.*
(iii) *If $\Delta_3 = 0$, one eigenvalue lies in the unit circle and the other two satisfy $\lambda_{2,3} = e^{\pm 2\pi i \theta}$; this case corresponds to a Hopf bifurcation.*

The conditions for local stability may be difficult to analyze in general. However, Proposition 2 indicates that loss of local stability is accompanied by a rich bifurcation structure, depending on which bifurcation boundary ($\Delta_1 = 0$, $\Delta_2 = 0$ or $\Delta_3 = 0$) is crossed.

4.3. The model with rational fundamentalists only

It is of interest to consider the limiting case in which there are only rational fundamentalists in the market. Thus setting $n_t^c = 0$, $n_t^f = 1$ and writing z_t instead of z_t^f the deterministic difference equations for q and Y become

$$q_{t+\Delta t} = q_t + \Delta t \beta_q \left[\frac{(1-u)Y_t/K - \delta}{q_t} + z_t^f - r_t \right] q_t \tag{10.37}$$

$$Y_{t+\Delta t} = Y_t + \Delta t \beta_y [-(1-c)Y_t + i(q_t - 1) + A] \tag{10.38}$$

In the notation of this subsection, Equation (10.20) reduces to

$$z_t^f = \beta_q^f \varepsilon_t^f = \beta_q \left[\frac{(1-u)Y_t/K - \delta}{q_t} + z_t^f - r_t \right]$$

from which

$$z_t^f = \frac{\beta_q}{1 - \beta_q} \left[\frac{(1-u)Y_t/K - \delta}{q_t} - r_t \right] \tag{10.39}$$

Hence, the dynamics of q are governed by

$$q_{t+\Delta t} = q_t + \Delta t \, \frac{\beta_q}{1 - \beta_q} \left[\frac{(1-u)Y_t}{K} - \delta - r_t q_t \right]$$

Setting

$$\bar{\beta}_q = \frac{\beta_q}{1 - \beta_q}$$

we may then write the dynamics in the case of rational fundamentalists only as

$$q_{t+\Delta t} = q_t + \Delta t \bar{\beta}_q \left[\frac{(1-u)Y_t}{K} - \delta - r_t q_t \right]$$

$$Y_{t+\Delta t} = Y_t + \Delta t \beta_y [-(1-c)Y_t - i(q_t - 1) + A] \tag{10.40}$$

The steady state of the system (10.40) is still given by Proposition 1.

Proposition 3. *The steady state E of the system (10.40) is locally stable if and only if*

(i) $\beta_y \bar{\beta}_q [\bar{r}(1-c) - iB] > 0$,
(ii) $2[2 - (\bar{\beta}_q \bar{r} + \beta_y (1-c)) \Delta t] + \beta_y \bar{\beta}_q [\bar{r}(1-c) - iB](\Delta t)^2 > 0$,
(iii) $\beta_y \bar{\beta}_q [\bar{r}(1-c) - iB](\Delta t) < \beta_y (1-c) + \bar{\beta}_q \bar{r}$,

where

$$B = \frac{1-n}{K} - \frac{k}{h_2} \bar{q}$$

In addition,

(i) *the eigenvalue $\lambda = 1$ occurs if*
$$\bar{r}(1-c) - iA = 0,$$

(ii) *the eigenvalue $\lambda = -1$ occurs if*
$$2[2 - (\bar{\beta}_q \bar{r} + \beta_y (1-c)) \Delta t] + \beta_y \bar{\beta}_q [\bar{r}(1-c) - iB](\Delta t)^2 = 0$$

(iii) *a Hopf bifurcation occurs if*
$$\beta_y \bar{\beta}_q [\bar{r}(1-c) - iB](\Delta t)^2 = 2 - \rho$$

where $\rho = 2\cos 2\pi\theta$, and the corresponding eigenvalues are given by
$\lambda_\pm = e^{\pm i2\pi\theta}$.

Proof. Set

$$F_1(q, Y) = q + \Delta t \bar{\beta}_q \left[\frac{1-n}{K} Y - \delta - \frac{kY + h_1 - m}{h_2} q \right]$$

$$F_2(q, Y) = Y + \Delta t \beta_y [-(1-c)Y - i(q-1) + A]$$

Then, at the steady state E, we calculate the partial derivatives

$$\frac{\partial F_1}{\partial q} = 1 - \Delta t \bar{\beta}_q \bar{r}$$

$$\frac{\partial F_1}{\partial Y} = \bar{\beta}_q B \Delta t$$

$$\frac{\partial F_2}{\partial q} = i \beta_y \Delta t$$

$$\frac{\partial F_2}{\partial Y} = 1 - \beta_y (1 - c) \Delta t$$

so that the Jacobian at steady state is given by

$$J = \begin{pmatrix} 1 - \Delta t \bar{\beta}_q \bar{r} & \bar{\beta}_q B \Delta t \\ i \beta_y \Delta t & 1 - \beta_y (1 - c) \Delta t \end{pmatrix}$$

The characteristic equation is given by

$$\Gamma(\lambda) = |\lambda I - J| = \lambda^2 + p_1 \lambda + p_2 = 0$$

where

$$p_1 = -2 + [\bar{\beta}_q \bar{r} + \beta_y (1 - c)] \Delta t$$

$$p_2 = 1 - [\beta_y (1 - c) + \bar{\beta}_q \bar{r}] \Delta t + \beta_y \bar{\beta}_q [\bar{r}(1 - c) - iB](\Delta t)^2$$

The steady state E is stable if and only if

(i) $\Gamma(1) \equiv 1 + p_1 + p_2 > 0$,
(ii) $(-1)^2 \Gamma(-1) = 1 - p_1 + p_2 > 0$,
(iii) $|p_2| < 1$.

Note that

$$\Gamma(1) = 1 + p_1 + p_2 = \beta_y \bar{\beta}_q [\bar{r}(1 - c) - iB]$$

$$\Gamma(-1) = 1 - p_1 + p_2$$
$$= 2[2 - (\bar{\beta}_q \bar{r} + \beta_y (1 - c)) \Delta t] + \bar{\beta}_q \beta_y [\bar{r}(1 - c) - iB]$$

and $|p_2| < 1$ is equivalent to (using $\Gamma(-1) > 0$)

$$\beta_y \bar{\beta}_q [\bar{r}(1 - c) - iB](\Delta t) < \beta_y (1 - c) + \bar{\beta}_q \bar{r}. \quad \blacksquare$$

4.4. Simulating the global dynamics

In this section, we seek to gain some insight into the global dynamics of the deterministic skeleton of the model.

Table 10.1.   Parameter set for simulations of the deterministic skeleton

h_1	3	h_2	55
m	5.5	k	0.25
c	0.7	i	10
A	10	δ	0
u	0.7	K	94.2857
β_y	0.9	β_{z_c}	5
β_q^+	1.4	β_q^-	0.7
ε^+	0.12	ε^-	−0.08

Figure 10.2.   Simulations of the noiseless underlying nonlinear mechanism

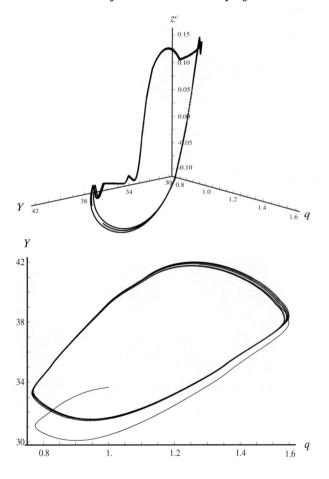

First we consider the case of fixed proportions of agents and simulate directly the 3D dynamical system (10.14),(10.18),(10.19) and (10.21). We have used the numerical values displayed in Table 10.1. Some of these (in particular $C, i, \beta_y, \beta_z, h_2$) have been chosen in line with estimated values obtained in Chiarella *et al.* (2002); the others have been obtained by numerical experimentation. These parameter values yield the steady state $q_0 = 1$, $Y_0 = 33.3$ and $z_0 = 0$. Note also that unless otherwise stated we assume that both groups have common values for the set of parameters β_q^+, β_q^-, ε^+ and ε^-.

Figure 10.3. ***Bifurcation diagram of q as a function of n***

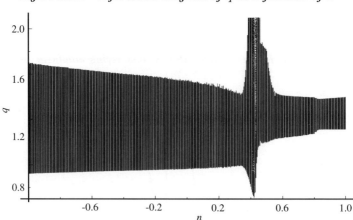

Figure 10.4. ***Bifurcation diagram of q as a function of β_{z_c}. Here $n = -0.5$ and*** ***$\beta_q^- = 0.7$***

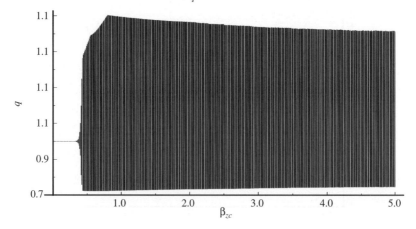

Figure 10.2 shows the long-run cycle in the 3-D phase space (a) and the projection onto the $q - Y$ phase plane (b) for the case of equal proportions of fundamentalists and chartists, i.e. $n = 0$; the economy converges to this cycle after about $t = 100$. The rapid changes in expectations of capital gains (z_c) on the part of the chartists that accompany the end of an upswing or downswing of the stock market (q) are clearly evident. This is of course a consequence of our

Figure 10.5. *The effect of increasing levels of optimism with $\beta_{z_c} = 5$ and $n = 0.76$ ($\beta_q^+ - \beta_q^- = 0.7$)*

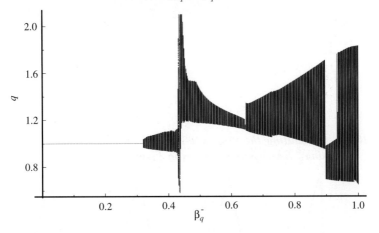

Figure 10.6. *Bifurcation diagram of q as function of β_{z_c}. The case of fluctuating proportions. Here $\beta_q^- = 0.7$, $\beta_q^+ = 1.4$, $\lambda = 40$, $\kappa^c = 0.01$, $\kappa^f = 0.02$*

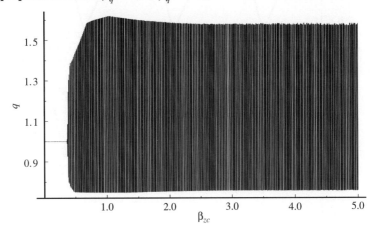

Figure 10.7. *Bifurcation diagram of q as function of β_q^-. The case of fluctuating proportions. Here $\beta_{z_c} = 5$, $\lambda = 40$, $\kappa^c = 0.01$, $\kappa^f = 0.02$*

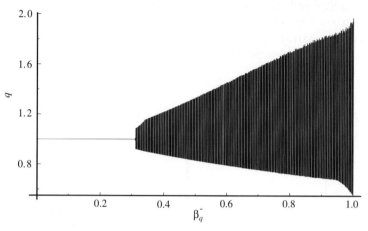

Figure 10.8. *Calculating the time series of q and n over phases of booms and recessions. Same parameters as in Figure 10.7 with $\beta_q^- = 0.7$*

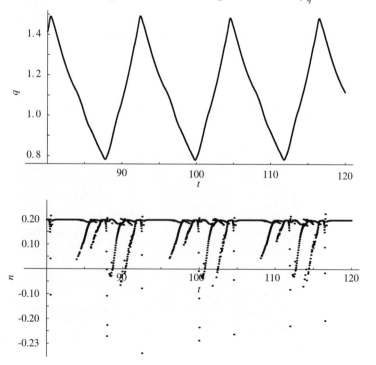

choice of a relatively large value of β_{z_c} (the chartist expectations adjustment coefficient). Lower values of β_{z_c} tend to smooth out this effect and ultimately lead to stability. The values of q range from about 0.8 in the depression phase to about 1.6 in the boom phase. Generally the three-dimensional phase plots are similar to the one in Figure 10.2, so we do not reproduce them for the subsequent simulations. Figure 10.3 gives a bifurcation diagram for q as a function of n. By and large the fluctuations in q do not vary greatly across the range of n values. The amplitude of the fluctuations are somewhat larger when the chartists dominate the market, as we might expect. In Figure 10.4 we see the influence of changing β_{z_c} on the bifurcation diagrams for q when $n = -0.5$, so that the market consists of 75% chartists. We see that once the steady state become locally unstable at around $\beta_{z_c} = 0.5$, the amplitudes of the fluctuations remain similar for a wide range of β_{z_c}.

Figure 10.5 studies the influence of the optimism/pessimism variables (β_q^+, β_q^-), with the chartists adjusting expectations fairly rapidly ($\beta_{z_c} = 5$). We maintain a constant difference $\beta_q^+ - \beta_q^- = 0.7$ and obtain a bifurcation diagram for q as a function of β_q^-. Once local instability occurs, the fluctuations seem to display some sensitivity to the optimism/pessimism variables, with fluctuations increasing as the base level β_q^- increases.

Figures 10.6 and 10.7 give an impression of the dynamics behaviour when the proportion of agents is allowed to switch according to Equations (10.22)–(10.24). Figure 10.6 gives a bifurcation diagram for q as a function of β_{z_c}. Interestingly, as in Figure 10.4, there seem to be two basic phases – the steady state is stable or there is a cyclical pattern of booms and recessions that remains much the same for

Figure 10.9. *A stochastic simulation of q. The darker (lighter) curve is for the case when the noiseless model is locally stable (unstable)*

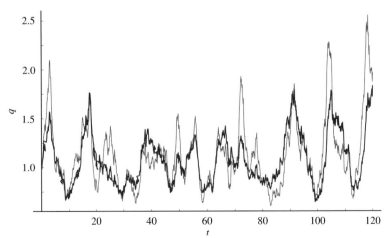

a large range of β_{z_c}. Figure 10.7 shows that, as in the case of fixed proportions, changes in the optimism/pessimism parameters (β_q^-, β_q^+) have a significant impact on the gap between the boom and recession phases. Figure 10.8 shows the typical evolution of $q(t)$ and $n(t)$ in the case $\beta_q^- = 0.7$ and $\beta_q^+ = 1.4$.

The main impressions gained from these simulations are as follows. First, once the chartists' speed of adjustment of expectations goes past the critical value leading to local instability, the fluctuations remain qualitatively similar with respect to further increases in β_{z_c}. Second, in the case of fixed proportions, variation in n does not greatly change the qualitative features of the fluctuations in the locally unstable situation. Third, the optimism/pessimism variables,

Figure 10.10. **Distribution of booms (*a*) and busts (*b*) for various β_q and** $n^c = 0.12,\ n^f = 0.88,\ \beta_{z_c} = 5$

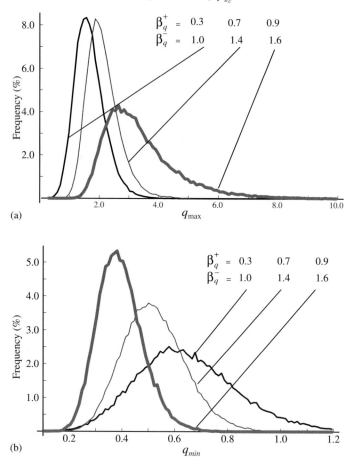

(a)

(b)

(β_q^+, β_q^-) seem to have the largest influence on the qualitative features of the fluctuations. Fourth, the observations on the qualitative behaviour with regard to β_{z_c} and (β_q^+, β_q^-) also hold for the case of fluctuating proportions of fundamentalists and chartists.

5. Analysis of the nonlinear stochastic model

In this section, we simulate the model with Wiener process noise (in (10.18) we set $\sigma_q = 0.1$) over a 120-year period using a weekly time interval. We have compared the time path of q when the underlying deterministic model is stable $(\beta_q^+ = 1.0, \beta_q^- = 0.3)$ with that when the underlying deterministic model is unstable $(\beta_q^+ = 1.4, \beta_q^- = 0.7)$ using the same sequence of Wiener increments. Figure 10.9 shows the result of such a simulation and, at least for this simulation, the unstable deterministic case generates more stock market booms

Figure 10.11. *Distribution of booms* **(a)** *and busts* **(b)** *for various* β_q *and* $n^c = 0.88, \; n^f = 0.12, \; \beta_z = 5.0$

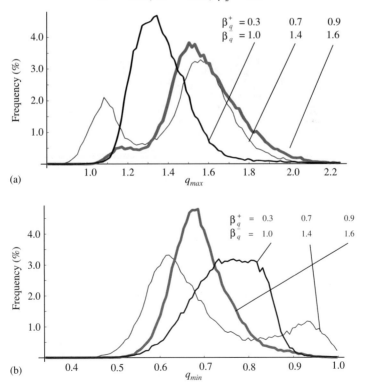

354   *Carl Chiarella et al.*

and crashes compared to the stable case. A similar pattern has been observed in
a number of simulations. Of course this could be a statistical abberation so we
have run 50,000 such simulations and for each simulated path have recorded the
max and min of q in both the stable and unstable cases. Figures 10.10 and 10.11
show the distributions of the max (i.e. the distribution of the highpoint of
booms) and the min (i.e. the distribution of the lowpoint of busts) for a range of
pairs (β_q^-, β_q^+). Here we took $n^c = 0.12$ and $n^f = 0.88$ so that fundamentalists
dominate the market, as well as $n^c = 0.88$, $n^f = 0.88$ so that chartists are more
dominant. These distributions indicate that the unstable model generates bigger
booms and crashes and this effect is somewhat more pronounced when chartists
dominate the market.

Figure 10.12 displays the distribution of booms and busts for the same
situation as Figure 10.11 but with the proportions of fundamentalists and
chartists evolving according to (10.22)–(10.24). Again, we see that the locally
unstable model generates bigger booms and crashes (Figure (10.13)).

Figure 10.12.   ***Distribution of booms (a) and busts (b) for various β_q. Here n^c
and n^f fluctuate according to the expected returns and $\beta_{z_c} = 5.0$***

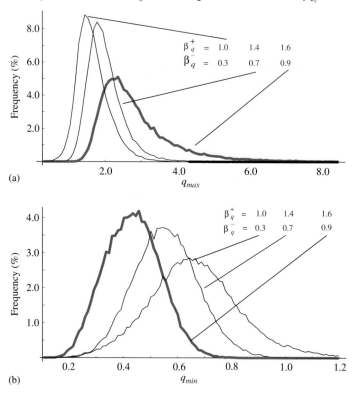

(a)

(b)

Figure 10.13.   Distribution of booms (a) and busts (b) for three scenarios with fluctuating n^c and n^f. Dashed line: $\varepsilon^- = -0.08$, $\varepsilon^+ = 0.12$, $\beta_q^- = 0.7$, $\beta_q^+ = 1.4$. Thin line: $\beta_{qf}^- = 0.7$, $\beta_{qf}^+ = 1.4$, $\beta_{qc}^- = 0.6$, $\beta_{qc}^+ = 1.5$, $\varepsilon^- = 0.08$, $\varepsilon^+ = 0.12$. Thick line: $\beta_q^- = 0.7$, $\beta_q^+ = 1.4$, $\varepsilon_f^- = -0.08$, $\varepsilon_f^+ = 0.12$, $\varepsilon_c^- = -0.06$, $\varepsilon_c^+ = 0.14$

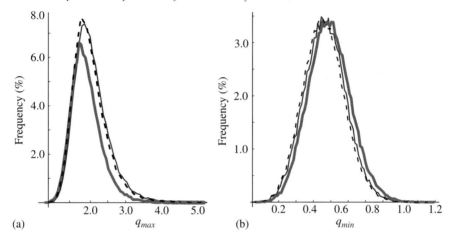

(a)   (b)

6. Conclusion

We have developed an extension to the Blanchard (1981) model of stock market–real market interaction. The key features of this extension are imperfect substitution between alternative assets, less than perfect foresight expectations and (most importantly) a state-of-market dependent coefficient of reaction to the expected return differential between different assets. The stock market of the model contains two groups rational fundamentalists and trend-chasing chartists. The original Blanchard model can be recovered as the limiting case when there is perfect substitution and the rational fundamentalists become the only agents.

Because the reaction coefficient is relatively high close to the steady state the model exhibits local instability. The trend-chasing chartists also play a role in bringing about local instability if they react sufficiently quickly to their expected capital gain. As there is movement away from the steady state the state-of-market dependent reaction coefficient of both the groups of agents operates in such a way that motion eventually is back towards steady state, where the reaction coefficient rises again. In this way the alternance between stock market upswing and downswing phases is established for the underlying deterministic driving mechanism of the model. We then added some background (steady news arrival) noise process to the dynamics for the stock market using the increments of a Wiener process.

We used numerical simulations to demonstrate that the effect of these noise processes interacting with the unstable underlying nonlinear mechanisms is to generate the booms and crashes characteristic of market economies. The simulations suggest that the distributions of peaks of booms and lows of recessions are affected by the local stability/instability of the underlying nonlinear deterministic mechanism. In particular local instability is associated with higher booms and deeper recessions.

Acknowledgment

The authors wish to acknowledge helpful comments from participants at the SNDE meeting in Atlanta in 2004, seminar participants in the Faculty of Economics at The University of Bielefeld and the School of Finance and Economics at University of Technology, Sydney. Chiarella and He acknowledge the financial support of Australian Research Council Discovery grant DP0450526.

References

Andresen, T. (1991), "A model of short- and long-term stock market behaviour", *Complexity International,* Vol. 6, www.csu.edu.au/ci/vol06/andresen/andresen.html.

Black, F. (1986), "Noise", *Journal of Finance*, Vol. 41(3), pp. 529–544.

Blanchard, O. (1981), "Output, the stock market, and interest rates", *American Economic Review*, Vol. 71, pp. 132–143.

Brock, W. and C. Hommes (1997), "A rational route to randomness", *Econometrica*, Vol. 65(5), pp. 1059–1095.

Chiarella, C. (1992), "The dynamics of speculative behaviour", *Annals of Operations Research*, Vol. 37, pp. 101–123.

Chiarella, C., P. Flaschel and W. Semmler (2004), "Real-financial interaction: a reconsideration of the blanchard model with a state-of-market dependent reaction coefficient", pp. 31–85 in: W. Barnett, C. Deissenberg and G. Feichtinger, editors, Economic Complexity, ISETE Series, Vol. 14, Amsterdam: Elsevier.

Chiarella, C., S. Mittnik, W. Semmler, and P. Zhu. (2002), "Stock market, interest rate and output: a model and estimation for us time series data", *Studies in Nonlinear Dynamics and Econometrics*, Vol. 6(1), Article 2.

Day, R. and W. Huang (1990), "Bulls, bears and market sheep", *Journal of Economic Behavior and Organization*, Vol. 14, pp. 299–329.

Kindleberger, C. (1978), *Manias, Panics and Crashes: A History of Financial Crises*, London: MacMillan.

Lux, T. (1995), "Herd behaviour, bubbles and crashes", *Economic Journal*, Vol. 105, pp. 881–896.

Lux, T. (1997), "Time variation of second moments from a noise trader/infection model", *Journal of Economic Dynamics and Control*, Vol. 22, pp. 1–38.

Lux, T. and M. Marchesi (1999), "Scaling and criticality in a stochastic multi-agent model of a financial markets", *Nature*, Vol. 397(11), pp. 498–500.

Simon, H. (1997), *Models of Bounded Rationality*, Vol. 3, New Haven: MIT Press.

Sornette, D. and W. Zhou (2002), "The US 2000-2002 market descent: how much longer and deeper?", *Quantitative Finance*, Vol. 2, pp. 468–481.

White, E.N. (1990), *Crashes and Panics: The Lessons from History*, New York: Dow Jones-Irwin.

Appendix

Variables:[6]

Y	output
Y^d	aggregate demand
p_e	share price
$q = p_e E/(pK)$	Tobin's average q
m^d	demand for real balances
r	short-term interest rate
p_b	bond price
Π	real profits
$\rho = \frac{\Pi}{K}$	rate of profit
L^d	labour demand
$p_e^e(\hat{p}_e^e)$	expected value of (rate of change in) the price of equities
q^e	expected value of
z	expected value of rate of change in Tobin's q
$\varepsilon = \frac{\Pi/K}{q} + \hat{p}_e^e - r$	expected return differential between equities and the short-term interest rate
n	the measure of the balance of fundamentalists and chartists

Parameters:[7]

$c(0 < c < 1)$	marginal propensity to consume
$i(>0)$	marginal propensity to invest
T	real taxes
G	real government consumption
M	money supply

---

[6] Units are in [ ]. Note T is the time and PG the physical good (e.g. steel).
[7] All parameters are assumed to be positive unless otherwise stated.

$p(= 1!)$ price level
w nominal wages
$k(>0)$ money demand parameter
$h_1(>0)$ money demand parameter
$h_2(>0)$ money demand parameter
m real balances
B number of long-term bonds
E number of equities
K real capital stock
$\delta(>0)$ depreciation rate of the capital stock
$x = Y/L^d$ labour productivity

$$u = wL^d/(pY)$$

$\quad = w/(px)$ wage share
I autonomous component of investment
C autonomous component of consumption
$\beta_x(>0)$ adjustment speed of a variable x
superscripts

f fundamentalists

c chartists

CHAPTER 11

A High-Dimensional Model of Real-Financial Market Interaction: The Cascade of Stable Matrices Approach

Carl Chiarella, Peter Flaschel, Reiner Franke and Willi Semmler

Abstract

This paper analyzes a high-dimensional macrodynamic model of the real-financial interaction. Regarding the financial sector it focuses on the stock market dynamics, while for the real sector it details goods market disequilibrium and two Phillips curves for prices as well as wages. The central link between the two sectors is constituted by Tobin's (average) q. The integrated dynamics of the model constitute a seven-dimensional system of differential equations, the stability analysis of which is the main contribution of the paper. The analysis proceeds by constructing a cascade of stable matrices and thus demonstrating that the long-run equilibrium is locally stable if certain adjustments are sufficiently sluggish. Large values of some reaction parameters, on the other hand, can destabilize the economy, while a Hopf bifurcation analysis shows the potential for cyclical motion in such circumstances.

Keywords: real-financial interaction, higher-order local stability analysis, cascade of stable matrices, Tobin's average q, wage-price dynamics, Hopf bifurcation

JEL classifications: E12

1. Introduction

This paper makes a contribution to descriptive non-market clearing macro-economics and to the systematic analysis of medium-scale dynamic models

CONTRIBUTIONS TO ECONOMIC ANALYSIS
VOLUME 277   ISSN: 0573-8555
DOI:10.1016/S0573-8555(05)77011-5

thus arising. Two strands of macroeconomic theory are linked together. On the one hand, we build on the basic working model of Chiarella *et al.* (2005) and Chiarella *et al.* (2000) by incorporating various feedback effects in the real sector that are associated, primarily, with the wage–price dynamics in an inflationary environment. On the other hand, the paper reconsiders an influential model by Blanchard (1981) and Blanchard and Fischer (1989, Ch. 10.4), which combines a dynamic Keynesian multiplier with a richer financial sector. Blanchard's treatment is, however, modified by relaxing his hypothesis of rational expectations and perfect substitutability of the non-money financial assets. The paper thus proposes a model of the real-financial interaction that merges in a consistent way these two approaches from the literature. The subsequent analysis seeks to uncover its basic dynamic properties and feedback mechanisms.[1]

The development of the model stresses the role of Tobin's average q in the investment function.[2] The real-financial interaction is built around it by modelling carefully the feedback loop from capacity utilization to profits and nominal interest rates, from there to Tobin's q through to investment and back to utilization again. As a consequence, also the role of the wage–price dynamics involved here goes beyond what is traditionally investigated in low-order macrodynamics of two or three dimensions.

The main methodological contribution of the paper arises from the fact that the dynamic system at which we finally arrive is of dimension 7. We present a systematic approach that allows us to derive a set of meaningful conditions on the behavioural parameters which ensure local stability of the long-run equilibrium position. It proceeds by considering dynamical subsystems of successively higher dimension for which stability can be established, in such a way that basically only the (well-behaved) determinants of the higher-order systems have to be computed. We call this proof strategy a cascade of stable

---

[1] Our framework is admittedly non-mainstream, in that it directly puts forward the structural equations and disregards the (so-called) microfoundations of the representative agent and its rational expectations. There are good reasons for now reconsidering this alternative approach to macroeconomic modelling, though at a more elaborated level, both conceptually and mathematically, than thirty years ago. This is not least to do with the extreme difficulty that the intertemporal optimizing procedures of microfounded approaches have in delineating in a clear-cut fashion the type of dynamic feedback mechanisms that we can study here. However, the present paper is not the appropriate forum to discuss this fundamental methodological issue.

[2] While economic theory focuses almost exclusively on marginal q as determining investment, the validity of this approach rests on very stringent assumptions concerning markets and adjustment costs. The use of Tobin's average q, by contrast, as *one* of the main explanatory variables of investment remains valid under a wide variety of scenarios. This point is emphasized by Caballero and Leahy (1996).

matrices, and we believe that it may also be of more general applicability to the analysis of high-dimensional dynamic economic models beyond the specific model of this paper.

The material is organized as follows. Section 2 presents the building blocks of the model. Section 3 translates these equations into intensive form, which yields a 7th-order differential equation system. Section 4 studies 2D subdynamics in the real and financial sector, respectively, thus highlighting the main positive and negative feedback loops. Section 5 returns to the full 7D dynamics and develops the techniques for examining the stability and instability conditions of the system's Jacobian matrix. Section 6 concludes the paper.

2. Formulation of the model

The core of the real-financial interaction is constituted by Tobin's q. It is here assumed that investment I varies, not with the real rate of interest, but with Tobin's average q. Regarding the financial sector, it is consequently the stock price dynamics that feeds back on the real sector. The influence of the (nominal) interest rate, i, is in this respect more indirect; it is only used by investors on the stock market, who compare the (inflation-augmented) equity rate of return to it. This difference, then, drives equity prices and ultimately Tobin's q. Regarding the real sector, output Y impacts on the interest rate through the usual transaction motive of money demand. In addition, Y, i.e. capacity utilization, affects the equity rate of return via the rate of profit, r, and the corresponding dividend payments of firms. The real-financial interaction to be studied may thus be concisely summarized by the feedback loop $Y \rightarrow (r, i) \rightarrow q \rightarrow I \rightarrow Y$.

This picture still leaves out the role of inflation and the wage–price dynamics. The relative adjustments of wages and prices, into which also inflationary expectations enter, determine income distribution in the form of the wage share and, partly, the rate of profit. Owing to differential savings of workers and asset owners, the wage share has an impact on aggregate demand via consumption expenditures. Its impact on investment is channelled through Tobin's q, since the profit rate is not a direct argument in the investment function but only co-determines the equity rate of return, which in turn has a bearing on the movements of equity prices and Tobin's q.

In the following the model is set up in extensive form, which still refers to the level variables. Much of the notation we adopt is standard, otherwise the symbols are introduced as the discussion of the modelling equations develops.

2.1. Constant growth rates

We begin by postulating constant growth rates for labour productivity $z = Y/L$, labour supply L^s, and money M:

$$\hat{z} = g_z = \text{const} \tag{11.1}$$

$$\hat{L}^s = g_\ell = \text{const} \tag{11.2}$$

$$\hat{M} = g_m = \text{const} \tag{11.3}$$

$$g^o = g_z + g_\ell \tag{11.4}$$

$$\pi^o = g_m - g^o \tag{11.5}$$

where g^o is the real growth rate that must prevail in a long-run equilibrium position, π^o the rate of inflation supporting this growth path.

When at a later stage of research the model is to be employed to study business cycle mechanisms, the technological assumption on the labour inputs can be augmented by allowing for procyclical variations of labour productivity (relative to some trend), such as was proposed in Franke (2001). The local stability analysis, however, would not be seriously impaired by this feature, so we may presently proceed with Equation (11.1) as it stands.

2.2. The goods market

The following equations specify the components of final demand Y^d: consumption C, net investment I, replacement investment δK (δ, the constant rate of depreciation), and government spending G. They are complemented by a simple tax rule and the laws of motions for capital and output.

$$Y^d = C + I + \delta K + G \tag{11.6}$$

$$pC = wL + (1 - s_c)(pY - wL - \delta pK + \iota B - T_c) \tag{11.7}$$

$$I = [g^o + \beta_I(q - 1)]K \tag{11.8}$$

$$G = \gamma K \tag{11.9}$$

$$T_c = \theta pK + iB \tag{11.10}$$

$$\dot{K} = I \tag{11.11}$$

$$\dot{Y} = g^o(Y - g^o\beta_n y^n K) + \beta_y[Y^d - (Y - g^o\beta_n y^n K)] + g^o\beta_n y^n I \tag{11.12}$$

Equation (11.7) states that wage income wL is fully spent on consumption, whereas asset owners save a constant fraction s_c of their non-wage income ($0 < s_c \leqslant 1$). The latter is made up of firms' profits, which are in their entirety distributed to shareholders, and interest payments at interest rate i for the presently outstanding fixed-price bonds B (the bond price being normalized at unity), minus (nominal) taxes T_c. As mentioned in the introduction, the investment function (11.8) focuses on the influence of Tobin's (average) q, which is defined as $q = p_e E/pK$ (E is the number of shares and p_e their price). As it is formulated, (11.8) implicitly presupposes that $q = 1$ is indeed supported as the economy's long-run equilibrium value of Tobin's q. This will have to be confirmed later on.[3] Equation (11.9) may be seen as a variant of neutral fiscal policy; γ is a constant. The tax rule (11.10) is conveniently aimed at making the term $iB - T_c$ in the expression for disposable income in (11.7) likewise proportional to the capital stock.

While the change in fixed capital in (11.11) is just the capacity effect of investment, Equation (11.12) for the change in output is a behavioural equation that requires some additional explanation. It arises from the implications of allowing for goods market disequilibrium. This means that a positive excess demand is served from the existing stock of inventories, and production in excess of demand fills up inventories. To keep the model simple we here neglect possible dynamic feedback effects from these inventories. Nevertheless, since the economy is growing over time, inventories even if remaining in the background must be growing, too. Accordingly, besides producing Y^{md} to meet final demand, firms produce an additional amount to increase a stock of desired inventories N^d. Adopting the equilibrium growth rate g^o for this purpose, we have $Y = Y^{md} + g^o N^d$.

The output component Y^{md} is adjusted to reduce the current gap between final demand Y^d and Y^{md}. Letting β_y be the corresponding adjustment speed and taking (trend) growth into account, Y^{md} evolves like $\dot{Y}^{md} = g^o Y^{md} + \beta_y(Y^d - Y^{md})$. On the other hand, desired inventories N^d may be proportional with factor β_n to productive capacity Y^n, which in turn is linked to the capital stock K by what may be called a 'normal' output–capital ratio y^n. Hence, $N^d = \beta_n Y^n = \beta_n y^n K$, where y^n itself is treated as an exogenous and constant technological coefficient. Differentiating the determined output Y with respect to time, then, yields eq. (11.12).

2.3. Wage-price dynamics

The adjustment of wages brings the employment rate λ into play, which is defined in (11.13). Labour demand and supply, L and L^s, are measured in hours, and L^s is thought to refer to normal working hours. Hence λ may well exceed unity, if workers work overtime or firms organize extra shifts. $\lambda = 1$ corresponds to normal employment.

$$\lambda = L/L^s \tag{11.13}$$

$$\hat{p} = \kappa_p(\hat{w} - g_z) + (1 - \kappa_p)\pi + \beta_p(y - y^n) \tag{11.14}$$

$$\hat{w} = g_z + \kappa_w \hat{p} + (1 - \kappa_w)\pi + \beta_w(\lambda - 1) \tag{11.15}$$

$$\dot{\pi} = \beta_{\pi p}(\hat{p} - \pi) \tag{11.16}$$

---

[3] The stability analysis would not be affected if also a (limited) capacity utilization effect on I is considered in (11.8), which could be easily represented by the output–capital ratio.

The subsequent two Equations (11.14) and (11.15) put the determination of prices and wages on an equal footing by positing a price as well as a wage Phillips curve, augmented by inflationary expectations π. In their core, both price and wage inflation respond to the pressure of demand on the respective markets. These are the deviations of capacity utilization from normal on the one hand (as they are captured by the difference between the output–capital ratio $y = Y/K$ and the normal ratio y^n), and the deviations of the employment rate from normal on the other hand. For price inflation, the cost-push term is a weighted average of expected inflation, π, and current wage inflation (corrected for labour productivity growth); in parallel, the cost-push term for wage inflation is a weighted average of the same rate of expected inflation and current price inflation. It goes without saying that the two weighting coefficients κ_p and κ_w are between zero and one.[4]

In Equation (11.16), the rate of expected inflation is supposed to be governed by adaptive expectations with adjustment speed $\beta_{\pi p}$. As π refers, not to the next (infinitesimally) short period, but to a longer time horizon of about a year, say, this rate may perhaps be better called a general inflation climate. With this interpretation, it also makes more sense that, as implied by (11.16), π systematically lags behind $\hat{p}$. In further support of such a mechanism it should be pointed out that a similar pattern is found in the survey forecasts made in the real world (see, e.g., Evans and Wachtel, 1993, fig. 1 on p. 477, pp. 481ff.).

2.3.1. The money market

The bond rate of interest i is determined by an ordinary LM schedule. With parameters $\beta_{mo}, \beta_{mi} > 0$, it is formulated as

$$M = pY(\beta_{mo} - \beta_{mi}i) \tag{11.17}$$

2.4. The stock market dynamics

The third financial asset besides money and government bonds are equities. In Equation (11.18) it is explicitly stated that they are issued by firms to finance investment (and there is no other source of internal or external finance). The next two equations put forward an elementary speculative dynamics on the stock market in two variables: the equity price p_e and expected capital gains π_e, i.e., the expected rate of stock price inflation. Equation (11.21) defines the real rate of

---

[4]Franke (2001) points out that, in their combination, the Phillips curves (11.14) and (11.15) have undesirable cyclical implications. It is shown there that the cyclical features can be improved upon by adding further adjustment mechanisms in the two equations, which are both channelled through the wage share. This idea may be taken up in a later version of the model.

return, r, in the real sector.

$$pI = p_e \dot{E} \tag{11.18}$$

$$\hat{p}_e = \beta_e(rpK/p_eE + \pi_e - \xi - i) + \kappa_e\pi_e + (1 - \kappa_e)\pi^0 \tag{11.19}$$

$$\dot{\pi}_e = \beta_{\pi e}(\hat{p}_e - \pi_e) \tag{11.20}$$

$$r = (pY - wL - \delta pK)/pK \tag{11.21}$$

The adjustment Equation (11.19) rests on the supposition that, unlike in the usual LM treatment, bonds and equities are imperfect substitutes. While perfect substitutability between bonds and equities conveys the notion that any difference in the rates of return of the two assets would immediately be eliminated by arbitrage sales or purchases and the corresponding price changes, imperfect substitutability implies that these price adjustments take place at a finite speed. The (nominal) rate of return on equities is given by the dividends which, as has already been mentioned above, are fully paid out to the shareholders. In addition, the expected capital gains π_e have to be considered, and a risk premium ξ may be deducted. Thus, $r_e := rpK/p_eE + \pi_e - \xi$ is compared to the bond rate i. If $r_e > i$ then equities have become more attractive than the alternative asset, the consequence being that the demand for equities increases and bids up the equity price; corresponding downward adjustments of p_e take place if $r_e < i$.

Equation (11.19) expresses this mechanism in growth rate form. The equation furthermore takes into account that the changes in stock prices have to be related to a general growth trend of p_e. This is specified as a weighted average of currently expected stock-price inflation π_e and inflation of stock prices in a long-run equilibrium, which as shown below must be equal to the long-run equilibrium rate of price inflation π^0.

A low value of β_e in (11.19) would indicate that equities, because of the risk associated with them, are only a weak alternative to the almost risk-free government bonds. Hence, even if equities offer a markedly higher rate of return, the pressure of demand on the stock market and the price increases resulting from it are only limited. With respect to a given (positive) differential in the two rates of return, a higher value of β_e would signify a greater pressure of demand on the share price, since agents are more easily willing to switch from bonds to equities, or to invest their current savings in equities rather than bonds. The limit in which $\beta_e = \infty$ would correspond to the situation of perfect substitutability.

Eq. (11.20) invokes adaptive expectations for the expected capital gains, which are therefore treated analogously to the general inflation climate in (11.16). The speed of adjustment $\beta_{\pi e}$, however, would typically be faster than $\beta_{\pi p}$.

It is not very hard to set up versions of speculative stock market dynamics that specify some of the relevant features in finer detail. They may, in particular, explicitly distinguish fundamentalists and chartists as the two prototype trading groups on this market (see, e.g., Franke and Sethi, 1998), or the speeds of adjustments in Equations (11.19) or (11.20) could be dependent on the recent history of returns (*ibid.*) or the economic climate in general (as in Chiarella *et al.*, 2005). The basic stabilizing and destabilizing feedback mechanisms, however, would be very similar, at least as far as the local dynamics is concerned. For this reason the elementary adjustment Equations (11.19) and (11.20) may for the present (but only for the present) suffice.

3. The model in intensive form

In order to analyze the dynamics generated by Equations (11.1)–(11.21), the model has to be translated into intensive form. In this way a 7D differential equation system comes about, with state variables:

$y = Y/K$ output–capital ratio
$v = wL/pY$ wage share
$q = p_e E/pK$ Tobin's q
π_e expected capital gains
$m = M/pK$ real balances ratio
$k = K/zL^s$ capital per head
π expected price inflation

Capital per head is a shorthand expression for capital per hour of labour supplied, measured in efficiency units (recall z is labour productivity).

3.1. The differential equations

We first sketch the way in which the differential equations for the state variables are obtained, including the composite expressions of some of the variables entering them. For a better overview, the complete equations are subsequently collected in a whole.

The time rate of change of the output–capital ratio is obtained from $\dot{y} = \hat{Y} - \hat{K}y$ and, in particular, Equations (11.12). Making use of (11.7)–(11.11), the aggregate demand term $y^d = Y^d/K$ in (11.22) is easily computed as stated in Equations (11.29). In order to determine the rate of inflation in (11.16) and also the changes in the wage share, the mutual dependence of $\hat{p}$ and $\hat{w}$ in the two Phillips curve has to be eliminated. Defining $\kappa := 1/(1 - \kappa_p \kappa_w)$, the reduced-form equations read

$$\hat{p} = \pi + \kappa[\beta_p(y - y^n) + \kappa_p \beta_w(\lambda - 1)]$$
$$\hat{w} = \pi + g_z + \kappa[\kappa_w \beta_p(y - y^n) + \beta_w(\lambda - 1)]$$

On this basis, the changes in the wage share $v = wL/pY = w/pz$ derive from $\hat{v} = \hat{w} - \hat{p} - g_z$; see (11.23), with κ given in (11.34). Obviously, the two weights κ_p and κ_w must not both be unity simultaneously. Equation (11.30) makes explicit how the employment rate entering (11.23) can be expressed in terms of the state variables y and k. This formula is the simple decomposition $\lambda = (Y/K)(L/Y)(K/L^s) = (Y/K)(K/zL^s)$. The equation for the rate of inflation will also be referred to in the next steps and so is reiterated in (11.31).

To get the law of motion for Tobin's q, observe first that, with (11.18), the growth rate of the number of equities is $\hat{E} = p_e\dot{E}/p_eE = (pI/pK)(pK/p_eE) = \hat{K}/q$. Thus, $\hat{q} = \hat{p}_e + \hat{E} - \hat{p} - \hat{K} = \hat{p}_e - \hat{p} + [(1-q)/q]\hat{K}$. Equations (11.24) follows from substituting (11.19) for $\hat{p}_e$. As (11.32) shows, the rate of profit entering here is dependent on y and v. Furthermore, the bond rate i in (11.24) depends on y and m. It is the solution of the LM Equation (11.17) in intensive form, $m = y(\beta_{mo} - \beta_{mi} i)$, given in Equation (11.33).

The adjustments of the expected capital gains in Equation (11.25) combine Equation (11.20) with (11.19). The motions of the remaining three variables are less involved. Logarithmic differentiation of $m = M/pK$ and $k = K/zL^s$, together with the growth rate specifications (11.1)–(11.5), yields the differential equations (11.26) and (11.27) for these two variables. Lastly, (11.28) for the adaptive expectations of the inflation climate π is a restatement of (11.16).

$$\dot{y} = \beta_y[y^d - (y - g^o\beta_n y^n)] - (y - g^o\beta_n y^n)\beta_I(q - 1) \tag{11.22}$$

$$\dot{v} = v\kappa[\beta_w(1 - \kappa_p)(\lambda - 1) - \beta_p(1 - \kappa_w)(y - y^n)] \tag{11.23}$$

$$\dot{q} = q\left\{\beta_e\left[\frac{r}{q} + \pi_e - \xi - i\right] + \kappa_e\pi_e + (1 - \kappa_e)\pi^o - \hat{p}\right.$$
$$\left. + [(1-q)/q][g^o + \beta_I(q-1)]\right\} \tag{11.24}$$

$$\dot{\pi}_e = \beta_{\pi e}\left\{\beta_e\left[\frac{r}{q} + \pi_e - \xi - i\right] - (1 - \kappa_e)(\pi_e - \pi^o)\right\} \tag{11.25}$$

$$\dot{m} = m[\pi^o - \hat{p} - \beta_I(q - 1)] \tag{11.26}$$

$$\dot{k} = k\beta_I(q - 1) \tag{11.27}$$

$$\dot{\pi} = \beta_{\pi p}(\hat{p} - \pi) \tag{11.28}$$

$$y^d = y^d(y, v, q) = (1 - s_c)y + s_c vy + \beta_I(q - 1) + g^o + s_c\delta + \gamma - (1 - s_c)\theta \tag{11.29}$$

$$\lambda = \lambda(y, k) = yk \tag{11.30}$$

$$\hat{p} = \hat{p}(y, k, \pi) = \pi + \kappa[\beta_p(y - y^n) + \kappa_p\beta_w(\lambda - 1)] \tag{11.31}$$

$$r = r(y, v) = (1 - v)y - \delta \tag{11.32}$$

$$i = i(y, m) = \beta_{mo}/\beta_{mi} - m/(\beta_{mi}y) \tag{11.33}$$

$$\kappa = 1/(1 - \kappa_p\kappa_w) \tag{11.34}$$

3.2. Long-run equilibrium

A steady state position of the economy is constituted by a rest point of system (11.22)–(11.28). Proposition 1 ensures that it exists and that, at least if the system is not degenerate, it is unique. The steady state values of the variables are denoted by a superscript '0'. Note that expected inflation π in the steady state is indeed equal to π^o as defined in (11.5), which justifies the slight abuse of the notation for equilibrium inflation.

Proposition 1. *System* (11.22) – (11.28) *has a stationary point given by*

$$y^0 = y^n, \quad v^0 = 1 - [g^0(1 + \beta_n y^n) + s_c \delta + \gamma - (1 - s_c)\theta]/s_c y^n$$

$$q^0 = 1 \quad (\hat{p})^0 = (\pi)^0 = (\pi_e)^0 = \pi^0$$

$$k^0 = 1/y^n \quad m^0 = [\beta_{mo} - \beta_{mi}((1 - v^0)y^n - \delta + \pi^0 - \xi)]y^n$$

Provided that the parameters $\beta_I, \beta_p, \beta_w, \beta_{np}, \beta_e, \beta_{\pi e}$ *are all strictly positive, this position is uniquely determined.*

Proof. We proceed in a number of successive steps. Setting $\dot{k} = 0$ gives $q = q^0 = 1$; setting $\dot{m} = 0$ gives $\hat{p}^0 = \pi^0$; setting $\dot{\pi} = 0$ gives $(\pi)^0 = \hat{p}^0 = \pi^0$ for the inflation climate. Then, consider $\dot{q} = 0$ and $\dot{\pi}_e = 0$ (the terms in the curly brackets only). Subtracting the second equation from the first gives $[\kappa_e + (1 - \kappa_e)](\pi_e - \pi^0) = 0$, hence $(\pi_e)^0 = \pi^0$.

From $\dot{v} = 0$ we get $\beta_w(1 - \kappa_p)(\lambda - 1) - \beta_p(1 - \kappa_w)(y - y^n) = 0$, while from $\hat{p} = \pi$ in (11.31) we have $\beta_w \kappa_p(\lambda - 1) + \beta_p(y - y^n) = 0$. This can be viewed as two equations in the two unknowns $(\lambda - 1)$ and $(y - y^n)$. An obvious solution is $(\lambda - 1) = 0$, $(y - y^n) = 0$, and it is easily seen to be the only one if κ_p and κ_w are not both unity simultaneously. $\lambda = 1$ implies $k = k^0 = 1/y^n$ by eq. (11.30).

Putting $\dot{y} = 0$ and solving the resulting equation $y^n - g^0\beta_n y^n = (y^d)^0$ for v yields v^0 as stated in the proposition. Returning to $\dot{q} = 0$ and setting $r^0 = (1 - v^0)y^n - \delta$ in (11.32), this equation now amounts to $r^0 + \pi^0 - \xi - i = 0$, or $r^0 + \pi^0 - \xi = i(y^n, m) = \beta_{mo}/\beta_{mi} - m/(\beta_{mi}y^n)$ with (11.33). Solving this for m gives the proposition's expression for the equilibrium real balances.   q.e.d

4. Subdynamics in the real and financial sector

To get an impression of the basic stabilizing and destabilizing forces in the economy, it is instructive to study the dynamics of its underlying subsystems. One of them represents the stock market, the other the goods and labour market in the real sector.

4.1. Stock market subdynamics

Let us first consider the dynamics on the stock market in isolation of the rest of the economy. Two variables are here determined; Tobin's q reflecting the adjustments of equity prices, and expected capital gains π_e.

There is only one channel through which the stock market impacts on the real sector. This is Tobin's q in the investment function of the firms. Hence the real sector may continue to grow in its steady-state proportions if the investment coefficient β_I in (11.8) is set equal to zero. Freezing the five state variables y, v, m, k, π (that characterize the behaviour of the real sector) at their equilibrium values and denoting $r^0 = r(y^0, v^0)$, $i^0 = i(y^0, m^0)$, the differential Equations (11.24), (11.25) become

$$\dot{q} = q\left\{ \beta_e\left[\frac{r^0}{q} + \pi_e - \xi - i^0\right] + \kappa_e(\pi_e - \pi^0) + \frac{(1-q)g^0}{q}\right\} \tag{11.35}$$

$$\dot{\pi}_e = \beta_{\pi e}\left\{ \beta_e\left[\frac{r^0}{q} + \pi_e - \xi - i^0\right] - (1 - \kappa_e)(\pi_e - \pi^0)\right\} \tag{11.36}$$

An obvious destabilization mechanism is the positive feedback loop of expected capital gains. A rise in π_e increases the demand for equities and thus drives up share prices. If p_e rises sufficiently fast relative to general inflation, the gap between $\hat{p}_e$ and π_e in Equation (11.20) widens, so that π_e increases further. On the other hand, the resulting increase in Tobin's q lowers the rate of return on equities (the expression r^0/q), which tends to reduce equity demand. Whether the positive or negative feedback dominates depends on the speed at which expectations of capital gains are adjusted upward: instability (stability) should prevail if $\beta_{\pi e}$ is sufficiently high (low). Proposition 2 makes more precise the conditions under which this happens.

Proposition 2. *Suppose the equilibrium rate of profit exceeds the real growth rate, $r^0 > g^0$. Then the equilibrium q^0, π^0 of system (11.35), (11.36) for the stock market subdynamics is locally, asymptotically stable if either $\beta_e \leqslant 1 - \kappa_e$, or (with $\beta_e > 1 - \kappa_e$) if*

$$\beta_{\pi e} < (g^0 + \beta_e r^0)/(\beta_e + \kappa_e - 1).$$

The equilibrium is unstable if in the latter case ($\beta_e > 1 - \kappa_e$) the inequality for $\beta_{\pi e}$ is reversed.

The supposition of the relative size of the profit rate r^0 can be safely taken for granted.[5] Furthermore, overly sluggish reactions of equity prices, as represented by low values of β_e, do not really seem plausible. The proposition's inequality for the adjustment speed of expected capital gains, $\beta_{\pi e}$, is therefore the central stability condition for the stock market.

---

[5] Indeed, taxes must be extraordinarily (unless inconsistently) high for the inequality $r^0 > g^0$ to be violated. This can be seen from substituting the expression for v^0 from Proposition 1 in $r(y^0, v^0)$, which yields $r^0 = [g^0(1 + \beta_n y^n) + \gamma - (1 - s_c)(\delta + \theta)]$.

Proof. The Jacobian of (11.35), (11.36) is given by

$$
J = \begin{bmatrix} -(\beta_e r^o + g^o) & \beta_e + \kappa_e \\ -\beta_{\pi e}\beta_e r^0 & \beta_{\pi e}(\beta_e + \kappa_{e-1}) \end{bmatrix}
$$

$r^o > g^o$ is sufficient for the determinant to be positive, since det $J = \beta_{\pi e}[\beta_e(r^o - g^o)$ $+g^o(1 - \kappa_e)]$. The statements in the proposition then derive from the second stability condition that the trace be negative.   q.e.d

4.2. The income distribution subdynamics

Neglecting variations in fixed investment by putting $\beta_I = 0$ not only decouples the real sector from the stock market, but there is also no feedback of money balances m on the goods market, since we do not have to consider the impact of the bond rate $i = i(y,m)$ on Tobin's q. Furthermore, capital per head k remains constant in the employment rate $\lambda = \lambda(y,k)$. For simplicity, let us here also ignore the inflationary climate and its influence on current inflation $\hat{p}$ in Equation (11.31) by fixing π at π^o. In this way we concentrate on a (2D) subdynamics in output y and the wage share v, which reads,[6]

$$
\dot{y} = \beta_y[y^d(y, v, q^o) - y + g^o\beta_n y^n] \tag{11.37}
$$

$$
\dot{v} = v\kappa\{\beta_w(1 - \kappa_p)[\lambda(y, k^o) - 1] - \beta_p(1 - \kappa_w)(y - y^n)\} \tag{11.38}
$$

The stability of this reduced system crucially depends on the relative speeds at which wages and prices respond to the disequilibrium on the labour and goods market. To see this, suppose a positive shock on the wage side has raised the wage share above its steady-state level. The immediate effect is an increase in consumption demand on the part of workers. Since there are no possibly counterbalancing effects in investment, aggregate demand y^d and then total output y increases. The corresponding overutilization of the capital stock raises inflation in the price Phillips curve (11.14), while the correspondingly higher employment rate λ raises wage inflation in (11.15). If the price level rises faster than the nominal wage rate (discounting for the productivity growth rate g_z in the wage Phillips curve), the wage share falls back towards normal. In this way we identify a negative, stabilizing feedback loop. Otherwise the wage share increases and moves the economy further away from equilibrium.

This short chain of effects may be called the real wage effect, or the Rose effect, whereby we pay tribute to a seminal contribution on the stability implications of wage and price adjustments by Rose (1967) or, more

---

[6] Adopting the (otherwise useful) notation $y^d = y^d(\cdot, \cdot, \cdot)$ for aggregate demand, the supposition $\beta_I = 0$ is expressed by plugging in q^0. This nevertheless does not rule out that q may be actually moving on the stock market.

comprehensively later on, by Rose (1990). Normally this effect may be expected to be stabilizing, so we may speak of an adverse Rose effect in the destabilizing case. Schematically, the two cases may be summarized as follows, where ↑↑ indicates a faster rate of change than ↑:

Normal Rose effect:

$$v \uparrow \longrightarrow y^d \uparrow \longrightarrow \begin{cases} y \uparrow & \longrightarrow & \hat{p} \uparrow\uparrow \\ \lambda \uparrow & \longrightarrow & \hat{w} \uparrow \end{cases} \longrightarrow v \downarrow$$

Adverse Rose effect:

$$v \uparrow \longrightarrow y^d \uparrow \longrightarrow \begin{cases} y \uparrow & \longrightarrow & \hat{p} \uparrow \\ \lambda \uparrow & \longrightarrow & \hat{w} \uparrow\uparrow \end{cases} \longrightarrow v \uparrow$$

Proposition 3 shows that in the real sector subsystem the sign of the Rose effect is the decisive stability argument. The key expression for stability is α_{wp}, which contrasts the adjustment speeds β_w and β_p in the two Phillips curves,

$$\alpha_{wp} = \beta_w(1 - \kappa_p)/y^n - \beta_p(1 - \kappa_w) \tag{11.39}$$

Note, however, that α_{wp} not only involves β_w and β_p, but also the weighting parameters κ_w and κ_p in (11.14), (11.15).

Proposition 3. *The equilibrium point y^0, v^0 of the real sector subsystem (11.37), (11.38) is locally asymptotically stable if $\alpha_{wp} < 0$. It is unstable if the inequality is reversed.*

Proof. The Jacobian is

$$J = \begin{bmatrix} -s_c\beta_y(1 - v^o) & s_c\beta_y y^o \\ v^o \kappa \alpha_{wp} & 0 \end{bmatrix}$$

Its trace is always negative, and $\det J = -s_c\beta_y y^o v^o \kappa \alpha_{wp}$. Hence stability is given if and only if $\det J > 0$, that is, if and only if α_{wp} is negative.   q.e.d

In evaluating the Rose effect, the proposition warns against exclusively looking at the direct wage and price adjustment speeds. Though conceptually the weights κ_w and κ_p are of secondary importance, their dynamic implications for the real wage, or the wage share, are by no means innocent.[7] In particular, if price adjustments are independent of the inflation climate, i.e. if $\kappa_p = 1$, the Rose effect will always be normal, even if β_w itself might be excessively high.[8] A converse reasoning applies for $\kappa_w = 1$. The distorting effect of κ_w and κ_p is more directly expressed if (assuming $\kappa_p < 1$) the stability condition is rewritten as

$$\beta_w < \frac{(1 - \kappa_w)y^n}{1 - \kappa_p} \beta_p \tag{11.40}$$

---

[7] Empirical estimations of Phillips curves, however, do not seem to pay much attention to coefficients like κ_w and κ_p. They are possibly fairly sensitive to the specific proxy adopted for inflationary expectations.

[8] We recall that, for κ in (11.34) to be well-defined, κ_w cannot be unity, too, in this case.

It may finally be remarked that though it is tempting to relax the assumption $\beta_I = 0$ and merge the stock market dynamics (11.35), (11.36) with the real sector subdynamics (11.37), (11.38), the resulting 4D system would not be consistent, even if π were still kept at π^0. On the one hand, k is now being changed in (11.27) by the variations of Tobin's q, which feeds back in $\lambda = \lambda(y, k)$ in (11.38). On the other hand, the variable real balances m from (11.26) make themselves felt in the interest rate $i = i(y, m)$ in (11.35). In addition, such a combined system would not be easily tractable, either. Results going beyond what can also be obtained for the general system would be hard to come by. We therefore proceed directly to the stability analysis of the full 7th-order dynamics that integrates consistently the stock market and real sector dynamics.

5. Local stability analysis of the full 7D dynamics

5.1. Immediate instability results

The local stability analysis of the full 7D differential Equations system (11.22)–(11.28) is based on the Jacobian matrix J, evaluated at the steady-state values. It is useful in this respect to change the order of the differential equations. Maintaining the first three for y, v, q and rearranging the remaining four in the order m, k, π, π_e, the Jacobian is computed as

$$J = \begin{bmatrix} -s_c \beta_y (1-v) & s_c \beta_y y & \beta_I \alpha_{yn} & 0 & 0 & 0 & 0 \\ v\kappa\alpha_{wp} & 0 & 0 & 0 & v\kappa\alpha_{wK} & 0 & 0 \\ \beta_e \alpha_{vi} - \hat{p}_y & -\beta_e y & -(\beta_e r + g) & -\beta_e i_m & -\hat{p}_k & -1 & \beta_e + \kappa_e \\ -m\hat{p}_y & 0 & m\beta_I & 0 & -m\hat{p}_k & -m & 0 \\ 0 & 0 & k\beta_I & 0 & 0 & 0 & 0 \\ \beta_{\pi p}\hat{p}_y & 0 & 0 & 0 & \beta_{\pi p}\hat{p}_k & 0 & 0 \\ \beta_{\pi e}\beta_e \alpha_{vi} & -\beta_{\pi e}\beta_e y & -\beta_{\pi e}\beta_e r & -\beta_{\pi e}\beta_e i_m & 0 & 0 & \beta_{\pi e}(\beta_e + \kappa_e - 1) \end{bmatrix}$$

Here the superscript '0' is omitted and besides α_{wp}, which has already be defined in (11.39), the following abbreviations are used:

$$\alpha_{yn} = \beta_y - (1 - g\beta_n)y \quad \hat{p}_y = \partial\hat{p}/\partial y = \kappa[\beta_p + \beta_w \kappa_p k]$$
$$\alpha_{vi} = (1 - v) - \partial i/\partial y \quad \hat{p}_k = \partial\hat{p}/\partial k = \kappa\beta_w \kappa_p y$$
$$\alpha_{wK} = \beta_w(1 - \kappa_p)y \quad i_m = \partial i/\partial m = -1/\beta_{mi}y$$

One of the necessary conditions for local stability is a negative trace. With $\beta_e > 1 - \kappa_e$, this condition is obviously violated whenever $\beta_{\pi e}$ in the diagonal entry j_{77} of matrix J is large enough. We can thus immediately recognize that the stock market dynamics can always destabilize the whole economy: if the expected capital gains adjust sufficiently fast to the previously observed changes in the equity price.

Proposition 4. *Given that* $\beta_e > 1 - \kappa_e$, *the steady state of system* (11.22) – (11.28) *is unstable if* $\beta_{\pi e}$ *is sufficiently large.*

In many monetary growth models with adaptive expectations of an expected rate of inflation, the same type of result obtains if the speed of adjustment of inflationary expectations is sufficiently fast. In the present framework this would mean that $\beta_{\pi p}$, too, could destabilize the economy. However, $\beta_{\pi p}$ does not show up in the diagonal entry j_{66}, so that the straightforward argument involving the trace of J is no longer available. As a matter of fact, it can be shown below that low values of $\beta_{\pi p}$ are stabilizing, whereas we have so far not been able to prove that high values of $\beta_{\pi p}$ are (largely) sufficient for instability.

Another mechanism that, at least at a theoretical level, is likewise capable of destabilizing the whole economy is an adverse Rose effect. The mathematical argument refers to the principal minor of order 2 which is constituted by the determinant of the 2 × 2 submatrix in the upper-left corner. Denoting it by $D^{(2)}$, we have, as in the proof of Proposition 3, $D^{(2)} = -s_c \beta_y y^0 v^0 \kappa \alpha_{wp}$. One of the more involved Routh–Hurwitz conditions necessary for stability says that the sum of all second-order principal minors must be positive. Since α_{wp} enters no other of these principal minors, a negative $D^{(2)}$ can dominate the sum if α_{wp} is large enough. We thus obtain

Proposition 5. *Given that* $\kappa_p < 1$, *the steady state of system* (11.22) – (11.28) *is unstable if* β_w *is sufficiently large.*

After these negative results we should now inquire into the conditions for the long-run equilibrium growth path to be attractive.

5.2. The proof strategy: A cascade of stable matrices

Stability conditions for system (11.22)–(11.28) can be derived in a number of successive steps, where we proceed from lower-to higher-order matrices. Our method rests on the following lemma.

Lemma. *Let* $J^{(n)}(\beta)$ *be* $n \times n$ *matrices,* $h(\beta) \in \mathbb{R}^n$ *row vectors, and* $h_{n+1}(\beta)$ *real numbers, all three varying continuously with* β *over some interval* $[0, \varepsilon]$. *Put*

$$J^{(n+1)}(\beta) = \begin{bmatrix} J^{(n)}(\beta) & z \\ h(\beta) & h_{n+1}(\beta) \end{bmatrix} \in \mathbb{R}^{(n+1) \times (n+1)},$$

where z *is an arbitrary column vector,* $z \in \mathbb{R}^n$. *Assume* $h(0) = 0$, $\det J^{(n)}(0) \neq 0$, *and let* $\lambda_1, \ldots, \lambda_n$ *be the eigen-values of* $J^{(n)}(0)$. *Furthermore for* $0 < \beta \leqslant \varepsilon$, $\det J^{(n+1)}(\beta) \neq 0$ *and of opposite sign of* $\det J^{(n)}(\beta)$. *Then for all positive* β *sufficiently small,* n *eigen-values of* $J^{(n+1)}(\beta)$ *are close to* $\lambda_1, \ldots, \lambda_n$, *while the* $n + 1$st *eigen-value is a negative real number. In particular, if matrix* $J^{(n)}(0)$ *is asymptotically stable, so are these matrices* $J^{(n+1)}(\beta)$.

Proof. With respect to $\beta = 0$, it is easily seen that $J^{(n+1)}(0)$ has eigen-values $\lambda_1, \ldots, \lambda_n, h_{n+1}(0)$. In fact, if λ is an eigen-value of $J^{(n)}$ with right-hand eigen-vector $x \in \mathbb{R}^n$, the column vector $(x, 0) \in \mathbb{R}^{n+1}$ satisfies $J^{(n+1)}(x, 0) = \lambda \cdot (x, 0)$. (We omit reference to the argument β for the moment.) This shows that λ is an eigen-value of $J^{(n+1)}$, too. It is furthermore well-known that the product of the eigen-values of a matrix equals its determinant, which gives us $\det J^{(n)} = \lambda_1 \cdot \ldots \cdot \lambda_n$ and $\det J^{(n+1)} = \lambda_1 \cdot \ldots \cdot \lambda_n \cdot \lambda_{n+1}$. On the other hand, expanding $\det J^{(n+1)}$ by the last row yields $\det J^{(n+1)} = h_{n+1}(0) \cdot \det J^{(n)} \neq 0$. Hence $\lambda_{n+1} = h_{n+1}(0)$.

Then, consider the situation in the lemma and denote the $n + 1$ eigen-values of $J^{(n+1)}(\beta)$ by $\lambda_i(\beta)$. It has just been shown that $\lambda_i(0) = \lambda_i$ for $i = 1, \ldots, n$, while $\lambda_{n+1}(0)$ is a real number. Eigen-values vary continuously with the entries of the matrix.[9] As $\det J^{(n)}(0) \neq 0$, this implies that $\text{sign}[\lambda_1(\beta) \cdot \ldots \cdot \lambda_n(\beta)] = \text{sign}[\lambda_1 \cdot \ldots \cdot \lambda_n] = \text{sign}[\det J^{(n)}(0)]$ also for small positive β. The relationship $\det J^{(n+1)}(\beta) = \lambda_1(\beta) \cdot \ldots \cdot \lambda_n(\beta) \cdot \lambda_{n+1}(\beta)$ entails $\text{sign}[\det J^{(n+1)}(\beta)] = \text{sign}[\det J^{(n)}(0)] \cdot \text{sign}[\lambda_{n+1}(\beta)] \neq 0$. Since $\det J^{(n+1)}(\beta)$ and $\det J^{(n)}(0)$ have opposite signs, $\lambda_{n+1}(\beta)$ is a negative real number for all β sufficiently small (but, of course, β still positive, should $h_{n+1}(0)$ happen to be zero).

The final statement about the stability of $\det J^{(n+1)}(\beta)$ follows from the fact that, by hypothesis, the n eigen-values of $\det J^{(n)}(0)$ have all strictly negative real parts. So for small β the same holds true for the $\lambda_i(\beta)$.   q.e.d

We thus proceed with the above Jacobian matrix in the following manner. Suppose in the nth step, so to speak, a submatrix $J^{(n)}$ made up of the first n rows and columns of J, $n < 7$, has been established to be stable. Suppose moreover that there exists a parameter β such that all entries of the $n + 1$st row, except perhaps for the diagonal entry $j_{n+1, n+1}$, converge to zero as $\beta \to 0$. If we are able to verify that the determinant of the augmented matrix $J^{(n+1)} = J^{(n+1)}(\beta)$ has the opposite sign of $\det J^{(n)}(\beta)$, the lemma applies and we conclude that $J^{(n+1)}(\beta)$ is stable as well if only β is chosen sufficiently small.

In this way a collection of parameter values are found that render the submatrix consisting of the first $n + 1$ rows and columns of J stable. This result completes the $n + 1$st step and we can go over to consider matrix $J^{(n+2)}$, etc. On the whole, we therefore strive to obtain a cascade of stable matrices $J^{(n)}$, $J^{(n+1)}$, $J^{(n+2)}, \ldots$, until at $n = 7$ stability of the full system has been proved.

The argument, of course, equally applies if it is the $n + 1$st column that exhibits the property just indicated. Likewise, if β does not enter matrix $J^{(n)}$, the $n + 1$st column or row may also converge to zero as β itself tends to infinity.

---

[9] This proposition is so intuitive that it is usually taken for granted. Somewhat surprisingly, a rigorous proof, which indeed is non-trivial, is not so easy to find in the literature. One reference is Sontag (1990, pp. 328ff.).

5.3. Local stability of the full system

We are now ready to consider the full dynamical system (11.22) – (11.28) and put forward conditions on the behavioural parameters that ensure local stability of its long-run equilibrium.[10]

Proposition 6. *Consider the non-degenerate system* (11.22) – (11.28) (*in particular,* $\beta_p > 0$, $\beta_I > 0$). *Suppose that* $\kappa_w < 1$, $\beta_I < s_c r^0$, *and* $\beta_y > (1 - g^0 \beta_n) y^0$. *Then the steady-state position is locally asymptotically stable if* β_w, $\beta_{\pi p}$, $\beta_{\pi e}$ *are sufficiently small, while* β_{mi} *is sufficiently large.*

Proof. Our starting point is the submatrix $J^{(3)}$ given by the first three rows and columns of J. For the moment being, we assume that $\beta_w = 0$ (so that $\alpha_{wp} = -\beta_p(1 - \kappa_w) < 0$) and $\beta_{mi} = \infty$ (so that $\partial i / \partial y = 0$ and $\alpha_{vi} = 1 - v$). Given that $\beta_I < s_c r^0$, it has to be shown that $J^{(3)}$ satisfies the Routh–Hurwitz conditions. This demonstration may be summarized as 'steps 1–3'.

Steps 1–3. The Routh–Hurwitz conditions require that the following terms a_1, a_2, a_3, b are all positive. Again, here and in the rest of the proof superscripts '0' are omitted.

$$a_1 = -\text{trace } J \qquad = |j_{11}| + |j_{33}| = s_c \beta_y(1 - v) + (\beta_e r + g)$$

$$a_2 = J_1^{(3)} + J_2^{(3)} + J_3^{(3)} = 0 + [\beta_y \beta_e(1 - v)(s_c r - \beta_I) + \kappa \beta_p \alpha_{yn} + a_{21}] + v\kappa y s_c \beta_y |\alpha_{wp}|$$

$$a_3 = -\det J^{(3)} \qquad = |\alpha_{wp}| v\kappa y [\beta_y \beta_e(s_c r - \beta_I) + s_c \beta_y + \beta_e \beta_I(1 - g\beta_n)y]$$

$$= |\alpha_{wp}| v\kappa y \beta_y s_c(\beta_e r + g) - |\alpha_{wp}| v\kappa y \beta_e \beta_I \alpha_{yn}$$

$$= a_{31} - a_{32}$$

$$b = a_1 a_2 - a_3 \qquad = (|j_{11}| + |j_{33}|)(J_2^{(3)} + J_3^{(3)}) - a_{31} + a_{32}$$

Positivity of a_1 is obvious. a_{21} in the determination of $J_2^{(3)}$ is a positive residual term, while $\alpha_{yn} > 0$ by the assumption on β_y. Hence $a_2 > 0$ by virtue of $s_c r - \beta_I > 0$. The latter inequality also ensures $a_3 > 0$, as seen in the first line of the computation of a_3. Decomposing a_3 as indicated in the second line allows us to infer $b > 0$. It suffices to note here that $-a_{31}$ cancels against $|j_{33}| \cdot J_3^{(3)}$, so that only positive terms remain.

Step 4. Regarding $J^{(4)}$, consider its 4th column and take $i_m = \partial i / \partial m = -1/\beta_{mi} y$ as the relevant parameter when referring to the lemma. Since $i_m \to 0$ as $\beta_{mi} \to \infty$, and $\det J^{(3)} < 0$, we have to show that $\det J^{(4)} > 0$ for $i_m \neq 0$ (i.e., $\beta_{mi} < \infty$). In fact, expanding $\det J^{(4)}$ by the 4th column and the remaining

---

[10] Regarding the variations of the reaction coefficient β_{mi} in the money demand function (11.17), it is understood that they are accompanied by appropriate changes of the intercept β_{mo} that leave the equilibrium rate of interest i^o unaffected. Concretely, β_{mo} is assumed to be given by $\beta_{mo} = (M/pY)^o + \beta_{mi} i^o$.

determinant by the 2nd column, it is easily seen that $\det J^{(4)} = \beta_e i_m(-s_c\beta_I)v\kappa\alpha_{wp}$
$(-m\beta_I) > 0$ (recall $i_m < 0$, $\alpha_{wp} < 0$).

Step 5. Realize that in the 5th column of $J^{(5)}$, α_{wk} and $\hat{p}_k$ tend to zero as $\beta_w \to 0$. It therefore remains to verify that the determinant of $J^{(5)}$ is negative as $\beta_w > 0$. This can be seen by expanding $\det J^{(5)}$ by the 4th column, the newly arising determinant by the 4th row, and the next one by the 2nd column, which yields $\det J^{(5)} = \beta_e i_m(-k\beta_I)(-s_c\beta_y y)v\kappa m \cdot \det \tilde{J}^{(2)}$, where

$$\det \tilde{J}^{(2)} = \det \begin{bmatrix} \alpha_{wp} & \alpha_{wk} \\ -\hat{p}_y & -\hat{p}_k \end{bmatrix} = y\kappa\beta_p\beta_w(1 - \kappa_p\kappa_w) > 0$$

Step 6. For $J^{(6)}$, the lemma applies with respect to the 6th row and $\beta_{\pi p} \to 0$, so only $\det J^{(6)} > 0$ has to be shown. While the previous determinants could be computed directly, it is here useful to carry out certain row operations that leave the value of the determinant unaffected but lead to a convenient structure of zero entries in the matrix. Apart from that, a couple of multiplicative terms are factorized (they do not involve a sign change since they are all positive). To ease the presentation, we do all this directly for the final matrix $J^{(7)} = J$, the result being the determinant $D^{(7)}$. Observe, however, that none of the first six rows is modified by adding or subtracting the 7th row. Hence the determinant of the first six rows and columns in $D^{(7)}$ exhibits the same sign as $\det J^{(6)}$. In detail, $D^{(7)}$ is obtained as follows:

(1) Factorize $v\kappa$, m, k, $\beta_{\pi p}$, $\beta_{\pi e}$ in row 2, 4, 5, 6, 7, respectively.
(2) Add the 5th row to the 4th row, to let entry j_{43} vanish.
(3) Add the (new) 4th row to the 6th row, which makes entries j_{61} and j_{65} vanish, while j_{66} becomes -1.
(4) Subtract the (new) 4th row from the 3rd row, so that $\hat{p}_y$ disappears from j_{31}, and j_{35}, j_{36} both become zero.
(5) Subtract the (new) 3rd row from the 7th row, in which way $j_{71} = j_{72} = j_{74} = j_{75} = j_{76} = 0$, $j_{77} = -1$, and $j_{73} = g^0$.
(6) Subtract g^0/β_I times the 5th row from the 7th row, which renders j_{73} zero and leaves the other entries in that row unaffected.

$$D^{(7)} = \det \begin{bmatrix} -s_c\beta_y(1-v) & s_c\beta_y y & \beta_I\alpha_{yn} & 0 & 0 & 0 & 0 \\ \alpha_{wp} & 0 & 0 & 0 & \alpha_{wk} & 0 & 0 \\ \beta_e\alpha_{vi} & -\beta_e y & -(\beta_e r^0 + g^0) & -\beta_e i_m & 0 & 0 & \beta_e + \kappa_e \\ -\hat{p}_y & 0 & 0 & 0 & -\hat{p}_k & -1 & 0 \\ 0 & 0 & \beta_I & 0 & 0 & 0 & 0 \\ 0 & 0 & 0 & 0 & 0 & -1 & 0 \\ 0 & 0 & 0 & 0 & 0 & 0 & -1 \end{bmatrix}$$

Regarding $D^{(6)}$, the determinant of the first six rows and columns in $D^{(7)}$, it is easily checked that

$$D^{(6)} = (-1)(\beta_e i_m)(-s_c \beta_y y)(-\beta_I) v \kappa m \det \tilde{J}^{(2)}$$
$$= \beta_e |i_m| s_c \beta_y y \beta_I v \kappa m \, y \kappa \, \beta_p \beta_w (1 - \kappa_p \kappa_w)$$

and therefore $\det J^{(6)} > 0$.

Step 7. As for $J^{(7)} = J$, the lemma applies with respect to the 7th row and $\beta_{\pi e} \to 0$. Since $D^{(7)} = (-1)D^{(6)}$, $\det J^{(7)}$ if of opposite sign of $\det J^{(6)}$. Summarizing that β_{m_i} is sufficiently large in step 4 and β_w, $\beta_{\pi p}$, $\beta_{\pi e}$ are sufficiently small in steps 5–7, respectively, this completes the proof.   q.e.d

The condition $\beta_I < s_c r$ in Proposition 6 is reminiscent of similar formulations in many Keynesian-oriented macro models with explicit reference to a rate of profit and a propensity to save out of profit (or rental) income. There, for example, such an inequality ensures a negative slope of an IS curve. The analogy in somewhat surprising since not only in the present model more complex, but also the investment reaction coefficient β_I refers to a variable, Tobin's q, which is usually not considered in these lower-order macro models. On the other hand, a closer look at the Routh–Hurwitz terms a_2 and a_3 in the proposition's proof shows that the condition $\beta_I < s_c r$ is not a necessary one and, depending on the relative size of various other parameters, there is some room for relaxing it.

The main result of the stability analysis can be succinctly summarized by saying that slow reactions or adjustments of the following kind are favourable for stability: sluggish reactions of the bond rate of interest, as brought about by a high interest elasticity of money demand (captured by the parameter β_{mi}); sticky adjustments of nominal wages (low parameter β_w); slow revisions of the inflationary climate variable (low adjustment speed $\beta_{\pi p}$); and slow adjustments of expected capital gains (low adjustment speed $\beta_{\pi e}$).

5.4. A note on the role of interest rate effects

To put the stability conditions in perspective, they should be compared to results that have been derived in similar models. The most relevant model in this respect is the so-called Keynes–Metzler–Goodwin (KMG) model in its 6D version. It was put forward, together with a basic stability proposition, in Chiarella and Flaschel (2000, Ch. 6.3), Chiarella *et al.* (2000, Ch. 2.3.2); a very detailed investigation, which also includes a calibration of the model dynamics and an extensive numerical stability analysis, can be found in Chiarella *et al.* (2005, pp. 4ff.).

The KMG model is more ambitious than the present model in that it introduces sales expectations and inventory accumulation and studies their feedbacks on the production decisions of firms (the inventory feedback is the Metzlerian component). On the other hand, bonds and equities are still perfect substitutes, so that there is no role for Tobin's q. Investment is then directly driven by the spread between the profit rate and the real interest rate.

Clearly, there are several reaction coefficients that enter the stability conditions of the KMG model and not ours, and *vice versa*. Both conditions have nevertheless three coefficients in common: the slope β_w in the wage Phillips curve, the adjustment speed $\beta_{\pi p}$ of adaptive expectations of inflation, and the responsiveness β_{mi} of the money demand to variations of the interest rate. In the KMG model, too, low values of β_w and $\beta_{\pi p}$ are favourable for local stability, whereas the role of β_{mi} is reversed: in the KMG model it is low values of β_{mi} that are favourable for stability (Chiarella *et al.*, 2005, Ch. 4).

This difference in the stability statements appears to be puzzle, since in both models the main role of the interest rate is its negative effect on investment. In the KMG model it impacts directly on investment as an argument in the investment function; in the present model the effect is more indirect and invokes the stock market: a rise of i increases the spread of the return on equities and the interest rate, which increases equity prices and thus Tobin's q, and finally investment. While it may be said that these interest rate effects are more delayed than in the KMG model, is this already a satisfactory explanation of the opposite stability results?

Before proceeding with the discussion, a note of caution needs to be injected. One might be tempted to put a stronger statement in the short characterization of Proposition 6, interpreting it as saying that high values of β_{mi} are not only favourable for stability but also 'stabilizing', and the other way round in the KMG model. Unfortunately, this is not as far as the mathematical propositions go. In both models we have to content ourselves with a sufficient stability condition, which is not claimed to be a necessary one. In addition, it has to be read in combination with the conditions on the other parameters. Strictly speaking, the statement that high interest elasticities are stabilizing would just be a conjecture.

Though it is not warranted by the proposition itself, such a conjecture can nevertheless be reasonable.[11] So we may ask which of the two opposite conjectures make more economic sense. The standard argument in our context is the Keynes effect. Referring directly to inflation, a fall in the rate of inflation accelerates the growth of real money balances relative to output. This decreases

---

[11] Or one may be able to prove it mathematically in a suitable lower-dimensional submodel, which also would lend more credibility to it.

the nominal rate of interest and increases investment expenditures. As has been seen above, this mechanism basically works in both models. Then, via the two Phillips curves, the subsequent increase in production and employment causes inflation to rise again. In sum, we have a negative feedback loop in the rate of inflation, which acts as a stabilizer. According to this logic, stronger reactions of the interest rate, which are brought about by lower values of β_{mi}, should be stabilizing. It is thus the stability proposition of the KMG model that conforms more closely to what we expect, while the opposite result of Proposition 6 might even seem counterintuitive.

A thorough analysis of the KMG model, however, reveals that the concentration on the Keynes effect can be rather misleading. As it turns out, an important feature of the KMG model studied in Chiarella *et al.* (2005) is the abovementioned introduction of wage share effects in the wage and price Phillips curve, which when sufficiently strong can reverse the Keynes effect. Interestingly, the model's calibration supports such a 'perverse' Keynes effect, and so far one expects low values of β_{mi} to be destabilizing.

On the other hand, already in a 3D submodel of the monetary dynamics, β_{mi} can be seen to be involved in other, more indirect and less transparent effects whose net outcome is hard to assess. Fortunately, within the range of the numerical parameters considered, where, in particular, the values of β_w, $\beta_{\pi p}$ and others are not arbitrarily close to zero, the numerical stability analysis can derive rather unambiguous results concerning the interest elasticity: in the 3D submodel and in the full 6D KMG model it is, despite the perverse Keynes effect being present, low values of β_{mi} that are stabilizing (*ibid.*, Chs 7.4 and 7.5). This result is in the same spirit as the mathematical stability proposition for the KMG model, although – we emphasize – the latter has a non-perverse Keynes effect underlying.

Against this background, the result of Proposition 6 may be less amazing, supposed that the following statements are true: regarding their stabilizing potential, the (indirect) interest rate effects not acting through the Keynes effect work, on the whole, in the opposite direction and dominate the Keynes effect, in the KMG model as well as in the present model. If then, in the KMG model, the wage share effects in the Phillips curve are absent, the Keynes effect would again be normal and now high values of β_{mi} would be stabilizing – contrary to the mathematical result and in accordance with the present Proposition 6.

At this stage of the argument, the difference in the stability statements for the two models has shifted. The result in the KMG model is numerical and assumes that the other reaction coefficients are plainly bounded away from zero, while the result of Proposition 6 is of a mathematical nature and relies on several other coefficients being close to zero. This observation calls for the next step in the analysis of the present model, namely, a numerical investigation in which the small parameters are now set a more sensible, higher values. The question we are primarily interested in would then be whether these more appropriate circumstances leave the role of the interest elasticity basically unaffected.

We conclude our informal discussion by pointing out that we cannot reasonably expect a more handsome stability condition regarding the parameter β_{mi}, although the interest rate only enters the return differential in the dynamic equations for q and π_e. Stability effects could be most easily identified if they are represented by terms in the diagonal of the model's Jacobian matrix. In the Jacobian J of our 7D system, the two partial derivatives of the interest rate with respect to output and money, y and m, show up in no more than four entries of J, but all of them are off-diagonal. Hence, if we were to write down the Routh–Hurwitz stability conditions for J, β_{mi} in the expressions $\partial i/\partial y$ and $\partial i/\partial m$ would be combined with the other entries of J in quite complicated ways, which would not leave much to hope for in a purely mathematical treatment. It seems the limited information about the role of β_{mi} that is provided by Proposition 6 is as much as we can get analytically.

Elementary feedback loops have been fruitful to predict the implications for stability if some key reaction parameters of a model are varied. Prominent examples are normal or adverse Rose (real wage) effects, the Mundell effect (not discussed here), and the Keynes effect. Or the effects are happily referred to when one has to make sense out of formal stability conditions derived from a mathematical analysis. Often, it has to be added, there are also no other similarly insightful feedback mechanisms, while the less direct effects are more uncertain in their direction and easily tend to abound if one only begins to search for them.

However, by falling back on the few major feedback mechanisms one runs the risk of overestimating their significance. The risk increases if the low-dimensional models are augmented, or combined, and one arrives at, say, 6 or 7D models. The preceding discussion of the stability effects of the parameter β_{mi} has been an example for this kind of problem. In order to avoid over-interpretation of the well-known feedback arguments and to make further progress, we again make the point that it would now be time for a numerical underpinning of the present model. Besides, for several building blocks a sound basis already exists; see Chiarella *et al.* (2005, Chs 5 and 6).

5.5. *Cyclical dynamics*

As concerns the parameters whose stabilizing effects have just been discussed, it may be conjectured that values of them lying in the other extreme are conducive to instability. Propositions 4 and 5 have confirmed this with respect to high values of β_w and β_{π_e}, but it has been indicated that similar statements for other coefficients would be much harder to obtain. We nevertheless know what happens if the system loses its stability. As a side result of the stability proof it is easily inferred that the transition from the stable to the unstable case occurs by way of a Hopf bifurcation.

Proposition 7. *Let the steady state of (the non-degenerate) system* (11.22) – (11.28) *be locally asymptotically stable. Consider a parameter, generically denoted by* α, *and suppose that under continuous* ceteris paribus *changes of* α *the steady state becomes unstable at some critical value* α_H. *Then at* α_H *the system undergoes a Hopf bifurcation.*

Proof. Step 7 in the proof of Proposition 6 has established that the Jacobian *J* is non-singular for all admissible (non-zero) values of the parameters. This implies that if the eigen-value $\lambda = \lambda(\alpha)$ with largest real part crosses the imaginary axis in the complex plane, at $\alpha = \alpha_H$, we have a pair of purely imaginary eigen-values, $\lambda(\alpha_H) = \pm i\,b$ in the usual notation. This is the key condition for a Hopf bifurcation to occur. The (very) technical details connected with the Hopf theorem are largely avoided (in particular, the velocity condition) if one uses the version of theorem A presented in Alexander and Yorke (1978, pp. 263–266).   q.e.d

A Hopf bifurcation asserts that for some interval of parameter values close to α_H, strictly periodic orbits of the dynamical system exist (which may be attracting or repelling). While we do not wish to overstate this phenomenon as such, we emphasize the more general feature associated with this result, namely, that the dynamics is determined by complex eigen-values. We can therefore conclude that there is broad scope for the economy to exhibit cyclical behaviour, which at the present state of the investigation may be dampened or undampened.

6. Conclusion

The economic contribution of this paper is a model that combines a financial sector, with special emphasis on the stock market, and a real sector that allows for disequilibrium on the goods as well as labour market. The model is a Keynesian-oriented one that gives a greater role to income distribution, as it is determined by Phillips curves adjustments for both price and wage inflation, and it also drops the usual assumption that bonds and equities are perfect substitutes. The feedback mechanisms here involved are so rich that the dynamics are described by a 7th-order system of differential equations. The methodological contribution of the paper is to work out a systematic way of performing a stability analysis of such a high-order dimensional system. It was thus possible to derive economically meaningful conditions for the local stability of the long-run equilibrium position. The technique of the cascade of stable matrices developed here for that purpose could be applicable to a wide range of high-dimensional dynamic economic models.

On the whole, the model that we discussed provides a consistent framework for subsequent theoretical and empirical studies of the real-financial interaction. One aspect we should recall is that goods market disequilibrium, as we have perceived it, implies the presence of inventories as buffers for excess demand or supply. It has been assumed that deviations of inventories from some target level do not feed back on the production decisions of firms. This restriction is legitimate in simplifying the model, but it should be improved upon if it is desired to study the medium- and long-run evolution of the economy, especially if we are to turn to an analysis of the global dynamics. A proven model building block in this respect is a Metzlerian inventory mechanism along the lines of Franke (1996), Chiarella and Flaschel (2000, Ch. 6.3) and, most extensively, Chiarella *et al.* (2005, Chs 4 and 6).

Another important topic for further work on the model concerns the market for equities. It may be noted that a generalization of the standard Keynesian LM sector can go in two directions. One option is to use the Tobinian portfolio approach that formulates the demand for the additional assets (besides money and bonds) as stock magnitudes. Here Tobin's q as the variable that represents the stock market would be determined as a statically endogenous variable, within the temporary equilibrium solution of the financial sector.[12] Inspired by Blanchard (1981), we followed in this paper the second direction where equities are treated somewhat differently from money and bonds, such that specifically Tobin's q becomes a dynamic variable. The advantage of this approach is that the structure of the model would not be essentially affected if the present equity price adjustments are extended to a more clearly conceived speculative asset price dynamics. Thus, as indicated at the end of Section 2, the two prototype trading groups of fundamentalists and chartists and their formulation of demand could be explicitly incorporated into the present setting.

If in line with Propositions 2 and 4, a high responsiveness of expectations about capital gains is viewed as the main destabilizing force for the whole model, then suitable and economically well-motivated nonlinearities that prevent the stock market dynamics from diverging become particularly critical. An additional point is that already very elementary mechanisms working to that effect are also capable of generating complex ('chaotic') dynamics.[13] It would be interesting to see how this kind of speculative dynamics interacts with the ('normal') rest of the model. Clearly, these themes call for a global analysis, which has to be left for future research.

---

[12] For the integration of such a financial sector into the real sector of the economy with, in particular, the abovementioned Metzlerian inventory mechanism, see Köper and Flaschel (2000). A separate study of a similar (but more extensive) financial sector and its adjustments over the business cycle is conducted by Franke and Semmler (1999).

[13] Various approaches to tackle the issue of boundedness can be found in Sethi (1996), Franke and Sethi (1998), Chiarella and Khomin (2000) and Chiarella *et al.* (2004, 2005). Complex dynamics may be easily brought about by the mechanisms studied in the first two papers.

References

Alexander, J.C. and J.A. Yorke (1978), "Global bifurcations of periodic orbits", *American Journal of Mathematics*, Vol. 100, pp. 263–292.

Blanchard, O.J. (1981), "Output, the stock market, and interest rates", *American Economic Review*, Vol. 71, pp. 132–143.

Blanchard, O. and S. Fischer (1989), *Lectures in Macroeconomics*, Cambridge, MA: MIT Press.

Caballero, R.J. and J.V. Leahy (1996), "Fixed costs: The demise of marginal q", NBER Working Paper, No. 5508.

Chiarella, C. and P. Flaschel (2000), *The Dynamics of Keynesian Monetary Growth: Macrofoundations*, Cambridge, UK: Cambridge University Press.

Chiarella, C., P. Flaschel and R. Franke (2005), *Foundations for a Disequilibrium Theory of the Business Cycle: Qualitative Assessment and Quantitative Analysis*, Cambridge, UK: Cambridge University Press.

Chiarella, C., P. Flaschel, G. Groh and W. Semmler (2000), *Disequilibrium, Growth and Labor Market Dynamics: Macro Perspectives*, Berlin: Springer.

Chiarella, C., P. Flaschel and W. Semmler (2004), "Real-financial interaction: a reconsideration of the Blanchard model with a state-of-market dependent reaction coefficient", pp. 31–65 in: W. Barnett, C. Deissenberg and G. Feichtinger, editors, *Economic Complexity, ISETE Series*, Vol. 14, Elsevier.

Chiarella, C., P. Flaschel, X. He, and H. Hung (2005). "A stochastic model of real-financial interaction with boundedly rational heterogeneous agents", Chapter 10, this volume.

Chiarella, C. and A. Khomin (2000), "The dynamic interaction of rational fundamentalists and trend chasing chartists in a monetary economy", pp. 151–165 in: D. Delli Gatti, M. Gallegati and A. Kirman, editors, *Interaction and Market Structure:Essays on Heterogeneity in Economics*, New York: Springer.

Evans, M. and P. Wachtel (1993), "Inflation regimes and the sources of inflation uncertainty", *Journal of Money, Credit, and Banking*, Vol. 25, pp. 475–511.

Franke, R. (1996), "A Metzlerian model of inventory growth cycles", *Structural Change and Economic Dynamics*, Vol. 7, pp. 243–262.

Franke, R. (2001), Three wage-price macro models and their calibration, University of Bielefeld, Center for Empirical Macroeconomics (http://www.wiwi.uni-bielefeld.de/~semmler/cem/wp.htm#2001).

Franke, R. and W. Semmler (1999), "Bond rate, loan rate and Tobin's q in a temporary equilibrium model of the financial sector", *Metroeconomica*, Vol. 50, pp. 351–385.

Franke, R. and R. Sethi (1998), "Cautious trend-seeking and complex asset price dynamics", *Research in Economics (Ricerche Economiche)*, Vol. 52, pp. 61–79.

Köper, C. and P. Flaschel (2000). "Real-financial interaction: a Keynes–Metzler–Goodwin portfolio approach", University of Bielefeld, Department of Economics, Discussion paper no. 442.

Rose, H. (1967), "On the non-linear theory of the employment cycle", *Review of Economic Studies*, Vol. 34, pp. 153–173.

Rose, H. (1990), *Macroeconomic Dynamics: A Marshallian Synthesis*, Cambridge, MA: Basil Blackwell.

Sethi, R. (1996), "Endogenous regime switching in speculative markets", *Structural Change and Economic Dynamics*, Vol. 7, pp. 99–118.

Sontag, E.D. (1990), *Mathematical Control Theory: Deterministic Finite Dimensional Systems*, New York: Springer.

CHAPTER 12

Currency Crisis, Financial Crisis, and Large Output Loss

Peter Flaschel and Willi Semmler

Abstract

Given the volatility of exchange rates, there is a reemergence of interest in the effect of such volatility, in particular of large currency shocks, on the domestic financial markets and the output and investment decisions of firms. For small open economies where a large fraction of debt is denominated in foreign currencies, for example in dollars, exchange rate shocks have a strong impact on the liabilities of firms, households, banks and the government. We use a portfolio approach to model the impact of large exchange rate shocks on the asset allocation decisions of economic agents as well as on real activity. Following a model sketched by Krugman (1999, 2001) we show rigorously in a simple dynamic Mundell–Fleming–Tobin model that such large currency shocks set in motion financial market and investment reactions that can, due to the existence of multiple equilibria, lead to low-level equilibria and large output losses. This can occur despite significant improvements in the trade balance.

Keywords: small open economies, exchange rate dynamics, currency crisis, financial crisis, economic decline

JEL classifications: E31, E32, E37, E52

1. Introduction

With the end of the Bretton Woods system in the 1970s and the financial market liberalization in the 1980s and 1990s, the international economy has experienced

CONTRIBUTIONS TO ECONOMIC ANALYSIS
VOLUME 277   ISSN: 0573-8555
DOI:10.1016/S0573-8555(05)77012-7

several financial crises in certain countries or regions entailing, in most cases, declining economic activity and large output losses. This has occurred regardless of whether the exchange rates were pegged or flexible. There appear to be destabilizing mechanisms at work from which even a flexible exchange rate regime cannot escape.

Recent financial crises, such as the Asian crisis 1997–1998, were indeed triggered by a sudden reversal of capital flows and, after a retreat from pegged exchange rates, an unexpected strong depreciation of the currency.

There are typical stylized facts to be observed before and after the financial crises, which have been studied in numerous papers (see, for example, Milesi-Ferreti and Razin, 1996, 1998; Mishkin, 1998; Kamin, 1999). The empirical literature on financial crisis episodes may allow us to summarize the following stylized facts: (1) there is a deterioration of balance sheets of economic units (households, firms, banks, the government and the country), (2) before the crisis the current account deficit to GDP ratio rises, (3) preceding the currency crisis the external debt to reserve ratio rises; after the crisis the current account recovers, (4) there is a sudden reversal of capital flows and unexpected depreciation of the currency, (5) the foreign debt denominated in foreign currency of the economic agents suddenly rises due to a drastic depreciation of the currency, (6) domestic interest rates jump up, partly initiated by the Central Bank's policy, (7) subsequently stock prices fall, (8) a banking crisis occurs with large loan losses by banks and subsequent contraction of credit (sometimes moderated by a bail out of failing banks by the government), and (9) the financial crisis entails a large output loss due to large-scale investment declines and bankruptcies of firms and financial institutions.

In this paper we review some of the stylized facts that appear to be common to such financial crises, and develop a Mundell–Fleming–Tobin type model based on Rødseth (2000, Ch. 6) that takes up Krugman's (1999, 2001) largely graphical suggestions in order to study such real and financial crises generated by large exchange rate swings.

With respect to exchange rate shocks due to currency runs triggering financial and real crises, there are three views, in fact three generations of models that have been presented in the literature. A first view maintains that news on macroeconomic fundamentals (differences in economic growth rates, productivity differences and differences in price levels, in the short-term interest rates as well as in monetary policy actions) may cause currency runs. The second view maintains that speculative forces drive exchange rates where there can be self-fulfilling expectations at work, destabilizing exchange rates without deterioration of fundamentals. Third, following the theory of imperfect capital markets, it has recently been maintained that the dynamics of self-fulfilling expectations depend on some fundamentals, for example the strength and weakness of the balance sheets of the economic units such as households, firms, banks and governments. From the latter point of view we can properly study the connection between deterioration of fundamentals, exchange rate volatility, financial instability and declining economic activity. Although recently there have been proposed diverse micro- as well as macroeconomic theories to explain currency runs, financial crises and recessions, we think that those types of models are particularly relevant that show how currency crises may entail destabilizing mechanisms leading, possibly through non-linearities and multiple equilibria, to large output losses.

Such type of a model can be found in Miller and Stiglitz (1999), who base their model on the work by Kiyotaki and Moore (1995), the diverse papers by Krugman (1999, 2001) and Aghion *et al.* (2000). For a detailed survey of the literature on exchange rate volatility, financial crisis and large output loss, see Semmler (2003, Ch. 12). The work by Krugman (1999, 2001) is related closest to our paper. It, however, contains partly different motivations of Krugman's graphical analysis as to how the destabilizing mechanism, triggered through the currency crises, actually takes its course. Our model is narrower than the framework discussed in Krugman, and thus concentrates on a few but essential elements of the currency crises. This is due to the fact that many behavioral equations of the employed Mundell–Fleming–Tobin type model remain stable despite the occurrence of large currency depreciation, implied large declines in investment and large output losses.

Whereas the above theories, that build on imperfect capital markets, point to the perils of too fast liberalization of financial markets and to an important role of the government's bank supervisions and guarantees, Burnside *et al.* (1999) view government guarantees as cause for currency runs and financial crises. These authors argue that the lack of private hedging of exchange rate risk by firms and banks led, for example, to the financial crisis in Asia. Other authors, following the bank run model by Diamond and Dybvig (1983) (see, for example, Chang and Velasco, 1999) argue that financial crisis occur if there is a lack of short-run liquidity.

We will build up a model that attempts to explain some of the stylized facts, with particular stress of the impact of large currency depreciations on the breakdown of investment decisions and resulting large output loss. This can occur despite significant improvements in the trade balance. We will use a standard portfolio approach to describe the financial sector of the economy and concentrate on the balance sheets of firms, their investment behavior and the multiplier dynamics that derives from it in order to show how ongoing reallocation of assets into foreign bonds can imply a currency crisis, a breakdown of investment and a large output loss.

The remainder of the paper is organized as follows. Section 2 presents the basic model. Section 3 then adds the budget restrictions and considers the accounting relationships that characterize the model in order to provide a clear picture of the scope of the model. Section 4 studies the dynamics under flexible exchange rates and Section 5 discusses the breakdown of a fixed exchange rate system. Section 6 concludes the paper. In an appendix[1] to the paper, we present the details of the Mundell–Fleming–Tobin type model employed in Rødseth (2000, Ch. 6) for the study of a variety of exchange rate regimes and their comparative static properties. This is a type of a model that we have modified and simplified in the main body of this paper in our presentation of Krugman's (1999, 2001) currency crisis dynamics.

2. The basic model

It is stated in Krugman (2001, p. 83) that 'a fully fledged model of balance-sheet driven crisis is necessarily fairly complex'. This paper shows that Krugman's ideas can be represented in a coherent way if his type of investment function is assumed and if imperfect substitution between financial assets is modeled as in Tobin. We build on a simplified and modified version of the Mundell–Fleming–Tobin model developed by Rødseth (2000, Ch. 6.2). We aim at a fully fledged modeling of the balance-sheet-driven crisis considered in Krugman (1999, 2001). With respect to consumption and investment behavior, the model only contains the necessary variables to make Krugman's point and thus does not use wealth and interest rate effects in consumption and investment behavior. Instead, we make use of the following simple representation of consumption, investment and goods market equilibrium:

$$Y = C(Y - \delta\overline{K} - \overline{T}) + I(e) + \delta\overline{K} + \overline{G} + NX(Y, \overline{Y}^*, e) \qquad (12.1)$$

We assume behind this equation given price levels $\overline{p}, \overline{p}^*$ at home and abroad (n, given foreign output $\overline{Y}^*$ and given world interest rate $\overline{r}^*$) as is often done in Mundell–Fleming models of small open economies. We normalize the price levels to 'one' for reasons of simplicity, which allows to identify quantities and value terms in national accounting. We finally assume as usual $C' + NX_Y < 1$, $NX_e > 0$ and, as aforementioned, neglect the influence of the domestic rate of interest on consumption and investment. Since we presume that there is no inflation at home and abroad, we also do not need to consider real interest and real exchange rates in this model type. The assumed type of investment behavior is described in detail below.

Private households consume and save out of their disposable income $Y - \delta\overline{K} - \overline{T}$. We assume that $\overline{K}$ and δ, the rate of depreciation are given; and $\overline{T}$ is the lump-sum tax.[2] Feedbacks from the flow of savings into the asset holdings of households are still ignored, but could be added as in Rødseth (2000, Ch. 6.6) via the government budget constraint, which, however would add further laws of motion to the model; see our remarks in the next section. Here, however, we only

---

[1] The appendix can be obtained from the authors upon request.
[2] Here lump-sum taxes are calculated net of interest (see Rødseth, 2000, Ch. 6) for a similar assumption.

consider explicitly the stock constraint of private households and their portfolio demand functions as first proposed in Tobin and as modeled in Rødseth (2000):[3]

$$W_p = M_0 + B_0 + eF_{p0} \tag{12.2}$$

$$M = m(Y, r) \tag{12.3}$$

$$eF_p = f(\xi, W_p), \quad \xi = \bar{r}^* + \varepsilon - r \tag{12.4}$$

$$B = W_p - m(Y, r) - f(\xi, W_p) \tag{12.5}$$

Note again that we have normalized the price level to be equal to '1'. We here consider the reallocation of money holdings, M_0, fixed-price domestic bond holdings, B_0, and foreign fixed-price bond holdings of domestic households, F_{p0}, between money M, dollar-dominated (private) foreign bonds F_p and domestic bonds B (for simplicity the prices of these bonds are also assumed to be equal to '1' in terms of their currency).

We do not yet consider any specific exchange rate regime of Mundell–Fleming type, and thus do not yet state in detail which of the quantities M, i, B, F_p, F_c are to be considered as exogenously determined. Note that i is here the foreign bond holdings of the Central Bank. We presume here that domestic bonds are not or cannot be traded internationally. A fixed exchange rate regime will imply that $F_p + F_c$ can considered as fixed, while in a flexible exchange rate regime we even get that F_p can be considered as fixed, since the Central Bank need not intervene then in the foreign exchange market. Equation (12.2) provides the definition of private wealth currently held in the household sector, with e being the nominal exchange rate. Money demand equal to money supply is considered next as in the usual LM approach. Demand for dollar-denominated bonds eF_p, expressed in domestic currency, is assumed to depend on private wealth W_p and the risk premium ξ, which is defined by the difference of foreign and domestic interest rates augmented by capital gains or losses ε, with ε being the expected rate of depreciation or appreciation. We assume $f_\xi > 0$ and $F_{W_p} \in (0, 1)$ and of course $M_Y > 0, m_r < 0$. Demand for domestic bonds B is then determined residually by Walras' Law of Stocks. With respect to expected depreciation ε we assume

$$\varepsilon = \varepsilon(e), \quad \varepsilon' \leqslant 0, \quad \varepsilon(e_0) = 0 \quad \text{for the steady-state value of } e \tag{12.6}$$

which is a general formulation of regressive expectations; see Rødseth (2000, Ch. 1.4) for details.[4] Note here that we assume that economic agents have perfect knowledge of the relevant steady-state value of e of the model (denoted by e^f)

---

[3] We present the portfolio model using the gross substitute assumption in the way that asset demands always depend positively on their own rate of return and negatively on the other ones. We therefore define the risk premium on foreign bonds as the negative of the one considered in Rødseth (2000) in order to get a positive dependence of the demand for foreign bonds on the risk premium in place of negative one in his book, which however is but a change in the used conventions.

[4] A specific formulation would be $\varepsilon = \beta_\varepsilon(e^f/e - 1)$, where e^f denotes the steady-state value the economy is converging to.

and that they are therefore forward-looking in their behavior and expect that the actual exchange rate adjust, with possibly varying speed, to this steady-state value. Such an expectational scheme may also be characterized as asymptotically rational behavior and represents a very fundamental and tranquil type of expected exchange rate adjustments. Expectations are therefore not central in the explanation of the currency crises considered in this paper.

As the above portfolio demand approach is formulated, we have substitution between money and domestic bonds on the one hand and between domestic and foreign bonds on the other, the first determined in reference to the nominal rate of interest r and the second in reference to the risk premium ξ between domestic and foreign bonds. Furthermore, all domestic money and bonds are held by domestic residents. There is thus no international trade in domestic bonds, and private households are characterized by a simple consumption, and savings function and a standard portfolio approach to imperfect capital mobility.

Following the simplification by Krugman (1999, 2001), the sector of firms is represented by its net investment function $I(e)$. Thus, investment is here made dependent solely on the nominal exchange rate e. This dependence is represented in Figure 12.1.

Specifying the shape of the investment function, we assume here that investment depends negatively on the exchange rate e and this strongly in an intermediate range.

The story behind this assumption is that depreciation worsens the balance sheet of firms (see the next section) due to the fact that their past investment decisions are financed by foreign bonds – firm bonds denominated in foreign – dollar – currency. Depreciation thus increases the debt of firms when measured

Figure 12.1. A Krugman (2001) type of investment function

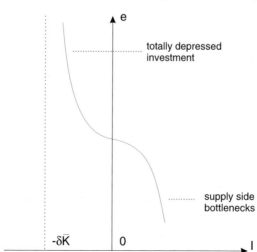

in domestic currency, and thus lowers the credit rating and the credit worthiness of the firms and their ability to finance current investment.

Investment is, therefore, reduced when depreciation of the domestic currency occurs and, by the assumption made below, in the considered middle range for the exchange rate, to a degree that dominates the positive (normal) reaction of net exports NX with respect to exchange rate changes:

$$-I'(e) > NX_e > 0$$

In this range we, therefore, get for the aggregate demand function,

$$Y^d(Y, e): \quad Y_Y^d \in (0, 1) \text{ and } Y_e^d < 0$$

The latter partial derivative represents a striking difference to the usual assumptions on aggregate demand in models of the Mundell–Fleming type. For very high and very low exchange rates we, however, assume that investment is not very sensitive to further exchange rate changes, on the one hand, since there are supply bottlenecks for very high investment demand and, on the other, since there are some investment projects that must and can be continued – despite severe credit rationing of firms – even for very high levels of the exchange rate. For extreme values of the exchange rate, we therefore have the usual positive dependence of goods market equilibrium on the level of the exchange rate.

We have already stated that the implications of the government deficit with respect to changes in the supply of money and domestic bonds are still ignored in the current short-term analysis of a small open economy. With respect to the Central Bank, finally, we assume that it not only can change the supply of money and domestic bond holdings instantaneously, through standard open market operations, but also the amount of the dollar-denominated bonds if it desires to do so. Following Rødseth (2000, Ch. 6) we however assume that the following constraint must hold true:

$$F_p + F_c = \overline{F}^*$$

with F_c the foreign bond holdings of the Central Bank and $\overline{F}^*$ the total amount of dollar-denominated bonds held in the domestic economy, treated separately from the credit given to firms. This assumption can be justified by considering regimes where money can only be exchanged against foreign currency in the domestic economy, through the monetary authority, and, as aforementioned, by assuming that domestic bonds cannot be traded internationally. This closes the short-run equilibrium description of the considered small open economy. Note again that we even get a fixed F_p value if the monetary authority is not required and not intervened in the foreign exchange market.

Finally, note again that the above feature of investment behavior has been chosen so that in its middle range the investment function is characterized as very elastic with respect to the exchange rate e. For very high and very low exchange rates, however, investment becomes very inelastic in this regard. If the currency is strong (low e), investment runs into a bottleneck and is limited by supply-side conditions. If the currency is very weak, net investment is reduced to its floor level (which may even be negative). In sum, we have an investment behavior, formally similar to the one considered in the Kaldor (1940) trade cycle model, but here based on net worth effects resulting from exchange rate changes, instead of an influence of economic activity Y on the net investment of firms.

As in Kaldor (1940), see also Blanchard and Fischer (1989, p. 532), we consider the following goods market adjustment process off the IS or goods market equilibrium curve (as simplification of a more general goods market adjustment process where inventories are also adjusted by firms):

$$\dot{Y} = \beta_y(Y^d - Y) = \beta_y(C(Y - \delta\overline{K} - \overline{T}) + I(e) + \delta\overline{K} + \overline{G} + NX(Y, \bar{Y}^*, e) - Y)$$

This dynamic multiplier process is a stable one for any given level of e, since $Y_Y^d - 1 < 0$ was assumed to hold true.

Next, we derive two equilibrium curves, for the goods and asset market equilibrium respectively, in the Y, e phase space and surrounded by the multiplier dynamics just introduced. We consider the IS-curve, defined by Equation (12.1), first and get by the implicit function theorem for the shape of this curve with Y the dependent and e the independent variable:

$$Y'(e) = -\frac{I' + NX_e}{C' + NX_Y - 1} \gtreqless 0$$

due to sign of the numerator, while the denominator is unambiguously negative. In the midrange of e values, discussed above, we thus have $Y'(e) < 0$ and thus a backward-bending IS-curve, since I' dominates NX_e in this range, while we have a positive slope for this curve outside of this range, since $|I'|$ becomes close to 0 then.

For the IS-curve we thus get a scenario as shown in Figure 12.2, where we have also added the output adjustment of firms when economic activity departs from the IS-curve. This shows that the IS-curve is a global attractor with respect to output adjustment whenever the economy is displaced from it by a shock.

Note also that the IS-curve should become very steep for very large and very small values of the exchange rate e, since investment and net exports may be very insensitive to further exchange rate changes then. Note also that this curve should cut the horizontal axis at a positive value of output Y, since $\dot{Y}$ is positive at $Y = 0$ by assumption.

Let us next consider the asset market equilibrium as described by Equations (12.2)–(12.6). From Equation (12.3) we get in the usual way, for any given M, a positive dependence of r on Y and a negative one with respect to M as is generally the case in such simple LM approaches to the money market:

$$r(Y, M), \quad r_Y > 0, \quad r_M < 0$$

Figure 12.2.   IS-equilibrium and output adjustment along the AA-curve in the case of an output and asset market determined exchange rate

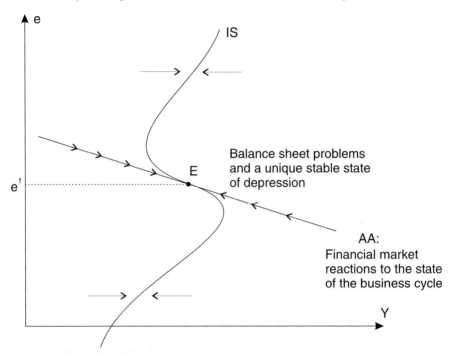

Inserting this reduced-form equation and Equation (12.6) into Equation (12.4) gives rise to[5]

$$eF_p = f(\bar{r}^* + \varepsilon(e) - r(Y, M), M_0 + B_0 + eF_{p0}), \quad M \text{ given.}$$

This condensed representation of full asset markets equilibrium will give rise (for flexible exchange rates and thus given F_p) to a strictly negatively sloped equilibrium curve AA (representing the influence of the business cycle on exchange rate determination) which – by assumption – cuts the vertical axis and which – for reasons of simplicity – we will always draw as a straight line in the following. Under Walras' Law of Stocks we thus have a well-defined single curve for the characterization of equilibrium in the financial market of the economy

---

[5] Note that the use made of this equation and the *F-restriction* in this paper assumes that domestic bonds are non-tradables, which implies that the tradable amount of foreign bonds is fixed to the domestic holdings of such bonds in each moment of time. In the case of a flexible exchange rate, this amount even reduces to F_p due to the non-intervention of the domestic Central Bank in this case.

for any given level of money supply M.[6] In the present modeling framework we have a new and extended type of IS–LM diagram, where LM-equilibrium is combined with an FF-equilibrium for dollar-denominated bonds to provide a strictly decreasing function in the Y, e phase space in the place of the usual output-interest phase space, the AA asset market equilibrium curve, and where the IS or goods market equilibrium curve is now placed in the same phase space. Its usually assumed strictly positive slope is, however, only valid for very high as well as very low values of the exchange rate e. We thus have to deal with new slopes of IS–LM curves in a newly defined economic phase space in the following.

3. Budget restrictions

Next we consider the dynamic adjustments of foreign reserves (or bonds) in the domestic economy, as well as flows into domestic money and bond holdings that occur due to the investment decision of firms, the saving decision of households, the decisions of the government and the Central Bank, taking also into account the net exports. We show that all the foreign account flows are in balance in the balance of payments, under certain consistency assumptions on new domestic money and bond supply, so that there is no need – beyond what happens in the stock markets – for the Central Bank to intervene in order to get equilibrium on the market for foreign exchange. We will, in particular, describe here the changes in foreign bond holdings of households and the Central Bank and the change in the foreign debt of firms.

First of all, we assume – as is usually the case – that all income generated by firms is transferred to the household sector, formally deducting, however, depreciation in order to arrive at net magnitudes. Since we allow for negative net investment, the amount representing depreciation need, however, not be kept back by and invested within firms. We thus assume here that there is a positive floor to gross investment I^g and that enough foreign credit is available to finance at least the minimum amount of investment projects, not scrapped within a currency crisis. This gives rise to the following budget equations of firms:

$$Y - \delta \bar{K} - e\bar{r}^* F_f = wL^d + \Pi_p, \quad I = e\dot{F}_f(e)$$

i.e., firms have to pay interest on their foreign debt and transfer all remaining proceeds to the household sector as wages wL^d and profits Π_p. Their investments

---

[6] This distinguishes our approach to the AA-curve from the one suggested in Krugman (2001), where a leaning against the wind strategy seems to be part of the AA-curve. Leaning against the wind in our model means shifting the AA-curve to the left by means of restrictive monetary policy (reduced money supply). This is indeed also stated in Krugman and Obstfeld (2003) where however the interest rate parity condition is used for the derivation of the AA-curve in the place of our explicit (imperfect substitute) portfolio representation of the asset markets.

I (if positive) thus have to be financed completely by new and here by assumption foreign debt. We here have to assume, however, that investment goods are completely purchased on the national goods markets. They thus represent domestic goods – measured in terms of the domestic currency. Due to the financing of investment, we get that the quantity demanded on the domestic market must depend on the exchange rate with an elasticity that is smaller than -1 in order to give rise to an investment schedule in the domestic currency with the assumed property $I'(e)<0$. This investment behavior may be due to credit constraints, but also be due to the fact that such investment is simply not profitable at the currently prevailing exchange rate.

Next, for the household sector we get as flow budget constraint:

$$Y - \delta\bar{K} - e\bar{r}^*F_f + e\bar{r}^*F_p - \bar{T} - C = \dot{M} + \dot{B} + e\dot{F}_p$$

Note that lump-sum taxes are here calculated as net of domestic interest payments (by the government), similar to the procedure applied in Rødseth (2000, Ch. 6). The government budget constraint simply reads

$$\bar{G} - \bar{T} = \dot{M} + \dot{B}, \quad \bar{T} = T - rB$$

We assume with respect to Central Bank behavior that all interest income on government bonds that are held by the Central Bank, due to past open market operations, is transferred back to the government sector and thus does not appear in the government budget constraint as an explicit item. We, therefore, represent explicitly only privately held government bonds, as is usually done in the literature. The above budget equation of households says that households' savings are spent on new money and new domestic bonds as they are supplied by the government, and the remainder then on new bonds denominated in foreign currency. This, in fact, represents a flow consistency assumption that guarantees that the balance of payments – showing here planned magnitudes solely – will always be balanced in the present framework. Note again that all prices, goods and assets, except to the exchange rate, are set equal to 1 in the present form of the model.

With respect to Central Bank behavior, we finally assume that its (remaining) income, equal to its savings, is spent on the acquisition of foreign reserves in the form of foreign bonds, i.e., we have

$$e\bar{r}^*F_c = e\dot{F}_c$$

Aggregating all (dis-)savings (of households, government and the Central Bank) gives the equation

$$Y - \delta\bar{K} - C - \bar{G} + e\bar{r}^*(F_p + F_c) - e\bar{r}^*F_f = e(\dot{F}_p + \dot{F}_c)$$

which in turn implies due to the assumed goods market equilibrium condition:

$$CA + I = NX + e\bar{r}^*(F_p + F_c) - e\bar{r}^*F_f + I = e(\dot{F}_p + \dot{F}_c) = S = S_p + S_g + S_c$$

Inserting the foreign bonds that finance firms' investment then gives rise to the equality between the current account deficit (or surplus) and the surplus (or deficit) in the capital account.

$$NX + e\bar{r}^*(F_p + F_c) - e\bar{r}^*F_f = e(\dot{F}_p + \dot{F}_c) - e\dot{F}_f$$

We thus have that the balance of payments is – under the assumption that households absorb the new money and the new domestic bonds shown in the government budget constraint – always balanced. All flows requiring foreign currency will be matched by foreign currency and the stock market – as assumed – is always in equilibrium. Net exports and net interest payments on foreign bonds are always equal in sum to net capital export or net foreign bond import, with households and the Central Bank as creditors and firms as debtors in the interest and foreign bond flows that are considered. Note though we have an equilibrate balance of payments, we have nevertheless included the possibility of credit rationing of firms, subsumed in the assumed shape of the investment function.

We note again that domestic money can only be exchanged against foreign currency in the domestic economy, which together with the assumption that domestic bonds are not traded internationally. It is sufficient to provide the constraint $F_p = F_{po}$ for asset reallocations in the case of a flexible exchange rate and an endogenous F_p determination, served by the domestic central bank, in the case of a fixed exchange rate system, see the next two sections. Note that the case of an exchange rate that is fixed by the domestic central bank exhibits as constraint on the reallocation of foreign bonds between households and the Central Bank the inequality $F_p \leqslant F_{po} + F_c$, which therefore characterizes the range in which the Central Bank may be capable to fix the domestic exchange rate.

Note finally that the balance sheet effect for firms, here issuing bonds in foreign currency only, with no retained earnings and with no equity financing, here simply reads:[7]

Note the actual change in this balance sheet – through (dis-)investment – is here simply represented by the assumption (Tables 12.1 and 12.2)

$$I(e) = e\dot{F}_f(e), \qquad I'(e)<0, \quad \text{i.e.,} \quad \frac{d\dot{F}_f}{\dot{F}_f} \bigg/ \frac{de}{e} < -1$$

In our model firms combine labor L^d and capital K, financed by bonds denominated in foreign currency, produce the output Y and the accounting net worth $pK - eF_f$. Portfolio markets determine the interest rate and the exchange rate (if flexible), r, e, for any given output level. The goods market determines the output level Y of firms for any given exchange rate, separately in a fixed

---

[7] This balance sheet is thus based on the historical (current) value of the capital stock and does not take into account any discounted cash flows here in its formulation of the net worth of firms (there are also not yet equities present in the model, the value of which may be measured by such discounted cash flows).

Table 12.1.   The balance sheet of firms

Tangible Assets	Liabilities
pK	eF_f
	Net worth (measuring credit-worthiness) W^n

Table 12.2.   The balance of payments

Debits	Credits
Trade account	
Imports	Exports
eIm	Ex
Interest income account	
Interest payments to the foreign economy	Interest payments from the foreign economy
$e\bar{r}^* F_f$	$e\bar{r}^* F_p + e\bar{r}^* F_c$
Capital account	
$e\dot{F}_p$	$e\dot{F}_f$
Official reserve transactions of the Central Bank	
$e\dot{F}_c$	

exchange rate system, where asset markets determine r, F_p, and jointly with the asset markets in the case of a flexible exchange rate. Financial flows caused by the savings and investment decisions of the considered sectors of the economy do not matter in this interaction, but have been considered here in addition for consistency reasons. Financial crisis in the proper sense results here from the pre-assumed investment behavior and its financing condition. Subsequently, we will add capital flight parameter, α, to be discussed in detail later. Consumption behavior and asset demands remain stable, bankruptcies are disregarded too.

There is finally the balance of payment which records the items concerning the current and the capital account, the latter also including the reserve changes of the Central Bank.

This balance of payment is always in balance, due to our treatment of the budget equations of the four sectors of the economy and thus does not represent a further restriction – besides the stock portfolio equilibrium equations – to the working of the economy.

This concludes our presentation of the flow conditions that characterize the considered small open economy. We stress in view of the above the situation here considered is still a fairly transparent one. Capital accumulation is financed by foreign bonds throughout and interest payments are always met at the world rate of interest. However, new credit will become rationed as expressed by the investment function if the balance sheet of firms worsens through depreciation. This credit rationing results in a Keynesian effective demand depression with large loss in domestic output and income due to large reduction in investment demand, but still with flow consistency in particular in the balance of payments. The crisis scenario is still a partial one with credit-rationed firms and a capital flight parameter indicating perception risk, to be introduced below, but otherwise stable portfolio demand equations, a stable expectations scheme, stable behavioral equations on the goods market and given wages and prices.

4. Dynamics under flexible exchange rates

We consider here exclusively the case of flexible exchange rates and thus the case where the Central Bank needs normally not to intervene in the market for foreign exchange and to conduct trade in foreign bonds. The equilibrium in the foreign exchange market can therefore be described by $F_{p0} = F_p$ being a constant.

The amount of dollar-denominated bonds that can be traded in this market is simply given by the amount of such bonds held by households. As aforementioned, we presume that domestic bonds cannot be traded internationally and M (or r) is assumed to be kept fixed by open market operations (concerning domestic bonds) by the monetary authority, for details see Asada *et al.* (2003, Ch. 4). The case of a flexible exchange rate will be used later on to describe the consequences of a breakdown of a fixed exchange rate regime.

Given the supply of foreign currency we can determine an asset market equilibrium curve $e(Y)$ from the reduced form asset market representation, which for any given output level determines the exchange rate e that clears the asset markets, the interest rate r being determined by $r = r(Y, M)$, the LM-curve of the model. According to the implicit function theorem, the slope of this curve is given by

$$e'(Y) = -\frac{-f_\xi r_Y}{-F_{p0} + f_\xi \varepsilon' + f_{W_p} F_{p0}}$$

We have $(f_{W_p} - 1)F_{p0} < 0$ and $f_\xi \varepsilon' \leq 0$, since $f_{W_p} < 1$ and $\varepsilon' \leq 0$ has been assumed.

Furthermore, the numerator of the fraction shown is always positive, which results in $e'(Y) < 0$. This asset markets equilibrium curve AA is always negatively sloped, as already shown in Figure 12.2. We note that the AA-curve is steep, the higher the capital mobility, as measured by f_ξ, the lower the interest rate elasticity of money demand, the more dominant the demand for dollar bonds is in the portfolio of asset holders (and also the more sluggishly are the regressively formed expectations).

Next, we investigate the implications of a steep AA-curve that under otherwise normal conditions gives rise to a situation as shown in Figure 12.3, exhibiting now three IS–AA equilibria.

Two of those are stable under the assumption of flexible exchange rates and the assumed sluggish adjustment of output through the dynamic multiplier process as Figure 12.3 reveals.

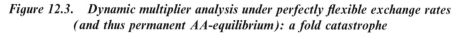

Figure 12.3. **Dynamic multiplier analysis under perfectly flexible exchange rates (and thus permanent AA-equilibrium): a fold catastrophe**

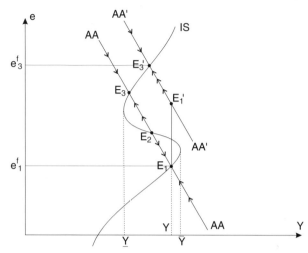

Below E_2, at a point on the AA curve (which is always binding if the exchange rate is perfectly flexible), we have expanding output according to the IS-curve and thus convergence to E_1, while the opposite holds for points above E_2 on the AA-curve. We stress that AA-equilibrium must here prevail by assumption, when e is treated as a statically endogenous variable), while the economy may temporarily be off the IS-curve however. As shown, this implies that E_1 and E_3 are attractors, while E_2 is a repeller in the considered graphical illustration of our small open economy.

Assume now that the AA-curve shifts to the right to AA' (see Figure 12.3) so that only the upper stationary equilibrium remains. Assume further that the economy was initially in E_1. Since output Y cannot react instantaneously, the economy must jump to the new asset market equilibrium E'_1 and will thus undergo an instantaneous process of strong currency depreciation. Yet, despite such strong depreciation, the economy will not expand its activity level thereafter, via the exchange rate affect on net exports, but will instead start to contract until the new stationary equilibrium E'_3 has been reached, a process which is accompanied by further depreciation of the currency, as Figure 12.3 shows.

The effects of the considered shift in the asset market equilibrium curve are therefore a sudden and then continuous further depreciation of the currency, a radical and then continuous improvement in the trade balance (due to rising e and falling Y), a radical and then continuous decrease in domestic investment near to its floor and as a result of this dominant change in aggregate demand, declining economic activity and declining domestic interest rates.

The question now is what the likely reasons may be that imply the considered rightward shift in the AA-curve (to AA′). To provide a possible explanation, we expand the asset demand curve f as follows:

$$eF_p = f(\bar{r}^* + \varepsilon(e) - r(Y, M), W_p, \alpha), \quad f_\alpha > 0$$

We use the new parameter α to express the risk, from the international perspective of domestic asset holders, of investing in domestic bonds – assuming that dollars represent the preferred currency and thus dollar bonds the preferred assets in the household sector – since a devaluation of the domestic currency deteriorates the international position of asset holders. If there is a potential threat of a depreciation of the domestic currency, asset holders may gradually decide (as expressed by an increase of the risk parameter α) to reallocate their asset holdings into dollar-denominated bonds. This process may be considered as capital flight from the domestic currency into the foreign one. An increasing α, expressing increasing dollar-liquidity preference,[8] therefore induces reallocation attempts into foreign bonds which, however, cannot succeed here, since $F_{p0} = F_p$ is fixed in a regime of flexible exchange rates, but which nevertheless moves E_1, since an increasing α shifts the AA-curve to the right; maybe even to the extent that this lower equilibrium completely disappears and gives way to the sole equilibrium E_3' shown in Figure 12.3. An increasing α thus indeed produces currency depreciations (but also output expansions as long as the lower equilibrium E_1 remains in existence) and may thus induce further increases in the shift parameter.

What can be done by the Central Bank to stop this tendency toward small, and (if E_1 gets lost) even large, depreciations of the domestic currency? One possibility is to increase the domestic rate of interest to counteract such capital flight – by way of a contractionary monetary policy. Reducing money balances by way of internal open market operations shifts the AA-curve to the left and thus may prevent that the AA-curves – under the assumed capital flight conditions – shift so much to the right that the lower equilibrium E_1 gets lost. There is then only some depreciation (if E_1 remains in existence), yet it still can expand output (if α is strong enough to overcome the contractionary impact of the restrictive monetary policy). Nevertheless, the economy may move closer to the output level where the strong currency equilibrium E_1 [the normal equilibrium in Krugman's (2001) words] may disappear. This leaning against the wind strategy thus may be of help if α increases, at least to some extent or for some time.

If, however, the economy becomes trapped in E_3', the monetary authority can nevertheless attempt to bring the economy back to the lower stable part of the IS-curve. Contractionary monetary policy moves the economy in the direction

---

[8] To be contrasted with $f\xi$, which measures capital mobility for a given state of dollar-liquidity preference.

toward E_3, and, if continued, thereafter eventually to a situation where the upper equilibrium gets lost. Exchange rate appreciation will then lead the economy vertically down until the asset market equilibrium curve is reached again. From there on we have a continuously rising exchange rate and rising output until a new stationary point of type E_1 is reached. It is questionable, however, that the capital flight parameter α will stay in place[9] in the early phase of such economic contraction, caused by restrictive monetary policy, though this policy tends to increase the domestic nominal rate of interest (counteracted, but not fully offset, by the output contraction it leads to).

Note that monetary policy can be made more direct, if the interest rate is directly set by the monetary authority, while M is then adjusted to money demand $M(Y,r)$ through appropriate technical instruments of the Central Bank. The expression $r(Y,M)$ in the asset market equilibrium equation is then replaced by an exogenously given r, which is called an interest rate peg, which obviously changes the qualitative results so far discussed considerably, since the AA-curve then becomes a horizontal one with only a unique intersection with the IS-curve under all circumstances.[10] Note that, for given α and an equilibrium position E_1, expansionary monetary policy may lead to a contraction, if the economy, via the AA-curve, is shifted thereby so much to the right that the equilibrium E_1 gets lost. As long as the economy is on the lower branch, lowering r leads to mild depreciation and goods market improvements, since the NX effect there dominates the investment effect. Yet, beyond $\bar{Y}$ we reach the region where depreciation accelerates and output contracts (since investment then dominates NX) until stationarity is reached again in a situation where output and investment are at very low levels, in a stable state of depression as the model is formulated.

Next we investigate the exchange rate dynamics in more detail; let us consider the excess demand function X on the market for foreign bonds which is given by[11]

$$X(e) = f(\bar{r}^* + \varepsilon(e) - r(Y,M), M_0 + B_0 + eF_{p0}) - eF_{p0}$$

The slope of this function is given by

$$f_\xi \varepsilon'(e) + f_{W_p} F_{p0} - F_{p0} < 0 \quad (f_{W_p} < 1)$$

Excess demand for foreign bonds basically means excess supply of domestic bonds and thus domestic demand for foreign currency. It is therefore natural to

---

[9] In particular, if the rapid depreciation (accompanied by restrictive monetary policy) leads to a significant degree of bankruptcy of firms.

[10] The AA-curve is again negatively sloped in the case of a Taylor rule, which uses the output gap on its right-hand side where therefore the interest rate responds again to the state of the business cycle. This implies that it may be wise in certain situations to avoid automatic interest rate movements and thus the possibility of multiple and, in particular, bad equilibrium selections.

[11] With $r(Y,M)$ given or simply $r = \bar{r}$ set by the monetary authority.

Figure 12.4.   The market for foreign bonds and exchange rate adjustments

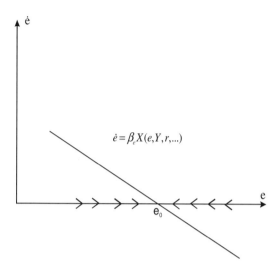

assume that

$$\hat{e} = \frac{\beta_e X(e)}{(eF_{po})} \quad \text{or slightly modified:} \quad \dot{e} = \beta_e X(e)$$

describes, here in a linear fashion, the reaction of the exchange with respect to such excess demand, when capital mobility is high and thus dominating exchange rate dynamics. This implies a stable adjustment process of the exchange rate to its equilibrium value e_0 as shown in Figure 12.4.

Using this additional law of motion, the dynamics along the asset market equilibrium curve AA can in fact now be extended to the whole Y, e phase space, as shown in Figure 12.5 (where we have returned for the moment to the consideration of a single stationary point E_1). Note that the AA-line is now crossed horizontally in these extended and thus modified dynamics and not characterized by the motion shown along the AA-line as in Figure 12.3.

This latter motion in fact solely characterizes the limit case of infinitely fast exchange rate dynamics, $\beta_e = \infty$, which instantaneously places the exchange e on the AA-curve, along which output still has to adjust, and thus represents a different dynamical system, as compared to the somewhat sluggish adjustment of the exchange rate that is now considered (the case $\beta_e = \infty$ is approached in a continuous fashion if β_e is approaching ∞; see the thick arrows in Figure 12.5). Note furthermore that the positive orthant is an invariant set of the now considered dynamics, which cannot be left, since the change in output (in the exchange rate) is always positive sufficiently close to the axis $Y = 0$ ($e = 0$).

We conjecture with respect to Figure 12.5 that the sole equilibrium, shown there, is globally asymptotically stable in the positive orthant of R^2, but do not

Figure 12.5.   *The Krugman dynamics extended to the whole Y, e phase space*

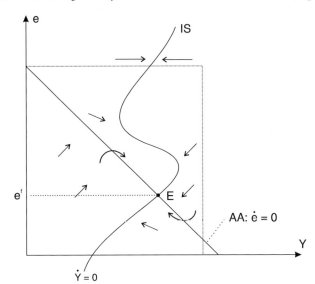

prove this here.[12] In fact the dynamics cannot leave the box shown in the Figure 12.5, but the occurrence of semi-stable limit cycles is not yet excluded thereby, unless the adjustment speed of the exchange rate is close to ∞, where the dynamics are then close to those of the limit case we considered beforehand.

Returning to the situation of Figure 12.3 with its multiple equilibria – embedded now into the dynamics just considered, see Figure 12.6 – implies again two locally asymptotically stable equilibria and one unstable one under the new dynamics as can easily be shown by calculating trace and determinant of the corresponding Jacobians. The process thus exhibits the equilibria E_1 and E_3 as (sole) stable equilibria under the now interacting dynamics of output Y and the exchange rate e.

Note also that Figure 12.6 suggests that the dynamics around E_2 is of saddle point type, with unstable arms leading to E_1 and E_3, respectively. It is even more difficult to determine the basins of attractions of the two attracting equilibria and to determine what may elsewhere happen in the phase space. Numerical investigations must here be used in addition to determine these basins explicitly. In the sequel we shall, however, simply assume that the dynamics is generally convergent to either of the two equilibria E_1 and E_3 after all shocks or disturbances. We justify this again with the limit case $\beta_e = \infty$, where global convergence along the AA-curve to either one or the other equilibrium is

---

[12] One could use an appropriate application of Olech's theorem on global asymptotic stability (see Flaschel, 1984).

Figure 12.6.   The extended dynamics in the Y, e phase space with three equilibria (two stable and one saddle)

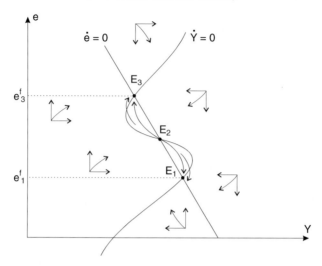

obvious (with the exception of the situation where the economy sits exactly in the unstable equilibrium E_2).

We observe finally that – in the case of flexible exchange rates, of course – the assumption of regressive expectations has to be interpreted and applied with care. If the economy converges to either E_1 or E_3 we know that the exchange rate will become stationary again, while the assumed type of regressive expectations $\varepsilon = \varepsilon(e)$, in particular with $\varepsilon'(e) < 0$, would imply that the expected rate of depreciation ε can only be 0 in at most one of the three considered equilibria. This however is implausible in an environment where rates of exchange settle down at stationary values. This situation can be remedied as follows. Assume that the shock shown in Figure 12.3 has hit the economy leading the economy to the point E_3' eventually. Imbedded into the new AA'-curve shown here is implicitly a second shock, namely a revision of the long-run reference value e^f, regressive expectations are implicitly referring to. This long-run reference value is here supposed to be always determined from the AA'-situation, where in the defining equation we have set ε identically equal to 0. It is therefore the value of the exchange rate where stationarity can be assured. We assume here that expectations formation immediately switches to this new long-run value when the α-shock has occurred, for example by way of the following explicit formula:

$$\varepsilon(e) = \beta_\varepsilon \left(\frac{e^f}{e - 1} \right)$$

with e^f now being the relevant long-run value of the exchange rate e. Regressive expectations are therefore always forward looking with respect to the long-run situation and thus change their schedule when an α-shock occurs. This means that the AA'-curve is subject to changes, the first caused by the parameter α (from which e^f can then be determined) and the second due to the shift in the ε schedule by means of e^f, which makes the AA'-curve steeper and guarantees that at E_3' we arrive at e^f and $\varepsilon = 0$.

There is another possibility to discuss the change in the long-run exchange rate. Assume that e_o is the stationary value which the economy is currently approaching. Assume furthermore – again for concreteness – that $\varepsilon(e)$ is given by $\varepsilon(e) = \beta_{\varepsilon}(e^f/e - 1)$ with $e^f \neq e_o$, but sufficiently close to e_o. Assume finally as additional law of motion

$$\dot{e}^f = \beta_{e^f}(e - e^f)$$

This adaptive mechanism says that the point of reference in the regressive expectations mechanism is a weighted average (with exponentially declining weights) of past observations of actual exchange rates and thus moving with the occurrence of new observations of actual exchange rates. Extending in this way our 2D dynamics to a 3D dynamical system implies for its stationary points (that are stable in the above 2D subdynamics) that they are also stable in the extended 3D system for all adjustment speed of the reference point e^f chosen sufficiently small. This follows easily from an application of the Routh–Hurwitz conditions for local asymptotic stability to the resulting 3D Jacobian, the added minors all having the correct sign (as can be shown by appropriate row operations) and since the determinant of the 3D system is dominated by the product of trace and the 2D principal minors if β_{e_1} is chosen sufficiently small.

We conclude that the considered equilibria E_1 and E_3 preserve the stability properties if the regressive expectations mechanism is assumed to only slowly take account of the new stationary value the actual exchange rate is converging to. This however is only a local argument. Furthermore, the alternative, i.e., partially forward-looking regressive expectations (on e^f) are known from the literature on Dornbusch type models and give the asset market equilibrium curve a refined underpinning that is not without interest. Finally, we will see in the next section that under such conditions currency crises may happen, though exchange rate expectations are of still very fundamental and tranquil type.

We next consider the case of a fixed exchange rate system, where $\varepsilon(e) = 0$ can be assumed to be 0, and where the amount of depreciation that takes place in the event of a currency crisis is not foreseen by the economic agents. The discussed dynamics of e therefore can then even be considered with $\varepsilon(e) \equiv 0$ and be viewed as being only implicitly present until the currency crisis in fact occurs (and modifies the expectations mechanism as discussed above).

5. Currency crisis in a fixed exchange rate regime

Flexible exchange rates do not represent the only exchange rate regime to which this model of large exchange rate swings and real crisis can be applied to. We now turn to the fixed exchange rate case in order to see for a normal situation of a seemingly fairly strong currency and high economic activity how the discussed tendency to capital flight may there gradually give rise to situations where the economy finally becomes trapped in a depressed stationary equilibrium of type E_3 with a weak currency and low economic activity. This can be accompanied by a significant reversal of net exports from a trade deficit to a trade surplus, despite the crisis state and large output loss of the economy after the initial depreciation shock. In the fixed exchange rate regime we again consider the cases of a fixed money supply. Now however the quantity F_p realized by households foreign bond demand can depart from the level households already own and can indeed rise beyond this level and indeed be realized until the foreign reserves F_c of the Central Bank become exhausted.

In order to investigate the possibility of an exchange rate crisis for the fixed exchange rate regime, let us first introduce as reference curve a balanced trade line in its relationship to the IS or goods market equilibrium curve of Figure 12.3. Obviously, the equation

$$0 = NX(Y, e), \quad NX_Y < 0, \quad NX_e > 0$$

defines an upward-sloping curve, representing balanced trade in the Y, e phase space. We have positive net exports on the upper part of the IS-curve and negative net exports on its lower part. We assume for this curve that Figure 12.7 holds true.

Figure 12.7 shows that output is completely fixed by the exchange rate in our model when a given exchange rate is assumed. In the depicted situation we have a high level of economic activity, a trade deficit due to a strong currency and, based on this high level of activity, a capital market curve AA that would imply slight currency depreciation and even higher economic activity (with a lower trade deficit in addition) in the case of perfect exchange rate flexibility. Note here that the AA-curve is, however, only implicitly present and that it determines in the background of Figure 12.7 the stock of foreign bonds demanded by the public (excess demand being met out of the stocks held by the Central Bank) and that this curve is based on the assumption of $\varepsilon = 0$ in the fixed exchange rate case. The equilibrium Y may be called a normal equilibrium as in Krugman (2001).

The dynamics shown in the next Figure 12.8 (case $\beta_e = \infty$ solely) is therefore only a shadow dynamics that would come into existence when the fixing of the exchange rate were abandoned by the Central Bank. As long as this is not the case we always have that the excess demand for foreign bonds $F_p - F_{po}$ of the private sector, determined by $\bar{e}F_p = f(\bar{r}^* - r(Y, M), M_o + B_o + \bar{e}F_{po}, \alpha)$, is always served by the Central Bank out of the foreign bond reserves F_c currently held by it and assumed to be sufficiently large to allow for this balancing of the market for foreign currency. This indeed allows then for the fixing of the exchange rate and implies in the course of time – when the capital flight parameter α starts to increase in a continuous fashion – that private households hold more and more foreign bonds in their portfolio without change in the total

Figure 12.7. Balanced trade line and a normal equilibrium in a fixed exchange rate regime (with 'excess demand' for the foreign asset)

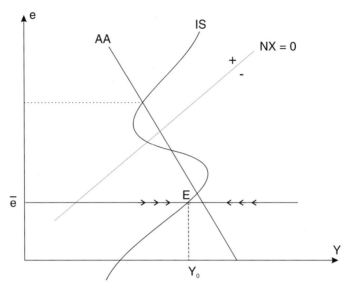

value of this portfolio, W_p, and thus their nominal wealth position, since the exchange rate is fixed.

We thus assume now that the expression F_p is slowly increasing through the influence (and solely through the influence) of the parameter α, since output is fixed by the given exchange rate. Only the IS-curve matters for the domestic equilibrium on the real markets, while the AA-curve only determines the position F_p of the stock of foreign bonds currently held in the private sector. Note here again that the expectations mechanism $\varepsilon(e)$ is not present in a system of fixed exchange rates, as long as people do not speculate about an exchange rate crisis in terms of exchange rates, which may nevertheless be approaching through increases in the capital flight parameter α.

Besides the $NX = 0$ curve shown in Figure 12.8 also the critical line AA_c where $\alpha = \alpha_c$ has become so large that $\bar{F}^* = F_p$ ($F_c = 0$) holds, i.e., the Central Bank has no longer any reserves of foreign currency. At this critical value of α – or even before this value has been reached – the fixed exchange rate system will break down and is likely to be replaced by the regime of flexible exchange rates as considered in the preceding section. We thus assume now that the ongoing process of a financial capital restructuring of private households – via further increases in the capital flight parameter α – has progressed to such a point that the foreign exchange reserves of the Central Bank are basically exhausted as represented by the line AA_c ($\varepsilon = 0$ still).

We already indicated in Figure 12.8 the dynamics that would then come about if the exchange rate would become flexible and determined by the asset

Peter Flaschel and Willi Semmler

Figure 12.8. *Normal real equilibrium, limited intervention range and shadow dynamics in a fixed exchange rate regime*

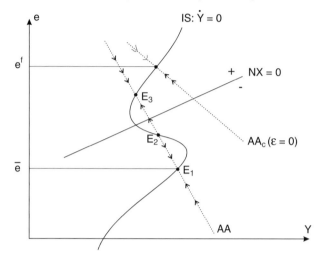

markets of our model. This would however then also reestablish the regressive expectations mechanism, based on the now sole equilibrium E_3 and would thus in addition rotate the line AA_c in a clockwise fashion around this equilibrium to the position AA_c', as explained in the preceding section and shown in Figure 12.9. In Figure 12.9, we therefore now go on from the potential situation shown in Figure 12.8 to what actually happens if the exchange rate is again the subject of market forces with an adjustment speed $\beta_e = \infty$.

When this situation is reached, the exchange rate – by assumption – becomes completely flexible and the shadow dynamics of Figure 12.8 comes into being, leading the economy in the way described in the preceding section to the bad equilibrium E_3 along the AA_c'-curve, which is steeper than the intervention limit curve AA_c shown, but also runs through the single equilibrium point E_3. The regressive expectations mechanism about the exchange rate dynamics is thus switched on in addition, with a long-run reference value for the exchange rate that is determined through E_3.[13]

The result of such a currency crisis will be (if Figure 12.9 applies): a large initial devaluation of the domestic currency, a large loss in output as the

---

[13] We thus in fact consider here some sort of asymptotically rational expectations which always know the long-run value of the exchange rate the economy will converge to. This presumes knowledge of the IS-curve and the AA-curve for $\varepsilon = 0$, at least for the ranges where investment is very unresponsive to the exchange rate. Under this assumption and the assumption that exchange rate dynamics must come to a rest again, the intersection of these two curves provide the agents with the long-run values of e to be put into their regressive expectations scheme.

Figure 12.9. The breakdown of the fixed exchange rate regime: Currency crisis, investment collapse and large output loss

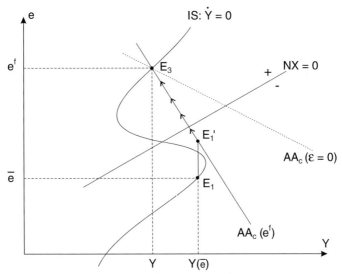

currency continues to depreciate toward the value e^f, due to the dominance of the investment crisis, and, along this way, a strong improvement in the trade balance (too weak however to overcome the loss of investment demand). All this happening on the background that the domestic central bank has (nearly) lost all of its currency reserves through the flight from domestic bond demand into foreign bonds. The economy thus tumbles into a real crisis with large output loss, based on a breakdown of investment, only partly counteracted by net exports due to the strong currency depreciation, with a Central Bank that has become powerless with respect to any further intervention into the foreign exchange market.

Next we consider in addition to the above – again for the case of fixed exchange rate $\bar{e}$ – a simple law of motion for the capital flight parameter α that by assumption shifts the AA-curve to the right if it increases. In the case of fixed exchange rates, we have in the place of Figure 12.9 again the Figure 12.8 which shows as dotted line the AA-curve as an attracting curve which could lead the economy to either E_1 or E_3 if exchange rates were completely flexible (still for $\varepsilon = 0$). We have excess demand for foreign bonds below the AA-curve and excess supply above it. We have assumed in Figure 12.9 that flexible exchange rates will come about when AA_c and immediately thereafter AA'_c applies in a situation where there is no longer a normal equilibrium point of type E_1.

We have pre-assumed that the demand function f for foreign bonds depends positively on the capital flight parameter α, since an increasing tendency to capital flight means that residents attempt to substitute domestic bonds by foreign ones. Excess demand, calculated before Central Bank intervention, increasing with α, may in fact give rise to a law of motion for α of the following type (presented in discrete time here solely):

$$\alpha_{t+h} = \alpha_t + \beta\alpha(f(\bar{r}^* - r(Y, M), W_p, \alpha_t) - f(\bar{r}^* - r(Y, M), W_p, \alpha_{t-h}))$$

where magnitudes $\bar{r}^*, r(Y, M), W_p = M_0 + B_{0,t} + \bar{e}F_{p0,t}$ are all given, despite the change in the composition of the bond holdings of the public. Note that we have inserted here $\bar{e}F_{p0,t} = f(\bar{r}^* - r(Y, M), W_p, \alpha_{t-h})$ as the result of the past foreign market intervention of the Central Bank at each point in time, in order to express excess demand by the change in demand that has happened from $t - h$ to t. Demand for foreign bonds and their actual holdings are changing in this manner through time (without any change in total private wealth). An initial increase in this demand may therefore set in motion a continuous increase in the parameter α, by way of contagion, as the situation can be interpreted. This may lead to an explosive movement of α if $\bar{e}$ and $\alpha(0)$ are such that there is a positive value for the excess demand function at these initial values.

Assume now again that some shock, for example coming from a neighboring country, shifts the AA-curve to the right to another curve AA'. In E_1, we now have excess demand for foreign bonds and thus an increasing α that continues to shift the AA'-curve to the right until AA_c is again reached. The normal equilibrium of the economy with flexible exchange rate shifts during this process toward higher output and exchange rate levels, until it finally disappears. During this process, excess demand for foreign bonds may be increasing in an accelerating fashion, so far always met by the Central Bank. When α continues to increase there may again arise the situation that the reserves of the Central Bank become exhausted:

$$F_c = \bar{F}^* - F_p \approx 0$$

The fixing of the exchange rate by the Central Bank will then break down and give rise to the exchange rate adjustments already discussed, leading the economy through a sudden depreciation to point E_1'. Here output will start to decrease and the exchange rate will continue to increase until the new stationary point E_3 is reached. The economy is now trapped in a bad equilibrium E_3 as discussed in Krugman (1999, 2001), but with a significant reversal from trade deficits to a trade surplus.

This outcome may depend to some extent on the way the above graph has been drawn and therefore only represents the one typical situation when the reserves of the Central Bank are so large and its intervention lasts so long that the AA_c-curve – where it stops its intervention – does exhibit only the upper bad equilibrium for the economy with a flexible exchange rate. An alternative situation that may arise in the case of only shorter intervention, for example, is provided in Figure 12.10 showing overshooting exchange rate depreciation and in fact an increase in economic activity as the currency starts to appreciate

Figure 12.10.   No currency crisis and output expansion in the case of a quick return to a flexible exchange rate regime

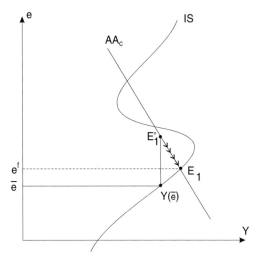

after the initial devaluation shock. There is still another possibility as indicated in Figure 12.11, where there is again no loss in output, neither large nor small.

The consequences of a return to a flexible exchange rate system due to the lack of reserves for a further fixing of the exchange rate, and the likelihood of exchange rate crisis, coupled with a dominant collapse in investment behavior and thus large output loss, reestablishes the importance of the AA_c-curve as a global attractor and the output movement along it – to the left if the bad equilibrium applies – until a new stationary point has been reached.

Since AA_c is now restricting again, the positions of the economy we return to $X = 0$ and thus possibly also to a stationary value for the capital flight parameter α.

The final consequence of the increasing propensity for capital flight is – if Figures 12.10 and 12.11 do not apply – that the exchange rate depreciates radically and that an severe economic depression will be induced, resulting from the balance sheet effect on investment, coupled with a pronounced reversal from a trade deficit to a trade surplus.

A leaning against the wind strategy of the Central Bank, i.e., an increase in domestic interest rates in order to stop the capital flight may, due to its shifting of the AA'-curves to the left, prevent the breakdown of the exchange rate system for some time, but will eventually fail due to the continuous increase in the parameter α as sketched above. This will then make the subsequent recession even more severe, since sooner or later the AA-curve will apply, where $\overline{F}^* = F_p$ ($F_c = 0$) has been reached.

Figure 12.11. *Overshooting exchange rate crisis and output improvements due to net export dominance*

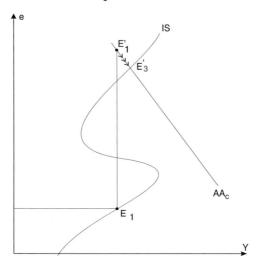

6. Conclusions

We have introduced in this paper an open economy portfolio model that allows us to study the channels that cause and the feedback effects that arise from large currency swings. We have demonstrated that large currency swings under flexible exchange rates, as well as slowly progressing and then sudden capital flights under fixed exchange rates, may lead to strong repercussions on the financial market when a large fraction of the domestic debt of firms is denominated in foreign currency. Those repercussions may in turn entail a low-level equilibria and large output losses for the economy. Following a model suggested by Krugman (1999, 2001), we showed rigorously in a dynamic model with multiple equilibria that there are mechanisms at work that indeed can give rise to such phenomena. Our results point to the dangers that may be brought about for a country if too fast financial and capital market liberalization without safety nets and sufficient financial market regulations are pursued, and we have shown that a flexible exchange rate does not exclude such dangers.

We have considered the small and sometimes very large effects of increasing dollar-liquidity preference in a setup where the exchange rate was moving – if flexible – countercyclically and where leaning against the wind policies were present via restrictive monetary policy that attempted to shift the financial markets equilibrium curve to the left toward reduced output, but stronger currency values, trying to neutralize increasing dollar-liquidity preference, may be supported by the IMF as lender of last resort. As discussed above, such efforts may or may not prevent the outbreak of the financial and real crisis of a small open economy exhibiting a high level of foreign debt.

The model was completely explicit with respect to budget conditions and the accounts of the four sectors of the economy and the balance of payments, showing however in this way the narrow foundations on which this type of crisis model still rests. We have flow consistency and the fulfillment of all plans of the agents of the economy – up to firms which may be credit of supply rationed in their pursuit of new investment goods. We still have fix-price bonds. Expectations thus solely concern changes in the exchange rate, depreciation or appreciation, and were assumed to be of asymptotically rational (regressive) type. Assuming fix-price bonds means that asset holders can indeed enforce a currency crisis – in a fixed exchange rate system – if they hold initially enough domestic bonds compared to the dollar-bonds held by the Central Bank.

Concerning expectations one might ask why we did not assume rational expectations (or myopic perfect foresight) in this paper. Presumably this would turn the two equilibria that were stable under regressive expectations into saddlepoint dynamics. Furthermore, the unstable equilibrium in the middle would then become a stable equilibrium, if the dynamic multiplier process is supposed to work with sufficient speed. We would therefore then obtain a situation that is not easily handled by means of the conventional jump variable technique. One could, furthermore, then assume that the economy always converges back to the stable equilibrium if displacements from this equilibrium are not too large. Capital flight however could again remove the economy from this equilibrium and the economy may then converge along the stable arm of the bad equilibrium to this weak currency situation and thus might repeat what we have done here for regressive expectations. One next step could then be to find the formula for regressive expectations that will place the economy exactly on this stable arm of the saddlepoint dynamics, an exercise that we will not pursue here any further.

Rather than pursuing this type of extension one might approach goods market behavior with more advanced behavioral functions (as in Rødseth, 2000, Ch. 6) or extend the asset market approach toward flex-price bonds and also add equity issuance of firms. A stock-flow interaction may then be added to the model. Finally, in the place of a fixed money supply or its discretionary changes, we could consider interest rate policy rules (Taylor rules) and also a Phillips-curve-driven price dynamics. The latter could in particular help to elaborate the issue of debt deflation, since firms are already formulated here as being highly indebted and thus also very vulnerable with respect to output price deflation, in particular if wages and foreign interest rates only slowly adjust. Contagion from and to neighboring countries may also become an issue here.

Acknowledgments

We wish to thank Alexander Karmann for comments on an earlier version of the paper. Financial support by the Ministry of Science, Education and Technology of the State of Northrine-Westfalia is gratefully acknowledged.

References

Aghion, P., P. Bacchetta and A. Banerjee (2000), "Currency crisis and monetary policy in an economy with credit constraints", Discussion paper no. 2529, Center for Economic Policy Research.

Asada, T., C. Chiarella, P. Flaschel and R. Franke (2003), *Open Economy Macrodynamics. An Integrated Disequilibrium Approach*, Heidelberg and New York: Springer.

Blanchard, O. and S. Fischer (1989), *Lectures on Macroeconomics*, Cambridge, MA: MIT Press.

Burnside, C., M. Eichenbaum and S. Rebelo (1999), "Hedging and financial fragility in fixed exchange rate regimes", Paper presented at the CEPR conference on Expectations, Economic Theory and Economic Policy, Perugia.

Chang, R. and A. Velasco (1999), "Liquidity crises in emerging markets: theory and policy", NBER Working Paper No. 7272, Cambridge, MA.

Diamond, P. and P. Dybvig (1983), "Bank runs, deposit insurance and liquidity", *Journal of Political Economy*, Vol. 93, pp. 211–248.

Flaschel, P. (1984), "Some stability properties of Goodwin's growth cycle. A critical elaboration", *Zeitschrift für Nationalökonomie*, Vol. 44, pp. 63–69.

Kaldor, N. (1940), "A model of the trade cycle", *Economic Journal*, Vol. 50, pp. 78–92.

Kamin, S.B. (1999), "The current international financial crisis: how much is new?", *Journal of International Money and Finance*, Vol. 18, pp. 501–514.

Kiyotaki, N. and J. Moore (1995), "Credit cycles", *Journal of Political Economy*, Vol. 105, pp. 211–248.

Krugman, P. (1999), "Balance sheets, the transfer problem and financial crises", in: P. Isard, A. Razin and A. Rose, editors, *International Finance and Finanacial Crisis*, Dordrecht: Kluwer Academic Publishers.

Krugman, P. (2001), "Crisis: the price of globalization, federal reserve bank of Kansas city", *Economic Review*, pp. 75–106.

Krugman, P. and M. Obstfeld (2003), *International Economics*, New York: Addison-Wesley.

Milesi-Ferretti, G.M. and A. Razin (1996), "Current account sustainability: selected East Asian and Latin American experiences", NBER Working Paper No. 5791, Cambridge, MA.

Milesi-Ferretti, G.M. and A. Razin (1998), "Sharp reduction in curent account deficits: an empirical analysis", NBER Working Paper No. 6310, Cambridge, MA.

Miller, M. and J. Stiglitz (1999), "Bankruptcy protection against macroeconomic shocks", The World Bank, mimeo.

Rødseth, A. (2000), *Open Economy Macroeconomics*, Cambridge, UK: Cambridge University Press.

Semmler, W. (2003), *Asset Prices, Booms and Recessions*, Heidelberg: Springer.

CHAPTER 13

Prosperity and Stagnation in Capitalist Economies

Toichiro Asada, Peter Flaschel and Peter Skott

Abstract

The Keynes–Metzler–Goodwin (KMG) growth dynamics in Chiarella and Flaschel (2000) assume that wages, prices and quantities adjust sluggishly to disequilibria in labor and goods markets. This paper modifies the KMG model by introducing Steindlian features of capital accumulation and income distribution. The resulting KMGS(teindl) model replaces the neoclassical medium- and long-run features of the original KMG model by a Steindlian approach to capital accumulation, as developed in a paper by Flaschel and Skott (2006). The model is of dimension 4 or 5, depending on the specification of the labor supply. We prove stability assertions and show that loss of stability always occurs by way of Hopf bifurcations. When global stability gets lost, a nonlinear form of the Steindlian reserve army mechanism can ensure bounded dynamics. These dynamics are studied numerically and shown to exhibit long phases of prosperity, but also long phases of stagnant growth.

Keywords: KMGS dynamics, accelerating growth, stagnant growth, normal/ adverse income shares adjustment, reserve army mechanisms

JEL classifications: E24, E31, E32

1. Steindlian views on prosperity and stagnation in integrated models of KMG growth

Building on Steindl's contributions, Flaschel and Skott (2006) derive a hierarchically structured sequence of Steindlian models. The present paper

CONTRIBUTIONS TO ECONOMIC ANALYSIS
VOLUME 277   ISSN: 0573-8555
DOI:10.1016/S0573-8555(05)77013-9

combines elements of these Steindlian models with the Keynes–Metzler–Goodwin (KMG) approach, developed in Chiarella and Flaschel (2000). Unlike the models in Flaschel and Skott, which assume goods-market (IS) equilibrium, the KMG approach includes explicit disequilibrium adjustment processes in goods and labor markets. The resulting KMGS(teindl) model has five markets: labor, goods, money, bonds and equities and three sectors: households (workers and asset holders, with differentiated saving habits), firms, and the fiscal and monetary authority. All budget equations are fully specified and stock-flow consistency is satisfied.

The KMG approach includes sluggish wage and price adjustment (by means of separate structural equations) as well as sluggish output adjustment via a Metzlerian process of active inventory adjustment.[1] Replacing goods market or IS equilibrium by this process of delayed responses may seem a minor improvement of the specification of the goods market. Mathematically, however, it is a big step, since it replaces an algebraic equation by two differential equations. Moreover, even when adjustments are fast, the properties of systems that incorporate these explicit adjustment mechanisms need not, in general, generate outcomes that are similar to those characterizing systems with instantaneous adjustment. Thus, the simpler system of instantaneous IS equilibrium may be misleading even if adjustment speeds are high. Explicit adjustment mechanisms increase the dimension of the dynamic system and this increase complicates the analysis. These complications, however, are partly offset by the simplifications of avoiding certain nonlinearities that arise in a static equilibrium formulation of the relationship between income distribution and capacity utilization.

While allowing for disequilibrium in real markets, the KMG approach assumes that all financial markets are in equilibrium.[2] The present paper simplifies the financial side and its interaction with the real side even further by assuming an interest rate peg (of the nominal rate) by the central bank and by excluding the conventional influence of the real rate of interest on aggregate demand. Thus, the emphasis is on the real markets and their disequilibrium adjustment processes.

A key difference between the present model and the KMG approach of Chiarella and Flaschel, 2000 concerns the determination of trend growth (steady-state growth). Chiarella and Flaschel assume that the trend rate of

---

[1] See Skott (1989a,b) for an alternative approach to the modelling of short-run disequilibrium in a process of cyclical growth.

[2] The KMG model analyses the financial markets by way of a simple liquidity preference approach to the money market and the assumption of perfect substitution among all other financial assets. Extensions of this formulations are pursued in Köper and Flaschel (2000).

growth is determined by the natural growth rate of the population. Changing participation rates, migration and the existence of hidden unemployment in backward sectors of the economy make this neoclassical closure of the model implausible. The supply of labor (to the modern or capitalist sector) may not be perfectly elastic in the short run but the growth rate of the labor supply is affected by the demand for labor. This Steindlian position motivates the alternative specification in this paper. We assume that investment determines the trend growth rate of the economy and that the labor supply adjusts endogenously to this trend. The specification of the growth rate of the labor supply in this paper gives rise to five-dimensional (5D) dynamics. An alternative specification yields a simpler 4D system which may be used if one wants to consider the dynamics without fluctuations in the labor–capital ratio; we reserve the analysis of this simpler system for future investigation.

The KMGS model may generate long waves of prosperity and stagnation. The Metzlerian inventory adjustment process can lead to local instability of the steady state, and in this case the destabilizing forces eventually drive the economy out of a neighborhood of the steady state. When this happens in an upward direction, high and increasing employment gradually undermines 'animal spirits' and generates a progressively decreasing trend in the investment function. This declining trend in turn implies that the model may produce recurrent phases of prolonged prosperity and subsequent stagnation. These results, which are confirmed by numerical simulation of the KMGS model, mirror Steindl's (1979) view of prolonged full employment in the 1950s and 1960s as a key factor behind the subsequent stagnation.

The KMGS model is introduced in detail in the next section. In Section 3, we present the reduced-form 5D version of the model and discuss its feedback structures: the dynamics of income distribution, the accelerator mechanism that characterize inventory adjustments, and the accelerator and reserve army mechanisms that are involved in the determination of the rate of accumulation. Section 4 provides the sketch of a proof of local asymptotic stability of the steady state (and its loss of local stability by way of Hopf bifurcations) in the special case of classical saving habits. This section shows how common components in the laws of motion can be manipulated or temporarily frozen in order to simplify the stability calculations in this case. The general case is considered in Section 5. In the main text of Section 5, we study eigenvalue diagrams that characterize the loss of stability from a numerical perspective and then show – also numerically – that the Kalecki/Steindl reserve army mechanism (whereby accumulation slackens systematically when the economy operates close to its full employment ceiling) can generate bounded fluctuations in a 5D dynamic system that is locally repelling in nature. A rigorous proof of local stability and uniquely existing Hopf-bifurcation points that accompany the loss of stability for faster disequilibrium adjustment processes is relegated to a mathematical appendix. Section 6 concludes the paper.

2. KMGS accumulation dynamics

In this section we start from a standard KMG approach to Keynesian monetary macrodynamics.[3] We then extend the model by introducing Steindlian aspects of capitalist accumulation dynamics, including in particular a new nonneoclassical determination of the steady state of the model.

The model has three types of agent: households (in their capacity as workers and asset holders), firms (that perform the role of production units and investors) and government (acting as the fiscal and monetary authority). These agents interact on markets for goods, labor and financial assets. We have sluggish wage adjustment on the labor market, and sluggish price and quantity adjustment on the market for goods. The price and wage adjustments are related to the employment rate and the degree of utilization of the capital stock, respectively,[4] while quantity adjustment takes place in response to goods market disequilibrium. The financial part of the model is simple and traditional. We use a conventional LM curve and assume that the central bank keeps the nominal interest rate constant.[5] The assumption of a constant interest rate, which is in line with other post-Keynesian work, implies that the money supply is fully endogenous and that the demand for money becomes proportional to aggregate income. Government bonds and equities of firms are perfect substitutes as in Sargent (1987), and standard specifications of tax and government expenditure policy allow us to characterize fiscal policy in terms of constant parameters on the intensive-form level of the model.

According to Steindl, deviations of the rate of capacity utilization from the desired level lead to changes in the markup. Unwanted excess capacity, he argued, exerted downward pressure on the markup. The KMG model, as introduced in Chiarella and Flaschel (2000), employs wage–price equations that can generate this Steindlian dynamics of the profit share. Thus, despite the different theoretical origins of its wage–price dynamics, we need not extend the KMG model in this respect.

When it comes to the investment behavior of firms, however, the Steindlian perspective introduces a significant change in the causal structure of the model. The trend rate of growth in the KMGS model is determined by the investment habits of firms, and not, as in Chiarella and Flaschel, by labor force growth. Furthermore, the long-run behavior of firms' investment decisions is influenced

---

[3] A detailed introduction to the baseline KMG approach and its significance within the conventional literature on Keynesian monetary growth models is given in Chiarella and Flaschel (2000). A thorough analytical, numerical and empirical investigation is provided in Chiarella *et al.* (2005).

[4] See Chiarella *et al.* (2000, Chapter 5) for an analysis that also allows variations in the utilization rate of the employed part of the labor force.

[5] The standard KMG model linearizes the LM curve. This linearization is unnecessary in the present setting since we assume a constant rate of interest.

by two reserve army mechanisms: a traditional Goodwin growth cycle mechanism via the distribution of income and an additional, direct mechanism. The second mechanism can be characterized by the Kaleckian phrase that 'bosses do not like full employment', see Kalecki's (1943) essay on the 'political aspects of full employment' for details. This Kaleckian mechanism is modeled as a direct but gradual effect of the rate of employment on the trend term in the accumulation function. The Kaleckian mechanism helps to ensure the boundedness of the fluctuations generated by the model and thus the economic viability of the model.

In the KMGS specification, investment determines the long-run trend in the growth of capital and output. Natural growth must therefore be endogenized in order to get steady state solutions around which the economy is fluctuating. This endogeneity of labor supply can be obtained in various ways, and we consider two specifications. The specifications are chosen with an eye to getting dynamic systems that are relatively simple and analytically tractable.

With respect to saving and consumption, finally, we follow Steindl and the post-Keynesian tradition and allow for differentiated saving habits.

Turning now to the structural equations of the KMGS model, we first introduce some definitions:

1. Definitions (remunerations and wealth):

$$\omega = w/p, \quad \rho^e = (Y^e - \omega L^d)/K \tag{13.1}$$
$$W = (M + B + p_e E)/p, \quad p_b = 1 \tag{13.2}$$

This set of equations define the real wage ω, the expected rate of profit on real capital ρ^e (based on expected sales Y^e) and real wealth W. Wealth is composed of money M, fixed price bonds B ($p_b = 1$) and equities E as in Sargent (1987). A full list of notation is given at the end of the paper.

Household behavior is described by the following set of equations:

2. Households (workers and asset-holders):

$$W = (M^d + B^d + p_e E^d)/p, \quad M^d = h_1 p Y \tag{13.3}$$

$$C = (1 - s_w)(\omega L^w + rB_w/p - T_w)$$
$$\quad + (1 - s_c)[(1 - s_f)\rho^e K + rB_p/p - T_p] \tag{13.4}$$

$$S_p = s_w(\omega L^a + rB_w/p - T_w)$$

$$\quad + s_c[(1 - s_f)\rho^e K + rB_p/p - T_p] = (\dot{M}^d + \dot{B}^d + p_e\dot{E}^d)/p \tag{13.5}$$

$$\hat{L} = n = a\left[\text{or} \quad n = a + i(u - \bar{u}) = \frac{I}{K}\right] \quad \text{see module 3} \tag{13.6}$$

We here start from Walras' Law of Stocks that states that real wealth W, in Equation (13.3), is the constraint for the stock demand for real money balances and real bond and equity holdings at each moment in time. Money demand is specified as a linear function of nominal income pY. The coefficient h_1 will, in general, depend on the interest rate, $h_1 = h(r)$, but by assumption the monetary authorities keep the interest rate constant.[6]

Consumption C, in Equation (13.4), is based on Kaldorian saving habits. It is assumed that workers' saving rate is lower than that of pure asset holders. Note that dividend payments to asset holders are given by a fraction $(1 - s_f)$ of expected profits. For simplicity, we assume that the real taxes T_w, T_p of workers and asset holders are paid in a lump-sum fashion and that taxes net of interest payments on government debt are proportional to the capital stock (see the government module below). These, or similar, simplifying assumptions are common when feedbacks from the government budget constraint and wealth accumulation are excluded from consideration and fiscal policy is treated in a parametric fashion.

Equation (13.5) provides the definition of aggregate personal saving S_p of workers and pure asset holders (in real terms). Personal saving, by definition, is equal to the sum of changes in the stock of money, bonds and equities held by the personal sector. The desired portfolio compositions and the composition of the changes in holdings of the different assets may be different for the two groups. We assume in line with earlier work on KMG modeling that workers only accumulate financial wealth in the form of short-term government bonds; we also use specific tax collection rules (see module 4) that allow us to ignore feedbacks from interest income.[7]

Equation (13.6), finally, describes the growth of the labor supply. One specification equates the growth of L to the trend rate of growth of the capital stock; the other specification equates it to the actual rate of accumulation I/K. In the latter case the rate of capacity utilization u and the rate of employment e will be strictly proportional – a particularly simple formulation of Okun's law in the case of a fixed proportions technology – and the labor–capital ratio $l = L/K$ is constant over time. A more satisfactory specification of the labor supply relates the growth of L to the employment rate e. This specification, used in Flaschel and Skott (2006), would increase the complexity of the system considerably, since growth in labor supply and the capital stock then have to interact in a way that allows for a common rate in the steady state. We therefore leave an examination of this case in a KMG context for future research.[8] Next,

---

[6] See Chiarella *et al.* (2000, part III) for the treatment of much more general situations.

[7] See again Chiarella *et al.* (2000, part III) for the treatment of much more general situations and note that the consideration of the allocation of the flow of savings to specific assets is here only presented for completeness and for clarity with respect to future extensions of the model.

[8] Sargent (1987) avoided this (Harrodian) problem by assuming that trend growth term in investment function is given by the natural rate of growth, while this paper takes to some extent the opposite view that labor supply growth (not necessarily natural growth) is adjusting perfectly to the trend growth rate a of the capital stock. Both assumptions relegate the treatment of the question what in fact synchronizes these two growth rates for future investigation.

the behavior of the production sector of the economy is described by the following set of equations:

3. Firms (production-units and investors):

$$Y^p = y^p K, \quad y^p = \text{const.}, \quad u = Y/Y^p = y/y^p \quad (y = Y/K) \tag{13.7}$$

$$L^d = Y/x, \quad \hat{x} = 0, \quad e = L^d/L = Y/(xL) \tag{13.8}$$

$$I/K = i(u - \bar{u}) + a \tag{13.9}$$

$$\hat{a} = \alpha_1(u - \bar{u}) - \alpha_2(\omega - \bar{\omega}) - \alpha_3(e - \bar{e}) \tag{13.10}$$

$$S_f = Y - Y^e + s_f \rho^e K = \mathcal{I} + s_f \rho^e K \tag{13.11}$$

$$p_e \dot{E}/p = I + \dot{N} - \mathcal{I} - s_f \rho^e K = I + \dot{N} - S_f \tag{13.12}$$

$$\hat{K} = I/K \tag{13.13}$$

$$I^a = I + \dot{N} \tag{13.14}$$

According to Equations (13.7) and (13.8), firms produce commodities using a fixed proportions technology characterized by the potential output/capital ratio $y^p = Y^p/K$ and a fixed ratio x between actual output Y and labor L^d. This simple concept of technology allows for a straightforward definition of the rate of utilization of capital u and the rate of employment e.[9]

In Equation (13.9) investment per unit of capital I/K is driven by two forces, the trend accumulation term and the deviation of the actual rate of capacity utilization from the normal rate of utilization. Unlike in the original KMG model, the trend term may change endogenously: the growth rate of a is determined in Equation (13.10) by capacity utilization, the wage rate (which determines the profit share) and the employment rate. This specification of investment implies that aggregate demand is wage led in the short-run, since consumption depends directly and positively on the real wage ω while the negative response of investment occurs with a time delay (through changes in the variable a).

Firms' saving, Equation (13.11), is equal to the excess of output over expected sales (caused by planned inventory changes) plus retained profits. It follows, as expressed in Equation (13.12), that the total amount of new equities issued by firms (their only source of external finance) must be equal to the sum of intended fixed capital investment and unexpected inventory changes minus retained earnings. (This specification may be compared with the formulation of the inventory adjustment mechanism in module 6.)

---

[9] Chiarella and Flaschel (2000, Chapter 5) show that the approach can be extended to the case of smooth factor substitution without much change to the qualitative behavior of the model. See also Skott (1989a) for an analysis of the choice of technique in the context of a Keynesian/neo-Marxian theory of cyclical growth.

The next Equation (13.13) states that firms' fixed investment plans are always realized. Output is predetermined in this model (cf. module 6) but accommodating changes in inventories make the realization of investment plans possible. Equation (13.14), finally, describes actual investment I^a as the sum of (actual = intended) fixed investment and actual changes in inventories.

We now turn to a brief description of the government sector:

4. Government (fiscal and monetary authority):

$$T = T_w + T_p, \text{ such that } t_w = \frac{T_w - rB_w/p}{K}, t_p = \frac{T_p - rB_p/p}{K}$$

both const.   (13.15)

$$G = \gamma K, \quad \gamma = \text{const.}$$ (13.16)

$$S_g = T - rB/p - G \ [= -(\dot{M} + \dot{B})/p, \text{ see below}]$$ (13.17)

$$r = r_o, \quad \dot{M} = \dot{M}^d = \hat{p} + \hat{Y}$$ (13.18)

$$\dot{B} = pG + rB - pT - \dot{M}$$ (13.19)

This part of the model is kept as simple as possible. In Equation (13.15), taxes net of interest payments are assumed proportional to the stock of capital; similar assumptions have been employed by Sargent (1987, part I) and Rødseth (2000). Real government expenditures are also taken to be constant per unit of capital (Equation (13.16)). Given these proportionality assumptions, fiscal policy is represented by simple parameters in the intensive form of the model. The definition of government saving, Equation (13.17), S_g is the obvious one. Money supply is used to peg the nominal rate of interest, and the growth of money supply μ is driven by the growth rate of output plus the price-inflation rate (cf. Equation (13.18)). The new issue of bonds by the government, finally, is determined residually via Equation (13.19) which states that money and bond financing must exactly cover the deficit in government expenditure financing. Note that the bond financing of government expenditure generates no feedback effects on the real part of the private sector of the economy (since interest rate effects are neutralized and wealth effects are excluded by the formulation of the model).

Our model of disequilibrium dynamics retains some static equilibrium conditions for the financial markets. These equilibrium conditions are given by:[10]

---

[10] Note that money demand could have been specified as follows: $M^d = h_1 pY + h_2(r_o - r)W$, by including interest and wealth effects into it, an extension that is irrelevant here due to the assumed interest rate peg.

5. Equilibrium conditions (asset-markets):

$$M = M^d = h_1 p Y \quad [B = B^d, E = E^d] \tag{13.20}$$

$$r_o = \rho^e p K / [p_e E] + \hat{p}_e \tag{13.21}$$

$$\dot{M} = \dot{M}^d, \quad \dot{B}^d = \dot{B} \text{ [which implies: } \dot{E} = \dot{E}^d, \text{ see Appendix 2]} \tag{13.22}$$

Asset markets are assumed to clear at all times. Equation (13.20) describes this assumption for the money market, given the constant interest rate. Bonds and equities are perfect substitutes, and we assume perfect share price expectations; these assumptions are captured by Equation (13.21) that determines the evolution of the price of shares. In the absence of wealth effects, however, share price expectations and the evolution of share prices have no influence on the rest of the model; Equation (13.21) is given for completeness. Given the perfect substitutability between equities and bonds and Walras' Law of Stocks, the clearing of the money market implies that the bond and equity market are then cleared as well. With perfect substitutability, the stock demands B^d and E^d are not unique when the expected returns are equal; asset holders are happy with any portfolio composition and the composition of demand for bonds and stocks simply accommodates to the composition of supply.

Note that this discussion concerns secondary asset markets (existing assets) and does not yet guarantee that the new asset demand generated by the flow of savings of households matches with the supply of new bonds issued by the government and the issue of new equities by firms on the primary markets which are separated from secondary ones in continuous time, see Sargent (1987, Chapter II.7) on this matter. Stock market equilibria are thus independent from the extent of the savings decision of households in this continuous time framework. Furthermore, due to the interest rate peg of the central bank, the stock demand for money of households is always fulfilled by the Central Bank and the growth in money supply therefore just given by the sum of current output growth and inflation. In Equation (13.22), it is finally assumed that wealth owners accept the new bond issue by the government for the current period, reallocating them only in the 'next period' by readjusting their portfolios then in view of a changed situation. It is easy to check by means of the saving relationships (budget equations) that the assumed (*ex post*) consistency between flow supplies and flow demands of money and bonds implies the consistency of the flow supply and demand for equities. These implied flow equalities only represent a consistency condition, implied by the budget constraints for households, firms and the government, but do not explain the forces that lead to their fulfillment on the primary or flow markets for financial assets. The working of these primary markets is not explained in the present approach to KMGS growth. Since flows are 'small' as compared to stocks, however, one may assume for simplicity that the rates of return on financial assets that clear the stock market are sufficient to clear the flow markets as well.

As financial markets are formulated here they do not matter at all for the evolution of the economy. Our formulations however show how they relate to the original KMG approach and its portfolio extension in Köper and Flaschel (2000) and how their working may be added to future extensions of the KMGS dynamics of this paper.

The goods-market adjustments are described by the following six equations:

6. Disequilibrium situation (goods-market adjustments):

$$S = S_p + S_g + S_f = I + \dot{N} \tag{13.23}$$

$$Y^d = C + I + G \tag{13.24}$$

$$N^d = \alpha_{n^d} Y^e, \quad \mathscr{I} = aN^d + \beta_n(N^d - N) \tag{13.25}$$

$$Y = Y^e + \mathscr{I} \tag{13.26}$$

$$\dot{Y}^e = aY^e + \beta_{y^e}(Y^d - Y^e) \tag{13.27}$$

$$\dot{N} = Y - Y^d = S - I \tag{13.28}$$

Equation (13.23) describes the *ex post* identity between saving S and investment I^a in a closed economy. Equation (13.24) defines aggregate demand Y^d, which is never constrained in the present model. In Equation (13.25), desired inventories N^d are assumed to be a constant proportion of expected sales Y^e. Intended inventory investment $\mathscr{I}$ is determined on this basis via the adjustment speed β_n multiplied by the current gap between intended and actual inventories $(N^d - N)$ and augmented by a growth term to capture the fact that this inventory adjustment rule is operating in a growing economy. Firms' output Y in Equation (13.26) is the sum of expected sales and planned inventory adjustments. Sales expectations are formed in a purely adaptive way, again augmented by a growth trend as shown by Equation (13.27). The trend terms in both expected sales and planned inventory dynamics are both given by a, the trend term in investment behavior and not by the natural rate of growth n as in the standard KMG model and the neoclassical approach to economic growth. Finally, in Equation (13.28), actual inventory changes are given by the discrepancy between output Y and actual sales Y^d, or alternatively, by the difference between total savings S and fixed business investment I.

The disequilibrium adjustment in the goods market is central for the dynamics of the economy. It is our conjecture that the implications of the disequilibrium formulation are different than those of a static IS equilibrium treatment of the goods market; in future research we shall try to prove that the use of an algebraic condition (IS equilibrium) in the place of the sluggish adjustment described by differential equations leads to quite different types of behavior and that the IS equilibrium situation cannot be conceived as the continuous limit of the quantity dynamics.

The final module of the model describes the wage–price spiral:

7. Wage–Price sector (adjustment equations):

$$\hat{w} = \beta_{w_1}(e - \bar{e}) - \beta_{w_2}(\omega - \bar{\omega}) + \kappa_w \hat{p} + (1 - \kappa_w)\hat{p}^c \tag{13.29}$$

$$\hat{p} = \beta_{p_1}(u - \bar{u}) + \beta_{p_2}(\omega - \bar{\omega}) + \kappa_p \hat{w} + (1 - \kappa_p)\hat{p}^c \tag{13.30}$$

$$\dot{\hat{p}}^c = \beta_{p^c}(\hat{p} - \hat{p}^c), \pi^c = \hat{p}^c. \tag{13.31}$$

These adjustment equations are based on symmetric assumptions concerning the causes of wage- and price-inflation. Our specification follows Rose (1967, 1990) and assumes that two Phillips curves (PCs) describe wage and price dynamics separately. The two equations include measures of demand pressure $e - \bar{e}$ and $u - \bar{u}$, in the markets for labor and for goods, respectively, and a feedback effect from the level of the real wage ω (or the wage share) as obtained in Blanchard and Katz (1999) and Chiarella *et al.* (2005). Both PCs are expectations augmented to allow for expected changes in cost. We assume a weighted average of myopic perfect foresight and a backward looking measure of the prevailing inflationary climate, symbolized by $\hat{p}^c$. The inflationary climate measure of expected inflation in the medium term is determined by adaptive expectations in Equation (13.31). The wage PC uses a weighted average of the current price inflation $\hat{p}$ and a longer-run concept of price inflation, $\hat{p}^c$, based on past observations. Similarly, cost pressure perceived by firms is given as a weighted average of the current wage inflation $\hat{w}$ and this measure of the inflationary climate in which the economy is operating. Thus, we have two PCs with very similar building blocks; the associated wage–price dynamics or wage–price spirals are discussed and estimated for the US Economy in Flaschel and Krolzig (2004).

The inflationary climate does not matter for the evolution of the real wage $\omega = w/p$ or, due to our assumption of no productivity growth, for the wage share ω/x. The law of motion of the wage share is given by:

$$\hat{\omega} = \kappa[(1 - \kappa_p)(\beta_{w_1}(e - \bar{e}) - \beta_{w_2}(\omega - \bar{\omega}))$$
$$- (1 - \kappa_w)(\beta_{p_1}(u - \bar{u}) + \beta_{p_2}(\omega - \bar{\omega}))] \tag{13.32}$$

where $\kappa = 1/(1 - \kappa_w \kappa_p)$.[11] As a special case (if $\beta_{w_1} = 0$ holds) we get (a linearized version of) the law of motion for the profit share π used in Flaschel and Skott (2006) to capture Steindl's views on the determination of the markup. The above more general formula produces a wage–price spiral in which demand pressures

---

[11] This result follows from the equivalent representation of the two PCs, 13.29 and 13.30,

$$\hat{w} - \hat{p}^c = \beta_{w_1}(\cdot) - \beta_{w_2}(\cdot) + \kappa_w(\hat{p} - \hat{p}^c) \tag{13.33}$$

$$\hat{p} - \hat{p}^c = \beta_{p_1}(\cdot) + \beta_{p_2}(\cdot) + \kappa_p(\hat{w} - \hat{p}^c) \tag{13.34}$$

by solving for the variables $\hat{w} - \hat{p}^c$ and $\hat{p} - \hat{p}^c$.

in the labor market also play a part in the law of motion for the real wage $\omega = w/p$.[12]

It should be noted perhaps that our specification of wage and price formation implies two cross-market or reduced-form wage and price PCs given by

$$\hat{w} = \kappa[\beta_{w_1}(\cdot) - \beta_{w_2}(\cdot) + \kappa_w(\beta_{p_1}(\cdot) + \beta_{p_2}(\cdot))] + \hat{p}^c \tag{13.35}$$

$$\hat{p} = \kappa[\beta_{p_1}(\cdot) + \beta_{p_2}(\cdot) + \kappa_p(\beta_{w_1}(\cdot) - \beta_{w_2}(\cdot))] + \hat{p}^c \tag{13.36}$$

These equations generalize the conventional view of a single-market price PC with only one measure of demand pressure, the one in the labor market. The reduced-form PCs synthesize the influence of the inflationary climate and demand pressures from labor and goods markets in a symmetric and general way.

Note, finally, that the restrictions $\beta_{w_1}, \beta_{w_2}, \beta_{p_2} = 0, \kappa_w = 1$ imply the following reduced-form PC:

$$\hat{p} = \beta_{p_1}(u - \bar{u})/(1 - \kappa_p) + \hat{p}^c$$

This special case of the wage–price spiral removes the role of income distribution from the dynamics, since real wages are held constant in this situation. The equation differs from a monetarist PC in that it is demand pressure on the market for goods that matters and that the expectations augmented part is captured by an adaptive climate expression.

This ends the description of the extensive form of our KMGS dynamics, its behavioral rules and the budget equations within which this behavior takes place.

3. The KMGS dynamics and their feedback structures

Combining the equations of module 6 of the model, the actual output–capital ratio is determined by

$$y = (1 + a\alpha_{n^d})y^e + \beta_n(\alpha_{n^d}y^e - v), \quad y^e = Y^e/K, \quad v = N/K \tag{13.37}$$

Aggregate demand per unit of capital is (using the consumption, investment and government expenditure functions of the model):

$$y^d = (1 - s_w)(\omega y/x - t_w) + (1 - s_p)(1 - s_f)(\rho^e - t_p) + a + i(u - \bar{u}) + g$$
$$= (1 - s_p)(1 - s_f)y^e + (s_p(1 - s_f) + s_f - s_w)\omega y/x + a + iu + \gamma \tag{13.38}$$

---

[12] Laws of motion for the profit share π of the type $\dot{\pi} = g(u, \pi, e)$ (with partial derivative that are positive, negative and negative, respectively) can be considered – using simple mathematical substitutions – as nonlinear extensions of the dynamics for the real wage in Equation (13.32); see also Flaschel and Skott (2006) in this regard.

where γ collects the given magnitudes in this aggregate demand expression. Using (13.1), (13.7), (13.8), the equations for the expected rate of profit ρ^e, the rate of employment e and the rate of capacity utilization u are

$$\rho^e = y^e - \omega y/x, \quad e = y/(xl) \quad (= L^d/L = xL^d/xL), \quad u = y/y^p$$

We use the following five state variables: sales expectations $y^e = Y^e/K$ and inventories $v = N/K$ per unit of capital (for the short run dynamics), trend growth a as part of investment behavior, the factor ratio l (in place of the rate of employment),[13] and the real wage ω. Unlike in the original KMG model, real balances per unit of capital $m = M/(pK)$ and the inflationary climate $\hat{p}^c$ no longer appear, and the so-called Keynes and Mundell-effects are excluded.

Taken together, the laws of motion of the KMGS dynamics read:

$$\dot{y}^e = \beta_{y^e}(y^d - y^e) - i(u - \bar{u})y^e, \tag{13.39}$$

the law of motion for sales expectations,

$$\dot{v} = y - y^d - (i(u - \bar{u}) + a)v, \tag{13.40}$$

the law of motion for inventories,

$$\hat{a} = \alpha_1(u - \bar{u}) - \alpha_2(\omega - \bar{\omega}) - \alpha_3(e - \bar{e}), \tag{13.41}$$

the trend growth dynamics,

$$\hat{l} = -i(u - \bar{u}) \quad \text{[or stationary and given by} \quad l \equiv l_o, \quad \text{if } n = I/K], \tag{13.42}$$

the evolution of the full employment labor intensity,

$$\hat{\omega} = \kappa[(1 - \kappa_p)(\beta_{w_1}(e - \bar{e}) - \beta_{w_2}(\omega - \bar{\omega})) - (1 - \kappa_w)(\beta_{p_1}(u - \bar{u}) + \beta_{p_2}(\omega - \bar{\omega}))], \tag{13.43}$$

the law of motion for real wages.

We assume that

$$0 \leqslant s_w < s_p \leqslant 1, \ 0 \leqslant s_f \leqslant 1, \quad \text{and} \quad 0 < \kappa_w, \kappa_p < 1.$$

Inserting the algebraic equations of this section into these laws of motion one obtains a nonlinear autonomous 5D system of differential equations. The properties of this system will be examined in the remainder of this paper. First, however, we briefly consider the important feedback chains.

The original KMG model contained four important feedback chains. The KMGS model excludes two of these chains but introduces two new feedback chains: a dynamic Harrodian accelerator mechanism and a Kalecki–Steindl reserve army mechanism. The feedback chains interact with each other in the full 5D dynamics, and different feedback mechanisms can become dominant, depending on parameter values.

---

[13] The employment rate $e = y/(lx)$ might seem a more obvious choice of state variable. The evolution of l, however, follows a particularly simple law of motion.

(1) *The Keynes and Mundell effects.* Neither the stabilizing Keynes effect nor the destabilizing Mundell effect is present in the KMGS model. The reason is simple: we have excluded any influence of the real rate of interest on investment and consumption and wealth effects on consumption are absent too. Thus, although price inflation appears implicity in the real wage dynamics, it does not affect aggregate demand.

(2) *A Metzler type inventory accelerator mechanism.* The Metzlerian inventory adjustment process defines two laws of motion; Equations (13.27) and (13.28). The crucial parameters in these adjustment equations are the adjustment speeds, β_{y^e} and β_n, of sales expectations and of intended inventory, respectively.

From the static Equation (13.37) it follows that output y depends positively on expected sales y^e and this effect is stronger the higher the speed of adjustment β_n of planned inventories. Using the static equation for y^d it then follows that the time rate of change of expected sales depends positively on the level of expected sales when the parameter β_n is chosen sufficiently large. Flexible adjustment of inventories coupled with a high speed of adjustment of sales expectations may therefore be expected to jeopardize economic stability through a refined multiplier–accelerator mechanism.

(3) *A Harrod-type investment accelerator mechanism.* This mechanism works through the parameters i and α_1 in the investment equations. Increased capacity utilization leads to higher investment (both directly and via the gradual changes in the trend of accumulation) and an increase in aggregate demand. As a result, sales expectations increase and produce a further rise in output and capacity utilization. Thus a dynamic Harrodian multiplier–accelerator process interacts with distribution effects and the Metzlerian inventory adjustment process. Trend investment can be seen as a utilization climate – like the inflation climate – or as slowly evolving 'animal spirits,' and it may be reasonable to assume that the direct effect on current investment is stronger than the indirect effect on trend investment.

(4) *A Goodwin/Rose-type reserve army mechanism.* The law of motion for the real wage, Equation (13.32), implies that the level of the real wage exerts a directly stabilizing influence via the Blanchard and Katz (1999) error correction expressions following β_{w_2} and β_{p_2}. But there are additional Goodwin–Rose mechanisms. The specification of aggregate demand in the model implies that the short-term effect of real wages on goods demand is positive (via workers' consumption). Hence, real wages will be further stabilizing through the expressions following β_{w_1} and β_{p_1} if price flexibility with respect to demand pressure on the market for goods is sufficiently high and wage flexibility with respect to demand pressure on the market for labor is sufficiently low (the delayed negative effect of real wages on investment behavior will of course just establish the opposite conclusions). Flaschel and Krolzig (2004) suggest that a situation where wage flexibility dominates price flexibility applies for the US economy in the period following World War II

and discuss the implied adverse real wage adjustments or adverse Rose effects in detail.[14]

This analysis suggests that if the rates e and u are positively correlated, income distribution may adjust in a stable manner when prices are more flexible than wages, while it may exhibit centrifugal forces in the opposite case. Investment demand will play a role in the dynamics as well, but it does so in a delayed form via the adjustment of the trend term a in the investment function. When considering the Jacobian of the dynamical system, the effects via consumption will appear in a clearly visible form in their minors of order 2, while the effects via investment on income distribution will be more roundabout.

(5) *A Kalecki/Steindl type reserve army mechanism (the conflict about full employment)*. Represented by the parameter α_3 we assume that 'bosses dislike high employment.' Increases in the rate employment e thus exert downward pressure on the a-component in the investment demand function, leading to reduced economic activity and providing a check to further increases in the rate of employment.

The feedback channels 2–5 are summarized in Table 13.1.[15]

Their interaction determines the stability of the interior steady-state position of the model. Based on our partial analysis of the feedback channels, we expect that wage flexibility (as measured by β_{w_1}), fast inventory adjustment and fast investment trend adjustment will be destabilizing, while price flexibility (as measured by β_{p_1}) will be stabilizing if the opposite Rose effect is tamed by assuming a low parameter α_2. Hence, the manipulation of the parameters β_{p_1} and α_3 may help to create local stability and/or to ensure the boundedness and economic viability of the trajectories in the case of local instability.

4. A simplified system

We are now in a position to formulate a baseline theorem on local asymptotic stability, instability and limit cycle behavior. Our approach to this theorem is based on 'feedback-guided stability analysis.' This methodology for the analysis of the high-dimensional dynamic models has been used extensively in Asada *et al.* (2003) and Chiarella *et al.* (2005). In the present case, the stability analysis again confirms expectations derived from the analysis of the constituent parts of the system.

---

[14] These effects are closely related to the presence of 'Robinsonian instability' as defined by Marglin and Bhaduri (1990); see also Flaschel and Skott (2006).

[15] There is also a tendency towards unstable capital accumulation, described by the feedback chain:
$l \overset{-}{\longmapsto} e \overset{+}{\longmapsto} \hat{\omega} \overset{+}{\longmapsto} \hat{u} \longmapsto l.$

Table 13.1.   The feedback structure of the KMGS model

1. Metzlerian accelerator mechanism:	$y^e \xrightarrow{+} y_l \xrightarrow{+} y^d \xrightarrow{+} y^e$
2. Harrodian accelerator mechanism:	$u_l \xrightarrow{+} \dot{a}_l \xrightarrow{+} \dot{u}$
3. Goodwin/Rose reserve army mechanism:	$\omega_l \xrightarrow{+:C(-:l)} u, e_l \xrightarrow{+/-} \dot{\omega}$
4. Kalecki/Steindl reserve army mechanism:	$e_l \xrightarrow{-} \dot{a}_l \xrightarrow{+} \dot{u}_l \xrightarrow{+} \dot{e}$

This section gives an intuitive account of the KMGS dynamics in the special case $s_w = 0, s_f = 0$; the general case is investigated rigorously in the Appendix A. In the special case, the static variables are given by:

$$y = (1 + a\alpha_{n^d})y^e + \beta_n(\alpha_{n^d}y^e - v)$$
$$y^d = \omega y/x - t_w + (1 - s_p)(\rho^e - t_p) + a + i(u - \bar{u}) + g$$
$$= (1 - s_p)y^e + s_p\omega y/x + a + iu + const.$$

while the laws of motion and the equations for the expected rate of profit ρ^e, the rate of employment e and the rate of capacity utilization u remain unchanged $(\rho^e = y^e - \omega y/x, e = y/(xl), u = y/y^p)$.

Theorem I. *Assume that labor supply growth fulfills $n = a$. The following statements then hold with respect to the 5D dynamical system* (16.7)–(16.12):

1. There exists a unique interior steady state of the model with $\omega_o = \bar{\omega}, e_o = \bar{e}, u_o = \bar{u}$. Moreover, this steady state is characterized by $y_o = \bar{u}y^p, y_o^d = y_o^e = y_o/(1 + a_o\alpha_{n^d}), v_o = \alpha_{n^d}y_o,$ and $l_o = y_o/(x\bar{e})$. Finally, the steady trend component in investment behavior a_o is the uniquely determined positive solution of the following quadratic equation, characterizing steady-state goods market equilibrium (if the left-hand side is larger than the right-hand side at $a_o = 0$):[16]

$$s_p y_o/(1 + a_o\alpha_{n^d}) = s_p\omega_o y_o/x - t_w - (1 - s_p)t_p + a_o + g$$

This equation implies that the steady-state value a_o of the term a depends positively on capitalists' savings rate, labor and capital productivity and the taxation rates, while it depends negatively on the real wage and the government expenditure ratio g (assuming in the case of s_p, y_o that the parameter α_{n^d} is chosen sufficiently close to zero).

2. The determinant of the Jacobian of the 5D dynamics at this steady state is always negative.

---

[16] In the opposite case we will have two negative roots, the larger of which may be used to discuss the case of an economy that is contracting in the steady state.

3. *Assume that the parameters β_{w_1}, α_2 and β_n are chosen sufficiently small and the parameters α_3 and β_{p_1} sufficiently large. Then: the steady state of the 5D dynamical system is locally asymptotically stable.*

4. *On the other hand, if any one of the parameters β_{w_1}, α_2 and β_n become sufficiently large (the latter for β_{y^e} sufficiently large), then the equilibrium is locally repelling and the system undergoes a Hopf bifurcation at an intermediate value of these parameters. In general, stable or unstable limit cycles are then generated close to the bifurcation value.*

Remark. The theorem says that increasing β_{p_1} and α_3 is good for economic stability, while α_1 and α_2 implement feedback chains (for quantity and real wage adjustment) that imply accelerating subdynamics and endanger the stability of the whole system. Note also that the investment functions (and $n = a$) enforce the steady-state value $\bar{u}$ of u, while the steady-state values of ω and e are jointly determined by the wage–price spiral and the accumulation trend function. The steady-state value of a finally follows from the steady-state goods-market equilibrium condition. We conjecture that the steady state will be locally unstable under reasonable assumptions on the parameters of the model, but that an increasing parameter α_3 may bound the dynamics far off the steady state (as will be shown below by way of a numerical example).

Sketch of Proof. 1. It is easy to show that the steady state value of the variable a is determined in the assumed situation by a quadratic function of the following type:

$$a^2 + \text{const}_1\, a - \text{const}_2 = 0, \quad \text{const}_1, \text{const}_2 > 0.$$

This quadratic function has exactly one positive and one negative real solution, as is obvious from the sign of its value at $a = 0$. Note that the unique positive solution of the equation can also be shown to exist by arguing that the left-hand side in its original presentation is a set of two hyperbola in a_o and the right-hand side a 45° line. These two curves intersect in the positive quadrant if and only if the 45° line starts below the intersection of the right-hand hyperbola on the vertical axis. The comparative statics then easily follow from the displacements of the two curves when parameters change.

2. The 5D determinant of the Jacobian of the dynamics at the steady state is easily computed by exploiting (removing) the many linear dependencies that exist in this Jacobian (evaluated at the steady state). This procedure can be applied informally directly on the level of the laws of motion by just removing step-by-step the reappearing expression from them. So for example, the law of motion for the ratio l can be used to remove the effect of capacity utilization from all other laws of motion, of course only in view of the objective of our analysis, i.e., without causing a change in the sign of the determinant of the then established Jacobian (which is thereby altered in their structure considerably). Next the remaining terms in the law of motion for a and ω, i.e., the influence of e, ω on these state variables, can be adjusted in such a way, again satisfying our

objective to get a new determinant that has the same sign as before, that only the influence of ω remains in the $\hat{\omega}$ equation and the influence of e in the a equation, which again restructures the newly obtained Jacobian considerably (without change in sign). The influence of ω where it is still present in the other laws of motion can now be suppressed without change in the sign of the considered determinants, and so on. In this way one finally arrives at the following system of differential equations that have been radically simplified and thus have not much in common with the original system, up to the fact that the sign of the determinant of the Jacobian evaluated at the steady state has not been changed through all the manipulations of the laws of motion we have considered:

$$\dot{y}^e = + \text{const } a$$
$$\dot{v} = - \text{const } v$$
$$\hat{a} = - \text{const } l$$
$$\hat{l} = - \text{const } y^e$$
$$\hat{\omega} = - \text{const } \omega$$

The determinant of these reduced dynamics is easily shown to be always negative.

3. Based on our partial knowledge of the working of the feedback channels of the 5D dynamics, we choose an independent 4D subsystem of the full 5D dynamics by setting the parameters β_{w_1}, β_n equal to zero:

$$\hat{\omega} = \kappa[-(1 - \kappa_p)\beta_{w_2}(\omega - \bar{\omega}) - (1 - \kappa_w)(\beta_{p_1}(u - \bar{u}) + \beta_{p_2}(\omega - \bar{\omega}))]$$
$$\dot{y}^e = \beta_{y^e}(y^d - y^e) - i(u - \bar{u})y^e$$
$$\hat{a} = \alpha_1(u - \bar{u}) - \alpha_2(\omega - \bar{\omega}) - \alpha_3(y/(xl) - \bar{e})$$
$$\hat{l} = - i(u - \bar{u})$$

Under the stated conditions on the parameters α_2, α_3 and β_{p_1} (which exclude Harrodian instability and Rose-type adverse real wage adjustment) one can show that the steady state is locally asymptotically stable, i.e., that the coefficients $a_i, i = 1, \ldots, 4$, of the Routh–Hurwitz polynomial (the characteristic polynomial of the considered Jacobian matrix) satisfies the conditions:

$$a_1 > 0, a_2 > 0, a_3 > 0, a_4 > 0, a_1 a_2 - a_3 > 0, (a_1 a_2 - a_3)a_3 - a_1^2 a_4 > 0$$

This result is obtained by exploiting again the many linear dependencies in the submatrices of the considered Jacobian (evaluated at the steady state) and by making use of the simple form of the aggregate demand function in Theorem I.

Since the full determinant is positive, we know from the continuity properties of eigen-values that small variations of the parameters β_{w_1} and β_n away from zero to positive values will preserve the negative real parts of the 4D subsystem, but push the remaining eigen-value from zero (since the determinant was zero beforehand) towards a negative value, since the determinant of the Jacobian at the steady state of the enlarged dynamics has been shown to be negative and is the product of the five eigen-values (four of which have already negative real parts) of the full dynamics.

4. Finally, since the determinant of the full Jacobian is always nonzero, loss of stability can only occur by way of (in general nondegenerate) Hopf bifurcations (where eigenvalues cross the imaginary axis with a positive speed). To complete the proof, it remains to be shown that the system loses its stability if the parameters considered in assertion 4 of the theorem become sufficiently large. This is shown in the case of the wage adjustment speed in the Appendix A of this paper. ∎

5. The general 5D KMGS accumulation dynamics

In the general version of the model the static variables are given by:

$$y = (1 + n\alpha_{n^d})y^e + \beta_n(\alpha_{n^d}y^e - v) \tag{13.44}$$

$$y^d = (1 - s_w)(\omega y/x - t_w) + (1 - s_p)(1 - s_f)(\rho^e - t_p) + a + i(u - \bar{u}) + g \tag{13.45}$$

The laws of motion and the equations for ρ^e, e and u are again unchanged.

Theorem II. *Assume that n is given by a, that $\alpha_1/y^p < \alpha_3/(xl_o)$ holds and that the parameters α_{n^d}, i, β_{w_1}, β_n and α_2 are all chosen sufficiently small. Then:*

1. There exists a unique interior steady state of the model with $\omega_o = \bar{\omega}, e_o = \bar{e}, u_o = \bar{u}$. Moreover, this steady state is characterized by $y_o = \bar{u}y^p, y_o^d = y_o^e = y_o/(1 + n\alpha_{n^d})$, $v_o = \alpha_{n^d}y_o^e$ and $l_o = y_o/(x\bar{e})$.

2. If $(1 - (1 - s_p)(1 - s_f))y_o/(1 + a_o\alpha_{n^d}) > (1 - s_w)(\omega_o y_o/x - t_w) - (1 - s_p)$ $((1 - s_f)\omega_o y_o/x + t_p) + a_o + g$ for $\alpha_0 = 0$, the steady-state component in investment behavior a_o is the uniquely determined positive solution of the following equation, characterizing steady-state goods-market equilibrium:

$$(1 - (1 - s_p)(1 - s_f))y_o/(1 + a_o\alpha_{n^d})$$
$$= (1 - s_w)(\omega_o y_o/x - t_w) - (1 - s_p)((1 - s_f)\omega_o y_o/x + t_p) + a_o + g.$$

3. The steady-state solution of the extended dynamics again fulfills the stability assertions 2–4 made in Theorem I in the preceding section.

Proof. The proof of this theorem is provided in the Appendix A of this paper.

Note that the last equation is again a quadratic equation to be solved for the positive value of a_o and that its solution must be used to determine y_o^e and $\rho_o^e = y_o^e - \omega_o y_o/x$. Note also that a unique positive solution for a_o under the stated condition will always exist, since the left-hand side is again composed of two hyperbolas in a_o and the right-hand side a 45° line in this variable (which starts below the intersection of the right-hand hyperbola with the vertical axis under the assumed circumstances). Note finally however that a_o will not be positive otherwise, that is the stated condition is also a necessary one for positive steady growth. The dynamics are well defined from the economic perspective as long as y^e, y^d and v stay positive.

Though intrinsically nonlinear, the above 5D growth dynamics are generally too weakly nonlinear to guarantee the boundedness of trajectories when the steady state is locally unstable. Indeed, the eigenvalue diagrams shown in Figure 13.1 (and also simple simulation runs of the dynamics not shown) by and large suggest that destabilizing forces can easily become very strong.[17] When this happens, the viability of the dynamics is quickly lost as the motions then violate economic boundary conditions or even lead to a sudden breakdown of the economy. The eigenvalue diagrams also illustrate the feedback mechanisms discussed in the preceding section and the partial stabilizing or destabilizing reaction patterns they imply. Top-left in Figure 13.1, for example, we see how the maximum real part of eigenvalues behaves when the parameter α_3, characterizing the strength of the Steindlian reserve army mechanism, is increased (all other parameters held constant). We see that the system is unstable if this influence is totally neglected, but is rapidly undergoing a Hopf bifurcation towards stability as this parameter is increased. For the given baseline set of parameter values, moreover, a_3 is the only parameter for which a sufficient increase is capable of enforcing local asymptotic stability.

Price flexibility with respect to demand pressure and the Blanchard and Katz (1999) error correction mechanism in the wage and price PC reduce the explosiveness of the dynamics when increased, but cannot – given the other benchmark parameters – enforce the local asymptotic stability over the ranges shown in Figure 13.1 (indeed, if increased beyond a certain point, a further increase in price flexibility may become destabilizing again, via effects on investment behavior as compared to the wage-led situation in consumption demand). As expected from our analysis of the adjustment processes, we see increasing instability if the parameters β_n (β_{y^e}), or α_1 are increased. In the numerical example we also find that an increase in α_2, characterizing the negative influence of real wages on trend accumulation, contributes to instability because an increase in this parameter can make the economy profit-led in the medium-run. Although this effect is working with a delay, it may give price flexibility a destabilizing role if it becomes sufficiently pronounced. Finally, wage flexibility with respect to demand pressure on the market for goods is – as expected – destabilizing.

---

[17] The parameters used in these eigenvalue calculations are $(s_w, t_w, s_f = 0)$: $\beta_{w_{1,2}} = 0.2, 0.2$, $\beta_{p_{1,2}} = 0.2, 0.2$, $\alpha_1 = 0.1$ $\alpha_2 = 0.1$, $\alpha_3 = 0.5$, $i = 0.2$, $\alpha_{n^d} = 0.1$, $\beta_n = 0.1$, $\beta_{y^e} = 0.5$, $\kappa_{w,p} = 0.5, 0.5$, $y^p = 1$, $x = 2$, $s_p = 0.8$, $t_p = 0.2$, $g = 0.2$, $\bar{e}, \bar{u} = 1$ and $\bar{\omega} = 1$. At this baseline parameter set the steady state is not locally asymptotically stable (otherwise all eigenvalue calculations would exhibit sections with negative values), i.e., the eigenvalue plots in Figure 13.1 test which parameters may enforce local asymptotic stability and which one cannot or even make the situation worse.

Figure 13.1.   Eigenvalue diagrams (maximum real part) for selected parameters of the model

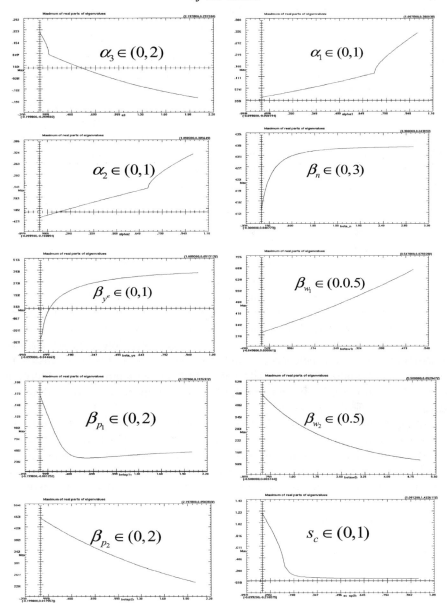

Overall, the example shows that most of the parameters that could be expected to enforce asymptotic stability may fail to establish this aim. The exception is the Metzlerian process as characterized by β_{y^e} and the parameter α_2 where local asymptotic stability is obtained when these adjustment speeds are chosen sufficiently small. Simple phase plot simulations (not shown) also suggest rapidly increasing amplitudes in the observed fluctuations that lead to the violation of economic nonnegativity constraints even for small deviations of the parameters from the Hopf Bifurcation point where the system loses its local asymptotic stability. Thus, extrinsic or behavioral nonlinearities may have to be added in order to ensure boundedness of the trajectories over longer time periods. In this respect increases in the value of α_3 may be the decisive mechanism to provide boundedness when the economy departs significantly from its steady-state position.

In Figure 13.2, we have therefore added to the dynamics a nonlinearity with respect to the term $\alpha_3(e - \bar{e})$ in the accumulation function. We now assume that α_3 is an increasing function of e of the form $\alpha_3(e) = \bar{\alpha}_3 e^b, b > 1$ to the right of the steady-state level $\bar{e} = 1,$[18] which is not necessarily a strong nonlinearity, depending on the choice of the parameter b. Thus, the value of α_3 now increases as the employment rate approaches the full employment ceiling (no longer explicitly specified), while to the left of the steady state $\alpha_3 = \bar{\alpha}_3$ is constant. This formulation captures the Kaleckian idea that 'bosses do not like full employment' in a simple way. We conjecture that this behavioral nonlinearity is sufficient to tame the strongly explosive nature of the 5D dynamics if the parameter b is chosen sufficiently large. Figure 13.2 shows that this is indeed the case. Note that the model tends to produce only long-phased cyclical fluctuations. This is to be expected since all parameters are kept time-invariant and since the stabilizing nonlinearity only affects the slow moving trend term in the accumulation function, and because the Metzlerian dynamics is weak in the considered numerical example.

The diagrams on the left-hand side of Figure 13.2 show the projection into the a, ω-plane of the attractor generated by the simulations of the KMGS dynamics. Top-left we employ the function $0.1e^5$ to the right of the steady-state rate of employment 1. In the middle we have changed the parameter b to the value 14, and the diagram at the bottom left is based on $\alpha_3 = 0.43e^7$. The diagram shows that less tension around the steady state (case 3) produces a simple limit cycle. Stronger centrifugal forces around the steady state (case 2) require a much stronger nonlinearity in order to generate this result ($b = 20$), while a weak nonlinearity leads to complicated fluctuations around the steady state as shown in case 2. In case 1 finally we have decreased the slope of the nonlinearity even more. In this case the tension between local repellers and the global stabilizer

---

[18] In our numerical example we have renormalized for expositional simplicity the steady-state rate of employment such that $\bar{e} = 1$ is now the benchmark for accelerating wage inflation, see the preceding footnote.

Figure 13.2. **Bounded irregular dynamics through increasing strength of the employment effect on trend accumulation (parameters as before, except α_3 which is 0.1 *now at the steady state*)**

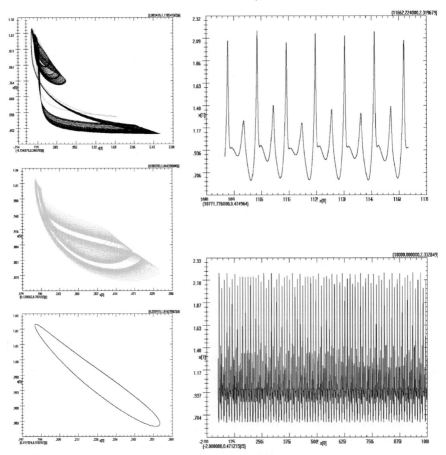

increases and leads to even more irregularity in the fluctuations, as is further exemplified for this first case on the right-hand side of Figure 13.2 (for a simulation run of 900 years and 10,000 years, respectively, with expected sales per unit of capital on the vertical axis). In this case we have a succession of smaller and larger cycles, each about 60 years long. These results are quite intuitive. Economies with a large $\bar{\alpha}_3$-value at the steady state need less nonlinearity in this function and are less volatile in amplitudes than economies with strong centrifugal forces around the steady state. These latter economies are tamed through stronger nonlinearities in the e^b function.

All phase plots share a common feature. They show a largely negative relationship between the trend growth of the capital stock and the real wage. The relation is almost linear when local instability is relatively weak but becomes nonlinear when the local tensions increase by a decrease of the parameter in front of the e^b function.

It should be noted, finally, that we did not impose supply bottlenecks with respect to labor or capital on the shown trajectories. Thus, implicitly it is assumed that capacity ceilings are absent, despite the large fluctuations in the sales–capital ratio. The additions of such ceilings and the treatment of quantity rationing and implied nonlinearities for wage and price adjustments are not the subject of this paper; see Chiarella *et al.* (2000, Chapter 5) on this matter.

6. *Conclusions*

In this paper we have combined elements of the Steindlian models of prosperity and stagnation in Flaschel and Skott with the KMG framework developed by Chiarella and Flaschel. The resulting KMGS model leads to significant modifications of the feedback structure of the KMG approach, and our analysis has focused on the real wage channel, two reserve army mechanisms and two quantity accelerator processes of Metzlerian and Harrodian type. The short-term Metzlerian mechanism, however, was not at the center of interest; it was but used for consistency reasons in the place of an incomplete, but simpler dynamic multiplier process.

We obtained local asymptotic stability of the steady state when – broadly speaking – inventory adjustments and the wage–price–spiral were sufficiently sluggish and the Kaleckian/Steindl reserve army mechanism operated with sufficient strength close to the steady state. These conditions, however, are unlikely to be met; the wage–price spiral may be destabilizing close to the steady state and the negative employment effect on trend investment may be weak. Thus, the more interesting case is one of local instability. We have shown by means of numerical simulations that in this case of local instability the economy may exhibit long waves of prosperity and stagnation if the Kalecki/Steindl reserve army mechanism becomes dominant close to full employment.

The KMGS model has obvious weaknesses and limitations in its present form. One problem concerns the specification of the growth of the labor supply. The endogeneity of this growth rate is justifiable, both theoretically and empirically, but our specification is less than satisfactory. It has the virtue of tractability and we have some confidence that many of the qualitative properties of the system may be robust to more satisfactory specifications. This conjecture, however, still has to be checked in future work. Another weakness of the model is the near-exclusive focus on real dynamics. The real-rate-of-interest channel, for instance, was excluded by assumption. The model should be extended to include greater interaction between real and financial variables. The financial side, moreover, should go beyond the simple Hicksian LM extension of the original KMG approach of Chiarella *et al.* This extension, again, is a topic for future research.

6.1. *Notation*

The KMGS model of this paper is based on the following macroeconomic notation:

A. Statically or dynamically endogenous variables:

Y	Output
Y^d	Aggregate demand $C + I + \delta K + G$
Y^e	Expected aggregate demand
N	Stock of inventories
N^d	Desired stock of inventories
$\mathscr{I}$	Desired inventory investment
L^d	Level of employment
C	Consumption
I	Fixed business investment
I^a	Actual total investment ($= I + \dot{N}$ total investment)
r	Nominal rate of interest (price of bonds $p_b = 1$)
p_e	Price of equities
$S_p = S_w + S_p$	Private savings
S_f	Savings of firms ($= Y_f$, the income of firms)
S_g	Government savings
$S = S_p + S_f + S_g$	Total savings
$T = T_w + T_p$	Real taxes
G	Government expenditure
ρ, ρ^e	Rate of profit, expected rate of profit
$e = L^d / L$	Rate of employment
Y^p	Potential output
$u = Y / Y^p$	Rate of capacity utilization
K	Capital stock
w	Nominal wages
p	Price level
$\hat{p}^c$	Inflationary climate (medium-run expectations)
M	Money supply (index d: demand)
L	Normal labor supply
$B = B_w + B_p$	Bonds (index d: demand)
E	Equities (index d: demand)
W	Real wealth
$\omega = w / p$	Real wage ($u = \omega / x$ the wage share)
$v = N / K$	Inventory–capital ratio
$y = Y / K$	Output–capital ratio
a	Trend or investment climate component in investment behavior
$n = a$	Endogenous natural growth

B. Parameters

$\bar{e}$	NAIRU-type normal utilization rate concept (of labor)
$\bar{u}$	NAIRU-type utilization rate of the capital stock concept (of capital)
i	Investment parameter
h_1	Money demand parameter
β_{w_1}, β_{w_2}	Wage adjustment parameters
β_{p_1}, β_{p_2}	Price adjustment parameters
β_{p^c}	Inflationary expectations adjustment parameter
α_{n^d}	Desired inventory output ratio
β_n	Inventory adjustment parameter
β_{y^e}	Demand expectations adjustment parameter
κ_w, κ_p	Weights for short- and medium-run inflation
κ	$= (1 - \kappa_w \kappa_p)^{-1}$
y^p	Potential output–capital ratio ($\neq y$, the actual ratio)
x	Output–labor ratio
g	Government expenditures per unit of capital
s_p	Savings-ratio (out of profits and interest)
s_w	Savings-ratio (out of wages and interest)
s_f	Savings-ratio of firms (out of expected profits)
b	Nonlinearity parameter in the numerical simulations
t_p	Tax to capital ratio of workers (net of interest)
t_w	Tax to capital ratio of asset holders (net of interest)
$\alpha_1, \alpha_2, \alpha_3$	Parameters of the trend investment function
$\bar{\omega}$	Target real wage of firms

C. Mathematical notation

$\dot{x}$	Time derivative of a variable x
$\hat{x}$	Growth rate of x
x', x_w	Total and partial derivatives
$x_o, etc.$	Steady state values
$y = Y/K, etc.$	Real variables in intensive form
$m = M/(pK), etc.$	Nominal variables in intensive form

References

Asada, T., C. Chiarella, P. Flaschel and R. Franke (2003), *Open Economy Macrodynamics. An Integrated Disequilibrium Approach*, Berlin: Springer-Verlag.

Asada, T. and H. Yoshida (2003), "Coefficient criterion for four-dimensional Hopf bifurcations: a complete mathematical characterization and applications to economic dynamics", *Chaos, Solitons and Fractals*, Vol. 18, pp. 525–536.

Blanchard, O. and X. Katz (1999), "Wage dynamics. Reconciling theory and evidence", *American Economic Review Papers and Proceedings*, Vol. 89, pp. 69–74.

Chiarella, C. and P. Flaschel (2000), *The Dynamics of Keynesian Monetary Growth: Macro Foundations*, Cambridge: Cambridge University Press.

Chiarella, C., P. Flaschel, G. Groh and W. Semmler (2000), *Disequilibrium, Growth and Labor Market Dynamics. Macro Perspectives*, Heidelberg: Springer-Verlag.

Chiarella, C., P. Flaschel and R. Franke (2005), *Foundations for a Disequilibrium Theory of the Business Cycle. Qualitative Analysis and Quantitative Assessment*, Cambridge: Cambridge University Press, to appear.

Flaschel, P. and H.-M. Krolzig (2004), "Wage and price Phillips curves. An empirical analysis of destabilizing wage–price spirals", Working Paper, Oxford University.

Flaschel, P. and P. Skott (2006), "Steindlian models of growth and stagnation", *Metroeconomica*, Vol. 57.

Kalecki, M. (1943), "Political aspects of full employment", Reprinted in: Kalecki, M. (1971), *Selected Essays on the Dynamics of the Capitalist Economy*, Cambridge: Cambridge University Press.

Köper, C. and P. Flaschel, (2000), "Real-financial interaction. A Keynes-Metzler-Goodwin portfolio approach", Working Paper, Bielefeld University.

Marglin, S.A. and A. Bhaduri (1990), "Profit squeeze and Keynesian theory", in: S.A. Marglin and J.B. Schor, editors, *The golden age of capitalism*, Oxford: Clarendon Press.

Rødseth, A. (2000), *Open Economy Macroeconomics*, Cambridge: Cambridge University Press.

Rose, H. (1967), "On the non-linear theory of the employment cycle", *Review of Economic Studies*, Vol. 34, pp. 153–173.

Rose, H. (1990), *Macroeconomic Dynamics*, Oxford: Basil Blackwell.

Sargent, T. (1987), *Macroeconomic Theory*, New York: Academic Press.

Skott, P. (1989a) *Conflict and effective Demand in Economic Growth*, Cambridge: Cambridge University Press.

Skott, P. (1989b), "Effective demand, class struggle and cyclical growth", *International Economics review*, Vol. 30, pp. 231–247.

Steindl, J. (1979), "Stagnation theory and stagnation policy", *Cambridge Journal of Economics*, Vol. 3, pp. 1–14.

A. Appendix

A.1. Proof of Theorem II

In this appendix we provide a rigoros and detailed proof of Theorem II considered in Section 5 of the paper. In accordance with the post-Keynesian or Kaleckian–Kaldorian macroeconomic tradition we start from the basic assumptions on differential saving habits.

Assumption 1. $0 \leq s_w < s_p \leq 1$, $0 \leq s_f \leq 1$. Under this assumption, we have

$$s_p(1 - s_f) + s_f - s_w = (s_p - s_w) + s_f(1 - s_p) > 0. \tag{A1}$$

In this case, Equations (13.44) and (13.45) in Section 5 give rise to:

$$y = (1 + a\alpha_{n^d})y^e + \beta_n(\alpha_{n^d}y^e - v) \equiv y(y^e, v, a); \tag{A2}$$
$$y_{y^e} = 1 + (a + \beta_n)\alpha_{n^d} > 0,$$
$$y_v = -\beta_n < 0,$$
$$y_a = \alpha_{n^d}y^e > 0$$
$$y^d = (1 - s_p)(1 - s_f)y^e + \{s_p(1 - s_f) + s_f - s_w\}\{\omega y(y^e, v, a)/x\} + a$$
$$\qquad + i\{y(y^e, v, a)/y^p - \bar{u}\} + \gamma \equiv y^d(y^e, v, a, \omega); \tag{A3}$$
$$y^d_{y^e} = (1 - s_p)(1 - s_f) + [\{s_p(1 - s_f) + s_f - s_w\}\omega/x + i/y^p]$$
$$\qquad \{1 + (a + \beta_n)\alpha_{n^d}\} > 0,$$
$$y^d_v = -[\{s_p(1 - s_f) + s_f - s_w\}\omega/x + i/y^p]\beta_n < 0,$$
$$y^d_a = 1 + [\{s_p(1 - s_f) + s_f - s_w\}\omega/x + i/y^p]\alpha_{n^d}y^e > 0,$$
$$y^d_\omega = \{s_p(1 - s_f) + s_f - s_w\}y(y^e, v, a)/x > 0$$

where $y_{y^e} = \partial y/\partial y^e$, $\quad y_v = \partial y/\partial v$ etc.

Substituting (A2) and (A3) into the equations (13.39)–(13.43) in the text, we obtain the following nonlinear 5D system of differential equations.

(i) $\dot{y}^e = \beta_{y^e}\{y^d(y^e, v, a, \omega) - y^e\} - i\{y(y^e, v, a)/y^p - \bar{u}\}y^e \equiv F_1(y^e, v, a, \omega)$

(ii) $\dot{v} = y(y^e, v, a) - y^e - [i\{y(y^e, v, a)/y^p - \bar{u}\} + a]v \equiv F_2(y^e, v, a)$

(iii) $\dot{a} = a[\alpha_1\{y(y^e, v, a)/y^p - \bar{u}\} - \alpha_2(\omega - \bar{\omega}) - \alpha_3\{y(y^e, v, a)/(xl) - \bar{e}\}],$
$$\qquad \equiv F_3(y^e, v, a, \omega, l)$$

(iv) $\dot{\omega} = \kappa\omega[(1 - \kappa_p)\{\beta_{w_1}(y(y^e, v, a)/(xl) - \bar{e}) - \beta_{w2}(\omega - \bar{\omega})\}$
$$\qquad - (1 - \kappa_w)\{\beta_{p1}(y(y^e, v, a)/y^p - \bar{u}) + \beta_{p2}(\omega - \bar{\omega})\}],$$
$$\qquad \equiv F_4(y^e, v, a, \omega, l)$$

(v) $\dot{l} = -li\{y(y^e, v, a)/y^p - \bar{u}\} \equiv F_5(y^e, v, a, l) \tag{A4}$

where $i \geqq 0$, and the case of $i = 0$ corresponds to the case of the degenerated 4D system with $l \equiv l_0$.

We can easily show that there exists a unique interior steady state that satisfies the following conditions (cf. also Theorem II in the text).

$$y^d(y^e, v, a, \omega) = y^e, \quad y(y^e, v, a)/y^p = \bar{u}, \quad y^e = y(y^e, v, a) + av, \omega = \bar{\omega},$$
$$y(y^e, v, a)/(xl) = \bar{e} \tag{A5}$$

Next, let us investigate the local stability of the equilibrium point (interior steady state) in the special case of $i = 0$. We can write the Jacobian matrix of the system, which is evaluated at the equilibrium point as follows:

$$J = \begin{bmatrix} F_{11} & F_{12} & F_{13} & F_{14} \\ F_{21} & F_{22} & F_{23} & 0 \\ F_{31} & F_{32} & F_{33} & F_{34} \\ F_{41} & F_{42} & F_{43} & F_{44} \end{bmatrix} \tag{A6}$$

where

$$F_{11} = \beta_{y^e}(y_{y^e}^d - 1)$$
$$= \beta_{y^e}[\{s_p(1 - s_f) + s_f\}\{(\bar{\omega}/x)(1 + (a_0 + \beta_n)\alpha_{n^d}) - 1\}$$
$$\quad - s_w(\bar{\omega}/x)\{1 + (a_0 + \beta_n)\alpha_{n^d}\}]$$
$$F_{12} = \beta_{y^e}y_v^d = -\beta_{y^e}\beta_n\{s_p(1 - s_f) + s_f - s_w\}(\bar{\omega}/x) < 0$$
$$F_{13} = \beta_{y^e}y_a^d = \beta_{y^d}[1 + \{(s_p(1 - s_f) + s_f - s_w)\bar{\omega}/x]\alpha_{n^d}y_0/(1 + a_0\alpha_{n^d}) > 0$$
$$F_{14} = \beta_{y^e}y_\omega^d = \beta_{y^e}\{s_p(1 - s_f) + s_f - s_w\}y_0/x > 0$$
$$F_{21} = y_{y^e} - 1 = (a_0 + \beta_n)\alpha_{n^d} > 0$$
$$F_{22} = y_v - a_0 = -(\beta_n + a_0) < 0$$
$$F_{23} = y_a - v = \alpha_{n^d}y_0\{1/(1 + a_0\alpha_{n^d}) - 1\} < 0$$
$$F_{31} = a_0\{\alpha_1/y^p - \alpha_3/xl_0\}\{1 + (a_0 + \beta_n)\alpha_{n^d}\}$$
$$F_{32} = -a_0\beta_n\{\alpha_1/y^p - \alpha_3/xl_0\}$$
$$F_{33} = a_0\{\alpha_1/y^p - \alpha_3/xl_0\}\alpha_{n^d}y_0/(1 + a_0\alpha_{n^d})$$
$$F_{34} = -a_0\alpha_2 < 0$$
$$F_{41} = \kappa\bar{\omega}\{(1 - \kappa_p)(\beta_{w_1}/xl_0) - (1 - \kappa_w)(\beta_{p1}/y^p)\}\{1 + (a_0 + \beta_n)\alpha_{n^d}\}$$
$$F_{42} = -\kappa\bar{\omega}\beta_n\{(1 - \kappa_p)(\beta_{w_1}/xl_0) - (1 - \kappa_w)(\beta_{p1}/y^p)\}$$
$$F_{43} = \kappa\bar{\omega}\{(1 - \kappa_p)(\beta_{w_1}/xl_0) - (1 - \kappa_w)(\beta_{p1}/y^p)\}\alpha_{n^d}y_0/(1 + a_0\alpha_{n^d})$$
$$F_{44} = -\kappa\bar{\omega}\{(1 - \kappa_p)\beta_{w2} + (1 - \kappa_w)\beta_{p2}\} < 0.$$

We furthermore have

$$\lim_{\alpha_{n^d}\to 0} F_{11} = \beta_{y^e}[\{s_p(1-s_f)+s_f\}\{\bar{\omega}/x-1\} - s_w(\bar{\omega}/x)<0 \tag{A7}$$

because $\bar{\omega}/x = \bar{\omega}L^d/Y$ is the equilibrium wage share, and it is less than one.

We now make the following additional assumptions.

Assumption 2. α_{n^d} is so small that we have $F_{11}<0$.

Assumption 3. The inequality $\alpha_1/y^p < \alpha_3/xl_0$ is satisfied.

Assumption 4. β_n, α_2, β_{w2}, and β_{p2} are sufficiently small.

Assumption 3 implies that α_3 is sufficiently large relative to α_1. It is easy to see that we have the following set of inequalities under Assumption 3.

$$F_{31}<0, \quad F_{32}>0, \quad F_{33}<0. \tag{A8}$$

We shall select the parameter β_{w_1} as bifurcation parameter. In this case, we have the following relationships.

$$F_{41} = F_{41}(\beta_{w_1}); \quad F_{41}(0)<0, \quad F'_{41}(\beta_{w_1}) = \text{constant}>0 \tag{A9}$$

$$F_{43} = F_{43}(\beta_{w_1}); \quad F_{43}(0)<0, \quad F'_{43}(\beta_{w_1}) = \text{constant}>0 \tag{A10}$$

Next, let us investigate the local stability/instability of the equilibrium point of this four-dimensional system. In the limiting case of $\beta_n = \alpha_2 = 0$, we have

$$F_{12} = F_{32} = F_{34} = F_{42} = 0. \tag{A11}$$

Under a set of conditions (A11), we can write the characteristic equation of the Jacobian matrix as follows.

$$\Delta(\lambda) \equiv |\lambda I - J| = \lambda^4 + b_1\lambda^3 + b_2\lambda^2 + b_3\lambda + b_4 = 0 \tag{A12}$$

where

$$b_1 = -\text{trace } J = \underset{(-)}{-F_{11}} \underset{(-)}{- F_{22}} \underset{(-)}{-F_{33}} \underset{(-)}{- F_{44}} >0 \tag{A13}$$

$b_2 = $ sum of all principal second-order minors of J

$$= \begin{vmatrix} F_{11} & 0 \\ F_{21} & F_{22} \end{vmatrix} + \begin{vmatrix} F_{11} & F_{13} \\ F_{31} & F_{33} \end{vmatrix} + \begin{vmatrix} F_{11} & F_{14} \\ F_{41}(\beta_{w_1}) & F_{44} \end{vmatrix}$$

$$+ \begin{vmatrix} F_{22} & F_{23} \\ 0 & F_{33} \end{vmatrix} + \begin{vmatrix} F_{22} & 0 \\ 0 & F_{44} \end{vmatrix} + \begin{vmatrix} F_{33} & 0 \\ F_{43}(\beta_{w_1}) & F_{44} \end{vmatrix}$$

$$= \underset{(-)\ (-)}{F_{11}F_{22}} + \underset{(-)\ (-)}{F_{11}F_{33}} - \underset{(+)\ (-)}{F_{13}F_{31}} + \underset{(-)\ (-)}{F_{11}F_{44}} - \underset{(+)\ \ (?)}{F_{14}F_{41}(\beta_{w_1})}$$

$$+ \underset{(-)\ (-)}{F_{22}F_{33}} + \underset{(-)\ (-)}{F_{22}F_{44}} + \underset{(-)\ (-)}{F_{33}F_{44}}$$

$$\equiv -A\beta_{w_1} + B; \quad A>0, \quad B>0 \tag{A14}$$

$b_3 = -(\text{sum of all principal third-order minors of } J)$

$$= - \begin{vmatrix} F_{22} & F_{23} & 0 \\ 0 & F_{33} & 0 \\ 0 & F_{43}(\beta_{w_1}) & F_{44} \end{vmatrix} - \begin{vmatrix} F_{11} & F_{13} & F_{14} \\ F_{31} & F_{33} & 0 \\ F_{41}(\beta_{w_1}) & F_{43}(\beta_{w_1}) & F_{44} \end{vmatrix}$$

$$- \begin{vmatrix} F_{11} & 0 & F_{14} \\ F_{21} & F_{22} & 0 \\ F_{41}(\beta_{w_1}) & 0 & F_{44} \end{vmatrix} - \begin{vmatrix} F_{11} & 0 & F_{13} \\ F_{21} & F_{22} & F_{23} \\ F_{31} & 0 & F_{33} \end{vmatrix}$$

$$= \underset{(-)\,(-)\,(-)}{- F_{22} F_{33} F_{44}} \underset{(-)\,(-)\,(-)}{- F_{11} F_{33} F_{44}} \underset{(+)\,(-)\,(-)}{+ F_{13} F_{31} F_{44}} \underset{(-)\,(-)\,(-)}{- F_{11} F_{22} F_{44}} \underset{(+)\,(-)\,(?)}{+ F_{14} F_{22} F_{41}(\beta_{w_1})}$$

$$\underset{(-)\,(-)\,(-)}{- F_{11} F_{22} F_{33}} \underset{(+)\,(-)\,(-)}{+ F_{13} F_{22} F_{31}} \equiv -D\beta_{w_1} + E; \quad D > 0, \quad E > 0 \qquad (A15)$$

(because we have $F_{14} F_{43}(\beta_{w_1}) F_{31} = F_{14} F_{33} F_{41}(\beta_{w_1})$)

$$b_4 = \det J = \begin{vmatrix} F_{11} & 0 & F_{13} & F_{14} \\ F_{21} & F_{22} & F_{23} & 0 \\ F_{31} & 0 & F_{33} & 0 \\ F_{41}(\beta_{w_1}) & 0 & F_{43}(\beta_{w_1}) & F_{44} \end{vmatrix}$$

$$= F_{22} \begin{vmatrix} F_{11} & F_{13} & F_{14} \\ F_{31} & F_{33} & 0 \\ F_{41}(\beta_{w_1}) & F_{43}(\beta_{w_1}) & F_{44} \end{vmatrix}$$

$$= \underset{(-)\,(-)}{F_{22} F_{44}} (\underset{(-)\,(-)}{F_{11} F_{33}} - \underset{(+)\,(-)}{F_{13} F_{31}}) > 0 \qquad (A16)$$

We shall consider the following function in the following:

$$\Phi(\beta_{w_1}) \equiv b_1 b_2 b_3 - b_1^2 b_4 - b_3^2 \equiv G\beta_{w_1}^2 + H\beta_{w_1} + T \qquad (A17)$$

where all of A, B, D, E, G, H and T are constants.

We shall make use of the following mathematical results to prove the main proposition in this appendix.

Lemma 1 (*Routh–Hurwitz conditions for a 4D system*). *All of the real parts of the roots of the characteristic Equation (A12) are negative if and only if the set of inequalities*

$$b_j > 0 \quad (j = 1, 2, 3, 4), \quad b_1 b_2 b_3 - b_1^2 b_4 - b_3^2 > 0 \qquad (A18)$$

is satisfied.

Lemma 2 (*Asada and Yoshida, 2003*). (i) *The characteristic Equation (A12) has a pair of purely imaginary roots and two roots with nonzero real parts if and only if either of the following set of conditions (A) or (B) is satisfied.*

(A) $b_1 b_3 > 0$, $b_4 \neq 0$, and $b_1 b_2 b_3 - b_1^2 b_4 - b_3^2 = 0$.

(B) $b_1 = 0$, $b_3 = 0$, and $b_4 < 0$.

(ii) *The characteristic Equation (A12) has a pair of purely imaginary roots and two roots with negative real parts if and only if the following set of conditions (C) is satisfied.*

(C) $b_1 > 0$, $b_3 > 0$, $b_4 > 0$, and $b_1 b_2 b_3 - b_1^2 b_4 - b_3^2 = 0$.

Now, we can prove the following proposition.

Proposition 1. *Under Assumptions 1–4, we have the following properties.*

(i) *There exists a parameter value $\beta_{w_1}^0 > 0$ such that the equilibrium point of the system (A4) with $i = 0$ is locally asymptotically stable for all $\beta_{w_1} \in [0, \beta_{w_1}^0)$, and it is unstable for all $\beta_{w_1} \in (\beta_{w_1}^0, +\infty)$.*

(ii) *The point $\beta_{w_1} = \beta_{w_1}^0$ is the unique Hopf-bifurcation point of the above system. In other words, there exist some nonconstant periodic solutions at some parameter values β_{w_1}, which are sufficiently close to $\beta_{w_1}^0$.*

Proof of the Proposition.

Step 1. First, we shall prove the proposition in the special case of $\beta_n = \alpha_2 = 0$. In this case, we can make use of the relationships (A13)–(A17).

(i) From (A13)–(A16), we have the following properties.

(P_1) b_1 and b_4 are always positive.

(P_2) $b_2 > 0$ for all $\beta_{w_1} \in [0, \beta_{w_1}^1)$, $b_2 = 0$ for $\beta_{w_1} = \beta_{w_1}^1$ and $b_2 < 0$ for all $\beta_{w_1} \in (\beta_{w_1}^1, +\infty)$, where $\beta_{w_1}^1 \equiv B/A > 0$.

(P_3) $b_3 > 0$ for all $\beta_{w_1} \in [0, \beta_{w_1}^2)$, $b_3 = 0$ for $\beta_{w_1} = \beta_{w_1}^2$ and $b_3 < 0$ for all $\beta_{w_1} \in (\beta_{w_1}^2, +\infty)$, where $\beta_{w_1}^2 \equiv E/D > 0$.

Since $\lim\limits_{\substack{\beta_{w_2} \to 0 \\ \beta_{p_2} \to 0}} F_{44} = 0$, we have

$$\lim_{\substack{\beta_{w_2} \to 0 \\ \beta_{p_2} \to 0}} \Phi(0) = \{ \underset{(+)}{F_{14}} \underset{(-)}{F_{22}} \underset{(-)}{F_{41}(0)} - \underset{(-)}{F_{11}} \underset{(-)}{F_{22}} \underset{(-)}{F_{33}} \}$$

$$\{ (\underset{(-)}{-F_{11}} \underset{(-)}{-F_{22}} \underset{(-)}{-F_{33}})(\underset{(-)}{F_{11}} \underset{(-)}{F_{22}} + \underset{(-)}{F_{11}} \underset{(-)}{F_{33}})$$

$$+ (\underset{(-)}{-F_{22}} \underset{(-)}{-F_{33}}) \underset{(-)}{F_{22}} \underset{(-)}{F_{33}} + (\underset{(-)}{F_{11}} \underset{(-)}{+F_{33}})(\underset{(+)}{F_{13}} \underset{(-)}{F_{31}}$$

$$+ \underset{(+)}{F_{14}} \underset{(-)}{F_{41}(0)} \} > 0, \tag{A19}$$

which means that we have $T > 0$ if β_{w_2} and β_{p_2} are sufficiently small. In this case, we have

(P_4) $\Phi(\beta_{w_1})$ is a quadratic function of β_{w_1} with $\Phi(0) > 0$. By the way, we have the following inequalities because of the properties (P_1)–(P_3).

$$\Phi(\beta_{w_1}^1) = -b_1^2 b_4 - b_3^2 < 0, \quad \Phi(\beta_{w_1}^2) = -b_1^2 b_4 < 0 \tag{A20}$$

These inequalities together with (P_4) imply that there exists the unique parameter value $\beta_{w_1}^0$ such that $0 < \beta_{w_1}^0 < \min[\beta_{w_1}^1, \beta_{w_1}^2] \equiv \bar{\beta}_{w_1}$, which satisfies the following properties.

(P_5) $\Phi(\beta_{w_1}) > 0$ for all $\beta_{w_1} \in [0, \beta_{w_1}^0)$, $\Phi(\beta_{w_1}) < 0$ for all $\beta_{w_1} \in (\beta_{w_1}^0, \bar{\beta}_{w_1})$, $\Phi(\beta_{w_1}^0) = 0$, and $\Phi'(\beta_{w_1}^0) < 0$.

Properties (P_1)–(P_3) and (P_5) imply that all of the inequalities (A18) in Lemma 1 are satisfied for all $\beta_{w_1} \in [0, \beta_{w_1}^0)$. In this case, the equilibrium point of the system is locally asymptotically stable.

On the other hand, we have $\Phi(\beta_{w_1}) < 0$ for all $\beta_{w_1} \in (\beta_{w_1}^0, \bar{\beta}_{w_1}]$, and we have $b_2 < 0$ or $b_3 < 0$ (or both) for all $\beta_{w_1} \in (\bar{\beta}_{w_1}, +\infty)$. This means that the equilibrium point of the system is unstable for all $\beta_{w_1} \in (\beta_{w_1}^0, +\infty)$.

(ii) It is apparent that a set of conditions (C) in Lemma 2 is satisfied at $\beta_{w_1} = \beta_{w_1}^0$. This means that the characteristic equation (A12) has a pair of purely imaginary roots and two roots with negative real parts at $\beta_{w_1} = \beta_{w_1}^0$. Furthermore, we have $\Phi'(\beta_{w_1}^0) < 0$ because of the property (P_5). In other words, the real part of a pair of the complex roots is not stationary with respect to the changes of the parameter value β_{w_1} at $\beta_{w_1} = \beta_{w_1}^0$. These properties ensures that the point $\beta_{w_1} = \beta_{w_1}^0$ is in fact the Hopf-bifurcation point (cf. Theorem A10 in the mathematical appendix of Asada *et al.* (2003)).

We can prove the uniqueness of the Hopf-bifurcation point as follows. It follows from Lemma 2 (i) that in our model a set of *necessary* conditions of the Hopf bifurcation is given by

$$b_3 > 0, \quad \Phi(\beta_{w_1}) = 0 \tag{A21}$$

because we always have $b_1 > 0$ in our model. However, we already know that only one point (namely, the point $\beta_{w_1} = \beta_{w_1}^0$) satisfies a set of conditions (A21).

Step 2. Next, let us extend the above results to the case in which both of β_n and α_2 are positive but sufficiently small. Suppose that β_n and α_2 slightly increased from zero. We can easily see that even in this case, all of the qualitative results, which were derived in Step 1 are unchanged due to the continuity of the considered relationships, except that the critical parameter value $\beta_{w_1}^0$ slightly changes according to the slight increase of the parameter values β_n and α_2. This completes the proof of the proposition.

A.2. Investment-saving identities and flow consistency

From the side of income generation, we get on the one hand for sectoral savings as well as aggregate savings the expressions:

$$S_w = \omega L^d + r_o B_w/p - T_w - C_w$$
$$S_p = (1 - s_f)\rho^e K + r_o B_p/p - T_p - C_p$$
$$S_f = Y - Y^e + s_f \rho^e K$$
$$S_g = T_w + T_p - r_o(B_w + B_p)/p - G$$

and hence

$$S = S_w + S_p + S_f + S_g = Y - \delta K - C - G = I + \dot{N} = I^a.$$

For allocations of savings of the four sectors we have on the other hand by way of the postulated budget equations:

$$S_w = \dot{B}_w/p$$
$$S_p = (\dot{M}_p + \dot{B}_p + p_e\dot{E}^d)/p$$
$$S_f = I + \dot{N} - p_e\dot{E}/p$$
$$S_g = -(\dot{M} + \dot{B})/p$$

that is we in sum get

$$S = S_w + S_p + S_f + S_g = p_e\dot{E}^d/p - p_e\dot{E}/p + I + \dot{N}$$

and thus – due to $S = I + \dot{N}$ – the consistency condition:

$$p_e\dot{E}^d/p = p_e\dot{E}/p,$$

which always holds as long as government can sell the newly issued bonds (and of course the new issue of money). We thus have that the new issue of equities must be in line with the demand for them at all points in time, if this holds true with respect to money and bonds.

PART IV
MONETARY POLICY AND INFLATION TARGETING

CHAPTER 14

Keynesian Dynamics without the LM Curve: Implications of Underlying Open Market Operations

Reiner Franke

Abstract

The paper relates to the burgeoning literature that combines an interest-rate reaction function of the central bank with an IS equation and a Phillips curve relationship. It takes up the deterministic prototype model advocated by J.B. Taylor and D. Romer and, under the assumption of open market operations, makes the implied dynamics of bonds and high-powered money explicit. As a minor extension, consumption, via disposable income, is supposed to depend on the interest payments on bonds. The resulting dynamic system is possibly totally unstable, that is, no coefficients in the Taylor rule are able to achieve local stability. A numerical investigation demonstrates that stability as well as instability can be brought about by fairly reasonable parameter values. On the other hand, full convergence and divergence are both extremely slow. This implies that, practically, there is a whole continuum of stable equilibria, such that the bond dynamics can be said to exhibit near-hysteresis.

Keywords: Taylor rule, government budget restraint, bond dynamics, local stability, hysteresis

JEL classifications: E12, E32, E52

1. Introduction

The traditional IS–LM model and its various dynamic extensions have been designed to understand macroeconomic fluctuations. Regarding monetary policy (MP), this framework is based on the supposition that the central bank

CONTRIBUTIONS TO ECONOMIC ANALYSIS
VOLUME 277   ISSN: 0573-8555
DOI:10.1016/S0573-8555(05)77014-0

targets the money supply. In recent times, however, a broad consensus has emerged that most central banks follow an interest rate rule. This observation calls for an alternative to the IS–LM approach that reverses the causality in the money-market equilibrium condition. Rather than use money as an instrument and have the money-market determined the rate of interest, MP now sets the interest rate and the equilibrium condition serves to determine the corresponding quantity of the money supply. It is evident that the LM curve, which on the basis of a given money supply relates the market clearing interest rate to the output levels, becomes obsolete in this way. In a recent paper, Romer (2000) emphasizes the advantages of this "Keynesian macroeconomics without the LM curve". Besides addressing the weakness of IS–LM that it assumes money targeting, he, in particular, argues that the new approach also makes the treatment of MP easier, in that it reduces the amount of simultaneity and gives rise to dynamics that are simple and reasonable.

Romer's discussions and graphical illustrations amount to a condensed deterministic version of the (stochastic) models underlying a burgeoning branch of investigations surrounding the Taylor rule, which in addition to this rule employ a dynamic IS equation and a Phillips curve relationship. In fact, this outlines "a distinctive modern form of macroeconomics that is now being used widely in practice" (Taylor, 2000a, p. 93). All these systems have in common that they do not include the movements of money and bonds that are implied by the open market operations enforcing the time path of the interest rate. These variables remain in the background since possible feedbacks from them on the rest of the economy are considered of secondary importance.

The present paper puts this assumption under closer scrutiny. Our starting point is a slight extension of the simple deterministic model put forward by Romer (2000) and Taylor (2000a, 2001), which exhibits a stable steady-state position. In this context, the paper first makes the bond dynamics explicit, as it is derived from a government budget restraint and the motions of the monetary base. Asking for the conditions under which, in the appendix to the main system, bonds and money, too, converge to their steady-state values, it is readily established that this should not be a great problem. Matters become more involved when subsequently aggregate demand in the model is differentiated by supposing that consumption depends on disposable income, part of which in turn is given by the interest payments. Though this provides a minimal feedback of bonds on the demand side, it turns out that local stability of the steady state is no longer easily warranted. There are meaningful sets of numerical parameters that cause the steady state to be unstable, regardless of how strong the interest rate reactions in the central bank's policy function may be chosen.[1] Even more

---

[1] By construction, the model admits of no variable that might jump on the stable branch of a saddle point.

important, however, is the medium-run behaviour of the economy. Whether in the long-run stability prevails or not, here it is appropriate to characterize the dynamics of bonds as (near-)hysteresis.

The material is organized as follows. The next section recapitulates the Romer–Taylor setting in continuous time. Section 3 introduces bonds and high-powered money together with a money multiplier, a money demand function, and the government budget restraint. Section 4 derives the bond dynamics in intensive form, which is still a mere appendix to the inflation dynamics of the Romer–Taylor model, and establishes a condition for its stability. Section 5 modifies the IS equation; as has just been mentioned it makes consumption, via disposable income, dependent on the interest payments on bonds. In this way, the dynamics of bonds and the rate of inflation are interrelated. The analysis of the resulting two-dimensional system of differential equations leads to conditions for the local stability, or instability, of its steady-state position. Since the corresponding inequalities are rather complicated, Section 6 takes some trouble to set up a numerical scenario. The subsequent investigation in Section 7 is first concerned with *ceteris paribus* parameter variations and how they affect local stability, and then with the system's dynamic properties over the medium-run. Section 7 concludes. An appendix finally collects the mathematical computations.

2. The IS–MP–IA model

In this section, we formalize in a continuous-time framework the elementary adjustment mechanisms set forth in Romer (2000), or likewise in a recent textbook by Taylor (2001, Chapters 24 and 25). Romer christens this approach the IS–MP–IA model, where the acronyms MP and IA stand for monetary policy and inflation adjustments, respectively. As Taylor (2001, p. 554) writes, this model combines Keynes's idea that aggregate demand causes departure of real GDP from potential GDP with newer ideas about central banking and how expectations and inflation adjust over time.

Let us begin with monetary policy MP, which means that the central bank sets the interest rate according to a Taylor rule (Taylor, 1993, p. 202). Romer (2001, p. 13) and Taylor (2001, p. 559) consider reactions of the interest rate to inflation only, but here we may just as well add an influence of economic activity. Thus, denote the nominal rate of interest by i, the rate of inflation by π, the output–capital ratio, which is invoked as a measure of capacity utilization, by y, and let r^o be the equilibrium real rate of interest, π^o the target level of inflation, and y^o the output–capital ratio in long-run equilibrium. α_π being a positive, α_y a nonnegative coefficient, we then have

$$i = r^o + \pi + \alpha_\pi(\pi - \pi^o) + \alpha_y(y - y^o) \tag{14.1}$$

In many (quarterly) discrete-time models or empirical estimations of interest-rate reaction functions, expected inflation is used rather than the current inflation rate

π. Usually these expectations refer to the next quarter and are supposed to be rational. As we are working in continuous time where the next period is infinitesimally near, this concept of inflationary expectations may presently be left aside. Another difference to the literature is that economic activity is commonly represented by the output gap. Since, however, the output gap and the (detrended) output–capital ratio show strong comovements over the business cycle, employing the output–capital ratio y in (14.1) fulfills the same role.[2]

Regarding the IS part of the model, we treat $i - \pi$ as the real rate of interest and suppose that the temporary equilibrium condition for the goods market is already solved for the output–capital ratio. y may thus be represented as a decreasing function of $i - \pi$,

$$y = f_y(i - \pi), \quad f'_y < 0 \tag{14.2}$$

To ensure existence of a long-run equilibrium, the central bank must set the real interest rate r^o in (14.1) at a suitable level that makes it compatible with this IS curve. In detail, with $i^o := r^o + \pi^o$, the function f_y is required to satisfy $f_y(r^o) = f_y(i^o - \pi^o) = y^o$.

Equations (14.1) and (14.2) give rise to an inverse relationship between inflation and output. Accordingly, y can be directly conceived as a decreasing function of π,

$$y = y(\pi), \quad \text{where } y(\pi^o) = y^o, \ y_\pi := dy/d\pi < 0 \tag{14.3}$$

The negative slope is obvious for $\alpha_y = 0$, where (3) is immediately inferred from substituting (14.1) in (14.2). With $\alpha_y > 0$, (14.3) follows from a straightforward application of the Implicit Function Theorem (see the Appendix).

The third building block of the model is IA. It assumes an accelerationist Phillips curve, which is to say that the rate of inflation is given at any point in time and shifts up (down) when real output is above (below) its natural level (Romer, 2000, p. 16; Taylor, 2001, pp. 566ff). In continuous time, the concept reads,

$$\dot{\pi} = f_\pi(y - y^o), \quad f_\pi(0) = 0, \ f'_\pi > 0 \tag{14.4}$$

Incidentally, it is readily checked that this specification of inflation adjustments implies countercyclical motions of the price level around its trend, which by now appears to be a well established stylized fact of the business cycle in many industrialized countries.[3]

Equation (14.4) completes the model. Clearly, $y = y^o$, $\pi = \pi^o$, $i = i^o = r^o + \pi^o$ constitute a long-run equilibrium position. The return of the economy

---

[2] Adopting the Hodrick–Prescott filter, we have computed a correlation coefficient of 0.97 over the four major US cycles between 1961 and 1991.

[3] See, for example, Cooley and Ohanian (1991), Backus and Kehoe (1992), Fiorito and Kollintzas (1994).

from disequilibrium back to steady-state growth is also evident: a positive departure of the output–capital ratio from normal causes an increase in the rate of inflation, which causes the central bank to raise the real interest rate, which then moves the output–capital ratio back to normal. Substituting (14.3) in (14.4), the dynamics is formally described by one differential equation in the inflation rate π,

$$\dot{\pi} = F(\pi) := f_\pi[y(\pi) - y^o] \tag{14.5}$$

By (3), π^o is a stationary point of (14.5). It is stable, even globally so, since $F'(\pi) = f'_\pi y_\pi < 0$. As Romer (2000, p. 18) concludes with his "Advantage 6" of the IS–MP–IA model: "The model's dynamics are straightforward and reasonable."

3. Bonds and high-powered money

With this section we begin to consider the implications of the interest rate variations for the monetary sector. Romer (2000, pp. 20–24) as well as Taylor (2001, pp. 559f) entertain the view that the central bank changes the interest rate through open market operations. In addition, Romer (p. 24) states explicitly that the corresponding adjustments of the stock of money, i.e., of the monetary base, have no further effect on aggregate demand, and the same holds true for the bonds that are bought or sold in the open market. In a first step, we accept this hypothesis and study the resulting bond dynamics, which is thus a mere appendix to the system of the previous section.

Let H be the stock of high-powered money and $1/\mu$ the (constant) money multiplier, so that the money supply is given by $M^s = H/\mu$. M denotes money and B the outstanding fixed-price bonds with their variable interest rate i (the bond price normalized at unity). M and B may be the only financial assets in the economy. Money demand M^d is specified as a fraction f_m of $M + B$ that decreases in the interest rate and (possibly) increases with economic activity as it is measured by the output–capital ratio:

$$M^d = f_m(i, y)(M + B), \quad f_{mi} < 0, \ f_{my} \geq 0 \tag{14.6}$$

where $0 < f_m < 1$ and $f_{mi} = \partial f_m/\partial i$, $f_{my} = \partial f_m/\partial y$. Hence, the money-market equilibrium condition $M^s = M^d$ reads $H/\mu = f_m(i, y)(H/\mu + B)$.

As the discussion takes place in a growth context, the equilibrium condition has to be given in intensive form. Designating $h = H/pK$, $b = B/pK$ (p is the price level and K the capital stock) and multiplying through by μ, the equation becomes

$$(h + \mu b)f_m(i, y) - h = 0 \tag{14.7}$$

Since MP uses the interest rate as its instrument, equality in (14.7) is not brought about by i, but by suitable combinations of the bond ratio b and the ratio of high-powered money h. For the further analysis it is useful to treat h in (14.7) as a function of i, y, and b. Denoting it by f_h, we have

$$h = f_h(i, y, b), \quad \text{with } f_{hi} < 0, \, f_{hy} \geqslant 0, \, f_{hb} > 0 \tag{14.8}$$

The signs of the reactions to the *ceteris paribus* changes in these variables are obvious (similar as above, $f_{hi} = \partial f_h / \partial i$, etc.). The precise formulae are provided in the appendix.

Bonds and the monetary base are linked together in a second relationship, which is of a dynamic form. This is the government budget restraint, $\dot{H} + \dot{B} = pG + iB - T$. To reflect the idea of automatic stabilizers, though in a simple way, we allow for countercyclical movements of government spending G; with two nonnegative parameters γ_k, γ_y and $Y^o = y^o K$ the level of normal output, it is given by $G = \gamma_k K - \gamma_y(Y - Y^o)$. As for nominal taxes T, a proportional tax rate τ levied on total income $pY + iB$ is assumed.[4] The intensive form of the budget identity is then calculated as

$$\dot{h} + \dot{b} = \gamma_k + \gamma_y y^o - (\gamma_y + \tau)y + (1 - \tau)ib - (h + b)(\pi + g) \tag{14.9}$$

where g designates the growth rate of the capital stock K.

To derive an ordinary differential equation from (14.9), a reduced-form representation of h has to be established, such that h is a function of the dynamic state variables of the system to be considered. For example, if the state variables are π and b and $\dot{\pi} = F_\pi(\pi)$ as in (14.5), we have $h = h(\pi, b)$ with partial derivatives h_π and h_b, which gives rise to $\dot{h} = h_\pi \dot{\pi} + h_b \dot{b} = h_\pi F_\pi(\pi) + h_b \dot{b}$. Substituting this expression in (14.9) finally allows one to resolve it into a differential equation of the form $\dot{b} = F_b(\pi, b)$. This is spelled out and subsequently examined for stability in the next section.

As this procedure appears rather technical, we may before briefly discuss the determination of bonds and high-powered money in a discrete-time setting; for simplicity with respect to original levels. Let H_t, B_t be the beginning-of-period stocks and $D = D(p_t Y_t, i_t B_t)$ the period t nominal deficit. Then the government budget restraint for period $t - 1$ is

$$(H_t - H_{t-1}) + (B_t - B_{t-1}) = D(p_{t-1} Y_{t-1}, i_{t-1} B_{t-1})$$

On the analogy to (8), H_t satisfies a functional relationship

$$H_t = f_h(i_t, Y_t, B_t)$$

Thus, there are two interrelated equations to compute the stocks H_t and B_t: one is the condition for money-market equilibrium, the other the financing of the government deficit. A problem may be that H_t cannot be represented by an explicit function; H_t and B_t would then only be implicitly determined.

---

[4] Output Y may be thought of as net of capital depreciation.

4. Bond dynamics in the IS–MP–IA model

When the IS–MP–IA model is augmented by high-powered money and bonds, in an appendix to Equation (14.5), we get another state variable besides the inflation rate π, namely, the bond ratio b. To establish the differential equation for b, we first take the output function $y = y(\pi)$ in (14.3) and substitute it in the Taylor rule (14.1). In this way the interest rate is expressed as a function of π,

$$i = i(\pi) := r^o + \pi + \alpha_\pi(\pi - \pi^o) + \alpha_y[y(\pi) - y^o] \tag{14.10}$$

Although $dy/d\pi$ is negative, it is easily shown that the real interest rate always increases in response to an increase in inflation: $di/d\pi > 1$ for all values of $\alpha_y \geqslant 0$.[5]

The two functions $y = y(\pi)$ and $i = i(\pi)$ can be plugged into (14.8), to the effect that the ratio of high-powered money h can be expressed as a function of π and b,

$$h = h(\pi, b) := f_h[i(\pi), y(\pi), b] \tag{14.11}$$

After differentiating (14.11) with respect to time, $\dot{h} = h_\pi \dot{\pi} + h_b \dot{b}$, it remains to substitute the derivative in the government budget restraint (14.9) and solve the resulting equation for $\dot{b}$. In Equation (14.9) we assume that the capital growth rate g, like the output–capital ratio in (14.2), depends solely on the real interest rate, so that g, like y in (14.3), can also be expressed as a function of the rate of inflation, $g = g(\pi)$. Taking finally account of Equation (14.4) for $\dot{\pi}$, we obtain

$$\dot{b} = F_b(\pi, b) := \frac{1}{1 + h_b}\{-h_\pi f_\pi[y(\pi) - y^o] + \gamma_k + \gamma_y y^o$$
$$- (\gamma_y + \tau)y(\pi) + (1 - \tau)i(\pi)b - (h + b)[\pi + g(\pi)]\} \tag{14.12}$$

The long-run equilibrium level of b, which renders $\dot{b} = 0$, is computed as follows. Denote, to this end, all steady-state values by a superscript 'o', in particular, $g^o = g(\pi^o)$ and $f^o_m = f_m(i^o, y^o)$ (recall $i^o = r^o + \pi^o$). Equation (14.7) gives $h^o = \mu f^o_m b^o / (1 - f^o_m)$, while with $y(\pi^o) = y^o$, the time derivative $\dot{b}$ vanishes if $\gamma_k - \tau y^o + (1 - \tau)i^o b^o - (h^o + b^o)(\pi^o + g^o) = 0$. Solving the latter equality for b^o yields

$$b^o = \frac{\gamma_k - \tau y^o}{[1 + \mu f^o_m/(1 - f^o_m)](\pi^o + g^o) - (1 - \tau)i^o} \tag{14.13}$$

As it is made more precise in Section 6 below, $\gamma_k - \tau y^o$ is reasonably positive. A positive value of b^o then requires the denominator in (14.13) to be positive. Given that $\mu f^o_m/(1 - f^o_m)$ is fairly low, we may directly posit that the equilibrium nominal growth rate of the economy, $\pi^o + g^o$, exceeds the after-tax equilibrium

---

[5] With y_π as computed at the beginning of the appendix, one has $di/d\pi = 1 + \alpha_\pi + \alpha_y y_\pi$ $= 1 + \alpha_\pi[1 - \alpha_y|f'_y|/(1 + \alpha_y|f'_y|)] = 1 + \alpha_\pi/(1 + \alpha_y|f'_y|)$.

rate of interest $(1 - \tau)i^o$. Since this supposition will also be invoked later on in the analysis, we set it up as

Assumption 1. *The tax rate τ is less than γ_k/y^o. For the steady-state values of the rates of interest, inflation, and real growth, the following inequality is satisfied,*

$$(1 - \tau)i^o < \pi^o + g^o$$

The bond dynamics converges locally to b^o if $\partial F_b/\partial b < 0$ in (14.12). This partial derivative results like $\partial F_b/\partial b = [(1 - \tau)i^o - (1 + h_b)(\pi^o + g^o)]/(1 + h_b)$, where $h_b = \partial h/\partial b$ is calculated as $h_b = f_{hb} = \mu f^o_m/(1 - f^o_m)$ (cf. the appendix). Hence $1 + h_b > 0$, and $\partial F_b/\partial b < 0$ if Assumption 1 applies. Considering Equations (14.5) and (14.12) together as a two-dimensional differential equations system in π and b, we have for the entries of its Jacobian matrix: $j_{11} = \partial \dot{\pi}/\partial \pi < 0$, $j_{22} = \partial \dot{b}/\partial b < 0$, and $j_{12} = \partial \dot{\pi}/\partial b = 0$. Irrespective of the sign of the fourth entry $j_{21} = \partial \dot{\pi}/\partial b$, $\partial F_b/\partial b < 0$ ensures that the Jacobian has a negative trace and a positive determinant. These findings are summarized in Proposition 1, which allows us to conclude that the dynamics of bonds and the monetary base that takes place in the background of the IS–MP–IA model, is no great problem.

Proposition 1. *Suppose Assumption 1 holds true. Then the equilibrium point (π^o, b^o) of the IS–MP–IA model, Equation (14.5), with its associated bond dynamics, Equation (14.12), is locally asymptotically stable.*

5. Interest payments and their impact on stability

So far, bonds had no feedback on the real sector. On the other hand, bonds are bought by agents because of the interest receipts, which are an income item and so have an effect on demand, most prominently on consumption. If furthermore total income is taxed proportionately as laid out in the government budget restraint above, then it is not seen how these interest payments should cancel out in the determination of aggregate demand. From this point of view it is almost a consistency requirement that interest payments, and thus bonds, enter explicitly into the model's IS equation.[6]

---

[6] Another tax rule in macroeconomic modelling is to define (nominal) tax collections T net of transfers, and to include interest payments as part of those transfer payments. If additionally T/pK = const. is postulated and that it is after-tax income on which aggregate demand depends, bonds again disappear from the IS equation. This simplifying device is, for example, adopted by Sargent (1987) in his textbook on macroeconomic theory (cf. pp. 16f, 113f) and by many Keynesian-oriented macro models in its wake.

Besides better tractability of the model, an economic reason for disregarding the income effects of interest payments on aggregate demand is that they are a small part of total income and so may be expected to have a minor bearing on the dynamics only. With this section we embark on checking this intuition.

To set the stage, decompose aggregate demand into consumption, investment and government spending. Consumption C is supposed to be made up of a basic component that grows with the capital stock and a component that varies in line with disposable income, where the latter includes the interest payments. With a constant $c_k > 0$ and c_y the marginal propensity to consume out of disposable income, $0 < c_y < 1$, we have

$$C = c_k K + c_y(1 - \tau)(Y + iB/p) \tag{14.14}$$

This type of consumption function that allows bonds to enter aggregate demand will be the only essential amendment to the IS–MP–IA model considered above.

For notational simplicity, the real interest rate is supposed to act merely on investment I. Other factors related to current output levels that may influence investment are likewise neglected.[7] The investment function is thus

$$I = f_g(i - \pi)K, \quad f_g' < 0 \tag{14.15}$$

As government spending has already been specified before, clearing of the goods market, $Y = C + I + G$, is fully determined. To obtain the IS equilibrium value of the output–capital ratio y, we first abbreviate the interest rate reaction function (1) as

$$j = j(y, \pi) := r^o + \pi + \alpha_\pi(\pi - \pi^o) + \alpha_y(y - y^o) \tag{14.16}$$

and then define excess demand for goods, normalized by the capital stock, as a function $E_y = E_y(y, \pi, b)$, so that the IS equilibrium condition reads,

$$E_y(y, \pi, b) := c_k + c_y(1 - \tau)[y + j(y, \pi)b] + f_g[j(y, \pi) - \pi] + \gamma_k - \gamma_y(y - y^o) - y$$
$$= 0 \tag{14.17}$$

Equilibrium in (14.17) is brought about by variations of y. Accordingly, let $y = y(\pi, b)$ be the value of the output–capital ratio at which, given π and b, excess demand $E_y(y, \pi, b)$ vanishes. In this way, the accelerationist Phillips curve from Equation (14.5) becomes

$$\dot{\pi} = F_\pi(\pi, b) := f_\pi[y(\pi, b) - y^o] \tag{14.18}$$

that is, the motions of the rate of inflation are no longer independent of the evolution of government debt.

---

[7] The only effect of adding an accelerator argument by making investment dependent on Y would be an increase in the multiplier. More precisely, the partial derivatives y_π and y_b in Equation (14.20) below would be higher since the term A_c defined in (14.19) would be lower.

For negative reactions of output to inflation as they previously prevailed in Equation (14.3), it proves necessary that investment is rather sensitive. In detail, the negative effect on investment from an increase in the interest rate i must dominate the positive effect, through higher interest payments, on consumption:

Assumption 2. $|f'_g| > c_y(1 - \tau)b^o$

Defining the terms

$$A_c := 1 - c_y(1 - \tau) + \gamma_y, \quad A_g := |f'_g| - c_y(1 - \tau)b^o \tag{14.19}$$

both of which are positive under Assumption 2, the partial derivatives of the IS output–capital ratio (evaluated at the steady-state values) are computed as

$$y_\pi = \frac{c_y(1 - \tau)b^o - \alpha_\pi A_g}{A_c + \alpha_y A_g}, \quad y_b = \frac{c_y(1 - \tau)i^o}{A_c + \alpha_y A_g} \tag{14.20}$$

(these and the formulae to follow are again derived in the appendix). A *ceteris paribus* increase of the bond ratio b unambiguously raises output, because of the corresponding rise in interest receipts and thus consumption demand. In contrast, the effect of an increasing rate of inflation could go either direction. The function $\pi \mapsto y(\pi, b)$, which is the counterpart of the above function $y = y(\pi)$ in Equation (14.3), is downward-sloping if and only if the inflation targeting coefficient α_π in the Taylor rule is sufficiently high. Nevertheless, the numerical inspection in the next section demonstrates that the critical value of α_π from when on, with α_π increasing, $y_\pi < 0$ obtains, tends to be relatively low unless the investment responsiveness $|f'_g|$ is not too small. Hence the observation that weak reactions of monetary policy to inflation might be destabilizing, in that they do not avert a spiral of rising inflation and output, is remarkable, but it is not worrying since the interest rate reactions can be reasonably believed to be strong enough. For better reference, we summarize this discussion in an extra proposition.

Proposition 2. *Given that Assumption 2 is fulfilled, so that $A_g > 0$ in (14.19), the MP rule diminishes the IS equilibrium output–capital ratio if, and only if, the inflation targeting coefficient α_π exceeds a certain critical value α_π^c. That is,*

$$y_\pi = \partial y / \partial \pi < 0 \quad \text{if, and only if,} \quad \alpha_\pi > \alpha_\pi^c := c_y(1 - \tau)b^o / A_g$$

When the interest rate function (14.1) or (14.16) is restricted to apply to the temporary equilibrium situations, one gets the reduced-form representation

$$i = i(\pi, b) := r^o + \pi + \alpha_\pi(\pi - \pi^o) + \alpha_y[y(\pi, b) - y^o] \tag{14.21}$$

whose partial derivatives are given by

$$i_\pi = 1 + \alpha_\pi + \alpha_y y_\pi > 1, \quad i_b = \alpha_y y_b \geqslant 0 \tag{14.22}$$

It is thus seen that, irrespective of the concrete coefficients α_π, α_y, the policy rule always leads to an increase in the real rate of interest if the inflation rate increases, even if $y_\pi < 0$ and α_y is large (this is verified in the appendix). As has just been shown, however, this property as such is not sufficient to cut down economic activity as a whole.

The next step in the analysis is to determine the ratio of high-powered money in its dependency on π and b. Referring to the function $f_h = f_h(i, y, b)$ in (14.8), the reduced-form representation of h is

$$h = h(\pi, b) := f_h[i(\pi, b), y(\pi, b), b] \tag{14.23}$$

The procedure is very much the same as in Section 4, Equation (14.23) being a generalization of (14.11). Likewise, the motions of bonds are derived from substituting the time derivative $\dot{h} = h_\pi \dot{\pi} + h_b \dot{b}$ in the government budget identity (14.9), solving it for $\dot{b}$, and using (14.18) for $\dot{\pi}$:

$$\dot{b} = F_b(\pi, b) := \frac{1}{1 + h_b} \{ -h_\pi f_\pi [y(\pi, b) - y^o] + \gamma_k + \gamma_y y^o - (\gamma_y + \tau) y(\pi, b)$$
$$+ (1 - \tau) i(\pi, b) b - (h + b)[\pi + f_g(i(\pi, b) - \pi)] \} \tag{14.24}$$

which may be compared with Equation (14.12) for $\dot{b}$ in the previous section. To sum up, Equations (14.18) and (14.24) constitute a two-dimensional differential equations system in the inflation rate π and the bond ratio b, whose dynamics are now interrelated. The steady-state position (π^o, b^o), of course, remains the same.

To inquire into the local stability of the steady state, the Jacobian matrix of (14.18) and (14.24) has to be set up. Define to this end,

$$A_y := -h_\pi f_\pi' - (\gamma_y + \tau) + \alpha_y [(1 - \tau) b^o + (h^o + b^o)|f_g'|]$$
$$A_b := (1 - \tau) i^o - (1 + h_b)(\pi_o + g^o)$$
$$A_\pi := (1 + \alpha_\pi)(1 - \tau) b^o + (h^o + b^o)(\alpha_\pi |f_g'| - 1) - h_\pi(\pi_o + g^o) \tag{14.25}$$

The Jacobian J can then be written as

$$J = \begin{bmatrix} f_\pi' y_\pi & f_\pi' y_b \\ \dfrac{A_y y_\pi + A_\pi}{1 + h_b} & \dfrac{A_y y_b + A_b}{1 + h_b} \end{bmatrix} \tag{14.26}$$

The reaction of the time rate of change of π to an increase in the level of inflation continues to be negative if, as pointed out in Proposition 2, the central bank in its policy rule pays adequate attention to inflation; $j_{11} = \partial F_\pi / \partial \pi = f_\pi' y_\pi < 0$ then, which is the same result as in Equation (14.5) for the IS–MP–IA model. The response of inflation to changes in b indicates a possible source of destabilization, since higher government debt accelerates inflation; $j_{12} = \partial F_\pi / \partial b = f_\pi' y_b > 0$.

The partial derivatives of the function F_b in (14.24) are apparently more complicated than those of F_π. For the stability analysis it is also necessary to assess the sign of the denominator of the entries j_{21} and j_{21}. Actually, the derivative h_b turns out to be comparatively small. It is established in the appendix that $1 + h_b$ is positive if the the money demand is not excessively responsive to the interest rate. In explicit terms, $1 + h_b > 0$ if Assumption 3a is satisfied, while, considering more strictly h_b itself, $h_b > 0$ if Assumption 3b is fulfilled. In particular, these statements hold regardless of the values chosen for the policy parameters α_π, α_y. Note also that the denominator in Assumptions 3a and b contains the product of two terms, i^o and $h^o + \mu b^o$, which should be quite small. The expressions on the right-hand side will therefore be easily rather high.

Assumption 3a.

$$|f_{mi}| < \frac{[1 - (1 - \mu)f^o_m]A_g}{c_y(1 - \tau)(h^o + \mu b^o)i^o}$$

Assumption 3b.

$$|f_{mi}| < \frac{\mu f^o_m A_g}{c_y(1 - \tau)(h^o + \mu b^o)i^o}$$

As for the second diagonal entry of the Jacobian, j_{22}, it can be concluded that Assumptions 1 and 3b imply $A_b < 0$. This type of inequality amounted to $\partial \dot{b}/\partial b < 0$ in the IS–MP–IA model. Now, however, the additional term $A_y y_b$ has to be taken into account, where A_y may take on either sign. In our numerical investigations there was nevertheless a strong tendency for j_{22} to be negative. The reason is that high values of α_y increase A_y, but simultaneously decrease y_b at the same order of magnitude; cf. Equation (14.20). On this basis we may say that normally both auto-feedbacks, π on $\dot{\pi}$ and b on $\dot{b}$, are negative and thus stabilizing, just as they were in the IS–MP–IA model.

If we take $j_{22} < 0$ for granted and concentrate on $\alpha_\pi > \alpha^c_\pi$, which implies $y_\pi < 0$ and thus also $j_{11} < 0$ and trace $J < 0$, the sign of the determinant of J becomes the decisive criterion for stability. Here the term A_y plays no more role since it cancels out:

$$\det J = f'_\pi(A_b y_\pi - A_\pi y_b)/(1 + h_b) \tag{14.27}$$

The sign of $h_\pi = f_{hi}i_\pi + f_{hy}y_\pi$ in the term A_π is given by $f_{mi}i_\pi + f_{my}y_\pi$. Hence $h_\pi < 0$ under the condition on α_π just stated. A_π itself, which is increasing in α_π, is consequently positive if α_π exceeds the value $\tilde{\alpha}_\pi$ that renders the sum of the first two terms in A_π zero. In short, $A_\pi > 0$ if $\alpha_\pi > \max\{\alpha^c_\pi, \tilde{\alpha}_\pi\}$. Computing $\tilde{\alpha}_\pi = (h^o + \tau b^o)/[(1 - \tau)b^o + (h^o + b^o)|f'_g|]$, it is furthermore easily verified that $\alpha^c_\pi > \tilde{\alpha}_\pi$ at least if $c_y \geqslant (h^o + \tau b^o)/(1 - \tau)b^o$, an inequality that will be reasonably satisfied. It then follows that $j_{11} < 0$ as an almost necessary condition for stability leads to $A_\pi > 0$ in $\det J$. Thus, on the whole, both products $A_b y_\pi$ and $A_\pi y_b$ in (14.27) are positive.

The determination of the sign of $\det J$, therefore, requires a more detailed investigation of the single terms A_b, A_π and y_b, y_π. The task is impeded by the fact that y_π and A_π on the one hand, and y_b and A_b on the other hand, are of a similar order of magnitude and involve rather lengthy expressions. To handle them it is useful to introduce the terms ϕ_o and ϕ_π, into which in turn enter the abbreviations A_1, A_2:

$$A_1 := \pi^o + g^o - (1 - \tau)i^o + \mu f_m^o(\pi^o + g^o)/(1 - f_m^o) > 0$$
$$A_2 := (h^o + \mu b^o)(\pi^o + g^o)|f_{mi}|/(1 - f_m^o) > 0$$
$$\phi_o := -c_y(1 - \tau)[A_1 b^o - i^o(h^o + \tau b^o - A_2)]$$
$$\phi_\pi := A_g A_1 - c_y(1 - \tau)i^o[(1 - \tau)b^o + (h^o + b^o)|f_g'| + A_2] \tag{14.28}$$

where for the positive sign of A_1, Assumption 1 has been presupposed. After some tedious calculations the determinant of J can be decomposed as

$$\det J = f_\pi'(\phi_o + \phi_\pi \alpha_\pi)/\{(1 + h_b)|E_{yy}|\} \tag{14.29}$$

It may be observed that the slope f_π' of the Phillips curve, a possible responsiveness of money demand to output (the derivative f_{my}), and the degree γ_y of countercyclicality in government expenditure have disappeared from the core expression $\phi_o + \phi_\pi \alpha_\pi$ in (14.29). Even more important is the phenomenon that the sign of the determinant is independent of the policy coefficient α_y, so only the inflation coefficient α_π has a bearing on it.[8] On this basis we arrive at Proposition 3.

Proposition 3. *Suppose Assumptions 1, 2, and 3a are satisfied. Then the following holds for the dynamic process* (14.18) *and* (14.24).

(a) *If $\phi_\pi > 0$, there exists a benchmark value $\alpha_\pi^s > 0$ such that $\alpha_\pi < \alpha_\pi^s$ implies instability of the steady state for all values of $\alpha_y \geq 0$, whereas $\alpha_\pi > \alpha_\pi^s$ implies local asymptotic stability for all values of $\alpha_y \geq 0$.*

(b) *If $\phi_o < 0$, $\phi_\pi < 0$, the steady state is unstable for all nonnegative values of α_π and α_y.*

The main result is that the MP rule (14.1) can turn out to be completely unable to stabilize the local dynamics, although the bond dynamics has a negative feedback on itself ($\partial \dot{b}/\partial b < 0$) and the central bank, by setting α_π sufficiently high, achieves a negative feedback of inflation on itself ($\partial \dot{\pi}/\partial \pi < 0$). Hence, it is the interaction between the inflation dynamics, that is, the interest rate–inflation–output nexus, and the consequences of monetary and fiscal policy in the financial sector, that is responsible for the instability of the long-run equilibrium. The feedbacks here involved are quite complex, which is also reflected in the irritating terms defined in (14.28). While this is an interesting theoretical finding, one might nevertheless question the practical relevance of the

---

[8] α_y has not been made explicit in Equation (14.27) for the determinant, but it is present in the derivatives h_π and h_b entering A_π and A_b, respectively. It is thus not obvious that α_y eventually cancels out in $\phi_o + \phi_\pi \alpha_\pi$.

instability result, in the sense that only special and not too plausible sets of numerical parameters would actually produce it. This issue is taken up in the next section.

Another property of the model is that only the inflation targeting coefficient α_π can stabilize the economy, whereas output targeting via the coefficient α_y has no effect in this respect. This is somewhat surprising, just when he have pointed out the complex interactions in the model. In addition, there is a general tendency that ϕ_o is negative and that the value of α_π at which, with $\phi_\pi > 0$, the determinant of J becomes positive exceeds the value α_π^c of Proposition 2. This means it is not sufficient for the central bank to accomplish negative reactions of output to an increase in inflation, $y_\pi < 0$, targeting of inflation must be stronger to also take account of the effects from the induced bond dynamics. However, rather than dwell into the troublesome algebraic details for this result to come about, we leave it to the next section's numerical investigations.

It is furthermore worth mentioning that the sign of $\det J$ in (14.29) remains also unaffected by fiscal policy in the form of the countercyclical expenditure coefficient γ_y. On the other hand, the coefficient does have some influence on the trace of J via the partial derivative y_π in j_{11}; see Equations (14.19) and (14.20). Since, however, this effect is not very strong, it can be said that the strength of the government's expenditure policy has practically no bearing on the stability question; certainly not if both ϕ_o and ϕ_π are negative.

Note finally that if $y_\pi < 0$ and also trace $J < 0$, but α_π not high enough to stabilize the steady state, instability will be of the saddle point type. Nevertheless, as the model is constructed there is no scope for the rate of inflation to jump on the stable branch of the saddle point dynamics.

6. Setting up a baseline scenario

In this section we propose a scenario of numerical parameter values, which can then be used to get a feel for the algebraic expressions that entered the stability proposition in the previous section, and to inquire into the system's medium-run dynamics. Beginning with the equilibrium rates of interest, inflation, and real growth, they may be set at

$$i^o = 4.5\% \quad \pi^o = 2\% \quad g^o = 3\% \tag{14.30}$$

2% is the usual level for the target rate of inflation, while the bond rate is above the 4% equilibrium value of the federal funds rate in Taylor's original formula (Taylor, 1993, p. 202). With a view to the later results it is, however, only a little bit higher. Equation (14.30) clearly respects Assumption 1.

Next, consider the steady-state ratios to output of money, bonds, and government expenditure as they result from US data. We choose $M/pY = 0.15$ (see, for example, the diagram in Blanchard, 2000, p. 63), $B/pY = 0.40$ (cf. Blanchard, 2000, p. 524, quoting from OECD Economic Outlook), $G/Y = 0.20$ (cf. Table 1 in Alesina, 2000, p. 7). Furthermore, adopting the numbers for the reserve requirement ratio (0.10) and the proportion in which people hold money in currency (0.40) that are mentioned in Blanchard (2000, pp. 69, 71), and computing the corresponding money multiplier (which amounts to 2.17; *ibid*, p. 73), we work with $\mu = 0.46$.

To relate M, B, and G to the capital stock rather than output, we also need to have an idea about the output–capital ratio (though y nowhere shows up in the stability analysis itself). Here we make use of the capital stock series that can be extracted from the database provided by Ray Fair on his homepage[9] and set $y^o = 0.90$. Decomposing the ratio of high-powered money as $h = H/pK = \mu(M/pY)(pY/pK)$, and similarly so for the bond ratio $b = B/pK$ and the ratio $\gamma_k = G/Y$ when output is on its trend path ($Y = Y^o = y^o K$), we so far have:

$$y^o = 0.90 \quad \gamma_k = 0.18 \quad \mu = 0.46 \quad h^o = 0.0621 \quad b^o = 0.360 \quad f_m^o = 0.2727$$
(14.31)

The equilibrium proportion of the money holdings in (14.6) derives, of course, from $f_m = M/(M + B) = (M/pY)/[(M/pY) + (B/pY)]$. The reason for invoking γ_k, although it plays no role either in the stability analysis, is that it serves us to compute the tax rate τ that, given the steady-state values already determined, is consistent with $\dot{b} = 0$. Equating the right-hand side of (14.12) to zero and solving it for τ yields (omitting the steady-state indication)

$$\tau = [\gamma_k + ib - (h + b)(\pi + g)]/(y + ib) = 19.11\%$$
(14.32)

This figure is close to the actual share of the government's total revenues to GDP (cf. Alesina, 2000, Table 2 on p. 8, which is quoted from the Congressional Budget Office), just as it should be.

We can thus turn to the reaction coefficients. The first one is the expenditure coefficient γ_y of the 'automatic stabilizer' in the government budget restraint. An orientation mark is provided by the rule of thumb that a 1% decrease in output leads to an increase in the deficit of 0.5% of GDP.[10] As the direct effect of output on the deficit is given by $-(\gamma_y + \tau)Y$ and the tax rate τ is approximately 20%, a reasonable value for γ_y is $\gamma_y = 0.30$.

The slope f'_π of the accelerationist Phillips curve (14.4) is determined as follows. Referring to the countercyclical variations of the price level around a Hodrick–Prescott trend, to capacity utilization u (which fluctuates around unity), and to the empirical standard deviations σ_u and σ_p of these time series, Franke (2001) argues for a ratio $\sigma_p/\sigma_u = 0.50$ as a stylized fact of the business cycle. Countercyclical movements of the price level are generated by a differential equation $\dot{\pi} = \tilde{\beta}_\pi(u - 1)$. Simulating it under exogenous regular sine

---

[9] The URL is http://fairmodel.econ.yale.edu.
[10] cf. Blanchard (2000, p. 526). In his regressions, Taylor (2000b, pp. 34ff) computes somewhat lower numbers.

wave oscillations of u, the desired ratio of 0.50 is brought about by $\tilde{\beta}_\pi = 0.45$. Since $u = y/y^o$, the linear specification $\dot{\pi} = \beta_\pi(y - y^o)$ of (14.4) is just a rescaling of the former equation, with $\beta_\pi = \tilde{\beta}_\pi/y^o$. These relationships motivate us to set $f'_\pi = \beta_\pi = \tilde{\beta}_\pi/y^o = 0.45/0.90 = 0.50$.

To infer the derivative f_{mi} of money demand with respect to changes in the rate of interest, we make reference to the interest elasticity $\eta_{mi} = (\partial M^d/\partial i)/(M/i)$. In this way, $f_{mi} = \eta_{mi}f_m^o/i^o$. Going back to the material discussed in Goldfeld (1976) and the short compilation in Boorman (1976, pp. 328–335), we decide on $\eta_{mi} = -0.20$, so that $f_{mi} = -1.21$. As has been noted above with respect to Equation (14.29), the reactions of M^d to changes in economic activity, f_{my}, are completely missing in the determinant of J. Because they only have a minor, almost negligible, bearing on the trace via the partial derivative h_b in entry j_{22}, we may just as well put $f_{my} = 0$.

A familiar order of magnitude for the marginal propensity to consume is $c_y \approx 0.70$. Regarding Equation (14.14), this intuition squares quite well with regressions of trend deviations of C/K on trend deviations of Y/K. Employing the Hodrick–Prescott filter, one obtains a slope coefficient $\beta_c = 0.542$ over the sample period 1961–1991.[11] Since the interest payments are only a small part of total income, the estimate would not be much affected if iB/pK were included in the regression. We may thus assume $c_y(1 - \tau) = \beta_c$ and, taking the tax rate $\tau = 19.11\%$ from (14.32) into account, settle on $c_y = 0.67$.

A clue to setting the responsiveness of investment f'_g to variations of the real interest rate can be obtained from the literature. For example, Ball (1997, pp. 3 and 5) in his discrete-time annual model works with the dynamic IS equation $x_{t+1} = 0.80x_t - 1.00(i_t - \pi_t)+$ error term, where x denotes the output gap (and the coefficients are justified by reference to further literature). The corresponding static relationship would be $(1 - 0.80)x = -1.00(i - \pi)$, so that a one-point rise in the interest rate diminishes the output gap by 1.25%. The outcome of the estimates employed by Rudebusch and Svensson (1999, pp. 207f) in their quarterly model is similar. They get $x_{t+1} = 1.16x_t - 0.25x_{t-1} - 0.10(i_t - \pi_t)+$ error term (the rates of interest and inflation are measured at annual rates). The multiplier of the real interest rate is here computed as $-0.10/(1 - 1.16 + 0.25) = -1.11$.

To relate these findings to the present framework, it does not suffice to note the strong correlation between the output gap and the output–capital ratio, but the fluctuations have also to be compared in size. If both $y = Y/K$ and $\ln Y$ are detrended by the usual Hodrick–Prescott filter, then over the period 1961–1991 the output gap exhibits a standard deviation of 1.81 percentage points, while the standard deviation of the output–capital ratio is 1.85. The numerical reactions of

---

[11] Slightly higher values of β_c, however, would allow the time series $\beta_c Y/K$ to better trace out the turning points of C/K.

x and y to changes in the interest rate can therefore be directly compared with each other.[12]

The multipliers $y_i:=\partial y/\partial i$ mentioned above do not yet invoke the Taylor rule. The same kind of multiplier as it results from the IS Equation (14.17) is given by $y_i = -A_g/A_c = -[|f'_g| - c_y(1-\tau)b]/[1 - c_y(1-\tau) + \gamma_y]$. Adopting for c_y, τ, b, and γ_y the values already determined, we look for a value f'_g such that y_i lies between -1.11 and -1.25. This leads us to set $f'_g = -1.10$, which brings about $y_i = -1.19$. For a better overview, this and the other coefficients are collected in an extra equation:

$$\gamma_y = 0.30 \quad f_{my} = 0.00 \quad f_{mi} = -1.21 \quad (\eta_{mi} = -0.20)$$
$$f'_\pi = 0.50 \quad c_y = 0.67 \quad f'_g = -1.10 \tag{14.33}$$

It is immediately seen that the coefficients f'_g and c_y satisfy Assumption 2. Furthermore, with the resulting $A_g = 0.905$ in (19), the right-hand sides of Assumptions 3a and b are as high as 139 and 20, respectively. That is, the money demand function with its interest coefficient f_{mi} has no trouble at all to pass the required inequalities. It is also clear that Assumptions 2 and 3 tolerate a great variety of deviations from Equations (14.31) and (14.33).

Given that the interest rate variations of the central bank take effect via the investment function, the investment reaction coefficient f'_g is of particular importance. Our choice of $f'_g = -1.10$ has relied on translating the core of a dynamic IS relationship into a static IS equation. The consequences when the output solutions to the latter are fed into the accelerationist Phillips curve with $f'_\pi = 0.50$ may thus not be exactly clear. At the end of this section we therefore evaluate this part of our numerical scenario by fixing the bond ratio, simulating the convergence of the (linearized) partial system $\dot{\pi} = f_\pi[y(\pi, b^o) - y^o]$, and comparing it to the quantitative adjustments as they result from another system studied in the literature.

To begin with the linear differential equation $\dot{\pi} = f'_\pi[y(\pi, b^o) - y^o]$, let us first adopt Taylor's (1993, p. 202) common reference values $\alpha_y = \alpha_\pi = 0.50$ in the MP function. With the above setting of, especially, f'_g and c_y one computes $y_\pi = -0.2126$ in Equation (14.20). This gives rise to an eigen-value $\lambda = f'_\pi y_\pi = -0.50 \times 0.2126 = -0.1063$, which indicates a fairly slow convergence speed. The bold line in the upper-left panel of Figure 14.1 illustrates the long adjustment time for π after a one-point shock to the rate of inflation at time $t = 0$ (time on the horizontal axis is measured in years). The lower-left panel shows the time path of the corresponding output gap $[y(\pi, b^o) - y^o]/y^o$. In contrast, the thin lines in the two panels are the inflation rate and the output gap

---

[12] Going into the details of footnote 6 in Rudebusch and Svensson (1999, p. 207), it might be inferred that the measure of the output gap underlying their regressions displays somewhat wider oscillations. This would mean that the coefficient f'_g established in a moment may also be taken a bit higher.

Figure 14.1.   Convergence paths after shock to inflation π

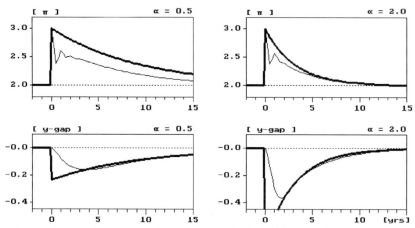

Note: 'y-gap' denotes the output gap (in percentage points). Bold lines are the time paths of system $\dot{\pi} = f_\pi[y(\pi, b^o) - y^o]$, thin lines are those of the Rudebusch–Svensson model. $\alpha = 0.5$ (and 2.0) indicates $\alpha_y = \alpha_\pi = 0.5$ (and 2.0, respectively).

that are obtained, after the same shock, from the quarterly model estimated by Rudebusch and Svensson (1999) mentioned above, which exhibits four lags of the inflation rate in the Phillips curve and two lags of the output gap in the IS equation (the numerical equations are reproduced in the appendix). Here convergence of the inflation rate is somewhat faster, though it still takes a veritable lapse of time. On the other hand, after a transi tional phase of about 3 years the time path of the output gap is remarkably close to that of our model.

One result of the Rudebusch–Svensson paper is that a Taylor-type interest rate reaction function like Equation (14.1) performs nearly as well in minimizing a central bank's loss function as more ambitious rules (cf. *ibid*, pp. 227ff). This, however, requires considerably higher coefficients α_y and α_π.[13] We thus did a second simulation with both α_y and α_π raised to a value of 2.00. As is seen in the two right-hand panels of Figure 14.1, these coefficients speed up convergence. Moreover, apart from the first few years, our differential equation and the Rudebusch–Svensson model generate very similar convergence paths. These sketches may serve to gain more confidence in the numerical parameters underlying our IS equation and the Phillips curve.

---

[13] Their exact size depends on the particular weights in the loss function for the variability of inflation, output, and changes in the interest rate.

7. Numerical analysis

On the basis of the numerical scenario (14.30)–(14.33), we can now assess the scope for local stability or instability of system (14.18) and (14.24) in greater detail. First, the condition for the derivative y_π to become negative is not very restrictive; α_π^c from Proposition 2 is given by 0.216. So, in words, the policy rule induces a decline in output in response to an increase in the rate of inflation as soon as the inflation targeting coefficient α_π exceeds $\alpha_\pi^c = 0.216$. By the same token, entry j_{11} in the Jacobian will be negative if $\alpha_\pi > 0.216$.

Turning to the trace of J, consider next the second diagonal entry j_{22}. At the critical value $\alpha_\pi = \alpha_\pi^c$, j_{22} is already negative – for all nonnegative values of the other policy parameter α_y. For example, j_{22} increases from -0.0261 to -0.0031 as α_y rises from 0 to 10 (j_{22} still remains below zero at $\alpha_y = 100$). The reason for $j_{22} \cong A_y y_b + A_b < 0$ is that though A_y (defined in (14.25)) changes from negative to positive as α_y rises, the composite term $A_y y_b$, which thus turns positive, too (since $y_b > 0$ from (14.20)), is always dominated by the expression A_b, which is negative (cf. (14.25) and the remark on Assumption 3b).[14]

Since, as we may just claim for brevity, things for j_{22} are not very different for other values of α_π, a negative trace of J may be taken for granted for at least all $\alpha_\pi \geqslant \alpha_\pi^c = 0.216$. So we have to study the determinant of J, that is, the expression $\phi_o + \phi_\pi \alpha_\pi$ from Equation (14.29). Numerically, one here computes $\phi_o = -0.0016$, $\phi_\pi = 0.0012$ (rounded). $\det J$ is therefore an increasing function of α_π, which is negative at $\alpha_\pi = 0$ and becomes positive when $\alpha_\pi = -\phi_o/\phi_\pi = 1.314$.

In conclusion, the central bank succeeds in stabilizing the steady-state equilibrium, if it sets $\alpha_\pi > 1.314$. Notice that $\alpha_\pi^s = 1.314 > 0.216 = \alpha_\pi^c$. This means it is not sufficient for the policy rule to take care of $y_\pi < 0$, inflation targeting must rather be stronger. In fact, in the present example the central bank must raise α_π above Taylor's reference value of $\alpha_\pi = 0.50$.

Before proceeding with a sensitivity analysis of this kind of result, we notice that the critical value $\alpha_\pi^c = c_y(1 - \tau)b^o/A_g$ does not change much, if at all, under a very wide range of parameter variations. It, moreover, turns out that ϕ_o remains negative. Consequently, $\phi_\pi > 0$ is required for the determinant in Equation (14.29) to become positive, and for the steady state to become locally stable. If $\phi_\pi > 0$, then, except for extremely large deviations of some of the parameters from the scenario (14.30)–(14.33), the above phenomenon is maintained. We may thus point out:

---

[14] In finer detail, A_b increases marginally from -0.0222 for $\alpha_y = 0$ to -0.0218 when $\alpha_y = 10$. At the same time, the increase of A_y from -0.260 to 7.295 is mainly offset by the corresponding decrease of y_b from 0.0322 to 0.0025, such that $A_y y_b$ increases relatively weakly, from -0.0084 over 0.0024 (at $\alpha_y = 0.50$) to 0.0181.

Observation 1. *The borderline value α_π^s (if it exists), from when on local stability prevails, tends to exceed the value α_π^c from Proposition 2, from when on the output reactions y_π are negative. That is, $\alpha_\pi > \alpha_\pi^c$ is a necessary, but not a sufficient, condition for the stability of the steady-state position.*

Because of its central role for stability, let us have a closer look at the 'slope' coefficient ϕ_π of the determinant, which perhaps appears to be somewhat low. By (14.28), ϕ_π is the difference between two positive terms $\phi_{\pi g} := A_g A_1 = 0.0201$ and $\phi_{\pi c} := c_y(1 - \tau)i^o[(1 - \tau)b^o + (h^o + b^o)|f_g'| + A_2] = 0.0189$ (rounded). There should be several coefficients or steady-state values a modest change of which yields $\phi_{\pi g} - \phi_{\pi c} < 0$. One example is a reduction of the investment reaction intensity. If it happens to be $f_g' = -0.90$ (instead of -1.10), A_g in (14.19) decreases and one computes $\phi_{\pi g} = A_g A_1 = 0.0157$. $\phi_{\pi c}$ decreases, too, but less so; $\phi_{\pi c} = 0.0168$. The outcome is $\phi_\pi = \phi_{\pi g} - \phi_{\pi c} = -0.0012$. Since the 'intercept' term ϕ_o is not affected by variations of f_g', det J as determined in (14.29) is negative for all $\alpha_\pi \geqslant 0$. Under these circumstances, the central bank is no longer able to accomplish convergence towards the steady state.

A stronger responsiveness of investment, on the other hand, contributes to a stabilization of the economy. Thus, consider $f_g' = -1.30$. Here $\phi_{\pi g}$ increases more than $\phi_{\pi c}$: $\phi_{\pi g} = 0.0250$ and $\phi_{\pi c} = 0.0209$, so that the difference ϕ_π rises from the previous 0.0012 to 0.0036. ϕ_o remaining unchanged, the ratio $\alpha_\pi^s = -\phi_o/\phi_\pi$ declines by a factor of almost 3, down to $\alpha_\pi^s = 0.445$. This threshold is now slightly below Taylor's reference value of 0.50.

Already with the information given, it can be critically asked for the speed of convergence or divergence. Before we turn to this issue, we investigate the stabilizing or destabilizing implications of other *ceteris paribus* parameter variations. A first set of reaction coefficients is presented in Figure 14.2. The upper-left panel extends the selective calculations for the investment responsiveness f_g'. To each value f_g', the bold line indicates the corresponding value of the inflation targeting coefficient α_π^s, if it exists, that ensures local stability for $\alpha_\pi > \alpha_\pi^s$. Hence the dotted area is the set of all pairs $(|f_g'|, \alpha_\pi)$ that, given the other numerical parameters in (14.30)–(14.33), render the steady state locally stable. As α_π^s decreases with $|f_g'|$ rising, a higher responsiveness of investment to changes in the real interest rate is certainly stabilizing, while at a responsiveness not much less than the baseline value $f_g' = -1.10$, the economy is always unstable.

Once the possibility of total instability is recognized, the stabilizing potential of a higher investment responsiveness might seem intuitively clear, because the same change in the interest rate has a stronger impact on aggregate output (in the first round, so to speak) and on the adjustments of the rate of inflation (in the second round). However, given the complicated expressions in Equation (14.29) for det J, which reflect the interaction of the inflation and bond dynamics, there

Figure 14.2. **Local stability under variations of** $|f'_g|$, c_y, $|\eta_{mi}|$, μ

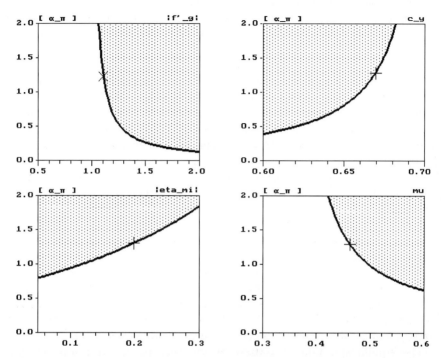

Note: Other parameters as set in scenario (14.30)–(14.33). Points in dotted area imply stability (instability otherwise), cross indicates α^s_π when all parameters are taken from (14.30)–(14.33).

are additional mechanisms at work that are eventually responsible for the stabilizing effects of $|f'_g|$.

Another parameter that directly influences the reactions of aggregate output in response to changes in the real interest rate is the marginal propensity to consume, c_y. Since a higher propensity increases the Keynesian multiplier, c_y might be expected to have similar effects as $|f'_g|$. The upper-right panel of Figure 14.2 reveals that this presumption is false: higher values of c_y are destabilizing rather than stabilizing. Furthermore, already at a familiar propensity like $c_y = 0.70$ there are no more realistic coefficients α_π by which the central bank could bring about stability ($\alpha^s_\pi = 9.16$ in this case).

The lower-left panel of Figure 14.2 demonstrates that a higher (modulus of the) interest elasticity of money demand, η_{mi}, is destabilizing. In comparison to the former two examples, however, the effect is quite moderate. The reason is that in the Jacobian matrix, the coefficient f_{mi} that corresponds to η_{mi} only shows up in the partial derivatives h_π and h_b, whose impact on the entries j_{21} and j_{22} (via A_y and A_π) proves to be relatively minor.[15]

According to the lower-right panel of Figure 14.2, the economy is destabilized by a higher money multiplier, i.e., a lower value of μ. This observation could have some significance for a more explicit modelling of the financial sector. Recall that setting the money multiplier at $1/\mu = 2.17$ was based on the standard formula that includes the reserve requirement ratio and the proportion in which people hold money in currency. If, for simplicity, the modelling of a banking sector disregards money holdings in currency, the money multiplier would directly be given by the reciprocal of the reserve requirement ratio, so that $\mu \leqslant 0.10$. At least in the present limited framework, this value would be much too low to possibly give rise to stability.

In a second set of experiments we study *ceteris paribus* variations of steady-state magnitudes. To begin with the upper-left panel in Figure 14.3, which considers government debt, it is seen that higher indebtedness endangers stability. For better comparability, reference is made to the equilibrium ratio of bonds to nominal output rather than to the bonds-capital ratio b^o. It can thus be said that certainly total instability would prevail if government debt were at a European scale, with B/pY being at a 50 or 60% level.

Regarding the other financial asset, the ratio of money holdings $M/pY = 0.15$ can perhaps be deemed to be somewhat low. The second panel in the upper-right corner of Figure 14.3 shows that higher ratios would be no problem; they would, mildly, enhance the stability prospects of the economy.

The equilibrium rate of interest of the baseline scenario was set quite arbitrarily at $i = 4.5\%$. The lower-left panel makes us aware that this choice is not innocent: a few basis points more destabilize the economy completely. Incidentally, the problem is not Assumption 1, which remains satisfied for $i \leqslant 6.2\%$. Referring to the terms $\phi_{\pi g}$ and $\phi_{\pi c}$ that were introduced above, a higher interest rate ($i^o = 4.7\%$, say) rather decreases $\phi_{\pi g}$ (from 0.0201 to 0.0187) and increases $\phi_{\pi c}$ (from 0.0189 to 0.0197), such that $\phi_\pi = \phi_{\pi g} - \phi_{\pi c}$ quickly becomes negative (the 'intercept' ϕ_o raises slightly but stays below zero).

Lastly, the lower-right panel of Figure 14.3 could be viewed against recent debates on whether the central bank may have a target rate of inflation of less than 2%. The main apprehension is here the risk of a 'liquidity trap', when at low inflation or even deflation the central bank, owing to the nonnegativity constraint on i, can no longer sufficiently reduce the real rate of interest. These problems are, of course, completely absent in the local analysis of the present economy. The panel shows that targeting for lower inflation can also destabilize the economy in very different ways.

---

[15] For example, reducing the interest elasticity to $|\eta_{mi}| = 0.10$ only changes j_{21} from 0.2064 to 0.2187 and j_{22} from -0.0162 to -0.0186.

Figure 14.3. **Local stability under variations of** $(B/pY)^o$, $(M/pY)^o$, i^o **and** π^o

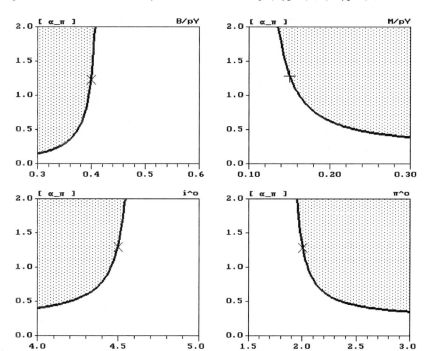

The findings of this numerical stability analysis may be briefly summarized in a second 'observation'.

Observation 2. *With respect to the local stability of the steady-state position, the following parameter changes are stabilizing: a higher responsiveness of investment to interest rate variations,* $|f'_g|$*; a lower propensity to consume,* c_y*; a lower interest elasticity (in absolute value) of money demand,* $|\eta_{mi}|$*; a lower money multiplier, i.e., higher values of* μ*. As for the steady-state magnitudes, stabilizing are also: a lower ratio of government debt* b^o *or* $(B/pY)^o$*; a higher money-output ratio* $(M/pY)^o$*; a lower rate of interest* i^o*; a higher target rate of inflation* π^o*.*

Local stability as well as instability can be brought about by fairly reasonable sets of parameter values.

The analysis so far was concerned with checking the stability conditions, whether local stability prevails or not. These results should, however, be complemented by an investigation of the speed of convergence or divergence. As a matter of fact, it might be suspected that the adjustments are rather slow. One easily infers from the above numerical examples that det $J \cong \phi_o + \phi_\pi \alpha_\pi$ is very close to zero, which means that likewise one of the eigen-values of the Jacobian, designate it λ_1, is nearly zero. In addition, the second eigen-value λ_2 always falls short of this one, so that, after possibly a phase of transition, the speed of convergence or divergence is eventually determined by λ_1. To take up the example with the three investment reaction coefficients $f'_g = -0.90, -1.10, -1.30$, and setting α_π as high as $\alpha_\pi = 2$, the leading eigen-value is computed as $\lambda_1 = 0.0027, -0.0004, -0.0023$, respectively (while α_y discernibly changes the second eigen-value, it has no effect on the first four significant digits of λ_1). A similar order of magnitude obtains for alternative values of α_π and also for quite different values of the other parameters. It must therefore be concluded that convergence of π and b towards the equilibrium, as well as divergence from it, takes place at a speed that is far below any time scale worth thinking of.

We have thus to ask for the economy's dynamic behaviour in the medium-run. Consider to this end the phase diagram in the (b, π)-plane of the linearized system (14.18) and (14.24) in the upper-left corner of Figure 14.4, which has the baseline scenario with the Taylor coefficients $\alpha_y = \alpha_\pi = 0.50$ underlying. As is already known, the steady state is still a saddle point at these values. The unstable manifold is drawn as the solid thin line with the outward-pointing arrows, the dashed thin line is the stable manifold given by the (translated) eigen-vector associated with the second eigen-value λ_2.

The bold lines depict two trajectories that are initiated by a positive and negative shock to the rate of inflation in the equilibrium position. The trajectories run over 10 years, where the arrow heads give the state of the economy after 5 years. It is thus seen that it takes more than 10 years to reach the unstable manifold. In the meantime, the trajectories are determined by the second eigen-value, in the sense that the speed of change is basically given by $\lambda_2 < 0$, i.e., by a factor $e^{\lambda_2 t}$, and (b, π) moves parallel to the corresponding eigen-vector. Consequently, after the supply shock assumed, the rate of inflation adjusts back towards its target level, while the bond ratio begins to diverge from the steady-state value. Over a reasonable span of time, this is what characterizes the dynamics.

When, eventually, the system approaches the unstable eigen-vector and the eigen-value λ_1 takes over, the motions are so slow that hardly any significant change is visible over the next few decades. So, for all practical reasons, the solid thin line can be regarded as a continuum of equilibria. Observe that even for larger deviations of b from b^o, the corresponding 'equilibrium' rate of inflation remains close to π^o.

Things are essentially the same if α_y and α_π are raised to 2.0, which renders the steady-state stable. This situation is represented in the upper-right panel of Figure 14.4. The eigen-vectors associated both with λ_1 and λ_2 change very little. Though in the long run all trajectories (except those starting on the dashed thin line) are attracted by the solid thin line, which then carries the economy back to (b^o, π^o), these adjustments are again completed only over an extremely long period of time. Practically this locus can again be viewed as an equilibrium set. Indeed the main difference to the first panel is the more rapid convergence to this set.

Figure 14.4. **Phase diagrams of the linearized system (14.18) and (14.24)**

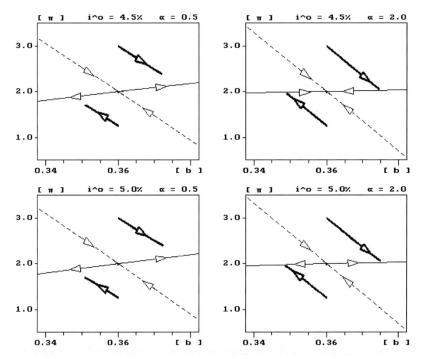

Note: Bold lines are trajectories over 10 years (over 5 years at tip of arrow); solid (dashed) thin lines are the paths given by the leading eigen-value λ_1 (by λ_2, respectively). $\alpha = 0.5$ (2.0) stands for $\alpha_y = \alpha_\pi = 0.5$ (2.0).

The lower two panels of Figure 14.4 are based on a higher equilibrium rate of interest, $i^o = 5\%$, which implies an unstable steady state for all α_π. The dynamic features are nevertheless very similar. For $\alpha_y = \alpha_\pi = 2.0$ the movements on the eigen-vector associated with λ_1 now point outward, but this hardly matters because they are still so slow. Note also that the eigen-vectors as well as the time paths are almost indistinguishable from those in the upper row of Figure 14.4. We thus summarize:

Observation 3. *The trajectories of system (14.18) and (14.24) in the (b, π)-plane are attracted by a set E, which can practically (i.e., over several decades) be regarded as a continuum of equilibria. The values of the inflation rate on this geometric locus are all close to the target level π^o.*

The speed at which (b, π) approaches the set E is basically governed by the policy parameter α_π, where higher values of α_π speed up convergence.

The dynamic features of the baseline scenario may finally be illustrated by the time series diagrams in Figure 14.5, where the bold lines depict the time paths

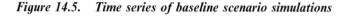

Figure 14.5.   Time series of baseline scenario simulations

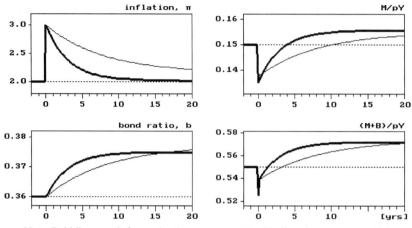

Note: Bold lines result from adopting $\alpha_y = \alpha_\pi = 2.0$, thin lines from $\alpha_y = \alpha_\pi = 0.5$.

obtained for $\alpha_y = \alpha_\pi = 2.0$. To put them into perspective, the thin lines are the time series resulting from $\alpha_y = \alpha_\pi = 0.5$. They show the same qualitative behaviour, though the adjustments are somewhat slower. So let us consider the bold lines, which correspond to the trajectory in the upper half-plane of the upper-right panel in Figure 14.4. They, in particular, demonstrate that all motions have nearly ceased after 10 years (when the trajectory in Figure 14.4 has almost reached the quasi-equilibrium set E given by the eigen-vector of λ_1). A comparison of the inflation time series in Figure 14.5 with the upper-right panel in Figure 14.1 shows that the two adjustment paths of π with the bond dynamics frozen (in Figure 14.1) and integrated (in Figure 14.5) are virtually identical. The same holds true for the output gaps, $[y(\pi, b) - y^o]/y^o$ (not shown) vis-à-vis $[y(\pi, b^o) - y^o]/y^o$ in Figure 14.1, since the partial derivative $y_b = \partial y / \partial b$ are really small.

   Figure 14.5 makes it once again clear that after the supply shock to the inflation rate that disturbs the economy from the steady-state position, inflation is led back to its target level, whereas bonds persistently diverge. That is, the bond ratio settles on a seemingly new equilibrium value, which is quite distinct from b^o. To which one, it is easily conceivable, depends on the size of the shock to π. Likewise, if another shock occurs to π in the course of its adjustment towards π^o, the bond ratio will converge to still another quasi-equilibrium level, depending also on the specific value b has attained when the shock occurred. What has thus been briefly described is the phenomenon of hysteresis ("history matters"). Technically, near-hysteresis could have already been inferred from recognizing the near-zero eigen-values of the Jacobian.

   The two panels on the right of Figure 14.5 demonstrate that what has been said about the bond ratio similarly applies to the alternative financial asset, money, as well as to total wealth (within our limited setting) $M + B$, both here related to nominal output.[16] Interestingly, the shock to π first diminishes the money-output ratio. In the sequel, M/pY rises and eventually overshoots the steady-state ratio, without returning to it. The same pattern is obtained for the sum of the two assets, $(M + B)/pY$.

8. Conclusion

The present paper relates to the burgeoning literature that combines an interest rate reaction function of the central bank with an IS equation and a Phillips curve relationship. For simplicity, this approach disregards the dynamics of bonds and high-powered money that are implied by this type of monetary policy, and possible feedbacks that may emanate from them. By contrast, taking up the deterministic prototype model of Taylor (2000a, 2001) and Romer (2000) and supposing in line with their background discussion that the interest rates are enforced by open market operations, we have made the evolution of these financial assets explicit. A channel was furthermore introduced through which bonds act on aggregate demand, the assumption being that consumption depends on disposable income, and that the latter comprises the interest payments on bonds.

The integration of these concepts into the Taylor–Romer framework gave rise to a two-dimensional differential equations system. A first result of the subsequent local stability analysis was the possibility of total instability. That is, whatever values for the inflation and output coefficients in the Taylor rule the central bank may adopt, the steady-state position is always unstable. The outcome is somewhat surprising since the (one-dimensional) Taylor–Romer model is unambiguously stable, our innovation of the feedback of bonds on the demand side is minimal, and also the auto-feedback of bonds themselves is a negative one. A careful numerical investigation established that both stability and instability can be brought about by meaningful parameter configurations.

A second main finding of the numerical analysis was a near-zero eigen-value of the Jacobian matrix, which in fact prevailed over all parameter variations considered. It is also the maximal eigen-value, the other one being distinctly negative. So, in the medium-run, the trajectories are attracted by a set that can be characterized as continuum of quasi-equilibria, since the motions have then virtually ceased on it. Consequently, the dynamics can be said to exhibit (near-)hysteresis.

Specifically, if the economy experiences a supply shock in the steady-state position, the rate of inflation turns back towards its target level, at a speed

---

[16] The time path of M/pY is obtained from the decomposition $M/pY = (H/\mu pK)(pK/pY) = h/\mu y$ and the linear approximation $z = z^o + z_\pi(\pi - \pi^o) + z_b(b - b^o)$, $z = y, h$.

roughly comparable with that in the models alluded to above. Over the same time horizon, however, bonds and money diverge from their steady-state ratios. We take this behaviour as an indication that the neglect of possible feedbacks of the financial assets on the real side of the economy (other than the interest payment effects here considered) may not be fully consistent. Larger variations of the array of financial assets are likely to affect other financial rates of return, in addition to the bond rate of interest, and some of them, or wealth variables themselves, should finally impact on aggregate demand. Feedbacks from a financial sector modelled in greater detail may therefore not just be interesting, they may also be important in assessing the virtues of (alternative) monetary policy rules.[17]

In conclusion, we may refer to the "Keynesian macroeconomics without the LM curve" mentioned in the title of the paper and likewise to the more general (discrete-time and stochastic) approach based on IS mechanisms, some Phillips curve and an interest rate reaction function. When introducing money and bonds into this framework, the implicit question was for possible destabilization effects. This question can now be answered at three different levels. First, in the long-run, the economy is not safe from instability, as there are realistic parameter scenarios of even total instability. This long-run was, however, found to be unduly long. Second, with respect to the medium-run and the usual key variables, convergence of output back towards normal and inflation back towards its target value is not essentially endangered by the present feedbacks from the bond dynamics. Third, these adjustments imply larger deviations of bonds and money. From this feature it can be suspected that also models with a richer financial sector will generate significant variations of the financial assets, which eventually should affect the rest of the economy. This third level provides a field for future research concerning the efficiency of monetary policy rules.

References

Alesina, A. (2000), "The political economy of the budget surplus in the United States", *Journal of Economic Perspectives*, Vol. 14(3), pp. 3–19.

Backus, D.K. and P.J. Kehoe (1992), "International evidence on the historical properties of business cycles", *American Economic Review*, Vol. 82, pp. 864–888.

Ball, L. (1997), "Efficient rules for monetary policy", NBER Working Paper 5952, published in *International Finance*, Vol. 2, pp. 63–83.

---

[17] Strictly speaking, the present assets are still a short-cut because the concept of the money multiplier usually presupposes the existence of loans granted to the private sector by commercial banks.

Blanchard, O. (2000), *Macroeconomics*, 2nd edition, Upper Saddle River: Prentice-Hall.

Boorman, J.T. (1976), "The evidence on the demand for money: theoretical formulations and empirical results", pp. 315–360 in: T.M. Havrilesky and J.T. Boorman, editors, *Current Issues in Monetary Theory and Practice*, Arlington Heights, IL: AHM Publishing Group.

Cooley, T.F. and L.E. Ohanian (1991), "The cyclical behavior of prices", *Journal of Monetary Economics*, Vol. 28, pp. 25–60.

Fiorito, R. and T. Kollintzas (1994), "Stylized facts of business cycles in the G7 from a real business cycle perspective", *European Economic Review*, Vol. 38, pp. 235–269.

Franke, R. (2001), "Three wage-price macro models and their calibration", Mimeo, University of Bielefeld, Center for Empirical Macroeconomics (http://www.wiwi.uni-bielefeld.de/~semmler/cem/wp.htm#2001).

Goldfeld, S. (1976), "The case of the missing money", *Brookings Papers on Economic Activity*, Vol. 3, pp. 683–739.

Romer, D. (2000), "Keynesian macroeconomics without the LM curve", NBER Working Paper 7461, published in *Journal of Economic Perspectives*, Vol. 14:2, pp. 149–169.

Rudebusch, G. and L.E.O. Svensson (1999), "Policy rules for inflation targeting", pp. 203–246 in: J.B. Taylor, editor, *Monetary Policy Rules*, Chicago: Chicago University Press.

Sargent, T. (1987), *Macroeconomics*, New York: Academic Press.

Taylor, J.B. (1993), "Discretion versus policy rules in practice", *Carnegie-Rochester Conference Series on Public Policy*, Vol. 39, pp. 195–214.

Taylor, J.B. (2000a), "Teaching modern macroeconomics at the Principles level", *American Economic Review, P.P.*, Vol. 90, pp. 90–94.

Taylor, J.B. (2000b), "Reassessing discretionary fiscal policy", *Journal of Economic Perspectives*, Vol. 14(3), pp. 21–36.

Taylor, J.B. (2001), *Economics*, Boston, NY: Houghton Mifflin.

Appendix

To show $y_\pi = \mathrm{d}y/\mathrm{d}\pi < 0$ in Equation (14.3), write $j(y, \pi)$ for the right-hand side of (14.1) and define the function $F_y = F_y(y, \pi) := y - f_y[j(y, \pi) - \pi]$, which has partial derivatives $\partial F_y/\partial y = 1 - \alpha_y f'_y > 0$, $\partial F_y/\partial \pi = -\alpha_\pi f'_y > 0$. Applying the Implicit Function Theorem to the equation $F_y(y, \pi) = 0$ yields $\mathrm{d}y/\mathrm{d}\pi = -(\partial F_y/\partial \pi)/(\partial F_y/\partial y) < 0$.

The formulae for the partial derivatives in (14.8) are most easily derived by applying the Implicit Function Theorem to Equation (14.7). Omitting here and in the following the superscript 'o' that indicates the steady state values, this yields,

$$f_{hi} = \frac{(h+\mu b)f_{mi}}{1-f_m} \qquad f_{hy} = \frac{(h+\mu b)f_{my}}{1-f_m} \qquad f_{hb} = \frac{\mu f_m}{1-f_m}$$

To obtain the partial derivatives of the IS output–capital ratio $y = y(\pi, b)$ from Equation (14.17), compute the partial derivatives of the excess demand function E_y,

$$E_{yy} = -A_c - \alpha_y A_g \qquad E_{y\pi} = c_y(1-\tau)b - \alpha_\pi A_g \qquad E_{yb} = c_y(1-\tau)i$$

and get $y_\pi = -E_{y\pi}/E_{yy}$, $y_b = -E_{yb}/E_{yy}$ from, again, the Implicit Function Theorem. To verify that $i_\pi = 1 + \alpha_\pi + \alpha_y y_\pi > 1$ in (14.22), observe that $\alpha_\pi + \alpha_y y_\pi > \alpha_\pi + \alpha_y \alpha_\pi A_g/(A_c + \alpha_y A_g) > \alpha_\pi - \alpha_\pi = 0$.

The partial derivatives of the function $h = h(\pi, b)$ in (14.23) are

$$\begin{aligned}
h_\pi &= f_{hi} i_\pi + f_{hy} y_\pi \\
&= (h+\mu b)[(1+\alpha_\pi)f_{mi} + (f_{my} + \alpha_y f_{mi})y_\pi]/(1-f_m)
\end{aligned}$$

$$\begin{aligned}
h_b &= f_{hi} i_b + f_{hy} y_b + f_{hb} \\
&= [(h+\mu b)(f_{my} + \alpha_y f_{mi})y_b + \mu f_m]/(1-f_m)
\end{aligned}$$

To determine the sign of h_b and $1 + h_b$, abbreviate $A_i := c_y(1-\tau)i$ and consider the expression $a = a(\alpha_y) := \alpha_y y_b = \alpha_y A_i/(A_c + \alpha_y A_g)$. The function $a(\cdot)$ is increasing with an upper limit A_i/A_g as $\alpha_y \to \infty$. With $f_{my} \geq 0$ we then have $1 + h_b \geq [1 - f_m + (h+\mu b)a(\alpha_y)f_{mi} + \mu f_m]/(1-f_m)$, and the term is square brackets is positive if $|f_{mi}| < [1 - (1-\mu)f_m]/(h+\mu b)a(\alpha_y)$. The right-hand side of this inequality is decreasing in α_y, and for $\alpha_y \geq 0$ is larger than $[1 - (1-\mu)f_m]A_g/(h+\mu b)A_i$. This proves $1 + h_b > 0$ if Assumption 3a is fulfilled.

Similarly, $h_b > 0$ if $(h+\mu b)a(\alpha_y)f_{mi} + \mu f_m > 0$, or $|f_{mi}| < \mu f_m/(h+\mu b)a(\alpha_y)$, which is satisfied if $|f_{mi}| < \mu f_m A_g/(h+\mu b)A_i$, the expression in Assumption 3b.

To verify (14.29) for $\det J$, we take up Equation (14.27) and prove that $|E_{yy}|(y_\pi A_b - y_b A_\pi) = \phi_o + \alpha_\pi \phi_\pi$. Define to this end $A_{i\pi} := (1-\tau)i - (\pi+g)$ and $A_{cg} := c_y(1-\tau)b - \alpha_\pi A_g$. Then, with Equations (14.20), (14.25) and E_{yy} as determined above,

$$\begin{aligned}
|E_{yy}|y_\pi A_b &= A_{cg}[A_{i\pi} - h_b(\pi+g)] \\
&= A_{cg}A_{i\pi} - A_{cg}\mu f_m(\pi+g)/(1-f_m) \\
&\quad - A_{cg}(h+\mu b)(f_{my} + \alpha_y f_{mi})c_y(1-\tau)i(\pi+g)/(1-f_m)|E_{yy}| \\
&= A_{cg}[A_{i\pi} - \mu f_m(\pi+g)/(1-f_m)] \\
&\quad - \frac{A_{cg}(h+\mu b)(f_{my} + \alpha_y f_{mi})c_y(1-\tau)i(\pi+g)}{(1-f_m)|E_{yy}|}
\end{aligned}$$

$$-|E_{yy}|y_\pi A_b = -c_y(1-\tau)i[(1+\alpha_\pi)(1-\tau)b + (h+b)(\alpha_\pi|f'_g|-1)$$
$$+ (h+\mu b)(1+\alpha_\pi)|f_{mi}|(\pi+g)/(1-f_m)$$
$$- (h+\mu b)(f_{my}+\alpha_y f_{mi})A_{cg}(\pi+g)/(1-f_m)|E_{yy}|]$$
$$= -c_y(1-\tau)i\{-\tau b - h + \alpha_\pi[(1-\tau)b + (h+b)|f'_g|]$$
$$+ (h+\mu b)(\pi+g)|f_{mi}|/(1-f_m)$$
$$+ \alpha_\pi(h+\mu b)(\pi+g)|f_{mi}|/(1-f_m)\}$$
$$+ \frac{c_y(1-\tau)i(h+\mu b)(f_{my}+\alpha_y f_{mi})A_{cg}(\pi+g)}{(1-f_m)|E_{yy}|}$$

The two fractions cancel out. Then, referring to (26), note that $A_{i\pi} - \mu f_m(\pi+g)/(1-f_m) = -A_1$. We thus remain with

$$|E_{yy}|(y_\pi A_b - y_b A_\pi) = -c_y(1-\tau)bA_1 + \alpha_\pi A_g A_1 + c_y(1-\tau)i(h+\tau b - A_2)$$
$$- \alpha_\pi c_y(1-\tau)i[(1-\tau)b + (h+b)|f'_g| + A_2]$$
$$= -c_y(1-\tau)[A_1 b - i(h+\tau b - A_2)]$$
$$+ \alpha_\pi\{A_g A_1 - c_y(1-\tau)i[(1-\tau)b + (h+b)|f'_g| + A_2]\}$$
$$= \phi_o + \alpha_\pi\phi_\pi$$

Finally, to turn to the Rudebusch–Svensson model mentioned at the end of Section 6, its quarterly equations for the inflation rate and the output gap read, in their deterministic part (*ibid*, p. 208):

$$\pi_{t+1} = 0.70\pi_t - 0.10\pi_{t-1} + 0.28\pi_{t-2} + 0.12\pi_{t-3} + 0.14y_t$$
$$y_{t+1} = 1.16y_t - 0.25y_{t-1} - 0.10(\bar{i}_t - \bar{\pi}_t)$$

where the bar over i and π indicates backward-looking four-quarter averages, $\bar{i}_t = (1/4)\sum_{k=0}^{3} i_{t-k}$ (i and π are measured at annual rates). The coefficients result from an estimation over the sample period 1961:1–1996:2 (the standard errors are reported as 1.009 for π and 0.819 for y, the Durbin–Watson statistic is in both cases close to 2).

CHAPTER 15

Nonlinear Phillips Curves, Endogenous NAIRU and Monetary Policy

Willi Semmler and Wenlang Zhang

Abstract

The recent literature on monetary policy has questioned the shape of the Phillips curve and the assumption of a constant NAIRU. In this paper, we explore monetary policy considering nonlinear Phillips curves and an endogenous NAIRU, which can be affected by the monetary policy. We first study monetary policy with different shapes of the Phillips curve: linear, convex and convex–concave. We find that the optimal monetary policy changes with the shape of the Phillips curve, but there exists a unique equilibrium no matter whether the Phillips curve is linear or nonlinear. We also explore monetary policy with an endogenous NAIRU, since some researchers, Blanchard (2003) for example, have proposed that the NAIRU may be influenced by monetary policy. Based on some empirical evidence and assuming that monetary policy can influence the NAIRU, we find that there may exist multiple equilibria in the economy, different from the results of models presuming a constant NAIRU.

Keywords: nonlinear Phillips curve, endogenous NAIRU, Kalman filter

JEL classifications: E0, E5

1. Introduction

Recently, an important topic in studies of monetary policy has been the shape of the Phillips curve. The shape of the Phillips curve plays an important role in monetary policy and has important implications for policymakers, because the

CONTRIBUTIONS TO ECONOMIC ANALYSIS
VOLUME 277   ISSN: 0573-8555
DOI:10.1016/S0573-8555(05)77015-2

IS and Phillips curves have been the core model for monetary policy studies from a Keynesian perspective.

In earlier studies the Phillips curve has been proposed to be linear. But most of the recent literature has casted doubt on the linearity of the Phillips curve. Dupasquier and Ricketts (1998a), for example, survey several models that explore why the Phillips curve may be nonlinear. It has been argued that the Phillips curve may have three shapes. The first group of researchers propose that the Phillips curve is convex. This possibility has been considered by Clark *et al.* (1996), Schaling (1999) and Bean (2000), for example. A convex Phillips curve appears in an economy subject to capacity constraints. The second group of researchers propose that the Phillips curve is concave. Eisner (1997), for example, reports some results concerned with this possibility. A concave Phillips curve may exist in an economy where firms are not purely competitive. Besides these two shapes of the Phillips curve, Filardo (1998), on the basis of some empirical research with U.S. data, proposes that the Phillips curve is not purely convex or concave, but instead convex–concave. He finds that the Phillips curve is convex if the output gap is positive and concave if the output gap is negative. Therefore, he points out that the supporters of a convex or concave Phillips curve have studied only one case and overlooked the other. The shape of the Phillips curve has crucial implications for central banks, since the optimal monetary policy may change with the shape of the Phillips curve.

Another important topic of monetary policy is whether the NAIRU is constant. In the 1960s Friedman and Phelps proposed a vertical long-run Phillips curve. The traditional view is that money cannot influence the unemployment rate in the long run and therefore the unemployment rate returns to the natural rate or the NAIRU over time, which is presumed to be constant. The recent literature has put this view into question and proposes that the long-run Phillips curve may be non-vertical and the NAIRU non-constant. That is, the NAIRU can be affected by the inflation rate and monetary policy. Gordon (1997), for example, estimates the time-varying NAIRU for the U.S. with and without the supply shocks. Some other researchers have also tried to estimate a time-varying NAIRU. An earlier survey on the estimation of the NAIRU is given by Staiger *et al.* (1996). Blanchard (2003), moreover, remarks that the natural rate of unemployment has been affected by the real interest rate in Europe in the 1970s and 1980s in different directions. He further proposes several mechanisms in which the real interest rate may influence the natural rate of the unemployment. On the other hand, some researchers, Stiglitz (1997) for example, maintain that the NAIRU may have feedback effects on policies in the sense that it might produce a moving target for monetary policy. Therefore, an economic model with an exogenous NAIRU might not explore monetary policy properly.

The remainder of this paper is organized as follows. In second section, we explore monetary policy in a traditional model with a linear Phillips curve and a constant NAIRU. In Section 3, we study monetary policy with different shapes of the nonlinear Phillips curve, maintaining the assumption of a constant

NAIRU. In fourth section, however, we study the monetary policy with an endogenous NAIRU, which can be affected by the monetary policy and the last section concludes the paper.

2. Monetary policy in a traditional model: linear Phillips curve with and without expectations

The traditional IS curve reads as

$$\dot{\mu}(t) = \alpha r(t) + \vartheta \mu(t), \quad \alpha > 0$$

where $\mu(t)$ denotes the gap between the actual unemployment $u(t)$ and the NAIRU $u_n(t)$, namely $u(t) - u_n(t)$, $r(t)$ is the monetary policy instrument. Assuming $\vartheta = 0$ for simplicity, we obtain

$$\dot{\mu}(t) = \alpha r(t) \tag{15.1}$$

In the traditional model the NAIRU is assumed to be an exogenous variable, which remains constant because of the neutrality of money. "·" denotes the derivative with respect to time t. The equation above implies

$$\dot{\mu}(t) = \dot{u}(t) - \dot{u}_n(t) = \dot{u}(t) = \alpha r(t) \tag{15.2}$$

since the NAIRU is constant. Let π denote the deviation of the actual inflation rate from its target (assumed to be zero here). Following Walsh (1999), Ball (1999) and Hall (2000) who assume that the inflation rate is affected by the real interest rate as well as the unemployment gap, we write the Phillips curve without expectation as[1]

$$\pi(t) = -\beta r(t) - \theta \mu(t), \quad \beta, \theta > 0 \tag{15.3}$$

---

[1] In fact, the Phillips curve above is equivalent to an open economy Phillips curve with

$$\pi(t) = -\tau e(t) - \theta \mu(t)$$

with $e(t)$ denoting the real exchange rate and τ the share of imports in domestic spending. A higher $e(t)$ means appreciation. Such a Phillips curve can be found in Walsh (1999) and Guender (2001). Ball (1999) employs a similar equation except that the change of $e(t)$ is included in the open-economy Phillips curve. Moreover, following Ball (1999) we can link the real exchange rate and the real interest rate by

$$e(t) = \omega r(t) + v(t)$$

with $v(t)$ being a white noise, which captures other effects on the exchange rate. The Phillips curve in Equation (15.3) is then obtained by substituting the deterministic version of the exchange rate equation into the above Phillips curve. Hall (2000) also includes the real interest rate in the Phillips curve. Furthermore, we follow Ball (1999) and take the real interest rate as the policy instrument. Although McCallum casts doubt on Ball (1999) for the use of the real rate as a policy instrument, Ball (1999, footnote 2), however, correctly argues that policy makers can move the real interest rate to their desired level by setting the nominal rate equal to the desired real rate plus the inflation rate. Ball (1999) also considers the exchange-rate effect in the IS equation. Given the exchange rate equation above, Equation (15.1) can also be considered as the IS equation in the open economy. Another justification for this Phillips curve is the so-called P-star model in which inflation rate turns out to be a function of the real interest rate.

Suppose the central bank has the following loss function

$$L(t) \equiv \pi^2(t) + \lambda \mu(t)^2 \tag{15.4}$$

where $\lambda(>0)$ denotes the weight of unemployment stabilization. We will drop the notation "t" in variables in the remainder of the paper just for simplicity. Suppose the goal of the monetary policy is to minimize the loss function with an infinite horizon, the central bank's problem turns out to be

$$\min_{r} \int_0^\infty e^{-\rho t} L \, dt$$

subject to

$$\dot{\mu} = \alpha r \tag{15.5}$$

where $\rho \, (0 < \rho < 1)$ is the discount factor and L defined by (15.4). The current-value Hamiltonian of the above problem reads as

$$H_c = [\beta r + \theta \mu]^2 + \lambda \mu^2 + \gamma \alpha r \tag{15.6}$$

where γ is a costate variable. The optimal conditions for this problem turn out to be

$$\frac{\partial H_c}{\partial r} = 0 \tag{15.7}$$

$$\dot{\gamma} = -\frac{\partial H_c}{\partial \mu} + \rho \gamma \tag{15.8}$$

with the following transversality condition

$$\lim_{t \to \infty} \gamma e^{-\rho t} = 0 \tag{15.9}$$

From (15.7), we get the optimal monetary policy

$$r = -\frac{\alpha \gamma}{2\beta^2} - \frac{\theta}{\beta} \mu \tag{15.10}$$

from which we know

$$\dot{\gamma} = -\frac{2\beta}{\alpha} (\beta \dot{r} + \theta \alpha r) \tag{15.11}$$

Some rearrangement of (15.8), (15.10) and (15.11) gives us the following dynamic system of r and μ

$$\dot{r} = \rho r + \left[\frac{\theta \rho}{\beta} + \frac{\alpha}{\beta^2} (\theta^2 + \lambda^2) \right] \mu \tag{15.12}$$

$$\dot{\mu} = \alpha r \tag{15.13}$$

Setting $\dot{r} = \dot{\mu} = 0$, we obtain the unique equilibrium

$$r^* = 0, \quad \mu^* = 0 \quad (u^* = u_n)$$

The Jacobian matrix of the dynamic system evaluated at the equilibrium is

$$J = \begin{pmatrix} \rho & \dfrac{\theta\rho}{\beta} + \dfrac{\alpha}{\beta^2}(\theta^2 + \lambda^2) \\ \alpha & 0 \end{pmatrix}$$

If x_1 and x_2 are two characteristic roots of J, it is obvious that

$$x_1 + x_2 = \rho > 0, \quad x_1 x_2 = -\alpha \left[\frac{\theta\rho}{\beta} + \frac{\alpha}{\beta^2}(\theta^2 + \lambda^2) \right] < 0$$

We find that x_1 and x_2 are both real with opposite signs. This indicates that the unique equilibrium $(0, 0)$ is a saddle point.

Above, we have explored monetary policy in a traditional model with a linear Phillips curve without expectation considered. Next, we explore monetary policy with expectation in the Phillips curve. The expectation-augmented Phillips curve is written as:

$$\pi = -\beta r - \theta\mu + \pi_e \tag{15.14}$$

with π_e denoting the expectation of the inflation rate. Following the traditional literature we assume that the expectation evolves in an adaptive way[2]

$$\dot{\pi}_e = \kappa(\pi - \pi_e), \quad \kappa > 0 \tag{15.15}$$

The loss function L now looks like

$$L = [\pi_e - \beta r - \theta\mu]^2 + \lambda\mu^2 \tag{15.16}$$

After some rearrangement the problem of a central bank turns out to be

$$\min_r \int_0^\infty e^{-\rho t} L \, dt$$

subject to

$$\dot{\pi}_e = -\kappa[\beta r + \theta\mu] \tag{15.17}$$

$$\dot{\mu} = \alpha r \tag{15.18}$$

The current-value Hamiltonian of this problem reads

$$H_c = [\pi_e - \beta r - \theta\mu]^2 + \lambda\mu^2 - \gamma_1\kappa[\beta r + \theta\mu] + \gamma_2\alpha r \tag{15.19}$$

where γ_1 and γ_2 are costate variables. The optimal conditions turn out to be

$$\frac{\partial H_c}{\partial r} = 0 \tag{15.20}$$

---

[2] We follow here Turnovsky (1981) and use an adaptive expectation dynamics. This is in line with Rudebusch and Svensson (1999) in the sense that only past information is used in the inflation equation.

$$\dot{\gamma}_1 = -\frac{\partial H_c}{\partial \pi_e} + \rho \gamma_1 \tag{15.21}$$

$$\dot{\gamma}_2 = -\frac{\partial H_c}{\partial \mu} + \rho \gamma_2 \tag{15.22}$$

$$\lim_{t \to \infty} \gamma_1 e^{-\rho t} = 0 \tag{15.23}$$

$$\lim_{t \to \infty} \gamma_2 e^{-\rho t} = 0 \tag{15.24}$$

From (15.20) we know

$$r = \frac{1}{\beta} \left[\pi_e - \theta \mu + \frac{\kappa \gamma_1}{2} - \frac{\alpha \gamma_2}{2\beta} \right] \tag{15.25}$$

After substituting (15.25) into (15.17), (15.18), (15.21) and (15.22), we obtain the following dynamic system

$$\dot{\pi}_e = -\kappa \left(\pi_e + \frac{\kappa}{2} \gamma_1 - \frac{\alpha}{2\beta} \gamma_2 \right) \tag{15.26}$$

$$\dot{\mu} = \frac{\alpha}{\beta} \left[\pi_e - \theta \mu + \frac{\kappa}{2} \gamma_1 - \frac{\alpha}{2\beta} \gamma_2 \right] \tag{15.27}$$

$$\dot{\gamma}_1 = (\rho + \kappa)\gamma_1 - \frac{\alpha}{\beta} \gamma_2 \tag{15.28}$$

$$\dot{\gamma}_2 = \left(\rho + \frac{\alpha \theta}{\beta} \right) \gamma_2 - 2\lambda^2 \mu \tag{15.29}$$

Let $\dot{\pi}_e = \dot{\mu} = \dot{\gamma}_1 = \dot{\gamma}_2 = 0$, we obtain the unique equilibrium:

$$\pi_e^* = 0, \mu^* = 0 \, (u^* = u_n), \gamma_1^* = 0, \gamma_2^* = 0$$

and therefore $r^* = 0$ and $\pi^* = 0$. In order to consider the out-of-steady-state dynamics around the equilibrium, we compute the Jacobian matrix of the system (15.26)–(15.29) evaluated at the equilibrium

$$J = \begin{pmatrix} -\kappa & 0 & -\dfrac{\kappa^2}{2} & \dfrac{\alpha \kappa}{2\beta} \\[2mm] \dfrac{\alpha}{\beta} & -\dfrac{\alpha \theta}{\beta} & \dfrac{\alpha \kappa}{2\beta} & -\dfrac{\alpha^2}{2\beta^2} \\[2mm] 0 & 0 & \rho + \kappa & -\dfrac{\alpha}{\beta} \\[2mm] 0 & -2\lambda^2 & 0 & \rho + \dfrac{\alpha \theta}{\beta} \end{pmatrix}.$$

The characteristic equation of J can be written as:

$$\Delta(x) \equiv |xI - J| = x^4 + b_1 x^3 + b_2 x^2 + b_3 x + b_4 = 0 \tag{15.30}$$

The Routh–Hurwitz sufficient and necessary condition for local stability in this case is[3]

$$b_i > 0 \ (i = 1, 2, 3, 4), \quad b_1 b_2 b_3 - b_1^2 b_4 - b_3^2 > 0$$

But it is obvious that

$$b_1 = -2\rho < 0$$

therefore, we conclude that the equilibrium is unstable. This is consistent with the results from the case without expectation. For example, if we take $\alpha = 0.6$, $\kappa = 0.9$, $\beta = 0.6$, $\theta = 0.5$, $\rho = 0.1$ and $\lambda = 0.5$, the eigenvalues of J turn out to be

$$x_1 = -1.060, x_2 = -0.421, x_3 = 1.160, x_4 = 0.521$$

This indicates that the unique equilibrium is unstable, since two characteristic roots are positive.

3. Monetary policy with nonlinear Phillips curve

In the previous section, we have explored monetary policy in a traditional model with a linear Phillips curve. There exists a unique saddle point equilibrium, no matter whether the expectation is taken into account or not.

Recently most of the literature, however, casts doubt on the linearity of the Phillips curve. Dupasquier and Ricketts (1998a), for example, survey several models of the nonlinearity in the Phillips curve. The five models surveyed are the *capacity constraint model*, the *mis-perception* or *signal extraction model*, the *costly adjustment model*, the *downward nominal wage rigidity model* and the *monopolistically competitive model*. These models explain the nonlinearity of the Phillips curve from various perspectives. As also mentioned by Akerlof (2002), the nonlinearity of the Phillips curve has been an important issue of macroeconomics, since it has crucial implications for the monetary authorities.

Many empirical studies have been undertaken to explore the nonlinearity of the Phillips curve. Dupasquier and Ricketts (1998a), for example, explore the nonlinearity in the Phillips curve for Canada and the U.S. and conclude that there is stronger evidence of a nonlinearity for the U.S. than for Canada. Aguiar and Martins (2002), however, test three kinds of nonlinearities (quadratic, hyperbole and exponential) in the Phillips curve and Okun's law with the aggregate Euro-area macroeconomic data and find that the Phillips curve turns out to be linear, but Okun's law is nonlinear.

---

[3] The reader is referred to some advanced textbooks or papers on dynamic systems, Yoshida and Asada (2001) for example, for the computation of b_i.

Other studies on the nonlinearity of the Phillips curve include Gómez and Julio (2000), Dupasquier and Ricketts (1998b), Chadha *et al.* (1992), Laxton *et al.* (1995) and Bean (2000). Monetary policy with a nonlinear Phillips curve has also been explored, see Schaling (1999), Tambakis (1998), Flaschel *et al.* (2001) and Nobay and Peel (2000), for example.

The problem is, if the Phillips curve is nonlinear, what does it look like? Some researchers, Filardo (1998) for instance, have explored this problem both theoretically and empirically. One possible shape of the nonlinear Phillips curve is convex. This possibility has been explored by Clark *et al.* (1996), Schaling (1999), Tambakis (1998), Bean (2000), Zhang and Semmler (2005) and so on. A convex Phillips curve is shown in Figure 15.1A. Filardo (1998) describes the property of a convex Phillips curve as follows:

> "... . The convex Phillips curve is consistent with an economy subject to capacity constraints. ... As the economy becomes stronger and capacity constraints increasingly restrict firms' ability to expand output, an increase in demand is more likely to show up as higher inflation than as higher output." (Filardo, 1998)

Another possible shape of the nonlinear Phillips curve is concave. This possibility has been proposed, for example, by Stiglitz (1997). A concave Phillips curve is shown in Figure 15.1B. The property of a concave Phillips curve can be described as follows:

> " ... Theoretically, a concave Phillips curve is consistent with an economy where firms are not purely competitive. If firms have some pricing power and thus the ability and desire to influence their market share, they will be more reluctant to raise prices than to lower them." (Filardo, 1998)

Eisner (1997) also reports results that are consistent with a concave Phillips curve. Filardo (1998) further claims that the implications for the output cost of fighting inflation may be different for different shapes of the Phillips curve.

> "The concave Phillips curve implies that the cost of fighting inflation rises with the strength of the economy because as the economy strengthens its slope flattens. In contrast, the convex Phillips curve implies that the costs of fighting inflation falls with the strength of the economy because its slope steepens." (Filardo, 1998)

On the basis of these literature, Filardo (1998) explores evidence of a third shape of the nonlinear Phillips curve and proposes that the nonlinear Phillips curve is not purely convex or concave, but a combination of both, namely, convex–concave. He sets up a model as follows:

$$\pi_t = \pi_t^e + \beta_w y_{w,t-1} + \beta_b y_{b,t-1} + \beta_s y_{s,t-1} + \varepsilon_t \tag{15.31}$$

where π_t and π_t^e are actual and expected inflation rates, respectively; y_t is the output gap and ε_t the supply shock; and w, b and s stand for "weak,"

Figure 15.1. Possible shapes of nonlinear Phillips curve

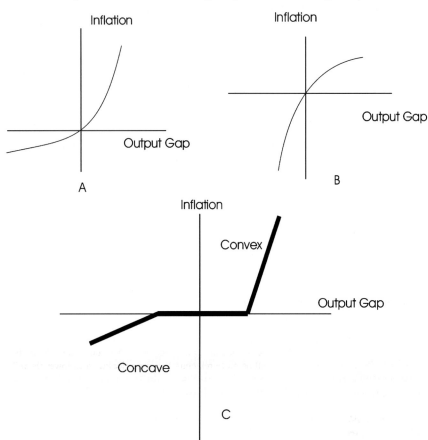

"balanced" and "strong," respectively. The slope coefficients on the output gap (β_w, β_b and β_s) measure the sensitivity of inflation to economic activity in the *weak, balanced* and *overheated* times. In the case of a linear Phillips curve, $\beta_w = \beta_b = \beta_s$. With the U.S. data from 1959–1997, Filardo (1998) finds that $\beta_w = 0.2$, $\beta_b = -0.02$ and $\beta_s = 0.49$. Therefore, he obtains a convex–concave Phillips curve as shown in Figure 15.1C. This nonlinear Phillips curve implies that when the output gap is positive, the Phillips curve is convex and when the output gap is negative, the Phillips curve is concave. Filardo (1998) further states that the researchers who have proposed a convex *or* concave Phillips curve have considered only one case and overlooked the other. The policy implication of a convex–concave Phillips curve is of course different from that of a convex or concave one. Recently, Orphanides and Wieland (2000) explore inflation-zone targeting in the context of a convex–concave Phillips curve.

Based on the literature of nonlinear Phillips curves, this section is devoted to the optimal monetary policy with nonlinear Phillips curves. We will explore monetary policy in two cases: a convex Phillips curve and a convex–concave one.[4] The expectation in the Phillips curve is not taken into account in this section, since the results in the previous section are similar no matter whether the expectation is considered or not. Moreover, the model without expectation is easier to study, since the dimension of the problem is then lower.

3.1. A convex Phillips curve

Some researchers, Schaling (1999) for example, assume that a convex Phillips curve can be defined through the following function

$$f(y) = \frac{\phi y}{1 - \phi \varphi y}, \quad f' > 0, \ f'' > 0, \ \phi > 0, \ 1 > \varphi \geqslant 0 \tag{15.32}$$

where y is the output gap and the parameter φ indexes the curvature of $f(\cdot)$. In case $\varphi = 0, f(\cdot)$ becomes linear. In line with Okun's law, we just assume $y = -\mu$ and then obtain the following convex Phillips curve[5]

$$\pi = -\beta r - \theta \Pi(\mu) \tag{15.33}$$

with $\Pi(\cdot)$ defined as

$$\Pi(\mu) = \frac{\phi \mu}{1 + \phi \varphi \mu} \tag{15.34}$$

In the research below, we assume $\theta = 1$ in the Phillips curve and $\alpha = 1$ in (15.1) just to simplify the analysis. With the above Phillips curve the current-value Hamiltonian of the optimal control now looks like

$$H_c = \left[\beta r + \frac{\phi \mu}{1 + \phi \varphi \mu} \right]^2 + \lambda \mu^2 + \gamma r \tag{15.35}$$

from which we obtain the optimal monetary policy

$$r = -\frac{\phi \mu}{\beta(1 + \phi \varphi \mu)} - \frac{\gamma}{2\beta^2} \tag{15.36}$$

and then by employing (15.8) and (15.36), we have the following dynamic system

$$\dot{r} = \frac{1}{\beta^2} \left[\frac{\phi^2}{\Omega^3} \mu + \lambda \mu + \frac{\beta \phi \rho}{\Omega} \mu \right] + \rho r \tag{15.37}$$

---

[4]Note that we use the unemployment rate instead of the output in the Philips curve. According to Okun's law, there exists a negative correlation between the unemployment and output, therefore, the convexity or concavity mentioned above will not be changed.

[5]In Okun's law ($\mu = -my$), the m is usually smaller than one. We take $m = 1$ just for simplicity since the result below will not be changed if we assume $m < 1$.

$$\mu = r \qquad (15.38)$$

with $\Omega = 1 + \phi\varphi\mu$. Setting $\dot{r} = \dot{\mu} = 0$, we know the equilibrium of r is

$$r^* = 0$$

and the equilibria of μ can then be solved from the equation

$$\Omega^3 \lambda\mu + \phi\beta\rho\Omega^2\mu + \phi^2\mu = 0 \qquad (15.39)$$

It is obvious that $\mu = 0$, therefore $u^* = u_n$ is a solution of (15.39). As a result, $u^* = u_n$ and $r^* = 0$ is an equilibrium of the system (15.37)–(15.38). This is consistent with the unique equilibrium with the traditional linear Phillips curve analyzed in the previous section. But in case $\mu \neq 0$, (15.39) becomes

$$\Omega^3 \lambda + \phi\beta\rho\Omega^2 + \phi^2 = 0, \qquad (15.40)$$

which has three solutions. Note that in order for the condition $f''(\cdot) > 0$ in (15.32) to be satisfied, μ must be larger than $-\frac{1}{\phi\varphi}$. We call this the *Convex Condition*. The *Convex Condition* implies $\Omega > 0$. But it is obvious that (15.40) has no solutions satisfying this condition and therefore $(0,0)$ is the only equilibrium of the above dynamic system. This is consistent with the results of the model analyzed in the previous section.

Next we explore the out-of-steady-state equilibrium dynamics around the equilibrium. The Jacobian matrix of the system (15.37)–(15.38) evaluated at the equilibrium is

$$J = \begin{pmatrix} \rho & \frac{1}{\beta^2}(\phi^2 + \lambda + \beta\phi\rho) \\ 1 & 0 \end{pmatrix}$$

It is obvious that the characteristic roots x_1 and x_2 of J satisfy

$$x_1 + x_2 = \rho > 0, \quad x_1 x_2 = -\frac{1}{\beta^2}(\phi^2 + \lambda + \beta\phi\rho) < 0$$

We find that x_1 and x_2 are both real with opposite signs, this implies that the equilibrium is a saddle point.

3.2. A convex–concave Phillips curve

We have explored monetary policy with a convex Phillips curve and find that there exists a unique equilibrium. As stated before, Filardo (1998) finds that the Phillips curve is convex–concave, depending on whether the output gap is positive or negative. A graph of such a curve is shown in Figure 15.1C. In this section, we will explore monetary policy with such a convex–concave Phillips curve. The Phillips curve in Figure 15.1C has breakpoints and moreover, it is assumed that the derivatives of the curve in the concave and convex zones are constant. This is in fact not consistent with the cases of the two graphs in 15.1A and B, where the derivatives of the curves are dependent on the sizes of the output gap. Filardo (1998) obtains such a non-smooth graph from the estimation of a simple model, in which he assumes the parameters β_w, β_b and β_s in (15.31) to be constant. But in reality the three parameters can be continuously state-dependent. If the parameters are continuously state-dependent, the Phillips curve is then smooth and convex–concave. In the research below, we assume that the Phillips curve is smooth and convex–concave. In order to consider this possibility, we have to design a function which is convex when the output gap is positive and concave when the output gap is negative, and moreover, the absolute values of the derivatives of the function with respect to the output gap are asymmetric around zero. That is, the graph is steeper when the output gap is positive than when the output gap is negative. Fortunately we can design a function with such properties.

Let y denote the output gap, we define the following function $f(y)$

$$f(y) = \delta(e^{ay} - ay - 1)\mathrm{sgn}(y), \quad \delta > 0, a > 0, \tag{15.41}$$

with

$$\mathrm{sgn}(y) = \begin{cases} 1, & \text{if } y \geqslant 0 \\ -1, & \text{if } y < 0 \end{cases}$$

$\delta(e^{ay} - ay - 1)$ is the so-called LINEX function proposed by Varian (1975) and applied, for example, by Nobay and Peel (1998) and Semmler and Zhang (2002). The LINEX function is non-negative and asymmetric around zero and, moreover, the parameter a determines the extent of asymmetry.[6] The parameter δ scales the function.

The graph of $f(y)$ is shown in Figure 15.2. From this figure we see $f(y)$ has the properties discussed above. Let $y = -\mu$, we obtain the following convex–concave Phillips curve

$$\pi = -\beta r - \theta[e^{-a\mu} + a\mu - 1]\mathrm{sgn}(\mu), \quad a > 0 \tag{15.42}$$

where $\mathrm{sgn}(\mu)$ equals 1 when $\mu \geqslant 0$ and -1 when $\mu < 0$. With the Phillips curve defined above the current-value Hamiltonian of the optimal control now looks like

$$H_c = \{\beta r + \theta[e^{-a\mu} + a\mu - 1]\mathrm{sgn}(\mu)\}^2 + \lambda\mu^2 + \gamma r \tag{15.43}$$

from which we obtain the following optimal monetary policy

$$r = -\frac{\theta}{\beta}[e^{-a\mu} + a\mu - 1]\mathrm{sgn}(\mu) - \frac{\gamma}{2\beta^2} \tag{15.44}$$

We have above derived optimal monetary policies from models with different Phillips curves. The optimal monetary policies without expectation are shown in (15.10), (15.36) and (15.44), respectively. The differences between these policies

---

[6] a can be either positive or negative, but in our model it is positive.

Figure 15.2.   *A convex–concave Phillips curve*

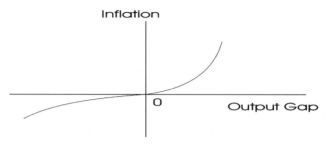

are obvious. Exactly speaking, when the Phillips curve is linear, the optimal monetary policy is also a linear function of the unemployment gap. When the Phillips curve is convex, the optimal monetary policy is a convex function of the unemployment gap. And finally, when the Phillips curve is convex–concave, the optimal monetary policy is a convex–concave function of the unemployment gap. Therefore, the optimal monetary reaction function of the central bank is dependent upon the shape of the Phillips curve.

3.2.1. Dynamics

Next we explore the dynamics of the model. By employing (15.8) and (15.44) we obtain the following dynamic system

$$\dot{r} = \frac{1}{\beta^2}\{a\theta^2(1 - e^{-a\mu})(a\mu + e^{-a\mu} - 1)$$

$$+ \beta\theta\rho(e^{-a\mu} + a\mu - 1)\mathrm{sgn}(\mu) + \lambda\mu\} + \rho r \qquad (15.45)$$

$$\dot{\mu} = r \qquad (15.46)$$

Setting $\dot{\mu} = 0$ we get the equilibrium of r, namely $r^* = 0$. With $r^* = 0$ and setting $\dot{r} = 0$, the equilibrium of μ can be solved from the following equation

$$a\theta^2(1 - e^{-a\mu})(a\mu + e^{-a\mu} - 1) + \beta\theta\rho(e^{-a\mu} + a\mu - 1)\mathrm{sgn}(\mu) + \lambda\mu = 0 \qquad (15.47)$$

$\mu = 0$, namely $u = u_n$ is the only solution of the above equation. This implies that the dynamic system has a unique equilibrium $r^* = 0$ and $\mu^* = 0$. This is consistent with the results in the previous sections. The Jacobian matrix of the system (15.45)–(15.46) evaluated at the equilibrium is

$$J = \begin{pmatrix} \rho & \dfrac{\lambda}{\beta^2} \\ 1 & 0 \end{pmatrix}$$

It is obvious that the equilibrium is a saddle point since the characteristic roots of J are both real with oppositive signs.

In this section, we have explored monetary policy with two nonlinear Phillips curves. There exists a unique equilibrium (a saddle point), no matter whether the

Phillips curve is convex or convex–concave. This is consistent with the results from a model with a linear Phillips curve. But the optimal monetary policy reaction function changes with the shapes of the Phillips curve.

4. Monetary policy with endogenous NAIRU

In the previous sections, we have explored monetary policy with linear and nonlinear Phillips curves with a constant NAIRU (like an exogenous variable). The difference of the results lies in the fact that the monetary policy functions change with the shapes of the Phillips curve. The similarity, however, is that there exists a unique equilibrium (a saddle point) despite of the shapes of the Phillips curve.

According to Friedman (1968) and Phelps (1968), monetary policy has no effects on the unemployment rate in the long run because of the so-called money neutrality. This implies a vertical long-run Phillips curve. The recent literature, however, has questioned this assumption. Stiglitz (1997), for example, surveys some factors that may lead to the movement of the NAIRU. Graham and Snower (2003) derive a microfounded long-run downward-sloping Phillips curve and show that a permanent increase in money growth incurs a permanent increase in the inflation rate and a permanent decrease in the unemployment level. Empirically, he shows that a 1% increase in the money growth rate can induce a long-run reduction in the unemployment from 15 to 0.5% below its steady-state level. They further claim that the effects can be large and have a long half-life in the short and medium run.

Karanassou *et al.* (2003) show that the changes in money growth can have long-run effects on the unemployment as well as inflation even if there are no money illusion and money neutrality. Akerlof *et al.* (2000) argue that the long-run Phillips curve is not vertical but instead bowed-inward and then forward-bending. Following Akerlof *et al.* (2000), Lundborg and Sacklén (2003), based on the Swedish data, show that there exists a negatively sloped long-run Phillips curve. Some researchers further propose that the NAIRU can be affected by the inflation rate and monetary policy.

Different from the traditional view of Friedman, Blanchard (2003) points out that monetary policy can and does affect the natural rate of unemployment. Blanchard and Summers (1988) argue that anything (e.g. a sustained increase in real interest rates) that increases the actual rate of unemployment for sufficiently long is likely to raise the natural rate. Blanchard (2003), moreover, explores several mechanisms in which the real interest rate may affect the natural rate of unemployment. He points out, for instance, that the capital accumulation mechanism plays an important role in accounting for the history of unemployment in Europe over 30 years:

"Low real interest rates in the 1970s probably partly mitigated the increase in labor costs on profit, limiting the decline in capital accumulation, and thus limiting the increase in the natural rate of unemployment in the 1970s. High real interest rates in the 1980s (and then again, as the result of the German monetary policy response to German reunification, in the early 1990s) had the reverse effect of leading to a larger increase in the natural rate of unemployment during that period. And the decrease in real interest rates since the mid-1990s is probably contributing to the slow decline in unemployment in Europe." (Blanchard, 2003)

Based on a microfounded model, Lengwiler (1998) finds that the NAIRU may be non-constant and can be influenced by the expected inflation. It can be downward-sloping or upward-sloping with a vertical long-run Phillips curve (a constant NAIRU) being only an exception. Perez (2000) explores why the NAIRU changes over time and finds that the NAIRU may change with the changes of productivity, minimum wage and so on. Tobin (1998) also points out that the NAIRU may vary over time because of the change of the relationships between unemployment, vacancies and wage changes.

Although it is still questioned whether the NAIRU can be precisely estimated, some economists have tried with different approaches. An earlier survey on the estimation of the NAIRU is given by Staiger, Stock and Watson (1996). Gordon (1997), for example, estimates the time-varying NAIRU with the U.S. data with and without supply shocks. Apel and Jansson (1999), estimate the potential output and NAIRU of Sweden with a system-based strategy.

Following Blanchard (2003), in this section we will explore optimal monetary policy with an endogenous NAIRU which can be affected by the monetary policy. Before exploring the optimal monetary policy with an endogenous NAIRU, we estimate the time-varying NAIRU for several countries with the model of Gordon (1997).

4.1. Estimates of time-varying NAIRU

Gordon (1997) estimates the time-varying NAIRU with the following state-space model:

$$\pi_t = a(L)\pi_{t-1} + b(L)(U_t - U_t^N) + c(L)z_t + e_t \tag{15.48}$$

$$U_t^N = U_{t-1}^N + \eta_t \tag{15.49}$$

where π_t is the inflation rate, U_t the actual unemployment rate and U_t^N the NAIRU, which follows a random walk path indicated by Equation (15.49). z_t is a vector of supply shock variables, L a polynomial in the lag operator, e_t a serially uncorrelated error term and η_t satisfies the Gaussian distribution with mean zero and variance σ_η^2. Obviously, the variance of η_t plays an important role in the estimation. If it is zero, then the NAIRU is constant and if it is positive, the NAIRU experiences changes. "If no constraints are imposed on σ_η^2 the NAIRU will jump up and down and soak up all the residual variation in the inflation variation (Gordon, 1997, p. 21)." This model can be estimated using maximum likelihood methods with the help of the Kalman filter.[7]

Gordon (1997) includes a z_t to proxy supply shocks, such as changes of relative prices of imports and the change in the relative price of food and energy. If no supply shocks are taken into account, the NAIRU is referred to as "estimated NAIRU without supply shocks." Although there are no fixed rules on what variables should be included as supply shocks, it seems more reasonable to take supply shocks into account than not, since there are undoubtedly other variables than the unemployment rate that affect the inflation rate. In this section the supply shocks considered include mainly price changes of imports (im_t), food ($food_t$) and fuel, electricity and water ($fuel_t$). As for which variables should be adopted as supply shocks for the individual countries, we undertake an ordinary least squares (OLS) regression for Equation (15.48) before we start the time-varying estimation, assuming that the NAIRU is constant. In most cases we exclude the variables whose t-statistics are insignificant. The data source is the International Statistics Yearbook 2000. As mentioned above, the standard deviation of η_t plays a crucial role. Gordon (1997) assumes it to be 0.2% for the U.S. for the period 1955–1996. There is little theoretical background on how large η_t should be, but since the NAIRU is usually supposed to be relatively smooth, we constrain the change of the NAIRU within 4%, which is also consistent with Gordon (1997).[8] Therefore we assume different values of η_t for different countries, depending on how large we expect the change of the NAIRU to be. The unemployment rates of the four EU countries are presented in Figure 15.3. The data used in this section are taken from International Statistics Yearbook.

As for Germany, the variance of η_t is assumed to be 7.5×10^{-6} and the price changes of foods, imports and fuel, electricity and water are taken as supply shocks. The estimates are shown below with t-statistics in parentheses

$$\pi_t = \underset{(0.056)}{0.004} + \underset{(10.982)}{1.052}\,\pi_{t-1} - \underset{(3.009)}{0.256}\,\pi_{t-2} + \underset{(0.153)}{0.008}\,\pi_{t-3} + \underset{(1.105)}{0.013}\,fuel_{t-1}$$

$$+ \underset{(1.994)}{0.061}\,food_{t-1} + \underset{(0.627)}{0.006}\,im_{t-1} - \underset{(0.993)}{0.042}(U_t - U_t^N) + e_t,$$

where $fuel_t$ indicates the price change of fuel, electricity and water; $food_t$ the price change of food; and im_t the price change of imports. The estimate of the standard deviation of e_t is 0.006 with t-statistic being 8.506. The time-varying NAIRU of Germany is shown in Figure 15.4A.

As for France, only one lag of the inflation rate is included in the regression, since the coefficient of the unemployment rate gap tends to zero when more lags

---

[7] The reader is referred to Hamilton (1994, Ch. 13) for the Kalman filter.
[8] Gordon (1997, pp. 21–22), however, discusses briefly the smoothing problem concerning the estimation of the time-varying NAIRU.

Figure 15.3. Unemployment rates of Germany, France, Italy and the U.K.

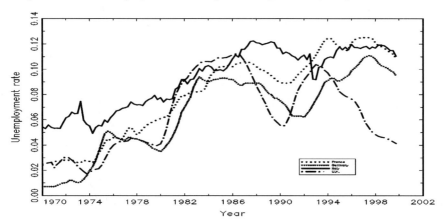

of the inflation are included. The price changes of food and intermediate goods are taken as supply shocks. Three lags of the price changes of intermediate goods are included to smooth the NAIRU. The result reads as

$$\pi_t = \underset{(0.312)}{0.004} + \underset{(27.967)}{0.989}\,\pi_{t-1} - \underset{(2.058)}{0.085}\,food_{t-1} + \underset{(2.876)}{0.132}\,in_t$$
$$- \underset{(1.313)}{0.090}\,in_{t-1} + \underset{(0.772)}{0.029}\,in_{t-2} - \underset{(1.889)}{0.054}(U_t - U_t^N) + e_t$$

where in_t denotes the price change of intermediate goods. The estimate of the standard deviation of e_t is 0.005 with t-statistic being 8.808, and the variance of η_t is predetermined as 1.3×10^{-5}. The estimate of the NAIRU of France is presented in Figure 15.4B.

For the same reason as for France, one lag of the inflation rate is included in the regression for the U.K. The estimation reads

$$\pi_t = \underset{(0.066)}{0.005} + \underset{(11.063)}{0.818}\,\pi_{t-1} + \underset{(2.768)}{0.130}\,food_{t-1} + \underset{(0.691)}{0.017}\,fuel_{t-1}$$
$$- \underset{(0.300)}{0.072}(U_t - U_t^N) + e_t$$

The estimate of the standard deviation of e_t is 0.013 with t-statistic being 8.764 and the variance of η_t is predetermined as 1.4×10^{-5}. The estimate of the NAIRU of the U.K. is shown in Figure 15.4C.

For Italy it seems difficult to get a smooth estimate for the NAIRU if we include only price changes of food, fuel, electricity and water and imports as supply shocks. The main reason seems to be that the inflation rate experienced drastic changes and therefore exerts much influence on the estimate of the NAIRU. Therefore, we try to smooth the estimate of the NAIRU by including the short-term nominal interest rate (nr_t) into the regression,

Figure 15.4.   Time-varying NAIRU of Germany, France, the U.K., Italy and the U.S.

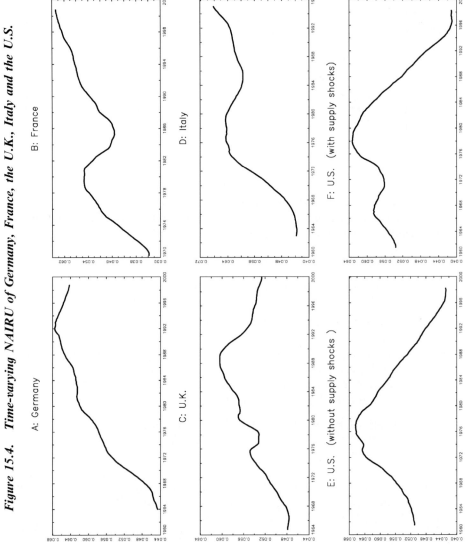

which makes the NAIRU more consistent with the actual unemployment rate. The result is

$$\pi_t = \underset{(0.001)}{0.0035} + \underset{(6.623)}{1.594}\,\pi_{t-1} - \underset{(4.961)}{0.832}\,\pi_{t-2} - \underset{(1.722)}{0.247}\,food_{t-1} + \underset{(2.255)}{0.322}\,food_{t-2}$$

$$\underset{(1.398)}{0.017}\,fuel_{t-1} + \underset{(1.599)}{0.030}\,fuel_{t-2} + \underset{(1.532)}{0.181}\,nr_t - \underset{(0.902)}{0.304}(U_t - U_t^N) + e_t$$

The estimate of the standard deviation of e_t is 0.010 with t-statistic being 8.982, and the variance of η_t is assumed to be 2.6×10^{-6}. The time-varying NAIRU of Italy is shown in Figure 15.4D.

We also undertake the estimation of the NAIRU for the U.S. with and without "supply shocks" for 1962:3–1999:4. In the estimation without supply shocks, only four lags of the inflation rate and unemployment gap are included in the regression and the result is

$$\pi_t = \underset{(0.002)}{0.002} + \underset{(16.045)}{1.321}\,\pi_{t-1} - \underset{(2.199)}{0.243}\,\pi_{t-2} - \underset{(61.971)}{0.121}\,\pi_{t-3} + \underset{(0.350)}{0.015}\,\pi_{t-4} - \underset{(8.864)}{0.065}(U_t - U_t^N) + e_t$$

The estimate of the standard deviation of e_t is 0.004 with t-statistic being 15.651 and the variance of η_t is predetermined as 4.5×10^{-6}. The NAIRU of the U.S. without supply shocks is presented in Figure 15.4E, very similar to the result of Gordon (1997). Considering supply shocks which include price changes in food, energy and imports, we have the following result for the U.S.:

$$\pi_t = \underset{(0.091)}{0.002} + \underset{(10.592)}{0.957}\,\pi_{t-1} - \underset{(1.350)}{0.151}\,\pi_{t-2} - \underset{(0.647)}{0.070}\,\pi_{t-3} + \underset{(1.822)}{0.120}\,\pi_{t-4} + \underset{(4.547)}{0.062}\,food_t$$

$$+ \underset{(0.468)}{0.007}\,fuel_{t-1} + \underset{(3.808)}{0.025}\,im_{t-1} - \underset{(3.036)}{0.060}(U_t - U_t^N) + e_t$$

The estimate of the standard deviation of e_t is 0.003 with t-statistic being 16.217 and the variance of η_t is predetermined as 4×10^{-6}. The time-varying NAIRU with supply shocks is shown in Figure 15.4F.

4.2. Monetary policy with endogenous NAIRU

Above, we have estimated the time-varying NAIRU with a model proposed by Gordon (1997). As stated before, Blanchard (2003) argues that monetary policy can and does affect the natural rate of unemployment. Therefore, the problem to tackle next is how monetary policy affects the NAIRU. Taking Europe as example, Blanchard (2003) argues that a tight monetary policy can raise the NAIRU and an expansionary policy may reduce the NAIRU. There seems to exist a positive correlation between the NAIRU and the real interest rate. Therefore, below we will analyze the relationship between the NAIRU and the real interest rate. In Table 15.1, we show the estimation of the following equation from 1982 to the end of the 1990s (t-statistics in parentheses):

$$u_{nt} = \tau_0 + \tau_1 \bar{r} \tag{15.50}$$

Table 15.1. **Regression results of Equation (15.50) and correlation coefficients of**
$\bar{r}$ (computed with the ex post real rate) and the NAIRU

Parameter	Country			
	Germany	France	U.K.	U.S.
τ_0	0.063 (130.339)	0.051 (24.263)	0.051 (57.513)	0.040 (29.076)
τ_1	0.064 (4.801)	0.085 (1.986)	0.128 (6.222)	0.322 (8.809)
R^2	0.250	0.056	0.356	0.526
Correlation	0.437	0.225	0.337	0.387

where $\bar{r}$ denotes the 8-quarter (backward) average of the real interest rate.[9] The real interest rate is defined as the short-term nominal rate minus the actual inflation rate. The reason that we use the 8-quarter backward average of the real interest rate for estimation is that some researchers argue that the NAIRU is usually affected by the lags of the real rate. The reason that the regression is undertaken only for the period after 1982 is that in the 1970s and at the beginning of the 1980s these countries experienced large fluctuations in the inflation, and therefore the real rate also experienced large changes. In Table 15.1 we find that τ_1 is significant enough. We also show the correlation coefficients of the NAIRU and $\bar{r}$ for the same period in Table 15.1.

The real rate above is defined as the gap between the nominal rate and the actual inflation. The real rate defined in this way is usually referred to as the *ex post* real rate. According to the Fisher equation, however, the real rate should be defined as the nominal rate (nr_t) minus the expected inflation, that is

$$r_t = nr_t - \pi_{t|t+1} \tag{15.51}$$

where $\pi_{t|t+1}$ denotes the inflation rate from t to $t+1$ expected by the market at time t. The real rate defined above is usually called the *ex ante* real rate. How to measure $\pi_{t|t+1}$ is a problem. Blanchard and Summers (1984), for example, measure the expected inflation by an autoregressive process of the inflation rate. Below, we will measure the expected inflation by assuming that the economic agents forecast the inflation by learning through the recursive least squares. Namely, we assume

$$\pi_{t|t+1} = c_{0t} + c_{1t}\pi_t + c_{2t}y_t \tag{15.52}$$

where y_t denotes the output gap. This equation implies that the agents predict the inflation next period by adjusting the coefficients c_0, c_1 and c_2 period by

---

[9] The interest rates of Germany, France, the U.K. and the U.S. are the German call money rate, 3-month interbank rate, 3-month treasury bill rate and the Federal funds rate, respectively. Data source: International Statistics Yearbook.

Table 15.2. *Regression results of Equation (15.50) and correlation coefficients of*
r̄ (computed with the ex ante real rate) and the NAIRU

Parameter	Country			
	Germany	France	U.K.	U.S.
τ_0	0.063 (162.748)	0.050 (22.663)	0.051 (59.251)	0.040 (31.278)
τ_1	0.073 (6.817)	0.097 (2.117)	0.131 (6.337)	0.329 (9.579)
R^2	0.410	0.065	0.371	0.574
Correlation	0.640	0.256	0.609	0.758

period. Following Sargent (1999), Orphanides and Williams (2002), Evans and
Honkapohja (2001) and Zhang and Semmler (2005), we assume that the
coefficients evolve in the manner of the recursive least squares

$$C_t = C_{t-1} + t^{-1}V_t^{-1}X_t(\pi_t - X_t'C_{t-1})$$
$$V_t = V_{t-1} + t^{-1}(X_tX_t' - V_{t-1})$$

with $C_t = (c_{0t}\, c_{1t}\, c_{2t})'$ and $X_t = (1\pi_{t-1}y_{t-1})'$. V_t is the moment matrix of
X_t.[10] With the output gap measured by the percentage deviation of the
industrial production index (IPI) from its HP-filtered trend and the $\pi_{t|t+1}$
computed by the equations above, we show the estimation results for Equation
(15.50) with the ex ante real rate and the correlation coefficients between the
NAIRU and $r̄$ computed with the ex ante real rate in Table 15.2.[11] The results in
Table 15.2 are not essentially different from those in Table 15.1 except that the
correlation coefficients between the NAIRU and $r̄$ in Table 15.2 are larger than
those in Table 15.1.

The ex ante- and *ex post* real rates of the U.S. from 1981:1 to 1999:4 are
shown in Figure 15.5. It is obvious that the two rates are not significantly
different.

The empirical evidence above indicates that there exists a positive relationship between the real rate and the NAIRU. The question then is whether the
path of the NAIRU is affected by r in a linear manner similar to that of the
actual unemployment given by (15.2) or in a nonlinear way. In the research
below, we assume that the the path of the NAIRU can be affected by the
monetary policy in a nonlinear manner because of adjustment costs in the

---

[10] The reader can refer to Harvey (1989, Ch. 7) and Sargent (1999) for the recursive least squares.

[11] The IPI has also been used by Clarida *et al.* (1998) to measure the output for Germany, France, the
U.S., the U.K., Japan and Italy. As surveyed by Orphanides and van Norden (2002), there are many
methods to measure the output gap. We find that filtering the IPI using the band–pass filter
developed by Baxter and King (1995) leaves the measure of the output gap essentially unchanged
from the measure with the HP-filter. The band–pass filter has also been used by Sargent (1999).

Figure 15.5.   *The ex ante- and ex post-real rates of the U.S.*

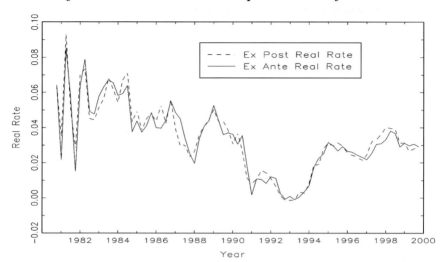

investment. Exactly speaking, we assume

$$\dot{u}_n = g(r) = a \tanh(br) \tag{15.53}$$

We know that $\tanh(x)$ is a function with upper and lower bounds 1 and -1, respectively. It equals zero when $x = 0$. The parameter a scales the function and b determines the slope of $g(r)$ around 0, the larger the b is, the steeper the function is around 0. In case b is relatively small, $g(r)$ tends to be linear. Two simulations of $g(r)$ with $a = 0.6$ and different b (1.2 and 0.2) are shown in Figure 15.6. This model implies that the change of the NAIRU increases with the increase of r and vice versa, but not proportionally. It increases or decreases faster when r is close to zero than when r is far from zero. The change of the NAIRU stops to increase or decrease in case r tends to positive or negative infinity. The reason for the nonproportional change of the NAIRU to the monetary policy is that there exist adjustment costs. Since the 1960s economists have been studying the implication of adjustment costs on the dynamic investment. An earlier study can be found in Jorgenson and Kort (1963). They derive the optimal path of the capital stock by assuming an exogenously given output. Lucas (1967) suggests that the adjustment costs can be thought of as a sum of purchase costs and installation costs, which are internal to the firm. Gould (1968) designs a quadratic function of adjustment costs and explores their effects on investment of the firm. Some other research on adjustment costs and their effects on the investment can be found in Eisner and Stroz (1963), Treadway (1969) and Feichtinger *et al.* (2001). Adjustment costs prevent firms from increasing or decreasing the investment proportionally with the decrease or increase of the interest rate. As a result, the aggregate demand does not decrease

Figure 15.6.   *g(r) with different b*

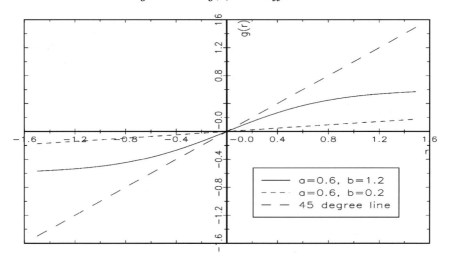

or increase proportionally with the increase or decrease of the interest rate, and therefore the change of the NAIRU does not increase or decrease proportionally with the interest rate either.[12]

We do not consider the effects of the adjustment costs on the actual unemployment, because there may exist idle capacity and the actual unemployment is supposed to be more affected by the capacity utilization than the NAIRU, which can be considered as the trend of the actual unemployment and may be mainly affected by the investment behavior.

Assuming that the path of the NAIRU can be affected by r as shown in (15.53), what is then the optimal monetary policy? Next we explore this problem with the model of a linear Phillips curve as given in Section 2, since it is more complicated to analyze the model with the nonlinear Phillips curve. With $\dot{u}_n = g(r)$ Equation (15.2) changes to

$$\dot{\mu} = \dot{u} - \dot{u}_n = \alpha r - g(r) \tag{15.54}$$

and the problem of the central bank with expectation taken into account in the Phillips curve reads

$$\min_{r} \int_0^\infty e^{-\rho t} L \, dt \tag{15.55}$$

subject to

---

[12] Of course $g(r)$ does not have to be symmetric around the origin $(0, 0)$ and we can modify $g(r)$ by using some parameters so that it becomes asymmetric around $(0, 0)$. We will not do so below because the results are not essentially changed no matter whether $g(r)$ is symmetric or not around the origin.

$$\dot{\pi}_e = -\kappa(\beta r + \theta\mu) \tag{15.56}$$

$$\dot{\mu} = \alpha r - g(r) \tag{15.57}$$

with L given by (15.16). The current-value Hamiltonian of the problem above reads

$$H_c = (\pi_e - \beta r - \theta\mu)^2 + \lambda\mu^2 - \gamma_1\kappa(\beta r + \theta\mu) + \gamma_2[\alpha r - g(r)] \tag{15.58}$$

From the first-order condition (15.20) we know the optimal monetary policy r is the solution of the following equation

$$-2\beta(\pi_e - \beta r - \theta\mu) - \gamma_1\kappa\beta + \gamma_2[\alpha - g'(r)] = 0 \tag{15.59}$$

Let $\check{r}(\Omega)$ denote the solution of r from the equation above, with Ω denoting the set of parameters and the variables μ, π_e, γ_1 and γ_2. Following (15.21)–(15.24) and (15.59), we obtain the following dynamic system

$$\dot{\pi}_e = -\kappa[\beta\check{r} + \theta\mu] \tag{15.60}$$

$$\dot{\mu} = \alpha\check{r} - g(\check{r}) \tag{15.61}$$

$$\dot{\gamma}_1 = -2(\pi_e - \beta\check{r} - \theta\mu) + \rho\gamma_1 \tag{15.62}$$

$$\dot{\gamma}_2 = 2\theta(\pi_e - \beta\check{r} - \theta\mu) - 2\lambda\mu + \gamma_1\kappa\theta + \rho\gamma_2 \tag{15.63}$$

$$0 = -2\beta(\pi_e - \beta\check{r} - \theta\mu) - \gamma_1\kappa\beta + \gamma_2[\alpha - g'(\check{r})] \tag{15.64}$$

Setting $\dot{\pi}_e = \dot{\mu} = \dot{\gamma}_1 = \dot{\gamma}_2 = 0$, we can compute the equilibria of the economy as follows:

$$0 = -\kappa[\beta\check{r} + \theta\mu] \tag{15.65}$$

$$0 = \alpha\check{r} - g(\check{r}) \tag{15.66}$$

$$0 = -2(\pi_e - \beta\check{r} - \theta\mu) + \rho\gamma_1 \tag{15.67}$$

$$0 = 2\theta(\pi_e - \beta\check{r} - \theta\mu) - 2\lambda\mu + \gamma_1\kappa\theta + \rho\gamma_2 \tag{15.68}$$

$$0 = -2\beta(\pi_e - \beta\check{r} - \theta\mu) - \gamma_1\kappa\beta + \gamma_2[\alpha - g'(\check{r})] \tag{15.69}$$

We will try some numerical solutions since it is difficult to get analytical solutions of this system. Before trying numerical solutions we explore whether there exist solutions of this system, starting with (15.66), since this equation contains only one variable, $\check{r}$.

Denote $\Theta(\check{r}) = \alpha\check{r} - g(\check{r})$ and let

$$\Theta(\check{r}) = 0 \tag{15.70}$$

It is clear that $\check{r} = 0$ is a solution of the above equation, but with some proper values assigned to the parameters, Equation (15.70) can have other

Figure 15.7. Θ(ř) with different sets of parameters

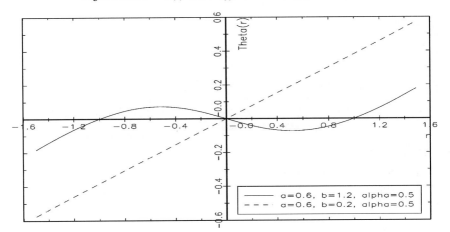

solutions, therefore the dynamic system (15.60)–(15.63) may have multiple equilibria.[13]

In Figure 15.7 we show two simulations of $\Theta(\check{r})$ with different parameters. It is clear that with $a = 0.6$, $b = 0.2$ and $\alpha = 0.5$ $\Theta(\check{r})$ cuts the horizontal axis once, but with $a = 0.6$, $b = 1.2$ and $\alpha = 0.5$ $\Theta(\check{r})$ cuts the horizontal axis three times, therefore there may exist two other equilibria in the dynamic system (15.60)–(15.63) besides the one with $r = 0$.

In order to explore whether the multiple equilibria are robust to parameters chosen, we will try numerical solutions of the system (15.65)–(15.69) with a different set of parameters from those employed in Figure 15.7. Let $a = 0.6$, $b = 6$, $\alpha = 0.75$, $\kappa = 0.9$, $\beta = 0.6$, $\theta = 0.5$, $\rho = 0.1$ and $\lambda = 0.0075$, the three sets of equilibria, a, b and c are given as follows:[14]

$$r_a^* = 0.800, \ \mu_a^* = -0.960, \ \pi_{ea}^* = -0.0012, \ \gamma_{1a}^* = -0.025, \ \gamma_{2a}^* = -0.0199$$

$$r_b^* = -0.800, \ \mu_b^* = 0.960, \ \pi_{eb}^* = 0.0012, \ \gamma_{1b}^* = 0.025, \ \gamma_{2b}^* = 0.0199$$

---

[13] As stated before, we do not consider the effects of adjustment costs on the path of the actual unemployment. But even if r can affect the path of the actual unemployment in a way similar to (15.53) instead of (15.2), the results of multiple equilibria should not be essentially changed. If we assume, for example, $\dot{u} = \varrho(r)$ with $\varrho(r)$ defined similarly to $g(r)$ with different parameters. The two functions $g(r)$ and $\varrho(r)$ can then cut each other once or more times, corresponding to one or multiple equilibria of the optimal control problem.

[14] Because the highly nonlinear system (15.65)–(15.69) is solved numerically, there might exist other equilibria, which are not detected. Therefore the model may have more than three equilibria.

Figure 15.8.   Numerical computation of the value function

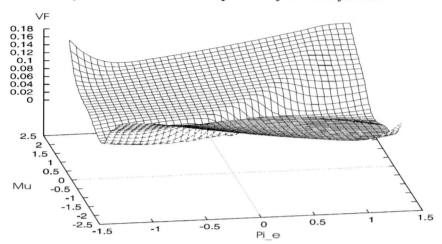

and

$$r_c^* = 0, \ \mu_c^* = 0, \ \pi_{ec}^* = 0, \ \gamma_{1c}^* = 0, \ \gamma_{2c}^* = 0$$

Substituting the π_e^*, μ^* and r^* into Equation (15.14), we can observe at least three equilibria values of π, $\pi_a^* = -0.0012$, $\pi_b^* = 0.0012$ and $\pi_c^* = 0$. Therefore, we have at least three steady states for inflation and unemployment, $(-0.0012, -0.960)$, $(0.0012, 0.960)$ and $(0, 0)$.[15]

Yet, we can hardly explore the stability of the equilibria because we cannot compute the Jacobian matrix without an explicit expression of $\check{r}$. Therefore, we will numerically compute the optimal control problem (15.55)–(15.57) with the algorithm developed by Grüne (1997) with the parameters given above. Grüne (1997) uses the Bellman equation and dynamic programing to compute numerically the optimal control problem with adaptive grids.[16]

The numerically obtained value function (VF) using the Grüne algorithm is shown in Figure 15.8, in which we observe that the value function is not smooth at the bottom. The vector field of the state variables with π_e on the horizontal axis and μ on the vertical axis is shown in Figure 15.9. In Figure 15.9, we indeed can observe three equilibria. As mentioned before, there may exist other equilibria which are difficult to observe in the vector field. In Figure 15.10, we show the vector field for the state variables with $\lambda = 0.5$, $a = 0.3$ and $b = 2$ and other parameters unchanged and find that there exists a unique equilibrium $(0, 0)$. In

---

[15] As above mentioned, given the strong nonlinearities in our functions there might exist other steady state equilibria as well.

[16] For further details of this algorithm see Grüne and Semmler (2004).

Figure 15.9.   Vector field with multiple equilibria

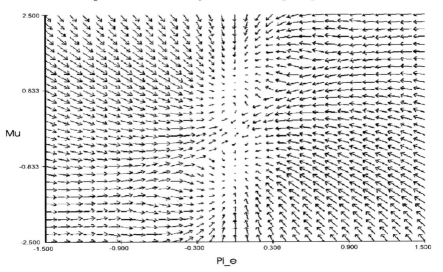

Figure 15.10.   Vector field with unique equilibrium

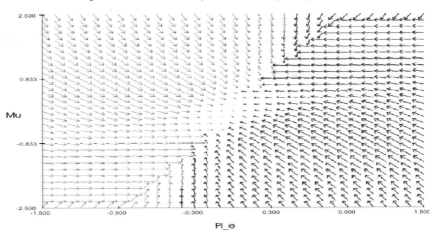

Figure 15.11, we show the optimal trajectories of π_e and μ with different initial values. The equilibria $(-0.0012, -0.960)$ and $(0.0012, 0.960)$ are stable. Note, however, that in the middle there might exist other fixed points besides $(0, 0)$. Numerically we can observe that the point $(0, 0)$ is unstable, but there seem to be two limit cycles close to $(0, 0)$, which can be detected with some initial values of π_e and μ close to $(0, 0)$. In Figure 15.12, we show the optimal trajectories of π_e and μ

Figure 15.11.   Optimal trajectories of π_e and μ

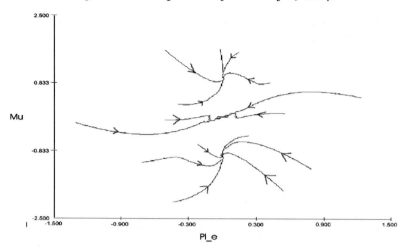

Figure 15.12.   Limit cycles with initial values close to (0,0)

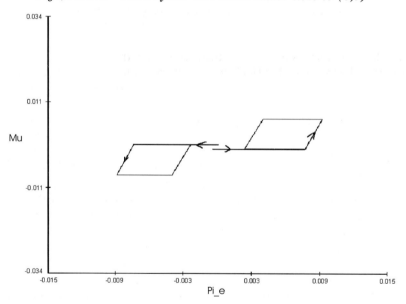

with initial values (0.0001, 0.0001) and (−0.0002, −0.0011). We observe indeed two limit cycles.

Based on some empirical evidence and assuming that the monetary policy affects the path of the NAIRU, in this section we have explored monetary policy with an endogenous NAIRU and find that there may exist multiple equilibria for such type of models. As stated before, Blanchard (2003) remarks that the monetary policy does and can affect the NAIRU. On the other hand, some researchers, Gordon (1997) and Stiglitz (1997), for example, maintain that the NAIRU has some feedback effects on the macroeconomic policy (monetary policy for instance) in the sense that it faces a moving target. Although we know that there are other forces affecting the NAIRU, a model of monetary policy with an exogenous NAIRU can probably not be considered a proper device to study monetary policy effects. Future research is likely to explore more extensively the way how monetary policy affects the NAIRU.

5. Conclusion

This paper is concerned with the optimal monetary policy with nonlinear Phillips curves and an endogenous NAIRU. Before exploring the optimal monetary policy with a nonlinear Phillips curve, we have studied the optimal monetary policy in a simple model with a linear Phillips curve and find that the optimal monetary policy is a linear function of the unemployment gap and that there exists a unique equilibrium, namely a saddle point. We have then explored the optimal monetary policy with two different shapes of the nonlinear Phillips curve: convex and convex–concave. We find that the optimal monetary policy changes with the shape of the Phillips curve, but there exists a unique equilibrium (a saddle point) despite of the different nonlinearities of the Phillips curve. Based on this result, we have then relaxed the traditional assumption of a constant and exogenous NAIRU. Recent literature has also proposed that the NAIRU can be influenced by the monetary policy. With some empirical evidence and assuming that the NAIRU can besides other forces be influenced by the monetary policy in a certain manner, we find that there may exist multiple steady-state equilibria in the economy, different from the results of models with a constant NAIRU.

The implications of a time-varying NAIRU for the central bank are as follows: first, if one considers a central bank's interest-rate reaction function, one should note that the gap between actual unemployment rate and a constant NAIRU is different from the gap between actual unemployment rate and a time-varying NAIRU, and as a result, the central bank may be misled in its monetary policy. Second, in case of the existence of multiple equilibria, the question of how the central bank can prevent the economy from falling into equilibria with inferior welfare becomes a crucial one.

Acknowledgments

The authors would like to thank Olivier Blanchard for his comments. This paper has been presented at the following conferences: Annual Meeting of the Austrian Economic Association 2004; 10th International Conference on Computing in

Economics and Finance; EEA annual meeting 2004; EcoMod 2004; Twelfth Annual Symposium of the Society for Nonlinear Dynamics and Econometrics 2004.

References

Aguiar, A. and M.M.F. Martins (2002), "Trend, cycle, and nonlinear trade-off in the Euro-area 1970–2001", CEMPRE.

Akerlof, G.A. (2002), "Behavioral macroeconomics and macroeconomic behavior", *American Economic Review*, Vol. 92, pp. 411–433.

Akerlof, G.A., T. Dickens and G.L. Perry (2000), "Near-rational wage and price setting and the optimal rates of inflation and unemployment", *Brookings Papers on Economic Activity*, Vol. 1, pp. 1–60.

Apel, M. and P. Jansson (1999), "A theory-consistent system approach for estimating potential output and the NAIRU", Sveriges Riksbank Working Paper No. 74.

Ball, L. (1999), "Policy rules for open economies", in: J.B. Taylor, editor, *Monetary Policy Rules*, Chicago: The University of Chicago Press.

Baxter, M. and R.G. King (1995), "Measuring business cycles: approximate band–pass filters for economic time series", NBER Working Paper, No. 5022.

Bean, C. (2000), "The convex Phillips curve and macroeconomic policymaking under uncertainty", Manuscript, London School of Economics.

Blanchard, O. (2003), Monetary policy and unemployment, remarks at the conference "Monetary policy and the labor market", in honor of James Tobin, held at the New School University, NY.

Blanchard, O. and L.H. Summers (1984), "Perspectives on high world real interest rates", *Brookings Papers on Economic Activity*, No. 2, pp. 273–324.

Blanchard, O. and L.H. Summers (1988), "Beyond the natural rate hypothesis", *American Economic Review*, Vol. 78(2), pp. 182–187.

Chadha, B., P. Masson and G. Meredith (1992), "Models of inflation and the costs of disinflation", *IMF Staff Papers*, Vol. 39(2), pp. 395–431.

Clarida, R., J. Gali and M. Gertler (1998), "Monetary policy rules in practice: some international evidence", *European Economic Review*, Vol. 42, pp. 1033–1067.

Clark, P.B., D.M. Laxton and D.E. Rose (1996), "Asymmetry in the U.S. output-inflation nexus: issues and evidence", *IMF Staff Papers*, Vol. 43(1), pp. 216–250.

Dupasquier, C. and N. Ricketts (1998a), "Price stability, inflation targets and monetary policy", Proceedings of a Conference, Bank of Canada, May 1997, pp. 131–173, Ottawa: Bank of Canada.

Dupasquier, C. and N. Ricketts (1998b), "Nonlinearities in the output-inflation relationship: some empirical results for Canada", Bank of Canada Working Paper 98–14.

Eisner, R. (1997), "New view of the NAIRU", in: P. Davidson and J.A. Kregel, editors, *Improving the Global Economy: Keynesian and the Growth in Output and Employment*, UK and Lyme, U.S: Edward Elgar Publishing Cheltenham.

Eisner, R. and R. Stroz (1963), "Determinants of business investment", *Impacts of Monetary Policy*, NJ: Prentice Hall.

Evans, G.W. and S. Honkapohja (2001), *Learning and Expectations in Macroeconomics*, Princeton, NJ: The Princeton University Press.

Feichtinger, G., F.H. Hartl, P. Kort and F. Wirl (2001), "The dynamics of a simple relative adjustment-cost framework", *German Economic Review*, Vol. 2(3), pp. 255–268.

Filardo, A.J. (1998), "New evidence on the output cost of fighting inflation", *Economic Review*, Vol. third quarter (June 22), pp. 33–61.

Flaschel, P., G. Gong and W. Semmler (2001), "Nonlinear Phillips curve and monetary policy in a Keynesian macroeconometric model", Working Paper 18, CEM, University of Bielefeld.

Friedman, M. (1968), "The role of monetary policy", *American Economic Review*, Vol. 58(1), pp. 267–291.

Gómez, J. and J.M. Julio (2000), "An estimation of the nonlinear Phillips curve in Colombia", Unpublished Manuscript, Bank of Republic of colombia.

Gordon, R.J. (1997), "The time-varying NAIRU and its implications for economic policy", *Journal of Economic Perspectives*, Vol. 11, pp. 11–32.

Gould, J.P. (1968), "Adjustment costs in the theory of investment of the firm", *Review of Economic Studies*, Vol. 35, pp. 47–55.

Graham, L. and D.J. Snower (2003), "The return of the long-run Phillips curve, Institute for the Study of Labor (IZA)", Discussion Paper, CEPR No. 3691.

Grüne, L. (1997), "An adaptive grid scheme for the discrete Hamilton–Jacobi–Bellman equation", *Numerische Mathematik*, Vol. 75, pp. 319–337.

Grüne, L. and W. Semmler (2004), "Using dynamic programming with adaptive grid scheme for optimal control problems in economics", *Journal of Economic Dynamics and Control*, Vol. 28, pp. 2427–2456.

Guender, A.V. (2001), "Inflation targeting in the open economy: which rate of inflation to target"?, Manuscript, Department of Economics, University of Canterbury.

Hall, R.E. (2000), "Monetary policy with changing financial and labor-market fundamentals", Manuscript, Hoover Institution and Department of Economics, Stanford University, NBER.

Hamilton, J.D. (1994), *Time Series Analysis*, Princeton, NJ: The Princeton University Press.

Harvey, A.C. (1989), *Time Series Models*, Oxford: Philip Allan Publishers Ltd.

Jorgenson, S. and P.M. Kort (1963), "Dynamic investment policy with installation experience effects", *Journal of Optimization Theory and Applications*, Vol. 77, pp. 421–438.

Karanassou, M., H. Sala and D. Snower (2003), "Unemployment in the European Union: a dynamic reappraisal", *Economic Modelling*, Vol. 20(2), pp. 237–273.

Laxton, D., G. Meredith and D. Rose (1995), "Asymmetric effects of economic activity on inflation: evidence and policy implications", *IMF Staff Papers*, Vol. 42(4).

Lengwiler, Y. (1998), "Certainty equivalence and the non-vertical long run Phillips curve", Manuscript, Board of Governors of the Federal Reserve System and Swiss Natioanl Bank.

Lucas, R.E. (1967), "Adjustment costs and the theory of supply", *Journal of Polotical Economy*, Vol. 75, pp. 321–334.

Lundborg, P. and H. Sacklén (2003), "Low-inflation targeting and unemployment persistence", FIEF Working Paper No. 188.

Nobay, A.R. and D.A. Peel (1998), "Optimal monetary policy in a model of asymmetric central bank preferences", Financial Markets Group, LSE.

Nobay, A.R. and D.A. Peel (2000), "Optimal monetary policy with a nonlinear Phillips curve", *Economics Letters*, Vol. 67, pp. 159–164.

Orphanides, A. and J.C. Williams (2002), "Imperfect knowledge, inflation expectations and monetary policy", NBER Working Paper 9884.

Orphanides, A. and S. van Norden (2002), "The unreliability of output gap estimation in real time", *The Review of Economics and Statistics*, Vol. 84(4), pp. 569–583.

Orphanides, A. and V. Wieland (2000), "Inflation zone targeting", *European Economic Review*, Vol. 44(7), pp. 1351–1387.

Perez, S.J. (2000), "Why does the NAIRU change across time"? Manuscript, Department of economics, Washington State University.

Phelps, E.S. (1968), "Money-wage dynamics and labor-market equilibrium", *Journal of Political Economy*, Vol. 76(2), pp. 678–711.

Rudebusch, G.D. and L.E.O. Svensson (1999), "Policy rules for inflation targeting", in: J.B. Taylor, editor, *Monetary Policy Rules*, Chicago: The University of Chicago Press.

Sargent, T.J. (1999), *The Conquest of American Inflation*, Princeton, NJ: The Princeton University Press.

Schaling, E. (1999), "The nonlinear Phillips curve and inflation forecast targeting", Bank of England.

Semmler, W. and W. Zhang (2002), "Asset price bubbles and monetary policy rules: a dynamic model and empirical evidence", Manuscript, Available at www.wiwi.uni-bielefeld.de/~Semmler/cem.

Staiger, D., J.H. Stock and M.W. Watson (1996), "How precise are estimates of the natural rate of unemployment"?, NBER Working Paper 5477.

Stiglitz, J. (1997), "Reflections on the natural rate hypothesis", *Journal of Economic Perspectives*, Vol. 11, pp. 3–10.

Tambakis, D.N. (1998), "Monetary policy with a convex Phillips curve and asymmetric loss", Working Paper 98/21, IMF.

Tobin, J. (1998), "Supply constraints on employment and output: NAIRU versus natural rate", International conference in memory of Fausto Vicarelli, Rome, Nov. 21–23.

Treadway, A.B. (1969), "On rational entrepreneurial behaviour and the demand for investment", *Review of Economic Studies*, Vol. 36, pp. 227–239.

Turnovsky, S. (1981), "The optimal intertemporal choice of inflation and unemployment: an analysis of the steady state and transitional dynamics", *Journal of Economics Dynamics and Control*, Vol. 3, pp. 357–384.

Varian, H.R. (1975), "A bayesian approach to real estate assessment", pp. 195–208. in: S.E. Fienberg and A. Zellner, editors, *Studies in Bayseian Econometrics and statistics in honour of Leonard J. Savage*, Amsterdam: New-Holland.

Walsh, C.E. (1999), Monetary policy trade-offs in the open economy, Santa Cruz and Federal Reserve Bank of San Francisco: University of California.

Yoshida, H. and T. Asada (2001), "Dynamic analysis of policy lag in a Keynes-Goodwin model: stability, instability cycles and chaos", Available at www.wiwi.uni-bielefeld.de/~Semmler/cem.

Zhang, W. and W. Semmler (2005), "Monetary policy under model uncertainty: Empirical evidence, adaptive learning and robust control", *Macroeconomic Dynamics*, Vol. 9, pp. 651–681. Available at www.wiwi.uni-bielefeld.de/~Semmler/cem.

CHAPTER 16

Inflation Targeting Policy in a Dynamic Keynesian Model with Debt Accumulation: A Japanese Perspective

Toichiro Asada

Abstract

In this paper, we investigate the macroeconomic impact of the inflation targeting policy by using the analytical framework of a dynamic Keynesian model with debt accumulation. We show that the monetary authority can stabilize an unstable economy by carrying out the sufficiently credible inflation targeting policy even in case of the liquidity trap, as long as the destabilizing Fisher debt effect is not extremely strong. We also show the existence of the cyclical fluctuation at some range of the parameter values by using the Hopf bifurcation theorem, and we provide some numerical examples which support our analysis.

Keywords: inflation targeting policy, Japanese economy, dynamic Keynesian model, Fisher debt effect, Mundell effect, liquidity trap, credibility, Hopf bifurcation

JEL classifications: E3, E4, E5

1. Introduction

After the prosperous 1980s which was accompanied by the stock bubble, the 1990s is called the 'lost decade' for the Japanese economy. We can understand

CONTRIBUTIONS TO ECONOMIC ANALYSIS
VOLUME 277   ISSN: 0573-8555
DOI:10.1016/S0573-8555(05)77016-4

the reason why it is called so if we cast a glance at the basic statistical data of the Japanese economy in Figures 16.1 and 16.2.[1] During this period, the rate of unemployment steadily rose, and the growth rate of the real GDP cyclically declined, which was accompanied by the sharp decline of the stock prices. In addition, the annual rate of inflation of the GDP deflator was mildly negative every year during the period 1995–2002.[2] A more remarkable fact is that the short-term nominal rate of interest became almost zero in the late 1990s and the early 2000s in Japan. This means that the Japanese economy fell into the notorious 'liquidity trap' which is accompanied by the mild deflation.

By the way, in traditional textbook interpretation of the static Keynesian model, the monetary policy becomes ineffective in case of the 'liquidity trap' in which nominal rate of interest is stuck at its lower bound. If this is true, in the depressed Japanese economy in the late 1990s and the early 2000s, the monetary policy must be ineffective, because nominal rate of interest already fell to nearly zero. In contrast to this traditional view, however, Krugman's (1998) constructed a formal model in which the 'inflation targeting policy' by the monetary authority is effective even in case of the liquidity trap. His paper had a practical purpose to present a policy recommendation to the Japanese central bankers. Although Japanese central bankers strongly opposed the inflation targeting policy, this policy has been adopted by the central banks of several countries (cf. Bernanke *et al.* (1999)), and recently this policy attracted attention of many economists in Japan and other countries partly due to the influence of Krugman's paper.[3]

Krugman's's (1998) model is one of the few existing formal models of the inflation targeting under liquidity trap, and his analytical framework is a microeconomically founded two-period 'representative agent' approach, which presupposes the existence of a representative agent who tries to maximize the present value of the utility in period 1, conditional on the agent's expectation concerning the price level in period 2. The credibility or the believability of the

---

[1] The source of Figure 16.1 is the Statistic Bureau and the Cabinet Office of Japan, and the source of Figure 16.2 is Nihon Keizai Shimbun-sha. Both data are quoted by Yoshida (2004).

[2] The annual rate of inflation of the GDP deflator was between – 2 percent and 0 percent every year during this period. See Hamada (2004) and Iwata, 2001, p. 13. By the way, unemployment rates in Japan in 2001 and 2002 were 5.0 percent and 5.4 percent, respectively. These numbers may not seem very high from the standard of the western countries. However, these are the extremely high numbers for Japan, since the Japanese economy never experienced the unemployment rate which is greater than 4 percent during such a long period as 1960–1997.

[3] For the controversy between the critics and the defenders of the Bank of Japan, see Komiya and Research Center of Japanese Economy (2002). Hamada (2004), Ito (2001), and Iwata (2001) contain very persuasive criticisms of the Bank of Japan.

Figure 16.1.   Rates of unemployment and real growth rates in Japan (u = rate of unemployment and g = annual growth rate of real GDP)

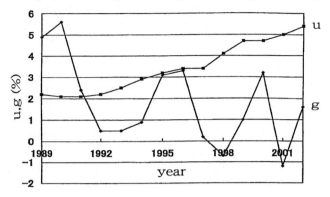

Figure 16.2.   Average stock prices in Japan (E = Nikkei stock average price)

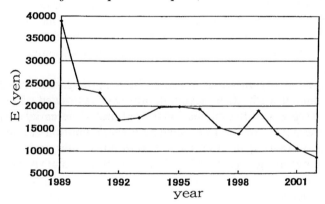

central banker's behavior plays a crucial role for the effectiveness of the monetary policy in his model.[4]

In this paper, we reconsider the macroeconomic impact of the inflation targeting policy by adopting another modeling strategy. Our analytical framework is a high-dimensional dynamic Keynesian model with debt accumulation, which was developed by Chiarella and Flaschel (2000),

---

[4]Yoshida (2004) generalizes Krugman's (1998) model by constructing the infinite time horizon dynamic optimizing model with continuous time which has the same properties as those of Krugman's (1998) model.

Chiarella *et al.* (2000), Chiarella *et al.* (2001), Asada *et al.* (2003) and Asada
(2004). As noted by Asada *et al.* (2003), "macrodynamics must look for
progress from at least two perspectives" (p. 334). One approach seeks, like
Krugman's (1998), solid microeconomic foundations which are based on the
optimizing behavior of single agent (representative agent).[5] Usually, this
modeling strategy results in relatively small linear or loglinear models for
reasons of tractability. On the other hand, another approach tries to provide a
full picture of the economic interdependency by constructing high-dimensional
macrodynamic system. Usually this approach is not based on the explicit
treatment of the optimizing behavior of agents, but, this does not necessarily
mean that it contradicts the optimizing behaviors. In this paper, we adopt the
latter modeling strategy to investigate the effect of the inflation targeting
policy. Our model integrates the 'debt effect' on the investment expenditure
which is due to Fisher (1933), Keynes (1936), and Minsky (1986) (cf. Nasica
(2000)) into high-dimensional Keynesian dynamic model which was developed
by Chiarella, Flaschel, and others. The merit of our approach is that we can
make explicit some important stabilizing (negative feedback) and destabilizing
(positive feedback) causal chains which are embedded in the dynamic process.
We show that the monetary authority can stabilize an unstable economy by
carrying out the sufficiently credible inflation targeting policy even in case of
the liquidity trap, as long as the destabilizing Fisher debt effect is not extremely
strong. We also show the existence of the cyclical fluctuation at some range of
the parameter values.

   This paper is organized as follows. In Section 2, our basic dynamic
Keynesian model with debt accumulation is constructed. The model is
reduced to a system of five-dimensional nonlinear differential equations. In
Section 3, the nature of the long-run equilibrium solution is considered. In
Section 4, we investigate the local stability/instability of the long-run
equilibrium by using the Routh–Hurwitz criteria, and then detect the
condition for the existence of the cyclical fluctuation by using the Hopf
bifurcation theorem. In Section 5, we provide some numerical examples
which support our analysis. In Section 6, the economic interpretation of the
main analytical results is provided. The proofs of the main propositions are
contained in the appendices.

2. Formulation of the model

Our model consists of the following system of equations, where a dot over a
symbol denotes the derivative with respect to time.

$$\dot{d} = \phi(g(\beta y, \rho - \pi^e, d)) - s_f\{\beta y - i(\rho, d)d\} - \{g(\beta y, \rho - \pi^e, d) + \pi\}d \qquad (16.1)$$

---

[5] For the comprehensive treatment of such an approach, see Woodford (2003).

$$\dot{y} = \alpha[\phi(g(\beta y, \rho - \pi^e, d)) + (1 - s_r)\{\rho v + i(\rho, d)d\}$$
$$- \{s_f + (1 - s_f)s_r\}\beta y] \quad \alpha > 0 \tag{16.2}$$

$$\dot{e}/e = \dot{y}/y + g(\beta y, \rho - \pi^e, d) - n \tag{16.3}$$

$$\dot{m}/m = \mu - \pi - g(\beta y, \rho - \pi^e, d) \tag{16.4}$$

$$\dot{\pi}^e = \gamma\{\theta(\mu_0 - n - \pi^e) + (1 - \theta)(\pi - \pi^e)\}; \quad \gamma > 0, \quad 0 \leqq \theta \leqq 1 \tag{16.5}$$

$$\pi = \varepsilon(e - \bar{e}) + \pi^e; \quad \varepsilon > 0 \tag{16.6}$$

$$\rho = \rho_0 + (h_1 y - m)/h_2 \equiv \rho(y, m); \quad \rho_0 \geqq 0, \quad h_1 > 0, \quad h_2 > 0 \tag{16.7}$$

$$\mu = \mu_0 + \delta(\mu_0 - n - \pi); \quad \mu_0 > 0, \quad \delta \geqq 0 \tag{16.8}$$

The meanings of the symbols are as follows: $d = D/pK = $ debt/capital ratio, $y = Y/K = $ output/capital ratio, which is also called 'rate of capacity utilization', $D =$ nominal stock of firms' private debt, $p = $ price level, $K = $ real capital stock, $Y = $ real output (real national income), $g = \dot{K}/K = $ rate of capital accumulation, $\rho = $ nominal rate of interest of interest-bearing safe assets, $i = $ nominal rate of interest which is applied to firms' private debt, $\pi = \dot{p}/p = $ rate of price inflation, $\pi^e = $ expected rate of price inflation, $e = N/N^s = $ rate of employment $= 1 - $ rate of unemployment $(0 \leqq e \leqq 1)$, $N = $ labor employment, $N^s = $ labor supply, $n = \dot{N}^s/N^s = $ growth rate of labor supply (natural rate of growth)$= $ constant > 0, $m = M/pK = $ money/capital ratio, $M = $ nominal money supply, $\mu = \dot{M}/M = $ growth rate of nominal money supply. The function $\phi(g)$ is the adjustment cost function of investment which was introduced by Uzawa (1969) with the properties $\phi'(g) \geqq 1$ and $\phi''(g) \geqq 0$. We shall explain the economic meanings of the parameters $\alpha, \gamma, \theta, \varepsilon, h_1, h_2, \delta, v, s_f,$ and s_r later.

Next, we shall explain how these equations are derived. The dynamic law of the motion of private debt can be expressed as follows:

$$\dot{D} = \phi(g)pK - s_f(rpK - iD) \tag{16.9}$$

where $r = P/K$ is the rate of profit (P is the real profit), and $s_f \in (0, 1]$ is the rate of internal retention of firms, which is assumed to be constant. For simplicity, we assume that there are no issues of new shares, and we neglect the repayment of the principal of debt. Differentiating the definitional relationship $d = D/(pK)$, we have

$$\dot{d}/d = \dot{D}/D - \dot{p}/p - \dot{K}/K = \dot{D}/D - \pi - g \tag{16.10}$$

Substituting Equation (16.9) into Equation (16.10), we obtain

$$\dot{d} = \phi(g) - s_f(r - id) - (g + \pi)d \tag{16.11}$$

For the dynamic adjustment in the goods market, we assume the following Keynesian/Kaldorian quantity adjustment process (cf. Asada, 1991, 2001):

$$\dot{y} = \alpha(c + h - y) \quad c = C/K \quad h = E/K \tag{16.12}$$

where C is real-consumption expenditure, $E = \phi(g)K$ is real-investment expenditure including adjustment cost, and α is a positive parameter which represents the speed of adjustment in the goods market. For consumption expenditures, we shall assume as follows, the Kaleckian formulation of the two-class economy (cf. Kalecki (1971)):

$$C = C_w + C_r \tag{16.13}$$

$$C_w = W = Y - P \tag{16.14}$$

$$C_r = (1 - s_r)\{(1 - s_f)P + \rho(V/p) + i(D/p)\}; \quad s_r \in (0, 1] \tag{16.15}$$

where C_w, C_r, and W are workers' real consumption, capitalists' real consumption, and real-wage income, respectively, V is the nominal value of the interest-bearing safe assets, and s_r is the capitalists' propensity to save, which is assumed to be a constant. These equations imply the Kaleckian postulate that the workers do not save, while the capitalists save a part of their income.[6] Substituting Equations (16.13), (16.14), and (16.15) into Equation (16.12), we obtain the following expression:[7]

$$\dot{y} = \alpha[\phi(g) + (1 - s_r)\{\rho(V/pK) + id\} - \{s_f + (1 - s_f)s_r\}r] \tag{16.16}$$

Furthermore, we assume the following relationships:

$$i = \rho + \xi(d) \equiv i(\rho, d) \quad \xi(d) \gtreqless 0, \quad i_d = \xi'(d) > 0 \; for \; d > 0$$
$$i_d < 0 \; for \; d < 0 \tag{16.17}$$
$$g = g(r, \rho - \pi^e, d) \quad g_r = \partial g/\partial r > 0 \quad g_{\rho-\pi} = \partial g/\partial(\rho - \pi^e) < 0$$
$$g_d = \partial g/\partial d < 0 \tag{16.18}$$
$$P/Y = \beta = constant, \quad 0 < \beta < 1 \tag{16.19}$$
$$V/pK = v = constant > 0 \tag{16.20}$$

Equation (16.17) captures the fact that the rate of interest of the 'risky' asset i is greater than ρ, and the difference between them reflects the degree of risk. Equation (16.18) is the investment function with Fisher debt effect. We can derive this type of investment function theoretically from the optimizing behavior of firms by using both Uzawa's (1969) hypothesis of increasing cost (Penrose effect) and Kalecki's (1937) hypothesis of increasing risk of investment (cf. Asada, 1999, 2001).

---

[6] We can expect that in a 'normal' situation, corporate sector as a whole is a debtor and capitalists as a whole is a creditor. In this case, we have $D > 0$. However, the case $D < 0$ is also possible.

[7] In the formulae (16.12)–(16.16), income tax and government expenditure are neglected. We can introduce, however, these factors without changing the qualitative behavior of the model, at the cost of the complication of the notation, by assuming that the tax rates and the real government expenditure per capital stock are constant.

We can interpret Equation (16.19) as follows: By definition, we have

$$p = z(wN/Y) = zw/a \quad z > 1 \tag{16.21}$$

where z is the mark up and $a = Y/N$ is average labor productivity. Therefore, we can express the share of profit in national income as the increasing function of the mark up, namely,

$$\beta = P/Y = (Y - W)/Y = 1 - (W/Y) = 1 - \{(w/p)N/Y\} = 1 - (1/z) \tag{16.22}$$

We assume that the mark up is a constant which reflects the 'degree of monopoly' in the sense of Kalecki (1971), so that β also becomes a constant. In this case, we have

$$r = P/K = \beta Y/K = \beta y \tag{16.23}$$

Equation (16.20) is merely the simplifying assumption to avoid the unnecessary complications. Substituting Equations (16.17), (16.18), (16.19), (16.20), and (16.23) into Equations (16.11) and (16.16), we obtain Equations (16.1) and (16.2).

Wee can derive Equation (16.3) as follows: By definition, we have

$$N = \frac{(Y/K)K}{Y/N} = yK/a \tag{16.24}$$

so that we also have

$$e = N/N^s = yK/aN^s \tag{16.25}$$

We abstract from technical progress, so that we assume that the average labor productivity a is constant. In this case, differentiating Equation (16.25), we have the following equation, which is nothing but Equation (16.3).

$$\dot{e}/e = \dot{y}/y + \dot{K}/K - \dot{N}^s/N^s = \dot{y}/y + g(\beta y, \rho - \pi^e, d) - n \tag{16.26}$$

Next, differentiating the definitional equation $m = M/pK$, we have

$$\dot{m}/m = \dot{M}/M - \dot{p}/p - \dot{K}/K = \mu - \pi - g(\beta y, \rho - \pi^e, d) \tag{16.27}$$

which is Equation (16.4).

Equation (16.5) formalizes the expectation formation hypothesis of the public's expected rate of price inflation, which is a mixture of the forward-looking and the backward-looking (adaptive) types of expectation formations.[8] In case of $\theta = 0$, Equation (16.5) is reduced to $\dot{\pi}^e = \gamma(\pi - \pi^e)$, which is nothing

---

[8] This type of expectation formation was studied by Asada *et al.* (2003).

but the standard formulation of adaptive (backward-looking) expectation hypothesis. On the other hand, in case of $\theta = 1$, it is reduced to $\dot{\pi}^e = \gamma(\mu_0 - n - \pi^e)$, which implies that the expected rate of inflation is adjusted toward the target rate $\mu_0 - n$. We shall see in the next section that this target rate is in fact the long-run equilibrium rate of inflation in our model. We assume that this target rate is announced by the monetary authority (central bank), so that it affects the expectation formation of the private sectors in the forward-looking manner.

Next, let us consider the price dynamics. We assume the following standard type of the expectation-augmented wage Phillips curve.

$$\dot{w}/w = \varepsilon(e - \bar{e}) + \pi^e \tag{16.28}$$

where ε is the speed of wage adjustment, which is assumed to be a positive parameter. On the other hand, from Equation (16.21) we have

$$\pi = \dot{p}/p = \dot{w}/w \tag{16.29}$$

Therefore, we can transform the wage Phillips curve (16.28) into the price Phillips curve (16.6).

Equation (16.7) is nothing but the standard type of the Keynesian 'LM equation' which describes the equilibrium condition for the money market. We specify the nominal demand function for money as $L^D = h_1 pY + (\rho_0 - \rho)h_2 pK$, where ρ_0 is the lower bound of the nominal rate of interest.[9] In this case, the equilibrium condition for the money market $M = L^D$ becomes as follows:

$$m = M/pK = h_1(Y/K) + (\rho_0 - \rho)h_2 = h_1 y + (\rho_0 - \rho)h_2 \tag{16.30}$$

Solving this equation with respect to ρ, we have Equation (16.7).[10]

Equation (16.8) formalizes the monetary policy rule of the monetary authority (the central bank). This is a type of the 'inflation targeting rule' (cf. Krugman's (1998) and Bernanke *et al.* (1999)). Monetary authority announces the target rate of inflation $\mu_0 - n$ to the public, and adjusts the growth rate of the nominal money supply towards the realization of this target.

---

[9] This formulation is due to Asad *et al.* (2003).
[10] Needless to say, we must suppose $\rho = \rho_0$ in case of $h_1 y - m < 0$. This corresponds to the case of the so-called 'liquidity trap.'

We can reduce the system of Equations (16.1)–(16.8) to the following system of the five-dimensional nonlinear differential equations:[11]

$$
\begin{aligned}
\text{(i)} \quad \dot{d} &= \phi(g(\beta y, \rho(y,m)) - \pi^e, d)) - s_f\{\beta y - i(\rho(y,m), d)d\} \\
&\quad -\{g(\beta y, \rho(y,m)) - \pi^e, d) + \varepsilon(e - \bar{e}) + \pi^e\}d \\
&\equiv F_1(d, y, e, \pi^e, m; \varepsilon) \\
\text{(ii)} \quad \dot{y} &= \alpha[\phi(g(\beta y, \rho(y,m)) - \pi^e, d)) + (1 - s_r)\{\rho(y,m)v \\
&\quad + i(\rho(y,m), d)d\} - \{s_f + (1 - s_f)s_r\}\beta y] \\
&\equiv F_2(d, y, \pi^e, m; \alpha) \\
\text{(iii)} \quad \dot{e} &= e[F_2(d, y, \pi^e, m; \alpha)/y + g(\beta y, \rho(y,m)) - \pi^e, d) - n] \\
&\equiv F_3(d, y, e, \pi^e, m; \alpha) \\
\text{(iv)} \quad \dot{\pi}^e &= \gamma\{\theta(\mu_0 - n - \pi^e) + (1 - \theta)\varepsilon(e - \bar{e})\} \\
&\equiv F_4(e, \pi^e; \varepsilon, \gamma, \theta) \\
\text{(v)} \quad \dot{m} &= m[(1 + \delta)\{\mu_0 - \varepsilon(e - \bar{e}) - \pi^e\} - \delta n - g(\beta y, \rho(y,m)) \\
&\quad - \pi^e, d)] \\
&\equiv F_5(d, y, e, \pi^e, m; \varepsilon, \delta)
\end{aligned}
\tag{16.31}
$$

3. Nature of the equilibrium solution

First, let us study the nature of the equilibrium solution of the system (16.31) which satisfies the condition $\dot{d} = \dot{y} = \dot{e} = \dot{\pi}^e = \dot{m} = 0$. The equilibrium values of the endogenous variables are determined by the following set of equations, which defines the long-run equilibrium (steady state) of our system:

$$
\begin{aligned}
\text{(i)} \quad & \phi(n) - s_f\{\beta y - i(\rho(y,m), d)d\} - \mu_0 d = 0 \\
\text{(ii)} \quad & \phi(n) + (1 - s_r)\{\rho(y,m)v + i(\rho(y,m), d)d\} \\
& \quad - \{s_f + (1 - s_f)s_r\}\beta y = 0 \\
\text{(iii)} \quad & g(\beta y, \rho(y,m)) - \mu_0 + n, d) = n \\
\text{(iv)} \quad & e = \bar{e} \\
\text{(v)} \quad & \pi = \pi^e = \mu_0 - n
\end{aligned}
\tag{16.32}
$$

Equation (16.32) (iii) and (iv) imply that at the long-run equilibrium position, the rate of capital accumulation (the rate of investment) is equal to the exogenously determined 'natural rate of growth', and the rate of employment is equal to the exogenously determined 'natural rate of employment.' Because of this fact, at first glance, it seems that the monetary policy is irrelevant to the

---

[11] This system is in fact an extended version of the model which was presented by Asada (2004). In Asada (2004), the simpler three-dimensional model was studied.

determination of the long-run equilibrium. But, in fact, this is not true. Usually, a set of equations (16.32) can be considered as the determinant of the equilibrium values $(d^*, y^*, m^*, e^*, \pi^{e*})$ for a given long-run target value of the growth rate of money supply μ_0. These equilibrium values except e^* usually depend on μ_0. In particular, (d^*, y^*, m^*) are determined by the subsystem (16.32) (i)–(iii) for given μ_0, and the equilibrium value of real rate of interest is determined by

$$(\rho - \pi^e)^* = \rho(y^*, m^*) + n - \mu_0 \tag{16.33}$$

By the way, the nominal rate of interest has the nonnegative lower bound ρ_0, so that the inequality

$$(\rho - \pi^e)^* \geqq \rho_0 + n - \mu_0 \tag{16.34}$$

must be satisfied. Since the economically meaningful ranges of y and d are restricted, there may be the case in which relatively small real rate of interest is required to keep the natural rate of growth. This means that the long-run equilibrium may not exist because of too high real rate of interest if the monetary authority chooses too small value of μ_0. That is to say, the target rate of inflation $\mu_0 - n$ cannot be chosen completely arbitrarily, and there are some restrictions on the choice of its value, even if there remains some degree of freedom for the choice of μ_0.[12] In fact, it is quite likely that the mildly positive target rate of inflation, for example, 2 or 3 percent per year, rather than zero inflation is required to ensure the existence of the long-run equilibrium (cf. Krugman's (1998)). Henceforth, we assume that μ_0 is fixed at the level which ensures the existence of long-run equilibrium, and monetary authority announces its value to the public. It is assumed that the public uses this information for its expectation formation in the manner of Equation (16.5).

It is worth noting that the values of the parameters $\alpha, \varepsilon, \gamma, \theta$, and δ do not affect the long-run equilibrium values of the main variables. However, this does not mean that these parameter values are irrelevant to the dynamic behavior of the system. In fact, the changes of these parameter values can affect the dynamic stability of the system. We investigate this theme in the next section.

4. Local stability analysis and the detection of cyclical fluctuations

In this section, we study the local stability/instability of the equilibrium point by assuming that there exists an economically meaningful equilibrium point such that $d^* > 0$, $y^* > 0$, and $m^* > 0$. We can express the Jacobian matrix of the five-dimensional system (16.31) which is evaluated *at the equilibrium point* as

---

[12] We can show that in the special case of $1/h_2 = 0(h_2 \to +\infty)$, monetary authority has no freedom over the choice of μ_0. In this case, there is just one 'correct' μ_0 which is consistent with the steady state with natural rate of growth. This case corresponds to the so-called 'liquidity trap' in which the nominal rate of interest becomes insensitive to the changes of y and m.

follows:

$$
ptJ_5(1/h_2) = \begin{bmatrix} F_{11} & F_{12}(1/h_2) & F_{13}(\varepsilon) & F_{14} & F_{15}(1/h_2) \\ F_{21}(\alpha) & F_{22}(\alpha, 1/h_2) & 0 & F_{24}(\alpha) & F_{25}(\alpha, 1/h_2) \\ F_{31}(\alpha) & F_{32}(\alpha, 1/h_2) & 0 & F_{34}(\alpha) & F_{35}(\alpha, 1/h_2) \\ 0 & 0 & F_{43}(\varepsilon, \gamma, \theta) & F_{44}(\gamma, \theta) & 0 \\ F_{51} & F_{52}(1/h_2) & F_{53}(\varepsilon, \delta) & F_{54}(\delta) & F_{55}(1/h_2) \end{bmatrix}
$$

$$(16.35)$$

where

$$
F_{11} = \partial F_1/\partial d = \underset{(+)}{(\phi'(n) - d)} \, \underset{(-)}{g_d} - \mu_0 + \underset{(+)}{s_f(i_d d - i)}
$$

$$
F_{12}(1/h_2) = \partial F_1/\partial y = \beta\{\underset{(+)}{(\phi'(n) - d)} \, \underset{(+)}{g_r} - s_f\} + [\underset{(+)}{\{\phi'(n) - 1\}} \, \underset{(-)}{g_{\rho-\pi}}]
$$

$$
+ \underset{(+)}{s_f \, i_\rho \, d}](h_1/h_2)
$$

$$
F_{13}(\varepsilon) = \partial F_1/\partial e = -\varepsilon d < 0
$$

$$
F_{14} = \partial F_1/\partial \pi^e = -\underset{(+)}{(\phi'(n) - d)} \, \underset{(-)}{g_{\rho-\pi}} - d
$$

$$
F_{15}(1/h_2) = \partial F_1/\partial m = -[\underset{(+)}{\{\phi'(n) - 1\}} \, \underset{(-)}{g_{\rho-\pi}} + \underset{(+)}{s_f \, i_\rho \, d}](1/h_2)
$$

$$
F_{21}(\alpha) = \partial F_2/\partial d = \alpha[\underset{(+)}{\phi'(n)} \, \underset{(-)}{g_d} + \underset{(+)}{(1 - s_r)(i_d \, d + i)}]
$$

$$
F_{22}(\alpha, 1/h_2) = \partial F_2/\partial y = \alpha\beta[\underset{(+)}{\phi'(n)} \, \underset{(+)}{g_r} - \{s_f + (1 - s_f)s_r\}] + \alpha[\underset{(+)}{\phi'(n)} \, \underset{(-)}{g_{\rho-\pi}}]
$$

$$
+ \underset{(+)}{(1 - s_r)(v + i_\rho d)}](h_1/h_2)
$$

$$
F_{24}(\alpha) = \partial F_2/\partial \pi^e = -\alpha \, \underset{(+)}{\phi'(n)} \, \underset{(-)}{g_{\rho-\pi}} > 0
$$

$$
F_{25}(\alpha, 1/h_2) = \partial F_2/\partial m = -\alpha[\underset{(+)}{\phi'(n)} \, \underset{(-)}{g_{\rho-\pi}} + \underset{(+)}{(1 - s_r)(v + i_\rho \, d)}](1/h_2)
$$

$$
F_{31}(\alpha) = \partial F_3/\partial d = \bar{e}[\underset{(-)}{F_{21}(\alpha)/y + g_d}]
$$

$$
F_{32}(\alpha, 1/h_2) = \partial F_3/\partial y = \bar{e}[\underset{(+)}{F_{22}(\alpha, 1/h_2)/y + \beta \, g_r}]
$$

$$
F_{34}(\alpha) = \partial F_3/\partial \pi^e = \bar{e}[\underset{(-)}{F_{24}(\alpha)/y - g_{\rho-\pi}}]
$$

$$
F_{35}(\alpha, 1/h_2) = \partial F_3/\partial m = \bar{e}[\underset{(-)}{F_{25}(\alpha, 1/h_2)/y - g_{\rho-\pi}(1/h_2)}]
$$

$$
F_{43}(\varepsilon, \gamma_2) = \partial F_4/\partial e = \gamma(1 - \theta)\varepsilon \gtreqqless 0
$$

$$F_{44}(\gamma_1) = \partial F_4/\partial \pi^e = -\gamma\theta \leqq 0$$

$$F_{51} = \partial F_5/\partial d = -m\, g_d > 0$$
$$\quad\quad\quad\quad\quad\quad\quad {\scriptstyle(-)}$$

$$F_{52}(1/h_2) = \partial F_5/\partial y = -m[\beta\, g_r + g_{\rho-\pi}(h_1/h_2)]$$
$$\quad\quad\quad\quad\quad\quad\quad\quad\quad {\scriptstyle(+)}\quad\quad {\scriptstyle(-)}$$

$$F_{53}(\varepsilon, \delta) = \partial F_5/\partial e = -m(1+\delta)\varepsilon < 0$$

$$F_{54}(\delta) = \partial F_5/\partial \pi^e = m[-(1+\delta)+g_{\rho-\pi}] < 0$$
$$\quad\quad\quad\quad\quad\quad\quad\quad\quad\quad\quad {\scriptstyle(-)}$$

$$F_{55}(1/h_2) = \partial F_5/\partial m = m\, g_{\rho-\pi}(1/h_2) \leqq 0$$
$$\quad\quad\quad\quad\quad\quad\quad\quad\quad {\scriptstyle(-)}$$

For a moment, we shall concentrate on the special case of $1/h_2 = 0 (h_2 \to +\infty)$, which corresponds to the case of the 'liquidity trap' in which the nominal rate of interest is fixed at its lower bound ρ_0. In this case, the Jacobian matrix at the equilibrium point becomes as follows:[13]

$$J_5(0) = \begin{bmatrix} F_{11} & F_{12}(0) & -\varepsilon d & F_{14} & 0 \\ \alpha G_{21} & \alpha G_{22} & 0 & \alpha G_{24} & 0 \\ \bar{e}[\alpha G_{21}/y + g_d] & \bar{e}[\alpha G_{22}/y + \beta g_r] & 0 & \bar{e}[\alpha G_{24}/y - g_{\rho-\pi}] & 0 \\ 0 & 0 & \gamma(1-\theta)\varepsilon & -\gamma\theta & 0 \\ F_{51} & F_{52}(0) & F_{53}(\varepsilon, \delta) & F_{54}(\delta) & 0 \end{bmatrix}$$

$$(16.36)$$

where

$$F_{12}(0) = \beta\{(\phi'(n)-d)\}\, g_r - s_f\} \quad G_{21} = \phi'(n)\, g_d + (1-s_r)(i_d\, d + i)$$
$$\quad\quad\quad\quad {\scriptstyle(+)}\quad\quad\quad {\scriptstyle(+)}\quad\quad\quad\quad\quad {\scriptstyle(+)\,(-)}\quad\quad\quad\quad {\scriptstyle(+)}$$

$$G_{22} = \beta[\phi'(n)\, g_r - \{s_f + (1-s_f)s_r\}] \quad \text{and} \quad G_{24} = -\phi'(n)\, g_{\rho-r} > 0.$$
$$\quad\quad\quad {\scriptstyle(+)\,(+)}\quad\quad\quad\quad\quad\quad\quad\quad\quad\quad\quad\quad\quad {\scriptstyle(+)}\quad\quad {\scriptstyle(-)}$$

Throughout the paper, we posit the following assumptions:

Assumption 1.

$$F_{11} < 0 \quad F_{12}(0) > 0 \quad F_{14} > 0 \quad G_{21} < 0 \quad \text{and} \quad G_{22} > 0$$

Assumption 2.

$$F_{11} G_{22} - F_{12}(0)G_{21} > 0$$

---

[13] Obviously, it is implicitly assumed that the monetary authority chooses the 'correct' value of μ_0 which is consistent with the existence of the long-run equilibrium with the natural rate of growth.

We can interpret the economic meanings of these assumptions as follows. Assumption 1 will be satisfied if $\phi'(n)$, g_r, $|g_{p-\pi}|$, and $|g_d|$ are sufficiently large at the equilibrium point. In other words, Assumption 2 will in fact be satisfied if the sensitivity of adjustment cost with respect to the changes of investment activity and the sensitivities of investment with respect to the changes of relevant variables are relatively large. On the other hand, it is easy to show that

$$\lim_{s_r \to 1} \{F_{11}G_{22} - F_{12}(0)G_{21}\} = \beta[\{-d\,g_d - \mu_0 + (d\,g_r + s_f)(\,i_d + i)\{\phi'(n)\,g_r - 1\}$$
$$\underset{(-)}{\qquad\qquad\qquad} \underset{(+)}{\qquad} \underset{(+)}{\qquad} \underset{(+)\ (+)}{\qquad}$$
$$+ s_f\,\phi'(n)\,g_r] \qquad\qquad\qquad\qquad (16.37)$$
$$\underset{(+)\ \ (+)}{\qquad\quad}$$

The right-hand side of Equation (16.37) becomes positive if $\phi'(n)$, g_r, $|g_d|$, and i_d are sufficiently large. This means that Assumption 2 will be satisfied if $\phi'(n)$, g_r, $|g_d|$, i_d, and s_r are sufficiently large at the equilibrium point. In other words, Assumption 2 will in fact be satisfied if capitalists' propensity to save as well as the sensitivities of investment etc. with respect to the relevant variables are relatively large.

The characteristic equation of the Jacobian matrix (16.35) becomes

$$\Delta_5(\lambda; 1/h_2) \equiv |\lambda I - J_5(1/h_2)| = 0 \qquad\qquad\qquad (16.38)$$

In particular, in case of $1/h_2 = 0$, this equation becomes

$$\Delta_5(\lambda; 0) = |\lambda I - J_4(0)|\lambda = 0 \qquad\qquad\qquad (16.39)$$

where

$$J_4(0) = \begin{bmatrix} F_{11} & F_{12}(0) & -\varepsilon d & F_{14} \\ \alpha G_{21} & \alpha G_{22} & 0 & \alpha G_{24} \\ \bar{e}[\alpha G_{21}/y + g_d] & \bar{e}[\alpha G_{22}/y + \beta g_r] & 0 & \bar{e}[\alpha G_{24}/y - g_{p-\pi}] \\ 0 & 0 & \gamma(1-\theta)\varepsilon & -\gamma\theta \end{bmatrix}$$
$$(16.40)$$

The characteristic Equation (16.39) has a root $\lambda_5 = 0$, and the other four roots are determined by the following equation:

$$\Delta_4(\lambda; 0) = |\lambda I - J_4(0)| = \lambda^4 + a_1\lambda^3 + a_2\lambda^2 + a_3\lambda + a_4 = 0 \qquad (16.41)$$

where

$$a_1 = -trace\,J_4(0) = -\,F_{11} - \alpha\,G_{22} + \gamma\theta \equiv a_1(\alpha, \gamma, \theta) \qquad (16.42)$$
$$\underset{(-)}{\qquad\quad} \underset{(+)}{\quad}$$

a_2 = sum of all principal second-order minors of $J_4(0)$

$$\alpha \begin{vmatrix} F_{11} & F_{12}(0) \\ G_{21} & G_{22} \end{vmatrix} + \begin{vmatrix} F_{11} & -\varepsilon d \\ \bar{e}[\alpha G_{21}/y + g_d] & 0 \end{vmatrix} + \gamma\theta \begin{vmatrix} F_{11} & F_{14} \\ 0 & -1 \end{vmatrix}$$

$$+ \begin{vmatrix} \alpha G_{22} & 0 \\ \bar{e}[\alpha G_{22}/y + \beta g_r] & 0 \end{vmatrix}$$

$$+ \alpha\gamma\theta \begin{vmatrix} G_{22} & G_{24} \\ 0 & -1 \end{vmatrix} + \gamma \begin{vmatrix} 0 & \bar{e}[\alpha G_{24}/y - g_{\rho-\pi}] \\ (1-\theta)\varepsilon & -\theta \end{vmatrix}$$

$$= \alpha\{\underset{(-)}{F_{11}}\,\underset{(+)}{G_{22}} - \underset{(+)}{F_{12}(0)}\,\underset{(-)}{G_{21}}\} + \varepsilon d\bar{e}[\underset{(-)}{\alpha\,G_{21}/y} + \underset{(-)}{g_d}]$$

$$+ \gamma[\theta(-\underset{(-)}{F_{11}} - \underset{(+)}{\alpha\,G_{22}}) - (1-\theta)\varepsilon\bar{e}\{\underset{(+)}{\alpha\,G_{24}/y} - \underset{(-)}{g_{\rho-\pi}}\}$$

$$\equiv a_2(\alpha, \varepsilon, \gamma, \theta) \qquad\qquad (16.43)$$

$a_3 = -$ (sum of all principal third-order minors of $J_4(0)$)

$$= -\alpha\gamma\varepsilon\bar{e} \begin{vmatrix} G_{22} & 0 & G_{24} \\ \alpha G_{22}/y + \beta g_r & 0 & \alpha G_{24}/y - g_{\rho-\pi} \\ 0 & 1-\theta & -\theta \end{vmatrix}$$

$$- \gamma\varepsilon\bar{e} \begin{vmatrix} F_{11} & -d & F_{14} \\ \alpha G_{21}/y + g_d & 0 & \alpha G_{24}/y - g_{\rho-\pi} \\ 0 & 1-\theta & -\theta \end{vmatrix}$$

$$- \alpha\gamma\theta \begin{vmatrix} F_{11} & F_{12}(0) & F_{14} \\ G_{21} & G_{22} & G_{24} \\ 0 & 0 & -1 \end{vmatrix} - \alpha\varepsilon d\bar{e} \begin{vmatrix} F_{11} & F_{12}(0) & -1 \\ G_{21} & G_{22} & 0 \\ \alpha G_{21}/y + g_d & \alpha G_{22}/y + \beta g_r & 0 \end{vmatrix}$$

$$= \gamma[\alpha(1-\theta)\varepsilon\bar{e}(\underset{(+)}{G_{22}\,g_{\rho-\pi}} - \underset{(-)}{G_{24}\,\beta\,g_r}) + \varepsilon\bar{e}\{(\underset{(+)}{\theta d} - \underset{(+)}{(1-\theta)\,F_{14}})(\underset{(+)}{\alpha\,G_{21}/y} + \underset{(-)}{g_d})$$

$$+ (1-\theta)\underset{(-)}{F_{11}}(\underset{(+)}{\alpha\,G_{24}/y} - \underset{(-)}{g_{\rho-\pi}})\} + \alpha\theta\{\underset{(-)}{F_{11}}\,\underset{(+)}{G_{22}} - \underset{(+)}{F_{12}(0)}\,\underset{(-)}{G_{21}}\}]$$

$$+ \alpha\varepsilon d\bar{e}(\underset{(-)}{G_{21}}\,\underset{(+)}{\beta\,g_r} - \underset{(+)}{G_{22}}\,\underset{(-)}{g_d})$$

$$\equiv a_3(\alpha, \varepsilon, \gamma, \theta) \qquad\qquad (16.44)$$

$$a_4 = \det J_4(0) = \alpha\gamma\varepsilon\bar{e} \begin{vmatrix} F_{11} & F_{12}(0) & -d & F_{14} \\ G_{21} & G_{22} & 0 & G_{24} \\ \alpha G_{21}/y + g_d & \alpha G_{22}/y + \beta g_r & 0 & \alpha G_{24}/y - g_{\rho-\pi} \\ 0 & 0 & 1-\theta & -\theta \end{vmatrix}$$

$$= \alpha\gamma\varepsilon\bar{e}[\theta d(\underset{(-)}{G_{21}} \underset{(+)}{\beta} \underset{(+)}{g_r} - \underset{(-)}{G_{22}} \underset{(+)}{g_d}) - (1-\theta)\{\underset{(+)}{\beta} \underset{(+)}{g_r}(\underset{(-)}{F_{14}} \underset{(-)}{G_{21}} - \underset{(+)}{F_{11}} \underset{G_{24}})$$

$$- \underset{(-)}{g_{\rho-\pi}}(\underset{(-)}{F_{11}} \underset{(+)}{G_{22}} - \underset{(+)}{F_{12}(0)} \underset{(-)}{G_{21}}) + \underset{(-)}{g_d}(\underset{(+)}{F_{12}(0)} \underset{(+)}{G_{24}} - \underset{(+)}{F_{14}} \underset{(+)}{G_{22}})\}]$$

$$\equiv a_4(\alpha, \varepsilon, \gamma, \theta) \tag{16.45}$$

The characteristic Equation (16.41) governs the local dynamics of the four-dimensional subsystem (16.31) (i)–(iv) in case of $1/h_2 = 0$. Now, let us assume:

Assumption 3.

$$F_{11} + \alpha G_{22} < 0 \quad \text{and} \quad G_{21}\beta g_r - G_{22}g_d > 0$$

The economic interpretation of this assumption is as follows. This assumption implies that

$$F_{11}\alpha G_{22} = (\underset{(+)}{\phi'(n)} - d) \underset{(-)}{g_d} - \mu_0 + \underset{(+)}{s_f(i_d} d + i) + \alpha\beta[\underset{(+)}{\phi'(n)} \underset{(+)}{g_r}$$

$$- \{s_f + (1-s_f)s_r\}] < 0 \tag{16.46}$$

$$G_{21}\beta g_r - G_{22}g_d = (1-s_r)(\underset{(+)}{i_d} d + i)\beta \underset{(+)}{g_r} + \{s_f + (1-s_f)s_r\} \underset{(-)}{g_d} > 0. \tag{16.47}$$

The inequality (16.46) will be satisfied if the quantity adjustment speed in the goods market (α) is not extremely large. The inequality (16.47) will be satisfied if the debt effect on investment ($|g_d|$) is relatively small compared with the profit rate effect on investment (g_r). Therefore, Assumption 3 will in fact be satisfied if α is not extremely large and $|g_d|$ is relatively small compared with g_r.

By the way, it is well known that the Routh–Hurwitz conditions for the local stability of the system (16.41) can be expressed as follows (cf. Gandolfo (1996)):

$$a_j > 0 \quad (j = 1, 2, 3, 4), \quad \Phi \equiv a_1 a_2 a_3 - a_1^2 a_4 - a_3^2 > 0 \tag{16.48}$$

Let us denote the four-dimensional subsystem (16.31) (i)–(iv) in case of $1/h_2 = 0$ as the system (S_4). By utilizing the criteria (16.48), we can prove the following results under Assumptions 1–3.

Proposition 1. (i) *Suppose that θ and γ are fixed at arbitrary values such that $0 \leq \theta \leq 1$ and $\gamma > 0$. Then, the equilibrium point of the system (S_4) is locally unstable for all sufficiently large values of $\varepsilon > 0$.*

(ii) *Suppose that $\theta \in [0, 1]$ is fixed at a value which is sufficiently close to zero, and ε is fixed at an arbitrary positive value. Then, the equilibrium point of the system (S_4) is locally unstable for all sufficiently large values of $\gamma > 0$.*

(iii) *Suppose that $\theta \in [0, 1]$ is fixed at a value which is sufficiently close to 1, and γ is fixed at an arbitrary positive value. Then, the equilibrium point of the system (S_4) is locally asymptotically stable for all sufficiently small values of $\varepsilon > 0$.*

(iv) *Suppose that the equilibrium point of the four-dimensional system (S_4) is locally asymptotically stable. Then, the behavior of the variable m also becomes locally stable in the sense that we have $\dot{m}/m \to 0$ as $(e, \pi^e, g) \to (\bar{e}, \mu_0 - n, n)$.*

Proof. See Appendix A.

Proposition 2. *Suppose that $\theta \in [0, 1]$ is fixed at a value which is sufficiently close to 1, and γ is fixed at an arbitrary positive value. Then, there exist some non-constant closed orbits at some intermediate range of the parameter value $\varepsilon > 0$.*

Proof. See Appendix B.

We can summarize these propositions as follows:

(1) If the wage adjustment speed in the labor market (ε) is sufficiently large, the equilibrium point of the system (S_4) becomes unstable irrespective of the parameter values concerning the price expectations. In other words, *the price flexibility tends to destabilize the system.*

(2) If the value of a parameter which reflects the credibility of the inflation targeting policy by the monetary authority (θ) is so small that the public's formation of price expectation is highly adaptive (backward looking), the high speed of the expectation adjustment (γ) tends to destabilize the system.

(3) Suppose that the wage adjustment speed in the labor market (ε) is not excessively large. Suppose, furthermore, that the inflation targeting policy by the monetary authority is so credible that the public's formation of price expectation is sufficiently forward looking (θ is sufficiently close to 1). Then, the equilibrium point of the system (S_4) becomes locally stable even if the speed of the expectation adjustment (γ) is very large. If the subsystem (S_4) which consists of the variables d, y, e, and π^e is locally stable, then, the behavior of money/capital ratio (m) also becomes locally stable.

(4) Under certain conditions, endogenous cyclical fluctuation around the equilibrium point occurs at some intermediate range of the speed of wage adjustment (ε).

In the above formal analysis, we only considered the special case of $1/h_2 = 0$ ($h_2 \to +\infty$), which corresponds to the case of the so-called 'liquidity trap.' In this case, the five-dimensional dynamical system (16.31) becomes decomposable in the sense that the behavior of money/capital ratio (m) does not affect the dynamics of the remaining four variables d, y, e, and π^e, although the behavior of m depends on the behavior of the other four variables. In this special case, the value of the monetary policy parameter δ is irrelevant to the qualitative dynamics of the system. This fact may be related to the alleged 'ineffectiveness' of monetary policy in case of the liquidity trap. However, as we already noted, *the monetary policy becomes effective through another channel of the 'credibility effect' which influences public's formation of price expectation, even in case of the liquidity trap.*

How dynamics of the system are modified if we consider the general case of $1/h_2 > 0$ ($0 < h_2 < +\infty$) instead of the case of liquidity trap? In this case, the five-dimensional system (16.31) is no longer decomposable, and the value of the monetary policy parameter δ can affect the qualitative dynamics of the system through the changes of the nominal rate of interest ρ. Without committing to the formal analysis, we can see that the increase of the policy parameter δ has a stabilizing effect at least potentially in this case of variable nominal rate of interest, because of the following reason:

In case of the variable nominal interest rate, the following stabilizing negative feedback effect, which is called 'Keynes effect' (KE) will work.

$$(y \downarrow) \Rightarrow e \downarrow \Rightarrow \pi \downarrow \Rightarrow m = (M/pK) \uparrow \Rightarrow \rho \downarrow \Rightarrow (\rho - \pi^e) \downarrow \Rightarrow g \uparrow \Rightarrow (y \uparrow)$$

$$\text{(KE)}$$

The increase of the monetary policy parameter δ will reinforce the part $\pi \downarrow \Rightarrow m \uparrow$ of this process through another feedback chain $\pi \downarrow \Rightarrow \mu \uparrow \Rightarrow m \uparrow$, so that the increase of δ will have a stabilizing effect. However, this stabilizing 'Keynes effect' will be almost negligible if the sensitivity of the *nominal* rate of interest with respect to the changes of the money/capital ratio $(1/h_2)$ is very small. In fact, this will be the case if the *nominal* rate of interest is already nearly zero, as in the case of the Japanese economy in the late 1990s and the early 2000s. Needless to say, the liquidity trap approximates this particular case in which the KE effect is very weak.

Before closing this section, we shall make a remark on the 'Taylor rule' which is due to Taylor (1993). Taylor rule is the monetary policy rule which selects the nominal rate of interest rather than the growth rate of the nominal money supply as the control variable of the central bank. A typical formulation of such a rule may be as follows:

$$\rho = \bar{\rho} + \delta_1(\pi - \bar{\pi}) + \delta_2(e - \bar{e}) \equiv \varphi(\pi, e) \quad \delta_1 > 0 \quad \delta_2 > 0 \quad (16.49)$$

This equation implies that the central bank raises (reduces) the nominal rate of interest when the rate of inflation increases (decreases) or the rate of employment increases (decreases). If we replace Equation (16.8) with Equation (16.49), we can analyze the model with the Taylor rule of monetary policy. In this case, money supply becomes a totally endogenous variable. Usually Japanese central bankers assert that their control variable is not the growth rate of nominal money supply but the nominal rate of interest. Therefore, it seems that the Taylor rule is suitable for the description of the monetary policy in Japan. However, we must remember that the nominal rate of interest cannot become negative. This means that the Taylor rule does not work in case of $\varphi(\pi, e) < 0$ in Equation (16.49). In fact, as Iwata (2002) pointed out correctly, we must modify the formula (16.49) as

$$\rho = \text{Max}[\varphi(\pi, e), \rho_0] \tag{16.50}$$

where ρ_0 is the nonnegative lower bound of the nominal rate of interest, which will be nearly zero.[14] If $\varphi(\pi, e) \leqq \rho_0$, Equation (16.50) is reduced to $\rho = \rho_0$, which is nothing but the case of 'liquidity trap.' The analysis in this section also applies to this case.

5. A numerical illustration

In this section, we present some numerical examples which support our analysis. The purpose of this section is not to present the quantitatively realistic numerical analysis, but to illustrate the qualitative conclusion of the mathematical analysis in the previous section. We assume the following parameter values and the functional forms:

$$\left.\begin{array}{l} s_f = s_r = 1 \quad \beta = 0.2 \quad i = \rho + d^2 \quad \rho = 0.01 \\ \bar{e} = 0.97 \quad \phi(g) = g \quad n = 0.03 \quad \alpha = 0.2 \quad \gamma = 0.3 \quad \varepsilon = 0.1 \\ g = 0.1\{1.8y^{0.8} - (\rho - \pi^e) - 0.9d - 0.19\} + n = 0.18y^{0.8} + 0.1\pi^e \\ -0.09d + 0.01 \end{array}\right\} \tag{16.51}$$

We interpret $100n$, 100ρ, and $100\pi^e$ as the annual percentages of the natural rate of growth, the nominal rate of interest, and the expected rate of price inflation, respectively. This example corresponds to the so-called 'liquidity trap' in which the nominal rate of interest is stuck at its lower bound of the 1 percent annual rate. In this case, a system of equations (16.31) (i)–(v) becomes as follows:

$$\left.\begin{array}{ll} \text{(i)} & \dot{d} = (0.18y^{0.8} + 0.1\pi^e - 0.09d + 0.01)(1 - d) \\ & \quad -0.2y + 0.01d + d^3 - 0.1(e - 0.97)d - \pi^e d \\ \text{(ii)} & \dot{y} = 0.2(0.18y^{0.8} + 0.1\pi^e - 0.09d + 0.01 - 0.2y) \\ \text{(iii)} & \dot{e} = e[0.2(0.18y^{0.8} + 0.1\pi^e - 0.09d + 0.01 - 0.2y)/y \\ & \quad +0.18y^{0.8} + 0.1\pi^e - 0.09d - 0.02] \\ \text{(iv)} & \dot{\pi}^e = 0.3\{\theta(\mu_0 - 0.03 - \pi^e) + (1 - \theta)0.1(e - 0.97)\} \\ & \quad 0 \leqq \theta \leqq 1 \\ \text{(v)} & \dot{m} = m[(1 + \delta)\{\mu_0 - 0.1(e - 0.97) - \pi^e\} \\ & \quad -0.03\delta - (0.18y^{0.8} + 0.1\pi^e - 0.09d + 0.01)] \end{array}\right\} \tag{16.52}$$

---

[14] Iwata (2002) assumed that $\rho_0 = 0$, but whether ρ_0 is zero or slightly positive is not essential for our argument.

First, let us consider the long-run equilibrium solution. In this case, a system of equations (16.32) (i)–(v), which determines the long-run equilibrium values, becomes:

(i) $0.03 - 0.2y + 0.01d + d^3 - \mu_0 d = 0$

(ii) $y = 0.15$

(iii) $1.8y^{0.8} + \pi^e - 0.9d - 0.2 = 0$ (16.53)

(iv) $e = 0.97$

(v) $\pi = \pi^e = \mu_0 - 0.03$

Substituting $y = 0.15$ and $\pi^e = \mu_0 - 0.03$ into Equation (16.53) (i) and (iii), we have the following set of equations:

(i) $0.01d + d^3 - \mu_0 d = 0$ (16.54)

(ii) $\mu_0 - 0.9d + 0.164589 = 0$

This is a set of simultaneous equations which determines the equilibrium values of d and μ_0. This means that the equilibrium rate of growth of money supply μ_0 cannot be given exogenously, but it becomes an endogenous variable in the special case of the 'liquidity trap.' In other words, the central bank must choose the 'correct' value of μ_0 to sustain the long-run equilibrium in this case (see also footnotes (12) and (13)). On the other hand, in this case of the liquidity trap, the equilibrium value of the money/capital ratio m becomes indeterminate. In fact, m becomes a 'path-dependent' variable in the sense that $\lim_{t \to \infty} m(t)$ depends on the initial value $m(0)$ even if the long-run equilibrium point is stable.

From Equation (16.54) (i), we have

$$\mu_0 = 0.01 + d^2 \qquad (16.55)$$

Substituting this expression into Equation (16.54) (ii), we obtain

$$d^2 - 0.9d + 0.174589 = 0 \qquad (16.56)$$

Solving this equation, we have the following multiple solutions:

$$d_1^* \cong 0.282934 \quad d_2^* \cong 0.617066 \qquad (16.57)$$

Corresponding to the small equilibrium value of debt/capital ratio d_1^*, we have the following equilibrium values:

$$\mu_{01}^* \cong 0.090052 \quad \pi_1^* = \pi_1^{e*} = \mu_{01}^* - 0.03 \cong 0.060052 \qquad (16.58)$$

On the other hand, we have the following equilibrium values corresponding to the large equilibrium value d_2^*:

$$\mu_{02}^* \cong 0.39077, \quad \pi_2^* = \pi_2^{e*} = \mu_{02}^* - 0.03 \cong 0.36077 \qquad (16.59)$$

In the former equilibrium point, the annual rate of price inflation is about 6 percent, which is a believable value. On the other hand, in the latter equilibrium point, the annual rate of price inflation is unbelievably high as the rate of inflation in modern advanced capitalist countries such as the United States, Japan, and the Euroland. Therefore, we assume that the central bank selects μ_{01}^* which supports the lower equilibrium value π_1^*. In this case, the equilibrium values of the relevant variables become

$$d^* \cong 0.282934, \quad y^* = 0.15, \quad e^* = 0.97, \quad \pi^* = \pi^{e*} \cong 0.060052 \qquad (16.60)$$

corresponding to the 'properly' selected value $\mu_0 \cong 0.090052$.

Figures 16.3–16.7 are the results of our simulation of the 'out of equilibrium' dynamics corresponding to the following initial values:

$$d(0) = 0.15 \quad y(0) = 0.13 \quad e(0) = 0.94 \quad \pi^e(0) = 0 \qquad (16.61)$$

In these figures, the following three alternative scenarios are shown:

Case D (Debt deflation):	$\theta = 0$ for all $t \geq 0$
Case R (Reflation):	$\theta = 0$ for $0 \leq t < 15$, and $\theta = 1$ for $t \geq 15$
Case S (Stagflation):	$\theta = 0$ for $0 \leq t < 15$, and $\theta = 0.5$ for $t \geq 15$

where t denotes 'time', and the unit time interval is interpreted as a year.[15]

It is worth noting that the dynamical system (16.52) is a decomposable system, and Equation (16.52) (v) does not affect the dynamic behavior of the variables d, y, e, and π^e. This means that the changes of the value of the policy parameter δ can not affect the dynamic behavior of real debt, real income, employment, and rate of price change. As we noted previously, this fact corresponds to the alleged 'ineffectiveness' of monetary policy in case of the liquidity trap. However, we have another root of the effectiveness of monetary policy through the influence on the public's expectation formation even in this case. Figures 16.3–16.7 show this fact clearly.

Case D is a typical example of the debt deflation in which the expectation formation is purely adaptive for all times. In this case, initial prosperity which is due to the relatively low initial debt/capital ratio automatically transforms to the serious depression through the rapid increase of the debt/capital ratio and the serious price deflation. The long-run equilibrium with $e^* = 0.97$ and $d^* = 0.282934$ is strongly unstable in this case.

In case R, it is supposed that the drastic 'regime switching' from $\theta = 0$ to $\theta = 1$ occurs at the period $t = 15$ because of the believable change of the attitude of central bankers. In this case, the long-run equilibrium point becomes stable and the economy recovers rapidly. In this case, the debt deflation is not triggered off, but the rate of price inflation begins to rise toward the equilibrium level

---

[15] We adopted Euler's algorithm and the time interval $\triangle t = 0.1$ (years) for numerical simulations.

Figure 16.3. **Alternative time paths of** e.

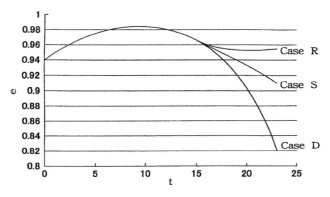

Figure 16.4. **Alternative time paths of** d

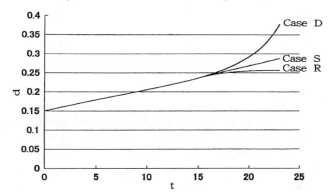

$\pi^* = 0.060052$ soon after the regime switching. This is the reason why we call this case 'reflation'.[16]

In case S, it is supposed that the incomplete regime switching from $\theta = 0$ to $\theta = 0.5$ occurs at the period $t = 15$. This means that the public only incompletely believes the announcement by the central bank. In this case, the long-run equilibrium is still unstable and the depression process continues in spite of the fact that the rate of price inflation begins to increase soon after the period

---

[16] In this numerical simulation, the nominal rate of interest is fixed at its lower bound $\rho_0 = 0.01$ for all time. But, in the real economy, the nominal rate of interest will begin to increase at the late stage of economic recovery. In this case, the speed of recovery will become less rapid at the late stage of economic recovery. However, the qualitative dynamics will not change seriously even if we introduce this effect explicitly.

Figure 16.5.   Time paths of π and π^e (Case D)

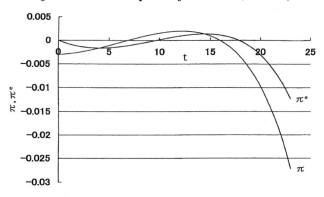

Figure 16.6.   Time paths of π and π^e (Case R)

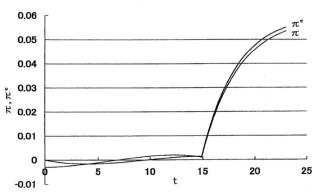

Figure 16.7.   Time paths of π and π^e (Case S)

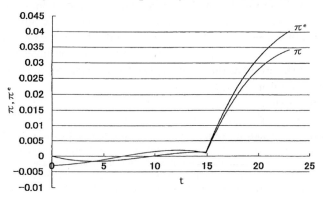

$t = 15$. This is the reason why we call this case 'stagflation'. Is this incomplete regime switching meaningless? It is not necessarily so, because the decline of the rate of employment and the increase of the debt/capital ratio become less rapid compared with the case D, so that the depression is mitigated considerably by this regime switching. In other words, the long-run equilibrium is relatively weakly unstable in this case.

It must be noted that in our three examples the structure of the economy is the same *except* the value of only one parameter θ, which governs the public's expectation formation of prices. This implies that the so-called 'structural reform' of the economy, which has nothing to do with the appropriate changes of the price expectation formation, is by no means a necessary condition for the economic recovery from debt deflation. Our findings apparently contradict the usual assertion by the 'structural reformists' in Japan, aside from the fact that the term 'structural reform' is rather vaguely used as a rhetoric and usually its content is not well defined in their argument.

6. Concluding remarks

The main destabilizing positive feedback mechanism in our dynamic Keynesian model is the so-called 'Fisher debt effect' (FDE), which can be represented schematically as follows.[17]

$$(y \downarrow) \Rightarrow e \downarrow \Rightarrow \pi \downarrow \Rightarrow d = (D/pK) \uparrow \Rightarrow g \downarrow \Rightarrow (y \downarrow) \qquad \text{(FDE)}$$

The strength of this effect will depend on the sensitivity of the rate of investment with respect to the changes of the debt/capital ratio ($|g_d|$) and the speed of the price adjustment (ε). The larger these parameter values, the stronger will be the FDE.

If the public's formation of price expectation is strongly backward-looking (adaptive), another destabilizing positive feedback effect through the changes of the expected *real* rate of interest, which is called 'Mundell effect' (ME), will also work. This effect can be represented as follows:

$$(y \downarrow) \Rightarrow e \downarrow \Rightarrow \pi \downarrow \Rightarrow \pi^e \downarrow \Rightarrow (\rho - \pi^e) \uparrow \Rightarrow g \downarrow \Rightarrow (y \downarrow) \qquad \text{(ME)}$$

The increase of the speed of the adaptation of price expectation (γ) will reinforce this process by reinforcing the part $\pi \downarrow \Rightarrow \pi^e \downarrow$.

On the other hand, we have a stabilizing negative feedback effect if the public's formation of price expectation is strongly forward-looking due to the credibility of the inflation targeting policy by the monetary authority (central bank).

---

[17] Needless to say, this name is associated with Fisher's (1933) classical paper on debt deflation.

Even if the causal chain $(y \downarrow) \Rightarrow e \downarrow \Rightarrow \pi \downarrow \Rightarrow \pi^e \downarrow$ works in the early stage of the depression process, the counteracting stabilizing process which is represented by

$$\mu_0 - n > \pi^e \Rightarrow \pi^e \uparrow \Rightarrow (\rho - \pi^e) \downarrow \Rightarrow g \uparrow \Rightarrow (y \uparrow) \tag{ITE}$$

will begin to operate if the inflation targeting policy becomes sufficiently credible so that the weight of the forward-looking expectation (θ) becomes sufficiently close to 1. We shall call this stabilizing effect 'Inflation targeting effect' (ITE).

Even if the stabilizing KE is very weak because of the downward rigidity of the nominal rate of interest at its nearly zero level, the monetary authority can transform the depression process into the prosperity by carrying out the sufficiently *credible* inflation targeting policy, as long as the destabilizing FDE is not extremely strong. Subtle factors such as public's expectation and credibility or believability of the attitude of central bankers play crucial roles which govern the dynamic behavior of the macro economy. This is the main conclusion of the present paper.

Acknowledgments

An earlier version of this paper was presented at the ACE 2004 (Australian Conference of Economists) which was held at the University of Sydney, Australia in September 29, 2004. This research was financially supported by the Japan Ministry of Education, Culture, Sports, Science and Technology (grant-in-aid for Scientific Research (B) 15330037) and Chuo University Joint Research Grant 0382. The author is grateful to Mr. Masahiro Ouchi for preparing the LATEX version of this paper.

References

Asada, T. (1991), "On a mixed competitive-monopolistic macrodynamic model in a monetary economy", *Journal of Economics*, Vol. 54, pp. 33–53.

Asada, T. (1999), "Investment and finance: a theoretical approach", *Annals of Operations Research*, Vol. 89, pp. 75–89.

Asada, T. (2001), "Nonlinear dynamics of debt and capital: a post-Keynesian analysis", (pp. 73–87) in: Y. Aruka and Japan Association for Evolutionary Economics, editors, *Evolutionary Controversies in Economics: A New Transdisciplinary Approach*, Tokyo: Springer.

Asada, T. (2004), "Price flexibility and instability in a macrodynamic model with a debt effect", *Journal of International Economic Studies*, Vol. 18, pp. 41–60.

Asada, T., C. Chiarella, P. Flaschel and R. Franke (2003), *Open Economy Macrodynamics: An Integrated Disequilibrium Approach*, Berlin: Springer.

Asada, T. and H. Yoshida (2003), "Coefficient criterion for four-dimensional Hopf bifurcations: a complete mathematical characterization and applications to economic dynamics", *Chaos, Solitons and Fractals*, Vol. 18, pp. 525–536.

Bernanke, B., T. Laubach, F. Mishkin and A. Posen (1999), *Inflation Targeting: Lessons from the International Experience*, Princeton: Princeton University Press.

Chiarella, C. and P. Flaschel (2000), *The Dynamics of Keynesian Monetary Growth*, Cambridge, UK: Cambridge University Press.

Chiarella, C., P. Flaschel, G. Groh and W. Semmler (2000), *Disequilibrium, Growth and Labor Market Dynamics*, Berlin: Springer.

Chiarella, C., P. Flaschel and W. Semmler (2001), "Price flexibility and debt dynamics in a high-order AS-AD model", *Central European Journal of Operations Research*, Vol. 9, pp. 119–145.

Fisher, I. (1933), "The debt-deflation theory of great depressions", *Econometrica*, Vol. 1, pp. 337–357.

Gandolfo, G. (1996), *Economic Dynamics*, 3rd edition, Berlin: Springer.

Hamada, K. (2004), "Policy making in deflationary Japan", *The Japanese Economic Review*, Vol. 55, pp. 221–239.

Ito, T. (2001), *Inflation Targeting*, Tokyo: Nihon Keizai Shinbun-sya (in Japanese).

Iwata, Ka. (2002), "Possibility of the occurrence of the deflationary spiral", (pp. 121–156) in: R. Komiya and Research Center of Japanese Economy, editors, *Issues of the Controversy on Monetary Policy*, Tokyo: Nihon Keizai Shimbun-sha (in Japanese).

Iwata, Ki. (2001), *Economics of Deflation*, Tokyo: Keizai Shinpo-sha (in Japanese).

Kalecki, M. (1937), "The principle of increasing risk", *Economica*, Vol. 4, pp. 440–447.

Kalecki, M. (1971), *Selected Essays on the Dynamics of the Capitalist Economy*, Cambridge, UK: Cambridge University Press.

Keynes, J.M. (1936), *The General Theory of Employment, Interest and Money*, London: Macmillan.

Komiya, R. and Research Center of Japanese Economy, (eds) (2002), *Issues of the Controversy on Monetary Policy*, Tokyo: Nihon Keizai Shimbun-sha (in Japanese).

Krugman, P. (1998), "It's Baaack: Japan's slump and the return of the liquidity trap", *Brookings Papers on Economic Activity*, Vol. 2, pp. 137–205.

Minsky, H. (1986), *Stabilizing an Unstable Economy*, New Haven: Yale University Press.

Nasica, E. (2000), *Finance, Investment and Economic Fluctuations: An Analysis in the Tradition of Hyman P. Minsky*, Cheltenheim, UK: Edward Elgar.

Taylor, J.B. (1993), "Discretion versus policy rules in practice", *Carnegie–Rochester Conference Series on Public Policy*, Vol. 39, pp. 195–214.

Uzawa, H. (1969), "Time preference and the Penrose effect in a two-class model of economic growth", *Journal of Political Economy*, Vol. 77, pp. 628–652.

Woodford, M. (2003), *Interest and Prices: Foundations of a Theory of Monetary Policy*, Princeton: Princeton University Press.

Yoshida, H. (2004), "The possibility of economic slump with the liquidity trap: a monetary optimizing model with sticky prices", *Studies in Regional Science* (Journal of the Japan Section of the Regional Science Association International), Vol. 34(2), pp. 39–51.

Appendix A

A.1. Proof of Proposition 1

(i) Differentiating Equation (16.43) with respect to ε, we have

$$\partial a_2/\partial\varepsilon = d\bar{e}[\underset{(+)}{\alpha\, G_{21}}/y + \underset{(-)}{g_d}] - \gamma(1-\theta)\bar{e}\underbrace{\{\alpha G_{24}/y - g_{\rho-\pi}\}}_{(+)} < 0 \qquad (A1)$$

for all $\theta \in [0, 1]$ and $\gamma > 0$ because of Assumptions 1 and 3. This means that a_2 becomes a linear decreasing function of ε, so that we have $a_2 < 0$ for all sufficiently large values of $\varepsilon > 0$. In other words, one of the Routh–Hurwitz conditions for stable roots (16.48) is violated for all sufficiently large values of $\varepsilon > 0$.

(ii) Suppose that $\theta = 0$. Then, we have

$$\partial a_2/\partial\gamma = -\varepsilon\bar{e}\underbrace{\{\alpha G_{21}/y - g_{\rho-\pi}\}}_{(+)} < 0 \qquad (A2)$$

for all $\varepsilon > 0$. This means that we have $a_2 < 0$ for all sufficiently large values of $\gamma > 0$ even if $\theta > 0$ as far as θ is close to zero.

(iii) Suppose that $\theta = 1$. Then, the characteristic equation (16.41) becomes

$$\Delta_4(\lambda; 0) = |\lambda I - J_3(0)|(\lambda + \gamma) = 0 \qquad (A3)$$

where

$$J_3(0) = \begin{bmatrix} F_{11} & F_{12}(0) & -\varepsilon d \\ \alpha G_{21} & \alpha G_{22} & 0 \\ \bar{e}[\alpha G_{21}/y + g_d] & \bar{e}[\alpha G_{22}/y + \beta g_r] & 0 \end{bmatrix} \qquad (A4)$$

The characteristic equation (A3) has a negative real root $\lambda_4 = -\gamma$, and other three roots $\lambda_j(j = 1, 2, 3)$ are determined by the following equation:

$$|\lambda I - J_3(0)| = \lambda^3 + b_1\lambda^2 + b_2\lambda + b_3 = 0 \qquad (A5)$$

where

$$b_1 = -trace\, J_3(0) = -\underbrace{(F_{11} + \alpha G_{22})}_{(-)} > 0, \qquad (A6)$$

b_2 = sum of all principal second-order minors of $J_3(0)$

$$= \begin{vmatrix} \alpha G_{22} & 0 \\ \bar{e}[\alpha G_{22}/y + \beta g_r] & 0 \end{vmatrix} + \begin{vmatrix} F_{11} & -\varepsilon d \\ \bar{e}[\alpha G_{21}/y + g_d] & 0 \end{vmatrix} + \alpha \begin{vmatrix} F_{11} & F_{12}(0) \\ G_{21} & G_{22} \end{vmatrix}$$

$$= e d\alpha \underbrace{\{\alpha G_{21}/y + g_d\}}_{(-)} + \alpha \underbrace{\{F_{11}G_{22} - F_{12}(0)G_{21}\}}_{(+)}, \tag{A7}$$

$$b_3 = -\det J_3(0) = \varepsilon d\alpha\bar{e} \begin{vmatrix} G_{21} & G_{22} \\ \alpha G_{21}/y + g_d & \alpha G_{22}/y + \beta g_r \end{vmatrix}$$

$$= \varepsilon d\alpha\bar{e}\underbrace{(G_{21}\beta g_r - G_{22}g_d)}_{(+)} > 0. \tag{A8}$$

From these expressions, we obtain

$$\lim_{\varepsilon \to 0} b_2 = \alpha \underbrace{\{F_{11}G_{22} - F_{12}(0)G_{21}\}}_{(+)} > 0 \tag{A9}$$

$$\lim_{\varepsilon \to 0}(b_1 b_2 - b_3) = -\alpha\underbrace{(F_{11} + \alpha G_{22})}_{(-)}\underbrace{(F_{11}G_{22} - F_{12}(0)G_{21})}_{(+)} > 0 \tag{A10}$$

These inequalities imply that all of the Routh–Hurwitz conditions for stable roots of Equation (A5) ($b_1 > 0$, $b_3 > 0$, $b_1 b_2 - b_3 > 0$) are satisfied for all sufficiently small $\varepsilon > 0$ if $\theta = 1$. This means, by continuity, that all of the Routh–Hurwitz conditions for stable roots of the four-dimensional system (S_4) are in fact satisfied for all sufficiently small $\varepsilon > 0$ even if $\theta < 1$, as long as θ is sufficiently close to 1.

(iv) If we substitute $e = \bar{e}$, $\pi^e = \mu_0 - n$, and $g = n$ into Equation (16.31) (v), we have $\dot{m}/m = 0$. This implies that we have $\dot{m}/m \to 0$ in case of $(e, \pi^e, g) \to (\bar{e}, \mu_0 - n, n)$. ∎

Appendix B

B.1. Proof of Proposition 2

Suppose that the premises concerning the parameter values θ and γ are satisfied. Then, it follows from Proposition 1 (i) and (iii) that the equilibrium point of the system (S_4) is locally asymptotically stable for all sufficiently small values of $\varepsilon > 0$, and it is locally unstable for all sufficiently large values of $\varepsilon > 0$. Therefore, by continuity, there exists at least one 'bifurcation point' at which the local stability of the equilibrium point is lost as the parameter value ε increases. At such a bifurcation point, the characteristic equation (16.41) has at least one root with zero real part. By the way, from Equation (16.45) we have

$$\lim_{\theta \to 1} a_4 = \lim_{\theta \to 1} (\lambda_1 \lambda_2 \lambda_3 \lambda_4) = \alpha \gamma \varepsilon \bar{e} d \underbrace{(G_{21} \beta g_r - G_{22} g_d)}_{(+)} > 0 \tag{B1}$$

so that, by continuity, we have

$$\lambda_1 \lambda_2 \lambda_3 \lambda_4 > 0 \tag{B2}$$

if $\theta \in [0, 1]$ is sufficiently close to 1, where λ_j $(j = 1, 2, 3, 4)$ are four roots of the characteristic equation (16.41). The inequality (B2) means that the characteristic equation (16.41) does not have a root such that $\lambda = 0$. In this case, Equation (16.41) must have a pair of pure imaginary roots

$$\lambda_1 = i\omega \quad \lambda_2 = -i\omega \quad (i = \sqrt{-1}, \omega > 0) \tag{B3}$$

at the bifurcation point. Substituting Equation (B3) into the inequality (B2), we obtain

$$\omega^2 \lambda_3 \lambda_4 > 0 \tag{B4}$$

at the bifurcation point. On the other hand, it follows from the proof of Proposition 1 (iii) that the characteristic Equation (16.41) has a negative real root $\lambda_4 = -\gamma$ when $\theta = 1$. This means that Equation (16.41) has a negative real root $\lambda_4 < 0$ even if $\theta < 1$ as long as θ is sufficiently close to 1. In this case, the remaining root λ_3 also becomes real and negative from the inequality (B4).

In sum, the characteristic Equation (16.41) has a set of pure imaginary roots and two negative real roots at the bifurcation point. Furthermore, the imaginary part of a pair of complex roots increases as the parameter ε increases passing through the bifurcation parameter value ε_0, because of the loss of stability. This means that the bifurcation point in this case is in fact the Hopf bifurcation point, and we can apply the Hopf bifurcation theorem to establish the existence of the closed orbits at some values of the parameter $\varepsilon > 0$ which are sufficiently close to the bifurcation value ε_0 (cf. Gandolfo, 1996, Chapter 25).[18]   ∎

---

[18] For a more elaborate treatment of the four-dimensional Hopf bifurcations which are described here, see Asada and Yoshida (2003) and the mathematical appendix of Asada *et al.* (2003).

Subject Index